International Labour Standards and Platform Work

AF715563

Bulletin of Comparative Labour Relations

VOLUME 110

Founding Editor

The series started in 1970 under the dynamic editorship of Professor Roger Blanpain (Belgium), former President of the International Industrial Relations Association. Professor Blanpain, Professor Emeritus of Labour Law, Universities of Leuven and Tilburg, was also General Editor of the International Encyclopedia of Laws (with more than 1,600 collaborators worldwide) and President of the Association of Educative and Scientific Authors. He passed away in October 2016.

General Editor

In 2015 Frank Hendrickx, Professor of labour law at the Faculty of Law of the University of Leuven (Belgium) joined as a co-Editor. Frank Hendrickx has published numerous articles and books and regularly advises governments, international institutions and private organisations in the area of labour law as well as in sports law. He is the Editor-in-Chief of the European Labour Law Journal and General Editor of the International Encyclopaedia of Laws.

Introduction

The Bulletins constitute a unique source of information and thought-provoking discussion, laying the groundwork for studies of employment relations in the 21st century, involving among much else the effects of globalization, new technologies, migration, and the greying of the population.

Contents/Subjects

Amongst other subjects the Bulletins frequently include the proceedings of international or regional conferences; reports from comparative projects devoted to salient issues in industrial relations, human resources management, and/or labour law; and specific issues underlying the multicultural aspects of our industrial societies.

Objective

The Bulletins offer a platform of expression and discussion on labour relations to scholars and practitioners worldwide, often featuring special guest editors.

The titles published in this series are listed at the end of this volume.

BULLETIN OF COMPARATIVE LABOUR RELATIONS – 110

International Labour Standards and Platform Work

An Analysis of Digital Labour Platforms Based on the Instruments on Private Employment Agencies, Home Work and Domestic Work

Mathias Wouters

General Editor

Frank Hendrickx

Founding Editor

Roger Blanpain

Wolters Kluwer

Published by:
Kluwer Law International B.V.
PO Box 316
2400 AH Alphen aan den Rijn
The Netherlands
E-mail: international-sales@wolterskluwer.com
Website: www.wolterskluwer.com/en/solutions/kluwerlawinternational

Sold and distributed by:
Wolters Kluwer Legal & Regulatory U.S.
7201 McKinney Circle
Frederick, MD 21704
United States of America
Email: customer.service@wolterskluwer.com

ISBN 978-94-035-4024-5

e-Book: ISBN 978-94-035-4041-2
web-PDF: ISBN 978-94-035-4042-9

© 2022 Kluwer Law International BV, The Netherlands

All rights reserved. No part of this publication may be reproduced, stored in a retrieval system, or transmitted in any form or by any means, electronic, mechanical, photocopying, recording, or otherwise, without written permission from the publisher.

Permission to use this content must be obtained from the copyright owner. More information can be found at: www.wolterskluwer.com/en/solutions/legal-regulatory/permissions-reprints-and-licensing

Table of Contents

Acknowledgements

First and foremost, I want to thank the FWO, *Fonds voor Wetenschappelijk Onderzoek – Vlaanderen*, for funding Prof. De Stefano's Odysseus project "Employment rights and labour protection in the on-demand economy", of which this study is a part. Furthermore, I am particularly grateful to Prof. Valerio De Stefano and Prof. Frank Hendrickx. Not just for allowing me to embark on this project in the first place, but for being so understanding and supportive. I could not have wished for a better duo to bring this to a successful conclusion. It was an absolute pleasure to work at the Institute.

During this whole process, I have come across many others who likewise deserve credit and praise. In particular, Prof. Paul Schoukens and Prof. Auriane Lamine have given incredibly constructive comments over the years. Prof. Yvonne Erkens has likewise been of great support. The time they have devoted to this project is much appreciated, as is the kind contribution of Prof. Jacques Herbots. Furthermore, the staff of the INWORK department at the ILO deserve special mention. Martine Humblet, Janine Berg, Uma Rani, Claire Hobden, Najati Ghosheh and others have all been tremendously welcoming during my internship in 2018 and beyond. Also, Prof. Miriam Cherry has been of great help and support, as were all the other ILO interns.

At the risk of making this list too long, I cannot mention all the colleagues at the KU Leuven and elsewhere who have assisted me over the years. Nevertheless, some have been so essential that they deserve a separate page. Especially Josephine Van Rijmenant and Bettina Vander Eecken have always been there to aid my fellow PhD students and me, whatever happened. They have been magnificent. Likewise, I want to thank all other colleagues at the Institute for creating such a splendid atmosphere. It was fantastic to share the office with Pieter Pecinovsky, Miet Vanhegen, Ilda Durri, Harry Stylogiannis, Simon Taes, Frea De Keyzer, Stan Bruurs, Silvia Rainone and Alberto Barrio. All of whom are very warm persons.

Lastly, I owe a lot to my parents, who have always been there for me, come what may. This work is in no small way also their merit, as well as that of Elisabetta, who continues to keep my spirits up. Thank you for your confidence in me. It has been essential at times.

Introduction

1. The Subject

Digital labour platforms[1] – The platform economy is home to a wide range of platforms. Many of these provide a source of income for people who invest their time developing content, offering services and selling goods. If this platform-related income is predominantly earned in return for the performance of work, one could speak of "platform work". It is a rather vague descriptive term. For example, do YouTube creators not perform platform work for the benefit of the platform's users?[2] Airbnb hosts are another example. These "lessors" take the necessary steps to leave the house in a hospitable state and take time to provide and collect the keys. Although this generally does not turn Airbnb hosts into employees,[3] one should, nevertheless, acknowledge that they purposely work under the platform's clout. Hence, why not consider it platform work? 1

As illustrated by these two examples, both of which are generally not perceived as platform work, any description of this phenomenon inevitably ends up being somewhat arbitrary. Eurofound, for instance, describes these employment arrangements very concisely as "the matching of the supply of and demand for paid labour through an online platform". The primary traded good needs to be labour, according to Eurofound. Therefore, Airbnb and, arguably, also YouTube are excluded (lodging and video content).[4] As discussed more extensively in the First Chapter, this dissertation broadly aligns its inquiry with the scope of Eurofound's research. Digital labour platforms 2

1. This dissertation was written in the framework of the Odysseus project "Employment rights and labour protection in the on-demand economy" funded by the FWO, Fonds voor Wetenschappelijk Onderzoek – Vlaanderen.
2. "The [Youtube Partner Program] is no longer a 'partnership,' if it ever was; it is a labor contract in a new form, governing an enormous variety of creative work". Robyn Caplan & Tarleton Gillespie, *Tiered Governance and Demonetization: The Shifting Terms of Labor and Compensation in the Platform Economy*, 6 Social Media + Society 1, 8 n. 2 (2020).
3. Robert Sprague, *Are Airbnb Hosts Employees Misclassified as Independent Contractors?*, 59 University of Louisville Law Review 63, 63–88 n. 1 (2020).
4. Eurofound, *Employment and Working Conditions of Selected Types of Platform Work* 3 and 9 (Publications Office of the European Union 2018).

are algorithmically managed networks that aim to bring about interactions between workers, including jobseekers, and "users". Businesses, households and end-market consumers can all rely on these platforms as users. Platform operators are supposed to provide the workers and users with the autonomy needed to self-determine the key terms of their interactions on the platform. However, in reality, many platform operators will take central control of their platform, and constrain workers' and users' autonomy. Consequently, these platform operators come under scrutiny from the perspective of labour and social security law because the workers show characteristics of employment rather than self-employment.

3 **International labour standards** – The International Labour Organization (ILO) celebrated its centenary in 2019. For this occasion, the International Labour Conference adopted the Centenary Declaration for the Future of Work, reaffirming that "[t]he ILO must carry forward into its second century with unrelenting vigour its constitutional mandate for social justice by further developing its human-centred approach to the future of work, which puts workers' rights and the needs, aspirations and rights of all people at the heart of economic, social and environmental policies".[5] Indeed, the ILO has a long track record of representing working people's interests globally. Its advocacy on behalf of vulnerable people is a red line throughout its history.[6] To this end, the ILO's International Labour Conference has adopted almost 200 Conventions and over 200 Recommendations since its first gathering in 1919. These Conventions and Recommendations, as well as the Declarations, Protocols and Resolutions adopted by the Conference and Governing Body, are the international labour standards that make up the ILO's "International Labour Code".[7] As Kohiyama and Petrović argue, the International Labour Code "should constitute a resource for the broader international community in its search for guidance on the meaning of social justice and as well as its principles and methods".[8] This dissertation explores whether the Code also offers guidance on how to create platform work that is socially just.

2. Context and Background

4 **A square peg and round holes** – When a jury was asked to classify the working relationship of Lyft drivers in California, judge Chhabria remarked: "the jury in this case will be handed a square peg and asked to choose between two round holes".[9] According to many commentators at the time, platform workers, such as Lyft or Uber drivers, could hardly be considered employees or independent contractors, i.e.

5. ILO Centenary Declaration for the Future of Work, 21 June 2019.
6. Jean-Michel Bonvin, *Les Valeurs Fondatrices de l'OIT et la Promotion de la Citoyenneté Sociale – Jalons Historiques et Défis Contemporains* 31, 32–39 (George P. Politakis, Tomi Kohiyama & Thomas Lieby eds., *ILO100: Law for Social Justice*, ILO 2019).
7. It should be noted that especially during the 1950s, the ILO issued a real "International Labour Code" which was "simply an attempt to arrange in an orderly and convenient manner the provisions of the Conventions and Recommendations adopted by the International Labour Conference". ILO, *The International Labour Code* LXVII (ILO 1951).
8. Tomi Kohiyama & Dražen Petrović, *The International Labour Code – Myth or Reality?* 815, 857 (George P. Politakis, Tomi Kohiyama & Thomas Lieby eds., *ILO100: Law for Social Justice*, ILO 2019).
9. United States District Court: *Cotter v. Lyft, Inc*, 60 F.Supp.3d 1067, 1081 (N.D.Cal. 2015).

"two round holes". Instead, they were seen as "sub-entrepreneurs" who are legally self-employed but experience "less freedom than those with true entrepreneurial scope and autonomy in their work".[10] Similar to Lyft and Uber drivers, many more platform workers would operate in this "grey area" between the archetype of an employee and a self-employed worker.[11]

Since Chhabria's comments in 2015, courts worldwide have continued to issue rulings 5 on platform workers' employment status. These judgments have reached different outcomes: many courts classified platform workers as employees or protected under another employment status, whereas other platform workers have seen their claim for labour and social protections dismissed.[12] Among other things, this uncertainty incited governments and legislatures to reflect on how to clarify the employment rights of platform workers. One of the problems, however, is that they plan to do so along very different lines.[13] Considering this range of national developments and responses, Novitz rightly suggests that "inconsistencies in treatment of gig work in national legislation and domestic litigation indicate that international regulation is worth investigating".[14] This dissertation takes up this challenge, also because of the transnational nature of many platforms' business activities.

International regulation – Since the body of existing "international regulation" on 6 working conditions is vast, and parts have already been applied to platform work by others,[15] a choice had to be made. So far, research has not yet focused extensively on the interaction between platform work and ILO standards. This is why the present work focuses on international labour standards (ILS). As mentioned above, the ILO has adopted ILS ever since the High Contracting Parties at the Treaty of Versailles decided "that there are methods and principles for regulating labour conditions which all industrial communities should endeavour to apply, so far as their special circumstances will permit".[16] The ILO's "permanent machinery" was established to decide what "methods and principles" all "industrial communities" should pursue, capturing these in ILS. Due to the organisation's drafting procedures, with tripartite delegations contributing from across the globe, the entire process "grants them

10. Emmanuel Josserand & Sarah Kaine, *Different Directions or the Same Route? The Varied Identities of Ride-Share Drivers*, 61 Journal of Industrial Relations 549, 550 n. 4 (2019).
11. Giuseppe Casale & Mario Fasani, *Labour Law and Digital Platforms* (Adalberto Perulli & Tiziano Treu eds., *The Future of Work: Labour Law and Labour Market Regulation in the Digital Era*, Kluwer 2021).
12. *See* Uber in France, Cour de cassation: Case 374, *Uber France and Others v. M. A… X…*, 4 March 2020, ECLI:FR:CCAS:2020:SO00374; *see also* Glovo in Spain, Tribunal Supremo: Case 805/2020, *D. Desiderio v. Glovoapp23 SL*, 25 September 2020, ECLI: ES:TS:2020:2924; *see also* Foodora in Italy, Corte suprema di cassazione: Case 11629/2019, *Foodinho S. R. L. v. Pisano Marco and Others*, 24 January 2020; *see also* Uber in the United Kingdom, Supreme Court: Case [2021] UKSC 5, *Uber BV and Others (Appellants) v. Aslam and Others (Respondents)*, 19 February 2021.
13. Valerio De Stefano, Ilda Durri, Charalampos Stylogiannis & Mathias Wouters, *Platform Work and the Employment Relationship* 18–29 (ILO 2021).
14. Tonia Novitz, *The Potential for International Regulation of Gig Economy Issues*, 31 King's Law Journal 275, 286 n. 2 (2020).
15. *E.g.* Bartłomiej Bednarowicz, *Platform-Mediated Work in the Gig Economy Through the Lens of the EU Social Acquis* (University of Antwerp 2019).
16. Art. 427 Treaty of Peace of Versailles, 28 June 1919.

indisputable legitimacy, if nothing else due to the two-thirds majority that adoption represents".[17] To that extent, whereas platform operators have not refrained from stressing the need for labour law to change,[18] ILS symbolise the exact opposite. These standards usually impose minimum protections and core principles without getting into too many details. In theory, this should provide an excellent benchmark for a regulatory approach to platform work.

7 What is important to emphasise in this regard is how ILO instruments follow their own "logic". As will be discussed in more depth, ILS are drafted in an institutional setup dictated by the ILO Constitution and Standing Orders. As a result, each separate Convention and Recommendation has its own scope and purpose while, at the same time, being part of the ILO's overall project. Every standard is a piece of the puzzle, contributing to the ILO's conception of social justice in the world of work, also referred to as decent work. Member States' commitment to the ILO Constitution presupposes that countries subscribe to this overarching goal of reaching social justice.[19] ILS can broadly be seen as standards detailing how the Member States can work towards that goal. Each standard carries a message, one that is also potentially relevant in relation to platform work.

8 **Prospects of a standard on platform work** – An analysis of the ILO's existing standards and their relevance to platform work is timely. A tripartite Meeting of Experts on "decent work in the platform economy" will likely be held in the second quarter of 2022.[20] The conclusions of such a Meeting of Experts are essential for the orientation of potential standard-setting action from 2023–2024 onwards.[21] This dissertation highlights many of the issues and ILS that such discussions should consider. Moreover, it can be used in retrospect to evaluate the solutions advanced by the experts and ILO constituents.

17. Alain Supiot, *The Tasks Ahead of the ILO at its Centenary*, 159 International Labour Review 117, 126 n. 1 (2020).
18. *See, e.g.*, Dara Khosrowshahi, Logan Green & John Zimmer, *Open Forum: Uber, Lyft Ready To Do Our Part for Drivers*, San Francisco Chronicle (12 June 2019), https://www.sfchronicle.com/opinion/openforum/article/Open-Forum-Uber-Lyft-ready-to-do-our-part-for-13969843.php; Dara Khosrowshahi, *I Am the C.E.O. of Uber. Gig Workers Deserve Better*, The New York Times (10 August 2020), https://www.nytimes.com/2020/08/10/opinion/uber-ceo-dara-khosrowshahi-gig-workers-deserve-better.html. For a substantial analysis: *see* Rebeca Smith & Maya Pinto, *Rewriting the Rules: Gig Companies' Drive for Labor Deregulation* 189, 189–207 (Deepa Das Acevedo ed., *Beyond the Algorithm: Qualitative Insights for Gig Work Regulation*, CUP 2020).
19. *E.g.* "Calling upon all constituents of the ILO to reaffirm their unwavering commitment and to reinvigorate their efforts to achieve social justice and universal and lasting peace to which they agreed in 1919 and 1944"; Preamble of the ILO Centenary Declaration for the Future of Work, 21 June 2019.
20. ILO Governing Body, *Decision Concerning the Agenda of the International Labour Conference: Agenda of Future Sessions of the Conference*, GB.341/INS/3/1(Rev.2)/Decision (ILO 2021).
21. ILO Governing Body, *Agenda of the International Labour Conference: Agenda of Future Sessions of the Conference*, GB.338/INS/2/1 (ILO 2020); ILO Governing Body, *Agenda of the International Labour Conference: Agenda of Future Sessions of the Conference*, GB.341/INS/3/1(Rev.1) (ILO 2021).

3. Description of the Research

3.1. Assumptions, (Sub-)research Questions, Research Goals and Approach

Assumptions – One of the assumptions of this research is that platform work can be beneficial. Economists would argue that it can produce economic benefits, such as increased productivity or higher overall employment.[22] Furthermore, for instance, workers with care responsibilities or health problems admit that online platforms allow them to find valuable employment opportunities.[23] Additionally, even though there are marked differences in working conditions between platforms,[24] most platform workers seem rather satisfied.[25] Because these sources indicate that the overall impact of platform work may well be positive, this dissertation does not advocate banning these kinds of work arrangements. At the same time, since platform work seemingly creates both good and bad jobs,[26] the research also assumes that to do nothing is not a solution either. Indeed, platform work should be regulated in one way or another.[27] The question should be to what ends and to what extent. 9

Other assumptions of this dissertation relate to the ILO's international labour standards. Lawyers are quick to point out that ILS are barely enforced in front of the courts; hence, why bother? Why not focus on the European Union's secondary instruments or the European Convention on Human Rights, both of which have the judicial authorities needed to enforce these standards? One answer from, for instance, a European point of view is that many platforms originate elsewhere and intend to implement their business practices without paying much attention to local regulations. For this reason, however robust a domestic court system may seem, in practice, it remains challenging to make these companies comply with local standards.[28] In light 10

22. Cyrille Schwellnus, Assaf Geva, Mathilde Pak & Rafael Veiel, *Gig Economy Platforms: Boon or Bane?* 11–17 (OECD 2019).
23. Qualitative interviews indicate that care responsibilities for older family members and health problems are some of the reasons why people engage in crowdwork. Janine Berg et al., *Digital Labour Platforms and the Future of Work: Towards Decent Work in the Online World* 38–39 (ILO 2018). *See also*, Premilla D'Cruz & Ernesto Noronha, *Positives Outweighing Negatives: the Experiences of Indian Crowdsourced Workers*, 10 Work Organisation, Labour & Globalisation 44, 44–63 n. 1 (2016).
24. Fairwork, *Fairwork 2020: Annual Report* 14 and 18 (Oxford Internet Institute 2020).
25. ILO, *World Employment and Social Outlook: The Role of Digital Labour Platforms in Transforming the World of Work* 145–147 (ILO 2021).
26. Arne L. Kalleberg & Michael Dunn, *Good Jobs, Bad Jobs in the Gig Economy*, 20 Perspectives on Work 10, 10–14 (2016).
27. The idea that regulation is inherently bad for the development of platforms should be dismissed. *See e.g.*, Jovana Karanović, Hans Berends & Yuval Engel, *Regulated Dependence: Platform Workers' Responses to New Forms of Organizing*, 58 Journal of Management Studies 1070, 1097–1099 n. 4 (2021). Similarly, McGaughey argues that the gig economy heavily draws on unsound economic theories. These companies wrongly assume that employment protections are bad for economic outcomes. Ewan McGaughey, *A Human is not a Resource*, 31 King's Law Journal 215, 215–235 n. 2 (2020).
28. A good example is the court rulings on Uber in the United Kingdom. Uber only accepted a ruling by the Employment Tribunal from October 2016 after its confirmation by the UK Supreme Court in February 2021. Moreover, even though Uber has pledged to no longer fight drivers' classification as limb (b) workers, in contrast to what these rulings demand, Uber still seems

of this, a universal standard might help buttress local efforts to regulate platforms or enforce existing rules. Another answer to the question of why a focus on ILS is justified has to do with one of the primary forms of platform work, namely online crowdwork. This form of platform work in which digital tasks, such as cropping images, are being parcelled out to a global workforce spans continents. To oversimplify things, Indians perform digital tasks for companies in the Anglosphere, crowdworkers in French-speaking Africa may help out French companies, and Ukrainians offer their online services to Russian companies. This form of platform work is genuinely global, requiring a global outlook.

11 Additionally, the more complicated explanation of why the ILO's standards deserve attention in this debate has to do with the organisation's mission. Scholars tend to perceive the ILO as an organisation that intends to prevent a race to the bottom between enterprises in various countries that try to take the upper hand by downgrading employment conditions. However, this is, arguably, a very narrow take on its mission, making it particularly easy to discredit the organisation. The ILO has, after all, never been given the powers to act as an international legislature, nor did it receive forceful enforcement mechanisms. Apparently, that was not what the High Contracting Parties had in mind. Instead, as argued by Langille in particular, "the object of international labor law is not to constrain nations from acting in their self interest but to show them where it lies in the first place, and to assist them in achieving it".[29] This dissertation operates on the assumption that this is the proper role ILS fulfil, which has inevitable consequences. For example, even if the ILO were to disintegrate, this research retains its value. It would still contain lessons for the Member States about how to tackle platform work based on ILO constituents' collective experiences and decisions.

12 **The main research question** – Because a comprehensive account of how ILS suggest that platforms should be regulated is currently missing, an answer to the following question is of value to both scholars and policymakers:

> "Do current international labour standards sufficiently respond to digital labour platforms, taking into account the organisational structure of these platforms

---

unwilling to remunerate a driver's standby time as working time (i.e. the time waiting for a transport request). To be fair, this is a situation in which everything goes well for the workers. In many other countries, the courts have much less of an impact, for example, because of the slow administration of justice, or because the platform operator decides to suspend services since the local market is not crucial to their business (e.g. Foodora left Canada, partially in response to reclassification). Supreme Court: Case [2021] UKSC 5, *Uber BV and Others (Appellants) v. Aslam and Others (Respondents)*, 19 February 2021; Kate Ewing, *Don't be Fooled, Uber is Still Dodging the Minimum Wage*, Institute of Employment Rights (17 March 2021), https://www.ier.org.uk/comments/dont-be-fooled-uber-is-still-dodging-the-minimum-wage/; Josh O'Kane, *Foodora to Exit Canada Just Months After Workers Won the Right to Unionize*, The Globe and Mail (27 April 2020), https://www.theglobeandmail.com/business/article-foodora-to-exit-canada-three-months-after-workers-won-the-right-to/.

29. Brian A. Langille, *What is International Labor Law For?* 3 Law & Ethics of Human Rights 48, 68 n. 1 (2009). "Today, as in the past, the ILO's primary mission is not to impose the same labour conditions on all States, but rather to support the efforts of those wishing to improve their workers' conditions and to ensure that such efforts do not put them at a disadvantage compared with States that opt out of taking similar measures". Alain Supiot, *supra* n. 17, at 125.

and the demands made by platform workers, and if not, what role can the International Labour Organization play in regulating digital labour platforms?"

Sub-research questions – This research question requires an answer to the following sub-research questions: 13

a) What are digital labour platforms? What do they do? How different are digital labour platforms from other actors in the labour market?
b) What is the ILO? What is the ILO's mandate? How does this mandate relate to digital labour platforms? What are international labour standards? What is their function at the ILO?
c) Which ILS are highly relevant to the regulation of digital labour platforms?
d) What are the rules governing the interpretation of such instruments?
e) What is the purpose and scope of application of the instruments that are identified as highly relevant to the regulation of digital labour platforms?
f) If these instruments apply, what does that tell us? Are the guidelines in these instruments responsive to the challenges posed by platform work, taking into account platforms' operational structure and platform workers' demands?
g) If these instruments do not apply, or if there are other reasons why they are insufficiently responsive, what role can the ILO play in regulating digital labour platforms?

Research goals – A first objective is to grasp what digital labour platforms are and figure out how they are novel compared to older labour market phenomena (subquestion a). This conceptual clarity is needed before advancing to the second objective, which is to verify to what extent some of the most relevant standards from the International Labour Code already apply to platform work (subquestions c and e). For this purpose, the rules on how to interpret ILS must also be known (subquestion d), and the ILO's normative agenda has to be explored (subquestion b).[30] Other reasons to pose subquestion b relate to this research's third objective. The goal is to judge what role the ILO already plays in regulating digital labour platforms – through applicable instruments – and what role it could potentially play in the future (subquestions f and g). Answering the questions under subquestion b is necessary to make an informed assessment about what to expect in the future. 14

Limitations and approach – This research aims to clarify to what degree the International Labour Code is already responsive to platform work. With that goal in mind, as it would be impossible to thoroughly examine the scope of application of each standard in the International Labour Code, a selection was made of the instruments that seemed most relevant in light of what this dissertation understands a digital labour platform to be. The reasons why the Private Employment Agencies Convention, 1997 (No. 181), Home Work Convention, 1996 (No. 177), and Domestic 15

30. As suggested by the Vienna Convention on the Law of Treaties, in case of treaty interpretation, "any relevant rules of international law applicable in the relations between the parties" "shall be taken into account". These "relevant rules of international law" include the ILO Constitution, as reinterpreted through the recent Declarations (*infra* no. 216). Amongst others for this reason, the ILO's normative agenda is explored because it may influence treaty interpretation. Art. 31.3.(c) Vienna Convention on the Law of Treaties, 23 May 1969.

Workers Convention, 2011 (No. 189), were selected are described quite extensively below (*infra* nos. 179–192). The choice has to do, *inter alia*, with our understanding of what constitutes a digital labour platform. As Part I will show, a genuine platform can be expected not to exert the amount of control needed for the platform operator to be considered a regular legal employer. Even if some platform operators, like those engaged in transport, meet the threshold to be considered a legal employer, it will be much harder to find an employment relationship for other platforms, which remain much more faithful to the original template and continue to resemble labour market intermediaries. Based on that understanding – genuine platforms leave workers with significant autonomy – this research does not focus on the Employment Relationship Recommendation, 2006 (No. 198), or any other instrument that confers labour and social protection to standard employees. Other researchers are invited to clarify the implications of applying the ILS, which are solely applicable to legal employees, onto legally employed platform workers.

16 This research, instead, relies on Convention No. 177, No. 181 and No. 189 to make its arguments. Although not wholly unrelated to the legal concept of an "employment relationship", these three instruments have a unique purpose and scope of application that extends protections beyond the stereotypical employee in industry or commerce. These instruments, moreover, apply to some specific subcategories of workers that show remarkable similarities with platform workers. For instance, like platform workers, the job opportunities and working time of temporary agency workers, industrial homeworkers and domestic workers are strongly affected by labour demand.[31] These three categories of workers also struggle to have their work appreciated as a proper occupation. This is similar to platform workers, who are often believed to perform their work as a side-gig. Additionally, besides the similarities in how these various types of workers are treated, there are also parallels between each separate instrument and platform work. Convention No. 181, for example, targets triangular employment, which is a prevalent characteristic of platform work arrangements.[32] Convention No. 177 regulates certain types of home-based work, making it a relevant instrument because many online platform workers perform tasks from their own homes. Thirdly, Convention No. 189 regulates domestic work, which is interesting because many app-based platforms essentially help users with their household activities. Therefore, because of these instruments' scope of application, which extends beyond the standard concept of employment relationships, because of factual similarities between these types of workers and because of the expectation that these ILO standards focus on core features of platform work, these three instruments were chosen as a sample from the Code to verify whether international labour standards are responsive to platform work.

31. Agency workers and industrial homeworkers are a flexible workforce for employers; once household members no longer require the services of domestic workers, they are easily dismissed or replaced.
32. Triangular employment is a situation in which a worker is being placed or assigned to a third party through an entity that, to a greater or lesser extent, controls the worker's employment conditions. This is often what happens in the platform economy, when the platform operator connects workers to users or dispatches workers to users. It is rare for the platform operator not to limit how the worker and third party can work together.

The advantage of this selection is that contrary to what might have happened if other standards, such as Recommendation No. 198, had been the focal point, this research finds that ILS do, in fact, apply to significant parts of the platform economy. The Code's guidelines apply to many more platform operators than those that are legal employers under domestic law. However, despite these instruments' applicability, for reasons described in Part IV of this dissertation, the overall conclusion nonetheless seems to be that the Code is unresponsive to digital labour platforms. As a result, assuming the Meeting of Experts concludes - similar to this research - that some form of standard-setting action is recommendable, the question becomes what role the ILO can play in this respect. 17

Any answer to this question will inevitably be incomplete. Throughout this research, it will become clear that platform work is a challenging topic to regulate. As such, the goal of Part IV of this dissertation is not to advance a clear-cut solution but to offer insight. It indicates, for example, what issues ILO constituents might want to deal with and what solutions ILO constituents have accepted in prior instruments. This part of the research limits itself significantly. It relies on information derived from Part I of the dissertation about the issues that can be expected to arise in platform work. It uses Part II of the dissertation that, for instance, describes "decent work" in general, making it possible to picture what "decent work in the platform economy" would require. Finally, it uses the content of the instruments on private employment agencies, home work and domestic work to give concrete indications of what might be realistic to expect from ILO constituents, given their prior agreements in Convention No. 177, No. 181 and No. 189 and the affiliated Recommendations. 18

These three sources of information are blended to illustrate what role the ILO could play. In effect, the final part of this dissertation explores the centre of this Venn diagram: 19

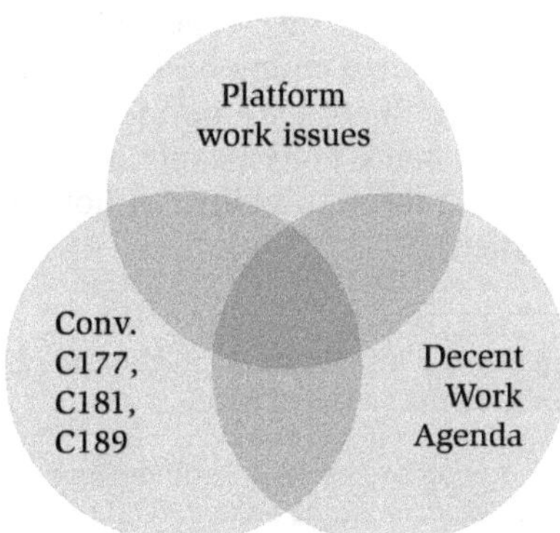

By doing so, Part IV intends to offer some guidance in terms of what to expect from a future instrument. All of the considerations in these final Chapters should be considered informative rather than prescriptive. In the end, the goal of this Fourth Part is not to argue that ILO constituents must do something, such as prohibiting platform operators from charging fees to workers because Convention No. 181 contains such prescriptions. The research merely indicates that it would make perfect sense for an ILO instrument on platform work to prohibit fee-charging, considering how platforms 20 operate, what platform workers complain about and what ILO constituents have agreed upon in the past. Whether ILO constituents reaffirm this principle and the other guidelines found in the instruments on private employment agencies, home, and domestic work depends on various factors, many of which might not even be mentioned here.

3.2. Societal Relevance and Scientific Innovation

21 **The prevalence of platform work** – It remains unclear how many platform workers there are exactly. Researchers rely on different concepts and methodologies, leading to various outcomes. In one notable contribution from 2020, Kilhoffer et al. evaluated the literature on platform work in the European Union. Notwithstanding ongoing uncertainty, their "research team" was "best persuaded by the more modest estimates for the prevalence of platform work".[33] These sources indicate that platform work takes up 1–3 per cent of total employment, with "indications that this share has been growing fast".[34] Months after this literature review, another team behind the EU's research project on the collaborative economy estimated that platform work is the "main" form of employment for around 1.4 per cent of the working-age population. The analysis covered sixteen EU Member States, with estimates "ranging from 2.6% in Spain to 0.6% in Finland".[35] Moving beyond the EU, information is arguably scarcer. In Australia, "7.1% of respondents were currently [in 2019] offering services or doing work mediated by a digital platform or they had done so within the last 12 months".[36] Zhou reports that in China, the number of "individuals providing services in one way or another through platforms" was 9.7 per cent of total employment in 2018.[37] According to Zhou, this high percentage stands in stark contrast to platform work's prevalence in, for example, the United States. The team behind the EU's research on the collaborative economy mentioned in 2018 that the situation in the United States is relatively similar to the EU.[38] Assuming this is true, platform work would, nevertheless, still affect a large chunk of the workforce in the EU and US. It would be the main form of employment for around 1–2 per cent of the working-age population; yet, it would affect many more people in total because most people in the West seem to rely on it as a form of additional household income (hence, not their main form of employment).[39]

33. Zachary Kilhoffer et al., *Study to Gather Evidence on the Working Conditions of Platform Workers* 45 (Publications Office of the European Union 2020).
34. Schwellnus, Geva, Pak & Veiel, *supra* n. 22, at 8.
35. Maria Cesira Urzì Brancati, Annarosa Pesole & Enrique Férnandéz-Macías, *New Evidence on Platform Workers in Europe. Results from the Second COLLEEM Survey* 17 (Publications Office of the European Union 2020).
36. Paula McDonald et al., *Digital Platform Work in Australia: Prevalence, Nature and Impact* 31 (Victorian Department of Premier and Cabinet 2019).
37. Irene Zhou, *Digital Labour Platforms and Labour Protection in China* 13 (ILO 2020).
38. Annarosa Pesole et al., *Platform Workers in Europe: Evidence from the COLLEEM Survey* 11–12 and 20 (Publications Office of the European Union 2018).
39. "Pesole et al (2020) estimate that 1.4% of the population in 16 EU Member States analysed do platform work as their main job, while another 10% do it at various levels of intensity and frequency next to other activities. Experts agree that this employment form and business model has been dynamically growing over the last decade and expect further growth in the future".

Platform work reflects general trends – In addition to the fact that platform work, therefore, affects many people in absolute numbers, it is also societally relevant because it reflects broad trends. The algorithmic management of the platform's workforce, for example, feels fresh and exciting. However, before long, many "regular" enterprises may also use algorithmic means to govern their workers.[40] As one report puts it: "[j]ust as the organisational design developed by Henry Ford came to characterise society more broadly, our research indicates that the techniques and tools of the platform economy have spread far beyond gig work, resulting in widespread 'gigification' and restructuring of workplace behaviours and relationships, jobs and communities".[41] To that extent, think of how platforms excel at handing out small tasks to a fluid workforce. Other employers may likewise master this craft,[42] as exemplified by just-in-time scheduling in warehouses.[43] Due to these links between platform work and broader trends, research into platform work can also provide valuable insights into more comprehensive phenomena. 22

Scientific innovation – The research is innovative for several reasons. The First Part will explain why this dissertation does not focus on the most hierarchical platforms, which exercise the kind of control labour law associates with subordination. For now, it suffices to note that this focus differs from most labour law scholars' perspectives because most tend to concentrate on the platform operators that – from a labour lawyer's point of view – closely resemble hierarchical firms. Secondly, as will become apparent in the dissertation's Third Part on the scope of application of ILS, this research does not take the concept of a "traditional employment relationship" as its focal point. To that extent, since an employment relationship is still the main gateway to labour protections for most workers, authors tend to discuss the criteria that characterise an employment relationship at the domestic or international level. However, for reasons that will become clear in the main text, this focus is not particularly fruitful at the ILO level. Many of the ILS governing digital labour platforms do not rely on a traditional employment relationship to frame their scope. As such, this research deviates from most other studies by not zooming in on subordination or the employer's means of control. A third reason why this research is, arguably, innovative relates to the limitations of other research. Many researchers only explore how platform work's complex reality can be captured under labour law's legal concepts. In other words, does this or that law apply? Often, these contributions do not discuss the implications of actually applying labour law. What would happen to these platform workers once working time regulations and wage protections are 23

Eurofound, *Back to the Future: Policy Pointers from Platform Work Scenarios* 1 (Publications Office of the European Union 2020).

40. Valerio De Stefano, *"Negotiating the Algorithm": Automation, Artificial Intelligence and Labor Protection*, 41 Comparative Labor Law & Policy Journal 15, 23–31 n. 1 (2019).
41. Abigail Gilbert et al., *The Amazonian Era: How Algorithmic Systems are Eroding Good Work* 3 (Institute for the Future of Work 2021).
42. Ursula Huws, *Labour in Contemporary Capitalism: What Next?* 156–157 (Palgrave Macmillan 2019). *See also*, Alex J. Wood, *Despotism on Demand: How Power Operates in the Flexible Workplace* (Cornell University Press 2020).
43. Sam Abbott & Alix Gould-Werth, *Unboxing Scheduling Practices for U.S. Warehouse Workers: Lessons from a Research and Advocacy Roundtable* (Washington Center for Equitable Growth 2020).

implemented, for example?[44] This research does venture into that area in its Fourth Part, albeit to a limited extent due to the instruments being used.[45]

24 A fourth and fifth reason that makes this research innovative relates to the choice of instruments. Most of the English literature relies on legal standards originating in the West. Although the ILO – a specialised agency of the United Nations – has been accused of Eurocentrism in the past,[46] it has broadened its outlook in more recent decades. Some examples are the organisation's interest in the informal economy since the 1980s and the explicit promotion of universal minimum standards since the 1990s. This research pulls in the direction of a more global analysis of platform work. It relies on relatively recent ILO instruments, which should take the experiences from developing countries into account, and uses platform work examples from, *inter alia*, Asia and South America. At the same time, the research's orientation towards continents other than Europe should also be taken with a grain of salt. Much of the research on platform work, labour law and the ILO is conducted by European researchers or, at the very least, is funded through institutions in high-income countries.[47] Digital labour platforms are, moreover, most active in North America, Europe and Asia.[48] Therefore, even if this research makes an effort to broaden the horizons, it will, nevertheless, refer to many scholars and views from the Global North. Finally, the research is also unusual in the way it deals with ILO standards. If used at all, most researchers only refer in passing to these instruments. By putting these instruments at the core of this research, the underlying message can be captured, sketching its implications for platform work.

4. Methodology

4.1. Legal Research and the Sources Used

25 **Legal research** – This work relies on legal research but takes a law in context approach. Labour law is a form of responsive law,[49] which often develops in light of events and shifting power relations.[50] Its responsive character makes it even more important not

44. A good article on this is: Anne C. L. Davies, *Wages and Working Time in the 'Gig Economy'*, 31 King's Law Journal 250, 250–259 n. 2 (2020).
45. As mentioned above, ILS tend to contain principles and broadly acceptable approaches. Applying an ILO Convention on working time is quite different from applying all domestic regulations on working time because the former has fewer details, typically making it less stringent than the latter. Therefore, when indicating what the implications are of applying Convention No. 181, No. 177 and No. 189 to certain platform workers, the discussion only sketches broad lines, without getting into detailed legal distinctions, as would happen domestically.
46. Gerry Rodgers, *India, the ILO and the Quest for Social Justice since 1919*, XLVI Economic & Political Weekly 45, 48 n. 10 (2011).
47. *E.g.*, Jasmien Van Daele, *The International Labour Organization (ILO) in Past and Present Research*, 53 International review of social history 485, 509 n. 3 (2008).
48. ILO, *supra* n. 25, at 242.
49. Frank Hendrickx, *Foundations and Functions of Contemporary Labour Law*, 3 European Labour Law Journal 108, 127 n. 2 (2012).
50. The fact that many governments and legislatures will reassess their regulation on telework in light of the COVID-19 pandemic, even if many forms of telework have been steadily developing

to lose touch with reality on the ground. For this reason, this legal research will also consider non-legal sources to various ends. First of all, it is essential to understand what a digital labour platform is, which implies using literature from multiple disciplines, such as management sciences and sociology. Secondly, it is necessary to grasp the state of affairs at the ILO. Non-legal sources concerning the ILO may be necessary, such as historians' accounts, to provide additional insight beyond what the ILO Declarations and Resolutions express. Thirdly, when trying to figure out an instrument's purpose, one needs to understand the situation it attempts to remedy. That, too, cannot be grasped satisfactorily using legal documents alone. It is helpful to rely on qualitative and quantitative research to show or confirm the actual issue. Lastly, an evaluation of ILS "responsiveness" to platform work benefits from the literature on platforms' business operations and workers' experiences. The research will, in other words, also use qualitative and quantitative insights about platform work to evaluate the content of ILO instruments.

Legal source material – Despite its frequent use of non-legal literature, the research 26
mainly draws on ILO related legal sources, such as the Conventions and Recommendations, and secondary sources, including the drafting committees' working documents or comments from the ILO Committee of Experts on the Application of Conventions and Recommendations. Academic contributions play a somewhat limited role at some points because scholarly writings are, in principle, of limited importance for treaty interpretation.[51] The dissertation needed to strike a balance in this respect. As this dissertation is the result of scientific work, it does incorporate academic reflections.[52] However, since the goal is to provide an honest account of these instruments' content, external commentators' opinions will only be relied upon to the degree they are reconcilable with the outcome reached under the rules of interpretation.

"External" legal writings that, unlike, for instance, working documents, do not 27
directly relate to an ILO instrument were chosen with this concern for neutrality in mind. Sometimes, there are particular reasons to attribute more credibility to one commentator's views over those of another. For example, an ILO official can generally be expected to give a neutral description because of the potential backlash when a group of ILO constituents feels wronged. Similarly, an external scholar who has written the Law and Practice Report leading up to an ILO instrument can be expected to have a clearer understanding of the instrument's background. Also, the means of publication can be relevant. For instance, ILO Working Papers tend to be reviewed by officials from the ILO Office and, from time to time, by staff from the Workers' and Employers' delegations. That should guarantee a relatively balanced account. Likewise, if an academic article is published in the *International Labour Review* – a journal issued by the ILO – it can be expected to give a relatively neutral account.

throughout the 21st century, is a case in point. Labour law springs from the heat of the moment, often characterised by pragmatic outcomes.

51. Arts. 31-32 Vienna Convention on the Law of Treaties, 23 May 1969.
52. Moreover, for instance, the International Court of Justice does rely on "the teachings of the most highly qualified publicists of the various nations, as subsidiary means for the determination of rules of law". Art. 38 Statute of the International Court of Justice, 26 June 1945.

28 Based on these reflections, it should not come as a surprise that around 45 per cent of the working papers and reports used in this dissertation are published through an ILO-affiliated source or have an ILO-affiliated author. At the same time, this percentage also indicates how much additional information was processed, turning this research into much more than a synthesis of existing ILO publications – especially because a significantly lower percentage of, for example, journal articles will have an ILO "affiliation".

29 The research has tried to approach the subject from a transnational perspective. However, at some points, country examples are used as illustrations. Those country examples might predominantly come from continental Europe, which partially explains why some source material is written in Dutch, French or another continental language. The aim has thereby been to use individual country examples solely as an illustration. The actual argument or analysis should derive from international sources or a comparative analysis of national examples.

4.2. Methodological Steps and Structure

30 **The methodology** – The First, Second and Third Parts of this thesis are descriptive and analytical. The First Part describes the object of this research: digital labour platforms (DLPs). It does so by, among other things, contrasting DLPs to similar labour market actors. The Second Part of this dissertation is likewise descriptive; it portrays the "cognitive framework"[53] for the ILO's work. It relies on various policy documents to describe what course the ILO has taken since the turn of the century, framing the ILO's actions on "decent work in the platform economy" in relation to the bigger picture. Subsequently, the Third Part of the dissertation analyses some specific ILS from the International Labour Code deemed crucial. It inquires what their purpose and scope of application are.

31 Only the Fourth Part of this dissertation breaks this mould. Since the instruments under consideration in Part III apply to platform work, their content is evaluated to verify whether the applicable instruments are responsive as well, considering the characteristics of labour platforms and the issues raised by platform workers. The outcome of this evaluation indicates that it is appropriate for the ILO to undertake additional steps to preserve decent work in the platform economy. After this evaluation, a more normative approach is taken, presenting a "blueprint" of sorts that can offer insight into what a future instrument regarding decent work in the platform economy might want to accomplish. As mentioned above (*supra* nos. 18–20), this blueprint draws on observations from the first three Parts of this dissertation. Therefore, it is inherently incomplete and should not be seen as binding or prescriptive. For example, although the sources analysed in this dissertation would suggest that platform operators need to be prohibited from charging fees to workers (*infra* nos. 459–460), there could be other overriding concerns. For this reason, Part IV of this research is best understood as an early contribution to a much broader regulatory discussion that will draw on many more authors and stakeholders.

53. Expression from Gerry Rodgers, Eddy Lee, Lee Swepston & Jasmien Van Daele, *The International Labour Organization and the Quest for Social Justice, 1919–2009* 7 (ILO 2009).

The research structure - As concerns Part I of the dissertation, first, a description is provided of what is considered a DLP for the purposes of this dissertation. Due to this description, it is asserted that genuine DLPs are similar to "labour market intermediaries" (LMIs). Consequently, the First Part compares the literature on DLPs and the literature on LMIs to ascertain whether DLPs indeed practise a form of labour market intermediation. These Subchapters serve two purposes. 32

- First, the comparison underpins the legal angle that is chosen to analyse platform work in the Third Part of this dissertation. If so many DLPs perform labour market intermediation, then why are the corresponding regulations not applied?

  Secondly, Part I also explores the purposes of labour market intermediation and how platforms practise this. This comparison provides a foundation for the Fourth Part of the dissertation, in which the content of certain applicable standards is evaluated in view of platforms' practices. The discussion in Part I, in other words, offers valuable information about the organisational structure of platforms, which is relied on in the Fourth Part of the dissertation to evaluate the existing instruments' utility and describe the possible role of the ILO in regulating DLPs.

- The Second Part of this dissertation predominantly looks at the ILO's "Decent Work Agenda" and all subsequent Declarations embedding that agenda. It contains two relatively short Subchapters on the ILO's characteristics and its original mandate, allowing readers who are unfamiliar with the organisation to make sense of it. Subsequently, the Chapters mainly discuss the ILO's three most recent Declarations from 1998, 2008 and 2019, which have reformulated its mandate. This is for two reasons.

  First, the Vienna Convention on the Law of Treaties stipulates that the "relevant rules of international law applicable in the relations between the parties" are part of the context taken into consideration when interpreting a treaty.[54] As highlighted in Part III, the ILO Constitution and the ILO Declarations that subsequently reinterpret the ILO Constitution are, therefore, part of the context when interpreting an ILO Convention. Secondly, Part IV of this dissertation cannot sketch what "decent work in the platform economy" might look like unless Part II has clarified the meaning of "decent work" as such. The Decent Work Agenda and the ILO Declarations that institutionalised the agenda are an essential component of the ILO's response to platform work, which is why it is included in this research design as well.

- Having detailed what DLPs are and what the ILO plans to do post-centenary, the Third Part of the dissertation turns its attention to some existing ILS. A first "preliminary" Subchapter explains the reasoning behind the choice for three ILO Conventions in particular: the Private Employment Agencies Convention, 1997 (No. 181), the Home Work Convention, 1996 (No. 177), and the Domestic Workers Convention, 2011 (No. 189). This choice has already

54. Art. 31 Vienna Convention on the Law of Treaties, 23 May 1969.

been explained briefly above (*supra* nos. 15–16) and will be discussed in more detail at a later stage (*infra* nos. 176–192).

Following this Subchapter, a second "preliminary" Subchapter discusses the rules of interpretation governing the interpretation of ILO Conventions. The Subchapter covers the general rules of interpretation found in the Vienna Convention on the Law of Treaties. However, it most notably points out what it means to implement those rules in relation to ILO instruments, and how the ILO's practices substantially deviate from these general rules.

Having clarified pursuant to which rules ILO Conventions should be interpreted, Chapters Two, Three and Four analyse the purpose and scope of application of each of the three Conventions individually. Chapter Four is followed by an interim conclusion.

- Each Chapter in Part III details what platform workers are covered by Convention No. 181, 177 and 189, respectively. The First Chapter of Part IV indicates what the implications are of applying some of the guidelines found in these Conventions and the associated Recommendations to the platform workers in question.[55] As it turns out, these instruments do contain relevant guidelines in light of platforms' practices and platform workers' complaints; however, these guidelines do not seem to materially influence the debate on platform workers' working conditions. Moreover, these instruments cover agency, home, or domestic workers in general, meaning the instruments do not contain instructions about issues that affect platform workers especially badly. For these reasons, the conclusion seems to be that these instruments from the International Labour Code are not responsive to platform work, even though they apply. More broadly, if this is the case for the instruments that address labour market phenomena that are pretty similar to platform work, then one might suspect this "unresponsiveness" to affect the Code as a whole.

  Hence, the final Chapters explore what an instrument in pursuance of decent work in the platform economy might cover, based on the findings of this research (i.e. a regulatory blueprint). One preliminary point is how, based on the instruments under consideration, the ILO has multiple "pathways" to adopt an instrument on platform work. There are options other than a Platform Work Convention or Recommendation. *Inter alia*, because of the various angles at the organisation's disposal, the last Chapter cannot make any determinative claims. After all, a Platform Work Convention will contain very different provisions from an instrument on digital employment services, home-based crowdwork or international labour recruitment. This makes it pointless to try to design a very concrete blueprint.

  At the same time, despite this uncertainty, it does not mean the final Chapter cannot say anything about what a future instrument might cover. To that end, the Chapter draws on Part II, which detailed the ILO's overall mandate and mission at this moment in time, to establish the framework for

55. Home Work Recommendation, 1996 (No. 184); Private Employment Agencies Recommendation, 1997 (No. 188); Domestic Workers Recommendation, 2011 (No. 201).

the discussion. The ILO's normative agenda, for instance, determines what components are fundamental to decent work and are, therefore, indispensable in any future instrument on decent work in the platform economy.

Once it is clear what topics a future instrument would likely discuss because of the ILO's overarching normative goals, the instruments from Part III can be used to illustrate how ILO constituents have dealt with these topics in the past. Information from Part I can be used to discuss whether it makes any sense to do the same again in the platform economy. The approach of this research entails that only three Conventions and Recommendations are used to illustrate what a future standard on platform work may advance. Although one could object that this limited selection is regrettable, it should be emphasised that these instruments are rather unusual. Most ILS only deal with one topic of labour protection, such as violence and harassment, wages, working time or minimum age. Convention No. 177, No. 181 and No. 189, on the other hand, deal with all these topics to the extent homeworkers, domestic workers and workers subjected to private employment services require it. What is more, these three instruments' protections can be expected to, by and large, correspond to the protections advanced by the ILO's general standards on occupational safety and health (OSH), wage-fixing, and so on. Therefore, since each of these three instruments extends a range of labour protections to one of these categories of workers, using all three actually gives us an effective way to see what protections ILO constituents consider particularly valuable and might want to extend across the platform economy (*infra* nos. 449–451).

Part I. Digital Labour Platforms and Labour Market Intermediaries

INTRODUCTION

The content of Part I – The First Chapter explores what a digital labour platform is. As discussed below, it could be described as a network that a platform operator algorithmically manages with the aim of bringing about interactions between workers, including jobseekers, and businesses, households and end-market consumers. In principle, a platform operator is expected to, on the one hand, implement features to foster such interactions, but on the other, refrain from controlling the critical terms of the interactions, such as prices and deadlines. Because of this description of DLPs in Chapter 1, Chapter 2 introduces the similar concept of labour market intermediaries (LMIs). As will become apparent, many - but not all - DLPs are LMIs. Also, many of the so-called benefits of platforms are already mentioned in the literature on LMIs. Chapter 3, subsequently, compares findings from the literature on DLPs to the literature on LMIs, aiming to deepen our understanding of what platforms do and the potential issues from a regulatory stance. Overall, this First Part substantiates other scholars' view that platform operators practise a modern form of labour market intermediation.[56] 33

Its purpose for the overall thesis – The First Part of the dissertation is used to justify the selection of international labour standards in the Third Part: if DLPs are often LMIs, what standards apply to labour market intermediation? Furthermore, this First Part also uncovers valuable information to evaluate applicable ILS's content in the dissertation's Fourth Part. This evaluation of the standards' content plans to take into account platforms' organisational structure, which is explored in this First Part of the dissertation. Moreover, the final, normative Chapter on the ILO's potential role in regulating platform work will also draw on the examples uncovered in this First Part. 34

56. In particular, Karolien Lenaerts et al., *Online Talent Platforms, Labour Market Intermediaries and the Changing World of Work* i (CEPS and IZA 2018).

Chapter 1. Digital Labour Platforms

SUBCHAPTER 1. THE CONCEPT OF A DIGITAL LABOUR PLATFORM

ILO terminology – Research within the ILO often uses the concept of a digital labour platform. As described in the organisation's report on digital labour platforms and the future of work, it includes "both web-based platforms, where work is outsourced through an open call to a geographically dispersed crowd ('crowdwork'), and location-based applications (apps) which allocate work to individuals in a specific geographical area".[57] In other words, the concept covers both "online platforms", such as Amazon Mechanical Turk, Freelancer.com and Upwork, as well as "location-based apps", such as Uber, Deliveroo, TaskRabbit and Care.com. The former category of platforms distributes digital work, cropping images or proofreading documents for example, to a crowd of platform workers, referred to as crowdworkers. The latter use a platform to organise local services, such as transport, caretaking, dog-walking or cooking. Although the concept of a DLP covers both categories of crowdwork platforms and location-based apps, the ILO report is predominantly concerned with crowdwork.[58] It makes a subdivision in this respect between crowdwork platforms that offer macro-tasks, more or less resembling consulting services,[59] and crowdwork platforms that predominantly source micro-tasks. Micro-tasking encompasses, for instance, collecting and processing information on the web, translating sentences, transcribing audio files, and writing or flagging online reviews. Translating an entire document instead of some sentences might be considered more of a macro-task. The boundaries between the micro- and macro-tasks can, therefore, become somewhat 35

57. Berg et al., *supra* n. 23, at xv.
58. The report describes crowdwork with a reference to Howe's description of "crowdsourcing", i.e. "[t]he act of taking a job once performed by a designated agent (an employee, freelancer or a separate firm) and outsourcing it to an undefined, generally large group of people through the form of an open call, which usually takes place over the Internet (Howe, quoted in Safire, 2009; see also Howe, 2006)". *Ibid.*, 3.
59. Macro-tasks are "defined as those that take more time and typically involve a higher skill set when compared with 'microtasks'". *Ibid.*, 83. For a concrete example: Yao Yao, *Uberizing the Legal Profession? Lawyer Autonomy and Status in the Digital Legal Market*, 58 British Journal of Industrial Relations 483, 483–506 n. 3 (2020).

blurred. This dissertation will use the term DLP to refer to platforms that support location-based services, online macro-tasking and micro-tasking.[60]

36 **What characterises a platform?** – In their study for the EU's Collaborative Economy research project (COLLEEM), Pesole et al. define platforms "as digital networks that coordinate transactions in an algorithmic way".[61] The COLLEEM survey's short definition contains several significant elements. First, it mentions the importance of algorithms. This is consistent with other scholars, including ILO researchers, who overall seem to agree that "[a]lgorithmic management of the workforce is a defining feature of digital labour platforms".[62] Algorithms are needed to track and manage market liquidity, ensuring that users are effectively matched to workers.[63] Secondly, Pesole et al.'s description of DLPs as "digital networks" that coordinate labour market transactions also confronts us with another question. One that is often avoided in the literature: what exactly is a platform?

37 Platforms are omnipresent these days. The word is used in various contexts, ranging from a civic or political platform and a collaborative platform for educational purposes to the kind of labour platforms this dissertation analyses. Even if we were to only focus on commercial platforms, the sheer variety remains remarkable. For instance, Wirtz et al. differentiate between search platforms such as Yahoo, communication platforms such as Skype, matching platforms such as Tinder, content and review platforms such as Tripadvisor, retail platforms such as eBay, payment platforms, booking platforms, social media platforms, crowdfunding platforms, sharing economy platforms and so forth.[64] In other words, this dissertation is only concerned with a relatively small subset of platforms. Nevertheless, since DLPs are part of this larger "platform revolution", it seems appropriate to at least deal with the question of what a platform is on a rudimentary level.

38 To this extent, the COLLEEM survey mentions that a platform "coordinates" transactions.[65] Legal scholarship seems to agree that "facilitation" or "intermediation" of transactions between separate sides on a network is a platform's core feature.[66] The same is true for non-legal scholars. For example, compared to other forms of work,

60. This "broader" use of the term digital labour platform is not out of the ordinary. *See e.g.*, Valerio De Stefano & Antonio Aloisi, *European Legal Framework for "Digital Labour Platforms"* 7–10 (Publications Office of the European Union 2018); Kurt Vandaele, *Will Trade Unions Survive in the Platform Economy?* (Etui 2018).
61. Pesole et al., *supra* n. 38, at 7.
62. Berg et al., *supra* n. 23, at 8. *See also, e.g.*, Jan Drahokoupil & Brian Fabo, *Outsourcing, Offshoring and the Deconstruction of Employment: New and Old Challenges* 33, 46 (Amparo Serrano-Pascual & Maria Jepsen eds., *The Deconstruction of Employment as a Political Question: 'Employment' as a Floating Signifier*, Springer International Publishing 2019).
63. Sangeet Paul Choudary, *The Architecture of Digital Labour Platforms: Policy Recommendations on Platform Design for Worker Well-Being* 5 (ILO 2018).
64. Jochen Wirtz et al., *Platforms in the Peer-to-Peer Sharing Economy*, 30 Journal of Service Management 452, 454 n. 4 (2019).
65. Pesole et al., *supra* n. 38, at 7.
66. Alain Strowel & Wouter Vergote, *Digital Platforms: To Regulate or Not to Regulate?* 3, 12 (Bram Devolder ed., *The Platform Economy*, Intersentia 2019); Quentin Cordier, *L'Économie de Plateforme: Description d'un Phénomène d'Intermédiation* 7, 10 (Jacques Clesse & Fabienne Kéfer eds., *Enjeux et Défis Juridiques de l'Économie de Plateforme*, Anthemis 2019); Céline

Kilhoffer et al. call the "'black box' of intermediation" the "most distinguishing feature" of platform work.[67] Others even claim that "[o]f course, gig work is only novel in the sense that labor supply is matched to labor demand by an online platform, and that each engagement of work is considered as a separate contract".[68] Based on such accounts, algorithmic "matching" or "intermediation" seems to be a core characteristic of DLPs. Platform operators are businesses that connect "external producers" or workers to consumers or users, enabling "value-creating interactions between them".[69]

Platform operators – For the sake of clarity and because it is helpful for analytical purposes, this dissertation will refer to the company that runs the platform and profits from its activities as the platform operator. If we take Uber as an example, the terms UberPOP, UberX, Uber Eats etc., refer to separate platforms. However, the platform operator is called Uber B.V. It can manage the operations of all these distinct platforms. This is important because every single platform may operate based on a different legal framework. In theory, at least in some countries, nothing would prevent UberPOP from relying on independent contractors, whereas UberX functions with legally employed drivers. Suppose Uber B.V. treats private individuals on UberPOP differently from professional drivers on UberX. In that case, Uber B.V. may well operate two similar services, one reliant on self-employed workers and another on employees. In fact, especially in the food-delivery business, some platform operators likely already rely on one governance system to direct labour when working with employed couriers and another system when working with independent contractors.[70] 39

Operators are network orchestrators – In addition to the need for algorithmic matchmaking, in order to speak of a DLP, the dissertation considers it necessary for the platform operator to do more than merely "facilitate" connections.[71] That is because platform operators follow a "network orchestrator model". They run "a 40

Wattecamps, *Quel Droit Social Pour les Travailleurs de Plateformes?* 29, 80 (Auriane Lamine & Céline Wattecamps eds., *Quel Droit Social pour les Travailleurs de Plateformes?*, Anthemis 2020).

67. Kilhoffer et al., *supra* n. 33, at 42. Graham and Woodcock similarly state how "[t]he common feature of all digital labour platforms is that they offer tools to bring together the supply of, and demand for, labour". Mark Graham & Jamie Woodcock, *Towards a Fairer Platform Economy: Introducing the Fairwork Foundation*, 29 Alternate Routes 242, 242 (2018).
68. Alex de Ruyter, Martyn Brown & John Burgess, *Gig Work and the Fourth Industrial Revolution: Conceptual and Regulatory Challenges*, 72 Journal of International Affairs 37, 39 n. 1 (2019).
69. Choudary, *supra* n. 63, at 1.
70. For instance, a Dutch court case on Deliveroo points out that the company used a "self-service booking tool" before March 2020 and a "Free Login" system afterwards. The former entails that days before the actual gig occurs, couriers can make reservations for specific time slots. The latter is the kind of system Uber relies on, in which case the platform worker simply logs in whenever it suits him or her. One can imagine the former kind of system to fit better if the platform operator relies on employees in a certain country. The latter system seems more adapted to the use of independent contractors, and, arguably, this second system is also deployed to justify the company's reliance on self-employed couriers. For the court case, *see* Gerechtshof Amsterdam: Case 200.261.051/01, *Deliveroo Netherlands B.V. v. Federatie Nederlandse Vakbeweging*, 16 February 2021, ECLI:NL:GHAMS:2021:392.
71. José van Dijck, *The Culture of Connectivity: A Critical History of Social Media* 29 (OUP 2013).

network of users whose activities in turn create value for the company".[72] The platform operator wants to effectively create value for its stakeholders, going beyond making it merely feasible to transact. This profit motive – success demands transactions – is relevant. For example, McAfee and Brynjolfsson emphasise that when platform operators "exercise control well", they remove barriers that have kept individuals from transacting and "influence the flow of transactions so that more benefits go to the platform owner".[73] As such, platforms are not neutral. All kinds of different mechanisms foster transactions, using psychological incentives,[74] reward systems,[75] automated search engines, and algorithmic support during the transaction.[76] These features largely operate in the background. However, the effect of this profit motive on the platform operator's orchestration of jobseekers should not be underestimated.[77]

41 Because a platform operator is supposed to implement a "network orchestrator model", the dissertation will not concern itself with networks that merely serve as conduits for information, and may incidentally be used to conclude employment or service contracts. For instance, the use of Facebook Messenger to agree on a service transaction does not turn it into a DLP.[78] Facebook Messenger was not designed to foster employment interactions between Facebook users. Furthermore, platform operators that do not aim to make a profit will not feature in this dissertation either. The research is limited to platforms developed to bring about interactions between workers and other users on the network for reasons of financial gain.

42 **Operators orchestrate but do not control the interactions** – In order to come up with an even more detailed description of a labour platform, the economics literature can be consulted. Zysman and Kenney, for instance, describe platforms in general,

72. Kellen Zale, *Scale and the Sharing Economy* 38, 40 (Nestor M. Davidson, Michèle Finck & John J. Infranca eds., *The Cambridge Handbook of the Law of the Sharing Economy*, CUP 2018). *See also*, Steven Engels & Monika Sherwood, *What if We All Worked Gigs in the Cloud? The Economic Relevance of Digital Labour Platforms* 9 (Publications Office of the European Union 2019).
73. Andrew McAfee & Erik Brynjolfsson, *Machine, Platform, Crowd* 206 (W. W. Norton & Company 2017).
74. Ognjen Scekic, Hong-Linh Truong & Schahram Dustdar, *Incentives and Rewarding in Social Computing: Praise, Pay, and Promote Crowd-Member Workers to Elicit Desired Behavioral Responses and Performance Levels*, 56 Communications of the ACM 72, 72–82 n. 6 (2013).
75. For instance, in Canada, Hyr uses a "UPoint" scheme in which workers obtain points by completing shifts. The points can be exchanged for USD 75 once the worker obtains 2,500 points. Julian Posada & Leslie Regan Shade, *Platform Labour Discourse: How Hyr Targets the "Bucket List Generation"*, 29 Democratic Communiqué 78, 85 n. 1 (2020).
76. Alex Rosenblat, *Uberland: How Algorithms are Rewriting the Rules of Work* 138–166 (University of California Press 2018); James Duggan, Ultan Sherman, Ronan Carbery & Anthony McDonnell, *Algorithmic Management and App-Work in the Gig Economy: A Research Agenda for Employment Relations and HRM*, 30 Human Resource Management Journal 114, 119–121 n. 1 (2020).
77. Diana Farrell & Friona Greig, *The Online Platform Economy: Has Growth Peaked?* 8 (JP Morgan Chase Institute 2016); Martin Kenney, Dafna Bearson & John Zysman, *The Platform Economy Matures: Pervasive Power, Private Regulation, and Dependent Entrepreneurs* 14 (Berkeley Roundtable on the International Economy 2019).
78. This is not to say that these networks cannot be used for these purposes. One survey found that "[s]everal respondents also indicated that they get their work through social networks (including specialized groups on Facebook.com, Odnoklassniki.ru and VKontakte.ru)". Mariya Aleksynska, Anastasia Bastrakova & Natalia Kharchenko, *Work on Digital Labour Platforms in Ukraine: Issues and Policy Perspectives* 18 (ILO 2018).

so going beyond labour platforms, as "multisided digital frameworks that shape or intermediate the terms on which participants - often, but not always, buyers and sellers - interact with one another". Platforms are "algorithm-enabled 'cyberplaces'" for interaction.[79] This portrayal seems to presuppose that platform participants have agency. Similarly, the OECD relies on the description provided by Hagiu and Wright.[80] These scholars have specified how multi-sided platforms differ from other intermediaries. According to Hagiu and Wright, pure multi-sided platforms, such as "Elance-oDesk" - nowadays called Upwork, allow users "almost complete freedom to set their own terms or negotiate them with employers".[81] What is more, multi-sided platforms have two key features. "They enable direct interactions between two or more distinct sides [and] [e]ach side is affiliated with the platform".[82] Crucial in this regard is the authors' subsequent clarification about what it means to have "direct interactions". This entails, "broadly speaking", "that the two or more distinct sides retain control over the key terms of the interaction, as opposed to the intermediary taking control of those terms".[83]

Diligent readers may discern a certain tension between this description of *pure* 43
multi-sided platforms and the previous paragraph on the platform operator's network orchestrator model. Earlier, it was argued that platform operators are not neutral, exerting influence to stimulate transactions between users.[84] The subsequent paragraph, on the other hand, seems to suggest that the users on the platform should, nevertheless, retain control over the key terms of the interaction, such as the quality of the services or how to market services.[85] Upon closer inspection, however, both perspectives are reconcilable. One way to look at it is to portray platform operators as "permissive potentates". According to Vallas and Schor, platforms "exercise power over economic transactions by delegating control among the participants".[86] A platform operator is a potentate in the sense that the operator is relatively free to decide the extent to which users, like you and me, are allowed to keep control over the key terms of their interactions. Unilateral changes to the terms and conditions will enable the platform to give and retake control. Uber could, for instance, design its platforms allowing passengers to handpick a driver,[87] but instead, it opts to dispatch drivers to

79. John Zysman & Martin Kenney, *The Next Phase in the Digital Revolution: Platforms, Abundant Computing; Growth and Employment* 5 (ETLA 2016).
80. OECD, *Tax Challenges Arising from Digitalisation – Interim Report 2018: Inclusive Framework on BEPS* 30 (OECD 2018).
81. Andrei Hagiu & Julian Wright, *Multi-Sided Platforms*, 43 International Journal of Industrial Organization 162, 162 (2015).
82. "By 'affiliation' we mean that users on each side consciously make platform-specific investments that are necessary in order for them to be able to directly interact with each other". *Ibid.*, 163.
83. *Ibid.*, 163.
84. *See also*, Ignasi Beltran de Heredia Ruiz, *Work in the Platform Economy: Arguments for an Employment Relationship* 13–14 (Huygens Editorial 2019).
85. *See also*, Cristiano Codagnone, Jacob Matthews & Athina Karatzogianni, *Platform Economics: Rhetoric and Reality in the Sharing Economy* 21 (Emerald Publishing Limited 2018).
86. Steven Vallas & Juliet B. Schor, *What Do Platforms Do? Understanding the Gig Economy*, 46 Annual Review of Sociology 273, 282 n. 1 (2020).
87. Belgian taxi companies are putting their weight behind "Wave-a-Cab" to compete with Uber. Wave-a-Cab wants passengers to choose their own carrier, instead of the platform dispatching one on the basis of parameters. X, *Nieuwe 'Vlaamse Uber' zet passagier aan de knoppen*, De

passengers based on several metrics automatically. Other app-based platforms, such as those that focus on cleaning or caring services, often do provide workers with more autonomy.[88] These platforms for household services typically permit workers and clients to select the opposite party to the transaction personally, and, frequently, allow them to negotiate the remuneration. To that extent, for instance, Care.com comes closer to a pure multi-sided platform; it is operated by a more permissive potentate than platforms such as Uber, Lyft, Postmates and Instacart. The latter more severely constrain workers' autonomy.[89]

44 Regarding the operators that run genuine platforms, such as Care.com, even when the platform's workers can personally choose the opposite party and negotiate the price, the platform operator can still implement new features to foster transactions. The operator can, for instance, develop more transparent payment methods or offer optional insurance packages. Such features benefit existing users and might even attract new users, but they do not significantly increase the platform's (direct) control over the interaction's key terms, e.g. the client's identity and price.[90] What is confusing, however, is that many platform operators decide to take it a step further. They effectively dictate the key terms of the interaction. In labour platforms' quest to reduce transaction costs, raise the quality of service or increase profit, some operators decide to, for example, impose stringent pricing systems. Like a potentate, they can subsequently alter the pricing system. An example is the operators' decision to allow or prohibit tips.[91] Although it might be too strong to claim that these businesses no longer operate "platforms", what is clear is that Uber, Lyft, Instacart, Postmates and others deviate sharply from the template of a pure multi-sided platform. Furthermore, confusingly, these ambivalent platforms are precisely the ones that have drawn the most attention from labour law scholars.

Tijd (24 February 2021), https://www.tijd.be/ondernemen/auto/nieuwe-vlaamse-uber-zet-passagier-aan-de-knoppen/10286716.html. Furthermore, as part of the effort to prevent drivers from being considered employees in California, Uber had allowed drivers to see passengers' destination before accepting the job, and to individually set their pricing. However, more recent reporting suggests that change might be reversed as it damages Uber's overall services. Carolyn Said, *Uber May Stop Letting Drivers See Destinations and Name Prices*, San Francisco Chronicle (5 April 2021), https://www.sfchronicle.com/business/article/Uber-may-stop-letting-drivers-see-destinations-16078491.php.

88. Julia Ticona, Alexandra Mateescu & Alex Rosenblat, *Beyond Disruption: How Tech Shapes Labor Across Domestic Work & Ridehailing* 20–24 (Data&Society 2018).

89. Ticona, Mateescu and Rosenblat call platforms which give users a lot of freedom to self-determine how, when and in return for what, to work "marketplace" platforms. Others, such as Lyft and Postmates, are "on-demand" platforms. *Ibid.*, 21.

90. "Where the interaction involves trading, the key terms of the interaction could be the pricing, bundling, marketing and delivery of the goods or services traded, the ability to determine the nature and quality of services offered, the terms and conditions, etc". Hagiu & Wright, *supra* n. 81, at 163.

91. Dave Lee, *Amazon Ordered to Pay Back $61.7m After Pocketing Delivery Drivers' Tips*, Financial Times (2 February 2021), https://www.ft.com/content/92abc0ac-1c58-46a6-94d9-2c16b31aa890.

SUBCHAPTER 2. THE IMPLICATIONS OF THIS DESCRIPTION

Information society services – The differentiation between platforms that enable users to set and control their own terms of service and platforms that do not is not only pertinent for academic purposes; it is also relevant under the law. Uber is a platform operator that exerts significant control over its workforce and is far from a pure multi-sided platform. As a result, the Court of Justice of the European Union ruled that, overall, Uber does not provide information society services under Directive 2000/31/EC.[92] Uber created a market for passenger transport and exercises decisive influence over that market.[93] The enterprise cannot be considered a mere provider of information society services but engages in transport services. This ruling differs from the judgment on Airbnb, which, according to the CJEU, does provide information society services. One of the reasons is that, unlike Uber, Airbnb does not exercise decisive influence over the conditions under which the services on the platform are provided.[94] 45

Van Acker has suggested that the distinction between the two platforms seems to hinge on whether the platform operator creates a market and exercises decisive influence over market participants, particularly by setting the price and picking the service provider.[95] Similarly, Grozdanovski argues that the critical difference is whether the platform operator only links the supply and demand of services (such as Airbnb) or actively intervenes by defining the service's economically relevant aspects (such as Uber).[96] To put it in Hagiu's and Wright's words, Airbnb comes closer to the ideal of a pure multi-sided platform than Uber. For economists, "[t]he real issue is related with control, i.e. whether there is direct interaction [e.g. Airbnb] or rather the control exerted by platform operators introduce [sic] an ambivalence between market and hierarchy".[97] As illustrated by the rulings of the CJEU, this issue is also relevant from 46

92. Directive (EU) 2000/31/EC of the European Parliament and of the Council of 8 June 2000 on certain legal aspects of information society services, in particular electronic commerce, in the Internal Market, OJ L 178, 17 July 2000.
93. Uber "provided an application without which those drivers would not have been led to provide transport services, and the persons who wished to make an urban journey would not have used the services provided by those drivers", and, Uber "exercised decisive influence over the conditions under which services were provided by those drivers, inter alia by determining the maximum fare, by collecting that fare from the customer before paying part of it to the non-professional driver of the vehicle, and by exercising a certain control over the quality of the vehicles, the drivers and their conduct, which could, in some circumstances, result in their exclusion". Court of Justice of the European Union: Case C-320/16, *Uber France SAS v. Nabil Bensalem*, 10 April 2018, ECLI:EU:C:2018:221. *See also*, Court of Justice of the European Union: Case C-434/15, *Asociación Profesional Elite Taxi v. Uber Systems Spain, SL*, 20 December 2017, ECLI:EU:C:2017:981.
94. Court of Justice of the European Union: Case C-390/18, *X v. YA, Airbnb Ireland UC, and others*, 19 December 2019, ECLI:EU:C:2019:1112.
95. Liesbet Van Acker, *C-390/18 – The CJEU Finally Clears the Air(bnb) Regarding Information Society Services*, 9 Journal of European Consumer and Market Law 77, 79–80 n. 2 (2020).
96. Ljupcho Grozdanovski, *Les Services Fournis par les Plateformes Numériques: Quelle Qualification Juridique Pour Quels Enjeux?*, 139 Journal des tribunaux 449, 455–456 n. 6818 (2020).
97. Francesco Bogliacino, Cristiano Codagnone, Valeria Cirillo & Dario Guarascio, *Quantity and Quality of Work in the Platform Economy* (Global Labor Organization 2019).

a legal perspective.[98] Only Airbnb provides information society services. Hence, only Airbnb hosts – not Uber drivers – can enjoy the protections under EU Regulation No. 2019/1150 on promoting fairness and transparency for business users of online intermediation services.[99]

47 **Ambivalent platforms** – Despite what has been said in the previous Subchapter, the dissertation will also refer to the enterprises that operate *ambivalent* platforms, such as Uber, as platform operators. Simultaneously, although ambivalent platforms are not entirely excluded from this research, the dissertation will, nonetheless, focus primarily on pure or *genuine* DLPs. This entails that, by and large, platform operators which exert the amount of control necessary to be accused of bogus self-employment are only discussed at the fringes. The research is, so to speak, more focused on LinkedIn than Uber.

48 Still, because the boundaries between genuine and ambivalent platforms are not all that clear, in the end, many of the platforms researched, such as online crowdwork platforms, might resemble more closely Uber than LinkedIn. Indeed, platform operators on the labour market seem inclined to minimise costs and maximise control.[100] This inclination, arguably, incites labour platforms to move away from the template of a pure multi-sided platform into the realm of labour law. However, among other things, because the classification of their workers as employees is perceived as a risk to their business model, platform operators will implement relatively obscure means of control.[101] Workers, for example, are left wondering how the system actually works.[102] Oftentimes, platforms also rely on multiple mechanisms, which add up to a form of fuzzy but unwavering control.[103] The fact that platform operators guard their systems like trade secrets further complicates things.[104]

98. Not only the CJEU considers this relevant for legal purposes. *See also, e.g.*, Denk Fabrik, *Eckpunte des BMAS: Faire Arbeit in der Plattformökonomie* (Bundesministerium für Arbeit und Soziales 2020).
99. Regulation (EU) No. 2019/1150 of the European Parliament and of the Council of 20 June 2019 on promoting fairness and transparency for business users of online intermediation services, OJ L 186, 11 July 2019; Pieter Van Cleynenbreugel, *Will Deliveroo and Uber be Captured by the Proposed EU Platform Regulation? You'd Better Watch Out...*, European Law Blog (12 March 2019), https://europeanlawblog.eu/2019/03/12/will-deliveroo-and-uber-be-captured-by-the-proposed-eu-platform-regulation-youd-better-watch-out/.
100. Codagnone, Matthews & Karatzogianni, *supra* n. 85, at 34.
101. Mirela Ivanova, Joanna Bronowicka, Eva Kocher & Anne Degner, *The App as a Boss? Control and Autonomy in Application-Based Management* 12–18 (Europa-Universität Viadrina 2018). *See also*, Aaron Shapiro, *Between Autonomy and Control: Strategies of Arbitrage in the "On-demand" Economy*, 20 New Media & Society 2954, 2959–2967 n. 8 (2018); Alex J. Wood, Mark Graham, Vili Lehdonvirta & Isis Hjorth, *Good Gig, Bad Gig: Autonomy and Algorithmic Control in the Global Gig Economy*, 33 Work, Employment and Society 56, 56–75 n. 1 (2019); Duggan, Sherman, Carbery & McDonnell, *supra* n. 76, at 119–121.
102. *E.g.* Dyna Rochmyaningsih, *"Only Gojek Knows this Mystery"*, Rest of World (18 May 2021), https://restofworld.org/2021/only-gojek-knows-this-mystery/.
103. Alex Veen, Tom Barratt & Caleb Goods, *Platform-Capital's 'App-etite' for Control: A Labour Process Analysis of Food-Delivery Work in Australia*, 34 Work, Employment and Society 388, 396–397 n. 3 (2020).
104. Janine Berg, *Protecting Workers in the Digital Age: Technology, Outsourcing, and the Growing Precariousness of Work*, 41 Comparative Labor Law & Policy Journal 69, 80 n. 1 (2019).

The platform narrative – For such reasons, the determination of platform workers' employment status in court will often be tricky. A challenge that becomes even more complicated due to platform operators' efforts to twist language in their favour. As observed by Gillespie – an information scientist – "[a] term like 'platform' does not drop from the sky, or emerge in some organic, unfettered way from the public discussion. It is drawn from the available cultural vocabulary by stakeholders with specific aims, and carefully massaged so as to have particular resonance for particular audiences inside particular discourses".[105] Many social media "platforms", for instance, initially embraced freedom of expression. Contrary to online news outlets, which are curated, people associate platforms with free speech.[106] However, the legal provisions that prevent these platforms from being held accountable for users' illegal content and hate speech have come under increasing pressure, both in the United States and in the EU.[107] Some argue that if the US Congress follows through and amends section 230 of the Communications Decency Act, "online platforms might effectively be required to proactively moderate their services for illegal content".[108] In short, if changes are implemented, soon, social media companies might have to take more responsibility for what happens on their platforms. 49

A similar process is underway within the area of labour law; indeed, as the ILO observes, "it is possible to detect considerable movement away from the 'no responsibility' pole in many countries".[109] Regulators seem less willing to stand by while platform operators wash their hands in innocence. As remarked by De Stefano and Aloisi in 2018, by now, many would agree that "a clean-up exercise is due. Using euphemisms such as 'Runners', 'Riders', 'Taskers', 'Clickers', 'Authors', 'Hourlies' or even 'Friends' is a clear attempt to hide the fact that human labour is at stake".[110] Similarly, many platforms have misused the word "sharing (economy)" to, for example, normalise precarious work.[111] Once this narrative of Uber and others being part of the sharing economy fell into disuse,[112] denominators like the "gig economy" 50

105. Tarleton Gillespie, *The Politics of 'Platforms'*, 12 New Media & Society 347, 359 n. 3 (2010).
106. Denis Masmejan, *Débat Public en Ligne et Protection des Libertés de Communication* 41 (Office fédéral de la communication 2020).
107. The European Commission is undertaking efforts to tackle illegal content on platforms. *See*, European Commission, *Proposal for Regulation of the European Parliament and of the Council on a Single Market for Digital Services (Digital Services Act) and Amending Directive 2000/31/EC* (European Commission 2020). There have been lively discussions in the United States about amending the Communications Decency Act. *See*, Alina Selyukh, *Section 230: A Key Legal Shield For Facebook, Google Is About To Change*, NPR (21 March 2018), https://www.npr.org/sections/alltechconsidered/2018/03/21/591622450/section-230-a-key-legal-shield-for-facebook-google-is-about-to-change.
108. Jeff Kosseff, *First Amendment Protection for Online Platforms*, 35 Computer Law & Security Review 1, 15 n. 5 (2019).
109. ILO, *supra* n. 25, at 237.
110. De Stefano & Aloisi, *supra* n. 60, at 11. *See also*, Jeremias Prassl, *Humans as a Service: The Promise and Perils of Work in the Gig Economy* 31–50 (OUP 2018); Sam Harnett, *Words Matter: How Tech Media Helped Write Gig Companies into Existence* 169, 169–188 (Deepa Das Acevedo ed., *Beyond the Algorithm: Qualitative Insights for Gig Work Regulation*, CUP 2020).
111. Daniel G. Cockayne, *Sharing and Neoliberal Discourse: The Economic Function of Sharing in the Digital On-demand Economy*, 77 Geoforum 73, 73–82 (2016).
112. Juliet B. Schor, *After the Gig: How the Sharing Economy got Hijacked and How to Win It Back* (University of California Press 2020).

and "platform economy" took over. Oei argues that these descriptions might likewise benefit platform operators.[113] As Eurofound rightly points out, the gig economy is associated with "trade in low-value, one-off exchanges".[114] Therefore, even if a courier works non-stop on a food-delivery platform, as long as the work remains framed as gig work, then, intuitively, that line of work does not seem to warrant extensive labour law protections. Regarding the use of the term "platform economy", as noted above, if Wright and Hagiu are to be believed, genuine platforms seem antithetical to labour law.[115] Consequently, this description might also stack the deck in a way that makes it easier to conclude that workers are self-employed rather than employed.

51 Due to these observations, it is appropriate to be somewhat critical of the narratives associated with platform work. The temporary staffing industry, for example, used to also portray itself as a "neutral facilitator of market forces, bringing enhanced efficiency, convenience and flexibility to both the workforce and employers".[116] This depiction is not so different from what platform operators argue nowadays. However, in time, as was the case for the temporary staffing industry, the opposite may likewise turn out to be the case for the platform economy. The contemporary legal structure surrounding temporary agency work is partially the result of these businesses' lobbying efforts. In the United Kingdom, Manpower actively lobbied to gain the legal status of an employer. This status was instrumental to its legitimacy.[117] In France, an agreement between Manpower and the *Confédération Générale du Travail* in 1969 "breached the hitherto unified political opposition to agency employment in France and enabled the codified legalisation of TEA activities".[118] Temporary work agencies have, in other words, explored pathways at the national level to become embedded in these local labour markets. Forty years after these initial efforts, Peck et al. conclude that due to the temporary staffing industry's global influence, the staffing industry "must be seen as an active agent in the process of labour market 'deregulation' [...]. Staffing companies have been gambling on, investing in and

113. "This essay therefore argues that scholars and policymakers should be vigilant about the ways in which 'gig talk' has been used to promote and shape legal outcomes". Shu-Yi Oei, *The Trouble with Gig Talk: Choice of Narrative and the Worker Classification Fights*, 81 Law and Contemporary Problems 107, 111 n. 3 (2018).

114. Eurofound, *Non-standard Forms of Employment: Recent Trends and Future Prospects* 21 (Eurofound 2018).

115. Platform operators like to present their services according to a "market logic", instead of a "corporation logic", even if, in reality, "gig workers are subject to HRM activities that are needed to control their actions, which is seen as necessary to grow the platform". Jeroen Meijerink, Anne Keegan & Tanya Bondarouk, *Having Their Cake and Eating it too? Online Labor Platforms and Human Resource Management as a case of Institutional Complexity*, The International Journal of Human Resource Management 1, 34 (2021).

116. Jamie A. Peck & Nikolas Theodore, *Temped Out? Industry Rhetoric, Labor Regulation and Economic Restructuring in the Temporary Staffing Business*, 23 Economic and Industrial Democracy 143, 157 n. 2 (2002).

117. Chris Forde, *"You know we are not an Employment Agency": Manpower, Government, and the Development of the Temporary Help Industry in Britain*, 9 Enterprise & Society 337, 362 n. 2 (2008).

118. Paul Brook & Christina Purcell, *The Resistible Rise of the Temporary Employment Industry in France*, 41 Economic and Industrial Democracy 121, 138 n. 1 (2020).

capitalizing upon the progressive 'deregulation' of first-world labour markets".[119] In the case of labour platforms, a similar trajectory may well unfold if platforms continue to receive preferential treatment, as happened, for instance, in Belgium and some states in the US.[120]

For the remainder of this dissertation, the term "DLP" will refer to a network that a platform operator algorithmically manages with the aim of bringing about interactions between workers and users. Businesses, households and end-market consumers can all be users of said platforms. Platform operators are expected to, in principle, allow the workers and users to control the key terms of their interactions. Nevertheless, in order to maximise their platforms' commercial success, platform operators may decide to centralise control on their platform and constrain workers' and users' autonomy. Depending on the techniques used by a platform operator, the law may, at some point, classify the platform operator as the legal employer of the platform worker. The point at which platform workers become regarded as bound by an employment relationship thereby varies between countries.[121] After all, "[t]he definition of the personal scope of application of any labour law system is an intensely and deeply political exercise. This exercise is shaped by fundamental decisions over the distribution of risks, rights, and duties between workers, employers, and society at large".[122] In the near future, it is pretty likely for ride-hailing companies, such as Uber and Lyft, to operate based on employment contracts in certain countries and with self-employed drivers in others. What remains to be seen, however, is whether, over time, Uber and Lyft for instance will accept to offer their services in legal systems where the competent authorities demand this type of work to be executed by employees.[123] Suppose such 52

119. Jamie Peck, Nik Theodore & Kevin Ward, *Constructing Markets for Temporary Labour: Employment Liberalization and the Internationalization of the Staffing Industry*, 5 Global Networks 3, 22–23 n. 1 (2005). *See also*, Neil M. Coe & David C. Jordhus-Lier, *Constrained Agency? Re-Evaluating the Geographies of Labour*, 35 Progress in Human Geography 211, 226–227 n. 2 (2010).

120. De Stefano, Durri, Stylogiannis & Wouters, *supra* n. 13, at 18–19.

121. For instance, in China, food-delivery couriers on Meituan and Ele.me are apparently self-employed even if they work full-time with minimum pay and fixed shifts. Once the order is accepted, couriers are given a challenging delivery time of, for example, 20–30 minutes. All kinds of circumstantial factors, such as the delivery being due under intense weather conditions or destined for an apartment in a skyscraper, could mean the workers arrive too late. As a result, workers are tempted to break traffic rules in order to accomplish the delivery in time. If couriers do not manage to succeed, they are called to order by their superiors, and may suffer pay cuts. X, *Delivery Workers, Trapped in the System*, Chuang (12 November 2020), https://chuangcn.org/2020/11/delivery-renwu-translation/. Although the Chinese courts sometimes do rule in favour of the workers, most courts seem to conclude that these couriers do not fall under the scope of labour and social laws. Zhou, *supra* n. 37, at 32. In case food-delivery platforms were to rely on similar mechanics in EU Member States, chances are high that courts would identify an employment relationship between the worker and platform operator.

122. Nicola Countouris & Valerio De Stefano, *New Trade Union Strategies for New Forms of Employment* 19 (ETUC 2019).

123. There are some indications that platform operators' threats that they will suspend their services if their drivers or couriers are legally classified as employees can be idle. Examples from Switzerland and the United Kingdom illustrate how even a company like Uber, which is radically opposed to its drivers being considered employees, will not necessarily withdraw if labour law is enforced. Matteo Ianni, *Le Canton de Genève Remporte une Victoire Face à Uber*,

conditions remain unacceptable to these individual enterprises. In that case, other companies may come in to provide similar services with employees, such as the Swedish ride-hailing "platform" Bzzt, the American "platform" Alto or the German "platform" CleverShuttle.

AGEFI (2 December 2020), https://agefi.com/actualites/entreprises/le-canton-de-geneve-remporte-une-victoire-detape-face-a-uber; Caroline Davies, *Uber "Willing to Change" as Drivers Get Minimum Wage, Holiday Pay and Pensions*, BBC (17 March 2021), https://www.bbc.com/news/business-56412397.

Chapter 2. Labour Market Intermediaries

SUBCHAPTER 1. THE CONCEPT OF A LABOUR MARKET INTERMEDIARY

A description – The definition given to DLPs is reminiscent of an older concept: labour market intermediaries (LMIs), a resemblance that has not escaped other researchers' attention and which can lead to new insights. Moreover, the similarity is also relevant from a legal perspective since labour market intermediaries are already regulated. For these reasons, Chapters 2 and 3 address how similar or different DLPs and LMIs are. 53

The concept of labour market intermediaries is rarely used in legal scholarship.[124] The law generally relies on different notions to refer to specific forms of LMIs, such as placement agencies, temporary work agencies, sports agents, payroll agencies or private employment agencies. The broader, mostly non-legal concept of LMIs does feature more prominently in economics literature and disciplines such as labour and economic geography. According to Benner et al., LMIs are "organizations – public, private, nonprofit, or membership-based – that help broker the employment relationship through some combination of job matching, training, and career support services".[125] In another notable publication on the topic, Autor defines LMIs as "entities or institutions that interpose themselves between workers and firms to facilitate, inform, or regulate how workers are matched to firms, how work is accomplished, and how conflicts are resolved".[126] 54

Although Benner's description refers to entities that broker an employment relationship, this reference does not seem intended in any legal sense, i.e. services aimed at concluding an employment contract. The researchers in question are preoccupied with how LMIs can affect disadvantaged workers' career opportunities. They ask 55

124. An exception is, *e.g.*, Kendra Strauss & Judy Fudge, *Temporary Work, Agencies and Unfree Labour: Insecurity in the New World* 1, 5-8 (Kendra Strauss & Judy Fudge eds., *Temporary Work, Agencies and Unfree Labour: Insecurity in the New World of Work*, Routledge 2014).

125. Chris Benner, Laura Leete & Manuel Pastor, *Staircases or Treadmills? Labor Market Intermediaries and Economic Opportunity in a Changing Economy* 10 (Russel Sage Foundation 2007).

126. David H. Autor, *Studies of Labor Market Intermediation: Introduction* 1 (David H. Autor ed., *Studies of Labor Market Intermediation*, University of Chicago Press 2009).

themselves, are LMIs staircases or treadmills? The "*sine qua non*" to speak of an intermediary, according to these authors, is the act of "job matching", which is also present in the case of "day-labor sites", for instance.[127] Therefore, the authors do not appear to deliberately limit the concept of LMIs to the brokerage of employment contracts. Their description seems to broadly correspond to the core of Autor's description. He also puts the matching of workers to firms at the centre. Autor does not make any explicit reference to the intermediated relationship's legal characteristics. However, both for Benner and Autor, what does seem to matter is the nature of the parties involved in the matchmaking. Autor explicitly mentions "firms" at the user-side of the interaction. Benner et al. speak of job matching. A "job" arguably connotes that a piece of paid work is being done for a principal or employer.

56 Scholars from various backgrounds have provided alternative descriptions of LMIs. Some economists include LMIs in the list of active matchmakers in a "bilateral search market", a function that would resemble a real estate broker on the housing market.[128] Others have given more precise descriptions. From the point of view of management sciences, Bonet et al. argue that "[t]he common element of all LMIs is that they take over basic aspects of HR management (HRM) that employers would previously have performed themselves".[129] For example, a staffing agency will take on essential aspects of an employer's HR department, even if it only advises on or executes new staffing arrangements. To that extent, whether the agency generates a payslip for an employee or an invoice for an independent contractor does not seem to alter the fact that basic aspects of HRM are passed on to an intermediary. Comparable to Autor and Benner et al., who seem to depict LMIs' demand side as made up of firms or principals/employers, Bonet et al. suggest that these users need to manage human resources.

57 **Platforms as LMIs** – As a result, in summary, an LMI can be described as an entity that interposes itself between a worker and a job provider to "help broker employment relationships",[130] or at least "facilitate, inform, or regulate" job matching,[131] thereby taking over "basic aspects of HR management (HRM) that employers would previously have performed themselves".[132] When thinking about platforms in light of this description, some points are important to stress.

58 First, some types of platforms are clear examples of LMIs. LinkedIn, for instance, has blended the functionalities of a job board with those of a social media platform.[133] This

127. Benner, Leete & Pastor, *supra* n. 125, at 11. *See also*, Enright on labour market intermediaries that are not in the business of generating employment relationships. Bryony Enright, *(Re) considering New Agents: A Review of Labour Market Intermediaries within Labour Geography*, 7 Geography Compass 287, 287–299 n. 4 (2013).

128. Abdullah Yavas,, *Middlemen in Bilateral Search Markets*, 12 Journal of Labor Economics 406, 407 n. 3 (1994).

129. Rocio Bonet, Peter Cappelli & Monika Hamori, *Labor Market Intermediaries and the New Paradigm for Human Resources*, 7 The Academy of Management Annals 341, 347 n. 1 (2013).

130. Benner, Leete & Pastor, *supra* n. 125, at 10.

131. Autor, *supra* n. 126, at 1.

132. Bonet, Cappelli & Hamori, *supra* n. 129, at 347.

133. "Work matters not just for a worker's own sense of meaning; it has an important social dimension as well, allowing people to show others that they live a purposeful life, and offering

is something that might become more prominent in the future,[134] whereby these platforms provide the infrastructure for other labour recruiters to exploit (e.g. "LinkedIn Talent Solutions").[135] Other platforms, such as Freelancer.com, Fiverr and Upwork, more blatantly match enterprises to freelancers than LinkedIn does. They even offer these companies systems to track work progress and payments. Along similar lines, micro-task platforms, such as Amazon Mechanical Turk, are heavily used by business users that systematically rely on crowdworkers' input for their business models.[136] Furthermore, as mentioned below (*infra* no. 61), "automated hiring platforms" are digital alternatives for recruitment agencies. Other "platforms", such as Temper and Wonolo, match "freelancers" to bars and warehouses, offering an alternative to temporary work agencies (*infra* no. 305). Additionally, within the group of what is commonly described as local app-based platform work, some platform operators clearly provide businesses with an external workforce. Customers on Instacart, for instance, buy groceries from affiliated retailers, after which Instacart dispatches a worker to do the shopping and deliver the groceries to the user's doorstep. Clic and Walk sends workers to a local business to photograph the shelves, for example, allowing the suppliers of these local businesses to verify whether their products are properly presented to the public.[137] In summary, many platform operators are not running peer-to-peer platforms; they are allowing businesses to recruit or make use of an external workforce. In the words of Autor: these platforms "interpose themselves between workers and firms to facilitate, inform, or regulate how workers are matched to firms, how work is accomplished, and how conflicts are resolved".[138]

Secondly, entities that solely provide intermediation between workers and end-market **59**
consumers are not LMIs. The obvious example is Uber. Uber passengers can hardly be considered as employers giving out jobs; in fact, Uber is the entity that hands out the work. There is also no chance of there ever being an employment relationship between an Uber driver and an individual passenger. Furthermore, these passengers have not passed any HR-related tasks on to the Uber platform either. Uber's taxi services, therefore, seem hard to characterise as labour market intermediation.

them a chance to gain status and social esteem. Today, social media has supercharged this phenomenon. It is no wonder that LinkedIn, which started as a networking tool to help people find new jobs, is now used by some to broadcast how successful they are and how hard they are working, turning it into a platform for a kind of conspicuous self-agrandizement instead". Daniel Susskind, *A World Without Work: Technology, Automation and How We Should Respond* 218 (Penguin Books 2021).

134. Ioannis Nikolaou, *Social Networking Web Sites in Job Search and Employee Recruitment*, 22 International Journal of Selection and Assessment 179, 187 n. 2 (2014).
135. Most of us use LinkedIn as if it is a professionally oriented social media platform. However, the platform operator offers a bunch of functionalities to businesses and recruiters under the branding "LinkedIn Talent Solutions". Of course, LinkedIn may well contend that it does not practice labour market intermediation itself, merely "facilitating" the process of others. Yet, in reality, it is clearly involved, for instance, when it allows employers to post vacancies on LinkedIn and provides them with access to its analytical tools.
136. Panagiotis G. Ipeirotis, *Analyzing the Amazon Mechanical Turk Marketplace*, 17 ACM Crossroads 16, 21 n. 2 (2010).
137. Clic and Walk's platform workers were reclassified as employees of the platform operator. Cour d'appel de Douai: Case 19/00137, *X v. SA Clic and Walk*, 10 February 2020
138. Autor, *supra* n. 126, at 1.

However, the same is not necessarily true for all of Uber's platforms. Uber Eats, in particular, provides restaurants with access to an external network of food-delivery couriers. It is an LMI that interposes itself between a courier and a restaurant, giving instructions to the courier who delivers the food to the restaurant's customer. The fact that some food-delivery platforms allow restaurants to rely on their personal employees to deliver food orders coming in through the app, moreover, illustrates how it is realistic for there to be an employment relationship between these couriers and restaurants. It is also possible for restaurants to have performed food delivery in the past using their personal employees, and directly responding to customers' orders over the phone. Nowadays, these restaurants may rely on food-delivery platforms to manage self-employed couriers who execute online delivery orders instead of picking up the phone and sending personal employees. In other words, these platforms might have taken over "basic aspects of HR management (HRM) that [restaurants] would previously have performed themselves".[139]

60 Thirdly, notwithstanding the relevance of DLPs needing business users to be an LMI, some platforms without affiliated business users might still qualify as an LMI. Most notably, there are many agencies providing households with access to domestic workers. The agencies thereby provide domestic workers with job opportunities.[140] In such cases, the heads of these households also manage human resources, not to conduct a business but to sustain the home and its members. Therefore, since a platform that matches gardeners, carers or cleaners to households is matching workers to job providers that manage these "human resources", it could likewise be considered an LMI. The example of Helpling in the Netherlands, furthermore, illustrates how each app-based cleaner on the platform can have a direct employment relationship with every separate householder.[141] In other words, by moving between households, Helpling's cleaners are involved in multiple direct employment relationships each week. To facilitate this process, the platform operator may take on specific HR-related tasks from these householders. The operator could, for example, generate automatic payslips or ensure households that the worker's accident insurance is in order, relieving the household from these tasks. To that extent, one could argue that this example of a cleaner on a platform such as Helpling is quite different from an Uber driver. Although householders will not always legally employ platform workers, as most notably shown by Helpling's reliance on self-employed cleaners in most other countries, at least the potential is there;[142] these platforms can relieve households of their obligations as employers/principals. Hence, when looking at DLPs through

139. Bonet, Cappelli & Hamori, *supra* n. 129, at 347.

140. *E.g.*, Simone Leiber, Kamil Matuszczyk & Verena Rossow, *Private Labor Market Intermediaries in the Europeanized Live-in Care Market between Germany and Poland: A Typology*, 65 Zeitschrift für Sozialreform 365, 365–392 n. 3 (2019).

141. Rechtbank Amsterdam: Case 7299840 CV EXPL 18-23708, *Federatie Nederlandse Vakbeweging v. Helpling Netherlands B.V.*, 1 July 2019, ECLI:NL:RBAMS:2019:4546.

142. Dutch law contains a specific type of employment contract that can be concluded between cleaners and households. Helpling relies on this unique employment contract to structure its activities in the country, by establishing such employment contracts between its cleaners and users. In contrast to the Netherlands, most other legal systems do not contain such a specific employment contract for cleaning personnel. In these other legal systems, Helpling tends to simply rely on self-employed cleaners. Yet, if these countries were to make adequate changes

the lens of LMIs, one should, arguably, differentiate between platforms that, on the one hand, match businesses or households to jobseekers and, on the other, platform operators that recruit workers to meet consumer demand for the platform's services.

SUBCHAPTER 2. THE RISE OF DIGITAL LABOUR MARKET INTERMEDIATION

Intermediation has gone digital – The market for private employment services was already quite diverse by the 1980s.[143] The incorporation of ICT technologies was a crucial subsequent development that has affected how employment services take place.[144] Job boards appeared in the 1990s, speeding up the application process compared to newspaper ads. Over time, the methods used to screen and filter jobseekers grew more sophisticated. For instance, Ajunwa and Greene argue that modern-day "automated hiring platforms" are a continuation of such developments. Persons who wish to apply for employment at Target or Walmart might have to do so through a platform.[145] Those platforms would be unlike earlier forms of LMIs. Automated hiring platforms are "implemented in similar fashion across different organizations and workplaces and [are distinct] in their constant, cloud-based connections to their designers – affording persistent adjustment and data analysis".[146] Supermarkets, retailers and other businesses rely on these platforms to recruit employees; they are the "platformed" successor to recruitment agencies.[147] 61

Notwithstanding such notable developments, little is actually being written on the connections between older forms of digital intermediation and its reiteration in the platform economy.[148] The OECD, for example, acknowledges the similarities, but it does not inquire into the differences. Its *Employment Outlook* from 2019 notes how digital platforms "can help employers find workers for tasks that their existing employees cannot perform, thereby enlarging the labour market by expanding opportunities in it", and, "[s]imilarly, digital intermediaries, such as commercial job boards, can provide access to a large number of vacancies and worker profiles, significantly reducing search costs for both workers and employers".[149] As such, the organisation stressed some of the benefits of digital intermediation, irrespective of 62

to their laws, cleaners on Helpling and other platforms could, theoretically, become engaged in some form of employment contract.

143. ILO, *Report VI The Role of Private Employment Agencies in the Functioning of Labour Markets* 9 (ILO 1994).
144. On the effects for public employment services, *see* IDB, WAPES & OECD, *The World of Public Employment Services* 114 and 132 (OECD 2015).
145. Ifeoma Ajunwa & Daniel Greene, *Platforms at Work: Automated Hiring Platforms and Other New Intermediaries in the Organization of Work* 61, 63 and 74–78 (Steve P. Vallas & Anne Kovalainen eds., *Work and Labor in the Digital Age*, Emerald Publishing Limited 2019). *See also*, Ifeoma Ajunwa, *The Paradox of Automation as Anti-Bias Intervention*, 41 Cardozo Law Review 1671, 1671–1742 n. 4 (2020), (1671).
146. *Ibid.*, 81.
147. ILO, *supra* n. 25, at 106.
148. A notable exception is Lenaerts et al., *supra* n. 56.
149. OECD, *OECD Employment Outlook 2019: The Future of Work* 155 (OECD 2019).

the entity being a digital platform or intermediary. Those benefits seem significant.[150] According to Autor, digital intermediation would, *inter alia*, allow LMIs: to make more information available, implement more effective search mechanisms, update the registers continually, and disperse job vacancies among a wider public while, at the same time, making it cheaper to do so.[151] Moreover, the information circulated online can remain directed at a wide audience and, simultaneously, become more customised to the individual, with more opportunities for interaction between interested parties.[152]

63 Based on a comparison of data from 2008–2009 and 1998–2000, an article titled "Is internet job search still ineffective?" also suggests that the effectiveness of online job-searching has increased significantly.[153] The researchers speculate that this might have something to do with network effects. The number of participants on these websites has increased, probably leading to more and better matches. The websites' designs have also improved, and websites have increased their specificity in the sense that they increasingly target niches, or manage to identify the right matches. Furthermore, readers of online job vacancies have become actors who can immediately apply for the job.[154] Along these lines, there is little to suggest that online job-searching has become any less effective since 2009. If anything, research from 2015 by the Boston Consulting Group and Recruit Works Institute pointed to job sites and standard referrals as the two most effective channels of finding a job.[155]

64 Longstanding private employment agencies and investors seem to recognise the potential of these digital services. Companies, such as Monster.com and LinkedIn, have transformed the recruitment industry.[156] Monster.com, one of the pioneers in

150. *E.g.*, on the (potential) benefits for young workers, *see* Christopher Stanton & Catherine Thomas, *Landing the First Job: The Value of Intermediaries in Online Hiring*, 83 Review of Economic Studies 810, 810–854 n. 2 (2016).
151. David H. Autor, *Wiring the Labor Market*, 15 Journal of Economic Perspectives 25, 26 and 30 n. 1 (2001).
152. Brian R. Dineen & David G. Allen, *Internet Recruiting 2.0: Shifting Paradigms* 383, 388–392 (Daniel M. Cable & Kang Yang Trevor Yu eds., *The Oxford Handbook of Recruitment*, OUP 2013).
153. Peter Kuhn & Hani Mansour, *Is Internet Job Search Still Ineffective?*, 124 Economic Journal 1213, 1230 n. 581 (2014). Earlier research from one of these authors had suggested that it was ineffective. Peter Kuhn & Mikal Skuterud, *Internet Job Search and Unemployment Durations*, 94 The American Economic Review 218, 230 n. 1 (2004).
154. This development has been associated with a move from web 1.0 to web 2.0. Maria De Hoyos et al., *Literature Review on Employability, Inclusion and ICT, Report 2: ICT and Employability* 49 (Publications Office of the European Union 2013).
155. Kazumasa Sakurai & Yukio Okubo, *Job Seeker Trends 2015: Channels, Search Time, and Income Change* 5 (The Boston Consulting Group & Recruit Works Institute 2015). "In Germany and South Korea, job seekers who used the internet had respectively 7.1 and 12.7 percentage points higher probability of being reemployed in the next 12 month". Farrukh Suvankulov, Marco Chi Keung Lau & Frankie Ho Chi Chau, *Job Search on the Internet and its Outcome*, 22 Internet Research 298, 313 n. 3 (2012).
156. Ken Sundheim, *The Internet's Profound Impact On The Recruiting Industry*, Forbes (2 April 2013), https://www.forbes.com/sites/kensundheim/2013/04/02/the-internets-profound-impact-on-the-recruiting-industry/?sh=6ee67a327070.

large scale digital job search, was acquired by the Dutch human resources company Randstad once Monster's market value had collapsed.[157] Other job boards such as Indeed or Glassdoor, all of which provide similar services, have been acquired by a big Japanese HR company. Moreover, of course, Microsoft got hold of LinkedIn in exchange for roughly USD 26 billion. The price tag signals how there is money to be made by digitally matching the supply and demand for labour, partly due to the data generated by these labour markets and the possibility of charging fees.[158] Big corporations seem to have taken notice. Also, Uber, for instance, announced in the second half of 2019 that it would launch Uber Works in Chicago, Miami and Dallas to match on-demand workers to enterprises.[159] As such, the company seems bent on diversifying its "platform portfolio", matching workers to work wherever possible.

Challenges - Although the widespread interest among jobseekers, employers and investors suggests these services have tremendous potential, it does not mean that they are without their challenges. The internet may make it easier, for instance, to advertise jobs that do not exist, aiming to find people who might prove helpful later.[160] This practice occurs, even though some legal systems consider such practices abusive, hence, prohibit the dispersal of fictitious jobs.[161] Another challenge has to do with businesses' reluctance to hire categories of workers that they expect might have hidden flaws. This mindset has, for example, been documented in relation to long-term unemployed people, who are sometimes assumed to remain unemployed for an unknown reason.[162] To limit this risk of adverse selection, among other things, businesses show a particular interest in so-called "passive jobseekers".[163] Passive jobseekers are workers who already have a job and have not necessarily decided 65

157. Monster Worldwide, Inc. was acquired in 2015 for a "meager" USD 429 million. Monster's former market caps had eclipsed USD 7 billion. Ingrid Lunden, *Randstad Buys Monster for $429M as Recruitment Consolidation Continues*, TechCrunch (9 August 2016), https://techcrunch.com/2016/08/08/randstad-buys-monster-for-429m-as-recruitment-consolidation-continues/.
158. Research on the Russian labour market indicates that "[t]he demand for online recruitment and job placement resources significantly increased over the last five to ten years: the share of companies who use the internet to recruit personnel has grown from 60% in 2010 to 76% in 2010–2014, while the share of job seekers using the internet to find employment in 2006– 2014 increased from 13% to 49%". Sergey Roshchin, Sergey Solntsev & Dmitry Vasilyev, *Recruiting and Job Search Technologies in the Age of Internet*, 11 Foresight and STI Governance 33, 41 n. 4 (2017).
159. The subsidiary has in the meantime been discontinued because COVID-19 forced the company to concentrate on its "core mobility and delivery platforms". Natasha Lomas, *Uber Launches a Shift-Work Finder App, Uber Works, Starting in Chicago*, TechCrunch (3 October 2019), https://techcrunch.com/2019/10/03/uber-launches-a-shift-work-finder-app-uber-works-starting-in-chicago/; X, *Uber to Close its Uber Works Staffing Operations*, Staffing Industry Analysts (19 May 2020), https://www2.staffingindustry.com/Editorial/Daily-News/Uber-to-close-its-Uber-Works-staffing-operations-53856.
160. Peter Cappelli, *Your Approach to Hiring Is All Wrong*, 97 Harvard Business Review 48, 50 and 52 n. 3 (2019).
161. ILO, *Report IV (1) Revision of the Fee-Charging Employment Agencies Convention (Revised), 1949 (No. 96)* 74 (ILO 1996).
162. John Atkinson, Lesley Giles & Nigel Meager, *Employment, Recruitment and the Unemployed* 128–129 (The Institute for Employment Studies, University of Sussex 1996).
163. Alice O. Nakamura et al., *Jobs Online* 27, 36–37 (David H. Autor ed., *Studies of Labor Market Intermediation*, University of Chicago Press 2009).

to give up on this job, but are in a state of mind that could have them transition to another employer. The ease with which employees can casually search for jobs online, or be approached by recruiters, may have boosted this phenomenon of "passive job-seeking".[164] Many registered users on business-oriented social networking sites are interested in access to new career opportunities.[165] Stevenson even contends that "[t]he vast majority of workers using the Internet to gather information about employment are those who are already employed".[166] Others remark that online job-searching risks excluding vulnerable groups in society who feel less at home in this digital environment, such as the less educated.[167] These three examples – fictitious jobs, eyeing passive jobseekers, "digital inequality" – illustrate how digital intermediation might exacerbate certain tendencies.

SUBCHAPTER 3. THE PURPOSES OF LABOUR MARKET INTERMEDIATION

66 **Three purposes of intermediation** – The previous paragraph suggests that technological developments and new forms of labour market intermediation may affect labour market dynamics in complex ways. However, the fact that new technology may, *inter alia*, give rise to new recruitment strategies does not necessarily mean that the underlying reasons why workers and employers use these intermediaries have changed. Therefore, we will turn our attention to the labour market intermediation's purpose, after which a comparison will be made with the literature on DLPs. An article written by Benner can serve as our starting point. He argues that LMIs have (at least) three functions for workers and employers. They reduce transaction costs, construe social and business networks, and manage the risk inherent in labour relations by reshuffling risks among labour market participants.[168]

67 **First purpose: Transaction costs** – The first function of LMIs is to reduce transaction costs. This observation draws, amongst others, on Coase's work and his theory on the nature of the firm.[169] The author asserted that using the market to coordinate human activities through its "price mechanism"[170] also involves costs. A clear component of this is the price paid to discover the relevant information, i.e. "search costs". In

164. Sam DeKay, *Are Business-Orientated Social Networking Web Sites Useful Resources for Locating Passive Jobseekers? Results of a Recent Study*, 72 Business Communication Quarterly 101, 102–103 n. 1 (2009).
165. Małgorzata Bartosik-Purgat & Barbara Jankowska, *The Use of Social Networking Sites in Job Related Activities: A Cross-cultural Comparison*, 5 Entrepreneurial Business and Economic Review 177, 180 n. 2 (2017).
166. Betsey Stevenson, *The Internet and Job Search* 67, 84 (David H. Autor ed., *Studies of Labor Market Intermediation*, Chicago University Press 2009). *See also*, Nikolaou, *supra* n. 134, at 187.
167. Gökçe Karaoglu, Eszter Hargittai & Minh Hao Nguyen, *Inequality in Online Job Searching in the Age of Social Media*, Information, Communication & Society 1, 1–19 (2021).
168. Chris Benner, *Labour Flexibility and Regional Development: The Role of Labour Market Intermediaries*, 37 Regional Studies 621, 622 n. 6–7 (2003).
169. Ronald H. Coase, *The Nature of the Firm*, 4 Economica 386, 386–405 n. 16 (1937).
170. Coase seems to describe this price mechanism by quoting Salter and referencing Hayek: "'The normal economic system works itself. For its current operation it is under no central control, it needs no central survey. Over the whole range of human activity and human need, supply is adjusted to demand, and production to consumption, by a process that is automatic, elastic

addition to these search costs, one must, subsequently, conclude a contract, which involves a cost to negotiate, a cost to enforce the negotiated contract etc. Williamson illustrates this line of thinking as follows: "[i]n mechanical systems we look for frictions: do the gears mesh, are the parts lubricated, is there needless slippage or other loss of energy? The economic counterpart of friction is transaction costs: do the parties to the exchange operate harmoniously, or are there frequent misunderstandings and conflicts that lead to delays, breakdowns, and other malfunctions?"[171] Coase argued that these transaction costs incited economic actors to establish vertically integrated firms.[172] Jobseekers are asked to sign an employment contract. The firm's managers, who are entitled to wield the managerial prerogatives of an employer, can then direct, monitor and discipline the employees if needed. No need for contract renegotiation or enforcement whenever misunderstandings or conflicts arise in the enterprise. The hierarchical structure imposed by the employment relationship allows for micromanagement; the associated disciplinary power presents "a mighty instrument of flexibility and transaction costs reduction".[173]

Although Coase predominantly focused on the firm and its role in diminishing transaction costs, the author also acknowledged that in specific markets, specialists that sell price information, such as commodity exchanges, may also reduce transaction costs.[174] Other scholars took a closer look at this idea. For example, Stigler contended that private employment agencies' "raison d'être is information, and they should have specialized in the occupations in which information is most difficult for the employer or worker to obtain".[175] A partial explanation for LMIs' presence in the labour market would, in other words, stem from their ability to aggregate information on labour supply and demand, including their capacity to deal with information asymmetries.[176] LMIs make it easier for workers and employers to find one another when required. 68

Information asymmetries – In view of this, DLPs' fixation on data might not come as a surprise when putting things into perspective. LMIs have always aimed at tackling information asymmetry – the worker or employer knowing more than the employer or worker – by developing methods to compel workers and employers to disclose 69

and responsive.' An economist thinks of the economic system as being co-ordinated by the price mechanism and society becomes not an organisation but an organism". *Ibid.*, 387.

171. Oliver E. Williamson, *The Economics of Organization: The Transaction Cost Approach*, 87 American Journal of Sociology 548, 552 n. 3 (1981).

172. The overall picture is much more complex. More modern accounts acknowledge that information processing benefits are only one consideration when deciding to vertically integrate production in a firm instead of contracting on the overall market. *E.g.*, Oliver E. Williamson, *The Vertical Integration of Production: Market Failure Consideration*, 61 The American Economic Review 112, 112–123 n. 2 (1971).

173. Renato Bignami, Giuseppe Casale & Mario Fasani, *Labour Inspection and Employment Relationship* 17 (ILO 2013).

174. Coase, *supra* n. 169, at 390–391.

175. George J. Stigler, *Information in the Labor Market*, 70 Journal of Political Economy 94, 102 n. 5 (1962).

176. Benner, Leete & Pastor, *supra* n. 125, at 13–17.

relevant yet obscure information.[177] These techniques are supposed to mitigate adverse selection, setting the scene for better-informed interactions.[178] DLPs build on this tradition, for instance, by using rate-and-review mechanisms to "collect information that is otherwise difficult to observe both because it is decentralized (in numerous geographic locations) and because service providers have every incentive to conceal low-quality activities".[179] Other methods, such as AI-powered background checks,[180] can similarly benefit the users of intermediation services, making LMIs' services more valuable. Moreover, because the quality of the data fed into a platform's algorithms influences how good the platform's services are,[181] DLPs have every reason to contest employers' and jobseekers' inclination to hide or misrepresent information on the web.[182] Jobseekers would, for example, "over-qualify" themselves in the initial stages.[183] In response, platform operators can establish skill tests to assess a new worker's abilities.[184] Employers may similarly promise many opportunities to advance one's career without sketching an accurate picture of current employees' career paths. This objective data might indicate that the potential for career advancement is modest at best. These days, job sites such as Glassdoor present information on employers' working conditions to inform prospective job applicants. It even publishes a list of "best places to work". So far, DLPs seem to largely refrain from screening their user base in this way. With a lack of such transparency, external initiatives, such as Turkopticon and the Fairwork Foundation, have taken it upon themselves to inform jobseekers about the pros and cons of working on certain online platforms or for specific platform users.

---

177. A straightforward method in this respect is to demand those who want to register on a website to fill in a lot more information than they would do if they were given the choice. The business that maintains the website could benefit from simply demanding an e-mail address and name as this may entice more people to create an account. However, in that case, other users on the website would not have any information about this new registrant except for this e-mail address and a name. In order to construe trust among its users, the website may opt to ask for much more information.
178. Adverse selection can occur, for example, whenever one party to the transaction uses private knowledge that is not shared with the opposite party, even though it is relevant. This gives the party that has the information the upper hand when trying to negotiate their way to the desired outcome. David Autor, *The Economics of Labour Market Intermediation*, VoxEU (30 October 2008), https://voxeu.org/article/economics-labour-market-intermediation.
179. Benjamin G. Edelman & Damien Geradin, *Efficiencies and Regulatory Shortcuts: How Should We Regulate Companies Like Airbnb and Uber?*, 19 Stanford Technology Law Review 293, 299–300 n. 2 (2016).
180. Rebecca Heilweil, *Beware of these Futuristic Background Checks*, Vox/Recode (11 May 2020), https://www.vox.com/recode/2020/5/11/21166291/artificial-intelligence-ai-background-check-checkr-fama.
181. Uma Rani & Parminder Jeet Singh, *Digital Platforms, Data, and Development: Implications for Workers in Developing Economies*, 41 Comparative Labor Law & Policy Journal 263, 271 n. 1 (2019).
182. Relying on untrustworthy information will have pernicious effects on the quality of the intermediary's services as a whole. This may eventually affect the LMIs' bottom line, for instance, because unsatisfied users might blame the mismatch on the intermediary.
183. Autor, *supra* n. 126, at 6.
184. Otto Kässi & Vili Lehdonvirta, *Do Digital Skill Certificates Help New Workers Enter the Market? Evidence from an Online Labour Platform* (OECD 2019).

Neutrality – As described in the previous paragraph, LMIs and DLPs need to deal with both jobseekers' and employers' propensity to hide or misrepresent the facts. To this end, employers and jobseekers are, for instance, provided with tools to effectively screen the information provided by the opposite party.[185] At the same time, by providing such tools, LMIs undertake aspects of HRM that the employers would have otherwise performed independently. If not for the LMI, these employers would have screened the jobseeker using their policies and the tools at their own disposal. Whenever the employer relies on the intermediary's methods to collect and filter information, the LMIs' policies shape the (potential) employer's perception of the situation. To put it bluntly, some fear that if the intermediary provides tool (a) instead of tool (b), the employer may hire employee (a) instead of employee (b). For instance, research on an online labour market concluded that workers who are recommended by the platform have to bid "about 16% higher to be just as preferred as that same seller without a platform recommendation".[186] Also, other studies "indicate that, confronted with the extreme heterogeneity of the labour pool that can be accessed through digital platforms, service requesters rely excessively on references and ratings".[187] When potential employers do this, the situation can become problematic; for example, once jobseekers know how to game the system and use the LMIs' or DLPs' systems to their own advantage.[188] Worker (a) may then have been selected because of prior knowledge about tool (a) instead of being the best match on the job board or platform. 70

More broadly, in terms of how LMIs operate, some have contended that LMIs are not entirely neutral. Job boards can compel jobseekers to make their profiles visible to any interested employer without giving them equal access to the job advertisements of their choice.[189] This disparity is one example of how job boards continuously frame the flow of information, deciding what information reaches employers and jobseekers, respectively, as well as how that information is presented.[190] Furthermore, other researchers are worried that LMIs might reflect and even uphold gender and racial biases through their screening and selection methods.[191] This could be the case, in particular, for LMIs that actively pursue matchmaking, such as headhunters. These 71

185. Carlo Gianelle, *Labor Market Intermediaries Make the World Smaller*, 24 Journal of Evolutionary Economics 951, 954 n. 5 (2014).
186. Moshe A. Barach, Joseph M. Golden & John J. Horton, *Steering in Online Markets: The Role of Platform Incentives and Credibility*, 66 Management Science 4047, 4048 n. 9 (2020).
187. Engels & Sherwood, *supra* n. 72, at 15.
188. Cappelli, *supra* n. 160, at 55–56. This is also relevant in the platform economy. Will Sutherland, Mohammad H. Jarrahi, Michael Dunn & Sarah B. Nelson, *Work Precarity and Gig Literacies in Online Freelancing*, 34 Work, Employment and Society 457, 470 n. 3 (2020).
189. Emmanuelle Marchal, Kevin Mellet & Géraldine Rieucau, *Job Board Toolkits: Internet Matchmaking and Changes in Job Advertisements*, 60 Human Relations 1091, 1110 n. 7 (2007).
190. Bonet, Cappelli & Hamori, *supra* n. 129, at 353. "LMIs play an active role in shaping how people are employed, who becomes employed and where people are employed". Enright, *supra* n. 127, at 295.
191. George F. Dreher, Jeong-Yeon Lee & Thomas A. Clerkin, *Mobility and Cash Compensation: The Moderating Effects of Gender, Race, and Executive Search Firms*, 37 Journal of Management 651, 675 n. 3 (2011). "We suggest that intermediaries' screening behavior can set gender segregation in motion even before the initial set of candidates is considered by the final employer, because by then the intermediary has already played a role in shaping the candidate pool". Isabel

intermediaries stock and restock their "pools of actual and potential candidates".[192] The individuals that do not feature in the headhunter's pool of candidates are excluded by default,[193] making it extremely important to guarantee that these processes are free from discriminatory biases.

72 **Second purpose: Network capabilities** – Although the *raison d'être* of LMIs, according to economists, may well relate to information processing, their role in society is much more complex. Attention should, among other things, also be paid to LMIs' network capabilities. One way to approach this subject is by first introducing the distinction between "internal" and "external" labour markets. An internal labour market has been described as "an administrative unit, such as a manufacturing plant, within which the pricing and allocation of labor is governed by a set of administrative rules and procedures".[194] Businesses of a significant size form these kinds of administrative units with their internal labour market. As an administrative unit, a firm's internal labour market can be distinguished from the overall labour market.[195] The external and internal labour markets are supposedly connected by "ports of entry and exit to and from the internal labor market".[196]

73 In the past, LMIs might have played a somewhat limited role in the labour market because the number of entry ports to, for example, "stereotypical unionised, blue-collar" internal labour markets was limited.[197] Once employed, employees mostly remained devoted to their employer and progressed along the employer's job ladder without much competition from external workers. Both a "psychological contract" between employees and employers, in which loyalty and willingness to learn was repaid with continuity of employment, and legal arrangements, such as seniority pay and notice periods that trailed seniority, underpinned this career within the internal labour market.[198] However, at some point, internal labour market structures began to

---

Fernandez-Mateo & Zella King, *Anticipatory Sorting and Gender Segregation in Temporary Employment*, 57 Management Science 989, 1006 n. 6 (2011).

192. William Finlay & James E. Coverdill, *The Search Game: Organizational Conflicts and the Use of Headhunters*, 40 The Sociological Quarterly 11, 16 n. 1 (1999).

193. Placement agencies for IT professionals would similarly function as gatekeepers that preselect candidate pools. Zella King, Simon Burke & Jim Pemberton, *The 'Bounded' Career: An Empirical Study of Human Capital, Career Mobility and Employment Outcomes in a Mediated Labour Market*, 58 Human Relations 981, 997–1003 n. 8 (2005).

194. Perter B. Doeringer & Michael J. Piore, *Internal Labor Markets and Manpower Analysis* 1–2 (D.C. Heath and Company 1971). At least two distinct types of processes affect these internal labour markets: the firm has procedures through which it creates, changes and eliminates jobs, and its management makes decisions concerning the recruitment of jobseekers and the promotion/demotion of already employed workers. Lawrence T. Pinfield, *The Operation of Internal Labor Markets: Staffing Practices and Vacancy Chains* 3 (Plenum Press 1995).

195. The overall labour market can be described as the entirety of processes that take place between labour demand and labour supply, as well as the associated rules and institutional provisions as a result of which both the allocation and pricing of labour is established. Paul F. van der Heijden et al., *Lexicon van Arbeidsrecht en Arbeidsverhoudingen* 29–30 (Sdu Uitgevers 1997).

196. Doeringer & Piore, *supra* n. 194, at 2.

197. Pinfield, *supra* n. 194, at 19.

198. Leah F. Vosko, *Managing the Margins: Gender, Citizenship, and the International Regulation of Precarious Employment* 59 (OUP 2011).

disintegrate.[199] Employers began to turn their attention to the external labour market. In the United States, according to Cappelli, "[i]n the era of lifetime employment, from the end of World War II through the 1970s, corporations filled roughly 90% of their vacancies through promotions and lateral assignments. Today the figure is a third or less".[200] Workers likewise started to rely on the external labour market to advance their careers instead of relying on the employer's job ladder.[201] Although, in retrospect, this might have been somewhat overblown, at the time, switching jobs became associated with career progression and wage gains.[202]

As labour mobility has increased, albeit more in some countries than in others,[203] 74
the contribution of LMIs has probably also become more substantial. These labour market actors create networks among citizens, either locally, as is the case with a job fair, or long-distance, for example through a competitive programming platform.[204] LMIs are well aware of ports of entry and assist workers who have reached ports of exit.[205] They can provide a partial substitute for jobseekers who lack the necessary connections to find a job through their personal networks.[206] What is more, these businesses have a clear interest in the pursuit of flexible labour markets. They benefit from a labour market that generates a steady demand for their services.[207] For instance, Kalleberg claims that the "growth of precarious employment relations has reduced workers' attachments to their employers and increased the salience of labor market

199. Katherine V.W. Stone, *From Widgets to Digits Employment Regulation for the Changing Workplace* 289 (CUP 2004); Arne L. Kalleberg, *Precarious Work, Insecure Workers: Employment Relations in Transition*, 74 American Sociological Review 1, 1–22 n. 1 (2009).
200. Cappelli, *supra* n. 160, at 51.
201. Peter Cappelli, *Career Jobs Are Dead*, 42 California Management Review 146, 162 n. 1 (1999); Luc Behaghel, Eve Caroli & Emmanuelle Walkowiak, *Information and Communication Technologies and Skill Upgrading: The Role of Internal vs External Labour Markets*, 64 Oxford Economic Papers 490, 490–517 n. 3 (2012); Ilana Gershon, *Down and Out in the New Economy: How People Find (or Don't Find) Work Today* 207–234 (University of Chicago Press 2017).
202. OECD, *supra* n. 149, at 96. The OECD report refers to Robert H. Topel & Michael P. Ward, *Job Mobility and the Careers of Young Men*, 107 The Quarterly Journal of Economics 439, 439–479 n. 2 (1992); and Joyce K. Hahn, Henry R. Hyatt & Hubert P. Janicki, *Job Ladders and Growth in Earnings, Hours, and Wages* (RePEc 2018).
203. Evidence on the decline of internal labour markets is not uncontroversial. For instance, Sels et al., who made a labour market prognosis for Belgium and the region of Flanders, emphasise that numerical flexibility remains limited, that average job seniority has not decreased significantly and that neither labour mobility nor the percentage of self-employed workers has significantly increased. The authors suggest that the largely Anglo-Saxon literature on these developments might not accurately reflect the experiences in other countries. Luc Sels, Sarah Vansteenkiste & Heidi Knipprath, *Toekomstverkenningen Arbeidsmarkt 2050 (Werk.Rapport 2017 nr.1)* 37 (HIVA - KU Leuven 2017).
204. "Competitive programming platforms do not charge fees to developers and programmers; they build communities of programmers and developers who can provide top-quality services while at the same time honing their skills". ILO, *supra* n. 25, at 84.
205. Benner, Leete & Pastor, *supra* n. 125, at 14.
206. Fabienne Liechti, *Connecting Employers and Workers: Can Recommendations from the Public Employment Servicer Act as a Substitute for Social Contacts?*, 34 Work, Employment and Society 587, 600–601 n. 4 (2019).
207. Enright, *supra* n. 127, at 288–289.

intermediaries that help to create channels for mobility between firms".[208] Wood et al. similarly suggest that also DLPs capitalise on this growth of, what Kalleberg calls, "market-mediated, open employment relations".[209] Career progression, then, becomes governed by "market mechanisms" instead of the rules accompanying a firm's internal labour market, for instance, regarding promotions. LMIs and DLPs create some of the "market mechanisms" in this realm, framing and forging working relationships between jobseekers and job providers through their recommendations and services in general.[210]

75 **Third purpose: Reshuffle risks** – A third institutional function of intermediaries has to do with their tendency to redistribute risks.[211] One of the most flagrant illustrations is the so-called "temp-to-perm construction", in which the agency employs a jobseeker with the aim of perhaps, eventually, being recruited directly by the user enterprise. The period of temporary employment by the agency is meant to serve as an alternative probationary period. Because there is no direct contractual relationship between the worker and user, the user enterprise retains a high degree of discretion to hire the agency worker after this initial period. Moreover, by having the agency serve as the legal employer, the agency is tied up in the risks associated with this initial employment arrangement.[212] This feature allows the user enterprise to shield itself, for instance, from having to pay severance pay.[213]

76 Scholarship suggests that the insertion of temporary work agencies not only transfers risks from the factual employer to the agency, such as the risks associated with work accidents, but can likewise transfer risks from the employer to the worker.[214] More specifically, the agencies would contribute to the presence of a contingent workforce.

208. Arne L. Kalleberg, *Good Jobs, Bad Jobs: The Rise of Polarized and Precarious Employment Systems in the United States, 1970s to 2000s* 191 (Russel Sage Foundation 2011).
209. Wood, Graham, Lehdonvirta & Hjorth, *supra* n. 101, at 59.
210. By doing so, LMIs and DLPs give rise to new work-related networks that might benefit freelancers, for example. LMIs, such as FlexJobs.com, can pitch in on freelancers' needs and assist workers at successfully developing an open, non-standard career path. Alessandro Gandini, *Digital Work: Self-branding and Social Capital in the Freelance Knowledge Economy*, 16 Marketing Theory 123, 127 n. 1 (2016); I-WIRE, *How Can Labour Market Intermediaries Secure Nonstandard Career Paths? An Exploratory Grid* 3–4 (Independent Workers and Industrial Relations in Europe 2016); Nadège Lorquet, Jean-François Orianne & François Pichault, *Who Takes Care of Non-standard Career Paths? The Role of Labour Market Intermediaries?*, 24 European Journal of Industrial Relations 279, 279–295 n. 3 (2018).
211. Strauss & Fudge, *supra* n. 124, at 17.
212. "While economic justifications are regularly advanced to explain the increase of these arrangements, it has been well recognized that some employers use contingent work arrangements precisely for avoiding employer-related responsibilities and in order to circumvent employment and labor laws". Orly Lobel, *The Slipperiness of Stability: Contracting for Flexible and Triangular Employment Relationships in the New Economy*, 10 Texas Wesleyan Law Review 109, 116 n. 1 (2003); Bonet, Cappelli & Hamori, *supra* n. 129, at 362–364.
213. Susan N. Houseman, *Why Employers Use Flexible Staffing Arrangements: Evidence From an Establishment Survey*, 55 Industrial and Labor Relations Review 149, 156–157 n. 1 (2001); David H. Autor, *Outsourcing at Will: The Contribution of Unjust Dismissal Doctrine to the Growth of Employment Outsourcing*, 21 Journal of Labor Economics 1, 1–42 n. 1 (2003).
214. Jamie Peck & Nikolas Theodore, *The Business of Contingent Work: Growth and Restructuring in Chicago's Temporary Employment Industry*, 12 Work, Employment and Society 655, 660–661 n. 4 (1998); *see also* Strauss & Fudge, *supra* n. 124, at 6.

Agency workers tend not to perform their work on a long-term, full-time basis.[215] In such a contingent work scenario, it is increasingly the individual workers who have to invest in developing their skills rather than employers.[216] By shifting such risks and costs among the parties, and given the respective size of the temporary work industry in certain countries, Peck and Theodore conclude that the industry "can now be seen as a purveyor of flexibility not just at the 'micro' level (meeting the needs of individual enterprises), but also at the 'macro' level – mediating macroeconomic pressures and socio-economic risks across the labour market as a whole".[217]

In this regard, although the literature sometimes blames intermediaries for dismantling 77
worker protections, the opposite can also be true. Certain LMIs have the explicit aim of limiting workers' socio-economic risks. A clear example is the French concept of *portage salarial*.[218] It concerns a legal structure in which a *société de portage* concludes a contract with the worker who will work for user enterprises under the conditions agreed upon between the worker and the enterprises. The difference with temporary agency work is that the worker has negotiated the assignment with the "user enterprise" instead of the agency having negotiated it with the user enterprise and merely offering it to the worker.[219] This legal structure is advantageous whenever the worker does not want or cannot perform services as an independent contractor, or if the principal does not want to or cannot operate as the employer of record. The *société* reconciles both parties' interests by placing itself between the worker and principal, potentially limiting some of the risks the worker would have endured as an independent contractor.[220] Because of its potential to balance these interests, French authorities explicitly wonder whether this concept can aid workers in the platform economy.[221] Furthermore, beyond this specific French example, intermediaries can more broadly, for instance, enhance social security coverage for workers engaged by multiple users.[222] So far, the problem remains, however, that many platform operators refuse to embrace such protective ambitions. Instead, other external intermediaries have developed to perform valuable support services for precarious platform workers.[223]

---

215. Stephen F. Befort, *Revisiting the Black Hole of Workplace Regulation: A Historical and Comparative Perspective of Contingent Work*, 24 Berkeley Journal of Employment & Labor Law 153, 158 n. 1 (2003).
216. King, Burke & Pemberton, *supra* n. 193, at 982.
217. Jamie Peck & Nik Theodore, *Flexible Recession: The Temporary Staffing Industry and Mediated Work in the United States*, 31 Cambridge Journal of Economics 171, 172 n. 2 2007.
218. Sections L1254-1 – L1254-31 Code du Travail.
219. Steve Gilson, Caroline Candito, Maureen Degueldre & Louise Harel, *Regards sur le Portage Salarial* 263, 264 (Charles-Éric Clesse & Steve Gilson eds., *Le Travail Temporaire, le Travail Intérimaire et la Mise à Disposition de Travailleurs: Les 30 Ans de la Loi du 24 Juillet 1987*, Anthemis 2017).
220. Vinciane Rysselinck, *Portage Salarial: une Idée Française Illicite en Belgique – Alternatives en Droit Belge*, 42 Oriëntations 2, 2 n. 6 (2012).
221. Jean-Yves Frouin & Jean-Baptiste Barfety, *Réguler les Plateformes Numériques de Travail* 46–50 (Rapport au Premier Ministre 2020).
222. Lobel, *supra* n. 212, at 133.
223. Anita Gurumurthy, Nandini Chami & Deppti Bharthur, *Platform Labour in Search of Value: A Study of Worker Organizing Practices and Business Models in the Digital Economy* 38–40 (ILO 2021).

78 As has been shown, what many agencies that shift risks have in common is how they establish an employment relationship between the worker and intermediary. Yet, although this is undoubtedly an effective means to shift employment-related risks, it is not required. There are also more subtle ways in which intermediaries can shift risks. Companies may, for example, contact an intermediary instead of directly contacting a worker because the intermediary can mitigate the risk of the work not being completed by quickly sending a replacement.[224]

224. Matthew Bidwell & Isabel Fernandez-Mateo, *Three's a Crowd? Understanding Triadic Employment Relationships* 142, 157 (Peter Cappelli ed., *Employment Relationships: New Models of White-Collar Work*, Cambridge, CUP 2008).

Chapter 3. Digital Labour Platforms' Involvement in Labour Market Intermediation

SUBCHAPTER 1. LABOUR MARKET INTERMEDIARIES AND PLATFORMS ARE HYBRIDS

A platform paradox – This Third Chapter takes another look at the claim that, in principle, "platforms function as labour market intermediaries that connect labour demand and supply in a triangular work relationship".[225] As emphasised earlier, algorithmic matching or intermediation are commonly highlighted as a characteristic feature of platforms. Among others, Prassl stresses that "the key function of platform economy operators as discussed in [his] report is Digital Labour Intermediation".[226] Still, the author goes on to clarify that many platforms do much more than mere matchmaking. This culminates in what he calls a "Platform Paradox".[227] In order to maintain a quality service, the platform operator moves beyond stimulating matchmaking and imposes clear standards with which the users on the platform must comply. It leads to a contradictory situation in which "[t]he position of the platform vis-á-vis the marketplace is more like that of a government that sets policies to encourage efficient market outcomes without dictating trades".[228] However, the catch is that platforms are not public entities in charge of their private marketplaces and can, in fact, exert their "network orchestrator" role in such a way that they become private entities that hierarchically control other market participants. Therefore, they may end up resembling traditional employers. Whether this control serves to achieve satisfactory market liquidity or to maintain a certain quality of service is irrelevant 79

225. Lenaerts et al., *supra* n. 56, at i.
226. Jeremias Prassl, *Collective Voice in the Platform Economy: Challenges, Opportunities, Solutions* 7 (ETUC 2018).
227. *Ibid.*, 8.
228. Ajay Agrawal, John Horton, Nicola Lacetera & Elizabeth Lyons, *Digitization and the Contract Labor Market: A Research Agenda* 219, 241 (Avi Goldfarb, Shane M. Greenstein & Catherine E. Tucker eds., *Economic Analysis of the Digital Economy*, University of Chicago Press 2015).

from a labour lawyer's perspective. The platform operator is ensnared in a "Platform Paradox": promising freedom as if it is a marketplace while practising control as if it is an employer.[229]

80 **Hybrids** – The tension between simply encouraging transactions and doing so by controlling participants has made it challenging to classify platforms conceptually. Platforms are not exactly markets, nor are they generally considered employers. Scholars have tried to make sense of platforms' paradoxical position in between markets and hierarchical firms. According to Sundararajan, platforms present a sort of "hybrid between a pure market and a hierarchy" in which the boundary between markets and hierarchies becomes blurred.[230] Most authors seem to concur with this assessment,[231] even though the labels vary. For instance, Acquier refers to platforms as "market organizations";[232] Möhlmann and Geissinger, in turn, use the term "firm-market hybrids".[233] Because these descriptions seem to suggest that platforms are exceptionally unusual, it is worthwhile stressing that before the platform revolution even took place, LMIs had already been described as "hybrid" in nature. Benner argued in 2003 that "[a]s labour markets have grown more volatile and unpredictable, LMIs have arisen as an efficient alternative to internal labour markets, while still also being more efficient than decentralized open market transactions".[234] Many DLPs seem to, in other words, compete in the same space as LMIs, effectively trying to provide a better hybrid solution for users than "traditional" types of LMIs. Instead of having to call the agency to send a replacement, for example, the user goes online on the platform to choose a replacement based on the presented information, such as workers' ratings and reviews. Technology might, furthermore, allow the user enterprise or householder to ask the worker to engage in a quick preliminary test or a short video chat. The worker can likewise receive an instruction video from the employer before accepting the job. In short, technology, arguably, increases the effectiveness of these hybrid solutions.

81 **Deepening functional integration** – In a similar vein, technology may also facilitate a more profound functional integration between platforms and users than previously

229. Moreover, if Vallas and Schor are right that "[t]he history of capitalism suggests that extracting profit from workers requires potent mechanisms of control", then, this balancing act between freedom and control might be an ongoing process, repeatedly triggering litigation in its way. Vallas & Schor, *supra* n. 86, at 284.

230. Arun Sundararajan, *The Sharing Economy: The End of Employment and the Rise of Crowd-Based Capitalism* 70 and 77 (MIT Press 2016).

231. *See, e.g.*, the subchapter "Between a firm and a marketplace" by Christophe Degryse, *Technological Disruption, Social Dereliction?* 11, 23–24 (Isabelle Daugareilh, Christophe Degryse & Philippe Pochet eds., *The Platform Economy and Social Law: Key Issues in Comparative Perspective*, Etui 2019).

232. Aurélien Acquier, *Uberization Meets Organizational Theory: Platform Capitalism and the Rebirth of the Putting-Out System* 13, 15 (Nestor M. Davidson, Michèle Finck & John J. Infranca eds., *The Cambridge Handbook of the Law of the Sharing Economy*, CUP 2018).

233. Mareike Möhlmann & Andrea Geissinger, *Trust in the Sharing Economy Platform-Mediated Peer Trust* 27, 31 (Nestor M. Davidson, Michèle Finck & John J. Infranca eds., *The Cambridge Handbook of the Law of the Sharing Economy*, CUP 2018).

234. Benner, *supra* n. 168, at 627. Subsequently, on page 628: "It is the hybrid nature of intermediaries, with close communication and ties with a diverse array of both employers and workers, which makes them especially important in this process of labour market adjustment".

possible between agencies and users. During prior decades, LMIs, such as temporary work agencies, have increasingly blurred the distinction between the user enterprise's internal labour market and the external labour market through "deepening functional integration". Agencies and users thereby continuously perform multiple functions in an integrated fashion.[235] For example, firms that rely on headhunters are advised to discuss their succession planning with the agency, or inform the agency early on to perform an "anticipatory search".[236] Temporary work agencies have supposedly also become integral to business strategy and a critical part of users' personnel strategies.[237] Take the example of Foxconn. Temporary work agencies have offices at its factory in the Czech Republic, where, contrary to what usually happens, not Foxconn itself but the agencies "were directly responsible for organizing, controlling and managing agency workers' performance on the assembly line".[238] Contemporary e-commerce giants offer another example of such an "integrated operation" involving agencies at the user's plant. Bol.com – probably the main competitor of Amazon in Belgium and the Netherlands – has a distribution centre in the Netherlands with around eight temporary work agencies permanently present at the workplace.[239] These agencies seemingly employ Bol.com's workforce, many of whom are migrants. The agencies, furthermore, provide housing for the workers and take care of the transport between the residences and the distribution centre.

For what concerns both local on-demand work and online crowdwork, ICT technology 82
may reinforce this process of functional integration. Regarding the former, nothing might be more emblematic of functional integration than a food-delivery platform.[240] The platform provides client-restaurants with the software (and sometimes hardware) to register orders, and to track food-delivery couriers on their way to deliver the meal to the restaurant's customer.[241] Another example is Instacart. This enables

235. Peck & Theodore, *supra* n. 214, at 666–667.
236. Nancy Garrison Jenn, *Headhunters and How to Use Them: A Guide for Organisations and Individuals* 34 (Economist Books 2005).
237. Stanley D. Nollen, *Negative Aspects of Temporary Employment*, 17 Journal of Labor Research 567, 567 n. 4 (1996); Courtney von Hippel et al., *Temporary Employment: Can Organizations and Employees Both Win?*, 11 The Academy of Management Executive 93, 93 n. 1 (1997).
238. Rutvica Andrijasevic & Devi Sacchetto, *'Disappearing Workers': Foxconn in Europe and the Changing Role of Temporary Work Agencies*, 31 Work, Employment and Society 54, 61–62 n. 1 (2017).
239. Jeroen van Bergeijk, *Binnen bij Bol.com: Undercover bij de Winkel van ons Allemaal* 13 (Querido Fosfor 2019).
240. For an explanation of restaurants' relationship with these platforms, *see* ILO, *supra* n. 25, at 114–115.
241. Consider the information provided by Deliveroo on how the restaurant's tablet works. "Inside each of the thousands of restaurants we work with, orders through Deliveroo are managed using a tablet. When a restaurant receives an order, the tablet will ping and a window will pop with the new order. When a restaurant taps 'Accept order', our technology matches this order to the best placed available rider, for the most efficient delivery. That's based on the rider's live location and the estimated time it will take a rider to travel to the restaurant – you can find out more about this here. Once you accept the order, the tablet lets the restaurant know how long it will take you to get there. It also gives a time for them to have the order ready, so that when you arrive at the restaurant, the food is prepared and ready for you to pick up". Deliveroo, *Tech Round-up: How the Restaurant Tablet Works*, Roocommunity (22 April 2020), https://roocommunity.com/tech-round-up-restaurants/.

customers to shop online at the "virtual storefront" of Instacart's affiliated retailers, after which a "personal shopper" is instructed to collect those items at the selected store and bring them to the customer's household. Similarly, crowdworkers are becoming an institutional part of platform users' businesses. They are, for example, already a "structural component of contemporary artificial intelligence production processes".[242] Corporaal and Lehdonvirta have likewise observed a tendency among Fortune 500 companies to integrate crowdwork platforms into their business strategies. According to their research from 2017, "[i]n most of the cases that we studied, firm adoption of platform sourcing was still at a relatively nascent stage. But managers leading organization-wide adoption efforts were in the process of creating internal infrastructures around platform sourcing that could scale up to hundreds or thousands of simultaneous engagements".[243] In a more recent report from 2020, this kind of practice is called "widespread".[244] Other research on Amazon Mechanical Turk, in particular, similarly points out how some companies seem to, indeed, use crowdworkers systematically. According to these findings, 1 per cent of requesters would post more than 50 per cent of "the dollar-weighted tasks".[245] Correspondingly, a CEO from a substantial micro-task platform has admitted that large businesses were the source of about 80 per cent of its revenue.[246]

SUBCHAPTER 2. PLATFORMS' LABOUR MARKET INTERMEDIATION

83 **First purpose: Transaction costs** – The previous paragraph illustrated platforms' potential as "connecting hubs"[247] for outsourcing work to an external workforce. This function derives from platforms' ability to reduce transaction costs and enhance the user's surveillance capabilities.[248] This ability to reduce transaction costs is a feature shared by all labour platforms.[249] Lobel contends that platforms may generally have a positive effect "in each of the three stages of pre-deal, deal-making, and post-deal – [on] 1) search costs; 2) bargaining and decision costs; and 3) policing and enforcement costs".[250] To this extent, for instance, listing directories and "direct matching algorithms" would reduce search costs. Platforms' "bidding and auction tools" and the systems that fix the service's price reduce bargaining and decision

242. Paola Tubaro, Antonio A. Casilli & Marion Coville, *The Trainer, the Verifier, the Imitator: Three Ways in Which Human Platform Workers Support Artificial Intelligence*, 7 Big Data & Society 1, 1 n. 1 (2020).
243. Greetje F. Corporaal & Vili Lehdonvirta, *Platform Sourcing. How Fortune 500 Firms Are Adopting Online Freelancing Platforms* 21 (Oxford Internet Institute 2017).
244. Joseph B. Fuller et al., *Building the On-demand Workforce* 2 (Harvard Business School and BCG 2020).
245. Ipeirotis, *supra* n. 136, at 21.
246. ILO, *supra* n. 25, at 108.
247. Antonio Aloisi, *Hierarchies Without Firms? Vertical Disintegration, Personal Outsourcing and the Nature of the Platform* 7 (Quaderni del Premio "Giorgio Rota" 2020).
248. Engels & Sherwood, *supra* n. 72, at 12–13.
249. Edelman & Geradin, *supra* n. 179, at 297; Drahokoupil & Fabo, *supra* n. 62, at 46.
250. Orly Lobel, *Coase and the Platform Economy* 67, 68–70 (Nestor M. Davidson, Michèle Finck & John J. Infranca eds., *The Cambridge Handbook of the Law of the Sharing Economy*, CUP 2018).

costs. Lastly, the provision of, among other things, escrow accounts diminishes enforcement costs.[251]

Information asymmetry – The fact that platforms can have these positive effects does not guarantee, however, that platforms are always developed to reduce transaction costs in a fair and balanced manner. Like LMIs (*supra* nos. 69–71), platform operators also decide what kind of information asymmetries they will condone between the workers and users,[252] and between the platform and its users.[253] Two issues stand out. First, the platform operator decides what information it wants to collect. Digitalisation allows platform operators to be quite intrusive in this regard. For instance, employers have shown great interest in social media to "weed out" individual job applicants, *inter alia*, based on their lifestyle choices.[254] When a DLP enables workers to integrate their Facebook, Twitter, and other accounts, potential employers are effectively stimulated to take recourse to these social media accounts.[255] In recent times, this kind of visibility has become normalised as a prerequisite to gain access to jobs,[256] yet, it may not stop at social media accounts. Employers are also interested in, for example, the financial situation of jobseekers.[257] **84**

Platforms' tendency to normalise this type of workers' visibility is particularly problematic whenever the same level of transparency is not demanded of users. Although the platform might perform a background check on workers,[258] the platform does not necessarily bother doing it for the employer, even if employers' balance sheets may be freely available on the internet. In other words, platform operators might be inclined not to demand reciprocal transparency. Some platform workers in domestic work, for instance, "often felt discomfort toward the visibility that carework platforms enabled, and the asymmetry that did not grant them reciprocal transparency in being able to scrutinize clients".[259] Similarly, one of the problems identified on Amazon Mechanical Turk (AMT) was the difficulty for workers to identify good clients because AMT did not allow workers to rate clients.[260] Six **85**

251. Engels & Sherwood, *supra* n. 72, at 11–12.
252. The worker may have information about the user through the platform, which the user does not have about the worker, and vice versa.
253. The platform may have information about the worker or user which it does not share with anyone until the moment has come when disclosing this information serves its own goals.
254. Seili Suder & Andra Siibak, *Employers as Nightmare Readers: An Analysis of Ethical and Legal Concerns Regarding Employer-Employee Practices on SNS*, 10 Baltic Journal of Law & Politics 76, 100 n. 2 (2017).
255. Ticona, Mateescu & Rosenblat, *supra* n. 88, at 26.
256. Andrea Mateescu & Julia Ticona, *Invisible Work, Visible Workers: Visibility Regimes in Online Platforms for Domestic Work* 57, 63 (Deepa Das Acevedo ed., *Beyond the Algorithm: Qualitative Insights for Gig Work Regulation*, CUP 2020).
257. Barbara Kiviat, *The Art of Deciding With Data: Evidence From How Employers Translate Credit Reports Into Hiring Decisions*, 17 Socio-Economic Review 283, 283–309 n. 2 (2019).
258. *E.g.* Abigail Hunt & Fortunate Machingura, *A Good Gig? The Rise of On-demand Domestic Work* 27 (ODI 2016).
259. Julia Ticona & Andrea Mateescu, *Trusted Strangers: Carework Platforms' Cultural Entrepreneurship in the On-demand Economy*, 20 New Media & Society 4384, 4397 n. 11 (2018).
260. Engels & Sherwood, *supra* n. 72, at 16.

Silberman and Irani, therefore, devised "Turkopticon" to address this deficit and straighten out the asymmetry.[261]

86 Secondly, in addition to platform operators' decisions about what information to collect, they also decide how to use it. Research suggests in this regard that platform operators may deliberately withhold information or strategically disclose it to benefit their operational goals.[262] For instance, Uber withholds information until a driver has accepted a transport request. Only then does the driver know how far the trip will be. "By creating this information asymmetry between itself and the worker, the platform uses its information advantage to remove workers' free agency [...]".[263] Likewise, before accepting the job, Deliveroo couriers may be unaware of the distance between the customer and the restaurant.[264] Many more platforms may rely on such features to constrain workers' agency and essentially entice them to accept bad gigs.[265]

87 These findings correspond to what has been remarked about LMIs. The way intermediaries collect and handle information is opaque and can be problematic. Similar to DLPs, also modern-day LMIs run on various sources of data.[266] Jobseekers might receive "dynamic customized job postings" generated not just based on the information provided by the individual but also on their overall online behaviour.[267] This dynamic makes it unclear which factors determine how job advertisements are targeted towards certain individuals. An issue that is further aggravated when LMIs rely on self-learning artificial intelligence. As explained by Cappelli, consider:

> "a variable that data scientists have found to have predictive value: commuting distance to the job. According to the data, people with longer commutes suffer higher rates of attrition. However, commuting distance is governed by where you live – which is governed by housing prices, relates to income, and also relates to race. Picking whom to hire on the basis of where they live most likely has an adverse impact on protected groups such as racial minorities".[268]

As illustrated by this example, depending on the algorithms running in the background, indirect discrimination may occur even when protected characteristics are

261. The application allows workers on AMT to browse through the various tasks and consult the ratings of the clients that have posted the task. M. Six Silberman & Lilly Irani, *Operating an Employer Reputation System: Lessons from Turkopticon, 2008–2015*, 37 Comparative Labor Law & Policy Journal 505, 526 n. 3 (2016).
262. Aaron Shapiro, *Dynamic Exploits: Calculative Asymmetries in the On-demand Economy*, 35 New Technology, Work and Employment 162, 163 n. 2 (2020).
263. Choudary, *supra* n. 63, at 10. *See also*, Ileen A. DeVault et al., *On-demand Platform Workers in New York State: The Challenges for Public Policy* 24–26 (ILR Worker Institute 2019).
264. Ivanova, Bronowicka, Kocher & Degner, *supra* n. 101, at 16. *See also*, Veen, Barratt & Goods, *supra* n. 103, at 397–398.
265. "Crucially, this type of transparency is not symmetrical; Care.com and other platforms don't allow workers to post reviews of families or display metrics about how responsive families are to messages, how many other workers they've hired, or other safety verifications". Ticona, Mateescu & Rosenblat, *supra* n. 88, at 28.
266. John J. Horton & Prasanna Tambe, *Labor Economists Get Their Microscope: Big Data and Labor Market Analysis*, 3 Big Data 130, 130–137 n. 3 (2015).
267. Dineen & Allen, *supra* n. 152, at 383.
268. Cappelli, *supra* n. 160, at 57.

taken out of the equation.[269] Indeed, jobseekers often have no idea what is taking place behind the screen of their ICT device,[270] even though it might subject them to age discrimination, for instance.[271]

Second purpose: Network capabilities – As noted in the previous Subchapter, many LMIs have an interest in establishing professional networks. This entails that "as intermediaries build relationships with multiple employers, they become centrally part of regional production networks".[272] The same seems partially true for platforms. LinkedIn and Facebook Business are clear examples of platforms that aim to establish professional networks, shaping relationships between jobseekers, recruiters and businesses through their algorithmic support. Platforms that provide freelancers with macro-tasks, such as Upwork, also generally fit this bill. From a worker's point of view, these platforms virtually extend workers' social and economic networks, enhancing their opportunities to obtain paid work on and off the platform.[273] **88**

What is particularly important in this respect, however, is how these platform freelancers can end up being "locked" into the platform. As argued by Zhu and Iansiti, a successful platform operator needs to counteract disintermediation, in which users take their business elsewhere. Operators do not benefit from their workers performing services on multiple platforms at once either.[274] Therefore, just like certain LMIs,[275] platform operators add clauses to their terms and conditions to prohibit the worker and user from disintermediating the triangular relationship.[276] The worker and user on the platform might, for example, have to pay the operator a fee if they want to **89**

269. Kenneth G. Dau-Schmidt, *The Impact of Emerging Information Technologies on the Employment Relationship: New Gigs for Labor and Employment Law*, University of Chicago Legal Forum 63, 67 (2017); De Stefano, *supra* n. 40, at 28–29.
270. "Facebook provides the option for advertisers to target their advertisements based on inter alia location, age, gender, sexual orientation, language, education, job, relationship status, financial status, home ownership, income, political interest and ethnic affinity. [...] Some of the targeting options have a potential for discriminatory usage". David J. Dalenberg, *Preventing Discrimination in the Automated Targeting of Job Advertisements*, 34 Computer Law & Security Review 615, 617 n. 3 (2018).
271. Ifeoma Ajunwa, *Age Discrimination by Platforms*, 40 Berkeley Journal of Employment and Labor Law 1, 1–27 n. 1 (2019); Miriam A. Cherry, *Age Discrimination in the On-demand Economy and Crowdwork*, 40 Berkeley Journal of Employment and Labor Law 29, 29–60 n. 1 (2019).
272. Benner, *supra* n. 168, at 628.
273. Sally-Anne Barnes, Anne Green & Maria de Hoyos, *Crowdsourcing and Work: Individual Factors and Circumstances Influencing Employability*, 30 New Technology, Work and Employment 16, 27 n. 1 (2015).
274. Feng Zhu & Marco Iansiti, *Why Some Platforms Thrive... and Others Don't*, 97 Harvard Business Review 118, 123 n. 1 (2019).
275. Bidwell & Fernandez-Mateo, *supra* n. 224, at 165.
276. *E.g.*, on Upwork, "Section 7 discusses your agreement to make and receive payments only through Upwork for two years from the date you first identify or meet your Client or Freelancer on the Site, unless you pay a Conversion Fee; violating this Section 7 is a serious breach and your Account may be permanently suspended for violations, as detailed below". Upwork, User Agreement, Upwork (30 August 2020), https://www.upwork.com/legal#NONCIRCUMVENTION. On Fiverr, "Users may not submit proposals or solicit parties introduced through Fiverr to contract, engage with, or pay outside of Fiverr". Fiverr, Fiverr's Terms of Service, Fiverr (30 August 2020), https://www.fiverr.com/terms_of_service?store = false. *See also*, Mohammad H. Jarrahi, Will Sutherland, Sarah B. Nelson & Steve Sawyer, *Platformic Management, Boundary Resources for*

pursue a bilateral relationship elsewhere. Consequently, even when crowdworkers manage to develop "long-term higher-trust personal relationships" with platform users, which workers consider very important,[277] the platform workers may effectively be "locked-in" by legal means, dissuading them from contacting the user directly.

90 Besides this legal aspect, other reasons of a more practical nature also explain why platform workers' labour mobility is constrained.[278] Realistically, workers can only devote enough attention to a couple of platforms because it requires time to perform the necessary number of tasks to build sufficient social capital.[279] Once this social capital is established, the worker will try to exploit it. In practice, the workers risk becoming "locked-in" unless they have a portable rating that they can carry with them when transitioning to another platform.[280] Other design features can similarly bind workers to the platform. One can think of systems that attribute upgrades based on the number of projects completed, or systems that solely allow veteran crowdworkers to bid for well-paid jobs.[281]

91 Furthermore, workers also complain about the "poor communication with requesters as a flaw in the system".[282] This difficulty communicating effectively with users is, arguably, another indication of how platform operators deliberately shape their platforms to limit labour mobility. Wood et al. even suggest that platforms purposely do not provide the architecture to develop "thick, strong, stable and durable ties". Over time, such high-trust relationships might lead users to bypass the platform.[283] This conflicts with operators' interests, as crowdwork platforms like to exert "substantial steering power" over their network.[284] This steering power can manifest itself both in an eye-catching way through recommendations for workers that pay for premium membership, or somewhat covertly, for instance, by valuing and devaluing certain social and cultural practices, "specifically in relation to freelancers' language use".[285] To conclude, many platforms are all but a neutral "cyberplace" for workers to extend their social and economic networks.

Gig Work, and Worker Autonomy, 29 Computer Supported Cooperative Work 153, 179 n. 1–2 (2020).

277. Alex J. Wood, Mark Graham, Vili Lehdonvirta & Isis Hjorth, *Networked but Commodified: The (Dis)Embeddedness of Digital Labour in the Gig Economy*, 53 Sociology 931, 938–939 n. 5 (2019).
278. Lenaerts et al., *supra* n. 56, at 82.
279. Aleksynska, Bastrakova & Kharchenko, *supra* n. 78, at 19.
280. Antonio Aloisi, Valerio De Stefano & Six Silberman, *A Manifesto to Reform the Gig Economy*, Regulating for Globalization (1 May 2019), http://regulatingforglobalization.com/2019/05/01/a-manifesto-to-reform-the-gig-economy/.
281. Philip Schörpf, Jörg Flecker, Annika Schönauer & Hubert Eichmann, *Triangular Love-Hate: Management and Control in Creative Crowdworking*, 32 New Technology, Work and Employment 43, 50–51 n. 1 (2017).
282. ILO researchers, furthermore, observed that "even where contact possibilities exist, [which is all but certain,] in many instances workers feel that this is a waste of time". Berg et al., *supra* n. 23, at 79.
283. Wood, Graham, Lehdonvirta & Hjorth, *supra* n. 277, at 939.
284. Barach, Golden & Horton, *supra* n. 186, at 4065.
285. Pelin Demirel, Ekaterina Nemkova & Rebecca Taylor, *Reproducing Global Inequalities in the Online Labour Market: Valuing Capital in the Design Field*, Work, Employment and Society 1, 14 (2020).

Networking among workers – In addition to limiting workers' mobility in relation to users and other platforms, platform operators are also hesitant to incentivise networking among workers. Crowdwork platforms often do not support crowdworkers' efforts to come together in search of a collective voice.[286] Efforts to mobilise may even be hampered by design. Choudary explicitly mentions that "[u]nlike social networks, labour platforms do not allow the creation of network connections between workers, as fostering connections between workers would seem to have little benefit for the platform".[287] Instead, the labour supply often remains unmitigated, leading to an oversupply of workers and severe price competition between them.[288] In such conditions, even when a crowdwork platform does provide a forum or other means to communicate among workers, results seem to be underwhelming.[289] **92**

Also, collective representation and action outside of the platform itself are not particularly welcomed by platform operators.[290] Some workers apparently fear that collective action might trigger retaliation.[291] The lack of support from platform operators to design their platforms so as to reinforce networks between workers may, moreover, be difficult to overcome. This is, among other reasons, because a large share of the workforce on platforms are not eager to bond and organise. Many perceive the other workers as competitors.[292] Only a minority of platform workers seem in favour of collective action.[293] This minority might, however, show significant overlap with the group of providers that rely on the platform as their primary source of income.[294] Research on the platform economy indicates that workers who are economically dependent on platforms seem to be less satisfied with the platform operators than casual platform workers,[295] giving economically dependent platform **93**

286. Berg et al., *supra* n. 23, at 79.
287. Choudary, *supra* n. 63, at 24.
288. "In the words of Chris, a Kenyan worker, 'the Filipinos will accept anything' (Interview Nairobi, October 2017), while a Nigerian respondent told us that Indians can be very intimidating because they can accept as low as US$1 for any job and work like 'camels'". Mohammad A. Anwar & Mark Graham, *Between a Rock and a Hard Place: Freedom, Flexibility, Precarity and Vulnerability in the Gig Economy in Africa*, 25 Competition & Change 237, 249–250 n. 2 (2021).
289. "The results suggest that, above all else, irrespective of the managerial strategy and type of crowdwork, many choose indifference, absenteeism or exit as individual coping strategies rather than contacting their peers. After all, interaction costs unpaid extra time and takes place in a context of competition". Christine Gerber, *Community Building on Crowdwork Platforms: Autonomy and Control of Online Workers?*, 25 Competition & Change 190, 208 n. 2 (2021).
290. Prassl, *supra* n. 226, at 14–15; ILO, *supra* n. 25, at 216.
291. Hannah Johnston & Chris Land-Kazlauskas, *Organizing On-demand: Representation, Voice, and Collective Bargaining in the Gig Economy* 14 (ILO 2018).
292. IPSOS, "High level summary of key findings", Prepared for KU Leuven, 2020.
293. Gemma Newlands, Christoph Lutz & Christian Fieseler, *Collective Action and Provider Classification in the Sharing Economy*, 33 New Technology, Work and Employment 250, 264 n. 3 (2018). For theoretical reflections in this respect, Vandaele, *supra* n. 60, at 11.
294. For what concerns platform workers in the Global North, "while most Uber drivers work few hours, a portion of long-hours drivers do the majority of the rides. There are similar distributions among Upworkers (Popiel 2017), etsy sellers (Etsy 2013), content providers, and crowd workers". Juliet B. Schor et al., *Dependence and Precarity in the Platform Economy*, 49 Theory and Society 833, 855 n. 5–6 (2020).
295. *Ibid.*, 855. The workers for whom working on AMT is supplemental income, similarly, report higher present and anticipated future life satisfaction. Melissa G. Keith, Peter Harms & Louis

workers more reason to take recourse to collective action. Casual platform workers' willingness to disregard the interests of heavily invested platform workers might, however, undercut the latter's bargaining position.[296]

94 **Third purpose: Reshuffle risks** – The third function of LMIs has to do with their capacity to redistribute risks. For instance, whereas a fast-food restaurant's delivery worker might have used a vehicle owned by the firm in the past,[297] the platform's couriers are lucky if they receive expenses for using their own bikes. It is also unlikely that the platform operator will repair the bike when broken.[298] This illustrates how, just as LMIs have been criticised for relieving user enterprises from their responsibilities under labour law, the same can be said for platforms. Think of Instacart. As noted by a CNBC documentary, one potential danger for the company's business model is that nothing prevents big supermarket chains from providing their customers with an app that allows them to forward their shopping lists to the supermarket's employees.[299] Such an app would bypass the services offered by Instacart. What it probably means is that unlike Instacart, which seemingly gets away with it, the supermarket will have a hard time claiming that this "shopper" is a self-employed worker. Even if the supermarket were to argue that the working time flexibility on the app is atypical of regular employment, it would seem absurd to think of Walmart's or any other retailer's "personal shoppers" as independent contractors casually receiving instructions through a Walmart app. Among other things, for this reason, the prediction in the CNBC documentary is unlikely to come true. Instacart and others managed to free supermarkets from taking up any responsibility for workers who shop on behalf of their customers. This led, for instance, to tensions during the COVID pandemic, when these Instacart shoppers were largely left to their own devices while shopping for clients too scared to visit the supermarket.[300] However cruel it might seem, from the supermarkets' perspective, the platform's ability to shield it from taking up responsibility for these workers' employment conditions

Tay, *Mechanical Turk and the Gig Economy: Exploring Differences Between Gig Workers*, 34 Journal of Managerial Psychology 286, 303 n. 4 (2019).

296. Platform operators such as Uber are aware of the diversity among their workforce, ranging from "recreational" to full-time drivers. Arguably, the operators do not hesitate to marginalise the most invested drivers whose dissent is not shared by the overall workforce, most of whom are less reliant on platform work. Rosenblat, *supra* n. 76, at 53–55 and 72. Similarly, in case of online crowdwork, workers have such different backgrounds that it is difficult for them to agree on priorities and bargain collectively with the platform operator. Vili Lehdonvirta, *Algorithms that Divide and Unite: Delocalisation, Identity and Collective Action in 'Microwork'* 53, 76 (Jörg Flecker ed., *Space, Place and Global Digital Work*, Palgrave Macmillan 2016).

297. Kirsten Korosec, *Domino's Launches E-Bike Delivery to Compete With Uber Eats, DoorDash*, TechCrunch (13 August 2019), https://techcrunch.com/2019/08/13/dominos-launches-e-bike-delivery-to-compete-with-ubereats-doordash/.

298. Eurofound, *supra* n. 4, at 34; Caleb Goods, Alex Veen & Tom Barratt, *"Is Your Gig Any Good?" Analysing Job Quality in the Australian Platform-Based Food-Delivery Sector*, 61 Journal of Industrial Relations 502, 511–513 n. 4 (2019).

299. CNBC, *The Rise of Instacart and Online Grocery Delivery*, YouTube (13 May 2020), https://www.youtube.com/watch?v=WRc3USp1RAQ.

300. Russell Brandom, *Sick Days: Instacart Promises a Safer Way to Shop, but Workers Tell a Different Story*, The Verge (26 May 2020), https://www.theverge.com/21267669/instacart-shoppers-sick-extended-pay-quarantine-leave-coronavirus.

is a valuable service provided by the intermediary. One that sees itself reflected, for example, in Albertsons' decision "to lay off delivery staff in many areas around the country and switch to 'third-party logistics providers.' The company has been partnering with the gig delivery service DoorDash since 2018".[301]

301. Eli Rosenberg, *Albertsons is Laying Off Employees and Replacing Them With Gig Workers, as App Platforms Rise*, The Washington Post (6 January 2021), https://www.washingtonpost.com/business/2021/01/06/vons-albertsons-doordash-prop-22-layoffs/.

Chapter 4. Interim Conclusion: A Focus on Genuine Digital Labour Platforms

Digital labour platforms – The First Chapter described the concept of a DLP. The platform operator's role as a network orchestrator was contrasted with another characteristic of pure or genuine platforms. According to Hagiu and Wright, platform operators are not supposed to control the key terms of the interaction between the users. As such, a platform operator aims to bring about transactions between distinct sides on the platform, yet conceptually, if it operates a genuine DLP, the operator leaves the parties the necessary control to self-determine the key terms of their interaction. 95

Assuming Wright and Hagiu have a point, certain platform operators seem to operate a hierarchical structure rather than a pure decentralised platform because they, for example, impose a price or automatically select the worker. However, by claiming to operate a platform nonetheless, even operators at this hierarchical end of the spectrum implicitly establish a presumption that their business lawfully relies on independent contractors. This is because genuine DLPs, which only broker contracts of/for service(s) between distinct sides on the platform and leave the parties to settle the conditions, are relatively peripheral to labour law. The rules on labour brokerage may apply, and, for instance, anti-discrimination law might as well, but a genuine platform will rarely be met with allegations of bogus self-employment. 96

Therefore, by extension, when any business claims to operate a platform, even though it does control the key terms of the interaction between its users, the word "platform" automatically lends credibility to the claim that most labour laws should not apply. To claim that labour law does apply to a business, such as Uber, roughly translates into claiming that the company does not operate a (genuine) platform, something that is difficult to argue, given the similar "digital aura" of all these businesses. Many of them come in the form of an app, allow for easy onboarding, rely on rate-and-review systems, etc. For such reasons, among others, it took some time to figure out that "the genuineness of the intermediation role is one of the key problems about platform companies: if they are not playing the role 97 as intermediary between the demand and supply of a service, then, they are most likely employers and their suppliers, drivers or riders are, in many legal systems, nothing but employees or workers".[302]

98 In the meantime, most attention has been devoted to a subset of the most hierarchical DLPs, such as Uber, which indeed hardly intermediate (*supra* no. 59).[303] Some might argue that these platforms are, in effect, hierarchical firms rather than firm-market hybrids.[304] Their business models have been selectively infused with market features and mechanisms.[305] Workers' interactions, nevertheless, occur via strictly controlled market-like architectures.[306] This architecture allows the platform operator to strive for complete control over the marketplace at the aggregate level, for instance, through "surge pricing",[307] albeit not necessarily at the individual level. This approach allows for "a façade of autonomy for the individual worker".[308] However, from an institutional perspective, these ambivalent platforms can, nevertheless, be perceived as "institutional alternatives to hierarchical governance [which] is also corroborated by several court rulings regarding Uber".[309] Indeed, many courts at the highest level have found the relationship between these hierarchical platforms and their workers to bear the hallmarks of an employment relationship.[310]

302. Vincenzo Pietrogiovanni, *Between Sein and Sollen of Labour Law: Civil (and Constitutional) Law Perspectives on Platform Workers*, 31 King's Law Journal 313, 314 n. 2 (2020).
303. Eurofound is of the opinion that "on-location platform-determined routine work" such as Uber and Deliveroo comes most close to a hierarchy. Instead, for example, "*online contestant specialist work*" is a form of platform work at the market end of the spectrum. Eurofound, *Platform Work: Maximising the Potential While Safeguarding Standards?* 6 (Publications Office of the European Union 2019).
304. For instance, Prassl and Risak argue that Uber "very clearly exercises the full range of employer functions: [...], it is little different from a traditional, unitary employer – with its drivers to be classified as employees". Jeremias Prassl & Martin Risak, *Uber, Taskrabbit, and co.: Platforms as Employers? Rethinking the Legal Analysis of Crowdwork*, 37 Comparative Labor Law & Policy Journal 619, 641 n. 3 (2016). The same might be true for some online platforms that engage crowdworkers. Tubaro contrasts Appen, Lionbridge and Pactera under the heading "*platforms as firms*" with Amazon Mechanical Turk under the heading "*platforms as markets*". Paola Tubaro, *Disembedded or Deeply Embedded? A Multi-Level Network Analysis of Online Labour Platforms*, Sociology 1, 8–11 (2021).
305. Teppo Felin & Todd R. Zenger, *Information Aggregation, Matching and Radical Market-Hierarchy Hybrids: Implications for the Theory of the Firm*, 9 Strategic Organization 163, 165 n. 2 (2011).
306. Aloisi, *supra* n. 247, at 14. For an example, Amanda Sperber, *Uber Made Big Promises in Kenya. Drivers Say it's Ruined Their Lives.*, NBC News (30 November 2020), https://www.nbcnews.com/news/world/uber-made-big-promises-kenya-drivers-say-it-s-ruined-n1247964.
307. When the supply of drivers is too low in a certain area, the platform operator can decide to raise the prices drivers will earn in that area to entice workers to come online, or to draw drivers out of other areas towards the "surge zone". Alex Rosenblat & Luke Stark, *Algorithmic Labor and Information Asymmetries: A Case Study of Uber's Drivers*, 10 International Journal of Communication 3758, 3768 (2016).
308. Shapiro, *supra* n. 262, at 163.
309. Kai Reimers, Xunhua Guo & Mingzhi Li, *Beyond Markets, Hierarchies, and Hybrids: An Institutional Perspective on IT-Enabled Two-Sided Markets*, 29 Electronic Markets 287, 298 n. 2 (2019).
310. De Stefano, Durri, Stylogiannis & Wouters, *supra* n. 13, at 30–40.

The dissertation's focus – The ongoing struggles between ambivalent DLPs and legislatures, trade unions and courts have contributed to companies such as Uber becoming the "poster-child of the sharing economy".[311] Yet, just as it has become clear that Uber has little to do with sharing,[312] perhaps in time, researchers may also conclude that these companies should not be seen as the "poster-child" of the "platform economy" either. In fact, one could argue that they have significantly strayed away from the original template by becoming unpermissive potentates (*supra* nos. 42–44). From that perspective, this dissertation is justified in primarily focusing on genuine DLPs, which are supposed to grant their users significant autonomy and control. 99

As Part IV of this dissertation will show, international labour standards cover even these more "decentralised" labour platforms. Before explaining why this is the case, though, the Second Part of the dissertation will first introduce the ILO. It aims to predominantly explore the organisation's normative agenda. This is necessary, among other reasons, to be able to sketch the context that needs to be taken into account when interpreting an ILO Convention. Most importantly, this information is also needed to give a realistic account of the ILO's potential regulatory responses in the Fourth Part of this dissertation. 100

311. Amanda Peticca-Harris, Nadia deGama & M. N. Ravishankar, *Postcapitalist Precarious Work and Those in the 'Drivers' Seat: Exploring the Motivations and Lived Experiences of Uber Drivers in Canada*, 27 Organization 36, 36 n. 1 (2020).

312. Giana M. Eckhardt & Fleura Bardhi, *The Sharing Economy Isn't About Sharing at All*, Harvard Business Review (28 January 2015), https://hbr.org/2015/01/the-sharing-economy-isnt-about-sharing-at-all.

Part II. The ILO's Normative Agenda: Decent Work

INTRODUCTION

The content of Part II. – The question of what the ILO might do in response to platform work cannot be answered without prior knowledge about the organisation. For this reason, the Second Part of the dissertation explores the ILO, and most notably, what its current mandate entails. To this end, the Chapters below connect the dots between the ILO's constitutional texts and its more recent Declarations, which reinterpret the organisation's founding treaties. By and large, Chapter 1 covers the constitutional texts, and Chapter 2 covers the Decent Work Agenda and Declaration on Fundamental Principles and Rights. Chapter 3 subsequently discusses the Social Justice Declaration, which is essentially the institutionalised version of the Decent Work Agenda. The final Chapters analyse the Centenary Declaration from 2019 and its connection to platform work. 101

The main goal is to explore the ILO's renewed mandate, and map out whether it has consequences for future discussions on decent work in the platform economy. Along the way, some of the tensions between ILO constituents are uncovered, which is also helpful for future Chapters to avoid making unrealistic proposals in this dissertation's Fourth Part. Also, since the Third Part will delve into specific ILO Conventions, this Second Part would like to situate the function of ILS in relation to the ILO's mandate. 102

Its purpose for the overall thesis – This Second Part is needed in order to understand that the individual instruments analysed in the Third Part of this dissertation are supposed to be building blocks that advance the ILO's overarching goals. Understanding that link is crucial. The instruments analysed in the Third Part advance principles and approaches that might be useful in dealing with platform work, yet those guidelines should be situated within the ILO's overall normative framework. A framework that still aims to provide: "decent work for all". 103

Furthermore, if Part IV plans to sketch what "decent work in the platform economy" might look like, Part II must uncover what "decent work" itself means. Decent 104 work and the ILO's normative agenda, more broadly, offer the foundation for this dissertation's Chapter on what the ILO can do to regulate digital labour platforms.

Chapter 1. The International Labour Charter and Declaration of Philadelphia

SUBCHAPTER 1. DEFINING CHARACTERISTICS OF THE INTERNATIONAL LABOUR ORGANIZATION

The struggle for peace – The ILO Constitution is a product of the Peace Conference 105
in Versailles. The High Contracting Parties intended to construct an infrastructure that would eradicate the causes of war.[313] Part XIII of the Versailles Treaty contains an International Labour Charter to that end. One of its core tenets is that universal peace "can be established only if it is based upon social justice".[314] To become a reality, the Treaty also founded an organisation guided by the convictions and principles engrained in this Charter, dedicated to social justice: the International Labour Organization.[315] It was a timely development, given recent events such as the end of World War I, the rise of an international workers' movement and the October Revolution of 1917.[316] As such, the High Contracting Parties were genuinely moved, as the Preamble of the ILO Constitution admits, "by the desire to secure the permanent peace of the world" because at that time, "conditions of labour exist[ed] involving such injustice, hardship and privation to large numbers of people as to produce unrest so great that the peace and harmony of the world are imperilled". Throughout the twentieth century, many have continued to approach the ILO's reason for existence from this perspective. Former ILO Director-General Hansenne, for example, stated that the organisation's *raison d'être* "can be summed up in few

313. Pierre-Olivier de Broux, *L'Internationalisation des Droits Sociaux Fondamentaux. De la Paix Mondiale à la Justice Sociale: Les Origines de la Charte Sociale Européenne* 15, 20 (Sébastien Van Drooghenbroeck, Filip Dorssemont & Guido Van Limberghen eds., *Europees Sociaal Handvest, Sociale Rechten en Grondrechten op de Werkvloer / Charte Sociale Européenne, Droit Sociaux et Droits Fondamentaux au Travail*, die Keure 2016).
314. Section I, part XIII. Labour, Treaty of Peace of Versailles, 28 June 1919.
315. Janelle M. Diller, *Social Justice, Rights, and Labour* 296, 308 (Dinah Shelton ed., *The Oxford Handbook of International Human Rights Law*, OUP 2013).
316. Werner Meng, *Article 57* 1611, 1628 (Bruno Simma et al. eds., *The Charter of the United Nations: A Commentary*, II, OUP 2012).

words: to contribute to universal and lasting peace through the promotion and development of social justice".[317]

106 **A specialised UN agency** – Regarding its position in the multilateral system, the ILO practically replaced the International Association for the Legal Protection of Workers and the International Association for Labour Legislation.[318] As an "autonomous partner" of the League of Nations,[319] once the ILO became fully operational, it systematically drafted and adopted international labour standards every year.[320] Moreover, partially because of a turn towards human rights in the 1940s, which 1944's Declaration concerning the Aims and Purposes of the International Labour Organization (Declaration of Philadelphia) contributed to,[321] the ILO's International Labour Conference adopted instruments that would later become designated as the Fundamental Conventions.[322] The adoption of the Freedom of Association and Protection of the Right to Organise Convention, (No. 87) 1948,[323] the Right to Organise and Collective Bargaining Convention, (No. 98) 1949,[324] the Equal Remuneration Convention, (No. 100) 1951, and the Discrimination (Employment and Occupation) Convention, (No. 111) 1958, was, arguably, an attempt by the ILO (and its constituents) to outshine the newly founded United Nations' Economic and Social Council.[325] An interesting observation, considering how the ILO became the first specialised agency of the United Nations in 1946.

107 As a specialised agency, the ILO remained autonomous, but cooperation became institutionalised under a relationship agreement.[326] The organisation is expected

317. ILO Director-General, *Defending Values, Promoting Change. Social Justice in a Global Economy: An ILO Agenda* 25 (ILO 1994). The organisation was clearly meant to, at least in part, reconcile social justice and capitalism so as to supress the threat of revolution. Guy F. Sinclair, *Managing the "Workers Threat": Preventing Revolution Through the International Labour Organization* 159, 159 (Michel Erpeldin, Burkhard Hess & Hélène Ruiz Fabri eds., *Peace Through Law: The Versailles peace treaty and dispute settlement after World War I*, Nomos 2019).
318. "Although its activities were interrupted by the [first world] war, the Association provided an important laboratory for the subsequent work of the ILO". Rodgers, Lee, Swepston & Van Daele, *supra* n. 53, at 4; Christian Deneve, *Internationaal Arbeidsrecht* 18–19 (die Keure 2010).
319. C. Wilfred Jenks, *Social Justice in the Law of Nations: The ILO Impact After Fifty Years* 16 (OUP 1970).
320. Bob Hepple, *Labour Laws and Global Trade* 25–29 (Hart Publishing 2005).
321. Alain Supiot, *L'Esprit de Philadelphie: La Justice Sociale Face au Marché Total* 21–24 (Seuil 2010); Adalberto Perulli, *The Declaration of Philadelphia (DoP)* 361, 363–364 (Edoardo Ales, Mark Bell, Olaf Deinert & Sophie Robin-Olivier eds., *International and European Labour Law Article-by-Article Commentary*, Nomos 2018).
322. Janice R. Bellace, *Achieving Social Justice: The Nexus Between the ILO's Fundamental Rights and Decent Work*, 15 Employee Rights and Employment Policy Journal 5, 11–12 n. 1 (2011).
323. Janice R. Bellace, *The ILO and Tripartism: The Challenge of Balancing the Three-Legged Stool* 289, 303 (George P. Politakis, Tomi Kohiyama & Thomas Lieby eds., *ILO100: Law for Social Justice*, ILO 2019).
324. Henner Gött, *Interactions Between International Organizations: Approaching a Neglected Governance Dimension*, 17 International Organizations Law Review 75, 83–84 n. 1 (2020).
325. Laurence R. Helfer, *Understanding Change in International Organizations: Globalization and Innovation in the ILO*, 59 Vanderbilt Law Review 649, 693 n. 3 (2006).
326. Protocol concerning the entry into force of the Agreement Between the United Nations and the International Labour Organization, 19 December 1946. Meng categorises the ILO's agreement as a rather "close relationship agreement", but without the organisation losing its "institutional

to, for instance, advance the aims of the UN Charter.[327] Furthermore, some have even argued that the ILO has a vital role in fulfilling the International Covenant on Economic, Social and Cultural Rights. Most notably, C. Wilfred Jenks, also a former ILO Director-General,[328] claimed that "[i]t is through the provisions of the International Labour Code that [the Covenant's] rights are given a specific content and become practically enforceable".[329] Nowadays, something similar could be argued about the UN's Sustainable Development Goals, and SDG 8, in particular. The ILO could, in theory, further substantiate these concepts and targets.[330]

The ILO's institutional infrastructure – Looking at the organisation itself, the ILO is composed of three main organs: a General Conference of representatives, known as the International Labour Conference (ILC), a Governing Body (GB) and the International Labour Office ("the Office").[331] The ILC is the yearly highlight. This is when ILO constituents, *inter alia*, accept the budget, scrutinise Member States' adherence to ILO standards and vote on adopting new ILO instruments. Traditionally, during June, all Member States are represented by a delegation that consists of two governmental delegates, a worker delegate and an employer delegate. A Credentials Committee supervises the composition of this delegation.[332] The ILO Constitution guarantees that "[e]very delegate shall be entitled to vote individually on all matters which are taken into consideration by the Conference".[333] 108

Like the ILC, the entire governance structure of the ILO is characterised by "tripartism".[334] Under the ILO Constitution, the GB must be made up of representatives from governments, workers and employers.[335] It is an essential feature because, in reality, 109

autonomy". Werner Meng, *Article 63* 1697, 1698 (Bruno Simma et al. eds., *The Charter of the United Nations: A Commentary*, II, OUP 2012).

327. Rosalyn Higgins et al., *Oppenheim's International Law: United Nations*, I, 232 (OUP 2017).
328. Jenks also had an important role in drafting the Declaration of Philadelphia in his prior capacity as Legal Adviser. Emmanuel Reynaud, *The International Labour Organization and Globalization: Fundamental Rights, Decent Work and Social Justice* 18 (ILO 2018).
329. Jenks, *supra* n. 319, at 71.
330. "In its 2019 report to the Conference, the Committee of Experts highlighted the fact that several targets in the 2030 Agenda for Sustainable Development had the potential to simultaneously benefit from and raise the profile of the standards supervisory work in the ILO's second century". ILO, *Monitoring Compliance With International Labour Standards: The Key Role of the ILO Committee of Experts on the Application of Conventions and Recommendations* 94 (ILO 2019). *See also*, Vitit Muntarbhorn, *Labour Rights, Human Rights and Challenges of Connectivity* 531, 541-543 (George P. Politakis, Tomi Kohiyama & Thomas Lieby eds., *ILO100: Law for Social Justice*, ILO 2019).
331. Art. 2 ILO Constitution.
332. Faina Milman-Sivan, *Freedom of Association in Deliberative Spaces: The ILO Credentials Committee* 204, 204-216 (Adelle Blackett & Anne Trebilcock eds., *Research Handbook on Transnational Labour* Law, Edward Elgar Publishing 2015).
333. Art. 4 ILO Constitution.
334. For instance, the Office has a Bureau for Employers' Activities (ACTEMP), which is related to the International Organisation for Employers, and a Bureau for Workers' Activities (ACTRAV), which is related to the International Trade Union Confederation. Both monitor the work of the Office and ILO more broadly. Also, the supervisory mechanisms of the ILO are largely tripartite. Both the Conference Committee on the Application of Standards and the Committee on Freedom of Association have a tripartite composition.
335. Art. 3 and 7 ILO Constitution.

the GB, which usually convenes three times a year, might be the most influential ILO organ.[336] It not only determines the agenda of the Conference, therefore giving it control over, for instance, the organisation's standard-setting activities, it also controls the Office and monitors the functioning of the ILO's supervisory bodies. Some have, therefore, portrayed the GB as the organisation's "linchpin". It wields the organisation's executive powers.[337]

110 The tripartite composition of both the ILC and GB has functional purposes: increasing both bodies' legitimacy and enabling effective action/implementation. The fact that the drafters managed to transpose tripartism and social dialogue from the domestic level to the international level is considered one of the ILO founders' most significant achievements.[338] Some have even called it "an historical and theoretical anomaly".[339] What might have had something to do with it were, for instance, "short-term political anxieties"[340] in the early twentieth century, and the governments' willingness to reward workers and employers for their suffering during the war.[341] According to Klabbers, Great Britain, in particular, would have been satisfied with how workers and employers had contributed to the war effort, making it a desirable prospect to implement tripartism on a broader scale domestically. However, Britain feared creating a comparative disadvantage if it would do so on its own. The ILO might have been a means to transpose tripartism beyond Britain's borders, attenuating this fear of a comparative disadvantage.[342]

111 Regardless of the original motives, tripartism has trickled down into all aspects of the organisation,[343] and the ILO has, in turn, actively promoted it at the domestic level. Moreover, its importance as a crucial feature of the organisation is not fading. Official ILO documents consistently highlight its importance.[344] Somavía, another former Director-General, has called it "the source of the ILO's strength and identity".[345]

336. Marieke Louis, *Who Decides? Representation and Decision-Making at the International Labour Organization*, 11 International Development Policy / Revue internationale de politique de développement 40, 40–58 (2019).
337. Victor-Yves Ghebali, *The International Labour Organisation: A Case Study on the Evolution of U.N Specialised Agencies* 141 (Martinus Nijhoff 1989).
338. Rodgers, Lee, Swepston & Van Daele, *supra* n. 53, at 14.
339. Jonathan Symons, *The Legitimation of International Organisations: Examining the Identity of the Communities that Grant Legitimacy*, 37 Review of International Studies 2557, 2574 n. 5 (2011).
340. Laurence R. Helfer, *supra* n. 325, at 679.
341. Hugo Stokke, *Decent Work: Principles, policies and programmes of the International Labour Organisation* 305 (University of Bergen 2015).
342. Jan Klabbers, *An Accidental Revolution: The ILO and the Opening Up of International Law* 132–133 (Tarja Halonen & Ulla Liukkunen eds., *International Labour Organization and Global Social Governance*, Springer 2021).
343. "Social dialogue, including collective bargaining and tripartite cooperation, provides an essential foundation of all ILO action and contributes to successful policy and decision-making in its member States". ILO Centenary Declaration for the Future of Work, 21 June 2019.
344. For example, Resolution and conclusions concerning the second recurrent discussion on social dialogue and tripartism, 107th Session of the International Labour Conference in 2018.
345. Juan Somavía, *A Stronger ILO: Meeting the Need for a Social Dimension of Globalization Through the Decent Work Agenda* v, vi (ILO ed., *Report V Strengthening the ILO's Capacity to Assist its Members' Efforts to Reach its Objectives in the Context of Globalization*, ILO 2007).

Academics similarly highlight how "the ILO's tripartite structure has been integral to its longevity and its continuing relevance".[346] Maupain, a former ILO Legal Adviser – the highest legal position in the organisation – has even argued that "[i]t is tripartism alone which gives gravitas and clout to the organisation's presence and advice, not least at forums like the G20".[347]

SUBCHAPTER 2. THE ORIGINAL ILO MANDATE

The ILO mandate – Article 1 of the ILO Constitution states that the organisation aims to promote the objectives set out in the Preamble and Declaration of Philadelphia. This mandate is largely spurred on by the Office, of which the staff "shall not seek or receive instructions from any government or from any other authority external to the Organization".[348] The Office, including its Director-General, can be understood to pursue the ILO mandate within the boundaries prescribed by the decisions of the GB and ILC. ILO constituents have a strong voice in this regard.[349] Their ability to steer the Office is partly the result of the ILO's original mandate, which has been written in vague terms to allow the ILO to take any action needed in the interest of social justice.[350] As such, the founding documents do not define or describe social justice.[351] The ILO seems to consider social justice a disposition rather than a defined, static concept.[352] It is a "guiding star" that can never be fully attained.[353] The Office pursues it in compliance with the instructions from ILO constituents. 112

346. Bellace, *supra* n. 323, at 289.
347. Francis Maupain, *The Future of the International Labour Organization in the Global Economy* 248 (Hart Publishing 2013). Along similar lines, tripartism would grant the ILO's international labour standards a particular legitimacy that other international instruments usually lack. Jean-Claude Javillier, *Presentation* v, v (Jean-Claude Javillier ed., *International Labour Standards: A Global Approach: 75th Anniversary of the Committee of Experts on the Application of Conventions and Recommendations*, ILO 2002).
348. Art. 9 ILO Constitution.
349. For instance, Murray has argued that the position of the Office should be reinforced, enabling it to impose itself when ILO constituents take decisions that are counterproductive in light of the constitutional mandate. Jill Murray, *Taking Social Rights Seriously: Is there a Case for Institutional Reform of the ILO?* 359, 377–378 (Colin Fenwick & Tonia Novitz eds., *Human Rights at Work: Perspectives on Law and Regulation*, Hart Publishing 2010).
350. ILO, *Dix Ans d'Organisation Internationale du Travail* 105–106 (ILO 1931).
351. Sandrine Kott, *L'OIT et la Justice Sociale (1919–2019)* 49, 50 (George P. Politakis, Tomi Kohiyama & Thomas Lieby eds., *ILO100: Law for Social Justice*, ILO 2019).
352. ILO, *supra* n. 350, at 106.
353. Marcelo G. Kohen, *Does General International Law Incorporate the Concept of Social Justice?* 91, 100 (George P. Politakis, Tomi Kohiyama & Thomas Lieby eds., *ILO100: Law for Social Justice*, ILO 2019). For example, Supiot argues that social justice or a "truly humane labour regime" manifests itself time and again based on both a specific combination of guiding principles and the "procedures that will allow the implementation of these principles to evolve in response to technical, economic or sociological changes". Alain Supiot, Sandrine Kott & Laure Piguet, *De l'"Esprit de Philadelphie" à la Responsabilité Sociale et Environnementale des Entreprises*, 263 Revue Le Mouvement Social 153, 159 n. 1 (2018). *See also*, Supiot, *supra* n. 17, at 118. The same is true for Maupain, who claims the ILO's understanding of social justice implies a process that gives the Constitution's values and principles a specific content and meaning in light of the circumstances. Francis Maupain, *A Second Century for What? The ILO at a Regulatory Crossroad*, 17 International Organizations Law Review 291, 297 n. 1 (2020).

113 These days, the ILO's constitutional mandate primarily derives from the Declaration of Philadelphia, which was annexed to the Constitution. The Declaration significantly expanded the original mandate of the ILO.[354] For instance, whereas the ILO was initially concerned with specific categories of workers, such as industrial workers in wage employment, in the Declaration of Philadelphia, the Conference affirmed that:

> "(a) all human beings, irrespective of race, creed or sex, have the right to pursue both their material well-being and their spiritual development in conditions of freedom and dignity, of economic security and equal opportunity;
>
> (b) the attainment of the conditions in which this shall be possible must constitute the central aim of national and international policy; [...]
>
> (d) it is a responsibility of the International Labour Organization to examine and consider all international economic and financial policies and measures in the light of this fundamental objective".[355]

114 In other words, the organisation aims to improve human beings' conditions of freedom, human dignity, economic security and equal opportunity in the world of work, enabling them to pursue their material well-being and spiritual development. With this goal in mind, the ILO is responsible for evaluating national and international policies to ensure that these policies contribute to social justice.[356] The fore-cited paragraphs are a reminder of the ILO's post-war endeavour to become "an economic and social 'master agency'" that would oversee other international organisations' policies.[357] Although this proved unachievable, evaluating economic and financial policies in light of social objectives still constitutes one of its main tasks in the multilateral system.[358] The ILO aims to re-embed the market into the social sphere, or, put in stronger terms, to subordinate the economy to social justice;[359] a goal that exceeds the organisation's capacities. For instance, in 2004, the World Commission on the Social Dimension of Globalization called out the imbalance between the economic power and influence of organisations involved in trade and finance compared to the organisations involved in social and development policies.[360] Because of this, the

354. Eddy Lee, *The Declaration of Philadelphia: Retrospect and Prospect*, 133 International Labour Law Review 467, 467 n. 4 (1994).
355. Declaration concerning the aims and purposes of the International Labour Organisation (Declaration of Philadelphia), 10 May 1944.
356. "The Declaration of Philadelphia sets forth the principle of the primacy of social objectives over those of economic policy". M. Humblet & M. Zakra-Matres, *ILO Standards Policy* 1, 6 (Jean-Claude Javillier ed., *International Labour Standards: A Global Approach: 75th Anniversary of the Committee of Experts on the Application of Conventions and Recommendations*, ILO 2002).
357. Gött, *supra* n. 324, at 81.
358. *Ibid.*, 88–91.
359. Tonia Novitz, *Past and Future Work at the International Labour Organization: Labour as a Fictitious Commodity, Countermovement and Sustainability*, 17 International Organizations Law Review 10, 10–40 n. 1 (2020); Emilios Christodoulidis, *The ILO and the New 'Common Sense': Reflections on a Centenary* 35, 39 (Marc Bungenberg, Markus Krajewski, Christian J. Tams & Jörg Philipp Terhechte eds., *European Yearbook of International Economic Law 2019*, Springer International Publishing 2020).
360. World Commission on the Social Dimension of Globalization, *A Fair Globalization: Creating Opportunities for All* 134 (ILO 2004). Some are optimistic, mentioning that the situation is slowly re-balancing. Joost Pauwelyn, *Is Globalization Finally Re-Balancing? Novel Ways of*

Commission recommended to, for example, also perform "regular national reviews of the social implications of economic, financial and trade policies" to complement the ILO's efforts.[361]

In light of its broad mandate and herculean assignment, Diller, a former Deputy Legal Adviser, has noted that the ILO developed into something akin to an "International Economic Organization".[362] The ILO thereby pursues its socio-economic aims based on a "strong ethical mandate" given to it by the Constitution.[363] The Constitution provides the ILO with the "cognitive framework for its work – the spectacles through which the ILO sees the world".[364] This cognitive framework is made up of, among other things, the Declaration of Philadelphia's fundamental principles: 115

> "(a) labour is not a commodity; (b) freedom of expression and of association are essential to sustained progress; (c) poverty anywhere constitutes a danger to prosperity everywhere; (d) the war against want requires to be carried on with unrelenting vigour within each nation, and by continuous and concerted international effort in which the representatives of workers and employers, enjoying equal status with those of governments, join with them in free discussion and democratic decision with a view to the promotion of the common welfare".[365]

A legalistic organisation – Under its mandate, the ILO swiftly adopted a broad range of ILS on subjects such as working time, young persons and maternity protection. The adoption of ILS used to be one of the organisation's main tasks.[366] ILS mostly come in two forms: ILO Conventions (or Protocols) and ILO Recommendations. Conventions are legally binding international treaties, whereas Recommendations provide for non-binding guidelines.[367] The ILC decides whether to pursue a Convention or Recommendation, or, as is often done, both a Convention and associated Recommendation on the same topic. As prescribed by the ILO Constitution, "[i]n either case a majority of two-thirds of the votes cast by the delegates present shall be necessary on the final vote for the adoption of the Convention or Recommendation, as the case may be, by the Conference".[368] Once adopted, the Member States are 116

Levelling the Playing Field for Labour 647, 647–659 (George P. Politakis, Tomi Kohiyama & Thomas Lieby eds., *ILO100: Law for Social Justice*, ILO 2019).

361. World Commission on the Social Dimension of Globalization, *supra* n. 360, at 134. *See also*, ILO Director-General, *A Fair Globalization: The Role of the ILO* 16 (ILO 2004).
362. Diller, *supra* n. 315, at 303.
363. ILO Director-General, *supra* n. 361, at 3.
364. Rodgers, Lee, Swepston & Van Daele, *supra* n. 53, at 7.
365. Declaration concerning the aims and purposes of the International Labour Organisation (Declaration of Philadelphia), 10 May 1944.
366. Lee Swepston, *International Labour Law* 155, 156 (Roger Blanpain ed., *Comparative Labour Law and Industrial Relations in Industrialized Market Economies*, Kluwer 2014). This even led to an "overproduction" of instruments, according to some. Efrén Cordova, *Some Reflections on the Overproduction of International Labor Standards*, 14 Comparative Labor Law Journal 138, 138–162 n. 2 (1993); Sean Cooney, *Testing Times for the ILO: Institutional Reform for the New International Political Economy*, 20 Comparative Labor Law & Policy Journal 365, 373 n. 3 (1999).
367. ILO, *Rules of the Game: An Introduction to the Standards-Related Work of the International Labour Organization* 18 (ILO 2019).
368. Art. 19 ILO Constitution.

obliged by the ILO Constitution to bring new Conventions and Recommendations before the competent authorities at the domestic level – mostly parliaments – to enact legislation or undertake other actions. The ILO Committee of Experts on the Application of Conventions and Recommendations verifies whether the Member States indeed comply with their duty to follow up on the adoption of standards.[369] Apart from this duty to reflect on implementation, the actual ratification of Conventions and the implementation of guidelines remains entirely voluntary. Only the Member States that decide to ratify a Convention are fully subjected to the ILO's supervisory system. Under the regular supervisory system, the Committee of Experts monitors States' compliance with ratified Conventions, after which a discussion may ensue at the Conference Committee on the Application of Standards (CAS) in case of grave violations. The fact that States remain free to ratify Conventions and even if they do not ratify the Convention in question can, nevertheless, scrutinise other countries' implementing measures at the CAS, contributes to the ILO's "legal powerlessness" to fulfil its mandate through its standard-setting machinery.[370] Many of the more recent developments at the ILO, some of which are discussed below, are in part a response to this problem. The ILO has been searching for mechanisms that can transcend Member States' inertia.

117 Beyond the original importance of ILS as a tool to forge social justice, other reasons also explain why the ILO can be called a "legalistic organisation". More specifically, its internal governance relies heavily on legal instruments that are, for the most part, adopted by the GB and ILC, such as programmes and budgets, resolutions and conclusions. These instruments often instruct the Office to do something. The Office, subsequently, reports back, referring to the earlier legal document that instructed it. This Office document, then, provides the input for a new decision by the GB or ILC and, as such, the wheel keeps turning.[371] It is worth looking at the three more recent ILO Declarations from this perspective. The ILO Declaration on Fundamental Principles and Rights at Work (1998 Declaration), the ILO Declaration on Social Justice for a Fair Globalization from 2008 (Social Justice Declaration), and the ILO Centenary Declaration for the Future of Work from 2019 (Centenary Declaration) offer authoritative references to incite new policy. They have the necessary clout to direct this legalistic process in new directions.

118 **Institutional layering** – Contrary to the Declaration of Philadelphia, none of these three Declarations has been annexed to the ILO Constitution. Therefore, the Constitution and Declaration of Philadelphia remain unchanged; these are the only "constitutional" documents. The latest Declarations merely contribute to "institutional layering", meaning that existing institutions are maintained – i.e. the constitutional documents – but new elements are attached to these institutions, allowing for gradual

369. *See, e.g.*, Direct Request on submission to competent authorities (CEACR) – adopted 2013, published 103rd ILC session (2014) – Mexico.
370. Alain Supiot, *supra* n. 17, at 125.
371. "The communications of the system, its decisions, are created only on the basis of what is legal, they make reference to previous legal decisions (e.g. standing orders, internal directives, etc.) and produce subsequent legal decisions". Carlos García Guzmán, *The International Labour Organization as an Autopoietic System* 797, 810 (George P. Politakis, Tomi Kohiyama & Thomas Lieby eds., *ILO100: Law for Social Justice*, ILO 2019).

institutional transformation.[372] Each of the three latest Declarations provides the ILO, including the Office, with a solid moral and legal foundation to pursue novel policies and objectives within the pre-established and unchanged boundaries of the original Constitution. The following Chapters cover these Declarations and their connection to digital labour platforms.

372. Velibor Jakovleski, Scott Jerbi & Thomas Biersteker, *The ILO's Role in Global Governance: Limits and Potential*, 11 Revue Internationale de Politique de Développement / International Development Policy 82, §50 (2019). On the concept: Jeroen van der Heijden, *Institutional Layering: A Review of the Use of the Concept*, 31 Politics 9, 9 n. 1 (2011).

Chapter 2. The Decent Work Agenda: A Blueprint for the Twenty-First Century

SUBCHAPTER 1. THE DECLARATION ON FUNDAMENTAL PRINCIPLES AND RIGHTS

Before the 1998 Declaration – The latest Declarations did not come out of the blue. **119**
The 1970s and 1980s were a difficult period for the ILO. Its work suffered from political tensions between the United States and the Soviet Union, and tensions regarding, among other subjects, apartheid in South Africa, Pinochet in Chile, Franco in Spain and Solidarność in Poland.[373] The United States even withdrew from the organisation in 1977, primarily for political reasons,[374] only to re-join it again in 1980.[375] In addition to this political instability, more fundamentally, "the 'Philadelphia consensus', based on an understanding of an intrinsic relationship of social and economic policies and the ultimate primacy of a social objective of all policies, began to crumble".[376] Industrialised economies intellectually distanced themselves from the ILO, opting for IMF, World Bank and OECD policies instead. The organisation was also largely ignored during the Uruguay Round of trade negotiations on the General Agreement on Tariffs and Trade (GATT). This indifference coincided with the opposition of developing countries to any ILO discussions on a social clause in trade agreements. Such a clause would have made it necessary for developing countries to comply with specific social standards in order to participate in international trade.[377] As a result of these developments,[378] the organisation and

373. Van Daele, *supra* n. 47, at 502–503; Daniel Maul, *The International Labour Organization: 100 Years of Global Social Policy* 219–240 (Walter de Gruyter 2019).
374. Christopher C. Joyner, *The United States' Withdrawal from the ILO: International Politics in the Labor Arena*, 12 International Lawyer 721, 721–739 n. 4 (1978).
375. Paul E. Masters, *The International Labor Organization: America's Withdrawal and Reentry*, 71 International Social Science Review 14, 23 n. 3–4 (1996).
376. Maul, *supra* n. 373, at 245.
377. Rodgers, Lee, Swepston & Van Daele, *supra* n. 53, at 213–216.
378. Diane F. Frey, *Social Justice, Neoliberalism, and Labor Standards at the International Labour Organization* 285, 287–289 (Gillian MacNaughton & Diane F. Frey eds., *Economic and Social*

its philosophy were side-lined in many significant discussions during the twentieth century's final decades.[379]

120 **World Summit for Social Development** – Although the organisation's position on the international scene remained shaky, a momentous turn of events came in 1995. The Programme of Action of the World Summit for Social Development in Copenhagen called on governments to safeguard and promote respect for "basic workers' rights". The Programme of Action pointed to forced labour and child labour, the need for freedom of association, the right to organise and bargain collectively, equal remuneration, and non-discrimination in employment. This selection of basic workers' rights echoed 1994's ILO Resolution concerning the 75th Anniversary of the ILO and its Future Orientation.[380] According to section 54 of the World Summit's Programme of Action, Member States needed to strive for full implementation if they ratified the ILO Conventions associated with these topics. Moreover, crucially, the States that had not ratified these Conventions should, nevertheless, take into account "the principles embodied in those conventions".[381] Soon after 1995's Social Summit, it became clear, furthermore, that the World Trade Organization would not deal with the linkage between trade and social standards. The Singapore WTO Ministerial Declaration from 1996 reasserted the ILO's role as the agency in charge of social justice on the global stage. The WTO Ministers renewed their "commitment to the observance of internationally recognized core labour standards".[382]

121 The ILO relied on these two international developments to reposition itself. Efforts to devise a social clause or social labels seemed to go nowhere,[383] bolstering the organisation to construe a Declaration on top of section 54(b) of 1995's Programme of Action. It was, arguably, a bold attempt to recover lost ground.[384]

Rights in a Neoliberal World, CUP 2018).

379. Guy Standing, *The ILO: An Agency for Globalization?*, 39 Development and Change 355, 361–365 n. 3 (2008); Yifeng Chen, *Proliferation of Transnational Labour Standards: The Role of the ILO* 97, 98–99 (Tarja Halonen & Ulla Liukkunen eds., *International Labour Organization and Global Social Governance*, Springer 2021).

380. "Noting the particular importance of ILO Conventions covering fundamental rights, including Conventions Nos. 87, 98, 100, 29 and 105, and 111". Resolution concerning the 75th anniversary of the ILO and its future orientation, 81st Session of the International Labour Conference in 1994.

381. Para. 54 Programme of Action of the World Summit for Social Development, 14 March 1995, A/CONF.166/9.

382. The paragraph continues: "The International Labour Organization (ILO) is the competent body to set and deal with these standards, and we affirm our support for its work in promoting them. We believe that economic growth and development fostered by increased trade and further trade liberalization contribute to the promotion of these standards. We reject the use of labour standards for protectionist purposes, and agree that the comparative advantage of countries, particularly low-wage developing countries, must in no way be put into question. In this regard, we note that the WTO and ILO Secretariats will continue their existing collaboration". Singapore Ministerial Declaration, 13 December 1996, WT/MIN(96)/DEC.

383. Huw Thomas & Peter Turnbull, *From a 'Moral Commentator' to a 'Determined Actor'? How the International Labour Organization (ILO) Orchestrates the Field of International Industrial Relations*, British Journal of Industrial Relations 1, 13 (2020).

384. Tapiola – a former Deputy Director-General – has said that "[t]he Office knew only too well that the moment there was a draft text on the table, a good number of actors would happily start

The 1998 Declaration - The core mechanism of the 1998 Declaration consists of two parts. First, the ILC "recalls" that Member States have endorsed the principles and rights in the ILO Constitution and Declaration of Philadelphia by becoming a member of the organisation. These constitutional principles and rights have come to expression throughout the decades in the so-called "Fundamental Conventions",[385] which are "recognized as fundamental both inside and outside the Organization".[386] Having recalled this, the ILC declares - and this is the innovative part: 122

> "that all Members, even if they have not ratified the Conventions in question, have an obligation arising from the very fact of membership in the Organization to respect, to promote and to realize, in good faith and in accordance with the Constitution, the principles concerning the fundamental rights which are the subject of those Conventions, namely: (a) freedom of association and the effective recognition of the right to collective bargaining; (b) the elimination of all forms of forced or compulsory labour; (c) the effective abolition of child labour; and (d) the elimination of discrimination in respect of employment and occupation".[387]

In other words, because the Member States have already accepted the rights and principles set out in the ILO Constitution and Declaration of Philadelphia, and these rights and principles have taken form in the Fundamental Conventions, as of 1998, the ILC declares that the ILO Member States have to respect, promote and realise, in good faith, "the principles concerning the fundamental rights which are the subject of those Conventions". This statement was a sweeping development. Member States' voluntary ratification of Conventions has long been a frustrating feature of ILO standard-setting because many States refuse to ratify Conventions,[388] even the fundamental ones.[389] The Declaration, which was preceded by a ratification campaign 123

shooting it down. For some time there was a draft of a kind in my office, which Government representatives and the constituents could read but which could not be copied or distributed. Such a cloak-and-dagger approach might not be possible with the technologies used twenty years later". Kari Tapiola, *The Teeth of the ILO – The Impact of the 1998 ILO Declaration on Fundamental Principles and Rights at Work* 32 (ILO 2018).

385. The eight Fundamental Conventions are the Forced Labour Convention, 1930 (No. 29), Freedom of Association and Protection of the Right to Organise Convention, 1948 (No. 87), Right to Organise and Collective Bargaining Convention, 1949 (No. 98), Equal Remuneration Convention, 1951 (No. 100), Abolition of Forced Labour Convention, 1957 (No. 105), Discrimination (Employment and Occupation) Convention, 1958 (No. 111), Minimum Age Convention, 1973 (No. 138), and Worst Forms of Child Labour Convention, 1999 (No. 182).
386. Art. 1 ILO Declaration on Fundamental Principles and Rights at Work and its Follow-up, 18 June 1998.
387. *Ibid.*, Art. 2.
388. ILO Director-General, *supra* n. 317, at 43–44.
389. For instance, the Republic of Korea only ratified 29 Conventions, including four of the eight Fundamental Conventions. It has not ratified the Fundamental Conventions on collective rights and forced labour. This is striking when compared to countries like Belgium, that have ratified 113 Conventions and two Protocols, including all Fundamental Conventions. Also, in particular, some of the more influential ILO Member States have a poor record of ratifying Conventions. The United States ratified 14 Conventions, including two Fundamental Conventions, which leaves 66 up-to-date Conventions and Protocols unratified. China ratified 26 Conventions, including four Fundamental Conventions. Indonesia, which has a higher population than France, Italy, Germany and Spain combined, ratified 20 Conventions, including all Fundamental Conventions.

concerning the Fundamental Conventions, gave the ILO a focus on fundamental principles and rights at work, which it could leverage to increase its visibility.[390]

124 **The fallout from the 1998 Declaration** – Because the 1998 Declaration was a bold move,[391] it is not surprising that it has drawn (constructive) criticism. Two lines of criticism are discussed because they are relevant to frame future discussions. The first one has to do with the Declaration's language, which is too vague. The second criticism relates to the choice of Fundamental Conventions and, hence, the selection of fundamental principles and rights.

125 **Vague terminology** – The Declaration, an example of realpolitik,[392] uses the language needed to get the Declaration approved. For instance, as noted by Maul, "[w]ithout the explicit statement in the Declaration that labour standards 'should not be used for protectionist trade purposes' and the pledge that 'the comparative advantage of any country should in no way be called into question by this Declaration and its follow-up', it is highly doubtful that it would have been adopted at all".[393] Similarly, for this instrument to see the light, the language used to describe the core mechanism probably had to remain sufficiently ambiguous. In her book on the topic, La Hovary mentioned in 2009 that no definitive answer had been given about potential differences between the Declaration's principles and the Fundamental Conventions' content. The vague linkage between the Declaration and the Fundamental Conventions left some room to interpret the 1998 Declaration's principles differently from the principles and rights in these Conventions.[394] In 2011, a significant development seemed to have taken place in this regard. In the context of corporate social responsibility, Foundational Principle 12 of the United Nations' Guiding Principles on Business and Human Rights prescribes that:

> "[t]he responsibility of business enterprises to respect human rights refers to internationally recognized human rights – understood, at a minimum, as those expressed in the International Bill of Human Rights and the principles concerning fundamental rights set out in the International Labour Organization's Declaration on Fundamental Principles and Rights at Work".

390. It provided, among other things, access to ongoing discussions at other international organisations. Janice R. Bellace, *The ILO Declaration of Fundamental Principles and Rights at Work*, 17 International Journal of Comparative Labour Law and Industrial Relations 269, 269–287 n. 3 (2001).
391. José E. Alvarez, *Frameworks for Understanding the ILO* 59, 64 (George P. Politakis, Tomi Kohiyama & Thomas Lieby eds., *ILO100: Law for Social Justice*, ILO 2019).
392. Kari Tapiola, *What Happened to International Labour Standards and Human Rights at Work?* 51, 56–58 (Tarja Halonen & Ulla Liukkunen eds., *International Labour Organization and Global Social Governance*, Springer 2021).
393. Maul, *supra* n. 373, at 261. This paragraph from the 1998 Declaration has received clarifications in the Social Justice Declaration. The Social Justice Declaration notes "that the violation of fundamental principles and rights at work cannot be invoked or otherwise used as a legitimate comparative advantage and that labour standards should not be used for protectionist trade purposes". Para. I.A.(iv) ILO Declaration on Social Justice for a Fair Globalization, 10 June 2008.
394. Claire la Hovary, *Les Droits Fondamentaux au Travail: Origines, Statut et Impact en Droit International* 206–209 (The Graduate Institute Geneva 2009).

Although it is noteworthy for the 1998 Declaration to be singled out together with the International Bill of Human Rights, it is the official commentary underneath Foundational Principle 12 that was surprising. The commentary mentions that:

> "[a]n authoritative list of the core internationally recognized human rights is contained in the International Bill of Human Rights [...], coupled with the principles concerning fundamental rights in the eight ILO core conventions as set out in the Declaration on Fundamental Principles and Rights at Work. These are the benchmarks against which other social actors assess the human rights impacts of business enterprises".[395]

Therefore, the commentary explicitly links the "fundamental rights" in the eight **126** Fundamental Conventions and the 1998 Declaration's principles. More broadly, regardless of the UN Guiding Principles, the Declaration's fundamental principles seem to have stayed more faithful to the content of the Fundamental Conventions than some might have anticipated. According to Frey, the fact that the bond between the Fundamental Conventions and the 1998 Declaration's principles endured was "[t]o the consternation of many countries and employers".[396] In a similar vein, according to Bellace, the UN Guiding Principles might have handed the Employers' group a reason to vehemently challenge the right to strike in 2011 and at 2012's ILO Committee on the Application of Standards.[397] The Employers' group claimed that the Freedom of Association and Protection of the Right to Organise Convention, 1948 (No. 87), which is a Fundamental Convention, does not contain principles regarding the right to strike, and even if it did, it could only give rise to a general right to strike. The Employers' group's opinion clashed with the views of the ILO's supervisory bodies, which have long held that the right to strike is protected under Convention No. 87.[398] From the Employers' perspective, however, if the supervisory bodies' views on this matter were left unchallenged, then, the commentary to the UN's Guiding Principles would suggest that the 1998 Declaration covers the right to strike. In turn, this would entail that businesses have the responsibility to respect the right to strike,[399] even if local governments do not acknowledge or protect this right.

---

395. United Nations, *Guiding Principles on Business and Human Rights: Implementing the United Nations "Protect, Respect and Remedy" Framework* 14 (UN 2011).
396. Frey, *supra* n. 378, at 291.
397. Janice R. Bellace, *ILO Convention No. 87 and the Right to Strike in an Era of Global Trade*, 39 Comparative Labor Law & Policy Journal 495, 524–525 n. 3 (2018). *See also*, Jeffrey Vogt et al., *The Right to Strike in International Law* 14 (Hart Publishing 2020).
398. The ILO Committee of Experts reaffirmed in 2012's general survey "that the right to strike derives from the Convention". ILO Committee of Experts on the Application of Conventions and Recommendations, *Giving Globalization a Human Face* 49 (ILO 2012). Similarly, the ILO Committee on Freedom of Association continues to see the right to strike as "an intrinsic corollary to the right to organize protected by Convention No. 87". ILO Committee on Freedom of Association, *Freedom of Association: Compilation of Decisions of the Committee on Freedom of Association* 143 (ILO 2018).
399. "The International Bill of Human Rights and the core ILO conventions provide basic reference points for businesses in starting to understand what human rights are; how their own activities may affect them; and how to ensure that they prevent or mitigate the risk of adverse impact". United Nations, *The Corporate Responsibility to Respect Human Rights: An Interpretative Guide* 11 (UN 2012).

Companies that do not see their workers going on strike because local governments do not safeguard the right to strike view this as a competitive advantage. One they would hate to lose. According to Bellace, "[t]his is the economic reality that may well underlie the 2012 rupture, with governments the primary cause of the instability of the tripartite arrangement".[400]

127 **Only eight Fundamental Conventions** – A second reason why the 1998 Declaration was criticised is the relatively limited list of fundamental principles and rights. The Declaration aimed to revitalise the ILO by singling out core labour standards and promoting those standards.[401] Overall, the 1998 Declaration has been quite successful in this respect. The Declaration, and broader ratification campaign, significantly boosted the rate of ratifications of the Fundamental Conventions. Even before the UN Guiding Principles were issued, Breining-Kaufmann had already argued that "the ILO formulation of core labour rights reflects a universal consensus, bringing these rights close to obligations erga omnes".[402] Furthermore, as evidenced by the UN Guiding Principles, the ILO's core labour rights are human rights, not just workers' rights.[403] This qualification implies that these core labour rights protect all workers, including informal workers and the self-employed, regardless of employment status.

128 Such observations make the critique that the selection of the four categories of principles and rights is arbitrary, even more poignant. Alston has called it a pragmatic political selection that disregarded many other ILS with a foundation in human rights law.[404] An often-cited example is a right to healthy and safe working conditions, which could also be considered fundamental.[405] This question has become particularly topical due to the proposal of the Global Commission on the Future of Work in 2019 to make safety and health at work a fifth category of fundamental principles and rights at work.[406] The ILO constituents subsequently watered down the Global Commission's proposal during 2019's ILC. They rephrased the Commission's wording in the Centenary Declaration, merely stating that "[s]afe and healthy working conditions are fundamental to decent work".[407] This formulation was acceptable for the Workers' group and the Member States on the condition that the Office was asked to send proposals to the ILO Governing Body to flesh out the Commission's

400. Bellace, *supra* n. 323, at 309.

401. Erika de Wet, *Governance Through Promotion and Persuasion: The ILO Declaration on Fundamental Principles and Rights at Work*, 9 German Law Journal 1429, 1448 n. 11 (2008).

402. Christine Breining-Kaufmann, *Globalisation and Labour Rights: The Conflict between Core Labour Rights and International Economic Law* 297 (Hart Publishing 2007).

403. Janice R. Bellace, *Labour Rights as the Means for Recognizing Human Rights at Work*, Universiteit Leiden (22 October 2018), https://www.universiteitleiden.nl/binaries/content/assets/rechtsgeleerdheid/instituut-voor-publiekrecht/sociaal-recht/bellace-leiden-lecture-22-oct-2018-.pdf. The author had already argued earlier on that the Declaration, for instance, speaks of fundamental principles and "rights at work" and not of "worker rights" because "they are rights that all persons possess by virtue of being human, and they are human rights with particular applicability at work". Bellace, *supra* n. 322, at 16.

404. Philip Alston, *"Core Labour Standards" and the Transformation of the International Labour Rights Regime*, 15 European Journal of International Law 457, 485–486 n. 3 (2004).

405. Hepple, *supra* n. 320, at 274.

406. Global Commission on the Future of Work, *Work for a Brighter Future* 39 (ILO 2019).

407. Para. II.D. ILO Centenary Declaration for the Future of Work, 21 June 2019.

proposal.[408] Interestingly, the Office report with proposals to incorporate safe and healthy working conditions into the ILO's framework of fundamental principles and rights at work mentions the reasons behind the differentiation between fundamental and non-fundamental rights at the ILO level. This differentiation is made based on: (i) the right's constitutional origin; (ii) its relevance to the fundamental principles on which the ILO is based, such as that labour is not a commodity; (iii) its nature as a human right; (iv) its status as an enabling condition or right that is instrumental in pursuing individual and collective conditions of work; and (v) the recognition of the right as fundamental both inside and outside of the organisation.[409]

SUBCHAPTER 2. THE DECENT WORK AGENDA

Director-General Somavía – Whereas the 1998 Declaration was, in the words of Standing, "the personal creation of the ILO's then Director-General, Michel Hansenne",[410] the Decent Work Agenda was his successor's opening shot. The incoming Director-General, Juan Somavía, had served as the Chairman of the Preparatory Committee for the Copenhagen Social Summit in 1995.[411] As noted above, the Summit's so-called "people's agenda" threw the ILO a lifeline, setting it on course to promote core labour standards through the 1998 Declaration.[412] ILO constituents felt that Somavía was, therefore, the right person to pursue the people's agenda at the ILO.[413] He was an ILO outsider who had served twice as the UN Economic and Social Council president, a person capable of raising the ILO's status on the global stage, and consolidating the organisation's position at the UN.[414] To this end, the Director-General launched the Decent Work Agenda in 1999 and, for instance, established the World Commission on the Social Dimension of Globalization in 2002. The point was no longer to work towards workers' rights within national frameworks but to "struggle for global social justice".[415] 129

Decent work – DG Somavía got off to a flying start. The Director-General's report to 1999's ILC argued that the organisation had too many priorities. The 1998 Declaration already allowed it to refocus on fundamental rights,[416] yet it needed a single message if it wanted to make a real impact.[417] As such, in the words of Somavía, "[t]he primary goal of the ILO today is to promote opportunities for women and men to 130

408. Resolution on the ILO Centenary Declaration for the Future of Work, 21 June 2019.
409. ILO, *Follow-up to the Resolution on the ILO Centenary Declaration for the Future of Work: Proposals for Including Safe and Healthy Working Conditions in the ILO's Framework of Fundamental Principles and Rights at Work* 4 (ILO 2020).
410. Standing, *supra* n. 379, at 366.
411. Maul, *supra* n. 373, at 265.
412. ILO Director-General, *Decent Work for Africa's Development* 15 (ILO 2003).
413. Rodgers, Lee, Swepston & Van Daele, *supra* n. 53, at 222.
414. Reynaud, *supra* n. 328, at 11.
415. Bob Deacon, *The International Labour Organization and Global Social Governance – The 100 Year Search for Social Justice within Capitalism* 45, 48 (Alexandra Kaasch & Kerstin Martens eds., *Actors and Agency in Global Social Governance*, OUP 2015).
416. Lee Swepston, *Introductory note by Lee Swepston*, 37 International Legal Materials 1233, 1234 n. 5 (1998).
417. Tapiola, *supra* n. 392, at 74.

obtain decent and productive work, in conditions of freedom, equity, security and human dignity".[418] This mission required a "converging focus of all its four strategic objectives: the promotion of rights at work; employment; social protection; and social dialogue". The goal to achieve decent work for all, moreover, demanded a comprehensive and inclusive approach. From the outset, these four strategic objectives were meant to benefit all workers. Furthermore, interestingly, Tapiola – a former Deputy Director-General – admitted that "'Decent Work' was a convenient way to express [the ILO's] aims – but especially after Amartya Sen's recognition of it as a development paradigm at the 1999 International Labour Conference, it became the framework for managing and carrying out ILO activities". [419]

131 **An inclusive approach** – Indeed, the significance of the Decent Work Agenda can hardly be overstated.[420] The concept has left deep marks. For example, some contemporary scholars argue that, unless the standard mentions otherwise, ILO Conventions and Recommendations apply to all workers, regardless of workers' employment status.[421] Even the preamble of the Domestic Workers Convention, 2011 (No. 189), to that extent, "recalls" "that international labour Conventions and Recommendations apply to all workers, including domestic workers, unless otherwise provided".[422] However, this expectation of "universal application" seems intertwined with the Decent Work Agenda because it sharply contrasts with ILO constituents' views during the organisation's first couple of decades.[423] The Permanent Court of International Justice had, for example, to issue Advisory Opinions in the 1920s on whether the ILO was competent to regulate persons employed in agriculture, and whether it could regulate the personal work incidentally performed by an employer.[424]

---

418. ILO Director-General, *Decent Work* (ILO 1999).

419. Tapiola, *supra* n. 392, at 74. "The case for a broader and more inclusive economic analysis and ethical examination is very strong in all these cases. Decent work is right to point in that comprehensive direction without falling prey to unexamined prejudices or premature pessimism". Amartya Sen, *Address by Mr Amartya Sen, Nobel Laureate in Economics*, International Labour Conference (15 June 1999), https://www.ilo.org/public/english/standards/relm/ilc/ilc87/a-sen.htm. *See also*: Amartya Sen, *Work and Rights*, 139 International Labour Review 119, 120 n. 2 (2000).

420. Decent work is not just a concept to reorient the organisation and mobilise ILO constituents and other international organisations. It even served to rearrange the Office. Rodgers, Lee, Swepston & Van Daele, *supra* n. 53, at 224.

421. Rudi Delarue, *De Rol van de Internationale Arbeidsorganisatie in de 21ste Eeuw* 20 (ILO Office for the European Union and the Benelux countries 2012).

422. The full title of this Convention is "Convention concerning decent work for domestic workers".

423. A dissenting opinion of Anzilotti at the Permanent Court of International Justice points this out very clearly. The question was whether women who did non-manual work were also prohibited from working at night. He writes: "[i]f the task allotted by Part XIII of the Treaty of Versailles to the Organization which it establishes is the regulation of conditions of manual labour, it is only natural to infer that any convention concluded under this Part is to be regarded as relating to manual labour and not to labour in general. Another and more general intention is conceivable but cannot be presumed: it must be proved". Opinion of Judge M. Anzilotti in Advisory Opinion No. 25, *Interpretation of the Convention of 1919 concerning Employment of Women during the Night*, 15 November 1932.

424. Permanent Court of International Justice: Advisory Opinion No. 2, *Competence of the ILO in regard to International Regulation of the Conditions of the Labour of Persons Employed in Agriculture*, 12 August 1922; Permanent Court of International Justice: Advisory Opinion No.

Since it was not even clear, by that time, whether the ILO could act in relation to these workers, it was entirely questionable to expect ILO instruments to cover all workers unless otherwise provided. Similar to domestic legal systems,[425] over time, the ILO gradually moved away from its original position in which it primarily focused on distinct categories of workers, such as female workers, industrial wage-earners or agricultural workers.[426] Notwithstanding some early instruments that might have always applied to all workers, the *general claim* that all ILO instruments apply to all workers unless otherwise provided completely overturns these initial dynamics. By looking at it from that angle, this general claim seems to largely find its legitimacy in the inclusive "Decent Work for All Agenda".[427]

Moreover, considering the ILO's initial inclination to focus on specific subsets of 132 workers, the Decent Work Agenda deserves credit for explicitly embracing all people's fate. For instance, Hepple has emphasised that "[t]he most innovative feature of the ILO's definition of Decent Work, as Amaryta [sic] Sen pointed out in his address to the 1999 ILC, is that it encompasses all kinds of productive work".[428] Blackett seemingly concurs, mentioning how perhaps the ILO's "most ambitious rethinking is found in its move beyond a narrow vision of its mandate, as that of regulating labour law through the prism of the employment relationship, to promoting 'decent work for all'".[429]

1998 Declaration / Decent work – In terms of the Decent Work Agenda's pedigree, 133 it was launched shortly after the ILO Member States' "hard-fought"[430] commitment to fundamental principles and rights at work. Routh points out that "rights at work", which is one of decent work's four strategic objectives, derives its substance from

---

13, *Competence of the ILO to Regulate Incidentally the Personal Work of the Employer*, 23 July 1926.

425. Thilo Ramm, *Laissez-faire and State Protection of Workers* 73, 88 (Bob Hepple ed., *The Making of Labour Law in Europe: A Comparative Study of Nine Countries up to 1945*, Hart Publishing 2010).
426. Peggie R. Smith, *Work Like any Other, Work Like no Other: Establishing Decent Work for Domestic Workers*, 15 Employee rights and employment policy journal 159, 171 n. 1 (2011).
427. ILO supervisory bodies have indeed tended to give a broad scope of application to specific ILO instruments since the early twentieth century, considering it irrelevant for workers to be employees or not. Yet, although this might have become an accepted practice throughout the decades, that itself does not legitimise it as the default rule. For example, Countouris has suggested that the ILO adopt "a horizontal instrument on the scope of application of ILO Conventions and Recommendations, perhaps in the form of a Recommendation for the ILO at large to interpret and apply its own instruments broadly, beyond the scope of formal salaried employment, subject only to specific instruments expressly requiring a narrower scope". If older ILO Conventions always apply to all workers unless provided otherwise, as some seem to suggest, there would be no reason to make this proposal. Nicola Countouris, *Defining and Regulating Work Relations for the Future of Work* 18 (ILO 2019).
428. Hepple, *supra* n. 320, at 64.
429. Adelle Blackett, *Introduction: Transnational Futures of International Labour Law*, 159 International Labour Review 455, 455 n. 4 (2020).
430. Brian A. Langille, *The ILO and the New Economy: Recent Developments*, 15 International Journal of Comparative Labour Law and Industrial Relations 229, 248–249 n. 3 (1999). *See also*, Laurence R. Helfer, *Monitoring Compliance with Unratified Treaties: The ILO Experience*, 71 Law & Contemporary Problems 193, 206 n. 1 (2008).

the 1998 Declaration. These rights at work "constitute the very heart of the concept of DW",[431] or at the very least, in Liukkunen's words, the fundamental labour rights "form a central pillar of the concept of decent work".[432] By embedding the 1998 Declaration into a broader framework for decent work, the ILO responded to a critique levelled at the 1998 Declaration: the Declaration had arguably downplayed the importance of the "non-Fundamental Conventions".[433] As such, from 1999 onwards, the Office's work was underpinned by the broader decent work paradigm, which "was built on what had been achieved with the adoption of the 1998 Declaration".[434] Henceforth, the organisation could advocate for more than just fundamental rights and principles for all people at work. Decent work for all allowed it to, for instance, systematically advocate in favour of adequate social security coverage and social dialogue for all, focusing on "people at the periphery of formal systems of labour and social protection".[435]

134 **Decent work remains ambiguous** – Despite the many policy documents related to the Decent Work Agenda, the specific content of decent work's four strategic objectives remains vague to this day. Identifying rights at work, employment promotion, social protection, and social dialogue as the organisation's four strategic objectives may have given the ILO renewed purpose, but the concept of decent work remains plain, with little actual content.[436] It offers a concept that everyone can appreciate, albeit for different reasons.[437] Decent work has even internalised a certain ambiguity. On the one hand, the Decent Work Agenda emphasises that economic and social development mutually sustain and reinforce one another and that the four strategic

431. Supriya Routh, *Informal Workers in India: Reconceptualizing Labour Law to Promote Capabilities* 156 (University of Victoria 2013).
432. Ulla Liukkunen, *The ILO and Transformation of Labour Law* 17, 27 (Tarja Halonen & Ulla Liukkunen eds., *International Labour Organization and Global Social Governance*, Springer 2021).
433. Supiot, *supra* n. 17, at 126.
434. Reynaud, *supra* n. 328, at 11. According to the Director-General, the ILC of 1999 showed "very wide support" for the Decent Work Agenda. Reply by the Director-General to the discussion of his Report, Record of proceedings of the International Labour conference, Geneva, ILO, 1999, 24/9.
435. Judy Fudge, *Regulating for Decent Work in a Global Economy*, 43 New Zealand Journal of Employment Relations 10, 12 n. 2 (2018). *See also*, Judy Fudge, *Blurring Legal Boundaries: Regulating for Decent Work* 1, 17 (Judy Fudge, Shae McCrystal & Kamala Sankaran eds., *Challenging the Legal Boundaries of Work Regulation*, Hart Publishing 2012).
436. "Senior ILO officials and policy-makers are themselves not sure of the appropriate import of the DW Agenda. While ILO officials sympathetic to the DW Agenda hold the view that the actual import of the DW Agenda is to be determined by respective member-states and societies that are working with the DW Agenda, ILO officials critical of the DW Agenda hold the view that the DW Agenda is, at best, political rhetoric, devoid of any practical meaning". Routh, *supra* n. 431, at 160. *See also*, Kirsten Sehnbruch, Brendan Burchell, Nurjk Agloni & Agnieszka Piasna, *Human Development and Decent Work: Why some Concepts Succeed and Others Fail to Make an Impact*, 46 Development and Change 197, 209–210 n. 2 (2015).
437. Thomas & Turnbull, *supra* n. 383, at 15. For instance, the "symbolic right to decent work" would have appealed to trade unions and NGOs, and the strategic objective devoted to employment creation as well as the prospect of reshaping the ILO institutionally convinced employers to give the agenda a chance. Felix Hauf, *The Paradoxes of Decent Work in Context: A Cultural Political Economy Perspective*, 6 Global Labour Journal 138, 141 n. 2 (2015).

objectives are interconnected.[438] However, on the other hand, ILO constituents wanted decent work to be a nationally determined concept, meaning it lacks a detailed and unified meaning (also *infra* nos. 144–145). Decent work was likened to "a moving target, a goal that evolves as the possibilities, circumstances and priorities of societies evolve".[439] A Member State could "set its own goals to reduce the decent work deficit with due regard to its specific circumstances and possibilities".[440]

Essentially, the Decent Work Agenda is a package deal with four components, but every component comes in different shapes and colours. When trying to picture the ILO's decent work framework, one could also think of an H_2O molecule. Rights at work (i.e. the Fundamental Conventions and the 1998 Declaration) form the oxygen atom at the molecule's core. It is where the hydrogen atoms bind. Rights at work are crucial for decent employment and social protection. Since it is the heaviest atom, "rights at work" is, moreover, described by some as the "organization's normative polestar".[441] Employment promotion and the advancement of social protection – the quantitative and qualitative aspect of employment – take the form of two hydrogen atoms. Despite evidence to the contrary,[442] it is frequently believed that these somewhat repel each other, yet at the same time, they belong together to form what has been called decent work (H_2O). Social dialogue and tripartism provide the bonds for the molecule. This strategic objective holds the entire structure together; however, it is, arguably, most prone to erosion. 135

SUBCHAPTER 3. INTERNATIONAL ACKNOWLEDGEMENT FOR THE DECENT WORK AGENDA

Poverty and fair globalisation – These days, decent work is very much entwined with the United Nations' development agenda. Sustainable Development Goal 8 calls for the promotion of sustained, inclusive and sustainable economic growth, full and productive employment and decent work for all. When looking back in time, this is actually quite surprising. Fukuda-Parr and Hulme have, for instance, claimed that the 136

438. ILO Director-General, *supra* n. 418, at 8.
439. ILO Director-General, *Reducing the Decent Work Deficit – a Global Challenge* (ILO 2001).
440. *Ibid.*
441. Helfer, *supra* n. 325, at 720. Something which, arguably, has not come to fruition in practice. Hyde claims that the 1998 Declaration has not really changed the ILO's focus. Alan Hyde, *The International Labor Organization in the Stag Hunt for Global Labor Rights*, 3 Law & Ethics of Human Rights 154, 169 n. 2 (2009).
442. Although employment promotion and employment protection are sometimes portrayed as opposites, some research has actually found no evidence to support the assumption that more protection for workers, for instance, reduces enterprises' demand for low-paid or low-skilled workers, or that "allowing insecure/unstable/lower quality jobs to proliferate is expected to help the unemployed move more quickly into employment". Silvia Avram, *Labour Market Flexibility and Unemployment Duration: Evidence from the UK* (Institute for Social and Economic Research, University of Essex 2020). *See also*, the following evidence that flexible employment and deregulation have little to offer in terms of economic performance: Simon Deakin, *The Contribution of Labour Law to Economic Development and Growth* (Centre for Business Research, University of Cambridge 2016); Zoe Adams et al., *The Economic Significance of Laws Relating to Employment Protection and Different Forms of Employment: Analysis of a Panel of 117 Countries, 1990–2013*, 158 International Labour Review 1, 1–35 n. 1 (2019).

top management of the ILO was sceptical about the Millennium Development Goals at first. They point to an ILO director of statistics who called it "a passing fad".[443] Perhaps partially because of this, the original MDGs – signed in 2000 – neglected the importance of decent work and employment creation for poverty reduction. Once the ILO had changed its opinion on the MDGs' relevance, this oversight would become one of the organisation's entry points.[444] The ILO argued that decent work was an important tool to reduce poverty and accomplish the MDGs.[445] The launch of the ILO's Global Employment Agenda in 2003, in response to a UN General Assembly decision from 2000, was well-timed in this respect.[446] It supposedly gave the ILO "a golden opportunity to restore its derailed position within the global governance framework".[447]

137 Another fortunate development was the launch of the World Commission on the Social Dimension of Globalization in 2002. The independent body, which was made up of prominent academics, politicians and others, but constituted by the ILO, had to devise policies to reduce poverty and make globalisation fairer. The Commission, most notably, noted that: "Decent Work for all should be made a global goal and be pursued through coherent policies within the multilateral system".[448] The ILO reacted by stressing that its constitutional mandate, which states that social objectives take precedence over economic objectives, provides a building block for a "fair globalisation".[449] The organisation argued, on the one hand, that decent work was not viable without a multilateral system geared towards fair globalisation and, on the other, that "the system as a whole won't achieve a fair globalization without responding to the democratic demand for decent work".[450] The United Nations' World Summit in 2005 took the Commission's message to heart, expressing support and resolve "to make the goals of full and productive employment and decent work for all [...] a central objective of our relevant national and international policies [...] as part of our efforts to achieve the Millennium Development Goals".[451] Along those

443. Sakiko Fukuda-Parr & David Hulme, *International Norm Dynamics and the "End of Poverty": Understanding the Millennium Development Goals*, 17 Global Governance 17, 27–28 n. 1 (2011).

444. ILO International Labour Office, *Report V: Strengthening the ILO's Capacity to Assist its Members' Efforts to Reach its Objectives in the Context of Globalization* viii (ILO 2007); Gillian MacNaughton & Diane F. Frey, *Decent Work, Human Rights and the Sustainable Development Goals*, 47 Georgetown Journal of International Law 607, 635–637 n. 2 (2016).

445. ILO Director-General, *Working Out of Poverty* 84 (ILO 2003). *E.g.* "[t]he foundations of a decent work approach to strategies for the reduction of poverty must be laid – and this is an urgent task". ILO Director-General, *supra* n. 412, at 41.

446. ILO International Labour Office, *Implementing the Global Employment Agenda: Employment Strategies in Support of Decent Work, "Vision" Document* 1 (ILO 2006).

447. Branka Likic-Brboric & Carl-Ulrik Schierup, *Asymmetric Governance, Labour Standards and Migrants' Rights* 220, 222 (Heidi Moksnes & Mia Melin eds., *Global Civil Society: Shifting Powers in a Shifting World*, Uppsala Universitet 2012).

448. World Commission on the Social Dimension of Globalization, *supra* n. 360, at xiii.

449. ILO Director-General, *supra* n. 361, at 6.

450. *Ibid.*, 9.

451. UN General Assembly, *2005 World Summit Outcome*, A/RES/60/1 11 (UN 2005).

lines, achieving full and productive employment and decent work for all, including women and young people, became a target under the goal of eradicating poverty.[452]

Although the ILO had advocated making decent work a new goal, not just a target under pre-existing goals,[453] the ILO Director-General interpreted the outcome as a ringing endorsement.[454] By 2005–2006, decent work became a relevant concept for both poverty reduction and fair globalisation within the broader international development agenda.[455] The effort to make decent work a part of this broader agenda was initiated well before 2008's Social Justice Declaration had been adopted at the ILO level. 138

Decent work, a UN concept? – Hence, by relying on decent work to gain a foothold on the international scene, the concept may have been tinged by these efforts early on. One example of this "cross-pollination" between decent work and the UN's development paradigm can be found in the area of statistics. As target 1.B of MDG 1 on poverty eradication was to "[a]chieve full and productive employment and decent work for all, including women and young people", statistical indicators had to be conceived to measure country-level progress. Even if the statistical measurement of decent work had been contested internally at the ILO,[456] the organisation had to now pay attention to the indicators and benchmarks associated with decent work in the MDGs. As a result, contrary to what would have been the case if the ILO constituents had accepted statistically measuring decent work at the ILO level, the ILO no longer had as much discretion about what indicators to use in the MDGs' framework.[457] This linkage between the ILO and the UN has only become more substantial in recent years. After a purposive campaign,[458] the ILO became the custodian agency for over ten indicators under 2015's Sustainable Development Goals. This responsibility put the ILO in a position in which it could leverage the need to improve its statistical work for the SDGs at the same time to expand its internal capabilities.[459] Yet, due to the funding that it receives to contribute to the SDGs, this might also entail that its 139

452. UN Economic and Social Council, *Creating an Environment at the National and International Levels Conducive to Generating Full and Productive Employment and Decent Work for All, and its Impact on Sustainable Development*, A/RES/64/135 (UN 2006).
453. MacNaughton & Frey, *supra* n. 444, at 635–637.
454. ILO Director-General, *Changing Patterns in the World of Work* x (ILO 2006).
455. ILO Director-General, *Consolidating Progress and Moving Ahead* (ILO 2005); ILO Director-General, *supra* n. 454, at 73.
456. The plans to create internal statistical indicators to measure progress on decent work were "hastily shelved" once they came under attack. Standing, *supra* n. 379, at 370. Constituents were especially opposed to the idea of launching a Decent Work Index that could rank countries. Richard Anker & Pascal Annycke, *Reporting Regularly on Decent Work in the World: Options for the ILO* 12–13 (ILO 2009).
457. To measure the percentage of vulnerable workers under target 1.B, for example, statistics focus on the proportion of own-account and contributing family workers in total employment. This resulted in the observation that 45 per cent of all workers provide their work in vulnerable conditions. Yet this criticised indicator provides only one way to measure the number of vulnerable workers in an economy. UN, *The Millennium Development Goals Report 2015* 19 (UN 2015); MacNaughton & Frey, *supra* n. 444, at 640.
458. ILO, *The Post-2015 Sustainable Development Agenda* (ILO 2013); *Ibid.*, 647–648.
459. Jakovleski, Jerbi & Biersteker, *supra* n. 372, at §36.

internal statistical work is somewhat locked into the SDG framework.[460] The ILO has, arguably, manoeuvred itself into a catch-22 in this regard. Some of its constituents are wary of measuring decent work through detailed statistical indicators because it threatens to upset the carefully crafted ambiguity surrounding decent work.[461] Through the United Nations' SDGs, the ILO, nevertheless, managed to find a way to move in this direction. However, the ILO's desire to leverage the UN may eventually result in it losing control over the content of decent work.[462]

140 According to Maupain, in a broader sense, "[i]t would thus seem that the 'strategic influence' [over the UN] that was enticingly depicted to the Governing Body in 2015 may ultimately boil down to a more modest sub-contracting role".[463] The Centenary Declaration contains a section that seemingly illustrates this tendency. The initial draft Declaration, which the Office drafted based on tripartite discussions, promoted "productive employment and decent work".[464] Due to ILO constituents' subsequent amendments, the adopted Declaration instead endorses "sustained, inclusive and sustainable economic growth, full and productive employment and decent work for all".[465] The adopted phrase is a copy of SDG 8; this was not yet the case for the draft Declaration. Although this amendment might seem like a minor detail, asking Member States to put SDG 8 at the centre of their macroeconomic policies instead of making "productive employment and decent work" the central objective is, in fact, a clear choice. A choice that, in time, might limit the ILO's discretion since it has little control over the content of SDG 8. This SDG has, for instance, been criticised for not being "people-centered" but "rather economy-centered".[466] SDG 8 turns economic growth into a goal, even though Sen and others consider economic growth to be a means to other ends like decent work.[467] This SDG, therefore, diverges from the

460. This despite, for instance, the realisation that "[a] broader set of core and associated targets – under an expanded goal that one might term 'SDG 8 + ' – arguably provides a more useful blueprint (and frame of analysis) for national and international policy-makers who are seeking to foster decent work and inclusive economic development". ILO, *World Employment and Social Outlook: Trends 2019* 58 (ILO 2019).
461. Lucio Baccaro & Valentina Mele, *Pathology of Path Dependency? The ILO and the Challenge of New Governance*, 65 Industrial & Labor Relations Review 195, 212–216 n. 2 (2012). This would also allow for comparisons between countries, meaning that countries might end up being criticised for their indecent working conditions. Sehnbruch, Burchell, Agloni & Piasna, *supra* n. 436, at 211–212 and 216.
462. "While the [Decent Work] Agenda has been adopted by bodies such as the UN Economic and Social Council (2006) as a policy instrument for achieving full and productive employment and decent work for all, we conclude that DW remains a contested notion and more than one 'agenda' is operating". Erica Di Ruggiero, Joanna E. Cohen, Donald C. Cole & Lisa Forman, *Competing Conceptualizations of Decent Work at the Intersection of Health, Social and Economic Discourses*, 133 Social Science & Medicine 120, 126 (2015).
463. Maupain, *supra* n. 353, at 326.
464. ILO, *Report IV ILO Centenary Outcome Document* 7 (ILO 2019).
465. Para. III.C. ILO Centenary Declaration for the Future of Work, 21 June 2019.
466. MacNaughton & Frey, *supra* n. 444, at 653 and 658–659. *See also*, Shirin M. Rai, Benjamin D. Brown & Kanchana N. Ruwanpura, *SDG 8: Decent Work and Economic Growth – A Gendered Analysis*, 133 World Development 368, 368–380 (2019).
467. Diane F. Frey, *Economic Growth, Full Employment and Decent Work: The Means and Ends in SDG 8*, 21 The International Journal of Human Rights 1164, 1175–1176 n. 8 (2017); Kaz Kobayashi, Shobod Nath, Michelle S. Chen & Josephine Malenga, *Decent Work and Economic Growth: Is*

ILO's own Decent Work Agenda. A people-centred agenda that underscores the ILO's responsibility "to examine and consider all international economic and financial policies in the light of the fundamental objective of social justice", or nowadays decent work.[468] Based on such considerations, as admitted by Cortebeeck, a former Chairperson of the ILO Governing Body, the United Nations' policies and reforms undoubtedly present the ILO with opportunities. However, at the same time, unless sufficient care is being taken, the ILO risks compromising its particularities and identity.[469]

NZ Business Progressing Well? 11, 13–14 (Gabriel Eweje & Ralph J. Bathurst eds., *Clean, Green and Responsible? Soundings from Down Under*, Springer International Publishing 2019).

468. Preamble of the ILO Declaration on Social Justice for a Fair Globalization, 10 June 2008.

469. Luc Cortebeeck, *Er is nog Werk: De Toekomst van Waardig Werk in de Wereld* 282–283 (Lannoo 2019). An example of this is the extent to which the ILO will give meaning to the concept of "social justice" by attaching universal statistical indicators to it, just like other international organisations have been doing (e.g. SDGs), or, on the contrary, continues to adhere to its original framework, in which the ILO constituents give a progressive interpretation to social justice in the form of the International Labour Code. Supiot, *supra* n. 321, at 122–129.

Chapter 3. The Second Stage: The Social Justice Declaration and Centenary Declaration

SUBCHAPTER 1. THE COMMITTEE ON STRENGTHENING THE ILO'S CAPACITY

One UN – The UN launched "One United Nations" in 2006.[470] The ILO Director-General's address to 2007's ILC made it clear that sustainable development served as the "overriding policy paradigm" for decent work.[471] Somavía publicly summarised what the ILO could "bring to the table" in light of the UN reform.[472] The address illustrates how the ILO was well aware of the significant changes a UN reform might bring. The organisation had, for instance, invested a lot of time and effort in developing Decent Work Country Programmes. These programmes are the ILO's flagship method to implement decent work on a country level. If the UN would strive for one programme, one budgetary framework and one leading office to pursue development policies at the country level,[473] it would inevitably affect the ILO's capacity to "independently" administer its Decent Work Country Programmes.[474] 141

An authoritative document – The ILO Director-General made his case on how to strengthen the ILO's institutional capacity under these circumstances. The aim was to deliver an authoritative document that "would in a certain sense retain the 'trademark' 142

470. "The essence of our vision is for the United Nations to deliver as one in the areas of development, humanitarian assistance and the environment". High-Level Panel on UN System-wide Coherence, *Delivering as One*, A/61/583 10 (UN 2006).
471. ILO Director-General, *Decent Work for Sustainable Development* 3 (ILO 2007).
472. *Ibid.*, 17.
473. UN General Assembly, *Resolution on System-wide Coherence*, A/RES/62/277 (UN 2008).
474. For instance, on the interaction between Decent Work Country Programmes and UN Development Assistance Frameworks, ILO Governing Body, *Update on the United Nations Reform*, GB.335/INS/10 3–4 (ILO 2019).

[i.e. decent work] and frame its meaning for use in other contexts".[475] In other words, the Social Justice Declaration also became a reaction of some sort to the success of decent work outside the ILO.[476] ILO constituents were asked to develop a response in which decent work remained "a synthetic and readily understandable expression of the ILO's objectives that are already well defined in its Constitution, which as such may have a greater value of persuasion".[477] The Office report stressed a couple of other features of decent work as well. For instance, "each of the constitutional objectives should be universally promoted" to the benefit of all people who work or look for work.[478] The Office's proposal with the building blocks for an outcome document confirmed this universality of the organisation's objectives.[479]

143 **Committee discussions** – The discussions held at 2007's ILC were mostly exploratory. Indeed, the outcome of these discussions was not set in stone. A general compromise seemed only to emerge as discussions went on. As had been suggested earlier by the GB, discussions focused on how the ILO could fulfil its mandate in an era of increased globalisation and how it could more effectively serve its Members.[480] Surprisingly, the Employers' members mentioned that "[t]he ILO should not change its mandate and call for reform in other organizations",[481] nor should the outcome of these discussions "increase its role in the multinational system".[482] Two remarkable reservations, considering how one important reason to adopt an authoritative document was to "reinforce the status of the ILO and tripartism within the framework of UN reform".[483] Along these lines, the Workers' group did consider the exercise opportune because "[t]o reaffirm the centrality of Decent Work was a means to maintain the ILO and its tripartite structure firmly anchored in the UN system".[484] The Director-General was instructed to facilitate extensive consultations and work on a report with a draft authoritative text for 2008's ILC.[485]

144 **Draft text** – As instructed by 2007's ILC, the Director-General issued a report that would form the basis for the second round of discussions. The report carried a dreadful title:

475. ILO, *Report V Strengthening the ILO's Capacity to Assist its Members' Efforts to Reach its Objectives in the Context of Globalization* 46 (ILO 2007).
476. For instance, the working documents hinted that "[stressing] the vital contribution that Decent Work would make towards attaining the MDGs, especially the eradication of poverty, would send out a very strong signal indeed". *Ibid.*, 46.
477. *Ibid.*, 4.
478. *Ibid.*, 4.
479. The sketch states that the objectives in the Constitution, the Declaration of Philadelphia and the 1998 Declaration, which are channelled through the four strategic objectives, are "of universal scope/applicability, irrespective of the status of the workers concerned". *Ibid.*, 54.
480. ILO Governing Body, *Strengthening the ILO's Capacity to Discharge its Core Missions and Promote Decent Work for All at the Outset of the Twenty-first Century*, GB.294/2/1(Add.) (ILO 2005).
481. Report of the Committee on Strengthening the ILO's Capacity at the 96th Session of the International Labour Conference, Geneva, ILO, 2007, 23/50.
482. *Ibid.*, 23/53.
483. *Ibid.*, 23/52.
484. *Ibid.*, 23/6.
485. Resolution concerning strengthening the ILO's capacity, 96th Session of the International Labour Conference in 2007, 23/65.

> "Report VI Strengthening the ILO's capacity to assist its Members' efforts to reach its objectives in the context of globalization: Continuation of the discussion on strengthening the ILO's capacity and possible consideration of an authoritative document, possibly in the form of a Declaration or any other suitable instrument, together with any appropriate follow-up, and the form they may take".

The title illustrates that 2008's ILC was anything but a formality. Based on the consultations held in between both Conferences, the "draft authoritative text" read:

> "The Conference recognizes and declares that:
>
> A. In the present context of accelerating change, Members' commitment and efforts to implement the ILO's constitutional mandate must be centred around four core objectives of recognized strategic importance, as follows:
>
> (i) placing full and productive employment at the centre of economic and social policies and creating a sustainable, institutional and macroeconomic environment in which:
>
> - individuals can develop and update the necessary capacities to be productively occupied for their personal fulfilment and the common well-being; and
> - both private and public enterprises can develop activities and initiatives offering greater employment and income opportunities and prospects for all;
>
> (ii) developing measures of social and labour protection which are sustainable and adapted to national possibilities, with a view to:
>
> - progressively extending social security to all and adapting its scope and coverage to meet the new needs and uncertainties generated by the rapidity of technological and economic changes;
> - ensuring healthy, safe and decent working conditions, bearing in mind the basic requirements spelled out in the 1919 "International Labour Charter", as well as the legitimate expectation of all those concerned to obtain a fair share of the wealth which they have helped to generate;
>
> (iii) promoting social dialogue and tripartism as the most appropriate method for:
>
> - adapting the implementation of the strategic objectives to the needs and possibilities of each country;
> - translating economic development into social progress and vice versa; and
> - facilitating consensus building on relevant national and international policies;
>
> (iv) guaranteeing fundamental principles and rights at work both as human rights and as the enabling condition without which none of the other objectives can be fully reached, and the violation of which cannot be invoked or otherwise used as a legitimate comparative advantage".[486]

486. ILO International Labour Office, *Report VI Strengthening the ILO's Capacity to Assist its Members' Efforts to Reach its Objectives in the Context of Globalization: Continuation of the Discussion on Strengthening the ILO's Capacity and Possible Consideration of an Authoritative Document, Possibly in the Form of a Declaration or Any Other Suitable Instrument, Together With Any Appropriate Follow-up, and the Form They May Take*, Geneva, ILO, 2008, 2–3.

Similar to the Decent Work Agenda (*supra* no. 134), the draft text initially stated that "[t]he specific content and relative importance to be given to these objectives is a matter to be determined by each Member, subject to its existing international obligations".[487] Employers and some governments were, furthermore, adamant about not defining the concept of decent work at the international level.[488]

145 This draft authoritative text would undergo further changes during 2008's Committee discussions. Many of the significant changes took place in a drafting group, hence behind closed doors. Therefore, it remains unclear why, for example, the reference to "human rights" was deleted from the fourth strategic objective. That it is difficult to find out why these changes were made is illustrated by the reason why "decent work" does not feature in the title of 2008's Declaration. According to the record of proceedings, the Employers insisted "that this was a concept to be determined by each State in accordance with its own needs and circumstances".[489] It had no place in the title. Instead, by using the title "ILO Declaration on Social Justice for a Fair Globalization", a term that harks back to the Constitution – "Social Justice" – was combined with "Fair Globalization"; the latter is associated with more contemporary thinking.[490] However, discussions dragged on because not all ILO constituents were eager to exclude "decent work" from the Declaration's title. Reynaud recalls in this regard that: "[a] turning point came when the Government member of Japan noted that there was no easy or obvious translation of 'decent work' in Japanese, it just did not translate directly. The Government member of China said it was also the case in Chinese".[491]

146 **A genuinely authoritative text** – At the end of the discussions, the Social Justice Declaration – or Decent Work Declaration, if you will – was considered to have a lot of political and symbolic value.[492] Constituents had been informed in advance that, according to ILO and UN practice, a Declaration could be described as "a formal and solemn instrument, suitable for rare occasions when principles of great and lasting importance are being enunciated".[493] In addition to its symbolic value, in terms of its legal effect, this Declaration only binds the ILO organs, serving as advisory guidance to the Member States. Moreover, it does not provide for an authoritative interpretation of Member States' constitutional obligations. That task remains in the hands of the International Court of Justice.[494]

487. *Ibid.*, 3.
488. *Ibid.*, 20.
489. Report of the Committee on Strengthening the ILO's Capacity at the 97th Session of the International Labour Conference, Geneva, ILO, 2008, 13/42.
490. *Ibid.*, 13/44.
491. Reynaud, *supra* n. 328, at 20.
492. "The Reporter [of the Committee] said that this was a visionary and historical moment. It was visionary in that it addressed what the ILO would be able to do with an eye to the future. It was the ILO's Declaration for the twenty-first century". Report of the Committee on Strengthening the ILO's Capacity at the 97th Session of the International Labour Conference, Geneva, ILO, 2008, 13/48.
493. Memorandum by the United Nations Office of Legal Affairs, 2 April 1962, E/CN.4/L.610.
494. ILO International Labour Office, *supra* n. 486, at 30–31.

SUBCHAPTER 2. THE ILO DECLARATION ON SOCIAL JUSTICE FOR A FAIR GLOBALIZATION

The States' commitment to decent work – Decent work's four "inseparable, inter-related and mutually supportive" strategic objectives are: 147

(i) "promoting employment by creating a sustainable institutional and economic environment";[495]
(ii) "developing and enhancing measures of social protection – social security and labour protection – which are sustainable and adapted to national circumstances";[496]
(iii) "promoting social dialogue and tripartism as the most appropriate methods" for certain purposes;[497]
(iv) "respecting, promoting and realizing the fundamental principles and rights at work, which are of particular significance, as both rights and enabling conditions that are necessary for the full realization of all of the strategic objectives".[498]

The fourth strategic objective is the most "foundational" one. Respecting fundamental principles and rights at work is an enabling condition without which the other three strategic objectives cannot be fully realised. This foundational role provides an additional reason why all Member States are constitutionally bound to comply with the 1998 Declaration. Without doing so, Member States cannot possibly keep their pledge to decent work, i.e. a people-centred version of social justice. Additionally,

---

495. This should be an environment in which "individuals can develop and update the necessary capacities and skills they need to enable them to be productively occupied for their personal fulfilment and the common well-being; – all enterprises, public or private, are sustainable to enable growth and the generation of greater employment and income opportunities and prospects for all; and societies can achieve their goals of economic development, good living standards and social progress". ILO Declaration on Social Justice for a Fair Globalization, 10 June 2008.
496. This includes: "the extension of social security to all, including measures to provide basic income to all in need of such protection, and adapting its scope and coverage to meet the new needs and uncertainties generated by the rapidity of technological, societal, demographic and economic changes; healthy and safe working conditions; and – policies in regard to wages and earnings, hours and other conditions of work, designed to ensure a just share of the fruits of progress to all and a minimum living wage to all employed and in need of such protection". *Ibid.*
497. These purposes are: "adapting the implementation of the strategic objectives to the needs and circumstances of each country; translating economic development into social progress, and social progress into economic development; facilitating consensus building on relevant national and international policies that impact on employment and decent work strategies and programmes; and making labour law and institutions effective, including in respect of the recognition of the employment relationship, the promotion of good industrial relations and the building of effective labour inspection systems". *Ibid.*
498. It is stressed: "– that freedom of association and the effective recognition of the right to collective bargaining are particularly important to enable the attainment of the four strategic objectives; and – that the violation of fundamental principles and rights at work cannot be invoked or otherwise used as a legitimate comparative advantage and that labour standards should not be used for protectionist trade purposes". *Ibid.*

gender equality and non-discrimination are "cross-cutting issues" relevant to all four objectives.[499]

148 **Constitution/Declaration/Standards** – Through these strategic objectives, the Social Justice Declaration provides a compass that details how to navigate the ILO Constitution. As stated by the Chairperson of the Committee on Strengthening the ILO's Capacity, "[w]e know what our destination is. Our destination is described for us in the Constitution of the ILO".[500] Historically, the ILO Conventions and Recommendations have been the main instruments on offer to take the Member States to this destination. These ILS aim to protect workers' human dignity and to achieve social justice.[501] However, this relationship between the ILO Constitution and its implementation through ILS might have slightly shifted due to the Social Justice Declaration. On this point, it is essential to highlight the governments' commitment in the second part of this Declaration. Member States committed themselves to implement "decent work".[502] They have not pledged to ratify all up-to-date ILO Conventions and comply with all relevant Recommendations. Because of this, one might ask, what is the link between decent work and the International Labour Code? The Centenary Declaration is particularly blunt in this respect: "[a]ll Members should work towards the ratification and implementation of the ILO fundamental Conventions and periodically consider, in consultation with employers' and workers' organizations, the ratification of other ILO standards".[503] Contrary to the ILO Constitution, which portrays the adoption of ILS as the ILO's main course of action, the Decent Work Agenda is unconcerned with how decent work is achieved. International labour standards, Decent Work Country Programmes and statistics all serve to propel the Decent Work Agenda at the national level. ILS are, in other words, only one tool in the ILO's twenty-first-century toolbox. Their importance for the organisation's future remains a subject of discussion.

---

499. *Ibid.*

500. Presentation of the Report of the Committee on Strengthening the ILO's Capacity to the plenary sitting at the 97th Session of the International Labour Conference, Geneva, ILO, 2008, 17/38.

501. Bellace, *supra* n. 322, at 11.

502. "Members have a key responsibility to contribute, through their social and economic policy, to the realization of a global and integrated strategy for the implementation of the strategic objectives, which encompass the Decent Work Agenda outlined in Part I of this Declaration. Implementation of the Decent Work Agenda at national level will depend on national needs and priorities and it will be for member States, in consultation with the representative organizations of workers and employers, to determine how to discharge that responsibility". ILO Declaration on Social Justice for a Fair Globalization, 10 June 2008. Some countries may have occasionally to be reminded of their commitment. Keith D. Ewing, *Regulating for Decent Work and the Effectiveness of Labour Law*, 39 New Zealand Journal of Employment Relations 3, 20–21 n. 2 (2014).

503. Para. IV.B. ILO Centenary Declaration for the Future of Work, 21 June 2019. *See also*, ILO Declaration on Social Justice for a Fair Globalization, 10 June 2008, 14. Scholars have long held that the Decent Work Agenda diminishes the importance of ILO Conventions and Recommendations within the ILO's overarching mandate. Baccaro & Mele, *supra* n. 461, at 196; Judy Fudge, *Regulating for Decent Work in a Global Economy*, 43 New Zealand Journal of Employment Relations 10, 13 n. 2 (2018).

SUBCHAPTER 3. THE ILO CENTENARY DECLARATION FOR THE FUTURE OF WORK

The ILO Centenary Initiative – The ILO was already sailing a new course based on the 1998 and Social Justice Declaration. Nevertheless, as these things go, a significant effort was undertaken to make the Conference's 108th Centenary Session stand out. Director-General Guy Ryder, who took office in 2012, proposed seven "centenary initiatives" in 2013: the governance initiative,[504] the standards initiative,[505] the green initiative,[506] the enterprises initiative,[507] the end to poverty initiative,[508] the women at work initiative,[509] and the future of work initiative.[510] The DG's report for 2015's ILC substantiated the "future of work centenary initiative". First, inclusive discussions would be held. The output of these "centenary conversations" would inform a high-level commission,[511] which was asked to submit a report to 2019's ILC. According to the 2015 report, "a crucial question is whether the Conference should adopt a solemn 'Centenary Declaration'. The occasion would seem to demand it. But if it is to be of more than symbolic or ceremonial value, serious advance consideration will need to be given to its substantive content and political purpose".[512] 149

The Global Commission on the Future of Work – The high-level commission was named the Global Commission on the Future of Work. Its report recommended giving "particular attention" to the "universality of the ILO mandate".[513] Many of the Commission's concrete proposals reflect this viewpoint. One can mention, for instance, the proposals for a universal entitlement to lifelong learning, for universal 150

504. "[T]he governance initiative to complete reform of the ILO's governance structures, to undertake the evaluation of the impact of the 2008 Declaration as set out in its final provisions, and to act on its findings".
505. "[T]he standards initiative to consolidate tripartite consensus on an authoritative supervisory system and to enhance the relevance of international labour standards through a standards review mechanism".
506. "[T]he green initiative to give practical application to the decent work dimension of the transition to a low-carbon, sustainable development path and to facilitate the tripartite contribution to it".
507. "[T]he enterprises initiative to establish a platform for ILO engagement with enterprises which would contribute to their sustainability and to ILO goals".
508. "[T]he end to poverty initiative to meet the urgent requirement for an adequate living wage for all workers, including through the employment and social protection components of the post-2015 development agenda".
509. "[T]he women at work initiative to survey the place and conditions of women in the world of work and engage tripartite constituents in concrete action to realize equality of opportunity and treatment".
510. ILO Director-General, *Towards the ILO centenary: Realities, Renewal and Tripartite Commitment* 28 (ILO 2013).
511. ILO, *Inception Report for the Global Commission on the Future of Work* (ILO 2017); ILO, *Synthesis Report of the National Dialogues on the Future of Work* (ILO 2017).
512. ILO Director-General, *The Future of Work Centenary Initiative* 3 (ILO 2015).
513. "This implies scaling up its activities to include those who have historically remained excluded from social justice and decent work, notably those working in the informal economy. It equally implies innovative action to address the growing diversity of situations in which work is performed, in particular the emerging phenomenon of digitally mediated work in the platform economy". Global Commission on the Future of Work, *supra* n. 406, at 14.

social protection, for a "Universal Labour Guarantee", and the proposal to make safety and health at work a fifth category of fundamental principles and rights at work. The GB decided that the outcome document of 2019's ILC should be a Centenary Declaration, meant to draw on the Global Commission's report. An agreement was reached before the ILC on the building blocks of a Centenary Declaration, subdivided into four parts. The first part was meant to reaffirm the ILO mandate and core principles, the second part would describe the current and future state of the world of work, both challenges and opportunities, and the third part calls "for the ILO and its constituents to commit to addressing specific priorities in the pursuit of the ILO mandate in its current and future context".[514] The last part addresses the organisation's means of action. Based on this document and additional consultations, the Office advanced a draft Declaration for consideration.

151 **The draft Centenary Declaration** – Building on the Social Justice Declaration, which predominantly describes how the ILO should implement the organisation's constitutional mandate along the lines of the Decent Work Agenda, this Centenary Declaration was meant to send a "political message". It needed to become action-oriented, highlighting what the ILO's twenty-first-century goals are. Something that, as the following paragraphs will show, is more easily said than done in a tripartite environment with diverging interests.

152 Some issues already arose in the Declaration's first part, which was solely intended to reaffirm established principles and describe the contemporary context. The draft Declaration's preamble called upon all ILO constituents "to reinvigorate the social contract for social justice and universal and lasting peace to which they committed in 1919".[515] Not an outrageous claim, one might think, considering, for instance, the UN Secretary-General's lecture in 2020 on "Tackling the Inequality Pandemic: A New Social Contract for a New Era".[516] Nonetheless, according to the Employer Vice-Chairperson, the concept of a "social contract" "was not commonly used in ILO texts and belonged more properly to the political philosophy of Jean-Jacques Rousseau or to trade union manifestos".[517] The Member States of GRULAC – the Group of Latin America and the Caribbean – supported deleting the reference. In contrast, the Workers' group, the Africa Group and the EU Member States hoped to maintain it.[518] The amendment was referred to the drafting group, where the reference to a social contract was deleted. Furthermore, in the Declaration's first part, the Government members of Brazil and the United States wanted to refer to "environmental change" instead of "climate change" as one of the factors driving

514. ILO Governing Body, *Outcome Document of the 108th (Centenary) Session of the Conference*, GB.335/INS/2/3 2 (ILO 2019).
515. ILO, *supra* n. 464, at 5.
516. UN Secretary-General, *Tackling the Inequality Pandemic: A New Social Contract for a New Era*, United Nations (18 July 2020), https://www.un.org/en/coronavirus/tackling-inequality-new-social-contract-new-era.
517. Report of the Committee of the Whole: Summary of proceedings at the 108th Session of the International Labour Conference, Geneva, ILO, 2019, 32.
518. The Worker Vice-Chairperson responded to the Employer Vice-Chairperson by stating that even the World Bank and OECD use this concept.

transformative change in the world of work.[519] Aided by the EU Member States, the Workers' group managed to maintain the reference to climate change. The adopted Declaration now refers to "environmental and climate change". The EU, Workers and others, also managed to add that the centenary comes "at a time of persisting inequalities".[520] A final noteworthy passage in the Declaration's first part is paragraph I.D. It asserts that the ILO must carry forward its constitutional mandate "by further developing its human-centred approach to the future of work, which puts workers' rights and the needs, aspirations and rights of all people at the heart of economic, social and environmental policies". The Employer Vice-Chairperson wanted the secretariat to reassure the constituents that this "human-centred approach" did not refer to the "human-centred agenda" of the Global Commission. In other words, it was important not to incorporate the Commission's recommendations into the Centenary Declaration unwittingly.[521] The representative of the Secretary-General assured the Employers' group that this was not the case. To this extent, it seems that the Centenary Declaration's new reference to a "human-centred approach to the future of work" does not have any distinct meaning. One reason is that it is hard to see where this terminology comes from if not the Global Commission's report; yet, as noted, the Declaration's human-centred approach should not be conflated with the Commission's human-centred agenda. Secondly, based on some of the ILO constituents' remarks, this human-centred approach seems to be the continuation of the decent-work approach;[522] in other words, decent work is, arguably, a human-centred approach to social justice.

In the second part of the Declaration, the EU Member States' suggestion to explicitly 153
refer to "collective bargaining" in paragraph II.B proved sensitive. The paragraph, as adopted, stipulates that social dialogue, including collective bargaining, provides an essential foundation for all ILO action. According to the record of proceedings, this reference "was a red line for the Employers' group that could not be crossed. The group could not accept singling out collective bargaining in the text. Either it was removed or the Employers' group would have to add other aspects of bipartite social dialogue".[523] The issue was referred to the drafting group, where ILO constituents seem to have agreed to retain the reference.

Subsequently, the topic of health and safety as a fundamental principle and right at 154
work came up. Although, for instance, the EU Member States proclaimed that "now was the time for a game-changer to include safety and health as a fundamental

519. Report of the Committee of the Whole: Summary of proceedings at the 108th Session of the International Labour Conference, Geneva, ILO, 2019, 34.

520. *Ibid.*, 34 and 37.

521. *Ibid.*, 47.

522. "With respect to the subamendment proposed by the Government member of Brazil to insert the words 'developing a' [human-centred approach], that suggested that the ILO did not already have a human-centred approach. [The Worker Vice-Chairperson] therefore proposed a further subamendment to read 'further developing its human-centred approach for the future of work'". Similarly, the Government member of Mexico "noted the shared language with the report of the Global Commission and observed that the human-centred approach had been a long-standing ILO mandate which featured in numerous other documents and discussions". *Ibid.*, 47.

523. *Ibid.*, 113.

principle and right at work in the ILO Centenary Declaration",[524] the opposition was strong enough to derail one of the draft Declaration's most prominent proposals. The Employer Vice-Chairperson argued that contrary to the 1998 Declaration's rights, such as the right to freedom of association, safe and healthy working conditions were "aspirational, not fundamental". "[I]f it was so fundamental, she wondered why so few member States ratified ILO Conventions on OSH".[525] The governments that intervened after the Employers' group's initial comments posed a series of questions regarding the impact of proclaiming health and safety a fundamental principle and right at work. These questions concerned, for instance, whether the Centenary Declaration could automatically "amend" the 1998 Declaration without the latter having to be revised separately. Another question was which ILO Conventions on OSH would come to mind as a potential Fundamental Convention. The Employer Vice-Chairperson cast doubt on the answers of the Legal Adviser to these questions. She disputed, for example, that the ILC could simply proclaim a new fundamental principle and right at work, leaving it up to the GB to select the relevant Fundamental Conventions.[526] Because of serious concerns, this discussion was also referred to the drafting group. A compromise was reached in the drafting group to insert "a statement of principle in the Declaration that read 'Safe and healthy working conditions are fundamental to decent work'".[527] The Employers' group obtained what it wanted.[528]

155 Quite similar to what had happened with health and safety, the Workers' group and the EU Member States again supported an aspirational Universal Labour Guarantee.[529] This part of the Declaration was likewise sent to the drafting group. There, the original Universal Labour Guarantee[530] evolved into something more akin to a reaffirmation of the Decent Work Agenda, with an emphasis on the importance of an adequate minimum wage and maximum limits on working time for all workers.[531]

---

524. *Ibid.*, 115.
525. *Ibid.*, 116.
526. *Ibid.*, 118.
527. *Ibid.*, 149.
528. The following interaction unfolded earlier during the Committee's discussions. "The Employer Vice-Chairperson announced that a news item on the official website of the United Nations Office of the High Commissioner for Human Rights (OHCHR) urged the ILO to immediately recognize and adopt safe and healthy working conditions as one of its fundamental principles and rights at work. In so doing, it claimed that some employers and their representative organizations were attempting to block that effort, calling into question the depth of the private sector's commitment to respect human rights. She expressed her dismay and displeasure at the public blaming of employers. In addition, some delegates had heard senior ILO officials suggesting that the Employers' group was trying to derail those efforts". *Ibid.*, 54.
529. *Ibid.*, 133.
530. "All workers, regardless of their employment status or contractual arrangements, should be guaranteed: (i) respect for their fundamental rights; (ii) an adequate living wage; (iii) limits on maximum working hours; (iv) safety and health at work; (v) privacy and personal data protection; and (vi) scope for achieving better work–life balance, by having greater influence over their working time, in ways that respect enterprise needs and promote productive efficiency and shared benefits". ILO, *supra* n. 464, at 7.
531. "All workers should enjoy adequate protection in accordance with the Decent Work Agenda, taking into account: (i) respect for their fundamental rights; (ii) an adequate minimum wage, statutory or negotiated; (iii) maximum limits on working time; and (iv) safety and health at work". Para. III.B. ILO Centenary Declaration for the Future of Work, 21 June 2019. ILO

The adopted Centenary Declaration – At the end of the discussions, the Worker Vice-Chairperson wondered what best symbolised the Committee's achievement. According to her, it was the phrase: "Calling upon all constituents of the ILO to reaffirm their unwavering commitment and to reinvigorate their efforts to achieve social justice and universal and lasting peace to which they agreed in 1919 and 1944".[532] To some extent, this observation says all one needs to know about the Centenary Declaration. The Employers' group was eager to draft a Declaration concerning the Aims and Purposes of the International Labour Organization in the 21st Century that predominantly expresses what they think is essential.[533] The Workers' group has managed to pay homage to the ILO's original aims and purposes.[534] No clear political message can be sent by adding the two together.[535] As such, some representatives expressed their disappointment at the Conference's plenary sitting.[536] Moreover, Thomas and Turnbull report that the centenary "was a disappointment for many in the Office. As an ILO official lamented, 'There's nothing from the Centenary that you'd want to put on a T-shirt' (field notes)".[537] 156

Based on these appraisals, one overall picture seems to emerge. Before the ILO Centenary Conference began, for instance, Van Der Heijden had claimed that "[a] powerful and unanimous signal on the occasion of the 100-year anniversary in 2019 is necessary if the organization is to survive in the 21st century".[538] The Centenary Declaration does not seem to carry that message, meaning that, at the very least, much work remains to be done. For example, as Alston and Gandour argue, "despite the 157

researchers nevertheless highlight the importance of a Universal Labour Guarantee to adequately protect all platform workers, for instance. Elva López Mourelo, *Work on Delivery Platforms in Argentina: Analysis and Policy Recommendations* 91 (ILO 2020).

532. Report of the Committee of the Whole: Summary of proceedings at the 108th Session of the International Labour Conference, Geneva, ILO, 2019, 158.
533. *Ibid.*, 154.
534. The ILO Centenary Declaration "is an instrument drafted to embed the triumph of neo-liberalism rather than promote social democracy, eclipsing the values of citizenship, redistribution and participation which we see in the Declaration of Philadelphia and the post-war initiatives of the ILO and its constituent parts". Keith Ewing, *Reflections on the ILO Centenary* 8, 9 (Caroline Kelly, Joo-Cheong Tham & Julian Sempill eds., *Papers from the Symposium on the Centenary of the ILO: Democracy, Labour Law and Trade Unions*, Centre for Employment and Labour Relations Law, Melbourne Law School 2019).
535. *See*, Nastazja Potocka-Sionek & Antonio Aloisi, *'Festina Lente': The ILO and EU Agendas on the Digital Transformation of Work*, 37 International Journal of Comparative Labour Law and Industrial Relations 35, 52 n. 1 (2021).
536. The Government representative from the United States: "On some issues, the Declaration does not delineate a clear sense of purpose, and much of the document falls short of providing the clarity and vision that it should provide". The employer representative from Australia: "Those of us who came here looking for a Declaration of ageless prose or a grand vision will be disappointed". The worker representative from Barbados: "But in addition to reinforcing the principles that undergird this house, the Centenary Declaration needed to be one that, when read by my daughter and other generations, would communicate the relevance of this house in language that could be easily understood. I think that we may not have achieved that". Presentation and discussion of the outcomes of the work of the Committee of the Whole at the 108th Session of the International Labour Conference, Geneva, ILO, 2019, 13–15.
537. Thomas & Turnbull, *supra* n. 383, at 21.
538. Paul van der Heijden, *The ILO Stumbling Towards Its Centenary Anniversary*, 15 International Organizations Law Review 203, 219 n. 1 (2018).

Declaration's opening reference to the various 'transformative changes' driven by inter alia 'environmental and climate change', its provisions are hardly at all responsive to the magnitude of the challenges posed in this regard".[539] Also, surprisingly enough, the Declaration barely says anything about multinational enterprises.[540] Both these gaps illustrate how the Declaration is not a daring attempt to revitalise the organisation in the present context.

158 **Remarkable aspects of the Declaration** – At the same time, despite its overall underwhelming content, the Declaration does contain a couple of pertinent elements. First, the Centenary Declaration might have the potential to address one of the critiques levelled at the concept of decent work. More specifically, decent work focuses on establishing decent working conditions, adequate social dialogue systems and satisfactory social security protection. It is unconcerned with the content of the work.[541] To put it crudely, irrespective of the harm done, if the work is performed under decent working conditions, the work seems to fulfil the criteria to be called decent work. The Centenary Declaration may be influential in this regard. It states that the ILO must carry forward "its constitutional mandate for social justice by further developing its human-centred approach to the future of work, which puts workers' rights and the needs, aspirations and rights of all people at the heart of economic, social and environmental policies".[542] Perhaps the latter part of this phrase enables the ILO to advance "a more ambitious vision of paid work, one in which work contributes to sustainable development in its economic, social and environmental dimensions".[543] A vision on decent work that, arguably, more closely resembles the spirit underlying the Declaration of Philadelphia.[544]

159 Besides touching on this "issue", the Centenary Declaration may also reinforce the relationship between the ILO and democracy. The preamble mentions the ILO

539. Philip Alston & Jackson Gandour, *The ILO's Centenary Declaration and Social Justice in the Digital Age* 565, 583 (George P. Politakis, Tomi Kohiyama & Thomas Lieby eds., *ILO100: Law for Social Justice*, ILO 2019). Likewise critical, Alexandra Kaasch & Amanda Shriwise eds., *Global Social Policy Digest 20.1*, 20 Global Social Policy 117, 129 n. 1 (2020).

540. *"Le non-dit de la Déclaration du centenaire sur cette question apparaît sans doute comme un des principaux points faibles du texte"*. Isabelle Daugareilh, *La Déclaration du Centenaire de l'OIT: Tout un Programme!*, Droit social 5 (2020).

541. Jean-Philippe Deranty & Craig MacMillan, *The ILO's Decent Work Initiative: Suggestions for an Extension of the Notion of "Decent Work"*, 43 Journal of Social Philosophy 386, 386–405 n. 4 (2012).

542. Para. I.D. ILO Centenary Declaration for the Future of Work, 21 June 2019.

543. S. J. Rombouts & N. Zekić, *Decent and Sustainable Work for the Future? The ILO Future of Work Centenary, the UN 2030 Agenda for Sustainable Development, and the Evolution of the Meaning of Work*, 24 UCLA Journal of International Law and Foreign Affairs 317, 354. n. 2 (2020).

544. The Declaration of Philadelphia already clarified that "[t]he Conference recognises the solemn obligation of the International Labour Organisation to further among the nations of the world programmes which will achieve: [...] (b) the employment of workers in the occupations in which they can have the satisfaction of giving the fullest measure of their skill and attainments and make their greatest contribution to the common well-being". Declaration concerning the aims and purposes of the International Labour Organisation (Declaration of Philadelphia), 10 May 1944. *See*, Alain Supiot, *Le Travail n'Est Pas une Merchandise: Contenu et Sens du Travail au xxie Siècle* §21 (Collège de France 2019).

constituents' desire "to democratize ILO governance by ensuring a fair representation of all regions and establishing the principle of equality among member States". Additionally, the Africa Group ensured the Centenary Resolution calls on Members to reach the number of ratifications needed for the Instrument of Amendment to the ILO Constitution, from 1986, to enter into force. The Resolution's goal is "to definitively democratize the functioning and composition of the governing bodies of the ILO".[545] A tripartite working group on full, equal and democratic participation in the ILO's tripartite governance has been established to this end.[546]

In addition to a desire to democratise the GB, the Conference also declared that: 160

> "[i]t is incumbent on the ILO to strengthen the capacity of its tripartite constituents to: (i) encourage the development of strong and representative social partner organizations; (ii) engage in all relevant processes, including with labour market institutions, programmes and policies, within and across borders; and (iii) address all fundamental principles and rights at work, at all levels, as appropriate, through strong, influential and inclusive mechanisms of social dialogue, in the conviction that such representation and dialogue contribute to the overall cohesion of societies and are a matter of public interest, and are crucial for a well-functioning and productive economy".[547]

It remains to be seen whether this provision can serve as a basis to move to a broader framework for economic democracy,[548] capable of addressing many scholars' call for more inclusive representation at the ILO.[549]

Fourthly, as mentioned above (*supra* no. 148), the Decent Work Agenda is not associated with decisive standard-setting action. However, the current Director-General, Ryder, might have somewhat diverted the organisation away from his predecessors' policy views. Hansenne wanted to give NGOs a more prominent role at the ILO and established the 1998 Declaration, which made the ILO less dependent on the Member States' (in)action. Somavía continued this process, launching decent work, which was also less State-centric than the original ILO Constitution. Ryder seems to, instead, attach more importance to the ILO Member States and their duty to implement a 161

545. Resolution on the ILO Centenary Declaration for the Future of Work, 21 June 2019.
546. ILO Governing Body, *Decision Concerning the Update on the Status of Ratification of the 1986 Instrument for the Amendment of the Constitution of the ILO and Follow-up to Paragraph 3 of the Resolution on the ILO Centenary Declaration for the Future of Work*, GB.340/INS/18/1/ (ILO 2020). Resolution on the principle of equality among ILO Member States and fair representation of all regions in the ILO's tripartite governance, 18 June 2021.
547. Para. IV.C. ILO Centenary Declaration for the Future of Work, 21 June 2019.
548. "Today, we need a broader understanding [than industrial or social democracy, one] of economic democracy to deal with the digital revolution, environmental threats and the plethora of forms of dependent self-employment ('informal', subcontracted, 'uberized' work, etc.) that exist". Supiot, *supra* n. 17, at 129.
549. For instance, more recently, Guy Mundlak, *Tri-Plus: Reflection on Opening the ILO's Tripartite Structure* 311, 311–336 (George P. Politakis, Tomi Kohiyama & Thomas Lieby eds., *ILO100: Law for Social Justice*, ILO 2019); Jakovleski, Jerbi & Biersteker, *supra* n. 372, at §51–52; Tonia Novitz, *Engagement with Sustainability at the International Labour Organization and Wider Implications for Collective Worker Voice*, 159 International Labour Review 463, 463–482 n. 4 (2020).

human-centred approach to the future of work.[550] This possible shift should be placed within its context. What happened at the Committee on the Application of Standards in 2012, when the Employers' group refused to hold discussions because they disagreed on the right to strike, was not just a shock for the ILO's supervisory system.[551] It put the ILO's entire standard-setting machinery under pressure.[552] Tensions cooled when the Workers' and Employers' groups reached an agreement in 2015 that was acceptable to the governments.[553] Nevertheless, the first three years were crisis years for Ryder, who was elected as the DG in 2012. For instance, the Standards Review Mechanism, which aims to keep the International Labour Code up to date, was established in 2011,[554] but its terms of reference were only accepted in 2015.[555] In this climate, the Director-General launched 2013's centenary initiatives, including a standards initiative "to consolidate tripartite consensus on an authoritative supervisory system and to enhance the relevance of international labour standards through a standards review mechanism".[556] The initiative paid off, at least on paper. In paragraph IV.A. of the Centenary Declaration, the Conference declares that:

> "The setting, promotion, ratification and supervision of international labour standards is of fundamental importance to the ILO. This requires the Organization to have and promote a clear, robust, up-to-date body of international labour standards and to further enhance transparency. International labour standards also need to respond to the changing patterns of the world of work, protect workers and take into account the needs of sustainable enterprises, and be subject to authoritative and effective supervision. The ILO will assist its Members in the ratification and effective application of standards".

162 **The constituents' Declaration** – Beyond these four examples of how the Centenary Declaration might make a difference, another significant feature of the Declaration is how it was drafted. The ILO constituents had a big hand in drafting the Centenary

550. Thomas & Turnbull, *supra* n. 383, at 1–25.
551. Lee Swepston, *Crisis in the ILO Supervisory System: Dispute over the Right to Strike*, 29 International Journal of Comparative Labour Law and Industrial Relations 199, 199–218 n. 2 (2013).
552. From the point of view of the Employers' group, the Committee of Experts' clarifications risked influencing the opinion of other courts, policymakers, etc. Most notably, the clarifications of the Committee on the meaning of rights and principles in the Fundamental Conventions risked having an impact on what the outside world thought the 1998 Declaration meant to say. "Seen from this perspective, what is perhaps ultimately at stake is therefore less the nature of the CEACR's pronouncements or even the future functioning of the supervisory body, but more broadly the influence, or existence, of ILS". Claire la Hovary, *The ILO's Supervisory Bodies' 'Soft Law Jurisprudence'* 316, 328 (Adelle Blackett & Anne Trebilcock eds., *Research Handbook on Transnational Labour Law*, Edward Elgar Publishing 2015).
553. ILO Standards Initiative–Joint Statement of Workers' & Employers' Groups (23.02.2015), TMFAPROC/2015/2.
554. ILO Legal Issues and International Labour Standards Section, *ILO Standards Policy: The Establishment and the Implementation of a Standards Review Mechanism*, GB.312/LILS/5 (ILO 2011).
555. ILO Legal Issues and International Labour Standards Section, *The Standards Initiative: Terms of Reference of the Standards Review Mechanism Tripartite Working Group*, GB.325/LILS/3 (ILO 2015).
556. ILO Director-General, *supra* n. 510, at 28.

Declaration. As mentioned by the Employer Vice-Chairperson in her opening remarks, "[t]he Declaration should not be limited to a cut and paste of the report of the Global Commission for the Future of Work, but should be based on the issues and aspirations of the constituents to ensure their full ownership".[557] As illustrated above, the Employers' group kept its word; possibly, to the dismay of some, who might have preferred to cut and paste the Commission's report. Once the Declaration was finished, the Secretary-General's representative acknowledged that it had been "the in-depth tripartite discussions themselves that had contributed to renewing the ILO".[558] Similarly, the Reporter of the Committee of the Whole stressed that their primary concern had been "to ensure the widest tripartite ownership of the ILO Centenary Declaration".[559]

As a result, the Centenary Declaration is quite different from the more articulate and cohesive Declaration of Philadelphia. The latter was drafted by ILO insiders and only slightly amended at the Conference, for instance, because constituents did not want the ILO to "scrutinize" national and international policies but to "examine and consider" them.[560] To put it in the words of the United States' Employer representative, "[t]he 1944 Declaration of Philadelphia was concise poetry; this [Centenary] Declaration properly reflects compromise and – with less than two months to consider drafts and nine days to address hundreds of amendments – it leans more to expedient prose".[561] The consequence of this difference between the two is that the Centenary Declaration is a text of the constituents, which has sometimes been negotiated on a knife-edge,[562] whereas the Declaration of Philadelphia is a text that has been presented to the constituents and was mostly embraced. This difference is significant. **163**

As noted by Chigara regarding the ownership and authorship of the International Labour Code, for a long time, many former colonies were asked to ratify or commit to ILS in which they had no hand.[563] Therefore, the importance of the Social Justice Declaration and Centenary Declaration also resides in the fact that tripartite delegations from developing countries have at last co-authored the authoritative framework **164**

557. Report of the Committee of the Whole: Summary of proceedings at the 108th Session of the International Labour Conference, Geneva, ILO, 2019, 4.
558. *Ibid.*, 160.
559. Presentation and discussion of the outcomes of the work of the Committee of the Whole at the 108th Session of the International Labour Conference, Geneva, ILO, 2019, 1.
560. Lee, *supra* n. 354, at 474–478.
561. Presentation and discussion of the outcomes of the work of the Committee of the Whole at the 108th Session of the International Labour Conference, Geneva, ILO, 2019, 16.
562. Employer Vice-Chairperson of the Committee of the Whole: "It is through our collective efforts, determination, goodwill and love for this institution and what it represents that we managed to reach a consensus on such an important occasion. The discussion was stretched right to the end with rumours about the possibility of not having consensus and what this would mean. I will not reveal a conversation that took place in a vehicle in which the President of the Conference kindly offered the two Vice-Presidents and myself a lift back from the last high-level lunch we had at our ILO building. I will leave it to you to guess, as rumours abounded and people were starting to panic". *Ibid.*, 4.
563. Ben Chigara, *Latecomers to the ILO and the Authorship and Ownership of the International Labour Code*, 29 Human Rights Quarterly 706, 706–726 n. 3 (2007).

that guides deliberations between ILO constituents.[564] This co-ownership of the more recent Declarations not only boosts the ILO's legitimacy, it is also helpful for more pragmatic reasons. According to governments in the Global South, "ILO standards were transformed from a means to achieve social justice across national borders into a protectionist tool used by the rich industrialized countries to maintain the inequalities of the international system".[565] In contrast, the Decent Work Agenda and the latest Declarations frame ILO standards as means to implement decent work, which contributes to sustainable development. In other words, in the more recent Declarations, developing countries have acknowledged that decent work is a fundamental part of sustainable development, implying ILS are not necessarily juxtaposed to their interests.[566] This affirmation opens the door for a more positive take on standard-setting and supervision.[567]

564. "It is particularly striking that, by contrast to less ambitious reforms that have indeed shown a frustrating record of slow progress if not plain failure, this complex and sweeping project [i.e. the Social Justice Declaration] has been adopted unanimously and in a relatively short period of time". Francis Maupain, *New Foundation or New Façade? The ILO and the 2008 Declaration on Social Justice for a Fair Globalization*, 20 The European Journal of International Law 823, 849 n.3 (2009).
565. Maul, *supra* n. 373, at 9.
566. For Daugareilh, what is significant about the Centenary Declaration is that it openly questions the democratic nature of the organisation's internal governance, and takes the form of a renewed and essential pact of mutual trust. Daugareilh, *supra* n. 540.
567. *See, e.g.*, Brian Langille, *'Hard Law Makes Bad Cases': The International Labour Organization (Nervously) Confronts New Governance Institutions*, 32 International Journal of Comparative Labour Law and Industrial Relations 407, 407–424 n. 4 (2016).

Chapter 4. Platform Work and the Centenary Declaration's Implementation

Commitments in the Centenary Declaration – The legal importance of ILO Declarations should be highlighted once more before mentioning the relevant paragraphs for platform workers in the Centenary Declaration. What applies to the Social Justice Declaration also holds true for the Centenary Declaration. As explained by the Office, "[i]n relation to the Organization, a solemn Declaration of the Conference is an act that commits the Organization as a whole. [...] In the form of a Declaration, such a document would have legal effects with regard to all the bodies of the Organization – the Conference, the Governing Body and the International Labour Office – at least equal to those of a resolution".[568] To that extent, since ILO Resolutions can have normative value,[569] the same is true for ILO Declarations. Hence, the Centenary Declaration is not without any legal effect. In part II of the Declaration, the Conference declares that: 165

> "the ILO must direct its efforts to: [...] (ii) harnessing the fullest potential of technological progress and productivity growth, including through social dialogue, to achieve decent work and sustainable development, which ensure dignity, self-fulfilment and a just sharing of the benefits for all; [...] (xii) ensuring that diverse forms of work arrangements, production and business models, including in domestic and global supply chains, leverage opportunities for social and economic progress, provide for decent work and are conducive to full, productive and freely chosen employment".

Moreover, part III of the Declaration adds that:

> "[t]he Conference calls upon all Members, [...], to further develop its human-centred approach to the future of work by: [...] C. Promoting sustained, inclusive and sustainable economic growth, full and productive employment and decent work for all through: [...] (v) policies and measures that ensure

568. ILO International Labour Office, *supra* n. 486, at 30–31.
569. Alain Pellet, *Le Rôle des Résolutions des Organisations Internationales à la Lumière de la Jurisprudence de la Cour internationale de Justice* 149, 155 and 158 (George P. Politakis, Tomi Kohiyama & Thomas Lieby eds., *ILO100: Law for Social Justice*, ILO 2019).

> appropriate privacy and personal data protection, and respond to challenges and opportunities in the world of work relating to the digital transformation of work, including platform work".

Based on these provisions, the Centenary Declaration contains the necessary leads to address platform work. The question is whether this issue will receive priority treatment.

166 **Implementation of these commitments** – The Centenary Declaration adheres to the inclusive approach advanced in the "Decent Work for All Agenda". This inclusivity is evident when looking, for example, at the ILO programme and budget for the biennium 2020–2021, which intends to "faithfully translate and operationalize the content of the Centenary Declaration".[570] Two of the programme's eight policy outcomes are called "adequate and effective protection at work for all" and "comprehensive and sustainable social protection for all". Under these policy objectives, the ILO has committed to researching how workers' labour protections in diverse forms of work arrangements can be strengthened. It highlights the example of platform work.[571] Furthermore, during the period 2020–2021, the ILO informs labour administrations about platform work,[572] and supports ILO constituents in "formulating and adopting measures integrating social protection with employment, wage or fiscal policies in order to effectively support transitions to the formal economy and the extension of social protection coverage to workers in diverse forms of work arrangements, including platform work".[573]

167 The COVID-19 pandemic broke out after the adoption of this programme. Evidently, the pandemic also required the ILO to adjust its priorities. The ILO's Strategic Plan for 2022–2025 was drafted to implement the Centenary Declaration, taking into account the pandemic's projected effects on labour markets. Its five policy outcomes are: (i) addressing change in the world of work, such as adjustments in global supply chains; (ii) addressing the need to leave no one behind; (iii) the global social protection deficit; (iv) safety and health at work; and, (v) the global recovery from the COVID-19 crisis. Again, the Strategic Plan highlights the need to strengthen protection across diverse forms of work, as part of this "need to leave no one behind". It mentions in this respect that "[i]f the pandemic results in the more rapid introduction of innovative work arrangements, for example in the form of remote and gig work mediated by digital technologies, then that need will become all the more pressing".[574]

168 Following this Strategic Plan, the programme and budget proposals for 2022–2023 mention that, among other things, "addressing regulatory gaps concerning digital platform work will be prioritized".[575] Research on platform work will continue, and the ILO will, in particular, "develop guidance to cover workers on digital platforms through adapted national social security legislation and enhanced compliance

570. ILO, *Programme and Budget for the Biennium 2020–21* xvii (ILO 2020).
571. *Ibid.*, 42.
572. *Ibid.*, 14.
573. *Ibid.*, 46.
574. ILO, *The ILO's Strategic Plan for 2022–25* 9 (ILO 2020).
575. ILO Director-General, *Programme and Budget Proposals for 2022–23* 44 (ILO 2021).

of digital platforms, and explore options for cross-national coordination".[576] This reference seems to follow up on the Global Commission's proposal regarding "an international governance system for digital labour platforms that sets and requires platforms (and their clients) to respect certain minimum rights and protections".[577]

To conclude, based on the latest policy documents, one could say that there is a **169**
sufficient basis for the ILO to consider standard-setting options concerning platform work. The ILC's Centenary Declaration, combined with the Governing Body's programme and budget proposals, indicates that platform work is a point of concern for both the Office and ILO constituents. Suppose the ILO indeed organises a Tripartite Meeting of Experts regarding "Decent Work in the Platform Economy" in the second quarter of 2022;[578] it will be interesting to see whether experts can reach clear-cut conclusions on how to pursue that goal.

576. ILO Director-General, *supra* n. 575, at 50.
577. Global Commission on the Future of Work, *supra* n. 406, at 44.
578. ILO Governing Body, *Composition, Agenda and Programme of Standing Bodies and Meetings*, GB.342/INS/10(Rev.2) (ILO 2021).

Chapter 5. Interim Conclusion: Concrete Prospects for a Future Standard

An open-ended mandate – The ILO's constitutional texts define its mandate in broad terms. It advances a framework within which ILO constituents can give substance to the concept of social justice. As discussed, social justice is a disposition rather than a defined concept. The same is true for decent work, which ILO constituents did not want to be given a concrete, universal definition. The Treaty of Versailles has equipped the ILO with "permanent machinery" to substantiate social justice throughout the decades, and the same applies to decent work. Discussions about how that machinery should be used are never-ending. 170

Due to these continuous struggles over the Conference's agenda, a critical topic of discussion is who gets to set the ILO's course. For instance, should the UN influence the ILO's decent work concept through the overarching SDG programme? Should not the developing world, for example the Africa Group, become more influential in the ILO's internal decision-making processes? Should NGOs, other than national trade unions and employers' associations, become an institutionalised actor in ILO deliberations? Moreover, perhaps most importantly, will the Office be allowed to set the future course, as happened with the Decent Work Agenda, or will the ILO constituents maintain tight control? The institutional tensions brought to the surface in the context of the right to strike, arguably, made the Office more cautious.[579] This restraint is a notable development given this organ's "key driving role" in the ILO.[580] 171

A human-centred approach to social justice – In the Centenary Declaration, the ILO constituents seem to have taken it upon themselves to outline the organisation's future. According to the constituents, the organisation should take a "human-centred approach to the future of work". For now, it is unclear what exactly this means. It is 172

579. Claire la Hovary, *The ILO's Mandate and Capacity: Creating, Proliferating and Supervising Labour Standards for a Globalized Economy* 37, 42 (Henner Gött ed., *Labour Standards in International Economic Law*, Springer 2018).

580. Maupain, *supra* n. 353, at 318.

hard to see how this new catchphrase is anything more than a continuation of the ILO's original mandate.[581]

173 For this reason, the ILO's twenty-first-century mission is still captured best by "decent work for all". In terms of the ILO's goals, the Centenary Declaration seems merely to have new emphases. Most notably, by highlighting that safe and healthy working conditions are fundamental to decent work. However, as shown in the excerpt from the draft Social Justice Declaration (*supra* no. 144), attributing particular importance to health and safety is not entirely new. The original draft Universal Labour Guarantee – as proposed by the Global Commission – would have made a significant difference; yet, that proposal was dismantled. Consequently, without really breaking new ground, the Centenary Declaration simply lists a range of topics that the ILO must work on, including "ensuring that diverse forms of work arrangements [...] provide for decent work and are conducive to full, productive and freely chosen employment".[582] Chapter 4 indicated that the Governing Body's programmes and budgets consider platform work to be a work arrangement captured under this objective. Furthermore, the Centenary Declaration called on the Member States to pursue "policies and measures that ensure appropriate privacy and personal data protection, and respond to challenges and opportunities in the world of work relating to the digital transformation of work, including platform work".[583]

174 **Labour standards' role** – Based on these references, the legal grounds to undertake action are present. Besides, the Centenary Declaration seems to confirm the role of ILS as one tool in the toolbox. As stated by the Chairperson of the Committee on Strengthening the ILO's Capacity (*supra* no. 148), the ILO Constitution contains the destination, and the Social Justice Declaration offers a compass to navigate the waters in contemporary times. One might add that the Centenary Declaration tweaks the compass. The International Labour Code, in turn, is the manual that accompanies the compass; it needs to be rewritten to match the compass. In the end, if the Fundamental Conventions are left out of the equation, one could say the International Labour Code has become a fundamentally important "guidebook" rather than a rulebook.

175 **Prospective action on platform work** – Time will tell whether the broader endeavour to rewrite the Code brings forth a standard on the platform economy. At the time of writing, ILO constituents are headed to the starting blocks to survey the possibilities. The Third Part of this dissertation covers some existing ILS that should not be overlooked in this regard.

581. *See*, Potocka-Sionek & Aloisi, *supra* n. 535, at 51.
582. Para. II.A.(xii) ILO Centenary Declaration for the Future of Work, 21 June 2019.
583. *Ibid.*, para. III.C.(v).

Part III. International Labour Standards Relevant for Platform Work

INTRODUCTION

The content of Part III. – When the ILO Governing Body decides to pursue a standard on a certain topic, the Office is tasked to write a Law and Practice Report on the situation worldwide. One component of that report succinctly discusses the relevance of already existing international labour standards for that topic. For example, in the case of a possible standard on privacy and personal data protection, the ILO Code of Practice on "protection of workers' personal data" would be mentioned. The report covers whether the instrument applies and briefly covers its implications. 176

The Third Part of this dissertation does the same to some extent. This Third Part focuses on applying some of the most relevant standards for platform work. However, it discusses the questions related to these instruments' scope far more extensively than any Law and Practice Report would. To this end, the First Chapter covers some preliminary observations: (i) what the particularly relevant standards are, and (ii) what the applicable rules of interpretation are. Chapter 2, 3 and 4, subsequently, analyse the scope of the Private Employment Agencies Convention, 1997 (No. 181), the Home Work Convention, 1996 (No. 177), and the Domestic Workers Convention, 2011 (No. 189). 177

Its purpose for the overall thesis – Knowing whether these standards apply to platform work is crucial to any future standard-setting action. Imagine they do apply and contain many relevant guidelines, then, the Governing Body might want to simply draft conclusions on decent work in the platform economy and issue them in the form of guidelines (soft law instrument). On the other hand, if they do not apply or offer inadequate protections, a new standard might be desirable. In such a case, knowing which instruments apply is also important because it establishes a benchmark. It would, for example, be hard to offer rights and protections to platform workers that are far below the protections applicable to domestic workers if many of the platform 178 workers in question also be classified as domestic workers.[584] Secondly, the already adopted instruments contain rules and guidelines that have been accepted in the past, indicating what might be politically feasible. That will be used in Part IV of this dissertation as source material for potential solutions.

584. See, for instance, Murray on the level of protection of part-time workers in light of the Fundamental Conventions. The author scrutinises the standards on part-time work for supposedly not meeting the threshold established in these Fundamental Conventions. Jill Murray, *Social Justice for Women? The ILO's Convention on Part-time Work*, 15 International Journal of Comparative Labour Law and Industrial Relations 3, 3–19 n. 1 (1999).

Chapter 1. Preliminary Observations

SUBCHAPTER 1. THE CHOICE FOR CONVENTION NO. 177, NO. 181 AND NO. 189

Standards applicable to self-employed workers – Most platform workers are contractually classified as self-employed workers. Therefore, traditionally at least, labour law does not apply to them. At the same time, this starting point has become increasingly nuanced over time. These days, many labour protections do apply to certain self-employed workers at the domestic level.[585] As hinted at earlier (*supra* no. 131), a parallel development from narrow standards for specific categories of workers to universal standards applicable to all workers has been taking place at the ILO. As such, multiple ILO Conventions also apply to self-employed and informal workers, particularly the Fundamental Conventions.[586] 179

Even certain non-fundamental Conventions apply to all workers.[587] For example, the Occupational Safety and Health Convention, 1981 (No. 155), is silent about its application to self-employed persons; hence, in line with the corresponding Recommendation,[588] "it is up to each country to determine what protective measures may be necessary and practicable to apply to this category of persons".[589] Some other 180

585. What are commonly described as "intermediate" categories of quasi-subordinate or economically dependent workers, such as "limb (b) workers", "*arbeitnehmerähnliche Personen*" and "*trabajadores autónomos económicamente dependientes*", can, arguably, be more accurately considered a sub-group of self-employed workers. These sub-groups are provided with many labour law protections. Countouris & De Stefano, *supra* n. 122, at 23. Domestic legal systems are also providing certain self-employed workers, like own-account workers, with collective rights. OECD, *Expert Meeting on Collective Bargaining for Own-Account Workers* (OECD 2020).
586. ILO Committee of Experts on the Application of Conventions and Recommendations, *supra* n. 398; Countouris & De Stefano, *supra* n. 122, at 29.
587. ILO, *supra* n. 25, at 203–205.
588. "Provision should be made for such measures as may be necessary and practicable to give self-employed persons protection analogous to that provided for in the Convention and in this Recommendation". Para. 1 Occupational Safety and Health Recommendation, 1981 (No. 164).
589. ILO Committee of Experts on the Application of Conventions and Recommendations, *ILO Standards on Occupational Safety and Health: Promoting a Safe and Healthy Working Environment*

instruments that aim to keep workers safe are more explicit about their application to the self-employed. The Violence and Harassment Convention, 2019 (No. 190), for instance, wants the Member States to prevent and eliminate violence and harassment in the world of work in general, which, of course, also benefits self-employed persons.[590] Furthermore, apart from OSH standards,[591] other ILS may similarly ask the Member States to improve self-employed workers' protections. This is the case in the area of social security, among others.[592] Consequently, as illustrated by these examples, even if platform workers would remain self-employed, the Home Work Convention, Private Employment Agencies Convention and Domestic Workers Convention are only some of the instruments relevant for the regulation of platform work. The relevance of these three instruments is partly due to the peculiarities associated with their scope of application. All three have a distinct approach to protecting a subset of workers that have proven challenging to cover under labour law in the past. Their scope is not construed around the notion of a regular "employment relationship", therefore, potentially applying to some of these contractually self-employed platform workers. In addition to their unusual scope, the selection of these three instruments is also based on the considerations detailed below.

181 **The rise of marginal part-time and casual work** – In addition to significant growth in "regular" part-time work, meaning that employees can be expected to perform about 30–90 per cent of a comparable full-time employee's working hours, the relatively high share of marginal part-time work has also become noticeable. Marginal part-time workers can be described as people working fewer than ten to fifteen hours per week for one employer.[593] These "marginal" working hours can be allocated on an irregular basis. When part-time work is performed with a high degree of variability, one might also consider it casual in nature. Casual work is characterised by irregularity and an *ad hoc* instead of a predictable work arrangement.[594] As such, casual work, marginal part-time work, and on-call work all share "important policy dimensions related to the short and unpredictable character of working hours".[595]

---

13 (ILO 2009).

590. Valerio De Stefano, Ilda Durri, Charalampos Stylogiannis & Mathias Wouters, *"System Needs Update": Upgrading Protection Against Cyberbullying and ICT-enabled Violence and Harassment in the World of Work* 19–20 (ILO 2020).

591. For instance, the Safety and Health in Agriculture Convention, 2001 (No. 184), and, most notably, the Safety and Health in Agriculture Recommendation, 2001 (No. 192), suggest protecting self-employed farmers. ILO Committee of Experts on the Application of Conventions and Recommendations, *Working Together to Promote a Safe and Healthy Working Environment* 176 (ILO 2017).

592. Social Security (Minimum Standards) Convention, 1952 (No. 102); Social Protection Floors Recommendation, 2012 (No. 202); Transition from the Informal to the Formal Economy Recommendation, 2015 (No. 204); Ippei Tsuruga, Quynh Anh Nguyen, Christina Behrendt & Judith van Doorn, *Extending Social Security to Self-Employed Workers: Lessons from International Experience* 3–4 (ILO 2019).

593. ILO, *Working Time in the Twenty-First Century: Report for Discussions at the Tripartite Meeting of Experts on Working-time Arrangements* 53 (ILO 2011).

594. Eurofound, *Casual Work: Characteristics and Implications* 4 (Publications Office of the European Union 2019).

595. ILO, *Non-standard Employment Around the World: Understanding Challenges, Shaping Prospects* 23 (ILO 2016).

Whereas casual work has been common for decades in some regions, such as the Asia-Pacific,[596] the increasing prominence of these "marginal" work arrangements has also become noteworthy in OECD countries. For example, in Germany, approximately five million people were exclusively employed on a "mini-job" in 2019.[597] According to the country's statistics, in New Zealand, about 5 per cent of all employees would be classified as casual workers.[598] This percentage contrasts with the 25 per cent of employees in Australia that work in casual arrangements. The difference leads Campbell to conclude that "casual work in Australia is almost five times as significant as a proportion of the waged workforce as the parallel category of casual work in New Zealand".[599] Although part of this gap might be attributable to different statistical methodologies, New Zealand's and Australia's example, nevertheless, suggests that the overall percentage of casual work arrangements shows marked differences between countries. To this extent, Eurofound's observation in 2019 that there has also been "a substantial increase of casual work during the last two decades" in the European Union must be complemented with a second observation. Namely, this is the case "except in countries where some regulation had been adopted aiming at curbing the trend".[600] 182

Platform work, a form of casual work – Researchers have suggested that platform operators seem to have latched on to this broader "casualisation trend".[601] The digital infrastructure of platform operators supposedly enables people to "work at any time or anywhere" and be their own boss.[602] However, being able to work anytime and anywhere is not always a blessing. Certain employers, for instance, prevent their staff from receiving e-mails after their working hours or explicitly reassure employees that 183

596. ILO Regional Office for Asia and the Pacific, *Asia-Pacific Labour Market Update, September 2017* (ILO 2017).
597. Additionally, two million people combined a mini-job with other forms of employment. Institut Arbeit und Qualifikation der Universität Duisburg-Essen, *Beschäftigte in Minijobs 2003 – 2019*, Sozialpolitik aktuell in Deutschland (28 April 2021), https://www.sozialpolitik-aktuell.de/files/sozialpolitik-aktuell/_Politikfelder/Arbeitsmarkt/Datensammlung/PDF-Dateien/abbIV91.pdf.
598. Iain Campbell, *On-call and Related Forms of Casual Work in New Zealand and Australia* 2 and 7 (ILO 2018).
599. *Ibid.*, 12. Farina et al. suggest that Australia might even be the "world leader" in zero-hours contract-like employment. Egidio Farina, Colin Green & Duncan McVicar, *Zero Hours Contracts and Their Growth* 9 (IZA Institute of Labor Economics 2019).
600. "Casual work is a type of work where the employment is not stable and continuous, and the employer is not obliged to regularly provide the worker with work, but has the flexibility of calling them in on demand". Eurofound, *supra* n. 594, at 7. Countries outside the EU also have legislation to limit the abusive reliance on casual work arrangements. An ILO report mentions examples of the Philippines, Papua New Guinea and Ghana. ILO, *supra* n. 595, at 257 and 261.
601. Valerio De Stefano, *Casual Work beyond Casual Work in the EU: The Underground Casualisation of the European Workforce – And What to Do about it*, 7 European Labour Law Journal 421, 421–441 n. 3 (2016); Valerio De Stefano, *The Rise of "Just-in-time workforce": On-demand Work, Crowdwork, and Labor Protection in the "Gig-economy"*, 37 Comparative Labor Law & Policy Journal 471, 480–483 n. 3 (2016); Eurofound, *supra* n. 594, at 35; Deirdre McCann, *Temporal Casualisation and 'Availability Time': Mencap, Uber and the Framed Flexibility Model* 1–9 (Decent Work Regulation, Durham University 2020).
602. Eurofound, *Telework and ICT-based Mobile Work: Flexible Working in the Digital Age* 5 (Publications Office of the European Union 2020).

they will not suffer any consequences when disconnecting during the weekends.[603] This reassurance is given out of concern for their employees' well-being. The thing about platform operators is that they do the complete opposite. Instead of advancing fixed working hours and making workers disconnect after those working hours, the platform's workforce is hardly ever obliged to come to work – at least on legal grounds – but remains connected, always within easy reach. Huws et al., therefore, call platform workers "logged" workers. They remain available to respond, can be enticed to come to work, and their actions are electronically logged.[604] Communication happens through e-mails, pop-up messages, or even phone calls.[605] For instance, Uber drivers are informed about when to expect activity on the platform due to an event in the city. Drivers can earn more when working at times or in areas of high-demand, so-called surge zones.[606] Among other things, because of the significance of such bonuses for drivers' overall income, Wu et al. argue that working time flexibility, as such, has itself become a "labor control strategy".[607] This volatility of working time provides a clear link between platform work and Convention No. 177, No. 181 and No. 189. Industrial homeworkers, temporary agency workers and domestic workers are all categories of workers whose working time is often flexible and subject to change; just like platform workers, their work is highly impacted by changes in labour demand.[608]

184 **"Pocket money"** – A significant share of fervent platform workers also experience other issues similar to those of day labourers, dock workers, homeworkers and agricultural workers from the past.[609] More specifically, they go online searching for intermittent work while hanging out at home or on the corner of the street, just like those other workers used to stand in line for a day's work. However, for policymakers, instead of concluding that these platform workers are "compound non-standard"

603. C. W. Von Bergen & Martin S. Bressler, *Work, Non-Work Boundaries and the Right to Disconnect*, 21 Journal of Applied Business and Economics 51, 55–56 n. 2 (2019).
604. Ursula Huws, Neil H. Spencer & Dag S. Syrdal, *Online, On Call: The Spread of Digitally Organised Just-in-time Working and its Implications for Standard Employment Models*, 33 New Technology, Work and Employment 113, 123 n. 2 (2018). *See also*, Ursula Huws, *Logged Labour: A New Paradigm of Work Organisation?*, 10 Work Organisation, Labour & Globalisation 7, 7–26 n. 1 (2016).
605. *E.g.* Alison Griswold, *This is the Script Uber is Using to Make Anti-union Phone Calls to Drivers in Seattle*, Quartz (22 February 2016), https://qz.com/621977/this-is-the-script-uber-is-using-to-make-anti-union-phone-calls-to-drivers-in-seattle/.
606. Rosenblat & Stark, *supra* n. 307, at 3768.
607. Qingjun Wu, Hao Zhang, Zhen Li & Kai Liu, *Labor Control in the Gig Economy: Evidence from Uber in China*, 61 Journal of Industrial Relations 574, 591–593 n. 4 (2019). Wood has similarly argued that flexible scheduling can be turned into a form of labour control. Wood, *supra* n. 42.
608. Employers sometimes need homeworkers to step up and complete additional orders. They sometimes require a temporary agency worker to arrive at short notice. Households may likewise demand a domestic worker to come when it suits their schedule. Platform technologies are being used to supercharge this type of flexibility. The technology facilitates the creation of a "just-in-time" workforce.
609. Aleksynska, Bastrakova & Kharchenko, *supra* n. 78, at 51. "With reference to two examples from the nineteenth century–outwork (or 'homework') and dock work–Prassl demonstrates quite convincingly that these aspects of gig work are anything but new". Ruth Dukes, *Regulating Gigs*, 83 Modern Law Review 217, 222 n. 1 (2020). *See*, Jeremias Prassl, *supra* n. 110, at 78–80.

workers, whose jobs combine various non-standard features, which makes them particularly precarious,[610] platform work is eagerly and often mistakenly[611] perceived as a pastime, side-gig, or source of supplemental income.[612] The fact is overlooked that, for instance, temporary agency work and industrial home work were also initially portrayed as a source of easy pin or pocket money.[613] In a similar vein to early employers of agency and homeworkers, operators continue to present platform work as a convenient source of a quick buck. In reality, this is sometimes true, of course.[614] Nevertheless, by doing so, "[t]his tale of 'additional income' [...] continues to crop up across the centuries" to justify low and insecure remuneration.[615] More broadly, just like industrial homeworkers, temporary agency workers and domestic workers, platform workers are another group whose occupation risks not being taken seriously. By conveniently depicting this work as pocket money, additional household income or an intermediate step towards something better, platform work, moreover, remains considered a relatively harmless labour market development.

Platform work, a reiteration of past practices? – As shown, platform work is not an 185
isolated phenomenon. It is related to the broader casualisation of the labour market, and platform operators draw on decades-old narratives to keep regulators at bay. Stanford, furthermore, claims that for the most part, operators' "new digital techniques of planning, allocation, supervision and payment [...] are simply facilitating the application of long-standing management labour extraction strategies that are as old as capitalism".[616] He notes how platform work is similar to: (i) on-call work, in which workers have no predictable hours and no predictable income; (ii) piece-work, in

610. Eurofound, *Labour Market Change: Trends and Policy Approaches Towards Flexibilization* 16–18 (Publications Office of the European Union 2020).
611. For instance, food-delivery couriers are often assumed to perform this work on the side. However, unlike in some other countries, for 89.4 per cent of respondents in Argentina, being a courier is their main source of income. López Mourelo, *supra* n. 531, at 74. Furthermore, 74.5 per cent of the food delivery couriers in China work full-time. Also, more than 20 per cent of ride-hailing drivers in China viewed it as a long-term occupation. Irene Zhou, *supra* n. 37, at 13–14. These percentages are not exceptional in the developing world either. ILO, *supra* n. 25, at 158.
612. "*Enfin, en dépit de la jurisprudence qui a reconnu dans le pilotage par algorithmes tous les traits de la subordination salariale, les travailleurs 'ubérisés' sont fermement maintenus dans un 'en deçà de l'emploi', par des dirigeants politiques soumis à l'intense lobbying des plateformes*". Supiot, *supra* n. 544, at §7.
613. Janine Berg, *Income Security in the On-demand Economy: Findings and Policy Lessons from a Survey of Crowdworkers*, 37 Comparative Labor Law & Policy Journal 543, 565–566 n. 3 (2016); Erin Hatton, *Gig Work: All Hustle and Little Gain*, 49 Contemporary Sociology 397, 398–399 n. 5 (2020); ILO, *Working from Home: From Invisibility to Decent Work* 18 (ILO 2021).
614. It is true that complementing pay is a major reason why some workers engage in platform work. However, for instance, a lack of alternative employment opportunities is likewise a "prime motivating factor". Moreover, many workers do not rely on this type of work to complement pay. One study indicates crowdwork is a primary source of income for about one third of crowdworkers. ILO, *supra* n. 25, at 143, 145 and 154.
615. Prassl, *supra* n. 110, at 82. *See also*, V. B. Dubal, *The Time Politics of Home-based Digital Piecework*, C4eJournal (15 May 2020), https://c4ejournal.net/2020/07/04/v-b-dubal-the-time-politics-of-home-based-digital-piecework-2020-c4ej-xxx/.
616. Jim Stanford, *The Resurgence of Gig Work: Historical and Theoretical Perspectives*, 28 The Economic and Labour Relations Review 382, 396 n. 3 (2017).

which workers are paid in return for their deliverables, instead of their time, which means that the risk of no available work is passed on to the worker; (iii) home work, with many platform workers being asked to use their personal equipment, albeit without compensation; and (iv) triangular employment, meaning the worker has difficulties identifying the entity responsible for his or her entitlements. All things considered, as Garben contends, "the online platform working arrangements can at times resemble very old working arrangements, presented in a new digital 'jacket'".[617] These holistic perspectives have influenced the choice for our three ILS. Indeed, the gig economy "is firmly rooted in structural labour market shifts".[618] Since the ILO has already adopted standards to address such shifts, those ILS may be particularly relevant to the regulation of platform work.

186 **A link with private employment services** – Contrary to the public's perception, some surveys indicate that most platform work might, in fact, take place online through crowdwork platforms and at the location of the household, e.g. cleaning and caring services.[619] As noted above (*supra* nos. 58–60), in many instances, these platforms function like LMIs, operating as "new players in the temporary staffing industry".[620] This similarity raises the question of why the regulation developed for labour market intermediation is not applied to these platforms. Moreover, beyond the many platforms of which the services resemble labour market intermediation, platform operators also regularly rely on external third parties to staff their platforms. For example, in Italy, Uber Eats relies on (affiliated) HR firms to recruit the workers, adding another intermediator to the mix.[621] Deliveroo in Belgium, Just Eat in Spain and Take Away in the Netherlands have also relied on third parties to recruit or hire the workers on their platform.[622] The same seems to be happening

617. Sacha Garben, *Tackling Social Disruption in the Online Platform Economy: Shifting the Narrative to the Benefits of (EU) Regulation* 7 (FEPS 2019).

618. Abigail Hunt & Emma Samman, *Gender and the Gig Economy: Critical Steps for Evidence-based Policy* 15 (ODI 2019). *See also*, Ursula Huws, *New Forms of Platform Employment or Crowd Work* 65, 66 (Werner Wobbe, Elva Bova & Catalin Dragomirescu-Gaina eds., *The Digital Economy and the Single Market*, FEPS 2016); Nick Srnicek, *Platform Capitalism* 37 (Polity Press 2017); Hatton, *supra* n. 613, at 397–401.

619. Ursula Huws, Neil H. Spencer, Matthew Coates & Kaire Holts, *The Platformisation of Work in Europe: Results from Research in 13 European Countries* 22 (FEPS 2019); Kilhoffer et al., *supra* n. 33, at 47.

620. Niels van Doorn, *Platform Labor: On the Gendered and Racialized Exploitation of Low-income Service Work in the "On-demand" Economy*, 20 Information, Communication & Society 898, 900 n. 6 (2017).

621. Uber Eats in Italy "is alleged to have been using small firms to recruit vulnerable migrant workers and asylum seekers, through practices that have been associated with the notorious model of 'caporalato' (i.e. 'unlawful labour intermediation and exploitation')". Antonio Aloisi & Valerio De Stefano, *Uber Eats Facing Criminal Charges in Italy: Are We Managers or Corporals?*, il Mulino (5 June 2020), https://www.rivistailmulino.it/news/newsitem/index/Item/News:NEWS_ITEM:5256.

622. Jan Drahokoupil & Agnieszka Piasna, *Work in the Platform Economy: Deliveroo Riders in Belgium and the SMart Arrangement* (Etui 2019); EFE, *Just Eat Prevé la Salida de su Competencia en España si se les Obliga a Contratar Riders*, elEconomista.es (4 October 2020), https://www.eleconomista.es/empresas-finanzas/noticias/10807488/10/20/Just-Eat-preve-la-salida-de-su-competencia-en-Espana-si-se-les-obliga-a-contratar-riders.html; FNV, *Wet Arbeidsmarkt in Balans: Een (Zoek)tocht naar meer Zekerheid*, FNV (14 January 2020), https://www.

in the UK.[623] In other words, when platform operators accept that their workers are entitled to labour protections, they often reach out to external agencies to staff their platforms. This offers another reason why the Private Employment Agencies Convention, 1997 (No. 181), is so relevant. Convention No. 181 regulates labour market intermediation and the employment of workers by "agencies" for the execution of work at user enterprises.[624] Therefore, especially in light of this dissertation's First Part, Convention No. 181 seems to present us with a justifiable starting point for our legal analysis of platforms.[625]

Formalising the platform economy? – In addition to Convention No. 181, two other instruments also have a clear connection to platform work. The Transition from the Informal to the Formal Economy Recommendation, 2015 (No. 204), refers to the Home Work Convention, 1996 (No. 177), and Domestic Workers Convention, 2011 (No. 189), as two instruments that apply to "specific categories of workers". Both of these Conventions were deemed necessary by the ILC to effectively formalise hard-to-reach parts of the labour market, which had remained underexposed to protective labour and social measures. Because home-based and domestic workers have long operated in the shadows, Convention No. 177 and Convention No. 189 advance two distinct approaches to establish formal relationships in these areas of the labour market. That could have interesting implications for platform workers, given how, as mentioned before, crowdworking from home and working at other people's households are significant forms of platform work.[626] Consequently, Convention No. 177 and No. 189 are relevant to any discussion on platform work. 187

Home-based work – The Home Work Convention, 1996 (No. 177), was drafted to regulate industrial home work and certain forms of digital telework. The instrument might likewise be relevant for home-based crowdwork. Consider, for instance, Acquier's central argument "that the emergence of platform capitalism should be understood as a digital reincarnation of the 'putting-out system,' a pre-industrial organizational form that preceded the emergence of manufacturing and the managerial corporation".[627] Such putting-out systems are very much associated with industrial home work.[628] This 188

fnv.nl/getmedia/929bd8d5-ffcf-4b64-a9f6-ecc27d745d0c/Notitie-FNV-Eerste-signalen-Wet-arbeidsmarkt-in-balans-jan2020.pdf.

623. Tim Bradshaw, *Just Eat Offers Hourly Wages in UK Gig Economy Shake-up*, Financial Times (9 December 2020), https://www.ft.com/content/352e3c09-7ce3-466a-b941-921f0d3906c7.
624. Luca Ratti, *Online Platforms and Crowdwork in Europe: A Two-step Approach to Expanding Agency Work Provisions?*, 38 Comparative Labor Law & Policy Journal 477, 494–495 n. 3 (2017).
625. This analytical angle has also been used by other scholars before, albeit with no emphasis on the Private Employment Agencies Convention, 1997 (No. 181). *Ibid.*; Thomas Haipeter, Dominik Owczarek, Michele Faioli & Feliciano Iudicone eds., *Final Report: Don't GIG Up!* 4–5 (Directorate-General for Employment, Social Affairs and Inclusion of the European Commission 2020).
626. Huws, Spencer, Coates & Holts, *supra* n. 619, at 22; Kilhoffer et al., *supra* n. 33, at 47.
627. Acquier, *supra* n. 232, at 14.
628. *See*, in particular, Matthew W. Finkin, *Beclouded Work, Beclouded Workers in Historical Perspective*, 37 Comparative Labor Law & Policy Journal 603, 603–618 n. 3 (2016); and Dubal, *supra* n. 615. But also: Sacha Garben, *Protecting Workers in the Online Platform Economy: An Overview of Regulatory and Policy Developments in the EU* 12 (Publications Office of the European Union 2017); David Mangan, *Labour Law: The Medium and the Message*, 100 Bulletin of Comparative Labour Relations 63, 69–70 (2018); Prassl, *supra* n. 110, at 74–75.

involves workers outside of the employer's workplace who ought to have – but often do not have – an employment relationship with the employer, subcontractor, agent or middleman. These "outworkers" usually have an ambiguous employment status, as "[i]n reality, sub-contracted home-based workers – or homeworkers – occupy an intermediate status in employment between fully independent self-employed worker and fully dependent employee".[629] The ambiguousness of their employment status has to do with the characteristics of home-based work. Homeworkers, for instance, make regular use of personal work tools. They are hard to organise because they operate in a decentralised way. Most of the interaction, moreover, occurs with or through intermediaries that operate between the employer and worker. And their remuneration is often calculated based on piece rates. Features such as these make it challenging to formalise these work arrangements along the lines of standard employment at the employer's premises.[630] That is why Convention No. 177 was adopted.

189 In light of this, it is vital to stress that crowdworkers share many of these characteristics. However, when compared to industrial home work, home-based crowdwork also shows some particular features. For example, while it is hard to instantly find people willing to make t-shirts from their homes, it is relatively easy to find someone willing to translate documents if a platform constantly highlights their availability. To that extent, although intermediaries and go-betweens have always been a crucial feature of putting-out systems,[631] the way platforms fulfil this role might have changed the dynamics. Non-digital intermediaries will not develop transcontinental work arrangements as quickly. They will not offer software to monitor the worker's screen and keystrokes either. Nor do they have the data needed to tailor piece-rate remuneration in the way DLPs do. Therefore, as Risak and Warter have argued, the Home Work Convention provides a relevant foundation to regulate crowdwork,[632] which the Committee of Experts also confirmed.[633] Yet, that does not mean current ILO instruments account for the new ways in which platforms, in particular, fulfil their role as intermediaries.

190 **Domestic work** – The third instrument, the Domestic Workers Convention, 2011 (No. 189), might also have significant consequences for platform workers' social protection. Domestic work is personally performed for a platform user's household

629. Martha Chen & Shalini Sinha, *Home-based Workers & Cities: India in Comparative Perspective* 9, 16–17 (*Empowering Home-based Workers in India: Strategies and Solutions*, Harvard University South Asia Institute 2016).
630. Gisela Schneider de Villegas, *Home Work: An Overview*, 8 Conditions of Work Digest 3, 4 n. 2 (1989).
631. Finkin, *supra* n. 628, at 616.
632. Martin Risak & Johannes Warter, *Decent Crowdwork Legal Strategies Towards Fair Employment Conditions in the Virtual Sweatshop*, Regulating for Decent Work 2015 Conference (8–10 July 2015). *See also*, *e.g.*, Phoebe V. Moore, *The Threat of Physical and Psychosocial Violence and Harassment in Digitalized Work* 31–32 (ILO 2018).
633. "[I]nsofar as digital platform work or crowdwork is carried out at home or in a place other than the employers' premises on a regular basis and for remuneration, it could fulfil the conditions to be considered a form of regular home work, and as such could be covered by the provisions of the Convention". ILO Committee of Experts on the Application of Conventions and Recommendations, *Promoting Employment and Decent Work in a Changing Landscape* 235 (ILO 2020).

by nannies, babysitters, nurses, cleaners, handypersons, technicians and others. Some researchers predict that these "on-demand platforms for domestic work are set for exponential growth over the years as Internet penetration and digitalisation takes further root in people's lives globally".[634] Such growth would have its implications. Belgian research on cleaning services performed through the country's system of subsidised service-vouchers has noted that, even though platforms' share of the market is small for now, both systems do compete. So far, the platforms seem to be primarily used for short-term services that are currently not on offer through the system of service-vouchers, such as dog-walking.[635] Outside of Belgium, domestic work platforms may increasingly replace traditional agencies.[636] That can be both good and bad. On a more positive note, "[i]n many cases, using a platform is directly substituting for more direct or casual means of obtaining these services that prevailed in the past".[637] Along those lines, domestic platform work presents a real opportunity to formalise the provision of largely informal household services.[638] However, caution is still advised;[639] whether platforms will formalise domestic work arrangements and improve domestic workers' working conditions will largely depend on the role platform operators decide to play.[640]

In summary, there are many other reasons to choose these three instruments, apart 191
from their unusual scope of application. Platform workers, home-based workers, temporary agency workers and domestic workers, for instance, regularly have: (i) flexible or casual work arrangements with vulnerability to changes in labour demand; and (ii) trouble convincing others that their work is a genuine occupation, not just a "side-hustle". Moreover, as explained in the First Part of this dissertation, many DLPs are LMIs; therefore, why not apply Convention No. 181, which regulates labour market intermediation? Furthermore, Convention No. 177 and No. 189 regulate relatively informal areas of the labour market. DLPs are very active in these areas. There are concrete similarities between crowdworkers and industrial homeworkers,

634. Hunt & Machingura, *supra* n. 258, at 34. *See also*, Huws, *supra* n. 42, at 135.

635. IDEA Consult, *De Dienstencheques 360° Doorgelicht* 74 (IDEA Consult 2018). Agencies that employ cleaners under the service-voucher scheme are not allowed to have domestic workers perform services for less than three consecutive hours at the household. This opens the door for platforms to provide the household services that have a short duration.

636. Ticona, Mateescu & Rosenblat, *supra* n. 88, at 19.

637. Ursula Huws, *The Hassle of Housework: Digitalisation and the Commodification of Domestic Labour*, 123 Feminist Review 8, 19 n. 1 (2019).

638. This could, for instance, improve the safety of domestic workers. Aurora Almendral, *For Domestic Workers, Apps Provide Solace – but not Justice*, Rest of World (4 August 2020), https://restofworld.org/2020/migrant-workers-virtual-solidarity/.

639. Frances Flanagan, *Theorising the Gig Economy and Home-based Service Work*, 61 Journal of Industrial Relations 57, 57–78 n. 1 (2019).

640. A study on nannies, home-based childcare providers, housekeepers and caregivers in New Jersey illustrates various differences between "large private platforms" and more worker-centred platforms. The former would, for example, readily accept an oversupply of workers, whereas the latter establish trust through "human interaction" between workers and clients, and/or only use unionised workers. Yana van der Meulen Rodgers & Elaine Zundl, *The Future of Work in New Jersey: Care Workers and the Gig Economy*, Future of Work Task Force New Jersey, https://fowtf.innovation.nj.gov/downloads/resources/Rodgers_Zundl_NJ_Care_Economy_Future_of_Work_RCS.pdf. *See*, in particular, Judy Fudge & Claire Hobden, *Conceptualizing the Role of Intermediaries in Formalizing Domestic Work* (ILO 2018).

as well as reasons to believe that app-based platform work has a lot to do with households who want to outsource domestic and care work. That is why these three instruments were selected.

192 Before delving into the scope of application of each individual instrument, Subchapter 2 clarifies the relevant "rules of interpretation". To that end, in order to point out why the interpretation of ILO instruments somewhat differs from the general rules of interpretation in the 1969 Vienna Convention on the Law of Treaties, the First Section clarifies what is atypical about ILO Conventions. Subsequently, the actual rules governing the interpretation of these atypical treaties are analysed.

SUBCHAPTER 2. THE RULES OF INTERPRETATION APPLICABLE TO ILO CONVENTIONS

1. ILO Conventions Are Atypical Treaties

193 **Law-making/contract-making treaties** – As mentioned earlier, Conventions are considered to constitute legally binding international treaties,[641] which mostly contain legal obligations addressed to the State.[642] Ratification obliges a State to take the measures necessary to render the provisions of the Convention effective,[643] yet full implementation is not guaranteed as the ILO lacks forceful enforcement mechanisms.[644] Recommendations are, on the other hand, perceived as non-binding guidelines. These are frequently used as standards of reference to supplement and clarify Conventions.[645]

194 Although these descriptions are generally accepted, there remains a lot more to say about the nature of ILO Conventions. After all, ILO Conventions look quite different from what the Vienna Convention on the Law of Treaties from 1969 (VCLT) describes as a treaty. The VCLT speaks of an "international agreement concluded between States". As illustrated in "Chapter 3. The second stage: The Social Justice Declaration and Centenary Declaration", ILO Conventions are developed through tripartite negotiations. These negotiations are regularly dominated by the Workers' and Employers' groups, after which a tripartite vote follows to adopt the draft

641. "While international labour Conventions are treaties in the sense of the Vienna Convention on the Law of Treaties, which are binding upon ratifying Members of the ILO, international labour Recommendations are non-binding instruments addressed to all ILO Member States". Constance Thomas, Martin Oelz & Xavier Beaudonnet, *The Use of International Labour Law in Domestic Courts: Theory, Recent Jurisprudence, and Practical Implications* 249, 253 (Jean-Claude Javillier, Bernard Gernigon & Georges P. Politakis eds., *Les Normes Internationales du Travail: Un Patrimoine pour l'Avenir. Mélanges en l'Honneur de Nicolas Valticos*, ILO 2004).
642. Nicolas Valticos, *International Labour Law* 44 (Kluwer 1979).
643. Art. 19 ILO Constitution.
644. For an excellent analysis of the supervisory system: Francis Maupain, *The ILO Regular Supervisory System: A Model in Crisis?*, 10 International Organizations Law Review 117, 117–165 n. 1 (2014).
645. ILO International Training Center, *Guide to International Labour Standards* 262 (ITC 2014).

instrument.[646] ILO Conventions are, therefore, anything but traditional "inter-state treaties".[647]

Moreover, the Permanent Court of International Justice has observed that the ILC is likewise very different from an "ordinary diplomatic conference". The Court sees differences, for instance, in terms of "the way in which conventions drawn up at such conferences are brought into force and from the method by which a contracting Party to any such convention can secure redress if his interests are prejudiced by a violation of its terms by another Party".[648] Related to this institutionalised fashion in which ILO Conventions are adopted and supervised, one of the discussions regarding ILO Conventions concerns the degree to which ILO Conventions are law-making (*traités-lois*) or contract-making treaties (*traités-contrats*). Law-making treaties generally refer to agreements that seemingly establish legislation and impose rules on all States, or at least a large number, rather than only the contracting parties. Contract-making treaties are of a contractual kind and only bind the parties to the treaty.[649] One of the reasons why this debate is relevant has to do with the view that *traités-lois* are more open to purposive interpretations than *traités-contrats*. The latter tend to be interpreted more restrictively.[650] 195

Concerning international labour standards, Valticos has argued that Conventions "represent a compromise between the notions of contract-making treaties and law-making treaties".[651] This compromise was engrained into the ILO Constitution. The draft Conventions are first developed "within an institutional law context". The drafting process in that institutional setup makes it seem like ILO constituents are negotiating a law-making treaty. Only subsequently, the standard-setting procedure "moves into a general treaty-making framework, with 'member States' turning into 'treaty parties'".[652] Consider, for example, the arguments made by Osieke. According to him, the ILO Constitution grants the General Conference the competence to issue 196

646. These procedures are considered an innovative feature of the ILO Constitution. Nicolas Valticos, *The ILO: A Retrospective and Future View*, 135 International Labour Review 473, 475 n. 3–4 (1996).
647. "As regards International Labour Conventions they are not inter-State treaties and can hardly be described even as agreements in the ordinary sense of the word. They are written instruments passed by resolutions of a two-thirds majority of the International Labour Conference in which employers, workers, and governments are represented. They can hardly be described therefore as agreements between governments in point of substance or 'negotiation', though they are certainly inter-governmental agreements in point of form and are 'ratified' by governments". J. Mervyn Jones, *International Agreements Other Than Inter-State Treaties – Modern Developments*, 21 British Year Book of International Law 111, 120 (1944).
648. Permanent Court of International Justice: Advisory Opinion No. 18, *Free city of Danzig / International Labour Organization*, 26 August 1930.
649. Catherine Brölmann, *Law-Making Treaties: Form and Function in International Law*, 74 Nordic Journal of International Law 383, 384 n. 3–4 (2005).
650. Eirik Bjorge, *The Convergence of the Methods of Treaty Interpretation: Different Regimes, Different Methods of Interpretation?* 498, 511 (Mads Andenas & Eirik Bjorge eds., *A Farewell to Fragmentation Reassertion and Convergence in International Law*, CUP 2015).
651. Valticos, *supra* n. 642, at 45.
652. Catherine Brölmann, *ILO Convention Practice: Mixed Methods in Norm-Setting for Social Justice* 137, 142 (George P. Politakis, Tomi Kohiyama & Thomas Lieby eds., *ILO100: Law for Social Justice*, ILO 2019).

international labour standards. This process follows pre-determined procedures in standard-setting committees. The committee eventually reaches a draft instrument, which is brought before the Conference's plenary session for a vote. Once the Convention is adopted, the Constitution obliges all Member States to submit the text to the competent authorities and consider ratification and implementation. To that extent, even Conventions that remain unratified exert significant influence on national law, Osieke claims. These considerations lead the author to conclude that:

> "[t]he important point which thus emerges from the present study is that the Conventions adopted by the ILO possess most of the essential elements of legislation in the national state, and represent a significant departure from the general situation in international law regarding treaties and conventions. It is thus permissible to conclude that the ILO exercises a unique legislative function for its Members".[653]

197 This conclusion makes sense to some degree. International labour regulation arose to, among other things, set international goals of, for instance, an eight-hour working day so that individual countries would be more inclined to work towards that goal.[654] Another purpose was to limit nonsensical competition between countries trying to take the upper hand by cutting back on labour standards.[655] Nothing would have been more effective in this respect than an international body that legislates global standards, period. However, things turned out quite different for the ILO. One could say the High Contracting Parties decided to retain their discretion to disregard ILS.[656] Therefore, as Jenks wrote in 1936, the organisation does not have "any direct legislative power"[657] because the Member States voluntarily ratify Conventions and, even when ratified, they mostly decide for themselves to what extent ILS are implemented. In essence, the organisation needs to persuade its Members to accept and implement its standards,[658] which is one of the reasons why strong domestic trade unions are crucial.

198 **Conventions' contractual character** – The ILO and its Member States, arguably, have a complicated back-and-forth relationship. On the one hand, Members have provided the organisation with the ability to issue standards beyond their control. Workers and employers can bond together, in theory, to issue standards with minimal governmental

653. Ebere Osieke, *Constitutional Law and Practice in the International Labour Organisation* 168 (Martinus Nijhoff Publishers 1985).

654. "The most striking example was the French decree of 1848 on the 10-hours working day which was promulgated by the provisional government and then abrogated after only five months because of the argument that it would be impossible to conclude an international treaty on this question". Thilo Ramm, *Epilogue: The New Ordering of Labour Law 1918–45* 277, 279 (Bob Hepple ed., *The Making of Labour Law in Europe: A Comparative Study of Nine Countries up to 1945*, Hart Publishing 2010).

655. Vosko, *supra* n. 198, at 37.

656. Prior to the founding of the ILO, trade unions and some European Member States had proposed to make Conventions that are adopted by the Conference immediately applicable in all ILO Member States, but, for instance, the United States opposed the proposal. Thilo Ramm, *supra* n. 654, at 279–284; Alain Supiot, *supra* n. 17, at 125.

657. C. Wilfred Jenks, *The Significance for International Law of the Tripartite Character of the International Labour Organisation*, 22 Transactions of the Grotius Society 45, 76 (1936).

658. Francis Maupain, *supra* n. 347, at 243–248.

support. For such reasons, some might argue that the ILO comes closest to a genuine global legislative procedure.[659] On the other hand, the Member States also remain vigilant not to hand ILO constituents the keys to their kingdom. ILO Conventions have the appearance of "international legislative texts", but at their core, they seem to have retained a "contractual character".[660] At the moment of their adoption at the Conference's plenary session, ILO Conventions are concluded between States, which - oddly enough - are represented by governmental and non-governmental delegates.[661] Subsequently, even when voting in favour of adoption, the State can still refuse to ratify.

The ILO's practices, therefore, do not seem to overturn the Conventions' contractual 199 character. Nevertheless, because of the unusual institutional context in which these instruments are drafted, the Governing Body and Conference do manage to express the ILO constituents' "collective will" in certain ways, regardless of an individual government's intentions. This sees itself reflected, for instance, in Member States' duty to report on efforts to implement unratified Conventions when asked to do so by the GB.[662] Furthermore, as Swepston notes, the ILO has allowed its standards to be revised since the beginning. This is unusual for international organisations.[663] As a result, once the revised Convention comes into force, typically, the Convention that has been revised can no longer be ratified by any State. The Member State that ratifies the revised Convention, moreover, immediately denunciates the previously ratified "original" Convention. These are only two examples of how the ILO's institutional framework leads the Conference to adopt Conventions somewhere in between contract-making treaties and law-making treaties. More broadly, features such as this trigger an "identity crisis over whether [the ILO] is a mere 'agent' of States or something more?"[664]

2. Unique Features of the ILO's Interpretative Rules

The Vienna Convention on the Law of Treaties – Although ILO Conventions are very 200 different from classic inter-State treaties, it seems undisputed that the VCLT applies to ILO Conventions. Indeed, among ILO actors, it seems broadly accepted that, in principle, the VCLT's provisions, including the ones on treaty interpretation, govern ILO Conventions.[665] The words "in principle" are in order due to Article 5 of the VCLT.

659. Cristina Hoss & Santiago Villalpando, *La Contribution de l'OIT au Droit des Traités* 169, 177 (George P. Politakis, Tomi Kohiyama & Thomas Lieby eds., *ILO100: Law for Social Justice*, ILO 2019).
660. Jean-Michel Servais, *International Labour Law* 47 (Kluwer 2011). *See also*, Jan Klabbers, *International Organizations and the Problem of Privity: Towards a Supra-Functionalist Approach* 629, 630 (George P. Politakis, Tomi Kohiyama & Thomas Lieby eds., *ILO100: Law for Social Justice*, ILO 2019).
661. Pellet, *supra* n. 569, at 160.
662. Art. 19, §5 (e) ILO Constitution.
663. Lee Swepston, *The Future of ILO Standards*, 117 Monthly Labor Review 16, 20 n. 9 (1994).
664. Alvarez, *supra* n. 391, at 89.
665. For example, when the ILO wanted to ratify 1986's Vienna Convention on the Law of Treaties between States and International Organizations or between International Organizations, the Office was asked for legal advice. According to the Office, it was necessary "to recall that the

It stipulates that the VCLT "applies to any treaty which is the constituent instrument of an international organization and to any treaty adopted within an international organization without prejudice to any relevant rules of the organization". In other words, Article 5 allows international organisations, such as the ILO, to set their own relevant rules, including their own rules of interpretation.[666] The rules of the ILO thereby take precedence over the VCLT.[667] However, one of the problems is that most of the organisation's own "rules of interpretation" seem to derive from internal circulars, manuals, etc.[668] The organisation does not have one single instrument that authoritatively explains the ILO's approach to treaty interpretation, making it difficult to determine how ILO rules precisely deviate from the VCLT.[669]

201 This lack of authoritative guidelines is quite problematic for this research because, as Servais points out in his book on international labour law, "there is nothing to authorize, except an express indication, anyone to go beyond the law governing classic treaties".[670] Therefore, this dissertation needs to find an appropriate set of rules. For instance, the Committee of Experts seems to use the "VCLT interpretation rule" as its "lodestone", yet it also extensively relies on working documents contrary to the VCLT's guidance.[671] Along those lines, the following paragraphs attempt to find a justifiable balance between the VCLT's rules of interpretation and the particularities that characterise ILO Conventions' interpretation.

1986 Convention does not apply to the ILO Constitution or to international labour Conventions; these are treaties to which only States may become parties. The 1969 Convention applies to them, as explicitly confirmed by Article 55 of that Convention". ILO International Labour Office, *Consideration of the 1986 Vienna Convention on the Law of Treaties between States and International Organizations or between International Organizations with a View to Formal Confirmation by the ILO*, 88th Session of the International Labour Conference in 2000, 5/3. Similarly, the ILO Committee of Experts has applied the rules of interpretation of 1969's VCLT in its general surveys. ILO Committee of Experts on the Application of Conventions and Recommendations, *Labour Standards on Merchant Ships* 43 (ILO 1990). The Committee relies on the working documents pursuant to the conditions prescribed in Arts. 31 and 32 of the VCLT. ILO, *supra* n. 330, at 23. The Employers at the ILC's Committee on the Application of Standards also seem to rely on the provisions of 1969's VCLT. ILO Committee of Experts on the Application of Conventions and Recommendations, *supra* n. 398, at 47; International Bar Association Global Employment Institute and International Organisation of Employers, *International Labour Standards in the Contemporary Global Economy* 18 (IBA 2018). The ILO's Legal Adviser and Standards Department would likewise base their interpretations on the VCLT, even though they additionally consider the *travaux préparatoires* and Committee of Experts' comments. ILO Committee on the Application of Standards, *Third Item on the Agenda: Information and Reports on the Application of Conventions and Recommendations* 16 Part I/11 (ILO 2010).

666. Thomas Lieby, *The Interpretation of International Labour Conventions and the Principle of 'Systemic Integration' – The Way Forward for an ILO Tribunal* 923, 938–939 (George P. Politakis, Tomi Kohiyama & Thomas Lieby eds., *ILO100: Law for Social Justice*, ILO 2019).
667. Vogt et al., *supra* n. 397, at 37.
668. Anne Trebilcock, *The International Labour Organization* 848, 871–873 (Michael J. Bowman & Dino Kritsiotis eds., *Conceptual and Contextual Perspectives on the Modern Law of Treaties*, CUP 2018).
669. Vogt et al., *supra* n. 397, at 41.
670. Servais, *supra* n. 660, at 90.
671. Trebilcock, *supra* n. 668, at 875. *See also*, Vogt et al., *supra* n. 397, at 40–42.

The Permanent Court of International Justice – First of all, only the International Court of Justice's decisions regarding the interpretation of ILO Conventions are binding.[672] Hence, the Advisory Opinions of its predecessor, the Permanent Court of International Justice, count as one of the most authoritative sources of information on how to interpret ILO Conventions. One Advisory Opinion gives a clear indication of how the Court proceeded in the past. Although dated, the Advisory Opinion of 1932 still has value because it somewhat approaches interpretation in the way the VCLT would.[673] As such, it gives us a couple of noteworthy indications in terms of what the Court considered relevant at the time. The Advisory Opinion concerned the interpretation of Article 3 in the now abrogated Night Work (Women) Convention, 1919 (No. 4). This Article stipulated that "[w]omen without distinction of age shall not be employed during the night in any public or private industrial undertaking, or in any branch thereof, other than an undertaking in which only members of the same family are employed [...]". The following question was asked to the Court: 202

> "Does the Convention concerning employment of women during the night, adopted in 1919 by the International Labour Conference, apply, in the industrial undertakings covered by the said Convention, to women who hold positions of supervision or management and are not ordinarily engaged in manual work?"[674]

The question was asked because some constituents were convinced the Convention only applied to women who were ordinarily engaged in manual work. The Court, however, immediately pointed out that the wording in Article 3 is general and free from ambiguity or obscurity. Therefore, "it is necessary to find some valid ground for interpreting the provision otherwise than in accordance with the natural sense of the words".[675] The Court considered the following items as a potential "valid ground" to contest the words' ordinary meaning. 203

- Whether the terminology of Article 3 was consistent with the title, the preamble and the Convention's other articles. This was indeed the case.
- The fact that the Convention was issued under the framework of part XIII of the Treaty of Versailles might affect its scope. In this regard, although considered relevant, the Constitution's preoccupation with "labour" did not suffice to interpret "women" in Article 3 of the Convention as confined to women doing manual work. The Advisory Opinion mentions that "the Court is not disposed to regard the sphere of activity of the International Labour Organization as circumscribed so closely, in respect of the persons with which it was to concern itself, as to raise any presumption that a Labour convention must be interpreted as being restricted in its operation to manual

672. Art. 37 ILO Constitution.

673. *"[L]a Cour se lance dans un exercice d'interprétation du traité qui reprend, presque mot pour mot, la plupart des éléments qui seront codifiés par la Convention de Vienne presque quarante ans plus tard".* Hoss & Villalpando, *supra* n. 659, at 169.

674. Permanent Court of International Justice: Advisory Opinion No. 25, *Interpretation of the Convention of 1919 concerning Employment of Women during the Night*, 15 November 1932, §1.

675. *Ibid.*, §31.

workers, unless a contrary intention appears".[676] The overarching framework that has led to the adoption of the instrument can, in other words, offer a valid ground, but in this particular instance, it was unconvincing. Important to note, one judge, Anzilotti, disagreed on this point. In his Dissenting Opinion, Anzilotti claimed that the task allotted to the ILO in the Treaty of Versailles was to establish the regulation of conditions of manual labour, which makes it "only natural to infer that any convention concluded under this Part is to be regarded as relating to manual labour and not to labour in general. Another and more general intention is conceivable but cannot be presumed: it must be proved".[677]

- In addition to the regulatory framework, also the broader circumstances surrounding the Convention were relevant. Reference was made to the older Berne Convention, which only covered manual workers. The Court, nevertheless, concluded that Convention No. 4, i.e. the Washington Convention, is not "so intimately linked with the Berne Convention as to require that the terms of the Washington Convention should bear the same meaning as the terms of the Berne Convention".[678] Again, the Court's reasoning suggests that earlier Conventions which cover the same topic are relevant for the interpretation of subsequent Conventions.
- Furthermore, "[t]he mere fact that, at the time when the Convention Work of Women was concluded, certain facts or situations, which the terms of the Convention in their ordinary meaning are wide enough to cover, were not thought of, does not justify interpreting those of its provisions which are general in scope otherwise than in accordance with their terms".[679] Conventions are not static. They are meant to endure and engage with new developments.
- Additionally, the Court mentioned as a rule "that there is no occasion to have regard to preparatory work if the text of a convention is sufficiently clear in itself".[680] Yet, despite this rule, it actually did decide to examine the preparatory work because it had been struck by several delegates' opinions. The Court seemingly wanted to verify these claims. This suggests that the threshold to take into account the working documents might be pretty low in the case of the ILO. As we will see below, the working documents are nowadays considered very important (*infra* nos. 205 and 237).
- Lastly, the Reporter's speech on behalf of the Drafting Committee at the International Labour Conference of 1919 indicated that multiple draft instruments adopted that year were supposedly drafted along uniform lines. This led the Court to point to a specific exemption in the articles of another Convention, the Hours of Work (Industry) Convention, 1919 (No. 1), that excluded "persons holding positions of supervision or management" and "persons employed in a confidential capacity" from the Convention's scope.[681]

676. *Ibid.*, §38.
677. *Ibid.*, §85.
678. *Ibid.*, §47.
679. *Ibid.*, §49.
680. *Ibid.*, §52.
681. Art. 2 Hours of Work (Industry) Convention, 1919 (No. 1).

Given that this exemption was not introduced in Convention No. 4, it would seem that Convention No. 4, indeed, applies to women who hold positions of supervision or management.[682] In building this argument, the Court first relied on the Reporter's opinion, expressing the parties' intention to rely on uniform language. Subsequently, the Court used this opinion to take the text of the other Conventions into account to clarify the interpretation of Convention No. 4. All this suggests that if the conditions are right, the language used in other Conventions might be relied on to contrast it with the standard under review.

Overall, this Advisory Opinion contains much interesting information, especially about the importance of an instrument's context. However, one cautionary note is that the Court did all of this to find "valid grounds" to refute the text's ordinary meaning. It did not go through these steps to construe a balanced interpretation. As subsequent paragraphs will point out, this methodology does not resemble how the general rule of interpretation in Article 31 VCLT is usually applied (*infra* no. 211). Before systematically discussing Article 31 VCLT, however, two features of ILO standard-setting are highlighted: the "will of the Conference" and the "International Labour Code".

The will of the Conference – The Dissenting Opinion of Anzilotti rebuked the Court's 204
methodology. According to him, "the question is not whether it is possible to find a valid ground for placing upon Article 3 of the Convention [...] an interpretation other than that which is consistent with the natural meaning of its terms";[683] instead, the subject and aim of the Convention have to be ascertained first. Only then is it "possible to say either that the natural meaning of terms used in a particular article corresponds with the real intention of the Parties, or that the natural meaning of the terms used falls short of or goes further than such intention".[684] As such, Anzilotti advanced a more teleological approach. Something which some contemporary scholars still view as a viable option when interpreting ILO Conventions.[685]

Along with this teleological take, Anzilotti attributed a central role to the intention 205
of the "Contracting Parties". His Dissenting Opinion speaks of the "intention of the (Washington) Conference". This is a crucial point. For instance, Jenks argued early on that, although the same principles of interpretation apply for ILO Conventions as is the case for "other international instruments of a legislative character", it would not be helpful to highlight the intention of single parties. In its place, the interpreter has to search for the intention of the International Labour Conference as a whole.[686] Therefore, in addition to the general rule in the VCLT, which only mentions the

682. Permanent Court of International Justice: Advisory Opinion No. 25, *Interpretation of the Convention of 1919 concerning Employment of Women during the Night*, 15 November 1932, §63-67.

683. *Ibid.*, §72.

684. *Ibid.*, §74.

685. Tineke Dijkhoff & Frans Pennings, *The Interpretation of International Social Security Standards* 149, 174 (Frans Pennings ed., *International Social Security Standards: Current Views and Interpretation Matters*, Intersentia 2007).

686. Jenks, *supra* n. 657, at 66-67.

importance of the "object" and "purpose" of an instrument, arguably, the "will" of the Conference also seems essential at the ILO.[687] Perhaps related to this, the working documents have long been considered vital.[688] The working documents often serve as a primary means of interpretation, if not the main one. This practice deviates from the VCLT's general rule of interpretation, which remains somewhat distrustful of working documents.

206 **The International Labour Code** – The ILO's institutional framework also gives rise to other peculiar dynamics. For instance, the "fundamental interconnectedness between ILO Conventions" may affect the interpretation given to a single Convention. According to the Advisory Opinion, earlier Conventions can influence the meaning of subsequent Conventions if they are "intimately linked". As we will discuss below, such an intimate link may be present between, for example, the Fee-Charging Employment Agencies Convention (Revised), 1949 (No. 96), and the Private Employment Agencies Convention, 1997 (No. 181). If the VCLT allows a similar argument to be made today, the various Conventions issued by the Conference, especially when they cover the same topic, might be helpful for interpretative purposes. What is more, the actual purpose of a Convention might only reveal itself by sketching how older instruments on the same topic have failed in certain respects, prompting the ILO constituents to take those failures into account when drafting new instruments.

207 Furthermore, perhaps, ILS do not have to cover the same subject matter for a comparison. Wolf, a former Legal Adviser, used to speak of a "network of international labour standards". According to him, Conventions and Recommendations were adopted pursuant to a similar standard-setting procedure, meaning all Conventions share the same legal characteristics. These Conventions have various interconnected aims that fit in with the ILO's overarching pursuit of social justice. Moreover, because the Office tries to maintain normative and linguistic consistency among these instruments,[689] the Code's various Conventions show a "fundamental interconnectedness".[690] The fact that the Permanent Court of Justice took the other Conventions from 1919 into account to interpret Convention No. 4 relates to this broader sense of interconnectedness. Even though the Advisory Opinion attributes importance to the fact that these instruments were adopted during the same Conference session, Wolf's comments seem to suggest that this might not be an essential condition. Linguistic differences between relatively unrelated ILS may, in fact, teach us something when interpreting individual instruments.

208 To that extent, although it might be tempting to compare the language of various ILS, there are also reasons why caution is warranted. At the ILO, context-specific political considerations can lead to minor amendments during the standard-setting

687. ILO Committee on Standing Orders and the Application of Conventions and Recommendations, *Article 37, Paragraph 2, of the Constitution and the Interpretation of International Labour Conventions*, GB.256/SC/2/2 14–15 (ILO 1993).

688. "In interpreting the provisions of Conventions the International Labour Office has placed great reliance upon the preparatory work". ILO, *supra* n. 7, at XIC.

689. Hoss & Villalpando, *supra* n. 659, at 182–184; Kohiyama & Petrović, *supra* n. 8, at 855–857.

690. Francis Wolf, *L'Interdépendance des Conventions Internationales du Travail*, 121 Recueil Des Cours 127, 127–144 n. 2 (1967).

procedures. Sweeping comparisons risk disregarding these nuanced differences between the separate instruments, hence ignoring the will of the Conference. Therefore, in principle, it is probably best to interpret ILO Conventions on an individual and case-by-case basis - as the VCLT suggests - because the will of a particular standard-setting committee should not be ignored by eagerly drawing on linguistic similarities or differences between Conventions.[691]

3. The Vienna Convention on the Law of Treaties: Interpretation of Treaties

Articles 31–32 VCLT - Previous paragraphs have indicated that, in so far as there **209**
are no deviations under Article 5, the Vienna Convention's rules of interpretation offer the template for the interpretation of ILS. With a lack of diverging guidelines from the ILO, these rules are, if not the only acceptable rules of interpretation for this dissertation, definitively the most authoritative ones.[692] The VCLT contains the following rules of interpretation:

> "Section 3. INTERPRETATION OF TREATIES
>
> Article 31, General rule of interpretation
>
> 1. A treaty shall be interpreted in good faith in accordance with the ordinary meaning to be given to the terms of the treaty in their context and in the light of its object and purpose.
>
> 2. The context for the purpose of the interpretation of a treaty shall comprise, in addition to the text, including its preamble and annexes: (a) Any agreement relating to the treaty which was made between all the parties in connexion with the conclusion of the treaty; (b) Any instrument which was made by one or more parties in connexion with the conclusion of the treaty and accepted by the other parties as an instrument related to the treaty.
>
> 3. There shall be taken into account, together with the context: (a) Any subsequent agreement between the parties regarding the interpretation of the treaty or the application of its provisions; (b) Any subsequent practice in the application of the treaty which establishes the agreement of the parties regarding its interpretation; (c) Any relevant rules of international law applicable in the relations between the parties.
>
> 4. A special meaning shall be given to a term if it is established that the parties so intended.
>
> Article 32. Supplementary means of interpretation
>
> Recourse may be had to supplementary means of interpretation, including the preparatory work of the treaty and the circumstances of its conclusion, in

691. *See also*, Valerio De Stefano, *Not as Simple as it Seems: The ILO and the Personal Scope of International Labour Standards*, 160 International Labour Review 387, 387–406 n. 3 (2021).
692. *See also*, Paolo Palchetti, *Halfway between Fragmentation and Convergence: The Role of the Rules of the Organization in the Interpretation of Constituent Treaties* 486, 496–497 (Mads Andenas & Eirik Bjorge eds., *A Farewell to Fragmentation Reassertion and Convergence in International Law*, CUP 2015).

order to confirm the meaning resulting from the application of article 31, or to determine the meaning when the interpretation according to article 31: (a) Leaves the meaning ambiguous or obscure; or (b) Leads to a result which is manifestly absurd or unreasonable".

210 **Primary and supplementary means of interpretation** – In short, Article 31 covers the primary means of interpretation. These can be summarised as the "conventional language, the context, and the object and purpose of a treaty".[693] Article 32 points to a non-exhaustive source of supplementary means of interpretation. These supplementary means cover most notably the use of working documents. Being supplementary, *travaux préparatoires* can, in principle, only be used for a couple of reasons. Either they serve to confirm the meaning resulting from the application of the primary means of interpretation. This function entails that working documents are used cumulatively with the application of Article 31's rule.[694] Alternatively, the working documents are relied on to determine the meaning of the provisions when the primary means have left the meaning of the text ambiguous, obscure, or have provided a manifestly absurd interpretation.[695] The condition that the meaning remains ambiguous or obscure would be fulfilled if the interpreter "is not able to extract a sufficiently clear and precise meaning from a provision" or is, for instance, presented with two contradictory interpretations.[696] To ensure that interpreters give Article 31's methodology a fair chance, they ought to assume that its methods provide an answer without a need for recourse to the supplementary means.[697]

211 **Article 31: Primary means of interpretation** – Conventional language, context, object and purpose form part of one general rule of interpretation. Article 31 presents a combined operation that reflects elements of a textual, subjective and teleological approach to treaty interpretation.[698] The Office has described it as seemingly giving "precedence to a textual approach (focus on the natural meaning of the words

693. Ulf Linderfalk, *Is the Hierarchical Structure of Articles 31 and 32 of the Vienna Convention Real or Not? Interpreting the Rules of Interpretation*, 54 Netherlands International Law Review 133, 135 n. 1 (2007).
694. Working documents can be used quite extensively and uncontroversially to confirm the meaning. Much more caution is needed when using these documents to determine the meaning. Richard Gardiner, *The Vienna Convention Rules on Treaty Interpretation* 459, 471 and 473–374 (Duncan B. Hollis ed., *The Oxford Guide to Treaties*, OUP 2020). To confirm does not imply the possibility to correct or displace the meaning. Makane M. Mbengue, *Rules of Interpretation (Article 32 of the Vienna Convention on the Law of Treaties)*, 31 ICSID Review – Foreign Investment Law Journal 388, 407 n. 2 (2016).
695. Linderfalk, *supra* n. 693, at 152–154.
696. Yves le Bouthillier, *Article 32 Convention of 1969* 841, 849 (Olivier Corten & Pierre Klein eds., *The Vienna Conventions on the Law of Treaties: A Commentary*, OUP 2011).
697. Donald H. Regan, *Sources of International Trade Law: Understanding What the Vienna Convention Says About Identifying and Using 'Sources for Treaty Interpretation'* (Samantha Besson & Jean d'Aspremont eds., *The Oxford Handbook of the Sources of International Law*, OUP 2017).
698. The conventional language, context, purpose and object of the treaty should settle the meaning of the treaty's words. This entails that the meaning of the text depends both on the object of the treaty, e.g. treaties can govern trade, foreign direct investment, taxation and so forth, as well as the aim of the treaty, in other words, for which problems does it try to find solutions, etc. Robert Kolb, *The Law of Treaties: An Introduction* 145 (Edward Elgar Publishing 2016); Shai Dothan, *The Three Traditional Approaches to Treaty Interpretation: A Current Application*

employed), which incorporates however the principle of effectiveness (aim towards effective achievement of the declared or apparent object and purpose of the treaty) and also takes into consideration subsequent practice (how the treaty is applied or operated by parties and authorized organs)".[699] Due to this range of considerations, which is, in reality, even broader, the VCLT's interpretation method is characterised by variability.[700] Taking into account that variability, the International Law Commission has clarified that treaty interpretation "consists of a single combined operation, which places appropriate emphasis on the various means of interpretation indicated, respectively, in articles 31 and 32".[701]

Sources of information – In addition to what information matters, another question is which sources can be used to discover the language, context, object and purpose of a Convention, as well as, for ILO purposes, the will of the Conference. Information can be deduced from the treaty's text, such as its provisions, preamble and title. Regarding the preamble of ILO Conventions, "[t]he Legal Adviser has consistently recalled that the preamble is non-binding in nature and that its primary function is to set out the context of the instrument".[702] It would generally not have a big impact on the interpretation given to the Convention's articles.[703] Beyond the instrument itself, scholars distinguish between sources that relate to the treaty's "narrow context", i.e. Article 31 §2, the "broader context" as described in Article 31 §3, and the third category of sources related to the supplementary means of interpretation in Article 32. Based on the VCLT, as such, the narrow and broader context *must* be taken into account. The sources in Article 32 may be used as appropriate. 212

The narrow context – The "narrow context" of an ILO Convention consists: (a) of instruments "relating to the treaty which [were] made between all the parties in connexion with the conclusion of the treaty"; and, (b) instruments which were "made by one or more parties in connexion with the conclusion of the treaty and accepted by the other parties as an instrument related to the treaty".[704] The legal form of these agreements or instruments is, apparently, of little importance. What counts is the act of agreement itself.[705] The instrument should contain an explicit agreement on how to interpret or apply the instrument's provisions. Consequently, even a joint 213

---

to the European Court of Human Rights, 42 Fordham International Law Review 765, 766–767 n. 3 (2019).

699. ILO International Labour Office, *Background Document for the Tripartite Meeting on the Freedom of Association and Protection of the Right to Organise Convention, 1948 (No. 87), in Relation to the Right to Strike and the Modalities and Practices of Strike Action at National Level (Revised) (Geneva, 23–25 February 2015)*, GB.323/INS/5/Appendix III 18 (ILO 2015).
700. This is captured by treaty interpretation's description as an art, rather than a science, giving the interpreter quite a lot of discretion. Regan, *supra* n. 697. More or less emphasis might be put on the text of the treaty or its object and purpose, depending, for instance, on the nature of the treaty. Georg Nolte, *First Report on Subsequent Agreements and Subsequent Practice in Relation to Treaty Interpretation* 6 (International Law Commission 2013).
701. Conclusion 2 International Law Commission, *Draft Conclusions on Subsequent Agreements and Subsequent Practice in Relation to the Interpretation of Treaties* (UN 2018).
702. ILO Office of the Legal Adviser, *Manual for Drafting ILO Instruments* 3 (ILO 2006).
703. Trebilcock, *supra* n. 668, at 867.
704. Art. 31 Convention on the Law of Treaties, 23 May 1969.
705. Gardiner, *supra* n. 694, at 467.

press release might, arguably, serve to clarify the meaning of the words.[706] These kinds of "agreements" between the ILO constituents about applying newly adopted Conventions seem unusual. Although it is not out of the question, e.g. the constituents could adopt conclusions or a Resolution alongside a Convention, these instruments seem not to be used for interpretative purposes.[707] ILO Recommendations that accompany an ILO Convention could also play a more significant role in this regard.

214 **The broader context** – The third paragraph of Article 31 details the broader context. It mentions additional instruments that can also make a significant difference, namely "any subsequent agreement between the parties regarding the interpretation of the treaty or the application of its provisions". One relevant question in this respect is whether a subsequent Resolution by the Conference concerning, for example, casual work could, in fact, clarify the Part-Time Work Convention's application to marginal part-time work. Kohiyama and Petrović observe that "[r]esolutions are usually of a technical and non-normative nature, but quite few of them, whether relating to an item on the Conference agenda or not, may be substantive and influence the understanding of the [ILO's] normative framework".[708] Resolutions can, in other words, have a substantial effect. However, whether they can also directly influence the meaning of an ILO Convention is a more specific and technical question. Nolte argues in this regard that under general international law, the subsequent agreement would have to express a common understanding among the parties.[709] In his view, the "Conferences of States Parties" would be able to issue an interpretative Resolution if this Resolution is sufficiently clear about the Conference's intention to influence the treaty's interpretation and indicates that it has legal consequences.[710] Whether the same might work at the ILO is not entirely clear.[711] Trebilcock, a former ILO Legal Adviser, seems to suggest that it is possible.[712] The author refers to the "Resolution concerning Gender Equality and the Use of Language of Legal Texts in the ILO" to illustrate this practice. The Resolution mentions that the General Conference resolves "that in the ILO Constitution and other legal texts of the Organization, in accordance with applicable rules of interpretation, the use of one gender includes in its meaning a reference to the other gender unless the context otherwise requires".[713] To this extent, ILO Resolutions might be an example of how a subsequent agreement about the interpretation of an earlier treaty does not necessarily require a second treaty.

---

706. Kolb, *supra* n. 698, at 150.
707. For instance, Resolution concerning efforts to make decent work a reality for domestic workers worldwide, 15 June 2011.
708. Kohiyama & Petrović, *supra* n. 8, at 831.
709. Georg Nolte, *Second Report on Subsequent Agreements and Subsequent Practice in Relation to the Interpretation of Treaties* 27–28 (International Law Commission 2014).
710. *Ibid.*, 39–40 and 43–44.
711. The Office did not seem all that sure in 1993. ILO Committee on Standing Orders and the Application of Conventions and Recommendations, *supra* n. 687, at 6–7.
712. "[T]he International Labour Conference – as the body having adopted a treaty – would theoretically have the implicit authority to interpret [a Convention], subject of course to Article 37 of the ILO Constitution, which does not attribute this power to the Conference". Trebilcock, *supra* n. 668, at 868.
713. Resolution concerning gender equality and the use of language in legal texts of the ILO, 9 June 2011.

Assuming it is possible to issue interpretative Resolutions at the ILO, this technique could be impactful. After all, there is a lack of hierarchy between the instruments mentioned in §2 of Article 31 (narrow context) and the instruments mentioned in §3 (broader context). Some scholars have suggested that sources from §2 have precedence over sources from §3, such as subsequent agreements, albeit "true only in general, since in a specific case an element under §3 may be decisive".[714] However, other scholars explicitly denounce this idea of a hierarchy between the narrow and broader context. They argue that all sources mentioned in Article 31 have "exactly the same status and authority".[715] As a result, the three sources mentioned in §3 become crucial for ILO Conventions' interpretation. To this extent, besides (a) subsequent agreements between the parties regarding the interpretation of a treaty, Article 31 §3 also refers to (b) "any relevant rules of international law applicable in the relations between the parties", and (c) "any subsequent practice in the application of the treaty which establishes the agreement of the parties regarding its interpretation". 215

The relevant rules of international law – The reference to "relevant rules of international law applicable in the relation between the parties" would allow constitutive treaties, such as the ILO Constitution, to influence the interpretation of the organisation's secondary instruments. Brölmann comments on this point, thereby citing Benzing, that in case of international organisations, a "principle favouring the 'paramount importance of contextual interpretation' is at work, meaning that 'legal acts always have to be construed by reference to and in accordance with the constitutive instrument of the organization'".[716] 216

The constitutive instruments notwithstanding, the reference to the "rules of international law that are applicable in the relations between the parties" is also crucial for another reason. It might allow us to take into account the phrasing in another international labour standard to interpret the instrument under review (e.g. the "fundamental interconnectedness" between ILS) (also see *supra* nos. 206–208).[717] This practice seems justified because ILO Conventions resemble what Gardiner calls "common form treaties". Such treaties do show individual variation "but use many of the same terms and approaches". They can be compared to one another.[718] Furthermore, since Article 31 §3 VCLT does not require "a precise congruence in the membership of multilateral conventions" for one instrument to be used to interpret another, it seems possible to rely on other Conventions for interpretative purposes, as was done by the Permanent Court of Justice in the example above (e.g. Convention No. 1 and No. 4).[719] 217

714. Kolb, *supra* n. 698, at 139.
715. Regan, *supra* n. 697. *See also*, Gardiner, *supra* n. 694, at 464–465; Nolte, *supra* n. 700, at 6.
716. Catherine Brölmann, *Specialized Rules of Treaty Interpretation: International Organizations* 524, 536 (Duncan B. Hollis ed., *The Oxford Guide to Treaties*, OUP 2020). This amounts to "a form of constitutional interpretation resulting from the hierarchy of norms" according to Benzing. Markus Benzing, *International Organizations or Institutions, Secondary Law* (Rüdiger Wolfrum ed., *Max Planck Encyclopaedia of Public International Law*, OUP 2007).
717. Richard K. Gardiner, *Treaty Interpretation* 325 (OUP 2015).
718. Gardiner, *supra* n. 717, at 324.
719. Lieby, *supra* n. 666, at 936–937.

218 **Subsequent practice / ILO Committee of Experts** – The last element of the broader context, i.e. "subsequent practice", also has exciting consequences for the ILO's legal system. The International Law Commission's Draft Conclusions on Subsequent Agreements and Subsequent Practice in Relation to the Interpretation of Treaties from 2018 indicate that subsequent practice can take various forms. Conclusion 13 refers to pronouncements of an "expert treaty body" as potentially giving rise to subsequent practice. The conclusions define an expert treaty body as "a body consisting of experts serving in their personal capacity, which is established under a treaty and is not an organ of an international organization".[720] At first sight, the ILO Committee of Experts seems eligible. However, the fact that the commentary to this conclusion explicitly refers to the ILO's Committee of Experts as an "organ of an international organization" is highly significant.[721] The reason why the ILO Committee is considered an organ of an international organisation, but, for instance, the UN Committee on Economic Social and Cultural Rights and UN Human Rights Committee are not, remains rather unclear.

219 The International Law Commission's draft articles on the responsibility of international organisations define an "organ of an international organization" as "any person or entity which has that status in accordance with the rules of the organization".[722] Whether it is explicitly called an organ or obtains this status from its functions would be irrelevant.[723] Regarding the ILO Committee of Experts, it should be noted that this is a supervisory body not envisioned in the ILO Constitution. Article 2 of the ILO Constitution mentions three organs: the Office, the GB and the ILC. Furthermore, contrary to the Committee on the Application of Standards, which is a standing committee of the ILC, or the Committee on Freedom of Association, which operates under the GB's wings, the Committee of Experts remains more institutionally detached. This institutional independence is essential to grasp. In the organisation's early years, the Office summarised Member States' reports about implementing measures without commenting on them. Because of the relatively small membership and the manageable number of instruments, it was feasible to discuss these reports at the annual Conference. Once the pile of reports became too large, a mechanism was needed to filter out Member States' reports.[724] The Office's functions were already established in the ILO Constitution, and ILO constituents understood that filtering reports might jeopardise the Office's neutral position. Therefore, as admitted in a report from 1926, "it seemed desirable that the Director should be aided in a task which must inevitably be at times difficult and delicate, by a completely impartial body which could not be subject to the suggestion that it might be affected by considerations other than those

720. International Law Commission, *supra* n. 701.

721. Footnote 989 of the Report of the International Law Commission, A/71/10 230 (UN 2016).

722. International Law Commission, *Draft Articles on the Responsibility of International Organizations* (UN 2011).

723. Mirka Möldner, *Responsibility of International Organizations – Introducing the ILC's DARIO* (Armin von Bogdandy & Rüdiger Wolfrum eds., 16 Max Planck Yearbook of United Nations Law 281, 291 n. 1 (2012)).

724. ILO, *Report of the Committee of Experts on the Application of Conventions and Recommendations* 2 (ILO 2019).

of a technical nature".[725] In other words, the Committee of Experts was established to fulfil a task with which none of the three official ILO organs could be burdened. From this perspective, the Committee of Experts is a subsequent addition to the ILO's supervisory system, deliberately set up to evade political tension. The Committee of Experts makes clarifications and observations based on the information contained in the reports that the GB demands from the Member States and the information brought to its attention by employers' and workers' associations. The Conference Committee on the Application of Standards decides which cases of non-compliance it wants to discuss publicly, taking into account the Committee of Experts' observations.

With this in mind, it seems reasonable to ask what makes, for instance, the Human Rights Committee that monitors the UN's International Covenant on Civil and Political Rights so different from the ILO Committee of Experts. Special Rapporteur Nolte clarified that the type of expert body he juxtaposes with the ILO's Committee of Experts consists of "experts who serve in their individual capacity", thereby referring to Article 28 of the ICCPR, which states that the members of the Human Rights Committee serve in their personal capacity.[726] However, the same is true for the experts who serve in the ILO's Committee of Experts and are appointed based on their external credentials.[727] The Draft Conclusions on Subsequent Agreements and Subsequent Practice in Relation to the Interpretation of Treaties, furthermore, clarify that experts should be free from governmental instructions.[728] This is likewise the case for the Committee of Experts. The experts – often (former) judges, professors, etc. – do not represent governments. They are recommended by the Director-General, in other words, the Office, for appointment by the GB.[729] 220

Considering these observations, the issue of what can be considered subsequent practice at the ILO is an interesting and important one. If the Committee of Experts is an institutional organ, its clarifications will constitute "materials that interpreters may (and are encouraged but not required to) take into account".[730] If it is not an institutional organ, its clarifications "shall" be taken into account. As such, this condition of not being an "organ of an international organization" should receive proper attention at the ILO level. One argument to differentiate between the UN Human Rights Committee and the ILO Committee of Experts may relate to how the ICCPR has directly established the Human Rights Committee (HRC). Therefore, it is not a Committee that has been established under the umbrella of the United Nations' general procedures, like the ILO Committee of Experts was at the ILO. The ILO's 221

725. Report of the Committee on Art. 408, 8th Session of the International Labour Conference in 1926, 406.
726. Georg Nolte, *Fourth Report on Subsequent Agreements and Subsequent Practice in Relation to the Interpretation of Treaties* 6 (UN 2016).
727. The ILO's handbook of procedures details that appointments to the Committee "are made in a personal capacity among completely impartial persons of technical competence and independent standing". ILO International Labour Standards Department, *Handbook of Procedures Relating to International Labour Conventions and Recommendations* 35 (ILO 2019).
728. Report of the International Law Commission, *supra* n. 721.
729. Eric Gravel & Chloé Charbonneau-Jobin, *The Committee of Experts on the Application of Conventions and Recommendations: Its Dynamic and Impact* 8 (ILO 2003).
730. Nolte, *supra* n. 726, at 24 and 26–28.

organs have established the Committee of Experts to supervise all ILO Conventions, not just one treaty. The difference is reflected, for instance, in the ratifying States' ability to nominate lawyers to sit in the HRC,[731] which is a very different process from that of the ILO's Committee of Experts. The HRC, furthermore, sets its own rules of procedure, even if the UN's General Assembly does set the terms and conditions of, for example, the Committee members' emoluments.[732] The terms of reference of the Committee of Experts are, on the other hand, revised by the GB, not the Committee itself.[733] It might, therefore, be more of an "organ of an international organization" than the HRC in the sense that, notwithstanding its independent nature, its terms of reference have been established and are framed by the ILO's main organs.

222 Still, it is hard to see how any of this affects the degree to which clarifications of the ILO's Committee of Experts are more directly attributable to the ILO, as an organisation, than the HRC's comments are attributable to the UN. In fact, due to the Committee of Experts' position at the ILO, its clarifications can be expected to represent subsequent practice fairly. The Workers' and Employers' permanent representation at the ILO – ACTRAV and ACTEMP – keep a close eye on the Committee of Experts' work.[734] This dynamic in which a tripartite constituency surveils an independent expert body can, arguably, increase the degree to which the Committee's clarifications are illustrative of subsequent practice.

223 Consider, for example, the crisis from 2011–2012, when the Employers' representatives openly confronted the organisation with their disagreement regarding the ILO Committee of Experts' views about the right to strike. One of the reasons why the Employers acted was the risk of the Committee of Experts *de facto* becoming considered a kind of interpretative tribunal of which the decisions are, in turn, relied upon by domestic and regional courts (another potential reason was CSR, *supra* no. 126).[735] The refusal of the Employers' group to discuss individual cases at the Conference's CAS, due to the alleged unobjective work of the Committee of Experts, sent a real shockwave through the organisation.[736] All the more because the Employers were intent on "correcting" the supervisory bodies' views on the right to strike. Cortebeeck, who served as the GB's Worker Vice-President at the time, has summarised the

731. Art. 29 International Covenant on Civil and Political Rights, 16 December 1966.
732. Arts. 35 and 39 *Ibid.*
733. ILO, *supra* n. 330, at 12 and 17.
734. For example, the factsheet of the International Organisation of Employers states that it is important for employers' associations to submit their comments to the Committee to "neutralize, balance or complement comments" by the trade unions on governments' reports. IOE, *Factsheet on Committee of Experts on the Application of Conventions and Recommendations (CEACR)*, International Organisation of Employers (14 August 2021), https://www.ioe-emp.org/index.php?eID=dumpFile&t=f&f=147483&token=9ded6f4a8ef5af953e3230072190122fd343d684.
735. Laurence R. Helfer, *Pushback Against Supervisory Systems: Lessons for the ILO from International Human Rights Institutions* 257, 272 (George P. Politakis, Tomi Kohiyama & Thomas Lieby eds., *ILO100: Law for Social Justice*, ILO 2019); Vogt et al., *supra* n. 397, at 12–13. For instance, the European Court of Human Rights relied on the clarifications of the ILO's supervisory bodies to point out that the ILO's Fundamental Conventions on collective rights cover the right to strike. Gött, *supra* n. 324, at 91–94.
736. Claire la Hovary, *Showdown at the ILO? A Historical Perspective on the Employers' Group's 2012 Challenge to the Right to Strike*, 42 Industrial Law Journal 338, 338–368 n. 4 (2013).

four main objections of the Employers as follows. The Employers' group wanted the reports of the Committee of Experts to stipulate that they served to advise the Conference's CAS and were not authoritative. Secondly, the Employers wanted to no longer discuss Convention No. 87 on Freedom of Association and Protection of the Right to Organise at the CAS, instead opting to discuss these issues at the tripartite Committee on Freedom of Association. The Employers' group, furthermore, wanted to stop issuing consensual conclusions at the CAS and, instead, issue separate comments from each of the tripartite groups. Fourthly, the Employers declared that the interpretations given to Convention No. 158 on the termination of employment, Convention No. 169 on indigenous and tribal peoples and Convention No. 183 on maternity protection might also be contested.[737] Based on these various concerns, the Committee of Experts' legitimacy in general was on the line, regardless of the right to strike. By extension, one might say the Employers' actions also challenged the overall influence of ILO Conventions outside of the organisation.[738] The gravity of the situation led to broad consultations across the organisation, after which workers' associations and employers' associations reached a "diplomatic truce" in 2015.[739] Since then, the ILO supervisory bodies' annual report contains what is effectively a mutually agreed description of the Committee of Experts' mandate. The 2020 edition mentions the Committee's mandate in bold:

> "The Committee of Experts on the Application of Conventions and Recommendations is an independent body established by the International Labour Conference and its members are appointed by the ILO Governing Body. It is composed of legal experts charged with examining the application of ILO Conventions and Recommendations by ILO member States. The Committee of Experts undertakes an impartial and technical analysis of how the Conventions are applied in law and practice by member States, while cognizant of different national realities and legal systems. In doing so, it must determine the legal scope, content and meaning of the provisions of the Conventions. Its opinions and recommendations are non-binding, being intended to guide the actions of national authorities. They derive their persuasive value from the legitimacy and rationality of the Committee's work based on its impartiality, experience and expertise. The Committee's technical role and moral authority is well recognized, particularly as it has been engaged in its supervisory task for more than 90 years, by virtue of its composition, independence and its working methods built on continuing dialogue with governments taking into account information provided by employers' and workers' organizations. This has been reflected in the incorporation of the Committee's opinions and recommendations in national legislation, international instruments and court decisions".[740]

737. Cortebeeck, *supra* n. 469, at 65.
738. La Hovary, *supra* n. 552, at 328; La Hovary, *supra* n. 579, at 45.
739. ILO Standards Initiative–Joint Statement of Workers' & Employers' Groups (23.02.2015), TMFAPROC/2015/2; ILO Standards Initiative–Government Group Statement (24.02.2015), TMFAPROC/2015/2.
740. ILO Committee of Experts on the Application of Conventions and Recommendations, *Report III (Part A) Application of International Labour Standards 2020* 11 (ILO 2020).

224 When considering this broadly accepted description of its function and the fact that ILO constituents can discuss, question and dispute the Committee's findings,[741] the Committee's clarifications could, in fact, be considered a balanced and credible source of subsequent practice. The actors surrounding the Committee force it to remain on point.[742] Moreover, the International Law Commission also leaves some room to consider the Committee's clarifications as subsequent practice. The comments of its draft conclusion indicate that organs of international organisations have been exempted as sources for subsequent practice, mainly for formalistic reasons. The exemption "does not exclude that the substance of the present draft conclusion may apply, mutatis mutandis, to pronouncements of independent expert bodies that are organs of international organizations".[743] In light of this, a strong case can be made in favour of considering some of the Committee of Experts' pronouncements as indicative of subsequent practice under Article 31. One can think, for example, of clarifications that the Committee repeats in several cases and incorporates in one of its general surveys without its opinion being disputed.[744] The quality of the Committee's arguments may also play a role in this respect.[745]

225 All in all, given the uncertainty that exists on this point, it would seem appropriate to assume that the clarifications and observations of the ILO's Committee of Experts can, in any case, constitute "other subsequent practice" under the supplementary means of interpretation of Article 32 VCLT. The clarifications may, furthermore, give rise to subsequent practice under Article 31 if certain conditions are fulfilled. However, it is unclear at which exact point its clarifications could be viewed as a primary means of interpretation. Does it, for instance, matter whether the ILO Member States implement the Committee's clarifications? Such implementing measures would signal that the Member States recognise that the instrument, indeed, intends to do what the Committee claims. Besides this form of "Member State-driven" subsequent practice, other forms might also exist. More specifically, the Conference's CAS can

741. See, for instance, the following interaction in relation to the Netherlands' commitment under Convention No. 177: "Further to its previous comment on this point, the Committee notes the Government's reply that because homeworkers are often persons enjoying the same protection as employees in an enterprise, no separate policy is required to offer them the protection resulting from the Convention. It is of the view, however, that this statement risks to be an oversimplification of the purpose of the Convention. The Committee draws the Government's attention to the clear obligation arising from this Article of the Convention to adopt, implement and periodically review, [...]". Direct Request (CEACR) – adopted 2009, published 99th ILC session (2010), Home Work Convention, 1996 (No. 177) – Netherlands (Ratification: 2002).

742. "Worker representatives have also expressed concern that the Committee 'has started to apply a certain degree of self-censorship due to the controversy'". Helfer, *supra* n. 735, at 273; Vogt et al., *supra* n. 397, at 185–186.

743. Report of the International Law Commission, *supra* n. 721.

744. "When the Committee repeats a given view in several cases concerning individual countries – especially as the Committee has stressed that the manner in which the implementation of Conventions is evaluated must be uniform – and also when that view is stated in one of its 'general surveys', the opinion of the Committee tends to acquire a more general and definitive character". Nicolas Valticos, *The Sources of International Labour Law: Recent Trends* 179, 192 (Wybo P. Heere ed., *International Law and its Sources: Liber Amicorum Maarten Bos*, Kluwer 1989).

745. Danae Azaria, *The Legal Significance of Expert Treaty Bodies Pronouncements for the Purpose of the Interpretation of Treaties*, 22 International Community Law Review 33, 59 n. 1 (2020).

play an innovative role in this dynamic. The CAS is made up of both governmental and non-governmental representatives. To the extent that they confirm[746] a settled position of the Committee of Experts, which is, for instance, expressed in a general survey, one can argue that it simulates a collective form of subsequent practice by the States. Indeed, "the intervention of a body [such as the CAS] with a political composition is not necessarily incompatible with the function of interpretation. 'Authentic' interpretations, that is, interpretations given by parties to a treaty or by the body that is the author of a treaty, are one possible method of interpretation in international law".[747]

Article 32: Secondary means of interpretation – When interpreting instruments adopted under the auspices of an international organisation, it is very convenient to take recourse to the working documents. Nevertheless, the VCLT considers this method as secondary, among other things, because it was perceived as unreliable.[748] That is particularly so whenever the interpreter relies on individual statements by participants.[749] *A contrario*, one could argue that when a credible individual such as the standard-setting committee's Reporter makes a public statement, this statement expresses a joint position of participants; thus, it should be given appropriate weight. As Gardiner notes, if a statement gives proof of the common understanding among participants, it can be seen as more reliable.[750] For ILO purposes, it is predominantly the Reporter who can be expected to present ILO constituents' common position accurately. Contributions by other participants have to be relied on more carefully, even if some individual contributions may be reliable, at least when weighed up against others. For instance, the Vice-Chairperson of the Employers' or Workers' group may stress that their group supports an amendment on the condition that the amendment has a specific meaning. If the group subsequently follows through and accepts the amendment, it most likely means that the Committee intended this amendment to have this specific meaning. These kinds of interactions can clarify the intention of the collective. They should be given sufficient attention. **226**

As pointed out by the phrasing of Article 32 VCLT, the secondary means of interpretation are non-exhaustive. At the same time, this would not allow the interpreter to have recourse to every type of document. Mbengue points out that, for example, previous court rulings and academic writings do not constitute a supplementary means of interpretation under Article 32.[751] For this reason, the secondary means of interpretation that seems most relevant within the ILO's legal system is the many working documents that are part of the drafting process and the Committee of Experts' clarifications that do not classify as subsequent practice under Article 31. The term "working documents" is considered to "include materials which document the negotiations and other circumstances that culminated in the formal conclusion **227**

746. Some caution is needed. The silence of ILO constituents should not be mistaken for consent. Conclusion 13 International Law Commission, *supra* n. 701.
747. ILO Committee on Standing Orders and the Application of Conventions and Recommendations, *supra* n. 687, at 6.
748. Mbengue, *supra* n. 694, at 400–402.
749. Le Bouthillier, *supra* n. 696, at 857.
750. Gardiner, *supra* n. 694, at 472–473.
751. Mbengue, *supra* n. 694, at 398–399.

of a treaty".[752] Although the precise boundaries of what is and is not a working document remain unclear,[753] this description, arguably, means that, for example, the conclusions of prior Meetings of Experts, which trigger a new draft instrument, might classify as an early working document.

228 **Decent work as a relevant rule of international law?** – As mentioned before, the ILO Constitution and Declaration of Philadelphia can be taken into account to interpret Conventions pursuant to Article 31, §3 VCLT (*supra* no. 216). One matter that remains unclear, however, is the degree to which the Social Justice Declaration and Centenary Declaration are subsequent agreements that reimagine the content of the ILO Constitution. Does the Social Justice Declaration have any influence on the interpretation of ILS adopted post-2008?[754]

229 Answering this question requires recalling that the ILO Constitution, including the annexed Declaration of Philadelphia, is the only constitutive instrument. Subsequent ILO Declarations have repackaged the ILO Constitution's mission. Although Article 1 of the Constitution still claims that the organisation promotes the objectives of the Labour Charter and Declaration of Philadelphia, it is evident the organisation nowadays focuses on the Social Justice Declaration's and Centenary Declaration's objectives, which are supposed to align with those of the Constitution. This leads to something of a dilemma. Usually, an instrument should not be interpreted so extensively that it amounts to an implicit amendment. The recent Declarations use very different language from that of the ILO Constitution, making it hard to interpret the latter along the lines of the former. However, in this particular situation, one has also to consider that "institutional treaties are more often than others interpreted in a purpose and aim-oriented way, that is, as living constitutions".[755]

230 On closer inspection, this observation covers two issues. The first one concerns the teleological interpretation of constitutive treaties. The second one concerns the "living" or evolutive character of constitutive treaties. Regarding the first, Brölmann notes that the interpretation of these institutional treaties follows the VCLT's framework, yet that framework is reasonably flexible. It leaves room for interpreters to apply supplementary approaches that accommodate the unique characteristics of these institutional treaties.[756] Gardiner credits Brölmann's view in this respect.[757] The

752. Martin Ris, *Treaty Interpretation and ICJ Recourse to Travaux Préparatoires: Towards a Proposed Amendment of Articles 31 and 32 of the Vienna Convention on the Law of Treaties*, 14 Boston College International and Comparative Law Review 111, 112 n. 1 (1991).

753. Jan Klabbers, *International Legal Histories: The Declining Importance of Travaux Préparatoires in Treaty Interpretation?*, 50 Netherlands International Law Review 267, 279 n. 3 (2003).

754. Servais seems to suggest that the concept of "decent work" might have a minor influence on interpretation. Jean-Michel Servais, *L'OIT et le Travail Décent. La Difficile Médiation entre Croissance, Création d'Emploi et Protection des Travailleurs*, Revue de droit comparé du travail et de la sécurité sociale 71, 77 n. 1 (2011).

755. Kolb, *supra* n. 698, at 164.

756. Brölmann, *supra* n. 716, at 525.

757. "The most helpful approach may be that of Brölmann who, in examining specialized rules of treaty interpretation in connection with international organizations, notes that: the [VCLT's] framework itself is famously broad, subsidiary and not very hierarchically structured. As a result, it may be best to approach treaty interpretation in this context, not as a separate regime, but

"special" characteristics of a constitutive instrument, such as the ILO Constitution, justify applying a somewhat skewed version of the VCLT pursuant to which, for instance, a more teleological interpretation could be allowed. Or, the subsequent practice of the organisation might more heavily influence the treaty's interpretation.[758]

The second issue relates to the use of interpretative techniques to achieve a "living constitution". While the use of a teleological method of interpretation may lend itself to evolutive treaty interpretation in the sense that "[t]he object and purpose of a treaty is sometimes used as a building block in order to establish the validity of evolutive interpretation",[759] these are interrelated but distinct questions. Considering what has been argued by Brölmann and Gardiner, who remain rather cautious, it seems advisable to verify whether the Constitution or the Treaty of Versailles provide indications about the Constitution's "teleological" and "living" nature. The Constitution's preamble tells a tale of a world in peril that requires the ILO (constituents) to improve labour conditions. The ILO is, in other words, an organisation on a mission.[760] Also, the Declaration of Philadelphia, for example, speaks about the "progressive application" of its principles, which is indicative of a certain motion.[761] Supiot's observations are also poignant. As he writes, at the ILO, social justice manifests itself time and again based on both a specific combination of guiding principles and the "procedures that will allow the implementation of these principles to evolve in response to technical, economic or sociological changes".[762] Hence, from an ILO perspective, the implementation of social justice is subject to change. Additionally, what is also relevant is that, as observed by the Permanent Court of Justice, "[t]he terms in which the objects committed to the International Labour Organization are stated are so general that, as the Court remarked in its second Advisory Opinion, 'language 231

rather as a version of the framework to which additional or supplementary approaches have emerged in light of the 'special' characteristics that these constitutive instruments possess". Gardiner, *supra* n. 717, at 127.

758. Brölmann, *supra* n. 716, at 528–533.

759. Panos Merkouris, *(Inter)Temporal Considerations in the Interpretative Process of the VCLT: Do Treaties Endure, Perdure or Exdure?*, 45 Netherlands Yearbook of International Law 121, 139 (2014).

760. Art. 427 of the Treaty of Versailles stipulates that the High Contracting Parties recognise "that the wellbeing, physical, moral and intellectual, of industrial wage-earners is of supreme international importance, [and] have framed, in order to further this great end, the permanent machinery provided for in Section I, and associated with that of the League of Nations".

761. "The conference affirms that the principles set forth in this Declaration are fully applicable to all peoples everywhere and that, while the manner of their application must be determined with due regard to the stage of social and economic development reached by each people, their progressive application to peoples who are still dependent, as well as to those who have already achieved self-government, is a matter of concern to the whole civilized world". Declaration concerning the aims and purposes of the International Labour Organisation (Declaration of Philadelphia), 10 May 1944.

762. "*La justice sociale se définit, d'une part, par la combinaison de quelques principes directeurs qui se trouvent formulés en termes généraux (le droit à la santé, à un salaire décent, au repos, etc.), et, d'autre part, au moyen de procédures qui vont permettre de faire évoluer la mise en œuvre de ces principes en fonction des changements techniques, économiques ou sociologiques*". Supiot, Kott & Piguet, *supra* n. 353, at 159. *See also*, Maupain, *supra* n. 353, at 297.

could hardly be more comprehensive'".[763] Suffice to note that this was purposively done to construe a mandate that could last.[764] Now, decades later, this open-ended language of the Constitution could be conducive to an evolutive interpretation.[765] Based on these elements, it can be argued that also in the case of the ILO, "[t]here is some authority for the proposition that a treaty of a constitutional character should be subject to different rules of interpretation to allow for the 'intrinsically evolutionary nature of a constitution'".[766] For instance, Butler, a Director-General during the 1930s, called the Constitution a "living institution", not "a static charter".[767]

232 Simultaneously, notwithstanding this relevant evidence, no obvious reference points seem present regarding the possibility of giving an evolutive interpretation to the Constitution. Actually, the most convincing argument in favour of an evolutive take seems to derive from Conclusion 8 of the Draft Conclusions on Subsequent Agreements and Subsequent Practice in Relation to the Interpretation of Treaties. It stresses that "[s]ubsequent agreements and subsequent practice under articles 31 and 32 may assist in determining whether or not the presumed intention of the parties upon the conclusion of the treaty was to give a term used a meaning which is capable of evolving over time".[768] Therefore, if the Social Justice Declaration and Centenary Declaration make clear that the terms in the ILO Constitution are given a new contemporary meaning, it would affect whether the Constitution can be given an evolutive interpretation. What is more, Conclusion 12 similarly points out that an international organisation's activities and practices may also express subsequent agreement or practice.

233 In view of this, it must be stressed that the Decent Work Agenda has received continued support since the first DG report in 1999. Subsequently, the 2008 Social Justice Declaration and the 2019 Centenary Declaration reaffirmed the legitimacy of this decent work framework as a modern-day re-creation of the Constitution's goals. The ILO Declaration on Social Justice for a Fair Globalization stipulates that:

> "the commitments and efforts of Members and the Organization to implement the ILO's constitutional mandate, including through international labour standards, and to place full and productive employment and decent work at the centre of economic and social policies, should be based on the four equally important

763. Permanent Court of International Justice: Advisory opinion No. 13, *Competence of the ILO to Regulate Incidentally the Personal Work of the Employer*, 23 July 1926, 17.
764. ILO, *supra* n. 350, at 105–106.
765. Merkouris, *supra* n. 759, at 141–142.
766. Philippe Sands & Pierre Klein, *Bowett's Law of International Institutions* 454 (Sweet & Maxwell 2009). *See also*, Daniel Moeckli & Nigel D. White, *Treaties as "Living Instruments"* 136, 170 (Michael J. Bowman & Dino Kritsiotis eds., *Conceptual and Contextual Perspectives on the Modern Law of Treaties*, CUP 2018).
767. Sinclair, *supra* n. 317, at 173. The author quotes from Harold Butler, *Past, Present, and Future of the International Labour Organization* 43 (Humphrey Milford ed., *Problems of Peace*, OUP 1930). The same quote can be found in Guy F. Sinclair, *To Reform the World: International Organizations and the Making of Modern States* 70 (OUP 2017).
768. International Law Commission, *supra* n. 701. *See also*, Malgosia Fitzmaurice, *Subsequent Agreement and Subsequent Practice: Some Reflections on the International Law Commission's Draft Conclusions*, 22 International Community Law Review 14, 28 n. 1 (2020).

> strategic objectives of the ILO, through which the Decent Work Agenda is expressed [...]".[769]

Similarly, constituents agreed in the Centenary Declaration that:

> "[t]he ILO must carry forward into its second century with unrelenting vigour its constitutional mandate for social justice by further developing its human-centred approach to the future of work, which puts workers' rights and the needs, aspirations and rights of all people at the heart of economic, social and environmental policies".[770]

This phrase, arguably, means as much as saying that the ILO must carry forward its constitutional mandate by developing decent work, a human-centred approach to social justice. From this point of view, both Declarations could be seen as subsequent agreements between the ILO Members regarding the Constitution's application.[771] Moreover, influencing the Constitution's interpretation in this way does not necessarily surpass the limits of the VCLT's general rule of interpretation in relation to constitutional treaties. According to Buga, a "wide range of dispute settlement bodies and the majority of legal scholars" even acknowledge the process of treaty modification by subsequent practice.[772] Furthermore, for example, Arato has remarked that the International Court of Justice "has relied upon the consistent practice of the [UN] organization to establish: an interpretation of the [UN] Charter; a reinterpretation of the Charter at odds with previous consistent practices; and even interpretations and reinterpretations at significant odds with the text, arguably amounting to the informal modification of the Charter's express terms".[773] Along these lines, whereas treaty modification through subsequent practice may still be the exception,[774] it does seem possible to at least understand the ILO Constitution through the lenses of the latest Declarations in so far as this does not contradict the Constitution.

769. ILO Declaration on Social Justice for a Fair Globalization, 10 June 2008, 9.
770. ILO Centenary Declaration for the Future of Work, 21 June 2019, 3.
771. The report of the Special Rapporteur mentions that it is essential for the Declaration to be "clear that the parties of the constituent instrument of an international organization acted [to express the attitudes of the States], and not, as they usually do, institutionally as members of the respective plenary organ". This is the case here. The constituents' interventions at the ILC indicate how the participants speak on behalf of the Member States, rather than institutionally. For instance, the Record of Proceedings of 2008's ILC notes that the Government member of the United States "confirmed her Government's support for a strong ILO", that the Ambassador and Permanent Representative of Slovenia stated on behalf of the European Union how the Union and its Member States "will make every effort to contribute to constructive dialogue with other constituents and to a successful follow-up that will result in a positive impact on the globe" and so forth. Report of the Committee on Strengthening the ILO's Capacity, 97th Session of the International Labour Conference in 2008, 13/46 and 17/39; Georg Nolte, *Third Report on Subsequent Agreements and Subsequent Practice in Relation to the Interpretation of Treaties* 26 (UN 2016).
772. Irina Buga, *Modification of Treaties by Subsequent Practice* 363 (OUP 2018).
773. Julian Arato, *Treaty Interpretation and Constitutional Transformation: Informal Change in International Organizations*, 38 The Yale Journal of International Law 289, 329 n. 2 (2013).
774. Fitzmaurice, *supra* n. 768, at 25.

234 Therefore, given the ILO's consistent subsequent practice, and Member States' repeated consent to the Decent Work Agenda,[775] it would seem that the ILO Constitution can no longer be used to imply that ILO Conventions only apply to "manual labour" (*supra* no. 203). At the same time, even when viewed through the lenses of the latest Declarations, the ILO Constitution does not evidently support an inclusive interpretation of ILO Conventions either. It would seem shaky, to say the least, to argue that "ILO Conventions apply to all workers unless otherwise provided" because of how the Declarations reinterpreted the ILO Constitution. In spite of everything, the ILO Constitution is still the constitutional text. While the Declarations might neutralise the former's orientation towards old-fashioned wage employment, that does not mean the ILO Constitution has all of a sudden become a contextual factor for arguing that, in principle, all instruments apply to all workers.

235 **Our interpretative scheme** – These concluding paragraphs draw on the discussions above. In summary, an ILO Convention shall be interpreted in good faith and in accordance with the ordinary meaning to be given to the terms of the treaty, in light of the instrument's context, object, purpose and the will of the Conference. As part of this context, attention must be paid to:

- the text, preamble and annexes of the ILO Convention itself;
- the Recommendation, Resolution, conclusions or other instruments that have been adopted by the same Conference and relate to the ILO Convention;
- any subsequent agreement regarding the interpretation of a Convention, such as a Protocol or possibly an interpretative Resolution;
- the applicable rules of international law; hence, the ILO Constitution as reinterpreted through the Social Justice Declaration, Centenary Declaration and the ILO's subsequent practice;
- under the right circumstances, the other international labour standards of the International Labour Code could also matter, in particular, the instruments that directly preceded the Convention under review;
- clarifications by the ILO Committee of Experts that meet the bar for "subsequent practice" under Article 31, §3 VCLT.[776]

236 Additionally, the Committee's clarifications that cannot be classified under Article 31 should be given appropriate weight as "other subsequent practice" under Article 32 VCLT. In that case, these clarifications should, in principle, only be consulted if Article 31's methods of interpretation do not provide any satisfactory solution. Relevant to highlight in this respect is that irrespective of theory, in reality, it seems that many national courts do consider the Committee's clarifications influential.[777]

775. For instance, Resolution on Advancing Social Justice through Decent Work, 9 June 2016.
776. It is extremely unclear right now to what extent this can be the case. It is a shame this matter is so sensitive at the ILO level, because it would be helpful to crystallise what impact the ILO's supervisory bodies ought to have on domestic authorities' and other international courts' use of ILS.
777. Xavier Beaudonnet, *Quelques Observations sur l'Utilisation des Normes de l'OIT par les Tribunaux Nationaux* 745, 762–763 (George P. Politakis, Tomi Kohiyama & Thomas Lieby eds., *ILO100: Law for Social Justice*, ILO 2019). *See also*, Teun de Vries, *Difficulties of the Interpretation of Conventions: A Judge's Point of View* 91, 91–100 (Frans Pennings ed., *International Social Security Standards: Current Views and Interpretation Matters*, Intersentia 2007). The degree

Similarly, also, the use of ILO working documents raises interesting questions. The VCLT merely depicts *travaux préparatoires* as a supplementary means of interpretation. However, some caveats are in order. Paragraph 4 of Article 31 VCLT, most notably, stipulates that "[a] special meaning shall be given to a term if it is established that the parties so intended". Therefore, it would seem unjustifiable to denounce such a "special meaning" because it is articulated in the preparatory work. All the more since the ILO Manual for Drafting ILO Instruments argues that: **237**

> "the ILC technical committees should indicate in their reports their own ideas as to how provisions framed in absolute terms in proposed texts must be interpreted. Such a paragraph would undoubtedly be part of the context within which the instrument would have to be interpreted, and would obviate any need to include such indications within the text of the instrument itself".[778]

In other words, it is somewhat of an institutional practice at the ILO to clarify the meaning of words and phrases in the Committee's reports, not in the standard itself. As explained, the ILO can deviate from the general rules of interpretation pursuant to Article 5 VCLT and has seemingly done so in this regard.[779] Such clarifications will, consequently, be fully taken into account. Now that the rules on treaty interpretation have been clarified, Chapter Two can dig into the purpose and scope of application of the Private Employment Agencies Convention. The Third Chapter will, subsequently, look at the Home Work Convention, and the Fourth Chapter considers the Domestic Workers Convention.

---

to which the Committee of Experts' clarifications matter in front of the national courts does depend on the legal system in question. For instance, in Japan, the standards are likely not to have much of an impact. Thomas Lieby, *Quelques Réflexions sur l'Interprétation des Conventions Internationales du Travail par le Juge National*, Revue internationale de droit économique 5, 5–31 n. 1 (2020).

778. ILO Office of the Legal Adviser, *supra* n. 702, at 42.
779. Trebilcock, *supra* n. 668, at 870–873.

Chapter 2. The Instruments on Labour Supply Services

SUBCHAPTER 1. THE INSTRUMENTS ON UNEMPLOYMENT AND FEE-CHARGING EMPLOYMENT AGENCIES

Labour supply was a matter for the State – Before analysing the scope of application 238 of the Private Employment Agencies Convention, 1997 (No. 181), a picture will be sketched of what happened to its predecessors. As mentioned above, such information can be relevant for interpretative purposes. Convention No. 181 originates from the ILO's earlier regulation on labour supply services. This subject has been at the forefront of ILO standard-setting ever since the organisation's inception. The ILO Constitution's preamble lists "the regulation of the labour supply" as one measure to improve labour conditions. It is, therefore, not entirely surprising that the Unemployment Convention, 1919 (No. 2), already contained an obligation for each Member to "establish a system of free public employment agencies under the control of a central authority". Where both public and "private free employment agencies" exist, the Convention continues, the Member States shall take steps to coordinate their operations on a national scale.[780] Moreover, in the accompanying Unemployment Recommendation, 1919 (No. 1), the General Conference recommended prohibiting the establishment of private employment agencies that charge fees or carry on their business for profit. If such commercial agencies already existed, "it is further recommended that they be permitted to operate only under Government licences, and that all practicable measures be taken to abolish such agencies as soon as possible".[781] Suffice to say that labour supply was a matter for the State at the beginning of the twentieth century. Only "private free employment agencies" could be condoned. Labour market intermediaries that would continually charge fees to workers, as some platforms do, were considered harmful.

780. Art. 2 Unemployment Convention, 1919 (No. 2).
781. Para. 1 Unemployment Recommendation, 1919 (No. 1).

239 **For-profit employment services** – One notable early exception to this general prohibition of commercial labour supply services were the "notices of situations vacant or situations wanted",[782] which were printed in newspapers and journals. Except for this particular practice, the prohibition of private employment services was considered absolute.[783] On behalf of the Commission on Unemployment, the Reporter warned against for-profit employment agencies, which he described as "employment bureaus which carry on the trade of finding employment for people". The Reporter did not hold back: "these agencies are very often merely a means of exploiting workers; and we recommend to the States that they keep such institutions under the strictest surveillance, and even as far as possible suppress them. In any case do not let them function except under a system of licensing".[784]

240 This negative view towards for-profit private employment agencies ("commercial agencies") would persist and leave its mark on 1933's and 1949's Fee-Charging Employment Agencies Conventions. If last century's advice is compared to today's policies and regulations, two different worlds emerge. During the final decades of the twentieth century, the State monopoly on employment services was, arguably, rightfully "pulverized", among others by the European Court of Justice in the 1990s.[785] Since State monopolies on employment services could not deliver effective services for labour market participants, they lost their legitimacy, so argued the Court.[786] Private enterprises should be allowed to administer these types of services. Furthermore, whereas commercial agencies were initially subjected to licensing and accreditation schemes, these schemes slowly unravelled. For example, unless it concerns temporary agency work,[787] the EU Directive 2006/123/EC on services in the internal market further cleared the obstacles that prevented commercial agencies from providing their services in the other EU Member States.[788] In Belgium, the explanatory memorandum of 2010's Flemish Decree on private employment services mentions that the regulation of mediation/placement agencies through authorisation schemes no longer

782. Report of the Commission on Unemployment at the first session of the International Labour Conference, Washington, ILO, 1919, 235.

783. This is, for instance, illustrated by Art. 1 of the Fee-Charging Employment Agencies Convention, 1933 (No. 34). It mentions that newspapers or other publications are allowed "unless they are published wholly or mainly for the purpose of acting as intermediaries between employers and workers".

784. Report of the Commission on Unemployment to the plenary at the 1st Session of the International Labour Conference, Washington, ILO, 1919, 133.

785. European Court of Justice: Case C-55/96, *Job Centre COOP. arl*, 11 December 1997, ECLI:EU:C:1997:603; Roger Blanpain, *Arbeidsmarktrecht* 30 (die Keure 2011).

786. ILO, *supra* n. 143, at 45.

787. Leah F. Vosko, *Less than Adequate: Regulating Temporary Agency Work in the EU in the Face of an Internal Market in Services*, 2 Cambridge Journal of Regions, Economy and Society 395, 405–407 n. 3 (2009).

788. Art. 2 Directive (EU) 2006/123/EC of the European Parliament and of the Council of 12 December 2006 on services in the internal market, OJ L 376, 27 December 2006. It should, nevertheless, be stressed that although temporary work agencies have been excluded from the Directive, Art. 56 TFEU is still operative in relation to temporary agency work. *E.g.* European Court of Justice: Case C-397/10, *Commission européenne v. Royaume de Belgique*, 30 June 2011, ECLI:EU:C:2011:444.

seemed tenable in light of Article 9 of this Directive.[789] The Decree, consequently, focuses on the protection of jobseekers by enforcing protective provisions through sanctions, whereas its predecessor, which was approved in the wake of the adoption of the Private Employment Agencies Convention, 1997 (No. 181), still contained an authorisation scheme.[790] Therefore, as the Committee of Experts also observed in Lithuania,[791] in many countries, the ILO Commission on Unemployment's initial idea to "in any case" not let commercial agencies operate "except under a system of licencing" is no longer tenable.

Labour is not a commodity – The increasingly privatised provision of labour supply services concerned the ILO. The notion that "labour should not be regarded merely as a commodity or article of commerce" has always been one of its guiding principles.[792] That principle was inextricably linked to the initial argument that public employment agencies should be given a monopoly.[793] The fact that this monopoly was no longer deemed suitable did not mean that the principle had lost its relevance. The opposite is probably closer to the truth;[794] private agencies, in particular, need to be reminded that jobseekers are not a commodity. Yet, with the breakdown of this monopoly, the boundaries of what is acceptable in labour brokerage, without violating the aforementioned principle, did become more fluid. 241

As observed by Hyman, the word "commodity" has a particular meaning. "[I]t is a good (or service) that is identical to any other of its type and can be made by anyone".[795] From this perspective, the phrase "labour is not a commodity" not only means that a person's labour is not just like any other input because labour cannot be separated from the human individual,[796] the phrase might also imply the idea 242

789. Memorie van toelichting bij het decreet van 10 december 2010 betreffende de private arbeidsbemiddeling. Available at: https://assets.vlaanderen.be/image/upload/v1590772336/WSE-uitzendbureaus-MvT-decreet-private-arbeidsbemiddeling_cxiumf.pdf (accessed: 28 April 2021).

790. Section 6 Décret du 13 avril 1999 relatif au placement privé en Région flamande (traduction) / Decreet 13 april 1999 met betrekking tot de private arbeidsbemiddeling in het Vlaamse Gewest. Similarly, the Walloon legislature abolished the prior system of conditional approval and replaced it by a requirement for prior registration combined with subsequent supervision. Projet de décret du 9 mars 2009 relatif à l'enregistrement ou à l'agrément des agences de placement, 11.

791. Direct Request (CEACR) – adopted 2014, published 104th ILC session (2015), Private Employment Agencies Convention, 1997 (No. 181) – Lithuania (Ratification: 2004).

792. Art. 427 Treaty of Peace of Versailles, 28 June 1919.

793. Leah F. Vosko, *Legitimizing the Triangular Employment Relationship: Emerging International Labour Standards From a Comparative Perspective*, 19 Comparative Labor Law & Policy Journal 43, 48–49 n. 1 (1997); Donna Koeltz, *Delivering Public Employment Services: Which Model Works Best?* 163, 164 (Jason Heyes & Ludek Rychly eds., *Labour Administration in Uncertain Times: Policy, Practice and Institutions*, ILO 2013).

794. Some might even argue that on the basis of the current rules on labour brokerage in the EU, including its regulation on temporary agency work, the "worker has become 'a commodity, no more, no less so than is the sugar'". Keith D. Ewing, *supra* n. 502, at 12.

795. Louis Hyman, *Temp: How American Work, American Business, and the American Dream Became Temporary* 37 (Viking 2018).

796. R. Blanpain, *Concluding Remarks* 537, 538 (W. Albeda, R. Blanpain & G. M. J. Veldkamp eds., *Temporary Work in Modern Society*, I, Kluwer 1978); Paul O'Higgins, *"Labour is not a Commodity" – an Irish Contribution to International Labour Law*, 26 Industrial Law Journal 225, 225–230 n. 3 (1997); Perulli, *supra* n. 321, at 365.

that the worker's labour is highly individual. Workers' performance, skills and ambitions differ; their labour is not identical to that of any other worker.[797] Therefore, the principle might also relate to what Bonvin considers an essential pillar of the Declaration of Philadelphia. Work is not just instrumental in generating an income. Work must contribute to individual fulfilment.[798] When applied in the context of employment services, workers should be matched with vacancies that correspond to their ambition, skill level, etc. The principle that labour is not a commodity is meant to oppose the use of LMIs to ship in replaceable workers as if everyone's labour is identical. This is a crucial point, considering how some platform operators have based their business model on breaking down jobs into tasks and matching fungible workers to those tasks. As such, the practices of these platform operators, which try to simplify the work to such an extent that it is irrelevant who performs the tasks, might fly in the face of the ILO's view that labour is not a commodity.

243 The Declaration of Philadelphia turned the "guiding principle" that labour is not a commodity into a "fundamental principle". The institutional importance granted to this principle partially explains why the original suppression of commercial agencies was largely sustained until the 1990s.[799] Private employment agencies were considered, *inter alia*, to make workers "buy jobs" in return for fees.[800] Such negative views about their brokerage services seemed widely shared. The first International Labour Conference agreed unanimously on 1919's Unemployment Convention and Recommendation.[801] Its recommendations stood for decades.[802] For instance, Mahaim, who at the time served as the Chairman of the Governing Body, stated in 1932 that the abolition of fee-charging employment agencies was "entirely in accordance with the principle of the Labour Charter, which lays down that labour should not be regarded as an article of commerce".[803] Similar thinking still influences contemporary

797. "We don't typically think of the jobs that we perform as commodities. The Merriam-Webster dictionary entry for commodity describes it as 'a massproduced unspecialized product.' [...] In fact, we'd probably argue that no one does exactly the same job we do – that we perform at least a slightly different set of tasks, or perform them in a slightly different way, than any coworker. We may well be right about that, but the world of business and management may feel otherwise. Jobs are increasingly viewed as undifferentiated and interchangeable across humans and machines – the very definition of a commodity". Thomas H. Davenport, *When Jobs Become Commodities*, 59 MIT Sloan Management Review 16, 16 n. 2 (2018).

798. Bonvin, *supra* n. 6, at 40.

799. The reason for this prohibition also had to do, for instance, with the belief that governments' experience in addressing manpower shortages during the war could, at least in theory, be consolidated. This experience would serve to advance public employment services, making private services redundant. ILO, *Employment Service Organisation*, Geneva 4 (ILO 1946).

800. George Gonos, *"Never a Fee!" The Miracle of Postmodern Temporary Help and Staffing Agency*, 4 Working USA 9, 10 n. 3 (2000–01).

801. Report of the Commission on Unemployment at the 1st Session of the International Labour Conference, Washington, ILO, 1919, 235.

802. Van Eck argues that the Private Employment Agencies Convention from 1997 has had a significant impact on South Africa's and Namibia's decision to regulate instead of ban employment agencies. Stefan van Eck, *Employment Agencies: International Norms and Developments in South Africa*, 28 International Journal of Comparative Labour Law and Industrial Relations 29, 29–44 n. 1 (2012).

803. Opening of the 16th Session of the International Labour Conference, Geneva, League of Nations, 1932, 5.

law. "Since, as stated in the Treaty of Versailles, labour is not a commodity, placing workers cannot be a commercial transaction", so wrote the ILO Office in 1994.[804] Consequently, the Private Employment Agencies Convention, 1997 (No. 181), for instance, stipulates that agencies shall not charge directly or indirectly, in whole or in part, any fees or costs to workers.[805]

Fee-Charging Employment Agencies - Looking back on Convention No. 181's predecessors, the original Fee-Charging Employment Agencies Convention, 1933 (No. 34), still overtly aimed to abolish private employment services. However, due to the instrument's flexibility clauses, in reality, the Convention only imposed a quasi-absolute prohibition on commercial agencies.[806] Agencies that were not conducted for profit received permission to operate because of their valuable, supplemental role to public employment agencies.[807] They needed to obtain authorisation and were only allowed to charge fees within a specific range fixed by governments. One notable element in 1932's Law and Practice Report on the "Abolition of Fee-Charging Employment Agencies" was the view that agencies' fraudulent and immoral practices victimised both employers and jobseekers.[808] Those immoral practices included, among others: **244**

> "exaction of exorbitant fees, charging of fees where no service is rendered, misrepresentation of the conditions of work, publication of false advertisements, advertising of posts or requests for employment without endeavouring to satisfy the requirements of persons already registered and who have paid a fee, the creation of a rapid turnover by splitting fees with employers or foremen, or by inducing workers on various pretences to change employment, [...], supply of substitute workers during industrial disputes, partiality and discrimination between organised and unorganised workers, pawnbrokerage and money-lending on usurious terms, [...], signing of contracts to the effect that applicants should retain the post for a limited period or resort in future to one and the same agent, [...], more or less forced purchase of clothes, articles of personal use, shipping and lottery tickets, etc".[809]

804. ILO, *supra* n. 143, at 7.
805. It provides an example of how the latest ILO Convention on labour supply at least somewhat adhered to the fundamental principle. Vosko, *supra* n. 793, at 60.
806. "[E]mployment agencies conducted with a view to profit, that is to say, any person, company, institution, agency or other organisation which acts as an intermediary for the purpose of procuring employment for a worker or supplying a worker for an employer with a view to deriving either directly or indirectly any pecuniary or other material advantage from either employer or worker; the expression does not include newspapers or other publications unless they are published wholly or mainly for the purpose of acting as intermediaries between employers and workers". Art. 1 Fee-Charging Employment Agencies Convention, 1933 (No. 34).
807. "[E]mployment agencies not conducted with a view to profit, that is to say, the placing services of any company, institution, agency or other organisation which, though not conducted with a view to deriving any pecuniary or other material advantage, levies from either employer or worker for the above services an entrance fee, a periodical contribution or any other charge". *Ibid.*
808. ILO, *Abolition of Fee-charging Employment Agencies* 9 (ILO 1932).
809. *Ibid.*, 9.

Although this list of abuses remains relevant to this day,[810] one must also be aware of the very different circumstances nowadays. For instance, Lee argues that before the 1930s, asymmetric information between jobseekers and agencies would explain why jobseekers were not in any position to distinguish between abusive (low-quality) agencies and good (high-quality) agencies. Jobseekers could not just pick up the phone to verify the agency's information by calling the fictional employer or some governmental agency. High-quality agencies would have felt pressure to lower their service quality and prices, leading to overall unfavourable conditions for jobseekers.[811] The situation is, therefore, somewhat different and better now. ICT allows us to easily search for alternative service providers, use multiple providers at once, and file complaints more quickly. The industry has also professionalised and adopted professional standards.[812]

245 **The goals of regulation on labour supply services** – Still, despite these improvements, it remains good to know what early regulations on the topic aimed to achieve. The ILO report highlights three goals in particular. Apart from preventing fraudulent and immoral practices, the ILO report claims that initial laws also meant to "provide for rational and economic organisation of the labour market" and implement the principle that services to jobseekers should be free of charge.[813]

246 In terms of achieving a "rational and economic" organisation of the labour market, at the time, the public agencies were entrusted with the task of matching labour supply and demand. The Employment Service Convention, 1948 (No. 88), gave public employment services the "essential duty" to ensure the best possible organisation of the employment market, in cooperation "where necessary" with other public and private bodies. This dynamic in which private agencies were engaged, as appropriate, was part of a "national programme for the achievement and maintenance of full employment and the development and use of productive resources".[814] In other words, the cooperation between private and public agencies was purposive. It had to contribute to this rational and economic organisation of the labour market. Along those lines, public employment services were entrusted with supervising the private agencies under the Revised Fee-Charging Employment Agencies Convention, 1949 (No. 96).[815] However, this cooperation was not without its flaws. It was felt that commercial agencies were, for instance, unwilling to share their vacancies and information on

810. Harris Freeman & George Gonos, *Taming the Employment Sharks: The Case for Regulating Profit-driven Labor Market Intermediaries in High Mobility Labor Markets*, 13 Employee Rights and Employment Policy Journal 285, 295–301 n. 2 (2009).

811. Woong Lee, *Private Deception and the Rise of Public Employment Offices in the United States, 1890–1930* 155, 155 and 159 (David H. Autor ed., *Studies of Labor Market Intermediation*, University of Chicago Press 2009).

812. *E.g.*, World Employment Confederation, *Promoting Fair Recruitment and Employment Practices: Code of Conduct*, Brussels, 2019.

813. ILO, *supra* n. 808, at 11–12.

814. Art. 1 Employment Service Convention, 1948 (No. 88).

815. ILO Committee of Experts on the Application of Conventions and Recommendations, *General Survey Concerning Employment Instruments in Light of the 2008 Declaration on Social Justice for a Fair Globalization* 52 (ILO 2010).

jobseekers with public agencies.[816] Both public and private agencies competed with one another over certain clientele.[817] Due to this "imperfect coordination", the ILO Office used to believe that "fee-charging employment agencies contribute to the existence of casual unemployment which is further accentuated by some of their abusive practices, such as too frequent a change of workers and the supply of posts and workers unsuitable one to another".[818] Moreover, public authorities did not succeed in compiling private agencies' scattered information, hence did not gain a complete picture of the labour market. This frustrated public authorities' "market-regulating roles", and still goes on to this day.[819] For instance, Dobson currently suggests that public services, such as Universal Jobmatch in the UK, scrape and collate individual tasks from different private platforms, "allowing jobseekers to efficiently assess the work currently available across multiple platforms".[820]

The third goal of maintaining a free labour exchange service would morph into a general "principle of free-of-charge" for the public as well as private employment services. One underlying reason has to do with the idea that jobseekers with an attractive profile and a robust social network do not commonly use employment services. These services are usually relied on by workers who struggle to find a job. Consequently, since many of these jobseekers may suffer from limited financial resources, employment services should be kept free of charge, allowing disadvantaged jobseekers to remain actively involved in the labour market. In short, job opportunities should not disappear behind a paywall. 247

The initial regulation's broad scope – Considering these broad principles and aims, it is not surprising for domestic law on labour supply services to seemingly have had a broad scope. The Law and Practice Report of 1932 mentions that "[t]here is a manifest tendency in recent legislative developments to extend the benefit of regulation to all occupations and all classes of labour and employment".[821] Perhaps linked to this, the Governing Body's evaluation of Convention No. 34 in 1948 noted that the original Fee-Charging Employment Agencies (FCEAs) Convention applied very broadly, namely "to all employment agencies which charge a fee in any form whatever for the placing of workers, […]. The definition of agencies conducted with a view to profit is very wide, including not only organised placing services such as employment agencies, but also persons or companies which, though without organised services as such, act as intermediaries between employers and workers".[822] The report does not clarify what is meant by the terms "worker" and "employer". It does mention 248

816. "The sole object of fee-charging employment agencies being profit-making, co-operation with public services which implies communication of information on available vacancies and applicants for employment becomes impossible, since it is precisely in the sale of such information that their business consists". ILO, *supra* n. 808, at 10–11.

817. Sergio Ricca, *Private Temporary Work Organisations and Public Employment Services: Effects and Problems of Coexistence*, 121 International Labour Review 141, 143–144 n. 2 (1982).

818. ILO, *supra* n. 808, at 10–11.

819. ILO, *supra* n. 143, at 51.

820. Ben Dobson, *Gainful Gigging: Employment Services for the Platform Economy* 20 (Reform 2017). *See also*, Marguerita Lane, *Regulating Platform Work in the Digital Age* 13 (OECD 2020).

821. ILO, *supra* n. 808, at 16.

822. ILO, *Report of the Governing Body of the International Labour Office upon the Working of the Convention (No. 34) Concerning Fee-charging Employment Agencies (1933)* 5 (ILO 1948).

how the Convention "applies to all placing activities conducted for profit, whatever the form of the activities or the nature of the organisations conducting them".[823]

249 **The German memorandum** – Along similar lines, a "memorandum"[824] of 1966, sent by the Office to the German Federal Ministry of Labour and Social Affairs, partially explains what was meant by the term "worker" in the Revised Fee-Charging Employment Agencies Convention, 1949 (No. 96). In this case, the German Ministry asked whether the term "worker" in Convention No. 96 only covered manual workers or also salaried employees. The memorandum suggests that the instrument covers both. It relied on the preparatory work of Convention No. 34, which has similar definitions as Convention No. 96. In those working documents, the Conference emphasised how "subject to the exclusion of seamen, 'the item on the agenda comprises within its range all occupations and forms of employment, e.g. industry, agriculture, commerce, domestic service and similar employment, professional occupations, theatrical and similar occupations, etc.'".[825] Furthermore, based on the information received from the ratifying Member States, it would seem "that in practice the term 'worker' has been regarded as applying to all categories of workers and not only to manual workers".[826] According to the Office, there was little reason to interpret the term "worker" narrowly. More generally, the ILO Office of the Legal Adviser's Manual for Drafting ILO Instruments from 2006 refers to this "German memorandum" to substantiate that "on many occasions, it has been emphasized that, if the subject matter of a given instrument is not limited only to employed workers, or the instrument does not provide for any specific exclusion in respect of one or more categories of workers, then 'worker' is understood to cover all workers".[827]

250 **The revised Fee-Charging Convention** – As this German memorandum suggests, the scope of Convention No. 34 and No. 96 is essentially the same; both seemingly had a broad scope. Therefore, what was this revision's aim? The documents on the revision of the original Fee-Charging Employment Agencies Convention indicate that, for instance, the United States wanted commercial agencies to be regulated instead of abolished, with the Employers' group favouring a similar outcome.[828] Most notably, France wanted to, on the other hand, revise the original Convention to make the quasi-absolute prohibition more effective.[829] As it stood, the Workers'

823. *Ibid.*, 5.
824. Although this practice was discontinued in 1983, in the past, this kind of memorandum was officially issued by the ILO Director-General. Memoranda were non-binding and not authoritative. Yet, since they were submitted to the GB and were subsequently published in the ILO's Official Bulletin, they did have value and merit because the Office had to draft them diligently. Jenks mentioned in 1970 that "they are accepted as good sense", in part because the only real "alternative" is to refer the matter to the International Court of Justice. Jenks, *supra* n. 319, at 46; ILO Committee on Standing Orders and the Application of Conventions and Recommendations, *supra* n. 687, at 5; Servais, *supra* n. 660, at 83.
825. ILO International Labour Office, *Memorandum Sent by the International Labour Office to the German Federal Ministry of Labour and Social Affairs*, XLIX ILO Official Bulletin 389, 390 n. 3 (1966).
826. *Ibid.*, 390.
827. ILO Office of the Legal Adviser, *supra* n. 702, at 43.
828. ILO, *Revision of the Fee-Charging Employment Agencies Convention, 1933* 7 (ILO 1948).
829. *Ibid.*, 14.

group and seemingly most Member States still favoured the progressive abolition of commercial agencies. In contrast, the Employers' group and, *inter alia*, New Zealand, Switzerland, the Union of South Africa and the United Kingdom followed the US Government's lead.[830] This discord explains why – contrary to Convention No. 34 – Convention No. 96 provides ratifying Members with the choice to either pursue progressive abolition or regulate the phenomenon.[831] Convention No. 96 reflects pragmatism and a clear preference to develop a broadly ratifiable instrument, offering a valid option for both sides.

Notwithstanding individual Member States' ability to still abolish commercial agencies, some Member States expressed disappointment. For instance, the Belgian Government adviser explained that "[t]he Belgian Government does not wish to take part in voting for a Convention which, in the first place, abandons a principle [of abolition] which was laid down in 1933, and, secondly, introduces an alternative which is very dangerous for the future".[832] The French Government delegate likewise called the revised Convention a "dangerous precedent".[833] The Government advisers of both Argentina and Israel called out the inconsistency between supposedly staying true to the principle that labour is not a commodity and allowing commercial agencies to operate.[834] 251

Despite these critical voices, Convention No. 96's formula has proven largely successful. Among the 23 States for which Convention No. 96 is still in force in 2021, 15 have agreed to abolish commercial agencies progressively. Furthermore, even if a Member State decides to regulate instead of progressively abolish these agencies, Convention No. 96 demands strict regulatory restrictions, such as a yearly renewable licence and fees that are approved by a competent authority. Commercial agencies are, moreover, supposed to be rigorously supervised.[835] According to its critics, Convention No. 96's stringent regulation suppresses private initiative and continues to underpin a monopoly for public employment services.[836] 252

SUBCHAPTER 2. THE RISE OF TEMPORARY WORK AGENCIES

Profit-seeking temporary work agencies – Although Convention No. 96 introduced significant and contentious changes, as its title suggests, it still operates using the concept of a "fee-charging employment agency". By and large, two criteria are essential to frame the scope of its regulations. First, does the agency charge a fee? Secondly, 253

830. *Ibid.*, 15.
831. Report of the Committee on Employment Agencies at the 32nd Session of the International Labour Conference, Geneva, ILO, 1949, 246.
832. *Ibid.*, 247.
833. *Ibid.*, 249.
834. *Ibid.*, 248 and 250.
835. For instance, Belgian correctional courts used to hand down judgments for non-compliance with the legislation on fee-charging placement agencies. André Beirlaen, *De Betekenis van de Conventies van de Internationale Arbeidsorganisatie in de Belgische Rechtssfeer 1919–1969*, II 297 (Centrum voor de studie van de Belgische betrekkingen met de internationale arbeidsorganisatie 1975).
836. ILO, *supra* n. 161, at 70.

if it does, is the agency intent on making a profit or are these fees simply charged to sustain the agency? As a result of this approach, profit-driven temporary work agencies (TWAs), and other more recent for-profit forms of labour market intermediation, came under scrutiny. For example, the Committee of Experts noted as late as 1992 that Argentina, having ratified 1933's Convention No. 34, was obliged to prohibit "'temporary employment enterprises', which appear to act as intermediaries in the recruitment of workers for temporary employment elsewhere", if these temporary employment enterprises are conducted with a view to profit.[837]

254 **The Swedish memorandum** – The question of whether TWAs, which recruit workers for temporary employment elsewhere, need to be prohibited or regulated under the FCEAs Conventions came to a head in the 1960s. Sweden had ratified part II of Convention No. 96, which meant it was supposed to abolish commercial agencies. However, the Government seemingly considered the services of, for instance, ambulatory typewriting agencies useful. Some of these typewriting agencies legally employed the workers and placed them at the disposal of end-users, which instructed the workers on the job and supervised them.[838] Because these kinds of arrangements also raised legal questions at the domestic level,[839] the Government asked the Office to form an opinion on the legality of these agencies under Convention No. 96. The Office did so in what we will call the "Swedish memorandum". Once the Office had checked whether these agencies conducted their services for a profit, it posed itself three questions. First, "[c]an an agency be considered to be a fee-charging employment agency within the meaning of the Convention where no direct contractual relationship is established between the worker and the person or undertaking for whom the services are performed and where there is [instead] a contractual relationship between the agency and the worker?"[840] Secondly, if the answer is affirmative, do the overall circumstances allow us to classify the agencies in question as fee-charging employment agencies? Thirdly, if the answer is again affirmative, what are the implications for Sweden?

255 The Office's answer gave serious consideration to the working documents of the original FCEAs Convention. At the time, the answers of the Member States to the preliminary questionnaire, which had been drafted based on the Conference's discussions in 1932, had led the Office to stress in the working documents that: (i) "it is generally contemplated that the term ' agency' should be used for the purpose of the draft Convention in its widest sense so as to comprise all forms or conditions in which placing operations are engaged in for profit"; and, (ii) that "it may be

837. Observation (CEACR) – adopted 1992, published 79th ILC session (1992), Fee-Charging Employment Agencies Convention, 1933 (No. 34) – Argentina (Ratification: 1950); Observation (CEACR) – adopted 1995, published 83rd ILC session (1996), Fee-Charging Employment Agencies Convention, 1933 (No. 34) – Argentina (Ratification: 1950).

838. ILO International Labour Office, *Memorandum Sent by the International Labour Office to the Ministry of Health and Social Affairs of Sweden*, XLIX ILO Official Bulletin 390, 391 n. 3 (1966).

839. "[T]he Supreme Court of Justice of Sweden had ruled in 1962 that agencies known as 'ambulatory typewriting agencies' were employment agencies within the scope of this legislation, which prohibits the carrying out of placing services by private persons for purposes of gain". *Ibid.*, 391 and 392.

840. *Ibid.*, 392.

taken to be implicit that all methods which are employed for this purpose should be covered by the draft Convention".[841] These and other documents, so argued the Office in 1966, would suggest the application of Convention No. 96 depends on "the actual nature of the transaction, rather than its form".[842] According to the Office, this idea of "nature over form" also shimmers through, for instance, in some of the Committee of Experts' clarifications from the 1950s and 1960s. This was, most notably, the case when the Committee clarified that labour contractors "whose activities consist in supplying workers for undertakings while generally remaining the formal employers of these workers"[843] fall within the scope of Convention No. 96.[844]

In view of these and other considerations, the Office concluded that "the Convention can apply to cases in which a contractual relationship is established between the worker and an agency, and not between the worker and the person or undertaking at whose disposal he is placed by that agency, the essential test being the nature of the transaction".[845] With regard to its second question, the Office observed that the primary purpose of many ambulatory typewriting agencies was to supply labour. "It would thus appear to be legitimate to conclude that the agency which places the worker at the disposal of the third party 'acts as an intermediary for the purpose of procuring employment for a worker or supplying a worker for an employer'".[846] Such ambulatory typewriting agencies are FCEAs. Therefore, in response to its third question, the Office reiterated that given Sweden's choice to ratify part II of the Convention, these agencies should be progressively abolished unless they fulfil the conditions for an exemption under Article 5 of Convention No. 96. 256

TWAs take on two roles: Employer and broker – The Swedish memorandum and the subsequent backlash it received illustrates how during the 1960s and 1970s, at least in European countries, the discussion was very much alive about whether TWAs should be abolished or regulated. The memorandum became an important reference point. In particular, because the ILO Committee of Experts relied on it as "the basis for its 'jurisprudence' on the subject".[847] As such, following the Office's memorandum, the Committee echoed that both "interim work enterprises" and "temporary work agencies" fall within the scope of Convention No. 96.[848] Member 257

841. *Ibid.*, 393.
842. *Ibid.*, 394.
843. *Ibid.*
844. ILO Committee of Experts on the Application of Conventions and Recommendations, *Report III (Part IV) Report of the Committee of Experts on the Application of Conventions and Recommendations* 75 (ILO 1955); ILO Committee of Experts on the Application of Conventions and Recommendations, *Report III (Part IV) Report of the Committee of Experts on the Application of Conventions and Recommendations* 55 (ILO 1959); ILO Committee of Experts on the Application of Conventions and Recommendations, *Report III (Part IV) Report of the Committee of Experts on the Application of Conventions and Recommendations* 127 (ILO 1962).
845. ILO International Labour Office, *supra* n. 838, at 394.
846. *Ibid.*
847. Direct Request (CEACR) – adopted 1995, published 82nd ILC session (1995), Fee-Charging Employment Agencies Convention (Revised), 1949 (No. 96) – Côte d'Ivoire (Ratification: 1992).
848. Direct Request (CEACR) – adopted 1995, published 82nd ILC session (1995), Fee-Charging Employment Agencies Convention (Revised), 1949 (No. 96) – Spain (Ratification: 1971); *Ibid.*

States that have ratified Convention No. 96 need to either abolish or regulate these entities, depending on their overall commitment.

258 Notably, some external legal scholars openly criticised the Office's initial memorandum. These scholars argued that the supply of temporary workers, with an agency that legally employs them, was "quite different" from traditional placement, as regulated by Convention No. 96. In the case of placement, the relationship between the agency and the jobseeker ends once a "work contract" is established between the jobseeker and the employer. Instead, in the case of TWAs, the relationship between the worker and agency is maintained, also when the worker is at the disposal of an end-user. This user is, moreover, not a party to any work contract between the agency and worker.[849] Hence, from a legal point of view, placement and agency work are very different. Similar discord arose at the domestic level. For example, in Belgium, Blanpain seemingly argued that temporary work agencies should be distinguished from placement agencies,[850] whereas Rigaux seemed to agree with the rationale behind the Office's decision (i.e. nature over form).[851]

259 In light of these disagreements, the chief of the ILO's International Labour Standards Department publicly defended the Swedish memorandum. According to Valticos, the actual nature of the transaction mattered rather than its legal form. Economists, for instance, consider TWAs to engage in labour market intermediation.[852] On the one hand, these agencies provide firms with readily employable pre-screened workers, and, on the other, they offer almost immediate employment for many jobseekers due to their semi-permanent relationships with user enterprises. For such reasons, the ILO's chief Legal Officer recapped in 1973 that: "as regards the scope of Convention No. 96, the opinion given in 1965 seems to follow necessarily both from the actual wording of the Convention and from the social purpose underlying its formulation. After all, the interpretation of an instrument should not be purely an exercise in intellectual ingenuity, with the attendant dangers that too much importance will be attached to a legal fiction and reality lost sight of".[853]

260 In this entire debate, two different logics seemed to be at odds with one another. Labour law scholars attributed significant importance to the agency's status as the jobseeker's legal employer, and the factual differences between traditional placement and the supply of temporary workers; therefore, the regulation on placement should not apply to TWAs.[854] In contrast, other scholars were reluctant to subject the laws

849. Gerhard Schnorr, *Le Travail Temporaire*, Cahier de Droit Européen 131, 132–135 (1973); G. M. J. Veldkamp & M. J. E. H. Raetsen, *Temporary Work Agencies and Western European Social Legislation*, 107 International Labour Review 117, 122 n. 2 (1973); G. H. Camerlynck, *Approaches to Temporary Work. Legal Sources. Definitions and Possible Channels* 443, 465–467 (W. Albeda, R. Blanpain & G. M. J. Veldkamp eds., *Temporary Work in Modern Society*, I, Kluwer 1978).

850. Roger Blanpain, *De Tijdelijke Arbeid*, 36 Rechtskundig Weekblad 509, 511 n. 11 (1972).

851. Marc Rigaux, *De Problematiek van de Uitzendarbeid*, Tijdschrift Sociaal Recht / Revue du Droit Social 57, 73 n. 2 (1976).

852. David H. Autor, *supra* n. 126, at 14–21.

853. Nicolas Valticos, *Temporary Work Agencies and International Labour Standards*, 107 International Labour Review 43, 50 n. 1 (1973).

854. These views may also have been influenced by a desire to legitimise these services, despite a public monopoly on employment services that was still in vogue in many European countries

governing labour supply to the binary logic of labour law. Whether the employment relationship is established between the worker and user or between the worker and agency, ultimately, these services fulfil a similar function in the labour market. Consequently, the laws governing labour supply should transcend the "legal fiction" created by temporary work agencies, namely that they are the legal employer instead of the user (e.g. Canada).[855] Many contemporary labour law scholars seem to have, likewise, become more sceptical in this respect. For instance, Theron explicitly calls the idea that the temporary work agency is an employer a legal fiction; as he states, the agency "is in fact an intermediary".[856] Also, in Europe, where these agencies are generally designated as the legal employer, scholars recognise the artificiality of current regulations on temporary agency work.[857]

To this extent, as the legal configuration of agency work is all but self-evident, it should be stressed that the designation of these agencies as workers' sole legal employer largely occurred on purpose. As explained by Freeman and Gonos, "[w]inning employer status for temp agencies was literally the key to success for the emerging temp industry".[858] This development was not only instrumental to their image as socially just enterprises, as mentioned before, it also provided one of the main arguments for why these agencies did not have to comply with the (stringent) regulation on 261

at the time.

855. For instance, in Canada, the decision over whether the agency or user is the "employer" of the worker used to depend on which entity "exercises 'fundamental control'". This is often considered to be the user. Guy Davidov, *Joint Employer Status in Triangular Employment Relationships*, 42 British Journal of Industrial Relations 727, 733–734 n. 4 (2004). Doorey summarised the situation as followed in 2009. "What's interesting in these cases is that almost invariably the placement agency and the client attempt to define the workers as employees of the placement agency, but those attempts are mostly ignored by the Board. [...] So, HR managers, don't assume that temp workers are not your employees just because you don't intend them to be, or a contract says so". David Doorey, *Who is the Employer of Temp Workers?*, Canadian LAW OF WORK Forum (27 October 2009), https://lawofwork.ca/who-is-the-employer-of-temp-workers/.

856. "The notion of the [temporary employment services provider] as employer, on the face of it, seems far-fetched and contrived". Jan Theron, *Intermediary or Employer – Labour Brokers and the Triangular Employment Relationship*, 26 Industrial Law Journal 618, 621 and 641 n. 4 (2005). *See also*, Nastazja Potocka-Sionek, *The Changing Nature of Labour Intermediation. Do Algorithms Redefine Temporary Agency Work?* 169, 175 (Jerzy Wratny & Agata Ludera-Ruszel eds., *News Forms of Employment: Current Problems and Future Challenges*, Springer 2020).

857. For example, McGaughey has argued that an agency worker is often both the employee of the agency and the end-user. Ratti presents the situation as if both the agency and user operate "a single employing entity". Luca Ratti, *Agency Work and the Idea of Dual Employership: A Comparative Perspective*, 30 Comparative Labor Law & Policy Journal 835, 873 n. 4 (2009); Ewan McGaughey, *Should Agency Workers be Treated Differently?* 33 (London School of Economics and Political Science 2010). Outside of Europe: Katherine Hannan Wears & Sandra L. Fisher, *Who is an Employer in the Triangular Employment Relationship? Sorting Through the Definitional Confusion*, 24 Employee Responsibilities and Rights Journal 159, 159–176 n. 3 (2012); Elsa Underhill, *Should Host Employers Have Greater Responsibility for Temporary Agency Workers' Employment Rights?*, 48 Asia Pacific Journal of Human Resources 338, 339 n. 3 (2010).

858. Harris Freeman & George Gonos, *Regulating the Employment Sharks: Reconceptualizing the Legal Status of the Commercial Temp Agency*, 8 Working USA 293, 300 n. 3 (2005). *See also*, George Gonos, *The Contest over 'Employment Status' in the Post-War United States: The Case of Temporary Help Firms*, 31 Law and Society Review 81, 81–110 n. 1 (1997).

placement agencies.[859] Furthermore, the establishment of a more profound relationship between the worker and agency also had its commercial benefits. Compared to placement agencies, the pre-established relationship between the worker and temporary work agency resulted in pre-screened workers. As such, these workers were readily available to be matched to an end-user.[860] The end-user had less or no work screening, selecting and contracting the agency worker. The direct contractual relationship between the user and the placement agency's jobseeker felt like a burden in comparison. Moreover, beyond the ease of onboarding a pre-employed worker, another benefit for the end-user was that the agency's status as the employer of record enabled user enterprises to frame temporary agency workers as a separate unit within their workforce. This distinction between a user's personal employees and external agency workers made it possible for users to provide these agency workers with a more limited set of rights. For instance, agency workers may lose out on the fringe benefits which users' regular employees receive.[861]

262 Of course, in time, policymakers in many countries have reacted by providing agency workers with a right to equal treatment in terms of pay and other basic working conditions. The aim is to ensure that agency workers' basic work and employment conditions are the same as those of the users' direct employees. However, this is essentially an *ex-post* measure to remedy a prior decision that has introduced a situation of inequality between agency workers and regular employees. By linking agency workers to a different legal employer, the gap between agency workers and the users' employees was created by law. Although it is very valuable, the right to equal treatment for agency workers can hardly be expected to remedy this inequality completely.[862] Moreover, in countries where agency workers do not enjoy equal treatment in practice,[863] agency workers remain "second-class workers" within the user's overall workforce.[864] As a result, the employment relationship between the worker and agency, in fact, continues to present a commercial asset for the agency.[865] It is advantageous for the agency to become the legal employer if this boosts the end-user's interest in its employment services (also see *supra* nos. 75–78). Therefore, Valticos was quite right. The agency's legal fiction as the jobseeker's employer should not blind us from what is happening underneath.

859. *Ibid.*, 301.

860. Autor, *supra* n. 126, at 16.

861. Consider in this respect how it became clear during the discussions on the regulation of temporary agency work at the EU level, that the Employers were not willing to accept that temporary agency workers would be treated "on an equal footing with staff in the user company". Ratti, *supra* n. 857, at 870. For an elaborate overview: Vosko, *supra* n. 787, at 400–404.

862. The right to equal treatment for agency workers is not always effective. *See, e.g.*, ILO, *supra* n. 595, at 254–255; Matthew Taylor, Greg Marsh, Diane Nicol & Paul Broadbent, *Good Work: The Taylor Review of Modern Working Practices* 47–48 and 58–59 (2017).

863. *E.g.*, Laura Padin & Maya Pinto, *Lasting Solutions for America's Temporary Workers* (NELP 2019).

864. Olaf Deinert, *Equal Treatment as a Problem: Germany and Agency Work* 25, 31 (Edoardo Ales, Olaf Deinert & Jeff Kenner eds., *Core and Contingent Work in the European Union: A Comparative Analysis*, Hart Publishing 2017).

865. Eklund described this point aptly, "the provider offers two kinds of services: recruitment services and legal responsibility as an employer". Ronnie Eklund, *A Look at Contract Labour in the Nordic Countries*, 18 Comparative Labor Law & Policy Journal 229, 242 n. 2 (1997).

A legal fiction – Regulating temporary agency work by constructing an employment relationship with the agency and imposing a duty of equal treatment in relation to the user's employees was a clear choice.[866] These days, human resources firms, such as Randstad, Adecco and Manpower, will provide factual "employers" with their preferred solution. Whether the employer/user enterprise wants the HR firm to search for a candidate for a bilateral employment contract, search for a professional freelancer, or wants the HR firm to serve as a TWA, thereby employing the worker, unless restricted by law, it is probably possible. From the HR firm's perspective, the last option is simply an alternative way to supply the end-user with the desired workers. And, in hindsight, it has proven to be a very successful one.[867] 263

By extension, as it regards the platform economy, for instance, the Adecco Group has developed two platforms: Adia and YOSS. Adia is a platform that allows enterprises to hire employed temporary agency workers. YOSS, on the other hand, allows enterprises to engage freelancers.[868] Randstad, in turn, seems likewise to have invested resources into developing Ploy and Randstad Go. Both platforms aid businesses that are on the lookout for temporary agency workers. A third Randstad-related platform is called YoungOnes. This enables freelancers to be matched to businesses.[869] In other words, as these examples show, HR conglomerates can be expected to develop digital alternatives to their existing services. As Adia and Randstad Go illustrate, established HR firms could be expected to willingly comply with the relevant regulations on agency work and placement services, even in the digital realm. One reason is that they are members of the World Employment Confederation, which represents private employment agencies at the global level. The Confederation's message is that platform operators offering similar services to their members need to comply with the same regulations.[870] Such messaging is only effective as long as Randstad, Adecco, and others continue to abide by the rules themselves. 264

At the same time, if comparable platform operators continue to skirt regulations, these established employment agencies find themselves between a rock and a hard place. So far, it has enticed them to simultaneously develop platforms such as YoungOnes 265

866. The Private Employment Agencies Convention, 1997 (No. 181), "was amongst the most controversial regulations introduced in the 1990s because it defined workers in triangular employment relationships as employees of private employment agencies whose services consist of making workers available to a third party responsible for assigning specific tasks and for direct supervision [...]". Vosko, *supra* n. 198, at 174.

867. Research in the United States indicates that in 2010, temporary help services accounted for 77 per cent of employment in the staffing services sector, professional employer organisations for 15 per cent, and employment agencies for 9 per cent. Only the latter kind of agencies do not employ the worker. Matthew Dey, Susan N. Houseman & Anne E. Polivka, *Manufacturers' Outsourcing to Staffing Services*, 65 Industrial & Labor Relations Review 533, 535 n. 3 2012.

868. Lenaerts et al., *supra* n. 56, at 6.

869. Commissie Platformeconomie en Werk, *Hoe Werkt de Platformeconomie?* 20 (Sociaal-Economische Raad 2020).

870. World Employment Confederation & UNI Global, *Joint Recommendations of the EU Sectoral Social Partners for Temporary Agency Work: Online Talent Platforms, Labour Market Intermediaries and the Changing World of Work* (WEC 2018); World Employment Confederation, *A Decent Level Playing Field for Platform Work: Policy Recommendations for Sustainable Growth of Platform Work and the Provision of Quality Online Talent Platform Services* (WEC 2020).

and YOSS; both connect businesses to freelancers. However, in light of what was described above, it might prove challenging to force platform operators that have no prior history as a TWA to abide by the same rules (e.g. Uber Works).[871] A first reason is that, from the operator's point of view, the legal incentives to establish an employment relationship between the agency/platform and the worker have mostly disappeared. Placement services are no longer as stringently regulated as in the past; a platform operator may well prefer being classified as a placement agency rather than a temporary work agency. In other words, the decision of TWAs to employ jobseekers might have been a child of its time; contemporary platform operators may be far more reluctant. Additionally, as long as businesses, such as restaurants or supermarkets, can rely on a self-employed platform worker without suffering the risk of being considered the worker's legal employer (e.g. Instacart, Deliveroo, etc., *supra* no. 94), why would these businesses bother relying on temporary agency workers instead. Thirdly, there are also practical reasons why platform operators may be less inclined to establish an employment relationship with their workers. Platforms have reduced transaction costs (*supra* no. 83); arguably, compared to traditional placement services, their automated systems made it far less cumbersome for businesses to conclude a contract for services with the platform worker directly. From the point of view of the user enterprise, that, too, diminishes the relative attractiveness of relying on a TWA that pre-employs the worker. In summary, both the legal and practical incentives to turn to employed agency workers seem to have been reduced. Hence, in light of these new circumstances, it seems unlikely that the temporary staffing industry will easily succeed in forcing platform operators to abide by their rules (also see *infra* nos. 302–306).

SUBCHAPTER 3. THE PRIVATE EMPLOYMENT AGENCIES CONVENTION

1. The Convention's Object and Purpose

266 **Setting the scene** – The regulatory object of the Private Employment Agencies Convention, 1997 (No. 181), is no longer the "fee-charging employment agency" but the "private employment agency". The focus on fee-charging and the commercial goals of the agency became less pronounced. According to Convention No. 181's preamble, a new instrument had to be adopted, "[c]onsidering the very different environment in which private employment agencies operate, when compared to the conditions prevailing when the above-mentioned Convention [No. 96] was adopted", considering the "importance of flexibility in the functioning of labour markets" and considering "the role which private employment agencies may play in a well-functioning labour market".[872] The new instrument was meant to give private employment agencies (PrEAs) the space needed to develop their services, even if policymakers should not neglect "the need to protect workers against abuses".[873]

871. Earlier we referred to how Uber was planning to enter the staffing industry (*supra* no. 64).
872. Preamble Private Employment Agencies Convention, 1997 (No. 181).
873. *Ibid.*

The preamble mentions some critical contextual factors, most importantly, ILO constituents' more positive attitude towards PrEAs. Nevertheless, some of the main reasons for adopting Convention No. 181 do not feature in the preamble. Several Member States had, for example, been frustrated by the Director-General's and Committee of Experts' views on temporary agency work and Convention No. 34 and No. 96. These Member States happily resorted to "the opinion of an influential school of jurists" to argue the contrary.[874] By 1994, Member States frequently carved out exemptions in national legislation on agencies to allow these TWAs to operate. Countries such as Australia, Switzerland, the United Kingdom and the United States, more broadly, exerted limited supervision over private employment services.[875] Furthermore, in addition to TWAs, other private agencies also claimed that they did not function as a typical employment mediator/placement agency.[876] Hence, they should not be prohibited either. A fine example of this arose in front of the Belgian *Cour de cassation* in 2002. The client of an agency had refused to pay for the agency's services. The client argued in court that this refusal was justified because the agency was an illegal employment mediator. The *Cour de cassation*, however, accepted the agency's defence. According to the agency, it was just a "selection agency" and not a placement agency. By carrying out activities to advise a client on the suitability of candidates, the agency did not genuinely match workers and employers; hence, its services were allowed.[877] The example illustrates how the scope of Convention No. 96, which was implemented under Belgian law, was also bypassed by agencies other than TWAs.[878] 267

Because of these developments, among others, it was clear that the FCEAs Conventions were becoming outdated. Multiple Member States even started to avail themselves of the possibility of denouncing Convention No. 96.[879] The ILO had to act. Efforts to put temporary agency work on the Conference's agenda as a separate topic had failed during the 1980s and 1990s. Instead, the organisation managed to arrange a general discussion on PrEAs, which could then include debates on TWAs.[880] Following the green light by the Governing Body, 1994's Law and Practice Report defined PrEAs as "service enterprises under private law which undertake, under contract and in exchange for financial compensation (a fee or subsidy), operations on behalf of individual clients or client enterprises with the aim of easing or speeding up access to employment or career progression or filling a vacancy".[881] The Office initially thought that both Convention No. 88 on public employment services and Convention No. 96 on FCEAs had to be replaced by a single, holistic standard. This new Convention 268

874. ILO, *supra* n. 143, at 1.
875. ILO, *supra* n. 161, at 3-4.
876. ILO, *supra* n. 143, at 46-47.
877. Cour de cassation: Case No. C.98.0125.N, *Wig Industrieinstandhaltung GmbH & Co. Benelux K.G. v. Cesba*, 17 January 2002.
878. ILO research described these types of service providers as "agencies with a contractual relationship in the form of performance of a service other than placement in the strict sense of the term". ILO, *supra* n. 143, at 12.
879. *Ibid.*, 46.
880. *Ibid.*, 3.
881. *Ibid.*, 11.

would implement a "shared labour market management" approach,[882] drawing on the strengths of both public and private employment services. This new instrument could, moreover, link up to existing standards on Member States' broader employment policy.[883] Despite this suggestion, however, it became clear during 1994's Conference discussions that the Workers' group, in particular, wanted only to revise Convention No. 96. They merely sought to deal with the growth in and diversification of PrEAs.[884] Since the Employers' group also expressed continued support for Convention No. 88,[885] the initially proposed revision of public employment services was taken off the table.

269 **1994's conclusions** – The discussions from 1994 led to the so-called "conclusions concerning the role of private employment agencies in the function of labour markets". The following statements were adopted both by the Committee on Private Employment Agencies and the General Conference [emphasis added]:

> "The Committee also found that there was still *total consent on the fundamental principle,* laid down in the Constitution of the International Labour Organization, that *labour is not a commodity* and that the freedom of jobseekers to search for jobs and the right for employers to take decisions concerning the recruitment of workers were fundamental elements in free market and mixed economies".[886]

> "The Committee acknowledged the fact that there were numerous *concerns regarding the ethics of PREA,* and that PREA were sometimes singled out for poor practices in relation to the interests of workers and jobseekers. During the Committee's deliberations this perception was frequently directed at temporary work agencies (TWAs). Whatever the circumstances, the behaviour of PREA called for rules to prevent or discourage them from engaging in conduct or practices that undermined workers' rights, be they in the areas of wages, general conditions of work, industrial relations or safety and health".[887]

> "The general approach that the Committee supported was for governments to adopt *a pragmatic attitude concerning the regulation of PREA.* Governments should rely on the laws and rules in force, whenever possible, before considering specific regulations".[888]

> "The overt objective of *Convention No. 96* was either to ban PREA or to place them under tight supervision by government authorities. As suggested in the preceding sections of this document, the Committee believed that *all these principles, except the one referred to in paragraph 53 below, no longer corresponded to today's reality* in modern labour markets. [...] **53.** The Committee believed however that one

882. "Shared management is a system by which the management of a market is organized under the influence of two institutions: public service institutions and, in particular, the public employment service; and private employment agencies, especially for-profit firms". *Ibid.*, 60.
883. *Ibid.*, 70.
884. Report of the Committee on Private Employment Agencies at the 81st Session of the International Labour Conference, Geneva, ILO, 1994, 21/16 and 21/18.
885. Vosko, *supra* n. 793, at 56.
886. Conclusions concerning the role of private employment agencies in the functioning of labour markets, 81st Session of the International Labour Conference in 1994, 21/23.
887. *Ibid.*, 21/28.
888. *Ibid.*, 21/29.

provision contained in Convention No. 96 should be maintained, namely that concerning the payment of services offered by PREA. It was indeed *essential to recall* that, with very few exceptions such as services provided to high-level professionals and executives, the Committee remained in favour of *the principle that fees should not be charged to the jobseeker*".[889]

Based on these conclusions, the GB decided to place an "item concerning the revision of the Fee-Charging Employment Agencies Convention (Revised), 1949 (No. 96)" on the agenda of 1997's ILC. The Law and Practice Report that preceded the Conference's single-discussion proceedings clarifies that PrEAs aim to provide an "employment service" on the labour market: "the feature that binds all PREA is that providing employment is their main aim or at least part of their secondary activities".[890] In terms of the goals of the new instrument, the Law and Practice Report indicated that it should: (i) protect workers and employers against abuse; (ii) acknowledge private agencies' contribution; (iii) achieve "an improvement in the functioning of labour markets";[891] and, (iv) achieve efficient cooperation between private agencies and the public employment services.[892] According to the Office's report, the instrument should, furthermore, allow enough space for the Member States to modify their legal framework, taking into account the level of development of their domestic labour market. If a country's labour market is not very developed with severe risks of abuse, a strict licensing system might be appropriate. "However, in a competitive market at the peak of development, [PrEAs] might be left more or less to regulate themselves".[893] At the end of 1997's Committee proceedings, when the Reporter of the Committee on the Revision of Convention No. 96 presented the draft instruments to the General Conference, the Reporter stated that the Member States had started to allow private employment agencies, including TWAs, to operate from the 1960s onwards. "It, therefore, became necessary for many governments to protect from exploitation the most vulnerable workers who were being placed by these agencies".[894] Sims claims along similar lines that "protecting workers in complex arrangements, such as subcontracting, which make them more susceptible to poor working conditions" was one of the "main objectives" of Convention No. 181.[895] 270

Extending the scope of labour supply regulation? – Clearly, the instruments on PrEAs also wanted to accommodate the overall diversification of employment services and satisfactorily deal with TWAs. Replying to the questions of governments, the ILO Legal Adviser stated in front of the standard-setting committee that "if TWA were not included, the proposed revised Convention would lose much of its raison d'être 271

889. *Ibid.*, 21/31.
890. ILO, *supra* n. 161, at 25.
891. ILO, *Report IV (2) Revision of the Fee-Charging Employment Agencies Convention (Revised), 1949 (No. 96)* 17 (ILO 1997).
892. ILO, *supra* n. 161, at 71–72.
893. *Ibid.*, 73.
894. Report of the Committee on the Revision of Convention No. 96 at the 85th Session of the International Labour Conference, Geneva, ILO, 1997, 267.
895. E. Sims, *Employment Policy* 195, 212 (Jean-Claude Javillier ed., *International Labour Standards: A Global Approach: 75th Anniversary of the Committee of Experts on the Application of Conventions and Recommendations*, ILO 2002).

because it would address only the private placement agencies".[896] Also, the Reporter of the Committee admitted in front of the General Conference that the inclusion of TWAs in the scope of the instrument saw itself "reflected" in Article 1 of Convention No. 181.[897] The Employer Vice-Chairperson, in turn, claimed that Convention No. 181 extends Convention No. 96's scope "very considerably" not only by taking on TWAs but also with regard to "other activities undertaken by private employment agencies".[898] In other words, one feature of Convention No. 181 is that it supposedly extends the scope of the FCEAs Conventions. However, the question remains, does this supposedly extended scope cover platform workers?

2. The Convention's Scope

The definitions in the Private Employment Agencies Convention, 1997 (No. 181):

> "Article 1
>
> 1. For the purpose of this Convention the term **private employment agency** means any natural or legal person, independent of the public authorities, which provides one or more of the following labour market services:
> (a) services for matching offers of and applications for employment, without the private employment agency becoming a party to the employment relationships which may arise therefrom;
> (b) services consisting of employing workers with a view to making them available to a third party, who may be a natural or legal person (referred to below as a "user enterprise") which assigns their tasks and supervises the execution of these tasks;
> (c) other services relating to jobseeking, determined by the competent authority after consulting the most representative employers and workers organizations, such as the provision of information, that do not set out to match specific offers of and applications for employment.
>
> 2. For the purpose of this Convention, the term **workers** includes jobseekers.
>
> 3. For the purpose of this Convention, the term **processing of personal data** *of workers* means the collection, storage, combination, communication or any other use of information related to an identified or identifiable worker.
>
> Article 2
>
> 1. This Convention applies to all private employment agencies.
>
> 2. This Convention applies to all categories of workers and all branches of economic activity. It does not apply to the recruitment and placement of seafarers.
>
> 3. One purpose of this Convention is to allow the operation of private employment agencies as well as the protection of the workers using their services, within the framework of its provisions.

896. Report of the Committee on the Revision of Convention No. 96 at the 85th Session of the International Labour Conference, Geneva, ILO, 1997, 16/5.
897. Report of the Committee on the Revision of Convention No. 96 at the 85th Session of the International Labour Conference, Geneva, ILO, 1997, 268.
898. *Ibid.*, 269.

4. After consulting the most representative organizations of employers and workers concerned, a Member may:
(a) prohibit, under specific circumstances, private employment agencies from operating in respect of certain categories of workers or branches of economic activity in the provision of one or more of the services referred to in Article 1, paragraph 1;
(b) exclude, under specific circumstances, workers in certain branches of economic activity, or parts thereof, from the scope of the Convention or from certain of its provisions, provided that adequate protection is otherwise assured for the workers concerned.

5. A Member which ratifies this Convention shall specify, in its reports under article 22 of the Constitution of the International Labour Organization, any prohibition or exclusion of which it avails itself under paragraph 4 above, and give the reasons therefor".

The term: Private employment agency – Considering the progression from Convention 272
No. 96 to Convention No. 181, arguably the principal description of a PrEA remains provided for in Article 1(1)(a), which interrelates with Article 1(1)(c). As such, whereas Convention No. 96 described commercial agencies as "any person, company, institution, agency or other organisation which acts as an intermediary for the purpose of procuring employment for a worker or supplying a worker for an employer" with a view to profit, Convention No. 181 describes PrEAs of type 1(1)(a) as "any natural or legal person, independent of the public authorities, which provides [...] (a) services for matching offers of and applications for employment, without the private employment agency becoming a party to the employment relationships which may arise therefrom". Instead of "procuring employment for a worker" or "supplying a worker for an employer" like a FCEA, a PrEA of type 1(1)(a) now provides "services for matching offers of and applications for employment". The similarly authoritative French text of the Convention seems to be even a little broader. It reads "*services visant à rapprocher offres et demandes d'emploi*", which means services "aimed at" matching offers and applications for employment.[899] For instance, selection advice could be considered to "aim" at matching offers of and applications for employment. Although this is not entirely clear, perhaps a transition took place from a concept of employment intermediation in a strict sense to employment intermediation in the broader sense of the word. The Flemish Decree that implemented Convention No. 181, for example, does not leave much room for doubt. If an intermediary provides services with a view to helping workers find a new job or helping employers look for suitable workers, the intermediary is an employment mediator in the sense of Article 1(1)(a) of Convention No. 181.[900]

Compared to Article 1(1)(a) of Convention No. 181, which resembles Convention No. 273
96's definition, Article 1(1)(b)'s definition is more of an outlier. Employment services of type 1(1)(b) presuppose "employing workers with a view to making them available to a third party, who may be a natural or legal person (referred to below as a 'user

899. Arts. 1 et 24 Convention sur les agences d'emploi privées, 1997 (No. 181).
900. Décret du 10 decembre 2010 relatif au placement privé / decreet 10 december 2010 betreffende de private arbeidsbemiddeling.

enterprise') which assigns their tasks and supervises the execution of these tasks". As mentioned and illustrated by this description, TWAs indeed shaped the structure and content of Article 1. However, not all agencies of type 1(1)(b) are necessarily temporary work agencies. The Committee of Experts also mentions leasing agencies, job shops, career management agencies and employment enterprises.[901] Art. 1(1)(b) includes but is, hence, not necessarily limited to TWAs. The three main criteria for an agency of type 1(1)(b) are an employment relationship between the worker and agency, an aim to put the worker at the disposal of third parties, and a third party that instructs and supervises the worker.

274 **The meaning of employment** – As discussed at length in earlier Subchapters, the Vienna Convention demands the interpretation of a treaty to be conducted in good faith with the ordinary meaning to be given to its terms. The "Swedish memorandum", which was mentioned in the discussion on Convention No. 96, relied on the *Oxford English Dictionary* and *Black's Law Dictionary* to sketch the ordinary meaning of "employ" and "employment".[902] A similar exercise is again relevant for Convention No. 181 to portray the ordinary meaning of the word "employment" in Article 1(1)(a). When trying to settle whether platforms can be considered PrEAs, the main issue is not whether the platform intermediates between jobseekers and users. Many platforms do this (*supra* nos. 58–60). Instead, the question is whether the Convention only regulates intermediation that results in employment contracts or also applies if these "job-matching services"[903] bring about a contract for personal services? The following clues need to be considered in this respect.

275 **The ordinary meaning of the words** – First, determining the ordinary meaning of the word "employment" is a confusing exercise. As Gardiner mentions, "there is commonly no single 'ordinary' meaning of a word and thus there is the need for a direct link to the context and the treaty's object and purpose".[904] The Office had stated in its Swedish memorandum that the fact that no employment relationship existed between the jobseeker and the agency's user, but instead between the jobseeker and the agency, did not preclude these ambulatory typewriting agencies from being considered FCEAs. In the Office's view, they still procure "employment" for the user. This reasoning was based, among other things, on the fact that "[t]he Oxford English Dictionary defines the words 'employ' and 'employment' to mean 'use the services of a person in a professional capacity or in a transaction of some special business' as well as 'have or maintain [a person] in one's service'".[905] Since *Black's Law Dictionary* gave a similar description, the ordinary meaning of the word employment allowed the TWA construction to fall within Convention No. 96's scope. Regarding the ordinary meaning of the word employment in Convention No. 181, given the context and object of the treaty, the use of law dictionaries seems more

901. ILO Committee of Experts on the Application of Conventions and Recommendations, *supra* n. 815, at 75.
902. ILO International Labour Office, *supra* n. 838, at 392.
903. This is the term used by the Committee of Experts in its general survey. ILO Committee of Experts on the Application of Conventions and Recommendations, *supra* n. 815, at 74.
904. Richard Gardiner, *supra* n. 694, at 465.
905. ILO International Labour Office, *supra* n. 838, at 392.

appropriate than reliance on regular ones.[906] *Ballentine's Law Dictionary* provides the following description of employment: "[t]he act of employing or being employed. The occupation, business, or profession to which one devotes his services, time, and attention, and which he depends upon for livelihood or profit".[907] *Black's Law Dictionary* clarifies that it concerns "[t]he quality, state, or condition of being employed; the condition of having a paying job".[908] As stated, the relevant part of the French text clarifies that agencies of type 1(1)(a) provide "*des services visant à rapprocher offres et demandes d'emploi*". Again, the word *emploi* does not require an employment contract. For instance, the *Dictionnaire juridique* by Puigelier et al. defines "*emploi*" as "*fonction, activité, poste*".[909] Based on these descriptions, it is possible to conclude that the word employment, in and of itself, as the Office observed decades ago, does not necessarily require the jobseeker to be employed in the legal capacity of the user enterprise's employee.[910]

Second subclause of Article 1(1)(a) – What makes things more complicated regarding 276
the meaning of "employment" in the first subclause of Article 1(1)(a), however, is the reference to "employment relationships" in the second subclause. An agency of type 1(1)(a) provides job-matching services "without the private employment agency becoming a party to the employment relationships which may arise therefrom". This reference to "employment relationships" is new compared to Convention No. 96, and, according to some of the law dictionaries, it does imply the state of being/becoming an employee.[911] Indeed, at least for labour lawyers, the notion of an employment relationship suggests a relationship that is underpinned by an employment contract. Therefore, we need to verify what the purpose of this second subclause is. Are scholars

906. The ordinary meaning of the word "employment" does not so much require us to understand how a layman would interpret the word. It is more appropriate to rely on the ordinary meaning of the word among those who actually use the instrument, i.e. legal practitioners.
907. *Ballentine's Law Dictionary*, 3rd edition, 2010 (accessed on LexisNexis).
908. *Black's Law Dictionary*, 11th edition, 2019 (accessed on Westlaw).
909. Catherine Puigelier, Jean-Louis Hérin & Jeanne Tillhet-Pretnar, *Dictionnaire Juridique* 372 (Bruylant 2017).
910. Besides, according to standard dictionaries, "employment" means having paid work or a paid job without necessarily implying an employment contract. For example, the *Cambridge Dictionary* defines employment as "regular paid work" or "the condition of having paid work". Available at: https://dictionary.cambridge.org/dictionary/english-french/employment. Lexico, which is powered by the University of Oxford, similarly mentions "the state of having paid work", "the action of giving work to someone" and "a person's trade or profession". Available at: https://www.lexico.com/definition/employment. *Macmillan Dictionary* describes employment as "work that you are paid regularly to do for a person or company", and *Collins Dictionary* as "the fact of having a paid job". Available at: https://www.macmillandictionary.com/dictionary/british/employment and https://www.collinsdictionary.com/dictionary/english/employment.
911. For instance, C. Puigelier et al. describe "*relations de travail*" as "*[r]apports existant entre un salarié et un employeur au cours de l'exécution du contrat de travail*". Puigelier, Hérin & Tillhet-Pretnar, *supra* n. 909, at 899. A standard dictionary such as the *Cambridge Dictionary*, on the other hand, describes the employment relationship more generally as "an official arrangement in which a business pays someone to work for them". Cambridge Dictionary, available at: https://dictionary.cambridge.org/dictionary/english/employment-relationship.

right to frame the scope of Convention No. 181 as if this international labour standard is only concerned with employees and not the self-employed?[912]

277 **Two scenarios** – Two scenarios seem to present themselves. The first scenario is that both Article 1(1)(a) and Article 1(1)(b) require an employment relationship, respectively, between the jobseeker and the user enterprise or between the jobseeker and the agency. The second scenario is that only Article 1(1)(b) requires an employment relationship, whereas Article 1(1)(a) does not. The second subclause of Article 1(1)(a), then, serves to ensure that agencies of type 1(1)(b) are not also considered agencies of type 1(1)(a). The significant degree of ambiguity justifies studying the working documents and the instrument's history. In this respect, it should be highlighted that TWAs were considered covered by the FCEAs Conventions (*supra* nos. 254–257) because "procuring employment for a worker or supplying a worker for an employer" does not presuppose the establishment of an employment relationship between the jobseeker and the user. Among other things, due to the controversy surrounding this, it makes sense for the Office and ILO constituents to have kept this in mind while drafting Article 1(1)(a) of Convention No. 181. TWAs perform "services for matching offers of and applications for employment", but because the TWAs become a party to an employment relationship, which may arise from these job-matching services, they cannot be considered agencies of type 1(1)(a). TWAs are only agencies of type 1(1)(b). From this history-sensitive perspective, the second subclause of Article 1(1)(a) operates as a switch between agencies of type 1(1)(a) and 1(1)(b), excluding agencies of type 1(1)(b) from also being considered type 1(1)(a). We will take a closer look at the narrow and broader context surrounding Convention No. 181 to determine whether either of these two scenarios find support.

278 **Convention's narrow context** – Paying attention to the Convention as such, its title "Private Employment Agencies Convention" immediately clarifies the Convention's regulatory object. The instrument concerns itself with agencies that provide private employment services on the labour market. Article 1 defines the scope of the Convention, together with Article 2. Entities that perform certain well-defined "labour market services" – Article 1 Convention No. 181 – are PrEAs. More precisely, entities that provide services of type 1(1)(a) or services of type 1(1)(b) are automatically considered PrEAs. Additionally, the national authority can determine that also "other services relating to jobseeking [...] that do not set out to match specific offers of and applications for employment" lead an entity of type 1(1)(c) to become considered a PrEA. This reference to "other services relating to jobseeking" in Article 1(1)(c) is particularly interesting. It gives resonance to the view that the Convention not only intends to regulate the act of matching offers of and applications for employment contracts but, more broadly, aims to regulate any activity that sets out to match offers of and applications for jobs. The term "job" does not reflect an employment status; self-employed workers also have jobs. Moreover, Article 1(2) of Convention No. 181 explicitly clarifies that the term "workers" includes jobseekers. This clarification was

912. Scholars seem to assume that the instrument is not applicable to self-employed workers. Roger Blanpain, *Belgian Report*, 36 Bulletin of Comparative Labour Relations 181, 182 (1999); Nicola Countouris, *The Changing Law of the Employment Relationship: Comparative Analyses in the European Context* 158 (Ashgate 2007).

not yet explicitly present in Convention No. 96. To this extent, when, for instance, the preamble of Convention No. 181 recalls the need to protect workers against abuse, one can conceive it as a call to protect jobseekers against abuse.

From this angle, because research has found that freelancers in search of jobs on an 279
international online labour market "act under a constant threat of malfeasance by clients",[913] the protection of these freelancers against abusive intermediation fits the purpose of Convention No. 181. In fact, if the treaty is read step by step, Article 1 first emphasises that "the term workers includes jobseekers", subsequently, Article 2 stresses that the Convention "applies to all categories of workers and all branches of economic activity". Therefore, arguably, the instrument also covers all categories of jobseekers. The references to jobseekers and jobseeking do not suggest that the definition of PrEAs, particularly the word "employment", should be construed any narrower than the personal scope of application of Convention No. 96.

Broader context – In terms of the broader context, a tripartite Meeting of Experts 280
convened in 2016 to negotiate draft principles and operational guidelines on fair recruitment. These guidelines aimed to respect the principles enshrined in the ILO's ILS, including Convention No. 181.[914] The outcome document comes across as a subsequent agreement, or at least subsequent practice, regarding the application of Convention No. 181's provisions. That is because the ILO constituents in the Governing Body authorised the Director-General to disseminate the principles and operational guidelines of this tripartite Meeting of Experts. The operational guidelines for the governments note, among other things, that "[t]he [national] legislation should apply to the act of recruitment and not only to some categories of labour recruiters but also to all recruiters operating outside any specific regulatory framework".[915] This is reminiscent of Convention No. 96's "nature over form"-approach (*supra* no. 255). Additionally, one of the main guidelines reads: "[g]overnments should ensure that relevant legislation and regulations cover all aspects of the recruitment process, and that they apply to all workers, especially those in a vulnerable situation".[916] This emphasis is similar to certain remarks that came up in the working documents regarding the protection of the most vulnerable workers by Convention No. 181 (*supra* no. 270). The outcome of the tripartite Meeting of Experts, as accepted by the Governing Body, in other words, gives no reason to suggest that Convention No. 181 has a narrow scope.

Subsequently, attention should be paid to the potential subsequent practice, as 281
evidenced by the ILO's supervisory bodies' work. An appropriate starting point is the Committee of Experts' general survey on employment instruments. In this report,

---

913. Andrey Shevchuk & Denis Strebkov, *Safeguards Against Opportunism in Freelance Contracting on the Internet*, 56 British Journal of Industrial Relations 342, 361 n. 2 (2018).

914. ILO Director-General, *Outcome of the Meeting of Experts on Fair Recruitment*, GB.328/INS/17/4 (ILO 2016).

915. "[T]he term recruitment includes the advertising, information dissemination, selection, transport, placement into employment and – for migrant workers – return to the country of origin where applicable. This applies to both jobseekers and those in an employment relationship". ILO Director-General, *supra* n. 914, at 4 and 6.

916. *Ibid.*, 6.

the Committee notes that "[t]he definition set forth in Article 1, paragraph 1, of Convention No. 181 generally encompasses any recruiter or direct service supplier outside the realm of public employment services".[917] The Committee goes on to describe services of type 1(1)(a) as "provision of job-matching services without becoming a party to the employment relationship", calling these agencies employment mediators.[918] Contrary to the Committee of Experts, the Committee on the Application of Standards has, so far, not produced any conclusions regarding Convention No. 181. Therefore, the only possible way to verify whether State practice indeed suggests Convention No. 181 regulates all job-matching services is by following up on Member States' reactions to the Committee of Experts' clarifications.

282 The Committee's direct requests and observations suggest that certain Member States seem to take a broad approach, whereas others do not. Direct requests in relation to Morocco claim that the country regulates both "the linking of job applications and job offers", also described as "the matching of job requests to vacancies", and "the provision of services to assist in the search for employment", elsewhere described as "the provision of services to help jobseekers find employment".[919] According to Georgia's 2006 labour code, "[p]rivate employment agency means any physical or legal person, which provides employment service to the unemployed (jobseeker)".[920] Albania offers licences for agencies to engage in "Mediation in the Labour Market".[921] Serbia's Government notes that PrEAs carry out employment activities, such as the "dissemination of information on employment opportunities and conditions, job matching in the country and abroad, professional orientation and career consulting".[922] An observation about Algeria even clarifies that the country's draft labour code aims to expand the scope of activities that certified PrEAs can conduct. The Government added that it "will also cover subcontracting activities with a view to combating informal work and illicit subcontracting activities".[923] The labour code in Mali stipulates that FCEAs regularly provide "services to match job offers with jobseekers, without the person carrying out this activity becoming a party to the labour relations that may result from it".[924] Based on this language, multiple countries seem to, indeed, take a rather broad regulatory approach to the issue.

917. ILO Committee of Experts on the Application of Conventions and Recommendations, *supra* n. 815, at 73.
918. *Ibid.*, 74.
919. Direct Request (CEACR) – adopted 2009, published 99th ILC session (2010), Private Employment Agencies Convention, 1997 (No. 181) – Morocco (Ratification: 1999); Direct Request (CEACR) – adopted 2014, published 104th ILC session (2015), Private Employment Agencies Convention, 1997 (No. 181) – Morocco (Ratification: 1999).
920. Direct Request (CEACR) – adopted 2010, published 100th ILC session (2011), Private Employment Agencies Convention, 1997 (No. 181) – Georgia (Ratification: 2002).
921. Direct Request (CEACR) – adopted 2018, published 108th ILC session (2019), Private Employment Agencies Convention, 1997 (No. 181) – Albania (Ratification: 1999).
922. Direct Request (CEACR) – adopted 2018, published 108th ILC session (2019), Private Employment Agencies Convention, 1997 (No. 181) – Serbia (Ratification: 2013).
923. Observation (CEACR) – adopted 2018, published 108th ILC session (2019), Private Employment Agencies Convention, 1997 (No. 181) – Algeria (Ratification: 2006).
924. Direct Request (CEACR) – adopted 2019, published 109th ILC session (2020), Private Employment Agencies Convention, 1997 (No. 181) – Mali (Ratification: 2016).

At the same time, the Committee's requests and observations are hardly conclusive. Regarding North Macedonia, the Committee did ask whether the regulation on employment agencies "applies to all categories of workers" but it failed to receive an answer the first time.[925] The second time, after the country's legislative changes in 2019, the Committee noted the Government's "indication that the Convention applies to all categories of workers and economic activities".[926] This phrasing does not tell us much. Moreover, the Committee does not frequently pose this question, even though it could do so, for instance, in relation to the following examples. In certain countries, the regulatory approach seems to remain relatively narrow. In Bulgaria, the Confederation of Independent Trade Unions of Bulgaria indicated that employment intermediation "consists of assisting and facilitating the establishment of an employment relationship between the employer and the jobseeker".[927] Also, Zambia mentions that it recognises employment agencies that intermediate "employees".[928] Despite these details, however, the Committee has not asked the governments in question whether the domestic regulation applies to all categories of workers. Moreover, in the Committee's own general survey, the Committee seems to associate (specific) employment mediators, such as "intermediaries," with the establishment of employment contracts.[929] It is unclear whether this is simply because most employment intermediation still involves employment contracts or because the Committee is convinced that employment services that lead to contracts for personal services are not regulated by Convention No. 181. Perhaps it is the former. During the discussion of 2010's general survey at the Committee on the Application of Standards, for example, the Chairperson of the Committee of Experts noted "that private employment agencies would no doubt play an increasingly important role in matching individuals to jobs and it was therefore to be hoped that more member States would seriously consider ratifying Convention No. 181".[930] "Matching individuals to jobs" is indicative of a broad scope. **283**

Overall, the interaction between the Committee of Experts' decisions and the Member States' actions does not offer conclusive findings. Certain ratifying Member States seem willing to move beyond the intermediation of employment contracts. This is the case in Belgium, for instance, where some of the regional decrees lend themselves **284**

925. Direct Request (CEACR) – adopted 2015, published 105th ILC session (2016), Private Employment Agencies Convention, 1997 (No. 181) – North Macedonia (Ratification: 2012); Direct Request (CEACR) – adopted 2019, published 109th ILC session (2021), Private Employment Agencies Convention, 1997 (No. 181) – North Macedonia (Ratification: 2012).

926. Direct Request (CEACR) – adopted 2020, published 109th ILC session (2021), Private Employment Agencies Convention, 1997 (No. 181) – North Macedonia (Ratification: 2012).

927. Direct Request (CEACR) – adopted 2011, published 101st ILC session (2012) Private Employment Agencies Convention, 1997 (No. 181) – Bulgaria (Ratification: 2005).

928. Direct Request (CEACR) – adopted 2015, published 105th ILC session (2016) Private Employment Agencies Convention, 1997 (No. 181) – Zambia (Ratification: 2013).

929. For instance, intermediaries are a kind of PrEA. "Although there are several sub-forms of intermediaries, they are the most typical and 'traditional' type of private agencies, bringing together vacancies and jobseekers without becoming a party to an employment contract". ILO Committee of Experts on the Application of Conventions and Recommendations, *supra* n. 815, at 74.

930. Report of the Committee on the Application of Standards at the 99th Session of the International Labour Conference, Geneva, ILO, 2010, 16 Part I/45.

to being applied beyond the intermediation of employment relationships. That could have significant implications for the platform economy.[931] In the Netherlands, Verhulp similarly argues that the Dutch Act on private employment services might apply to multiple platforms.[932] Some other Member States, however, seem to stick to a narrower scope. The Committee of Experts does not address these States to emphasise that the Convention applies to all categories of workers. This is surprising, to some extent, because the Committee has not shied away from highlighting the broad scope of application of other Conventions with language similar to that of Convention No. 181.[933]

285 **Working documents** – Because of the lasting ambiguity, it seems appropriate to reflect on the treaty's preparatory work before formulating a conclusion. The working documents of 1996 and 1997 were entitled "Revision of the Fee-Charging Employment Agencies Convention". The Law and Practice Report from 1996 provided the following definition:

> "a private employment agency means any natural or legal person, independent of the public administration, which provides one or more of the following labour market services: (i) services for matching demand and supply without the agency becoming a party to the employment relationship; (ii) services consisting of recruiting workers, who are employees of the agency, with a view to making these workers available [...]; (iii) services such as training, provision of information or any other employment-related services that are provided without seeking to match specific supply and demand".[934]

This is the definition with which the subject was presented to the Member States. A subsequent questionnaire asked the Members whether they wanted changes to the definition. The scope of application of Convention No. 181 was primarily settled based on Member States' responses to the Office's questionnaire. It led the Office to advance the following definition, which would subsequently receive further amendments at the Conference of 1997. PrEAs that provide the following labour market services as a "primary activity" are to be regulated:

---

931. Enguerrand Marique & Jonathan de Wilde d'Estmael, *La Fonction d'Intermédiaire des Plateformes: Une Nouvelle Clé pour Réglementer les Relations de Travail qu'Elles In-/produisent?* 241, 270–278 (Auriane Lamine & Céline Wattecamps eds., *Quel Droit Social pour Les Travailleurs de Plateformes?*, Anthemis 2020).
932. Evert Verhulp, *Platformwerkers Verdienen Meer!*, Arbeidsrecht n. 1 (2018).
933. Consider, for example, the Workers with Family Responsibilities Convention, 1981 (No. 156), which stipulates in Art. 2: "[t]his Convention applies to all branches of economic activity and all categories of workers". The Committee of Experts has clearly stated in the past that "it was intended that all workers should be covered, whether in full-time, part-time, temporary or other forms of employment, and whether they are in waged or non-waged employment. This point was of particular significance to many member States, due to the large number of workers in part-time and precarious forms of employment or self-employed, particularly in the developing countries". ILO Committee of Experts on the Application of Conventions and Recommendations, *Workers with Family Responsibilities* 18 (ILO 1993). The Committee has not adopted a similar position in relation to Convention No. 181, despite similar phrasing.
934. ILO, *supra* n. 161, at 72.

"(i) services for matching offers of and applications for employment, without the private employment agency becoming a party to the employment relationships which may arise therefrom;

(ii) services consisting of employing workers with a view to making them available to a third party, who may be a natural or legal person (referred to below as a 'user enterprise') which assigns their tasks and supervises the execution of these tasks;

(iii) other services relating to jobseeking, such as the provision of information, that do not set out to match specific offers of and applications for employment".[935]

A couple of things are noteworthy. First, the Office hardly gave any explanation about the reasons underlying its amendments. Therefore, it remains unclear if the new description in Article 1(1)(i), i.e. "services for matching offers of and applications for employment, without the private employment agency becoming a party to the employment relationships which may arise therefrom",[936] was meant to alter the scope of the original definition, or has the exact same meaning as "services for matching demand and supply without the agency becoming a party to the employment relationship".[937] One can only try to make a calculated guess based on ILO constituents' individual responses.[938] These individual responses do not suggest that the rephrasing aimed to restrict the instrument's scope. Many countries seemed to favour a broad approach, and very few States, e.g. Germany, apparently wanted to limit the Convention's scope to dependent employment. Because of the few references to this issue, it is unlikely for the word "employment" to be added to narrow the scope. This word might as well have been introduced to connect the unspecified activity of "matching demand and supply" to the overarching theme of the Convention, namely employment services. For instance, the Worker Vice-Chairperson indicated at the start of 1997's standard-setting committee that "it was vital that the new standards should provide adequate protection for all workers and jobseekers, regardless of their relationship with the various parties concerned".[939] In line with this remark, the questionnaire and Conference proceedings do not indicate an apparent effort to limit the instrument's overall scope to employment relationships.

In fact, the definition submitted after the questionnaire even points in the opposite **286**
direction. Before the changes from 1997's ILC, the definition of a PrEA designated three types of labour market services as constitutive of a PrEA. The most specific type of service is category (b), in which the agency employs a worker to make the worker available to a third party. A bit more general is category (a), in which the agency provides services for matching offers of and applications for employment, "without the private employment agency becoming a party to the employment relationships which may arise therefrom". Lastly, there is the broadest category (c), i.e. "other services relating to jobseeking, such as the provision of information, that do not set out to match

935. ILO, *supra* n. 891, at 131.
936. *Ibid.*
937. ILO, *supra* n. 161, at 72.
938. Those individual responses can be found here: ILO, *supra* n. 891, at 18–29.
939. Report of the Committee on the Revision of Convention No. 96 at the 85th Session of the International Labour Conference, Geneva, ILO, 1997, 16/4.

specific offers of and applications for employment". The last subclause of category (c) refers to category (a), whereas the last subclause of category (a) refers to category (b). In other words, the draft instrument advanced a definition with three stages. Agencies of type 1(1)(b), such as TWAs, were not agencies of type 1(1)(a) or 1(1)(c). Agencies of type 1(1)(a) were not agencies of type 1(1)(c). Agencies of type 1(1)(c) did not fulfil the conditions to be considered an agency of type 1(1)(a) or 1(1)(b), but were, nevertheless, a PrEA. Although the Office's reasoning cannot be traced, it would seem that at this point, the description given to agencies of type 1(1)(a) resembled the template of employment intermediation as regulated under Convention No. 96. Yet, as clarified earlier, Convention No. 181 aimed to extend its predecessor's scope.[940] As a consequence, it made sense to frame agencies of type 1(1)(b) around the template of a TWA, and to, additionally, develop a description for agencies of type 1(1)(c) that could extend the scope to agencies that support employment intermediation in the broadest sense of the word. Compared to Convention No. 96, the scope of Convention No. 181 is, then, explicitly extended along two dimensions. Moreover, the reference to "employment" and "employment relationships" in Article 1(1)(a) could not have been introduced to exclude self-employment from the draft instrument's scope. After all, at this stage, matching workers and clients through contracts for services would probably still have been considered a service related to jobseeking, in the sense of Article 1(1)(c). Therefore, when it was introduced, it is improbable for the phrasing of Article 1(1)(a) to have been explicitly intended to exclude self-employment from the scope of the draft instrument.

287 The "problem" is that the eventually adopted Convention might give another impression due to a chain of events at 1997's Conference. As pointed out, the third category (c) was initially just as crucial as the first and second categories. As the Workers' group put it, subparagraph (c) "reflected recognition that the revised Convention should not only address the present but also the future trends in the evolution of services in the labour market".[941] Article 1(1)(c) initially aimed at future-proofing the Convention. However, ILO constituents eventually decided to amend subclause (c), mainly due to the Employers' group's arguments. The Employers, for instance, maintained that "the Convention should not include activities of lesser significance".[942] Moreover, if Article 1(1)(c) remained unchanged, it would have meant that enterprises could not ask for any fees from jobseekers, even if it was to help the jobseekers improve their curriculum vitae. At that point, the scope of the instrument was so broad that many services which were not prone to abuse risked being regulated out of existence. These remarks persuaded many governmental delegates. By accepting the amendment, the ILO constituents effectively marginalised subclause (c). By inserting, as a condition, that the competent authority determines which "other" jobseeking activities are regulated, this category could no longer take on its initial role as an automatic safety net, capturing all (new) forms of employment intermediation *sensu*

940. Some commentators claim that Convention No. 181's scope has been expanded, compared to its predecessor. Vosko, *supra* n. 793, at 58; Thuy Phan, *ILO Convention on Private Employment Agencies (No. 181)*, 36 Bulletin of Comparative Labour Relations 77, 80 (1999).
941. Report of the Committee on the Revision of Convention No. 96 at the 85th Session of the International Labour Conference, Geneva, ILO, 1997, 16/12.
942. *Ibid.*, 16/12 and 16/34.

lato. Agencies of type 1(1)(c) became a residual category when compared to agencies of types 1(1)(a) and 1(1)(b). Due to the amendment, agencies are only automatically considered a PrEA if they deliver services of type 1(1)(a) or 1(1)(b); hence, the word "employment" became relevant.

With this in mind, we can discuss the changes that unfolded during the standard-setting committee's discussions. The constituents decided to delete the Office's condition that a PrEA's "primary activity" has to do with labour market services. The Member States that advanced the amendment wanted to cover all services provided to the labour market, even those provided as secondary activities. During these discussions on Article 1(1), the member of the secretariat explained that "[t]he Office wanted the Convention to be applicable to all those whose profession was to mediate in employment".[943] Once the reference to a "primary activity" was deleted, no single amendment was advanced in relation to Article 1(1)(a). Some interesting amendments were, on the other hand, advanced regarding Article 2. The Legal Adviser clarified that the flexibility provided therein allowed the Member States to exempt, for instance, seafarers and au pairs from the national law that implemented the Convention.[944] The Worker Vice-Chairperson gave examples of professional sportspersons, actors and artists.[945] Considering how many of these atypical categories of workers, such as au pairs,[946] are often not considered employees under national law, the discussions on exemptions seem to imply that the scope of the Convention might have been intended to, in principle, cover more than just salaried wage-employment. For instance, the Worker Vice-Chairperson suggested enabling the Member States to exclude "certain categories of workers" from the instrument's scope. The Government member of Sweden disagreed. "After all, the Convention set out to protect workers – it was therefore illogical to talk about exclusion. The focus should rather be on certain businesses or practices".[947] As a result of this, the eventually adopted Convention only allows to "exclude, under specific circumstances, workers in certain branches of economic activity, or parts thereof, from the scope of the Convention or from certain of its provisions, provided that adequate protection is otherwise assured for the workers concerned".[948] Furthermore, when discussing the possibility of exempting specific categories of workers from the principle that private employment services are free of charge, the Member States of the EU again pointed to artists and musicians.[949] Once more, these are also categories of workers that disproportionally operate outside the realm of labour and employment law.[950] 288

943. *Ibid.*, 16/10.
944. *Ibid.*, 16/14.
945. *Ibid.*, 16/18.
946. ILO, *Report IV(1) Decent Work for Domestic Workers* 34 (ILO 2010).
947. Report of the Committee on the Revision of Convention No. 96 at the 85th Session of the International Labour Conference, Geneva, ILO, 1997, 16/18.
948. Art. 2(4)(b) Private Employment Agencies Convention, 1997 (No. 181).
949. Report of the Committee on the Revision of Convention No. 96 at the 85th Session of the International Labour Conference, Geneva, ILO, 1997, 16/35.
950. Joanna Woronkowicz & Douglas S. Noonan, *Who Goes Freelance? The Determinants of Self-Employment for Artists*, 43 Entrepreneurship Theory and Practice 651, 651–672 n. 4 (2019); National Endowment for the Arts, *Artists and Other Cultural Workers: A Statistical Portrait* 21 (National Endowment for the Arts 2019).

289 Moving beyond the discussions at the standard-setting committee, the Employer Vice-Chairperson of the Committee on the Revision of Convention No. 96 mentioned in the Conference's plenary how the Employers' group regarded these instruments as good instruments for several reasons. One of which was that "the new Convention not only replaces Convention No. 96, it also extends its scope very considerably, including in its definition of actors the temporary work agencies as well as the other activities undertaken by private employment agencies".[951] The Convention strongly reflects a quid pro quo. Private employment agencies are, in principle, allowed to operate if the workers and jobseekers that rely on their services are protected. The Chairperson of the Committee phrased this sentiment as: "this is a balanced instrument. Private agencies find their legitimacy; workers get protection".[952]

290 **The case for a broad scope of application** – Overall, upon closer inspection of the entire text of the treaty, the narrow and broader context of the treaty as well as the working documents, a consistent interpretation of the Convention's scope seems to demand the word "employment" not to be given a restrictive meaning. Job-matching services of type 1(1)(a) do not require the service provider to bring about employment contracts. Entities that provide services for matching offers of and applications for jobs, or paid work, are not excluded from the regulation on PrEAs, just because these jobs are not performed in employment relationships. The reasoning is the following:

- the wording in Convention No. 181 with jobseekers, jobseeking, etc. is more inclusive than the phrasing used in its predecessor;
- nevertheless, as mentioned before, the Committee of Experts already considered its predecessor to apply to labour contractors;
- furthermore, the nature-over-form approach of Convention No. 34 and No. 96, in which the regulation targets all forms of employment intermediation, seems to prevail still, as evidenced in the guidelines on fair recruitment;
- to that extent, essentially, Convention No. 181 wants to regulate all entities that provide labour market services or employment services;
- as explained in detail, the word "employment" does not presuppose an employment relationship or contract.

The only defendable reason to restrict Convention No. 181's scope to employment relationships relates to this mentioning of "employment relationships" in the second subclause of Article 1(1)(a). However, that reference should not constrain Convention No. 181's scope for two reasons. First, in a history-sensitive perspective, this reference is needed to make sure that agencies of type 1(1)(b) are not also considered agencies of type 1(1)(a). That exemption is practical. It allows maintaining clarity when applying the various operative parts of the Convention and Recommendation to agencies of type 1(1)(a) and agencies of type 1(1)(b), respectively. Secondly, when looking at the working documents, arguably, when Article 1(1)(a) took shape, providing employment services that would result in contracts for services was still automatically covered under Article (1)(1)(c). Hence, the phrasing of Article 1(1)(a) cannot have had the purpose to, for instance, exclude employment services to freelancers. For

951. Report of the Committee on the Revision of Convention No. 96: Submission, Discussion and Adoption at the 85th Session of the International Labour Conference, Geneva, ILO, 1997, 269.
952. *Ibid.*, 271.

these reasons, it would be strange to let the reference to "employment relationships" in the second subclause affect the ordinary meaning of the word "employment" in the first subclause.

In addition to these arguments, a broad interpretation of Article 1 would, furthermore, fit in with the aim of the Chairperson of the Committee and Employer Vice-Chairperson who wanted to draft a "'living' Convention".[953] If the degree of self-employment in the labour market surges, it is only logical for employment agencies to increasingly cater to jobseekers looking for contracts for services. That is a development that Convention No. 181 should trail. Moreover, the Worker Vice-Chairperson also wanted the instrument to be future-proof and capable of absorbing "future trends in the evolution of services in the labour market".[954] Therefore, taking into account the text, purpose, context of the treaty and the will of the Conference, there is little to suggest this instrument is limited to the intermediation of employment relationships. All job-matching services seem targeted. 291

Applicability in the platform economy – Based on the preceding, Article 1(1)(a) of Convention No. 181 can be expected to capture platforms that provide services for matching offers of and applications for employment – i.e. paid work, for instance, in the form of "gigs" – unless the platform operator becomes a party to the employment relationships which may arise from these job-matching services. 292

As such, the main issue in determining whether a platform is covered seems to relate to the identity of the parties between which it operates. More specifically, for what kind of "client" does an employment mediator/platform have to perform its services in order to be covered? The client has not received any description in Convention No. 181. Article 1(1)(b) only refers to "user enterprises" in the context of agencies of type 1(1)(b). The following Section explores what qualities the platform user needs for the platform operator to be a PrEA of type 1(1)(a). 293

3. The User-Side of Convention No. 181

The "employer" – As already mentioned, Convention No. 181 describes the supply-side – jobseekers are workers – but not the demand-side of job-matching services. This differs from the FCEAs Conventions, which refer to an "employer".[955] As became apparent in the Swedish memorandum, the term employer was not interpreted as an entity that employed an employee through an employment contract. Otherwise, these ambulatory typewriting agencies could hardly have fallen under the scope of Convention No. 96. In view of this, we can safely assume that, in principle, a similar situation arises under Convention No. 181. The demand-side is not necessarily made up of "employers" in the word's narrow, legal sense. And yet, it would seem that, as pointed out in the remainder of this Subchapter, job-matching services do presuppose the demand-side to have certain characteristics. These characteristics 294

953. Report of the Committee on the Revision of Convention No. 96 at the 85th Session of the International Labour Conference, Geneva, ILO, 1997, 16/2 and 16/5.

954. *Ibid.*, 16/12.

955. Art. 1 Fee-Charging Employment Agencies Convention (Revised), 1949 (No. 96).

will be discussed by referring to Convention No. 181 as well as the never-adopted instrument on contract labour.

295 **Contract labour** – The draft instrument on contract labour was related to Convention No. 181; however, it was never adopted. The conclusions of 1994's Committee on Private Employment Agencies advised the ILO to establish general principles and provide guidance that protects workers' interests, considering "the concerns of some (but not all) Committee members with regard to triangular employment relationships, including contract labour, TWAs and staff-leasing arrangements".[956] From 1994 onwards, two separate standard-setting committees dealt with triangular employment relations. These proceedings resulted in Convention No. 181 and a draft instrument on contract labour. Both strived to make room for flexible forms of employment, and to provide protection for workers against abuse in triangular relationships.[957] The connection between both initiatives also becomes evident when reading the working documents and the discussions in these standard-setting committees.[958] The report of the Committee on Contract Labour points out that PrEAs were explicitly excluded from the instrument on contract labour.[959] This implies that without this exemption, the draft instrument on contract labour would probably have applied to PrEAs. Indeed, for instance, the Worker members argued during the Committee's discussions that temporary agency work should be considered a "specific type of contract labour requiring protection and regulation".[960] According to the Workers, irrespective of Convention No. 181, temporary agency workers should have been granted protection as contract workers, because if a Member State decided to ratify the instrument on contract labour but not the one on PrEAs, a situation would arise in which temporary agency workers are left without any protection, contrary to other forms of contract labour. For them, the exemption had to disappear. "The Employer members strongly opposed" this idea, according to the transcript of the proceedings. So did several government members.[961] At the same time, the Austrian Government, among others, "spoke in favour of the [Workers'] amendment on the ground that the two proposed Conventions at issue had different objectives: the revision to Convention No. 96 concerned licensing, while contract labour focused on protection".[962]

296 The Austrian Government's remark aligns with some scholars' observations. The draft instrument initially aimed to protect contract workers who were in a condition of

956. Conclusions concerning the role of private employment agencies in the functioning of labour markets, 81st Session of the International Labour Conference in 1994, 21/31.

957. Anne Trebilcock, *A Comment on "Legitimising the Triangular Employment Relationship"*, 19 Comparative Labor Law & Policy Journal 79, 83–84 n. 1 (1997).

958. ILO, *Report VI (1) Contract Labour* 75 (ILO 1996). For instance, the Government member of Sweden in the Committee on the revision of Convention No. 96 warned against confusion between the draft text on private employment agencies and the proposed text on contract labour. Report of the Committee on the Revision of Convention No. 96 at the 85th Session of the International Labour Conference, Geneva, ILO, 1997, 16/5.

959. Report of the Committee on Contract Labour at the 85th Session of the International Labour Conference, Geneva, ILO, 1997, 18/9 and 18/28.

960. *Ibid.*, 18/31.

961. *Ibid.*

962. *Ibid.*

substantial economic and/or organisational dependency on a user enterprise.[963] These contract workers could be engaged in both bilateral and triangular relationships. When engaged in a triangular relationship, the worker worked for a user enterprise through a subcontractor or intermediary. As such, the instrument showed a theoretical overlap with the instrument on private employment agencies because certain contract workers were engaged through intermediaries classified as PrEAs. What is more, because Convention No. 181's protective provisions, arguably, remained unsatisfactory,[964] some stressed the instrument on contract labour's potential to upgrade Convention No. 181's protective ambitions.[965] Furthermore, in addition to raising the level of protection for some of Convention No. 181's jobseekers, the instrument on contract labour could also have plugged a legal loophole in Convention No. 181. For instance, Belgium's National Labour Council responded to the Office's questionnaire on contract labour by indicating that the draft instrument was too broad and ambitious. According to the Council, "[t]he instrument to be adopted should, therefore, focus on the situation which is the most problematic and which therefore has the greatest need of a legal framework. The first Conference discussion suggested that this is the situation in which an 'intermediary' is involved (Article 1 (c)), i.e. a natural or legal person providing workers to a user enterprise, without the intermediary or user enterprise taking responsibility as an employer".[966] As discussed in greater depth below, this situation is one in which many platform workers find themselves. Neither the platform operator nor the end-user accepts any responsibility as the legal employer.

User enterprise – Considering that the draft instrument on contract labour was never **297**
adopted, this additional protective sphere was never established. Nevertheless, the non-adopted instrument can still sketch the boundaries of Convention No. 181 because the two were concomitantly drafted. The last draft of the Convention concerning contract labour covered workers who "personally" perform work for user enterprises "under actual conditions of dependency on or subordination to the user enterprise and these conditions are similar to those that characterize an employment relationship under national law and practice and where [...] the contract worker is provided for the user enterprise by a subcontractor or an intermediary".[967] For the purpose of analysing Article 1(1)(a) of Convention No. 181, it is the reference to a "user enterprise" in this definition that interests us. The term "user enterprise" was chosen because it points to the entity that ultimately uses the worker's labour.[968] The reference to a user enterprise in Article 1(1)(b) of Convention No. 181 can, similarly, be understood to imply that, despite the temporary work agency figuring as the legal employer of the worker, it is the "user enterprise" that ultimately relies on the labour of the agency worker.

963. ILO, *supra* n. 958, at 78.
964. Steven L. Willborn, *Leased Workers: Vulnerability and the Need for Special Legislation*, 19 Comparative Labor Law & Policy Journal 85, 95 n. 1 (1997).
965. Vosko, *supra* n. 793, at 73; Frances Raday, *The Insider-Outsider Politics of Labor-Only Contracting*, 20 Comparative Labor Law & Policy Journal 413, 421 n. 3 (1999).
966. ILO, *Report V (2A) Contract Labour* 32 (ILO 1998).
967. ILO, *Report V (2B) Contract Labour* 5 (ILO 1998).
968. "Between those two extremes, there are situations in which a worker is in an actual relationship of dependency on or subordination to another party who is using his or her labour (the 'user enterprise') but where the worker is not considered to be the employee of the user enterprise under national law". ILO, *Report V (2B) Add.* 2 (ILO 1998).

298 To this extent, whereas the user enterprise is not mentioned in Article 1(1)(a) of Convention No. 181, the concept of an intermediary in the draft instrument on contract labour was defined as "a natural or legal person who makes contract workers available to a user enterprise without becoming formally the employer of these workers".[969] This description suggests that, similar to Article 1(1)(b) of Convention No. 181, which explicitly refers to a user enterprise, Article 1(1)(a), which deals with intermediaries, might also presuppose a user enterprise's involvement. In other words, although it is not explicitly stated in Convention No. 181, without a user enterprise on the demand-side of the platform, it might be inappropriate to classify a platform operator as a PrEA of type 1(1)(a). At least, that is what the description of an intermediary in the draft instrument on contract labour suggests.

299 **The application of Convention No. 181 in the platform economy** – Based on this concept of a "user enterprise", one could argue about Article 1(1)(a) of Convention No. 181 that the services for matching offers of and applications for paid work occur between jobseekers/workers and natural or legal persons that use the worker's labour to undertake an entrepreneurial economic activity. This description entails that although a consumer on a platform such as Uber uses the worker's labour, this platform operator cannot be considered to undertake employment services because, in principle, the passenger does not rely on the worker to conduct an entrepreneurial economic activity.

Based on all the foregoing:

Platform operators, independent of the public authorities, which provide services for matching offers of and applications for employment – i.e. paid work – between jobseekers/workers and natural or legal persons, that use the workers' labour for entrepreneurial economic activities, classify as private employment agencies of type 1(1)(a). This is the case unless the platform operators become a party to the employment relationships, which may arise from their services, in which case Article 1(1)(b) of Convention No. 181 may apply.

300 **The impact** – Based on this description, platform operators such as Freelancer.com,[970] Upwork,[971] ZipRecruiter,[972] and Fiverr[973] may well be classified as agencies of type

969. ILO, *supra* n. 967, at 7. The Law and Practice Report also referred to user enterprises that are being serviced by intermediaries. ILO, *supra* n. 958, at 9–10.

970. Freelancer.com reached a total of 41.7 million users in 2019, adding 9.1 million users during 2019. A total of 17 million jobs had been posted on 31 December 2019. Freelancer.com, *Freelancer Limited: Financial Report & Directors' Report. For the Year Ended 31 December 2019*, Freelancer (31 December 2019), https://www.freelancer.com/about/investor-pdf.php?id=100734657&name=FLN%202019%20Financial%20Report%20v9%20FINAL.

971. "In 2018, our platform enabled $1.8 billion of [gross services volume], representing an increase of 28% over the prior year, and our total revenue was $253.4 million, representing an increase of 25% over the prior year". Upwork, *Annual Report 2018*, Upwork (14 August 2021), https://investors.upwork.com/static-files/8d67d7b3-1e42-48c0-92db-e839a6d323f2.

972. ZipRecruiter claims to have 7 million active jobseekers each month and over 40 million job alert email subscribers, with over 10.000 new enterprises subscribing every month. ZipRecruiter, *About us*, ZipRecruiter (16 September 2020), https://www.ziprecruiter.co.uk/about.

973. "In the year ended December 31, 2019, active buyers grew 17% y/y to 2.4 million, representing the fourth consecutive quarter of accelerating growth". Fiverr uses a confusing narrative of

1(1)(a). Of course, whether they indeed are employment mediators remains to be determined on a case by case basis, depending on the transposition of Convention No. 181 at the domestic level. Nevertheless, if these four platform operators were covered, this alone would impact millions of jobseekers. Add to this a service provider, such as LinkedIn, of which employment intermediation might not be the primary activity but is undoubtedly a secondary activity (e.g. LinkedIn Talent Solutions), and it affects tens of millions of potential jobseekers.[974] Moreover, classifying LinkedIn as a PrEA would have consequences. For instance, Article 13(3) of Convention No. 181 stipulates that PrEAs shall provide the competent authorities with the information required: "(a) to allow the competent authority to be aware of the structure and activities of private employment agencies in accordance with national conditions and practices; (b) for statistical purposes". To that extent, although LinkedIn advertises its collaborations with governments providing them with an analysis of their labour markets,[975] from the perspective of Convention No. 181, this is the natural course of events. If LinkedIn wants to continue operating, it is bound to provide the competent authorities with the information required to formulate their labour market policy. By not providing this information when required, LinkedIn would break the deal that underpins Convention No. 181.

Crowdwork and local platform work – In addition to freelance platforms and companies such as LinkedIn, the Convention, in principle, also covers crowdwork platforms that provide micro-tasks. Platforms such as Amazon Mechanical Turk or Clickworker offer companies, including universities, access to home-based workers to, for example, take surveys and train algorithms. The way these platform operators break down jobs into micro-tasks does not change anything about the fact that they intermediate between jobseekers and user enterprises that provide these gig-seekers with paid work. Furthermore, also, certain local on-demand apps are covered. Unlike ride-hailing platforms, many other platform operators have developed multi-sided platforms with more than just end-market consumers and workers on them. A "nature over form" approach would suggest that, for instance, Instacart offers services for matching offers of and applications for paid work.[976] Instacart and food-delivery 301

buyers and sellers for digital services, which are, in reality, simply enterprises or other users and service providers. Fiverr, *Q4 / 2019 Shareholder Letter*, Fiverr (14 August 2021), https://s23.q4cdn.com/749308338/files/doc_financials/2019/q4/Fiverr-Shareholder-Letter_vFF.pdf.

974. Recall that the ILO constituents at the standard-setting committee decided to delete the requirement that labour market services were a "primary activity". As explained by the Government member of the Netherlands, "agencies providing services to the labour market as a secondary activity should not be allowed to do so without falling within the scope of appropriate legislation". The amendment received tripartite support. Employer members feared unfair competition by corporations for which employment services were a secondary activity. In light of this amendment, LinkedIn is as much of a PrEA as the aforementioned platform operators, e.g. ZipRecruiter, which provide employment services as a primary activity. Report of the Committee on the Revision of Convention No. 96 at the 85th Session of the International Labour Conference, Geneva, ILO, 1997, 16/10.
975. Sue Duke, *LinkedIn Analytics Help Deepen and Enrich European Labour Market Policymaking*, LinkedIn Economic Graph (21 May 2018), https://economicgraph.linkedin.com/blog/linkedin-analytics-help-deepen-and-enrich-european-labour-market-policymaking.
976. The platform operator presents the customer with the "virtual storefronts" of its affiliated retailers. Once the customers place an order for groceries, they authorise the purchase and

platforms recruit self-employed workers to send them to retailers and restaurants, completing the delivery derived from the sales agreement between the customers and retailers/restaurants (*supra* no. 94). Therefore, when adding up all these platforms, Article 1(1)(a) of Convention No. 181 may, in fact, apply to a large segment of the platform economy.

4. Disguised Temporary Agency Work in the Platform Economy

302 **Article 1(1)(b) Convention No. 181** – Besides Article 1(1)(a), Article 1(1)(b) of Convention No. 181 is also relevant in the discussion on platform work. It should be recalled that Convention No. 181 aims to cover TWAs and, for instance, staff-leasing firms and job shops.[977] Due to the diverse range of agencies covered by Article 1(1)(b), Blanpain argued that the Convention applies to all kinds of situations in which workers are put at the disposal of a user enterprise, "involving some form of delegation of the employer's authority to the user regarding the workers, who are put at his disposal".[978] As a result, Article 1(1)(b) applies to two situations in the platform economy. First, it applies to the platform operator that legally employs workers with a view to making them available to the platform's user enterprises (e.g. Adia and Randstad Go). The user relies on the worker's labour to undertake an entrepreneurial economic activity and assigns tasks to the worker, supervising the execution. Secondly, the Convention also applies to any third party involved with the platform that employs workers with a view to making them available to the platform (users). In that case, it suffices for the platform or its users to assign tasks to the worker and supervise the execution. An example would be when staffing agencies legally employ Uber Eats couriers who, nonetheless, receive their directions from the Uber app when performing their delivery services, and are supervised through that app (*supra* no. 186).

303 **A rift between Article 1(1)(a) and 1(1)(b)** – Having described both platforms of type 1(1)(a) and 1(1)(b), one notable weak spot of Article 1 must be highlighted. As hinted at by the Belgian National Labour Council (*supra* no. 296), an issue the draft instrument on contract labour could have focused on was the situation in which neither the intermediary nor the end-user accepts any employer responsibilities. Convention No. 181 does not contain any safeguards against this. In particular, Davies has pointed out that there might, indeed, exist a legal grey zone in between the

---

delivery of those products from the retailer in question. According to the terms and conditions, the customer agrees "that retailer is the merchant of record, and that title to any goods passes to you when they are purchased at the applicable retailer's store". Therefore, one could argue that it is, in principle, the retailer that has committed to the sale, including its delivery. What Instacart does is provide the retailers with an external workforce to collect and deliver these purchase orders. This access is provided by the preliminary agreement between Instacart and the retailer, without which the retailer's "virtual storefront" would never have been presented to the customer. When depicted like this, why should these retailers not be considered users of these workers' labour for entrepreneurial economic activities? Instacart, *Terms of Service*, Instacart (16 September 2020), https://www.instacart.com/terms.

977. Phan, *supra* n. 940, at 80.

978. Blanpain, *supra* n. 912, at 182.

description of agencies of type 1(1)(a) and agencies of type 1(1)(b).[979] The extent to which this grey zone manifests itself depends on the national regulations on private employment services. Member States can draft their legislation about agencies of type 1(1)(b) to minimise the risk that agencies operate like an agency of type 1(1)(b), but without taking on any responsibilities as a legal employer.

Hybrids between 1(1)(a) and 1(1)(b) – This seems increasingly necessary (also see *supra* nos. 264–265). In the "platform economy", with its short-term engagements, platforms/agencies seem inclined to retain their relationship with the worker, yet without necessarily employing the worker, leading to various kinds of "hybrid" models.[980] Some platforms, such as Care.com and Fiverr, try to retain their link to the worker but limit themselves to generating a marketplace; they resemble technologically advanced job boards (agencies of type 1(1)(a)). Other platforms, such as Handy and TaskRabbit, which generally leave parties more negotiating room than, for instance, Uber nevertheless, use various metrics to surveil workers, leading them to move beyond simple job-matching.[981] In this respect, as observed by Jesnes et al., even if labour market intermediation is not a new phenomenon, "[w]hat is new is the reluctance of many [such] platforms to assume any employer responsibility for the workers, and to rely on algorithms in governing work, including determining prices, work schedules and remuneration".[982] 304

Some examples of platforms that might flaunt their obligations as employment agencies in this way are relatively clear. Wonolo provides "wonoloers" with both employment contracts at user enterprises and jobs for independent contractors, depending on the contract the user offers. Berg calls it "the tech version of the pickup truck on the street corner".[983] Based on its operations, Dubal claims that it "is essentially a next-generation, blue-collar temp staffing agency that specializes in warehouse work (but also advertises to companies seeking temporary labor for delivery work, event staffing, janitorial services; etc.)".[984] From the point of view of 305

979. "This may need to be addressed by broadening the language used to implement these provisions in national law". Anne C. L. Davies, *ILO Convention 181 Private Employment Agencies Convention, 1997 (No. 181)* 911, 912 (Edoardo Ales, Mark Bell, Olaf Deinert & Sophie Robin-Olivier eds., *International and European Labour Law Article-by-Article Commentary*, Nomos 2018). Countouris also highlights the "regulatory lacunae" in the scope of application of Convention No. 181. Nicola Countouris, *supra* n. 912, at 158.
980. Lenaerts et al., *supra* n. 56, at 6–8.
981. Ticona, Mateescu & Rosenblat, *supra* n. 88, at 21.
982. Kristin Jesnes et al., *Chapter 7. Conclusion* 79, 80 (Kristin Jesnes & Sigurd M. Nordli Oppegaard eds., *Platform Work in the Nordic Models: Issues, Cases and Responses*, Nordic Council of Ministers 2020).
983. Berg, *supra* n. 104, at 76.
984. Veena Dubal, *The Digitalization of Day Labor as Gig Work*, onlabor (7 May 2019), https://onlabor.org/the-digitalization-of-day-labor-as-gig-work/. Indeed, the case studies presented on its website speak volumes. One title reads, "Eyemart Express used Wonolo to source the best temp workers to help it scale fast". Other case studies suggest that most temp labor providers are inferior and that Wonolo provides excellent on-demand staffing services. Wonolo, *Eyemart Express Used Wonolo to Source the Best Temp Workers to Help it Scale Fast*, Wonolo (14 August 2021), https://www.wonolo.com/find-workers/case-studies/sourcing-the-best-temp-workers-to-help-eyemart-express-scale-fast; Wonolo, *AMP Printing Used Wonolo to Save Time it Would Have Spent Training New Workers*, Wonolo (14 August 2021), https://www.wonolo.com/

Convention No. 181, what would make sense is for Wonolo to employ the workers and then to put them at the disposal of Wonolo's clients. However, this is not what happens. Wonolo merely intermediates. Similarly, whereas Adecco Group and Randstad developed platforms for businesses to hire temporary agency workers, in other words, complying with all relevant rules (*supra* nos. 264–265),[985] other platform operators such as Temper do the same thing by providing businesses with access to freelancers through their platform.[986] Dutch trade unions have, therefore, sued Temper to enforce the regulations on temporary agency work.[987] A ruling has not been issued yet. Even if the labour inspectorate seemingly agrees with the trade unions that Temper is a disguised TWA,[988] whether the unions will succeed in court remains uncertain. First of all, the tax authorities continue to consider Temper's workforce self-employed.[989] Moreover, in an earlier lawsuit claiming that Helpling – another platform in the Netherlands – was a temporary work agency, a Dutch court of first instance ruled that this was not the case.[990] The Court of Appeal, on the other hand, was of the opinion that the court had made a mistake and that Helpling was, in fact, a TWA.[991] Although this second judgment indicates in black and white that platforms can indeed engage in disguised temporary agency work, the method by which the Court arrived at its decision is rather undeveloped.[992] In that sense, it remains to be seen whether a more refined method will be developed to identify disguised TWAs among the platforms, or whether, on the contrary, this is an isolated case. The importance of this should not be underestimated. For example, a temporary work agency in France that sued a digital labour platform for its breach of temporary work agency regulation lost the case.[993] This example illustrates "[t]he

find-workers/case-studies/wonolo-saved-amp-printing-time-it-would-have-spent-training-new-workers; Wonolo, *Choura Events Used Wonolo to Seamlessly Connect with Skilled Workers for Large-scale Events*, Wonolo (14 August 2021), https://www.wonolo.com/find-workers/case-studies/seamlessly-and-affordably-connecting-choura-events-with-skilled-workers-for-large-scale-events.

985. Lenaerts et al., *supra* n. 56, at 6–8.
986. Platforms are also being developed to this end in China. Zhou, *supra* n. 37, at 11.
987. Maarten Van Gestel, *Vakbonden Slepen Flexwerkapp Temper voor de Rechter*, Trouw (22 October 2020), https://www.trouw.nl/economie/vakbonden-slepen-flexwerkapp-temper-voor-de-rechter~b3379193/.
988. Barbara Vollebregt, *Flexwerkapp Gedraagt Zich als een Uitzendbureau, en dus ís het een Uitzendbureau*, Trouw (15 February 2021), https://www.trouw.nl/economie/flexwerkapp-gedraagt-zich-als-een-uitzendbureau-en-dus-is-het-een-uitzendbureau~b944edd1/.
989. ZiPredactie, "Modelovereenkomst platform Temper (voorlopig) verlengd", ZiPconomy (26 May 2021), https://www.zipconomy.nl/2021/05/modelovereenkomst-platform-temper-voorlopig-verlengd/.
990. Rechtbank Amsterdam: Case 7299840 CV EXPL 18-23708, *Federatie Nederlandse Vakbeweging v. Helpling Netherlands B.V.*, 1 July 2019, ECLI:NL:RBAMS:2019:4546. For an analysis: Valerio De Stefano & Mathias Wouters, *Triangulaire Arbeidsrelaties in de Platformeconomie: Een Voorstel tot een Vermoeden van Uitzendbureau*, 13 Arbeidsrechtelijke Annotaties 3, 3–38 n. 3 (2019).
991. Gerechtshof Amsterdam: Case 200.268.5 10/01, *Federatie Nederlandse Vakbeweging v. Helpling Netherlands B.V.*, 21 September 2021, ECLI:NL:GHAMS:2021:2741.
992. One could say that the Court took a rather intuitive approach, along the lines of "I know it when I see it", after which it verified whether all conditions were fulfilled for this arrangement to be considered temporary agency work.
993. Cour de cassation: Case 1026, *Staffmatch France et autres v. Brigad*, 12 November 2020, ECLI:FR:CCASS:2020:SO01026. "*D'une certaine manière, les juges en appellent à l'intervention*

fact that TWAs are overtaken by platforms that are not TWAs, thus undermining the regulatory framework envisaged for three-way relationships, [which] is a policy problem that needs to be urgently addressed".[994]

A gap in Convention No. 181 – Coming back to Davies' comment regarding the grey 306
zone between Article 1(1)(a) and 1(1)(b), although the ILO might want to address this issue, for the time being, it is up to the Member States to frame the kind of mechanisms that can effectively enforce regulations on agencies of type 1(1)(b) in a digital environment. One option could be to presume that every agency/platform with a lasting relationship with the worker is an agency of type 1(1)(b).[995] Another possibility could be to design a mechanism to distinguish platforms practising proper employment intermediation in the sense of Article 1(1)(a) from platforms that, first, settle the terms of employment with the user enterprise and, subsequently, find a platform worker willing to accept those terms. In other words, it is legitimate to question whether the agreement between the platform worker and user enterprise is based on genuine negotiations between these two, or whether the platform operator and user have pre-determined the essential conditions of the working relationship.[996] In the latter case, the jobseeker who does not even get to properly negotiate his or her contract with the user can hardly be seen as self-employed. Unless the platform user accepts serving as the legal employer, the agency would then be forced to take responsibility as the platform worker's legal employer by lack of the jobseeker's ability to effectively negotiate service contracts with the platform user.

étatique pour que soient clarifiées les conditions de mise en concurrence de deux modèles à la fois singuliers et analogues". Clément Couëdel, *Intérim et Plateforme Numérique de Mise en Relation: Les Enjeux des Nouvelles Formes d'Intermédiation*, Dalloz actualité (26 November 2020), https://www.dalloz-actualite.fr/flash/interim-et-plateforme-numerique-de-mise-en-relation-enjeux-des-nouvelles-formes-d-intermediati.

994. Potocka-Sionek, *supra* n. 856, at 187.
995. *See*, along those lines, Nicola Countouris & Rachel Horton, *The Temporary Agency Work Directive: Another Broken Promise?*, 38 Industrial Law Journal 329, 331–332 n. 3 (2009).
996. De Stefano & Wouters, *supra* n. 990.

Chapter 3. The Instruments on Home Work

SUBCHAPTER 1. THE CONVENTION'S OBJECT AND PURPOSE

A resurgence of home work – Industrial home work is often perceived as an outdated 307
system of production. An ILO Report from 1948 describes it as "a system of production under which work is carried on for an employer by an employee who works alone, or with one or two assistants, at a place of his own choosing (often his own home), upon materials which may or may not be furnished by the employer".[997] This type of work was associated with substandard working conditions.[998] In fact, 1934's Committee on Industrial Home Work in the United States even spoke about "evils" that could only be controlled through its abolition.[999] Decades later, the situation had arguably improved.[1000] It was expected that home work would continue to be phased out as a result of ongoing industrialisation. However, this never truly happened. On the contrary, industrial home work seemed to increase again in the 1980s. Investigative reports from 1978–1982, for example, "have pointed to the resurgence of industrial home work and sweatshop labor in the United States".[1001] Home work became a topic of notable concern again, even though it had existed throughout the twentieth century alongside factory work.[1002] This resurgence was, *inter alia*, associated with high levels of unemployment and cost-reduction strategies.[1003] The

997. X, *Industrial Home Work*, 58 International Labour Review 735, 735–736 n. 6 (1948).
998. *Ibid.*, 750; Schneider de Villegas, *supra* n. 630, at 3 and 10.
999. Ruth White, *Industrial Home Work in Chicago*, 10 Social Service Review 23, 57 n. 1 (1936).
1000. Arthur J. Goldberg, *Growth of Labor Law in the United States* 61 (U.S. Department of Labor 1962).
1001. Sandra L. Albrecht, *Industrial Home Work in the United States: Historical Dimensions and Contemporary Perspective*, 3 Economic and Industrial Democracy 413, 424 n. 4 (1982). *See also*, Nancy C. Jurik, *Getting Away and Getting By: The Experiences of Self-Employed Homeworkers*, 25 Work and Occupations 7, 7 n. 1 (1998).
1002. Gisela Schneider de Villegas, *Home Work: A Case for Social Protection*, 129 International Labour Review 423, 423 n. 4 (1990).
1003. *Ibid.*, 424; Economic Commission for Latin America and the Caribbean and International Labour Organization, *The Future of Work in Latin America and the Caribbean: Old and New Forms of Employment and Challenges for Labour Regulation, Employment Situation in Latin America and the Caribbean* 23–24 (2019).

ILO "Technical Background Document for the Meeting of Experts on the Social Protection of Homeworkers" from 1990, most notably, associated the increase with a change in enterprise structures. According to the report, the "model of the 'flexible firm'" might have stimulated a decentralisation of production towards low-wage areas in labour-intensive industries.[1004] More recent research, indeed, indicates that businesses mainly adopt home work to respond to fluctuations in labour demand.[1005] Furthermore, the profitability of decentralised production compared to centralised production was and probably still is an essential driver of home work as well.[1006] By having subcontractors and home-based workers sew garments, manufacturers could, for instance, avoid paying payroll taxes.[1007]

308 For such reasons, homeworkers became "an integral component" of, for instance, the garment and footwear supply chain.[1008] In terms of statistics, 14 per cent of urban employment in India, 6 per cent in South Africa and 3 per cent in Buenos Aires would be home-based.[1009] The ILO estimates that 7.9 per cent of global employment is home-based, with countries including Bangladesh, Indonesia and the Philippines hitting 15 per cent and over.[1010] Therefore, although Europeans tend to perceive these kinds of putting out processes as remnants of the past, the opposite is true. These practices still occur on a large scale, including at the outer end of global supply chains,[1011] such as IKEA's.[1012]

309 What is more, industrial home work is not only present in developing countries. Home work has long been present in some parts of Europe, such as the shoe industry

1004. ILO, *Technical Background Document for the Meeting of Experts on the Social Protection of Homeworkers* 7 (ILO 1990); Schneider de Villegas, *supra* n. 1002, at 424.
1005. ILO, *supra* n. 613, at 86. As the ILO Committee of Experts noted in light of the COVID-19 pandemic, homeworkers "are the first to be cut loose, with no income support and no social protection benefits". ILO Committee of Experts on the Application of Conventions and Recommendations, *Addendum to the 2020 General Survey: Promoting Employment and Decent Work in a Changing Landscape* 149 (ILO 2021).
1006. Finkin, *supra* n. 628, at 608–611.
1007. According to Hyman, companies that kept sewing garments using factory employees went out of business. Hyman, *supra* n. 795, at 272.
1008. OECD and ILO, *Tackling Vulnerability in the Informal Economy* 116 (OECD 2019).
1009. Martha A. Chen & Shalini Sinha, *Home-based Workers and Cities*, 28 Environment & Urbanization 343, 344 n. 2 (2016).
1010. ILO, *supra* n. 613, at 27–28.
1011. Conclusions concerning decent work in global supply chains, 10 June 2016, 14-1/2. *See also*, Dena Freeman, *Homeworkers in Global Supply Chains*, 43 Greener Management International 106, 106–119 (2003); Marlese von Broembsen, *Constitutionalizing Labour Rights: Informal Homeworkers in Global Value Chains*, 34 International Journal of Comparative Labour Law and Industrial Relations 257, 257–280 n. 3 (2018); Jenna Harvey, *Homeworkers in Global Supply Chains: A Review of Literature* (WIEGO 2019); Marlese von Broembsen & Jenna Harvey, *Decent Work for Homeworkers in Global Supply Chains: Existing and Potential Mechanisms for Worker-centred Governance* (Global Labour University 2019).
1012. Lin Lean Lim, *Employment Relationships and Working Conditions in an IKEA Rattan Supply Chain* (ILO 2015).

in Spain,[1013] and is still alive and well in Bulgaria, Turkey etc.[1014] Similarly, as the *New York Times* reported, women in the south of Italy receive one euro for every processed metre of fabric supplied to their homes by a factory that manufactures outerwear for luxury brands.[1015] According to some, the use of these European home-based workers and workshops might have to do with fast fashion. Because fast fashion trends change rapidly, the products need to be readily available, making it beneficial to produce them closer to home.[1016] This also allows manufacturers to sell the products as "made in Italy". Such factors put workers on the other side of the planet at a disadvantage.

While this might be true for manual labour, the same is not necessarily true when 310
talking about digital labour. Apart from, for instance, a difference in time zones, more limited access to digital infrastructure, and language barriers, there are few reasons not to have workers tag pictures in low-income instead of high-income countries.[1017] More generally, the outsourcing and offshoring of services to, for example, foreign call centres has already increased significantly.[1018] The outsourcing of digital labour through crowdwork platforms to home-based workers in more impoverished regions of the world, arguably, relates to these developments.[1019] As Berg writes, "digital labor platforms have permitted the real-time hiring of labor for a myriad of tasks from IT programming, web development, graphic design, copywriting, or routine clerical tasks".[1020] Some countries in the Global South even intend to ensure that their country attracts a fair share of this business in the hope of generating employment.[1021] Therefore, as evidenced by the rise of crowdwork, the massive use of telework during

1013. Lauren A. Benton, *Homework and Industrial Development: Gender Roles and Restructuring in the Spanish Shoe Industry*, 17 World Development 255, 256–258 n. 2 (1989); More broadly, *see* Mireia Baylina & Maria Dolors Garcia-Ramon, *Homeworking in Rural Spain: A Gender Approach*, 5 European Urban and Regional Studies 55, 55–64 n. 1 (1998).
1014. Marlese von Broembsen, *The European Union's Commodification of Bulgarian Homeworkers: Regulating Informal Labour in Global Production Networks* (WIEGO 2019); Saniye Dedeoğlu, *Home Bounded – Global Outreach: Home-based Workers in Turkey* (ILO 2020).
1015. Elizabeth Paton & Milena Lazazzera, *Inside Italy's Shadow Economy*, The New York Times (20 September 2018), https://www.nytimes.com/2018/09/20/fashion/italy-luxury-shadow-economy.html.
1016. Jerónimo Montero Bressán, *Local Sweatshops in the Global Economy: Accumulation Dynamics and the Manufacturing of a Reserve Army* 63, 71–72 (Maurizio Atzeni & Immanuel Ness eds., *Global Perspectives on Workers' and Labour Organizations*, Springer Singapore 2018).
1017. Right now, it is still difficult to access the internet in many parts of the developing world. Mohammad. A. Anwar & Mark Graham, *Hidden Transcripts of the Gig Economy: Labour Agency and the New Art of Resistance Among African Gig Workers*, 52 EPA: Economy and Space 1269, 1280 n. 7 (2020).
1018. Niccolò Pisani & Joan E. Ricart, *Offshoring of Services: A Review of Literature and Organizing Framework*, 56 Management International Review 385, 386 n. 3 (2016); Begoña Fuster, Adelaida Lillo-Bañuls & Carmen Martínez-Mora, *Offshoring of Services as a Competitive Strategy in the Tourism Industry*, 24 Tourism Economics 963, 966 n. 8 (2018).
1019. Jamie Woodcock, *Digital Labour and Workers' Organisation* 157, 165 and 169 (Maurizio Atzeni & Immanuel Ness eds., *Global Perspectives on Workers' and Labour Organizations*, Springer Singapore 2018).
1020. Berg, *supra* n. 104, at 74.
1021. Rani & Jeet Singh, *supra* n. 181, at 266.

the COVID-19 pandemic, as well as the high numbers of industrial homeworkers,[1022] home(-based) work is as relevant as ever.

311 **Home-based workers' particular conditions** – Given this production system's long history, regulating home work is nothing new. Nevertheless, despite the experience gained, it does remain challenging to this very day. This is, among other things, due to the place of work, which is always outside the employer's premises. Other characteristics, such as the form of payment, which often comes in the form of piece-rate remuneration, and the reliance on intermediaries to organise the work, likewise complicate things. Generally, these features can result in low levels of remuneration, health and safety issues, challenging working hours, and problematic access to social security.[1023] As illustrated by 1934's US Committee on Industrial Home Work, these working conditions even led to calls for a ban on industrial home work, because it simply seemed impossible to "enforce minimum wage, overtime and child labour laws".[1024] Such a ban cannot count on much support from contemporary scholars and homeworkers, however, who observe that home-based work is a lifeline for many.[1025] Instead, solutions must be found to improve their conditions, including, but not solely, through regulation.

312 What is crucial in this respect is that home-based work is not only tricky to regulate and supervise because of its inherently "invisible" nature. Some voices in the literature suggest that certain actors in society do their best to keep it invisible.[1026] Something similar is perhaps at play in the case of crowdwork.[1027] For instance, start-ups rely on crowdworkers to power their "artificial intelligence" systems but might like to keep the appearance of everything being automated.[1028] Also, more prominent companies engage crowdworkers to train their AI systems without necessarily acknowledging their crucial contribution.[1029] By downplaying the contribution made by home-based workers to these activities and the economy at large, governments do not enact targeted campaigns, and governmental agencies are not funded to go after

1022. Marc Bain, *A Huge Underclass of Ghost Workers Are Making your Shirts in their Homes*, Quartz (17 December 2015), https://qz.com/494818/in-much-of-the-world-the-sweatshop-isnt-a-factory-its-someones-kitchen-floor/.

1023. ILO, *supra* n. 1002, at 18–24.

1024. Janice R. Bellace, *The Changing Face of Capital: The Withering of the Employment Relationship in the Information Age*, 100 Bulletin of Comparative Labour Relations 11, 22 (2018).

1025. Annie Delaney, Rosaria Burchielli, Shelley Marshall & Jane Tate, *Homeworking Women: A Gender Justice Perspective* 81–106 (Routledge 2018); Amelita M. King-Dejardin, *Homeworking in the Philippines* 53 (ILO 2021).

1026. "Like other instances of homework around the world, such as India and Chile (Burchielli et al., 2008), there is evidence that Argentinian women's garment homework is trivialized and euphemized – invisibilization terminology – and ignored, normalized and renamed – denial terminology – through discourses, social relations and conditions that render it as non-work". Rosaria Burchielli & Annie Delaney, *The Invisibilization and Denial of Work in Argentinian Garment Homework*, 71 Relations industrielles / Industrial Relations 468, 480 n. 3 (2016).

1027. Mary L. Gray & Siddharth Suri, *Ghost Work: How to Stop Silicon Valley from Building a New Global Underclass* (Houghton Mifflin Harcourt 2019).

1028. Moritz Altenried, *The Platform as Factory: Crowdwork and the Hidden Labour Behind Artificial Intelligence*, 44 Capital & Class 145, 157 n. 2 (2020); ILO, *supra* n. 25, at 123.

1029. Paola Tubaro & Antonio A. Casilli, *Micro-work, Artificial Intelligence and the Automotive Industry*, 46 Journal of Industrial and Business Economics 333, 344 n. 3 (2019).

these practices. As the enforcement of existing regulation is already difficult due to home work's atypical characteristics, without sufficient political will, it becomes particularly problematic.[1030] Moreover, this lack of public enforcement coalesces with the difficulties experienced by trade unions, which regularly do not or fail to reach out to home-based workers.[1031] The relevance of the Home Work Convention must also be judged in this light. It was pretty remarkable for an international labour standard to explicitly acknowledge home work's importance in the world of work.

Home-based workers' "employment relationship" – The instruments provided an opportunity to attribute labour and social protections to home-based workers, raising awareness that "[m]any of those working at home may be counted, and may consider themselves, as self-employed but are essentially disguised wage earners".[1032] The determination of homeworkers' employment status on the grounds of subordination alone, especially when strictly based on the idea of supervision and control, obstructs homeworkers' access to protections.[1033] Unlike factory workers, who often perform their work under close supervision, industrial homeworkers are not directly monitored. Therefore, when the test used to identify bogus self-employment at an employer's premises is applied to home-based workers, it might indicate that the latter are self-employed. However, since these home-based workers may essentially perform repetitive work similar to factory workers' work, such as producing rattan for IKEA, they can more closely resemble employees than independent contractors. Many home-based workers effectively dance to the tune of an employer or subcontractor, but the employer is simply not there to supervise the dance. Because of home-based workers' particular position, the ILO Office believes that "[t]here thus appear to be grounds for considering the creation of a special employment status for homeworkers which would take into account the specific characteristics of homeworking".[1034] 313

The consequence of this line of thinking – creating a "special" employment status for homeworkers – is that at a domestic level, one has to constantly ask whether home-based workers are entitled to labour and social protection on account of their classification as employees, or because of such a "special employment status".[1035] 314

1030. "It will be clear from what has been said above that on the whole home work is a 'regulated' – and in some cases highly regulated – activity. So the basic problem is not so much the absence of legal provisions acknowledging its existence, as the deficient application of those rules already in force". Luz Vega Ruiz, *Home Work: Towards a New Regulatory Framework?*, 131 International Labour Review 197, 214 n. 2 (1992).

1031. Jane Tate, *Unions and Homeworkers: Organizing Homeworkers in the Informal Sector in Australia, the Netherlands and Canada* (ILO 1993).

1032. ILO, *supra* n. 1004, at 4.

1033. Luz Vega Ruiz, *supra* n. 1030, at 200–201.

1034. ILO, *supra* n. 1004, at 40.

1035. Bruno Veneziani, *New Technologies and the Contract of Employment*, 2 International Journal of Comparative Labour Law and Industrial Relations 117, 128 n. 4 (1986). *See, e.g.*, two different types of employment contract in Albania: the "home-based employment contracts" and "telework contracts". Direct Request (CEACR) – adopted 2020, published 109th ILC session (2021), Home Work Convention, 1996 (No. 177) – Albania (Ratification: 2002). Under Belgian law, the Employment Contracts Act of 3 July 1978 advances a separate "employment contract for home work" which to the extent industrial home work still exists, is mainly targeted towards that professional group. Additionally, separate collective agreements and laws have been adopted for employees who telework from home occasionally or structurally. These

During the COVID-19 pandemic, for example, many teleworkers enjoyed labour and social protection because of their employment status. These teleworkers do not require any special employment status for home-based work; oftentimes, specific labour laws become applicable to their regular employment contract when they (partially) perform their work at home. In contrast, the "special employment status for homeworkers" from Convention No. 177 was, arguably, primarily advanced to cover home-based workers that perform manual work at home, such as sewing garments, binding books or making pottery. Unlike teleworkers in the Global North, these workers were never given an employment contract, which the ILO instruments on home work try to rectify.

315 **Digital home work** – At the same time, although industrial home work may have been the main target of these ILS on home work, throughout Convention No. 177's drafting process (1990–1996), it also became clear that telecommuting or telework would become a major form of home-based work. From the 1990s onwards, the largest share of home-based workers in countries such as France, the United Kingdom and the United States have been engaged in the service industry, no longer performing manual home work in an industrial or agricultural setting.[1036] Based on data from 2019, this now seems true in all regions of the world, except for southern Asia and northern Africa.[1037] With telecommuting or telework, a new era of home-based work dawned.[1038] In the four decades since the 1980s, the immovable home office slowly but surely turned into a laptop-driven mobile office, which already at the turn of the century began to show signs of a cloud-stored virtual office.[1039] The latter is accessible anywhere, at any time, on any device. Digital home work has, therefore, become much more flexible in terms of space and time than industrial home work has. Digital labour platforms take full advantage of this opportunity by turning jobs into tasks and parcelling them out to workers worldwide.[1040] As such, we reach an odd observation. Industrial homeworkers are a category of workers that have historically been marginalised, having to fight to see their claims to social protections acknowledged.[1041] On the other hand, the word "telework" almost automatically connotes a proper employment status, at least from a European and North-American perspective.[1042] When thinking of a teleworker, most imagine an employee who

teleworkers are usually not considered to have an "employment contract for home work" but a "standard" employment contract. Employment contracts for home work: Arts. 119.1–119.12 Loi du 3 juillet 1978 relative aux contrats de travail; structural telework: Convention collective de travail no. 85 du 9 novembre 2005 concernant le télétravail; occasional telework: Arts. 22–28 Loi du 5 mars 2017 concernant le travail faisable et maniable.

1036. ILO, *supra* n. 1004, at 11–12.
1037. ILO, *supra* n. 613, at 36.
1038. Kathleen E. Christensen, *The New Era of Home-based Work: Directions and Policies* (Westview 1988).
1039. Jon C. Messenger, *Introduction: Telework in the 21st Century – An Evolutionary Perspective* 1, 4–8 (Jon C. Messenger ed., *Telework in the 21st Century: An Evolutionary Perspective*, Edward Elgar Publishing 2019).
1040. Dau-Schmidt, *supra* n. 269, at 69.
1041. Elisabeth Prügl, *Biases in Labor Law: A Critique from the Standpoint of Home-Based Workers* 203, 203–218 (Eileen Boris & Elisabeth Prügl eds., *Homeworkers in Global Perspective: Invisible no more*, Routledge 1996).
1042. For instance, US Telework Enhancement Act of 2010.

agrees with an employer to perform (some of) the work from a distance. These are not marginalised workers. Having the possibility of teleworking from home is considered desirable.[1043] Some have even suggested that it is a privilege.[1044] From this perspective, crowdworkers have little in common with traditional teleworkers, even if they both use ICT infrastructure. Crowdworkers resemble marginalised, industrial homeworkers much more closely. Both operate at the margins of the business. Similarly, crowdworkers' protection under the law may, therefore, come from their classification under a "special employment status for homeworkers" rather than from general labour law, as tends to be the case for stereotypical teleworkers.

The importance of intermediaries/platforms – In 1990, the Office envisaged "the organisational technique of geographical dispersal of the workforce on a global scale, known as 'off-shoring'" to become telework's "most spectacular advantage to the employer".[1045] Subsequently, for instance, a report from Huws et al. in 2004 observed the growing importance of "Internet-based intermediaries" when outsourcing ICT services. These intermediaries "facilitate outsourcing and offshoring of small projects or one-off tasks and provide access to offshoring to" small and medium-sized enterprises.[1046] Crowdwork platforms subscribe to this trend. According to Lehdonvirta et al., they present "new offshoring institutions"[1047] that put existing business process outsourcing companies under pressure.[1048] Instead of a business in the Global North contracting a business in the Global South, which employs local workers and manages their work, the work is now allocated directly from employers to workers and channelled through these platforms.[1049] 316

Like intermediaries in industrial home work, crowdwork platforms thereby obfuscate the home-based worker's employment relationship.[1050] The conclusions of the Meeting of Experts on the Social Protection of Homeworkers from 1991 emphasised that it was essential to determine the responsibilities of subcontractors or intermediaries 317

1043. "Second, of the employee-friendly alternatives we consider, working from home is the most valued. On average, job applicants are willing to take 8 percent lower wages for the option of working from home". Alexandre Mas & Amanda Pallais, *Valuing Alternative Work Arrangements*, 107 The American Economic Review 3722, 3726 n. 12 (2017).

1044. Alan Felstead, Nick Jewson, Annie Phizacklea & Sally Walters, *The Option to Work at Home: Another Privilege for the Favoured Few?*, 17 New Technology, Work and Employment 204, 221 n. 3 (2002). A clear digital divide exists between workers in the top wage quintile, of which three quarters can telework, and workers in the bottom wage quintile, where it is around one in twenty. Matteo Sostero et al., *Teleworkability and the COVID-19 Crisis: A New Digital Divide?* 62–63 (Eurofound 2020).

1045. ILO, *supra* n. 1004, at 25. *See also*, ILO, *Report V (1) Home Work* 15 (ILO 1994).

1046. Ursula Huws, Simone Dahlmann & Jorg Flecker, *Outsourcing of ICT and Related Services in the EU* 18 (Eurofound 2004).

1047. Vili Lehdonvirta et al., *The Global Platform Economy: A New Offshoring Institution Enabling Emerging-Economy Microproviders*, 45 Journal of Management 567, 567–599 n. 2 (2019).

1048. ILO, *supra* n. 25, at 118–121.

1049. Uma Rani & Marianne Furrer, *Digital Labour Platforms and New Forms of Flexible Work in Developing Countries: Algorithmic Management of Work and Workers*, 25 Competition & Change 212, 216 n. 2 (2021).

1050. On industrial home work, Manuela Tomei, *Home Work in Selected Latin American Countries: A Comparative Overview* 38 (ILO 2000). On crowdwork, Finkin, *supra* n. 628; and ILO Committee of Experts on the Application of Conventions and Recommendations, *supra* n. 633, at 208.

when drafting national laws and regulations that aim to protect homeworkers.[1051] A couple of years later, the Committee on Private Employment Agencies' conclusions similarly mentioned: "that certain types of agency that were scarcely mentioned in the ILO report, [...], deserved special attention and possible regulation by national governments in relation to abuses which are committed, particularly in the case of contract labour agencies which hire home workers for processing particular goods (e.g. cigarette rolling, hides, etc.)".[1052] Many crowdwork platforms can, likewise, be thought of as contract labour agencies of this kind. They hire home-based workers to process all kinds of digital tasks for user enterprises without assuming or imposing any employer responsibilities.

318 **The instrument's aim** – Looking at the text of the Home Work Convention, 1996 (No. 177), the preamble captures the eye. It mentions that many ILS lay down "standards of general application", which already apply to homeworkers. The preamble then points out that homeworkers' particular conditions make it desirable to improve the application of these standards and supplement them.[1053] In light of this, the ratifying Member States' "central obligation" is to adopt, implement and review a national policy on home work. This policy ought to cover certain forms of telework,[1054] and aims to improve homeworkers' and teleworkers' working conditions.[1055] According to the Committee of Experts, the policy's overall objective is for the protection of homeworkers to catch up to that of other workers at the employers' premises;[1056] the goal is to establish a level playing field between homeworkers and regular employees.[1057]

319 **National policy on crowdworkers?** – The following Subchapter's central question is whether this national policy on home work should also cover home-based platform workers. This question does not have an easy answer. Based on, for example, the Office's description of the 1990 Meeting of Experts, one would expect the instruments on home work to advance a broad scope of application.[1058] This broad

1051. ILO, *Social Protection of Homeworkers* 90 (ILO 1991).

1052. Conclusions concerning the role of private employment agencies in the functioning of labour markets, 81st Session of the International Labour Conference in 1994, 21/27.

1053. Preamble of the Home Work Convention, 1996 (No. 177).

1054. "The Committee wishes to recall, in this respect, that while it is true that the Convention does not apply to persons with employee status who occasionally perform their work as employees at home rather than at their usual workplaces, teleworking as a permanent arrangement, whether full-time or part-time – and not alternating with office-based work – is clearly covered by the definition of the term 'home work' set out in Article 1(a) of the Convention". Direct Request (CEACR) – adopted 2013, published 103rd ILC session (2014), Home Work Convention, 1996 (No. 177) – Netherlands (Ratification: 2002); ILO Committee of Experts on the Application of Conventions and Recommendations, *supra* n. 633, at 201.

1055. Reporter of the Committee on Home Work at the 83rd Session of the International Labour Conference, Geneva, ILO, 1996, 209.

1056. Equality of treatment between homeworkers and other wage earners is promoted as far as possible. ILO Committee of Experts on the Application of Conventions and Recommendations, *supra* n. 633, at 196 and 200.

1057. *Ibid.*, 199.

1058. "There was broad agreement that the lack of a clear definition of 'homeworkers' in labour legislation was a major impediment for extending social protection to such workers. Many experts from industrialized countries were of the opinion that the legal framework pertaining to

scope is necessary, amongst other reasons, in response to the various ways in which employers seek to keep home-based workers self-employed.[1059] However, despite this awareness, for the time being, uncertainty seems to still prevail concerning Convention No. 177's scope. Delaney et al. highlight that "[a] major weakness of Convention No. 177 [is] that it was largely modelled on an outdated model of the employment relationship and thus did not specifically mention or include self-employed workers, although the concept of economic dependence is included, thereby opening the door for other definitions and legislation".[1060] Since the Convention does not explicitly include self-employed workers in its scope, the fear is that it might not cover a large chunk of home-based workers. On the contrary, other scholars emphasise how the Convention potentially does have a broad scope. For instance, Davies suggests that the reference to "autonomy and economic independence" in Article 1 of Convention No. 177 "may be an attempt to ensure that, in those legal systems where 'sham' self-employment is an issue, only the truly independent are left outside the scope of the Convention".[1061]

The following Subchapters will explore this issue in full. First, the definition of the "employer" in Convention No. 177 is discussed. Section 1 subsequently explains the structure of Convention No. 177's definitions. As will be shown, the instrument implements a "basic definition", which presumes that workers with specific characteristics are "homeworkers". Only the homeworkers that show the degree of "autonomy" and of "economic independence" necessary to be considered an independent home-based worker are, in the next step, excluded from this "homeworker" concept and, therefore, from the scope of Convention No. 177 at large. 320

Having explained the definition itself in the First Section, Section 2 focuses explicitly on the meaning of "autonomy" and "economic independence" in the context of home work. This Second Section should not be understood to interpret the Convention as such. It discusses what a ratifying Member State might (not must!) consider relevant to settle whether a homeworker is rightfully considered self-employed. It tries to, in other words, give some reasonable substance to the concepts of "autonomy" and "economic independence" in this setting. However, that substance does not so much flow from the Convention but is primarily based on personal considerations. The Third Section concludes that based on the findings in Section 2, many crowdworkers might, in fact, be classified as homeworkers. It tentatively provides some indicators that can help us determine which crowdworkers are freelancers and which are covered under Convention No. 177. 321

homeworkers should be as broad as possible in order to cover the largest number of workers". ILO, *supra* n. 1045, at 55.

1059. Tomei, *supra* n. 1050, at 27–28 and 34.

1060. Annie Delaney, Jane Tate & Rosaria Burchielli, *Homeworkers Organizing for Recognition and Rights: Can International Standards Assist Them?* 159, 162 (Jill M. Jensen & Nelson Lichtenstein eds., *The ILO from Geneva to the Pacific Rim*, Palgrave Macmillan UK 2016).

1061. Anne C. L. Davies, *ILO Convention 177 Home Work Convention, 1996 (No. 177)* 909, 910 (Edoardo Ales, Mark Bell, Olaf Deinert & Sophie Robin-Olivier eds., *International and European Labour Law Article-by-Article Commentary*, Nomos 2018).

SUBCHAPTER 2. THE CONVENTION'S SCOPE

The definitions in the Home Work Convention, 1996 (No. 177):

> "Article 1
>
> For the purposes of this Convention:
>
> (a) the term **home work** means work carried out by a person, to be referred to as a homeworker,
>   (i) in his or her home or in other premises of his or her choice, other than the workplace of the employer;
>   (ii) for remuneration;
>   (iii) which results in a product or service as specified by the employer, irrespective of who provides the equipment, materials or other inputs used,
>
> unless this person has the degree of autonomy and of economic independence necessary to be considered an independent worker under national laws, regulations or court decisions;
>
> (b) persons with employee status do not become homeworkers within the meaning of this Convention simply by occasionally performing their work as employees at home, rather than at their usual workplaces;
>
> (c) the term **employer** means a person, natural or legal, who, either directly or through an intermediary, whether or not intermediaries are provided for in national legislation, gives out home work in pursuance of his or her business activity.
>
> Article 2
>
> This Convention applies to all persons carrying out home work within the meaning of Article 1".

1. The Basic Definition of a Homeworker

322 **Home-based workers and homeworkers** – One preliminary remark concerns the difference between "home-based workers" and "homeworkers". Together with the ILO Committee of Experts and the Office, the dissertation uses the concept of a home-based worker as an umbrella term to refer to anyone performing work from their home. This concept, for instance, includes independent freelancers and artisans who perform their work from home. Only home-based workers covered under Convention No. 177, because they lack autonomy or economic independence, will be called "homeworkers".[1062] The term homeworker is a legal concept, whereas the term home-based worker is a descriptive one. Precision is needed in this respect, among other reasons because the discussions at the standard-setting Committee on Home Work have indicated that the regulation of home work is a sensitive topic. In the words of Boris, when drafting the instruments, the Employers "[b]itterly opposed" the effort to reign in all forms of home work. Moreover, they still criticise the Home

1062. ILO Committee of Experts on the Application of Conventions and Recommendations, *supra* n. 633, at 201; ILO, *supra* n. 613, at 6.

Work Convention, 1996 (No. 177), to this day.[1063] This dissatisfaction may have something to do with a unique feature of Convention No. 177, namely its definition of the term "employer" in Article 1(c).

Employers and intermediaries – ILS rarely define or identify the employer. That is something that is generally left to domestic law to do. However, this time, the ILO constituents recognised the importance of defining the concept to regulate home work. In this regard, the initial descriptions given to the "employer" and "intermediary" caused concern.[1064] An intermediary was at first depicted as an entity that receives assignments and passes them on. An employer, on the other hand, gives out or causes home work. Because of these precise descriptions, some feared an intermediary might have become considered an employer, for example, if it altered the original assignment. In that case, it would no longer just "pass on" the work, perhaps becoming an employer. Other respondents to the questionnaire were apparently convinced that intermediaries, such as contractors and agents, should always be considered the employers of homeworkers. 323

Eventually, for these and other reasons, the Office decided to delete its definition of an intermediary. The Office, furthermore, clarified that the "responsibility is placed on the employer as the giver of work", making it unnecessary to be more precise about the differences between intermediaries.[1065] The ordinary meaning of an "intermediary" sufficed. According to the Office, an intermediary in this context is "someone acting between the parties", or as the Committee of Experts puts it, "a means of matching the supply and demand for [home] work".[1066] 324

Putting the spotlight on the "employer" meant that, contrary to what is the case for Convention No. 181 on private employment agencies, it is not the intermediary but the employer that is the critical figure for applying Convention No. 177. The Convention defines the employer as "a person, natural or legal, who, either directly or through an intermediary, whether or not intermediaries are provided for in national legislation, gives out home work in pursuance of his or her business activity". When reading Article 1(a)(iii) and Article 1(c) together, in order for a platform user to be 325

1063. Eileen Boris, *Mothers, Household Managers, and Productive Workers: The International Labor Organization and Women in Development*, 14 Global Social Policy 189, 203 n. 2 (2014). The Office noted based on the first questionnaire, before the discussions at the Conference had started, that "[r]eplies from workers' organizations overwhelmingly supported standards, while most employers' organizations opposed any standards on home work or had strong reservations about the adoption of national policies on home work which were not consistent with national custom and practice". ILO, *Report V (2) Home Work* 12 (ILO 1995).

1064. The Office initially asked the constituents: "Should the term 'employer' mean any physical or legal person who, either directly or through an intermediary, gives out or causes home work as defined below to be given out to a homeworker?" and "Should the term 'intermediary' mean a person who receives work assignments from an employer with a view to passing them on to a homeworker"? ILO, *supra* n. 1045, at 84–85.

1065. ILO, *supra* n. 1063, at 38. *See also*, Committee on Home Work at the 82nd Session of the International Labour Conference, Geneva, ILO, 1995, 25/22.

1066. *Ibid.*, 38; ILO Committee of Experts on the Application of Conventions and Recommendations, *supra* n. 633, at 208. The Committee's discussions point out that whether the intermediary is legal or illegal is irrelevant. Committee on Home Work at the 83rd Session of the International Labour Conference, Geneva, ILO, 1996, 10/23.

considered the "employer", the platform user must give out home work in pursuance of his or her business activity, providing the specifications of the product or service, which is to be delivered to the employer.[1067]

326 **A business activity** – In light of this description, clarity is needed about what constitutes a business activity. According to the French text of the Convention, the employer gives out home work "for the account of his or her business", furthermore, providing the "specifications". In terms of the ordinary meaning of a "business (activity)", according to *Black's Law Dictionary*, business means "[a] commercial enterprise carried on for profit; a particular occupation or employment habitually engaged in for livelihood or gain".[1068] The *Bouvier Law Dictionary* describes it as "[a]ny enterprise creating employment, service, or profit".[1069] To that extent, unless the working documents point out that "business (activity)" was supposed to have a special meaning, it would seem that also universities or think tanks that use crowdworkers for research purposes conduct a business activity in the sense of Convention No. 177.[1070] The working documents bear out the fact that the reference to business activities aimed to distinguish the interaction between a homeworker and employer from the interaction between an independent worker and customer. If the home-based worker makes a suit, for instance, and sells it to a customer for his or her personal use, the worker is an independent contractor. If instead the suit is made at home but eventually sold to the public in a shop, the enterprise running the shop might have given out "home work". The home-based worker might, then, be classified as a homeworker of this enterprise.[1071] Despite these clarifications, ILO constituents responded to the Office's second questionnaire that they remained uncertain about the exact consequences of the definition given to an employer. The Office, therefore, explicitly clarified in its commentary to the second questionnaire that "'[b]usiness' is sufficiently broad to cover the 'business' of governmental or non-profit organizations and is not restricted to private sector profit-making activities".[1072] Persons who give out "home work" for personal use or consumption are not covered.[1073]

327 **A two-step definition for homeworkers** – Having delineated which platform users can be an "employer" under Convention No. 177, the broader definition needs to be analysed. Article 1 relies on three criteria to describe home work. First, home work is carried out by a person on premises of his or her choice, other than the workplace of the employer. This location can be the worker's home, a workshop or

1067. Art. 1(a)(iii) states that home work "results in a product or service as specified by the employer, irrespective of who provides the equipment, materials or other inputs used". Home Work Convention, 1996 (No. 177).

1068. Definition of business in *Black's Law Dictionary* (11th ed. 2019) (accessed on Westlaw).

1069. Definition of business in *The Wolters Kluwer Bouvier Law Dictionary* Desk Edition (accessed on LexisNexis).

1070. On how crowdwork is utilised for research purposes, *see, e.g.*, Nathan Schneider, *Intellectual Piecework; Increasingly Used in Research, Platforms like Mechanical Turk Pose New Ethical Dilemmas*, 61 The Chronicle of Higher Education n. 23 (2015).

1071. ILO, *Report IV (1) Home Work* 5 (ILO 1995).

1072. ILO, *Report IV (2 A) Home Work* 39 (ILO 1996).

1073. ILO Committee of Experts on the Application of Conventions and Recommendations, *supra* n. 633, at 201.

any other premises of his or her choice.[1074] Secondly, the work is performed in return for remuneration, and thirdly, it results in a product or service as specified by the employer. These three criteria are the constitutive elements for the basic definition of home work.[1075] Subsequently, the last paragraph of Article 1(a) clarifies that even if these conditions are cumulatively fulfilled, this person is, nevertheless, an independent worker, hence excluded from the convention's coverage, if "this person has the degree of autonomy and of economic independence necessary to be considered an independent worker under national laws, regulations or court decisions".

In other words, the definition of a homeworker proceeds in two stages. As remarked by Vosko, the Convention introduces a presumption.[1076] If the worker fulfils the basic definition of home work, the home-based worker is presumed to be a homeworker covered by the Convention. Subsequently, even if the person has these characteristics, if "this person" is sufficiently autonomous and economically independent, the home-based worker is, nonetheless, rightfully considered independent. As a result of this two-step approach, Convention No. 177 contains what could be described as an autonomous "homeworker" concept. 328

Autonomous homeworker concept – The autonomous nature of the concept is illustrated in the definitions of Convention No. 177. For instance, whereas the Employment Relationship Recommendation, 2006 (No. 198) considers the use of personal tools as a valid indicator of self-employment, this is not the case for home-based work under Convention No. 177.[1077] As Convention No. 177 mentions, it does not matter whether the home-based worker uses his or her own tools; that should not affect the home-based worker's classification as a homeworker.[1078] Secondly, when looking at Article 1 of Convention No. 177, clause (a)(i)-(iii) provides the basic definition for a homeworker, after which the final clause makes clear that "this person" is covered "unless this person has the degree of autonomy and of economic independence necessary". Economic independence is not a criterion that the ILO Member States commonly use to distinguish between employees and self-employed workers. Therefore, the Conference's choice to require both a degree of autonomy 329

1074. *Ibid.*, 202.
1075. "This definition conformed to the majority of views expressed that the instruments should provide the basic definition of home work, but allow flexibility to take account of other criteria under national law which would distinguish homeworkers from truly independent workers". The representative of the Secretary-General during the Committee on Home Work at the 82nd Session of the International Labour Conference, Geneva, ILO, 1995, 25/3.
1076. Vosko, *supra* n. 198, at 173.
1077. The "provision of tools, materials and machinery by the party requesting the work" is one indicator listed by the Employment Relationship Recommendation, 2006 (No. 198), to settle the existence of an employment relationship. The Committee of Experts has put the importance of this indicator into perspective by clarifying that in certain cases, such as home work and platform work, other elements or indicators exist "that more clearly demonstrate the essence of the business and the true relationship that exists between the parties, and the manner in which workers are integrated in the main business". ILO Committee of Experts on the Application of Conventions and Recommendations, *supra* n. 633, at 111.
1078. Art. 1(a)(iii) Home Work Convention, 1996 (No. 177).

and economic independence matters.[1079] Although it is up to the Member States to determine the exact degree of autonomy and economic independence "necessary", the Convention obliges the Member State to consider both criteria.

330 In addition to these two examples, the working documents further illustrate how Convention No. 177 introduces an autonomous homeworker concept. In the first questionnaire, the Office asked the ILO constituents whether the term "homeworker" should "mean a person who, whether or not he or she has the status of employee, carries out home work as defined below".[1080] In its summary of the responses, the Office notes that even though some constituents insisted that only employees should be covered by the instruments, "consistent with numerous replies, the Office believes that the instruments should encompass those persons who are employees, those who are not employees but have a special status as homeworkers, and those whose status is unclear, but nonetheless more closely resemble an employee rather than an independent contractor".[1081] Later on, the Office again emphasised that the definitions in the draft instrument "reflected the view that the definition should be as inclusive as possible".[1082] These definitions were, subsequently, revised as a result of the discussions at the first Committee on Home Work.[1083] According to the Office, the revised text still meant that "a person who works at home for remuneration on work which results in a product or service specified by the employer can only be denied the status of homeworker if he or she has the degree of autonomy and of economic independence necessary to be considered an independent worker under national laws, regulations or court decisions".[1084] These features explain why the Employers' Vice-Chairperson complained about the Convention's definitions because they "amounted to an internationally imposed 'strait-jacket'".[1085]

331 **Occasional home-based work** – Another illustration of how Convention No. 177 introduces an autonomous concept can be found in Article 1(b). This clause is sometimes wrongly interpreted as people who only occasionally perform home work not constituting homeworkers. Initially, the Government member of the United States submitted a far-reaching amendment to make sure that "[a] person does not

1079. This is clear in some of the Committee of Experts' clarifications. For instance, "[t]he Committee notes therefore that the Convention may apply to wage earners who would not qualify as employees under national law but who are nevertheless in a relationship of economic dependence with another (a natural or legal person)". Observation (CEACR) – adopted 2018, published 108th ILC session (2019), Home Work Convention, 1996 (No. 177) – Bulgaria (Ratification: 2009).

1080. ILO, *supra* n. 1045, at 84.

1081. ILO, *supra* n. 1063, at 36.

1082. The representative of the Secretary-General during the Committee on Home Work at the 82nd Session of the International Labour Conference, Geneva, ILO, 1995, 25/3. When answering to the ILO constituents' responses to the second questionnaire, the Office confirmed that "the intent is to have a broad definition so as to include those who may not already be recognized as having employee status but who are not truly independent". ILO, *supra* n. 1072, at 37.

1083. Committee on Home Work at the 82nd Session of the International Labour Conference, Geneva, ILO, 1995, 25/20.

1084. ILO, *supra* n. 1071, at 4.

1085. Committee on Home Work at the 83rd Session of the International Labour Conference, Geneva, ILO, 1996, 10/36.

become a homeworker within the meaning of this Convention simply by performing incidental work for the employer in his or her own home".[1086] This broad exemption was, however, fine-tuned through subamendments. The Workers' group in particular wanted to clarify that the exemption only applied to home-based workers with employee status and not to all homeworkers. Furthermore, only if the home work was "incidental to his workplace-based work for his employer" could an exemption be allowed.[1087] In the end, the US Government's amendment, as subamended, was adopted as follows: "persons with employee status do not become homeworkers within the meaning of this Convention simply by occasionally performing their work as employees at home, rather than at their usual workplaces".[1088] Therefore, this exemption has become much narrower than the initial proposal. The occasional provision of home work is not covered under Convention No. 177, if and only if it concerns an employee who incidentally performs his or her work at home. So occasional teleworkers, who are employees, are not covered. Yet, whenever the home-based worker is not an employee of the "employer", even the incidental performance of home work for an "employer" in the sense of Convention No. 177 should, in principle, be protected under the Convention.[1089] These occasional home-based workers without employee status, such as many crowdworkers, are protected if they fulfil the basic definition;[1090] occasional homeworkers without employee status are covered unless they have the degree of autonomy and economic independence necessary to be considered self-employed workers under national law.

Therefore, since the frequency with which home work is performed, most likely, **332**
does not directly affect the crowdworker's classification as a homeworker, because crowdworkers are usually not employees, the following Section will only deal with the degree of (economic) autonomy necessary to be considered an independent home-based worker. The following discussion of "autonomy" and "economic independence" is merely illustrative. It aims to show that Convention No. 177 is most likely relevant for certain crowdworkers. Nothing in Convention No. 177 suggests that the concepts of autonomy and economic independence must be interpreted along the lines of the following Section.

1086. *Ibid.*, 10/21.

1087. *Ibid.*, 10/21.

1088. Art. 1(b) Home Work Convention, 1996 (No. 177).

1089. This would correspond with the recommendations of Huws and Podro. These authors issued some recommendations to stimulate the debate at 1996's Committee on Home Work. They proposed to not look at the number of working hours at home. What should be excluded from the scope are "'genuine freelancers' who work on their own account for a variety of different clients or sell their products directly to the general public". Ursula Huws & Sarah Podro, *Employment of Homeworkers: Examples of Good Practice* 2 (ILO 1995).

1090. The crowdworker that carries out work (i) in his or her home or in other premises of his or her choice, other than the workplace of the employer, (ii) for remuneration, (iii) which results in a product or service as specified by the platform user in pursuance of his or her business activity, is presumed to be a homeworker covered under Convention No. 177.

2. Autonomy and Economic Independence in Home-Based Work

333 **First criterion: A degree of autonomy** – One question regarding Convention No. 177's reference to a "degree of autonomy" is how it relates to the concepts of subordination and control. As argued above, Article 1 of Convention No. 177 presents a distinct description of the "homeworker" that is not identical to a "home-working employee", like a stereotypical teleworker. Arguably, because of the autonomous concept, the specific meaning of "autonomy" for the purpose of excluding independent home-based workers from the Convention's scope should be uncovered, not the meaning of autonomy for the distinction between regular employees and self-employed workers. Having said this, it is clear that even for home-based workers, their level of autonomy is somewhat related to the corresponding employer's level of authority to direct and control the home-based worker. After all, if an employer or intermediary directs and controls the home-based worker through certain mechanisms, the latter's autonomy likely decreases. So, direction and control are, to some extent, related to autonomy, even for home-based workers.

334 At the same time, as indicated by the example of "autonomous employees", employees can be legally subordinated and, thus, work under the control and authority of an employer while, nevertheless, performing their work with a high degree of autonomy. As such, autonomy relates to authority/supervision, but autonomy is not the opposite thereof.[1091] Consider the example of Uber. Some courts decided that Uber's workers are employees; others decided that the workers cannot be classified as employees. The courts that classify Uber drivers as self-employed often conclude that, overall, they are not working under Uber's control and authority. However, while this could be the court's overall conclusion, that same court might not necessarily agree with the claim that Uber drivers are "autonomous". Some courts might conclude that although these drivers are not employees under domestic law, they are in fact "sub-entrepreneurs" that are "operating under the legal classification of independent contractors but deprived of some of the key elements of control over their activity, with this type of work usually associated with low pay and minimal conditions".[1092] The driver has nothing to say about the price, very little control over the passengers to transport, runs the risk of having to financially compensate Uber and the passenger when taking an alternative route, and so forth. While at work, the Uber driver has little autonomy, even if the worker might not be legally subordinated. The driver supposedly belongs to the so-called "grey zone" between employment and self-employment. The crucial point to make in this respect is that, as evidenced by the Office's remarks above (*supra* no. 330), the Home Work Convention, 1996 (No. 177), aims to erase this grey zone for home-based workers in favour of their classification as homeworkers instead of independent home-based workers. Because of this, a non-subordinated, non-autonomous crowdworker should be covered.

335 For these reasons, the point is not to ask ourselves whether a crowdworker is subordinated or controlled. That would often leave crowdworkers in this grey zone

1091. Frank Hendrickx, *From Digits to Robots: The Privacy-Autonomy Nexus in New Labor Law Machinery*, 40 Comparative Labor Law & Policy Journal 365, 375–378 n. 3 (2019).
1092. Josserand & Kaine, *supra* n. 10, at 566.

outside of Convention No. 177's scope. Instead, the question must be what is the meaning of autonomy as such, because that criterion is supposed to signal the homeworker's truly independent nature. According to law dictionaries, the ordinary meaning of autonomy relates to the "individual's capacity for self-determination",[1093] for "self-governance",[1094] or the individual's independence.[1095] Researchers make similar findings. A group of workers was asked what they understood autonomy at work to mean. "The results indicate that the experience of autonomy includes not only the freedom to make decisions, but also an overall sense of authorship regarding decisions".[1096] Labour economists and sociologists similarly describe autonomy as "the extent to which employees exercise discretion in their work"[1097] or "the extent to which an employee is able to exercise discretion and initiative over what happens on the job".[1098]

Homeworkers' autonomy – In relation to Convention No. 177, the reference to a 336
"degree of autonomy" is embedded in Article 1(a), *in fine*, which reads: "unless this person has the degree of autonomy [...]". "This person" refers to the person that carries out home work along the lines of the basic definition found in Article 1(a) (i-iii).[1099] In other words, the point is not to settle whether any person has the degree of autonomy required to be considered an independent worker under national law; this question is contextualised. Does the *worker who performs home work* have the degree of autonomy necessary to be considered an independent home-based worker? This contextualisation might have certain consequences.

As mentioned before, the Employment Relationship Recommendation, 2006 (No. 198), 337
indicates that "the provision of tools, materials and machinery by the party requesting the work" can be considered an indicator of employment status.[1100] Convention No. 177, on the other hand, indicates that "who provides the equipment, materials or other inputs" is irrelevant in the context of home-based work.[1101] So whereas in general, one might think that using a personal laptop, instead of an employer's device, increases the worker's degree of autonomy when at work, this should not matter to assess the degree of autonomy for people who work home-based.

1093. *Black's Law Dictionary*, 11th edition, 2019 (accessed on Westlaw).
1094. *The Wolters Kluwer Bouvier Law Dictionary* Desk Edition (accessed on LexisNexis).
1095. *Ballentine's Law Dictionary*, 3rd edition, 2010 (accessed on LexisNexis).
1096. Ana L. S. V. Lopes & Adriana V. Garibaldi de Hilal, *Autonomy at Work: The Perspective of a Group of Brazilian Skilled Workers*, 17 Latin American Business Review 289, 307 n. 4 (2016).
1097. Jonas Estlund & Anne Grönlund, *Class and Work Autonomy in 21 Countries: A Question of Production Regime or Power Resources?*, 53 Acta Sociologica 213, 213 n. 3 (2010).
1098. Arne L. Kalleberg, Torstein Nesheim & Karen M. Olsen, *Is Participation Good or Bad for Workers?: Effects of Autonomy, Consultation and Teamwork on Stress Among Workers in Norway*, 52 Acta Sociologica 99, 101 n. 2 (2009).
1099. "*It is recalled that the original Office text provided that persons who met the requirements in the core part of the definition of home work (subparagraphs (a) (i), (ii) and (iii)) would be considered as homeworkers, unless they had the degree of autonomy and fulfilled other conditions (those in addition to (i), (ii), and (iii)), necessary to be considered independent workers under national laws, regulations or court decisions*". ILO, *supra* n. 1072, at 36.
1100. Para. 13 Employment Relationship Recommendation, 2006 (No. 198).
1101. Art. 1(a)(iii) Home Work Convention, 1996 (No. 177).

338 **Lack of direct supervision** – Along similar lines, one could argue that the Member States, which establish the indicators that evaluate the degree of autonomy necessary to be considered an independent home-based worker, should take all "special characteristics of home work" into consideration;[1102] not just the fact that employers will ask home-based workers to use their own tools if this counts as an indicator of their independent status. For example, the fact that the employer does not supervise the work directly is another factor that might be relevant to settling a worker's employment status at the employer's premises, but it is not pertinent in assessing the degree of autonomy enjoyed by a home-based worker. Since home-based work is performed away from the employer's workplace, it "implies that there is very little direct supervision or regulation of methods of work by the employer".[1103] The Office's working definition in its Law and Practice Report on home work explicitly mentioned that "[i]t is normally carried out without direct supervision by the employer or contractor".[1104] The (lack of) direct supervision on homeworkers was also briefly discussed during the first discussions at the Committee on Home Work. The Government member of Egypt proposed amending the description of home work to clarify that homeworkers lack "direct supervision" by their employer. The Employers' members supported the amendment, and the Workers' members did not oppose it, even though they considered it "superfluous". The representative of the Secretary-General clarified that the Office had not included such phrasing because modern forms of home work, such as telework, enable the employer to have direct control of the work. The Government members of Australia, Canada, Norway and the United States opposed the amendment in light of the representative's explanation.[1105] This entire discussion seems to reflect ILO constituents' implicit understanding that industrial homeworkers are, in principle, not directly supervised by their employers. In other words, just like the use of personal equipment, the lack of direct supervision should not be considered indicative of autonomous, independent home-based work.

339 **Indirect constraints on autonomy** – Given the lack of "direct" supervision, home work is characterised by structures that indirectly constrain home-based workers' autonomy. As explained by Benton, "[i]n the case of homework, the employer surrenders direct control over workers and relies on a combination of piecework incentives and indirect social controls to force workers to be productive".[1106] The employer and intermediary, most notably, maintain indirect control over homeworkers' productive activities by controlling the supply of work and the piece rate.[1107] Piece-rate pay, in which "workers are paid by the unit performed", "is a specific type of incentive

1102. Preamble of the Home Work Convention, 1996 (No. 177).
1103. Schneider de Villegas, *supra* n. 630, at 4.
1104. ILO, *supra* n. 1045, at 5.
1105. Committee on Home Work at the 82nd Session of the International Labour Conference, Geneva, ILO, 1995, 25/16.
1106. Benton, *supra* n. 1013, at 256.
1107. "Many surveys carried out in developing countries found that homeworkers complained of an inadequate and irregular supply of work. They were fearful of asking for higher rates because they did not want to risk losing the work, in view of the fact that there were many other homeworkers who would have been willing to do it for the rates offered". ILO, *supra* n. 1045, at 20; Baylina & Dolors Garcia-Ramon, *supra* n. 1013, at 59.

pay".[1108] Unless effectively regulated, reward systems that are based on incentive pay can be manipulated.[1109] Industrial homeworkers, for instance, report instances in which the piece rate goes down, arguably, because the worker's productivity goes up.[1110] Lower-paid workers in particular may perceive such performance-related pay as "controlling".[1111]

Platform operators are in a position to master this craft. Researchers have inquired 340
whether piece-rate systems can substitute for traditional forms of management and monitoring. This substitution seems more feasible in some cases than in others. For instance, when the cost of administering piece-rate systems diminishes, and when it is known how quickly a job can be executed, the substitution would be facilitated.[1112] Platforms may be in a relatively favourable position in this regard. Their algorithms can administer such systems rather efficiently, and because they may know how long it takes for other workers to perform similar tasks, e.g. workers tag x number of pictures or translate y number of sentences an hour on average, they may be capable of enhancing the level of control a piece-rate system can exert. In short, platform operators may have the information needed to adjust piece rates deliberately,[1113] and seemingly have the technological capacity to do it systematically. For example, Griesbach et al. report that "[m]any Instacart workers with whom [they] spoke believe that the algorithm 'learns' the lowest rate it can successfully offer for an order within a particular region at a particular time and day of the week". Some workers even believed "the algorithmic pricing system facilitates individual-level pay discrimination: that it learns each worker's reservation wage, the lowest rate each is likely to accept, and then tailors offers to each accordingly".[1114] Although Instacart generates local on-demand work, it is not hard to imagine how a crowdwork platform could similarly apply dynamic pricing. Clickworker, for instance, charges platform users 10 cents per word for translations by native speakers and 16 cents per word for translations with additional proofreading by a second clickworker.[1115] On platforms like these, the primary way to earn more money is to work more hours.[1116] Experience, better ratings, and improved skills seem to have little impact on the earnings of these workers.[1117] Such workers are largely at the mercy of platforms' piece-rate systems.

1108. Floriana Borino, *Piece Rate Pay and Working Conditions in the Export Garment Sector* 4 (ILO 2018).
1109. Alfie Kohn, *Why Incentive Plans Cannot Work*, 71 Harvard Business Review 54, 57 n. 5 (1993).
1110. Von Broembsen, *supra* n. 1014, at 9–10.
1111. W. D. McCausland, K. Pouliakas & I. Theodossiou, *Some are Punished and Some are Rewarded: A Study of the Impact of Performance Pay on Job Satisfaction*, 26 International Journal of Manpower 636, 653 n. 7/8 (2005).
1112. B. R. Skelton & Bruce Yandle, *Piece Rate Pay*, 3 Journal of Labor Research 201, 201–209 n. 2 (1982); Borino, *supra* n. 1108, at 4.
1113. Niels van Doorn, *From a Wage to a Wager: Dynamic Pricing in the Gig Economy* 9, 13–14 (James Muldoon & Will Stronge eds., *Platforming Equality: Policy Challenges for the Digital Economy*, Autonomy 2020).
1114. Kathleen Griesbach, Adam Reich, Luke Elliott-Negri & Ruth Milkman, *Algorithmic Control in Platform Food Delivery Work*, 5 Socius 1, 5–6 (2019).
1115. Clickworker, *Pricing*, Clickworker (17 November 2020), https://www.clickworker.com/pricing/.
1116. Mark Graham et al., *The Risks and Rewards of Online Gig Work At the Global Margins* 8 (Oxford Internet Institute 2017).
1117. Rani & Jeet Singh, *supra* n. 181, at 270.

341 More broadly, the point is that the autonomy of crowdworkers is restricted in a rather indirect manner, not through direct supervision and discipline. Vallas and Schor argue, in particular, that platform workers' limited autonomy is largely due to "the disciplining effect of the market rather than to high levels of centralized managerial control".[1118] Consider the following illustration: it is vital for high-skilled workers on platforms to have an excellent online reputation in order to obtain (good) jobs. Therefore, crowdworkers who are new and who have to still build a reputable profile "offer additional tasks, demand less payment or forfeit payment at all, do extra revisions or are constantly available in case the customers are not satisfied".[1119] In search of favourable ratings, this competition seems to foster wage dumping,[1120] thereby limiting established crowdworkers' chances of increasing their remuneration because new workers are willing to underbid. Rolandsson et al. observe, for example, how on a platform for online translators, "[e]ven with the education and skills necessary to join the crowd of online translators, the fierce competition on the platforms enables companies to demand that translators either accept job offers without unnecessary negotiations, or leave them to another willing to accept the pay, deadline or other conditions".[1121] This case study illustrates Vallas and Schor's point: the disciplining effect of the market limits workers' autonomy. Another somewhat dystopian example of how the dynamics on a platform's marketplace restrict workers' autonomy can be found on a Chinese platform. ZBJ.com – the "largest online aggregated labour platform in China" – uses a "big-data matching mechanism" that:

> "assigns the tasks to a workers [sic] who then has 15 minutes to respond to the invitation and accept the work or not. If a worker is non-responsive, the system will reassign the project to other available candidates. Given that this platform offers workers the option of paying different levels of 'fees and membership', it is likely that the algorithm will prioritize the amount of fees paid by the worker when allocating jobs, with workshop members given first priority, followed by the online members and the non-member registered workers".[1122]

342 Besides the potential manipulation of piece rates, and the "disciplining" effect of the market mechanics, another factor that might constrain home-based workers' autonomy is the employer's specifications.[1123] As the ILO Committee of Experts notes,

---

1118. Vallas & Schor, *supra* n. 86, at 284.

1119. "[W]hen trying to develop an online reputation, crowdworkers are completely and utterly at the clients' mercy and seem to be prepared to make any concessions in terms of payment, time, availability, number of revisions, etc". Schörpf, Flecker, Schönauer & Eichmann, *supra* n. 281, at 51 and 55.

1120. Georg Jäger, Laura S. Zilian, Christian Hofer & Manfred Füllsack, *Crowdworking: Working With or Against the Crowd?*, 14 Journal of Economic Interaction and Coordination 761, 783–786 n. 4 (2019).

1121. "In practice, it seems, the first translator who accepts an offer distributed via the platforms gets the job". Bertil Rolandsson, Antti Saloniemi & Tiina Saari, *High-skilled Platform Work in Finland and Sweden – The Case of Technical Translators* 47, 50 (Kristin Jesnes & Sigurd M. Nordli Oppegaard eds., *Platform Work in the Nordic Models: Issues, Cases and Responses*, Nordic Council of Ministers 2020).

1122. Yiu Por Chen, *Online Labour Platforms in China: Working Conditions, Policy Issues and Prospects* 10 and 37 (ILO 2021).

1123. ILO, *supra* n. 1063, at 36.

"[t]he requirement for products or services to respond to the specifications provided by the employer is an element that serves to determine the 'non-autonomous' nature of home work".[1124] For example, the mechanisms provided by Upwork challenge the autonomous nature of its freelancers. The worker and user on Upwork can decide to subdivide a fixed-price job into various phases, due dates and deliverables. This is achieved by allowing parties before and over the contract's course to add, edit, and rearrange so-called "milestones" through Upwork's website. Upon having accepted the project, the freelancer submits milestones for review. Upwork recommends to users that "[f]or each milestone, you'll detail exactly what your freelancer or agency agreed to provide in return for the funds you will deposit in escrow. [...] Be as specific as you can. This is your chance to formalize the agreement about what is to be delivered, when, and for how much money".[1125]

Working time autonomy – In addition to the systems above that limit home-based workers' functional autonomy, one can also reflect on the link between the home-based workers' autonomy and working time flexibility. After all, Wheatley subdivides workers' autonomy into "job control" and "schedule control". "Job control refers to autonomy over tasks and work conduct"; while "[s]chedule control reflects control over the timing and location of paid work".[1126] When thinking about homeworkers' particular circumstances, schedule control does not seem all too relevant in assessing home-based workers' autonomy. Ultimately, home-based workers are, by and large, expected to control the timing of their work. The European Framework Agreement on Telework, for instance, clarifies that teleworkers manage their own working time within the boundaries of applicable legislation, collective agreements and company rules.[1127] The Framework Agreement provides teleworkers with what is referred to as "time sovereignty".[1128] Enabling teleworkers to control their schedule – enjoy time sovereignty – avoids potential conflicts between working time and family/leisure time. It allows for a better work-life balance.[1129] Moreover, working time autonomy is also vital to ensure that telework is productive and benefits employers.[1130] To this extent, **343**

1124. ILO Committee of Experts on the Application of Conventions and Recommendations, *supra* n. 633, at 202.
1125. Upwork, *Milestones for Fixed-Price Jobs*, Upwork (27 September 2020), https://support.upwork.com/hc/en-us/articles/211068218-Milestones-for-Fixed-Price-Jobs.
1126. Daniel Wheatley, *Autonomy in Paid Work and Employee Subjective Well-being*, 44 Work and Occupations 296, 297 n. 3 (2017).
1127. Framework Agreement on Telework, 28 June 2006.
1128. ILO, *Teleworking During the COVID-19 Pandemic and Beyond: A Practical Guide* 5 (ILO 2020).
1129. Takao Maruyama, Peter G. Hopkinson & Peter W. James, *A Multivariate Analysis of Work-life Balance Outcomes from a Large-scale Telework Programme*, 24 New Technology, Work and Employment 76, 84–85 n. 1 (2009). Teleworkers that "are given a substantial degree of autonomy regarding where, when and how they work" are "happier, healthier and experience less stress". Jon C. Messenger, *Conclusions and Recommendations for Policy and Practice* 286, 305 (Jon C. Messenger ed., *Telework in the 21st Century: An Evolutionary Perspective*, Edward Elgar Publishing 2019).
1130. "This is an important finding because, as will be discussed later in this chapter, a Eurofound study points to the importance of working time autonomy in relation to the work–life balance of workers, particularly as regards the implications for productivity". ILO and Eurofound, *Working Anytime, Anywhere: The Effects on the World of Work* 25 (Publications Office of the European Union 2017).

if working time autonomy is needed to implement home-based work successfully, it would seem inappropriate to consider it an indicator of homeworkers' autonomous nature. As time sovereignty is needed for performative home work arrangements, the degree of home-based workers' schedule control is a skewed indicator for assessing homeworkers' autonomy. This is all the more so because governments and employers' representatives specifically wanted Convention No. 177 not to restrain homeworkers' working time flexibility through working time regulation.[1131] As such, it would be cynical to claim, on the one hand, that homeworkers' working time should remain flexible and largely unregulated and, on the other, that if home-based workers have schedule control, they are autonomous and should be seen as independent home-based workers instead of homeworkers.

344 **Focus on job control** – For these reasons, it would make more sense to assess the homeworker's degree of autonomy primarily based on job control, i.e. the homeworker's control over tasks and work conduct. As claimed by the Barbados Workers' Union during the Office's preliminary research, even "private contractors, they have no control over what to produce, how to produce and when to produce. They have to depend on work orders handed to them".[1132] In other words, they often have no job control. As far as working time autonomy is relevant to the evaluation of home-based workers' overall autonomy, the emphasis should be on the degree of flexibility envisaged while executing the work order. In any case, crowdworkers' nominal ability to reject job offers should not lead us to conclude that they have significant autonomy. The degree to which this ability to reject job offers bolsters workers' autonomy largely depends on personal circumstances.[1133] Since "[c]rowdworkers often do not find sufficient work and have to continuously look for it without any guarantee of finding any",[1134] if a worker is dependent on this source of income,[1135] the option to reject jobs becomes notional. Therefore, assuming schedule control matters at all, which, arguably, it should not, the inquiry should go much beyond this nominal ability to reject offers. Crowdworkers' "flexibility myth" is, for instance, illustrated by the 44 per cent of respondents who indicate that they lose sleep because "workers were expected to work at night to be in sync with their clients" in the US, UK and elsewhere.[1136] Other researchers observed that 43 per cent report working during the night (from 10 p.m. to 5 a.m.) and 68 per cent during the evening (from 6 p.m. to 10 p.m.).[1137] Some research has even found that the majority of micro-taskers in

1131. ILO, *supra* n. 613, at 189.

1132. ILO, *Part IV: Positions on Home Work*, 8 Conditions of Work Digest 159, 178 n. 2 (1989).

1133. "[T]he degree of control that the workers enjoyed in practice varied significantly between platforms and individuals". Vili Lehdonvirta, *Flexibility in the Gig Economy: Managing Time on Three Online Piecework Platforms*, 33 New Technology, Work and Employment 13, 23 n. 1 (2018); Dubal, *supra* n. 615; Anwar & Graham, *supra* n. 288, at 248.

1134. Berg et al., *supra* n. 23, at 62.

1135. Eurofound mentions that "click-workers" "tend to be pushed into platform work by necessity, either due to lack of other employment alternatives or because it is the simplest solution to earn money". Eurofound, *supra* n. 303, at 7.

1136. Wood, Graham, Lehdonvirta & Hjorth, *supra* n. 101, at 67.

1137. Berg et al., *supra* n. 23, at 67. Not all of this may be related to differing time zones, however. Research on Russian-speaking internet-based freelancers indicates that "[a]pproximately two-thirds of Internet-based freelancers in our sample work after 9 p.m. regularly, including

developing countries work at night,[1138] which, if confirmed, speaks volumes about the extent of schedule control these jobs enable.

Second criterion: A degree of economic independence – An independent crowdworker needs to have a certain degree of autonomy, as detailed above, and economic independence, as described below. The Office's initial draft of Article 1(a), *in fine*, referred to a degree of autonomy and "other conditions" necessary to be considered an independent worker under national law. The Workers' members brought up the concept of economic dependence to give substance to these "other conditions". They wanted the instrument to solely exclude home-based workers who perform "truly autonomous work not done in economic dependence on employers".[1139] Employers' representatives and certain governments objected to relying on economic independence, however, because the concept was not commonly used.[1140] Indeed, only some legal systems attribute labour and social protection to workers for reasons of economic dependence. Various criteria are thereby used to define economic dependence.[1141] **345**

A brief comparative overview is given in this regard to get a sense of what it might mean for a crowdworker to be economically independent. A good starting point to that end is a comparative study by Perulli. The author identified four characteristics of economic dependence that were used in the EU Member States' legislation. Economically dependent work entails, first, "mainly personal work" that is, secondly, performed continuously over time, whereby, thirdly, coordination occurs between the worker's performance and the client's business activity. Fourthly, the work is performed "mainly for one single client", turning the client into "a major source of worker's income".[1142] This research dates back to 2002. More recent legislation and case law provide, *inter alia*, the following descriptions of economic dependence: **346**

- Todolí-Signes noted in 2019 how section 11 of the Self-employed Workers' Statute in **Spain** describes economically dependent self-employed workers as "those who carry out an economic or professional activity on a lucrative basis and in a habitual, personal, direct and predominant manner for a natural or legal person, called a client, on whom they depend economically

31 % who apparently work nights for more than three hours per night". Andrey Shevchuk, Denis Strebkov & Shannon N. Davis, *The Autonomy Paradox: How Night Work Undermines Subjective Well-being of Internet-based Freelancers*, 72 ILR Review 75, 95 n. 1 (2019).

1138. ILO, *supra* n. 25, at 168.

1139. Committee on Home Work at the 82nd Session of the International Labour Conference, Geneva, ILO, 1995, 25/18.

1140. ILO, *supra* n. 1072, at 37.

1141. *See, e.g.*, Miriam A. Cherry & Antonio Aloisi, *"Dependent Contractors" in the Gig Economy: A Comparative Approach*, 66 American University Law Review 635, 635–689 n. 3 (2017).

1142. Adalberto Perulli, *Study on Economically Dependent Work/Parasubordinate (Quasi-subordinate) Work* 11 (European Parliament 2003); Zufiaur Narvaiza, *Opinion of the European Economic and Social Committee on "New Trends in Self-employed Work: The Specific Case of Economically Dependent Self-employed Work" (own-initiative opinion)*, European Economic and Social Committee (29 April 2010), https://www.eesc.europa.eu/en/our-work/opinions-information-reports/opinions/new-trends-self-employed-work-specific-case-economically-dependent-self-employed-work.

to receive at least 75 per cent of their income through income from work and from economic or professional activities".[1143]

- Section 213 of the **Slovenian** Employment Relations Act of 2013 defines economically dependent persons as self-employed persons who personally perform work, based on a civil law contract, for remuneration, independently and for a more extended period of time in circumstances of economic dependence, without employing workers. Economic dependence means that the person obtains at least 80 per cent of his or her annual income from the same client.[1144]
- According to Eurofound research from 2017, "[t]he status of economically dependent worker [in **Portugal**] has been defined in respect of the 'amount of the total value of the worker's yearly activity one collective entity benefits from'; when this amount is at least 80%, then the worker is considered economically dependent on the collective entity".[1145] The OECD reports the percentage was reduced to 50 per cent in 2018.[1146]
- **Italian** law has relied on the concept of economically dependent employment in the past. It had three main characteristics: "(a) continuance; (b) coordination; (c) the mainly personal nature of the work".[1147] More recently, legislation refers to work that is "hetero-organised", meaning "workers who continuatively collaborate by providing exclusively personal work in favour of a principal who organises the methods of execution of the activity also with reference to the time and place of work".[1148]
- In **Austria**, economic dependence is used to identify employee-like persons. Brameshuber clarified in 2019 how "this does not only refer to economic dependence stricto sensu, meaning that the person is dependent on the earnings she makes from working for one or very few persons, but the courts in their case law follow an overall-assessment, [...]. The most important one is that the employee-like working person does not offer her services on the market, but rather works for one or very few persons only". The author mentions other criteria as well, such as the economic fruits belonging to the principal and not the worker, the worker being "economically subordinated" in pursuance of the principal's business activity, and "[i]n some cases, the

1143. Ley 20/2007 del Estatuto del trabajo autónomo, de 11 de julio 2007; Adrián Todolí-Signes, *Workers, the Self-employed and TRADEs: Conceptualisation and Collective Rights in Spain*, 10 European Labour Law Journal 254, 258 n. 3 (2019).

1144. 213. člen Zakon o delovnih razmerjih, dne 5. Marca 2013.

1145. Eurofound, *Exploring Self-employment in the European Union* 40 (Publications Office of the European Union 2017).

1146. OECD, *Policy Responses to New Forms of Work* 27 (OECD 2019).

1147. The work meets "a long-term requirement of the other party", a connection exists "between the execution of the work and the organisation of the work by the beneficiary", and it has a "mainly personal nature". Adalberto Perulli, *Subordinate, Autonomous and Economically Dependent Work: A Comparative Analysis of Selected European Countries* 137, 166–167 (Giuseppe Casale ed., *The Employment Relationship: A Comparative Overview*, Hart Publishing 2011).

1148. Elena Gramano & Giovanni Gaudio, *"New Trade Union Strategies for New Forms of Employment": Focus on Italy*, 10 European Labour Law Journal 240, 243 n. 3 (2019).

courts also referred to a stronger integration into the contractual partner's organisation".[1149]

- Section 12a of the **German** statute on collective agreements provides employee-like persons with collective rights. As explained by Schlachter in 2019, "[t]hey must: qualify as economically dependent persons providing their services on the basis of any kind of civil law or commercial law contract for services; be obliged to provide their services in person primarily without the help of employees; provide their services to just one contracting party or generate more than 50% of their income from providing this type of service to just one contracting party".[1150] The OECD mentioned in 2019 that this percentage of 50 per cent had been reduced to 33 per cent for artists, writers and journalists.[1151]
- The Employment Status National Standard Order of 31 January 2012 in **Malta** describes economic dependence as well.[1152] Section 3 provides several criteria as part of a presumption of an employment relationship, which is triggered if at least five criteria are fulfilled. A first criterion is that the person who performs the work "depends on one single person for whom the service is provided for at least 75% of his income over a period of one year", a second that "he is integrated in the structure of the production process, the work organisation or the company's or other organization's hierarchy", and a third that "the person's activity is a core element in the organization and pursuit of the objectives of the person for whom the service is provided".[1153]
- Case law in **Canada** illustrates how open-ended the concept of "economic dependence" can be. Section 1 of the Labour Relations Act in Ontario defines dependent contractors, which, amongst other conditions, perform their services in a position of economic dependence.[1154] Pursuant to Canadian case law, this requires a type of economic dependence that is "closely analogous" to that of an individual employee.[1155] What counts is, "[c]an the individual contractor be said to be dependent upon the employer for the means of his or her livelihood. If so, then he or she is akin to an employee and so a dependent contractor".[1156] Although the test takes into consideration many factors, such as the possibility of substituting the worker, the Court of Appeal in Ontario has held that the dependent contractor status requires "a certain minimum economic dependency, which may be demonstrated by complete

1149. Elisabeth Brameshuber, *The "Personal Work Relationship" in Austria*, 10 European Labour Law Journal 187, 190 n. 3 (2019).
1150. Monika Schlachter, *Trade Union Representation for New Forms of Employment*, 10 European Labour Law Journal 229, 234 n. 3 (2019).
1151. The organisation does not clarify why or on what legal grounds it occurs. OECD, *supra* n. 149, at 143.
1152. Eurofound, *supra* n. 1145, at 41.
1153. Section 3 Employment Status National Standard Order, 31 January 2012.
1154. Labour Relations Act, 1995.
1155. Ontario Labour Relations Board: Case 1977 CanLII 422, *Adbo Contracting Company Ltd*, 6 April 1977.
1156. Ontario Labour Relations Board: Case 2001 CanLII 6537, *Toronto Star Newspapers Limited*, 2 February 2001.

or near-complete exclusivity".[1157] This degree of economic dependency would have to be assessed based on the "full history of the relationship".[1158] In *Thurston*, "near-complete exclusivity" had been considered to necessarily require "substantially more than 50% of billings. If it were otherwise, exclusivity – the 'hallmark' of dependent contractor status – would be rendered meaningless".[1159]

In a lawsuit concerning Foodora, however, the Ontario Labour Relations Board argued that this numerical measurement of "economic dependence" was not required under statutory law. The Court of Appeal in *Thurston* had ruled on the basis of the traditional common law test, which is different. Furthermore, the Ontario Labour Relations Board felt that relying on a numerical threshold carried risks, especially when people have multiple part-time jobs. For Foodora couriers, who are allowed to rely on another app such as Uber Eats, this "dual apping" is not a sign of entrepreneurialism. It would be more akin to a bartender deciding to work on Saturdays because customers during the weekend give better tips.[1160] According to the Board, having multiple sources of income does not necessarily preempt economic dependency, even if, for example, a more prolonged relationship does present a stronger case for economic dependence.[1161]

- Lastly, the **United Kingdom** provides another example of how economic dependence is not necessarily quantified. Section 230 of the Employment Rights Act defines the limb (b) worker, "whereby the individual undertakes to do or perform personally any work or services for another party to the contract whose status is not by virtue of the contract that of a client or customer of any profession or business undertaking carried on by the individual".[1162] The definition does not explicitly refer to economic dependence. Nevertheless, since the purpose would have been "to extend protection to [limb (b)] workers who are, substantively and economically, in the same position" as employees,[1163] economic dependence is not entirely irrelevant either.[1164] According to some, the definition would have, indeed, been

1157. Court of Appeal for Ontario: Case 2009 ONCA 916, *McKee v. Reid's Heritage Homes Ltd*, 23 December 2009.
1158. Court of Appeal for Ontario: Case 2016 ONCA 79, *Keenan v. Canac Kitchens Ltd*, 27 January 2016.
1159. Court of Appeal for Ontario: Case 2019 ONCA 640, *Thurston v. Ontario (Children's Lawyer)*, 31 July 2019.
1160. Ryan White & Amelia Philpott, *How the Ontario Labour Board Ruled Foodora Workers are "Employees" and Not Independent Contractors*, Canadian LAW OF WORK Forum (5 March 2020), https://lawofwork.ca/how-the-ontario-labour-board-ruled-foodora-workers-are-employees/.
1161. Ontario Labour Relations Board: Case 2020 CanLII 16750, *Foodora Inc. d.b.a. Foodora*, 25 February 2020.
1162. Section 230 Employment Rights Act 1996.
1163. Employment Appeal Tribunal: Case EAT/542/01, *Byrne Brothers (Formwork) Limited v. Baird*, 18 September 2001.
1164. Guy Davidov *Who is a Worker?*, 34 Industrial Law Journal 57, 60 n. 1 (2005). Some have argued to make economic dependence more important in the assessment under British law. *E.g.*, Nicola Countouris, *The Employment Relationship: A Comparative Analysis of National Judicial Approaches* 35, 64–65 (Giuseppe Casale ed., *The Employment Relationship: A Comparative Overview*, Hart Publishing 2011).

influenced by the phenomenon of economic dependence.[1165] Yet, at least for the time being, in order to determine who classifies as a limb (b) worker, much more relevant than any quantified take would be to verify "whether the purported worker actively markets his services as an independent person to the world in general [...], or whether he is recruited by the principal to work for that principal as an integral part of the principal's operations".[1166]

Personally performed work – If Perulli's work is interrelated with these more recent descriptions of economic dependence, a general picture can be drafted of when a home-based worker might be considered economically dependent. First, it would seem reasonable to expect the work to be performed personally. This entails "with a rather limited organization of means and/or human resources" (e.g. Germany, Italy, Slovenia, Spain, United Kingdom).[1167] To that extent, the Office, for instance, suggested excluding home-based workers from coverage if they employ other persons to assist them,[1168] except if they are family members.[1169] The Office's proposal was rejected, but it, nevertheless, supports the suitability of this indicator to evaluate home-based workers' economic independence. This indicator is, moreover, relevant in crowdwork, where individuals can decompose tasks into smaller subtasks and then redistribute them to their "own crowd".[1170] **347**

Continuous performance – The second feature of economic dependence relates to the continuous performance of work. For instance, Slovenia seemingly requires a longer period of time and significant dependence on one client for economic dependence to arise. Also, Spain requires, and Italy seemingly used to demand, performance over a more extended period of time. Other countries have made references to "stability", "continuity", or a "non-occasional nature".[1171] Countries such as Malta and Portugal seem to calculate the percentage of the income derived from one client over a period of a year. This might imply that the worker must at least work for this one client for one year before becoming economically dependent. Furthermore, the Canadian example shows how a longer relationship, in any case, increases the chances of the worker being considered economically dependent. **348**

Workflow coordination – The third feature of economic dependence would have to do with the coordination between the worker's services and the client's business. What should arise, according to Perulli, is a "functional link of the [economically dependent worker's] activity to a determinate productive context or cycle".[1172] Along similar lines, Casale speaks of economically dependent workers being "economically linked **349**

1165. Perulli, *supra* n. 1147, at 172.
1166. Employment Appeal Tribunal: Case UKEAT/0457/05, *Cotswolds Developments Construction Ltd v. Williams*, 21 December 2005; Employment Appeal Tribunal: Case UKEAT/0475/06/DM, *James v. Redcats (Brands) Ltd*, 21 February 2007.
1167. Perulli, *supra* n. 1147, at 175.
1168. ILO, *supra* n. 1071, at 4.
1169. ILO, *supra* n. 1063, at 37.
1170. David Durward, Ivo Blohm & Jan Marco Leimeister, *Principal Forms of Crowdsourcing and Crowd Work* 39, 50 (Werner Wobbe, Elva Bova & Catalin Dragomirescu-Gaina eds., *The Digital Economy and the Single Market*, FEPS 2016).
1171. Perulli, *supra* n. 1147, at 180.
1172. *Ibid.*, 179.

to the sphere of activity in which the person or enterprise that may be considered as the employer operates" (e.g. Italy and Malta).[1173] For instance, in Austria and the UK, the point is to verify whether the worker offers the service to the market, as such, instead of serving a couple of entities that, in turn, bring the final product or service to the market.

350 **Quantified dependency** – Fourthly, not all but many legal systems quantify the degree of dependence in relation to a main principal or client. The percentage of income required to be considered dependent can range around 75–80 per cent. However, countries such as Portugal, Germany and Canada show that the threshold can also be lower. In Germany, the exceptionally low mark of 33 per cent seems to be applied for specific purposes. Other countries, such as Austria, the United Kingdom and Italy, seem to paint a non-quantified picture.

351 **Economically dependent home-based workers** – Similar to what has been argued about the home-based worker's degree of autonomy (e.g. the relative importance of schedule control), the degree of economic independence required under Convention No. 177 might also have to be "recalibrated" to account for the particular characteristics of home-based work. To this extent, it appears that, although relationships between industrial homeworkers and employers can be more permanent, the working relationships usually have an unstable and fragile character.[1174] In terms of its fragility, think of "the case of a woman who worked as a salaried cleaning lady for a publishing house which also gave her binding work to do at home, as a homeworker".[1175] This woman might be formally employed as a cleaning lady while, at the same time, performing the binding work only occasionally as a self-employed or informal home-based worker.[1176] In addition to the rather casual nature of some homeworkers' work arrangement, it is "customary for homeworkers to carry out work for a number of employers simultaneously or during the course of their working lives. This is true both of workers who combine home work with other work modalities, and of those who are engaged in home working on a full-time and exclusive basis".[1177]

352 Two different situations have to be distinguished in this regard. On the one hand, persons can have multiple income sources in their capacity as a home-based worker, i.e. multiple employers that issue home work to them. On the other hand, they can also combine home work with an additional job in a factory or elsewhere. This difference matters when judging whether the homeworker runs a home-based business. Surprisingly enough, regarding the former, the simultaneous performance of home work for multiple employers seems relatively limited. Research on home-based work in Pakistan revealed that "[m]ost were highly dependent on a single work provider: 99

1173. Giuseppe Casale, *The Employment Relationship: A General Introduction* 1, 26 (Giuseppe Casale ed., *The Employment Relationship: A Comparative Overview*, Hart Publishing 2011).

1174. Tomei, *supra* n. 1050, at 28–29.

1175. *Ibid.*, 22. For instance, many garment workers in Bulgaria, and, perhaps, Eastern Europe more broadly, who already have a factory job, perform additional work as a homeworker out of economic necessity. Von Broembsen, *supra* n. 1012, at 7.

1176. This occurs, despite the binding work being much more "integral" to the business's primary activities than the cleaning services.

1177. Tomei, *supra* n. 1050, at 29.

per cent of workers who worked with contractors were reliant on just one contractor"; among the workers who subcontracted directly from godowns or small factories, "96 per cent had only one source of work. Among those who worked with middlemen, 98 per cent were entirely reliant on that one person".[1178] Pakistan seems to offer an extreme example. Nonetheless, earlier research in Peru had also found that 16 per cent of home-based garment makers worked for four or more employers and 28 per cent for two or three employers. "These figures permitted to conclude that 56 per cent of the garment-makers studied worked for a single employer".[1179] Research in Bulgaria indicated that 71 per cent of homeworkers worked for one factory, 17 per cent for three factories and a couple of workers for more than three factories.[1180] Therefore, irrespective of the continent, many industrial home-based workers seem to perform home work for just one employer, subcontractor or intermediary. When individuals' dependency is analysed without considering any other additional forms of work, such as factory work, these findings suggest an overall high percentage of these home-based workers are economically dependent homeworkers.

One question worth asking in this regard is whether the combination of home work **353**
with a cleaning, factory or commercial job matters for coverage under Convention No. 177. As indicated, relatively few Bulgarian homeworkers seem to perform services for multiple "factories". However, the same research on Bulgaria does clarify that when considering the possibility of combining home work with occupations other than home work, "the vast majority of homeworkers interviewed (86.2%) have more than one income source and several have professions inside or outside the factory".[1181] In the central area of Paraguay, workers likewise perform work for "a number of enterprises in different types of activity, combining self-employed work with home work and even paid employment". The further removed from the capital, the less pronounced the "phenomenon of combining different occupations" becomes.[1182] On the other hand, research in Thailand observed that only 22 per cent of the home-based workers would have a secondary source of income.[1183] These results suggest that, depending on the region, home work may predominantly be a primary or complementary source of income. Whereas home work might be a very significant source of income for many workers in Thailand or Pakistan,[1184] this may be less the case in, for instance, Bulgaria or Spain, where it might often be performed complementary to the individual's or household's other sources of income.[1185] Although this might generally make the Spanish or Bulgarian homeworkers less economically dependent on home work, as such, it says very little about their

1178. Mi Zhou, *Pakistan's Hidden Workers: Wages and Conditions of Home-based Workers and the Informal Economy* 33 (ILO 2017).
1179. Francisco Verdera, *Homeworkers in Peru* 15 (ILO 2000).
1180. Von Broembsen, *supra* n. 1014, at 8.
1181. *Ibid.*, 7.
1182. María Victoria Heikel, *Homeworkers in Paraguay* 30 (ILO 2000).
1183. Martha Alter Chen, *Informal Economy Monitoring Study Sector Report: Home-Based Workers* 10 (WIEGO 2014).
1184. In Lahore, about 27 per cent of industrial outworkers in the garment industry and about 31 per cent of industrial outworkers in other industries would have a second job. Bilal Naqeeb, Rubina Saigol & Ume-Laila Azhar, *Home-based Workers in Lahore, Pakistan* 19 (WIEGO 2014).
1185. Baylina & Dolors Garcia-Ramon, *supra* n. 1013, at 60.

entrepreneurial status. In fact, these Spanish or Bulgarian homeworkers are not any more of an independent home-based business than the homeworkers in Thailand or Pakistan; perhaps, quite the contrary.

354 To conclude, as the country examples of legislation and case law show (*supra* no. 346), the concept of economic (in)dependence is flexible. Furthermore, the role of home work in the local labour market seems to vary. To that extent, countries might want to define economic (in)dependence differently, depending on local conditions. At the same time, irrespective of local circumstances, if the goal is to identify homeworkers who conduct home-based businesses through the criterion of economic dependence, governments might want to disregard the way in which homeworkers combine home work with other forms of employment. Consider the example of the cleaning lady binding books at home for the same employer. She does not operate a home-based business. The criterion of economic dependence can measure her "entrepreneurial spirit" to the extent that it only looks at the income generated in this woman's capacity as a homeworker, disregarding her occupation as a cleaning lady.

355 **Economically dependent crowdworkers** – Since crowdwork is often combined with other jobs, the previous paragraph is also important for crowdworkers. According to a survey on Amazon Mechanical Turk and Crowdflower from 2015, many workers rely on crowdwork "to complement pay from other jobs".[1186] This has also been observed elsewhere. In China, about two-thirds of respondents have another paid job.[1187]

356 In contrast, although most seem to rely on crowdwork as a secondary source of income, a significant share of crowdworkers perceive it as a primary source of income. One survey mentions that 37 per cent of American and Indian crowdworkers consider crowdwork their primary source of income.[1188] Subsequent research measured even higher rates, "implying that for 56 per cent of the respondents, the main (personal) income source was crowdwork".[1189] In other words, even if many might not, another big chunk of crowdworkers rely on this work to make a living.

357 To that extent, contrary to industrial homeworkers who often seem to have only one client or subcontractor for whom they complete home work, among the 37–56 per cent of fervent crowdworkers, only a small percentage will be primarily working for one single platform user. For example, a survey in Ukraine, which has a significant digital freelancers market, observed that 11 per cent of freelancers on the country's platforms have one main client.[1190] Based on this percentage,[1191] requiring home-based crowdworkers to be economically dependent on individual clients would mean

1186. "For the 60% of AMT workers who do hold other jobs besides crowdwork, most of these are employees (81.6% of Americans and 84.3% of Indians) [...] Only 11.9% of Americans and 4% of Indians report that their other job is another form of 'freelance' work, and only 3.4% have other jobs in the 'gig' or 'on demand economy'". Berg, *supra* n. 613, at 556.

1187. Chen, *supra* n. 1122, at 17.

1188. Berg, *supra* n. 613, at 554–555.

1189. Berg et al., *supra* n. 23, at 41.

1190. Aleksynska, Bastrakova & Kharchenko, *supra* n. 78, at 32.

1191. The percentage measured in Ukraine might be relatively low. In the Philippines, researchers note how 35 per cent of online platform workers work for a single client on a platform. King-Dejardin, *supra* n. 1025, at 28.

around a tenth of these home-based "freelancers" are potentially homeworkers. This percentage seems far lower than that of industrial homeworkers working for just one factory. Therefore, assuming that about half of the crowdworkers have another primary job and that among the remainder of fervent crowdworkers, most derive their income from an array of platforms and users, very few crowdworkers will actually derive 30–80 per cent of their "total personal income" from one platform user. Furthermore, even if, on the grounds argued before, solely crowdwork-related income would count, i.e. discounting cleaning jobs, etc., it would still seem unlikely for the crowdworker to be economically dependent on one or two platform users.

In view of this, one could ask, is it appropriate to demand a crowdworker to be economically dependent on a couple of platform users before considering this worker to lack the economic independence necessary to constitute an independent home-based business? Ultimately, economic dependence on the intermediary/platform might also play a role in determining the degree of economic independence of home-based crowdworkers. 358

A cog in the machine - That is because, even if these crowdworkers technically work for multiple platform users, they, nevertheless, still operate like a short-term - even "anonymous"[1192] - cog in the machine of each of these other businesses. The crowdworker that cleans data or curates violent images for Microsoft, Google, Amazon and Facebook,[1193] because these companies dispatch this work through one or two platforms, that worker can hardly be characterised as a person who develops a business undertaking with its own clientele or customers.[1194] Although this might be different for online macro-taskers or those involved in design competitions,[1195] "clickworkers" on micro-task platforms, such as Amazon Mechanical Turk, arguably, partake in a cognitive assembly line.[1196] Another example is Testbirds, which relies 359

1192. For instance, workers on Amazon Mechanical Turk are identified using an alphanumeric ID. Christian Fieseler, Eliane Bucher & Christian P. Hoffman, *Unfairness by Design? The Perceived Fairness of Digital Labor on Crowdworking Platforms*, 156 Journal of business ethics 987, 989 n. 4 (2019).

1193. Phil Jones, *Rethinking Microwork: The Invisible Labour of the Platform Economy* 23, 25 (James Muldoon & Will Stronge eds., *Platforming Equality: Policy Challenges for the Digital Economy*, Autonomy 2020).

1194. Workers on, for instance, Amazon Mechanical Turk have limited opportunities to grow a "business". Indeed, "AMT leaves very little room for initiative, judgment or foresight". Alek Felstiner, *Working the Crowd: Employment and Labor Law in the Crowdsourcing Industry*, 32 Berkeley Journal of Employment & Labor Law 143, 177 n. 1 (2011).

1195. Durward, Blohm & Leimeister, *supra* n. 1170, at 48; Eurofound, *supra* n. 4, at 22 and 25. Some platforms can serve as an "entrepreneurial incubator". A worker starts on the platform, gets a sense of what it is like to run a personal "business" and, subsequently, branches out, developing a proper business on and off the platform. Francesca Bellesia, Elisa Mattarelli, Fabiola Bertolotti & Maurizio Sobrero, *Platforms as Entrepreneurial Incubators? How Online Labor Markets Shape Work Identity*, 34 Journal of Managerial Psychology 246, 246–268 n. 4 (2019).

1196. "Indeed, we suggest that many in the gig economy fall into the second group of workers in the new world of work identified by Spreitzer et al. (2017), namely, 'low-skill workers who struggle to make a living and are beholden to the needs of the organization'". Keith, Harms & Tay, *supra* n. 295, at 303.

on crowdworkers to hunt for software bugs in users' products.[1197] The workers that pitch in on this "assembly line" are presented as "micro-entrepreneurs". In reality, however, the workers simply try out apps and programs to inform a company how to improve its software. A "regular usability test" will earn you around twenty euros, with additional payments for the bugs and defects found.[1198] Crowdworkers committed to making a living on these cognitive assembly lines can only increase their efforts, searching, confirming and completing the work more swiftly.[1199] As Prassl writes, "[a]t its most extreme, the entrepreneurship narrative actively celebrates (self-)exploitation".[1200] In such a situation, the traditional quantitative approach to workers' economic independence probably does not deliver any substantial indication about the entrepreneurial spirit of the crowdworker. Signalling software bugs in one enterprise's mobile app in the morning and inconsistencies in another software developer's desktop application in the evening hardly proves economic independence as an independent home-based business. All these activities are outsourced through the same intermediary to workers, oftentimes irrespective of their capabilities and qualifications.

360 **Economic independence in relation to the platform** – If the condition of "economic independence" is meant to indicate whether the crowdworker has an entrepreneurial spirit, it might make as much, if not more, sense to analyse the degree of economic independence between the crowdworker and platform, instead of between the worker and platform user. For example, a crowdworker who services 300 clients each month, following those clients' instructions,[1201] on one single platform, probably works on a cognitive assembly line. Regardless of the number of "clients", that crowdworker is not the independent artisan or professional freelance consultant that Article 1(a), *in fine*, wants to exclude from coverage.[1202] While the crowdworker might not be economically dependent on any specific user, he or she is dependent on the platform's ecosystem to receive work offers. Does this kind of dependency turn the home-based crowdworker into an economically dependent homeworker? It could. The Committee of Experts recalls "that Convention No. 177 is applicable to all cases in which homeworkers work under some form of economic dependency, including workers in the informal economy".[1203]

361 In this regard, economic dependency on an intermediary potentially constitutes such a "form of economic dependency". As indicated in an ILO report on crowdwork,

---

1197. Sahil Deva & Veronika Wasza, *Testbirds Software Testing Solutions in the Crowdsourcing Industry* 56, 56–64 (Werner Wobbe, Elva Bova & Catalin Dragomirescu-Gaina eds., *The Digital Economy and the Single Market*, FEPS 2016).

1198. Testbirds, *Why be a Testbird?*, Testbirds (27 September 2020), https://nest.testbirds.com/home/tester.

1199. Juliet Webster, *Microworkers of the Gig Economy: Separate and Precarious*, 25 New Labor Forum 56, 60 n. 3 (2016).

1200. Prassl, *supra* n. 110, at 69.

1201. People who use a platform to, for example, sell products to 300 customers each month are not targeted by Convention No. 177 because they do not furnish the product or service pursuant to the instructions of the client.

1202. ILO Committee of Experts on the Application of Conventions and Recommendations, *supra* n. 633, at 203.

1203. *Ibid.*, 237.

when the work is submitted to the platform upon completion of the work order, the submission can be rejected for many reasons. Some platform operators provide requesters with much discretion in terms of why they accept or reject the finished product or service. Rejections can also be due to errors in the platform's features or methods, or software glitches. This usually means that the worker does not get paid. Frequently, no mechanisms ensure that the worker is informed about the reason why the work was rejected. Workers on Clickworker, CrowdFlower etc., are not even given the possibility of contacting the platform's users when this happens.[1204] Besides this example, crowdworkers' dependence on platforms, which could create communication channels with these users if they wanted to, also manifests itself in other ways. Platforms function based on "adhesion contracts" that tend to be unilaterally modified by the platform operator. The crowdworkers generally do not have any influence over the platform's future policies. Any change to the platform's operational features, such as removing support for Alipay or PayPal, may well impact the relationship between the crowdworker and clients or the future profitability of the platform for the worker.[1205]

From this perspective, one could argue that a crowdworker can be economically **362**
dependent on a platform. Economically dependent self-employed workers are generally protected because their dependency puts them in a vulnerable position. On a superficial level, for instance, the dominant client's - or in this case platform's - economic situation might deteriorate, in which case a dependent self-employed worker inevitably shares in the blows.[1206] However, entrepreneurial risks are also pushed to the worker at a deeper level. Lawyers, for example, are sometimes prohibited from being too dependent on one client because it prevents them from discontinuing their services if a dominant client asks the lawyer to break the law. When lawyers become dependent on clients and proceed to obey the client's requests, they fail to satisfy their occupational duties, and they can have their licence revoked, and so forth. For such reasons, some have argued that "[e]conomic dependence basically means that the dependent self-employed worker takes the entrepreneurial risk".[1207] As Davidov writes, placing "all the eggs in one basket" is the problem.[1208] When the basket starts to rot, the dependent worker suffers the brunt. A platform can constitute a basket, even if it provides the worker with access to multiple clients. The platform

1204. Berg et al., *supra* n. 23, at 75–79; Rani & Furrer, *supra* n. 1049, at 225 and 229. According to Eurofound, in case of Clickworker, the worker is selected by the platform, not the user, making the economic dependence on the platform particularly evident. Eurofound, *supra* n. 4, at 13.

1205. Berg et al. *supra* n. 23, at 23.

1206. Werner et al., *Social Protection Rights of Economically Dependent Self-employed Workers* 26 (European Parliament 2013).

1207. Ulrike Muehlberger & Silvia Pasqua, *Workers on the Border Between Employment and Self-Employment*, 67 Review of Social Economy 201, 202 n. 2 (2009). *See also*, René Böheim & Ulrike Muehlberger, *Dependent Forms of Self-employment in the UK: Identifying Workers on the Border between Employment and Self-employment* 3 (IZA 2006).

1208. Guy Davidov, *Freelancers: An Intermediate Group in Labour Law?* 171, 179–180 (Judy Fudge, Shae McCrystal & Kamala Sankaran eds., *Challenging the Legal Boundaries of Work Regulation*, Hart Publishing 2012).

operator, for instance, decides when it suspends or terminates a worker's account,[1209] and "in some cases, the platform declines to even provide the worker with a reason for the suspension or closure".[1210] When a permanent suspension or ban occurs, the worker loses contact with the employers on the platform and loses the social capital worked for on the platform. Such a ban can have profound implications. One-third of crowdworkers in China, for instance, only work on one platform.[1211] Other researchers in the Philippines found that over a period of three months, 83 per cent of online platform workers worked on only one platform.[1212]

363 The worker can, of course, start anew on another platform, but this is likely to have significant consequences for the worker's earning potential in any case. Furthermore, the potential risks of economic dependency increase when market failures prevent the worker from finding new clientele.[1213] Traditionally, home-based workers' isolation has made it difficult for them to recruit new clientele. Crowdworkers are in a similar position. The platforms create an environment in which users can cost-effectively work with crowdworkers at a distance; without access to the platform, that would not be the case. For example, Recital 2 of EU Regulation No. 2019/1150 argues that it is appropriate to protect small and medium-sized enterprises that are increasingly dependent on platforms' online intermediation services.[1214] If this is the case for SMEs, perhaps to an even greater extent, it would be appropriate to protect home-based crowdworkers dependent on the platforms that grant them access to (foreign) employers.

1209. Some platforms, for instance, indicate that disintermediation of the platform – workers and users working bilaterally outside of the platform – may result in a serious breach of the terms and conditions, leading to a permanent suspension. For instance, Upwork, *User Agreement*, Upwork (27 September 2020), https://www.upwork.com/legal. Platforms, furthermore, dissuade workers from working in certain ways, threatening that their account may be suspended or permanently banned. Alex C. Williams et al., *The Perpetual Work Life of Crowdworkers: How Tooling Practices Increase Fragmentation in Crowdwork*, 3 Proceedings of the ACM on human-computer interaction 1, 19 (2019).

1210. Michael Six Silberman & Hannah Johnston, *Using GDPR to Improve Legal Clarity and Working Conditions on Digital Labour Platforms* 6–7 (Etui 2020).

1211. Chen, *supra* n. 1122, at 21.

1212. King-Dejardin, *supra* n. 1025, at 28.

1213. Orsola Razzolini, *The Need to Go Beyond the Contract: Economic and Bureaucratic Dependence in Personal Work Relations*, 31 Comparative Labor Law & Policy Journal 267, 293–294 n. 2 (2010).

1214. "[T]he growing intermediation of transactions through online intermediation services, fuelled by strong data-driven indirect network effects, leads to an increased dependence of such business users, particularly micro, small and medium-sized enterprises (SMEs), on those services in order for them to reach consumers. Given that increasing dependence, the providers of those services often have superior bargaining power, which enables them to, in effect, behave unilaterally in a way that can be unfair and that can be harmful to the legitimate interests of their businesses users and, indirectly, also of consumers in the Union". Regulation (EU) No. 2019/1150 of the European Parliament and of the Council of 20 June 2019 on promoting fairness and transparency for business users of online intermediation services, OJ L 186, 11 July 2019.

Considering that, for instance, 40 per cent of AMT workers claim to work full-time on the platform,[1215] if dependency on the platform matters, one would expect many of these AMT workers, and other micro-taskers, to be homeworkers on account of their lack of economic independence. What is more, Convention No. 177 might have a broader reach beyond just micro-task platforms. For example, Aleksynska et al. describe intermediaries which rely on open-access platforms to recruit crowdworkers for "closed" platforms, where "[o]nce admitted, workers receive a constant stream of work and pay, and are requested to be available for work at regular times".[1216] These "intermediaries" might be related to the online platforms Tubaro associates with "deep embeddedness". On these platforms, according to the author, "the organization of the workflow is managed almost like in a firm or group of firms, which centralize most transactions and use contracts rather than the price system to ensure coordination".[1217] Such platforms might severely restrict the degree of (economic) autonomy experienced by crowdworkers, increasing the chances of them being classified as homeworkers. Researchers seem to have only paid limited attention to them so far, focusing on the more easily "accessible" platforms instead. 364

3. Certain Crowdworkers Are Homeworkers

Holistic assessment? – The Committee of Experts confirmed in 2020's general survey that: 365

> "[t]he only homeworkers who are explicitly excluded from the coverage of the Convention are those who, in accordance with Article 1(a), in fine, have a degree of autonomy and of economic independence necessary to be considered independent workers under national laws, regulations or court decisions. The coverage of the Convention is not confined to workers who are clearly in an employment relationship and, as indicated in Article 2, it applies to all persons carrying out home work".[1218]

To settle this exemption's boundaries, both the degree of autonomy and degree of economic independence need not be artificially separated and analysed in a cocoon, as 366

1215. Kristy Milland, *Crowd Work: The Fury and the Fear* 83, 84 (Werner Wobbe, Elva Bova & Catalin Dragomirescu-Gaina eds., *The Digital Economy and the Single Market*, FEPS 2016). Forty per cent of MTurk workers consider it their primary job. Alice M. Brawley & Cynthia L.S. Pury, *Work Experiences on MTurk: Job Satisfaction, Turnover, and Information Sharing*, 54 Computers in Human Behavior 531, 542 (2016). "We commenced our study with certain assumptions about the nature of the CS workforce (e.g., in terms of supplemental income and reasonable compensation levels), only to find that these assumptions were naïve at best. We found that many crowd workers are totally dependent on income arising from their microtask CS work, [...]". Xuefei N. Deng, K. D. Joshi & Robert D. Galliers, *The Duality of Empowerment and Marginalization in Microtask Crowdsourcing: Giving Voice to the Less Powerful Through Value Sensitive Design*, 40 MIS Quarterly 279, 298 n. 2 (2016). According to one survey, crowdwork is the only source of income for 43 per cent of crowdworkers in China. Zhou, *supra* n. 37, at 14.
1216. Aleksynska, Bastrakova & Kharchenko, *supra* n. 78, at 35.
1217. Paola Tubaro, *supra* n. 304, at 10.
1218. ILO Committee of Experts on the Application of Conventions and Recommendations, *supra* n. 633, at 237.

was done in the previous Section. After all, if the home-based worker is economically dependent, it seems logical for the home-based worker's degree of overall autonomy to decrease as well.[1219] The economically dependent worker might more readily accept instructions, or the principal with significant ties to an independent worker might also be more inclined to supervise this worker's activities because of the economic importance. In the case of platform work, for instance, the economically dependent worker seems to also more readily accept a gig at any point during the week, day or night, than an economically independent worker would.[1220] Therefore, economic dependency can also be thought of as an indicator of decreased overall autonomy.[1221] Both criteria, autonomy and economic independence, aim to distinguish homeworkers "from those persons who – on account of their truly independent and entrepreneurial status – should fall outside coverage".[1222] The following paragraphs attempt to illustrate what could be considered an independent crowdworker.

367 **First, a presumption** – A worker who carries out remunerated work through a digital labour platform from his or her home, or any other premises of his or her choice other than the platform user's workplace, is a presumptive homeworker if this work results in a product or service as specified by the platform user in pursuance of his or her business activity. These platform workers are genuine homeworkers unless they have the degree of autonomy and of economic independence necessary to be independent home-based workers.

368 **Economic independence** – So as to not be covered under Convention No. 177, a crowdworker needs to be economically independent. This will occur most notably when one or more of the following conditions are fulfilled.

- The crowdworker employs helpers, who are not family members, to assist in the employers' work. As such, for example, when crowdworkers take on

1219. "In terms of autonomy, Tables 30–32 show that the economically dependent workers always rank in between the self-employed, who are most able to choose their own order, methods and speed of work, and the employees, who are least able to do so. The same is true for the ability to influence the decisions that are important for their work (Table 36), and for the ability to apply their own ideas in their work (Table 34)". Agnès Parent-Thirion, Isabella Biletta, Adriaan Oostveen & Greet Vermeylen, *Self-employed or not Self-employed? Working Conditions of 'Economically Dependent Workers'* 4 (Eurofound 2013); D. Hunter & K. Leslie, *Statistical Definition and Measurement of Dependent "Self-employed" Workers: Rationale for the Proposal for a Statistical Category of Dependent Contractors* 2 (ILO 2018).

1220. Rebecca Florisson & Irene Mandl, *Platform Work: Types and Implications for Work and Employment – Literature Review* 70 (Eurofound 2018).

1221. Olivier Leclerc & Thomas Pasquier, *La Dépendance Économique en Droit du Travail: Éclairages en Droit Français et en Droit Comparé*, Revue de droit du travail 83 (2010). For instance, the European Court of Justice considers economic dependency as a criterion to verify the agent's degree of autonomy, when it evaluates pure agency agreements between a principal and agent. Ioannis Lianos, Nicola Countouris & Valerio De Stefano, *Re-thinking the Competition Law/ Labour Law Interaction: Promoting a Fairer Labour Market*, 10 European Labour Law Journal 291, 315 n. 3 (2019).

1222. ILO, *supra* n. 1063, at 37. The point is to figure out whether the home-based worker conducts his or her own business. Paul Benjamin, *Subordination, Parasubordination and Self-Employment: A Comparative Study of Selected African Countries* 95, 111 (Giuseppe Casale ed., *The Employment Relationship: A Comparative Overview*, Hart Publishing 2011).

tasks, aggregate those tasks into subtasks and pass them on to other crowdworkers, this aggregator or subcontractor becomes difficult to characterise as economically dependent.[1223]

- The crowdworker does not have a relationship with the employer or platform for a considerable period, i.e. at least a couple of months, but perhaps even a year. The fact that the relationship is intermittent does not mean that the relationship cannot last a considerable time.
- The work of the crowdworker is not coordinated with the economic activities of the employers. Typical for economic dependence is that the work forms "part of someone else's organizational scheme".[1224] If this is not the case, the crowdworker is not an economically dependent homeworker.
- Although a quantitative approach to the issue is not necessarily recommended, the crowdworker who does not earn a substantial part of his or her income from a dominant employer or platform might be independent. Based on a Ukrainian survey, about 11 per cent of digital freelancers have one main client.[1225] A survey in the Philippines, however, suggests this is the case for 35 per cent.[1226] These workers may well be economically dependent. The same is, arguably, valid for crowdworkers who work full-time on one platform and are economically dependent on this DLP, instead of on any particular user. Moreover, it is crucial to decide whether, for instance, factory or cleaning jobs are taken into account for the determination of economic dependency on crowdwork (*supra* nos. 353–354). If not, one could look at the income generated at home, which needs to be sufficiently diverse if the crowdworker is to be seen as an independent home-based business.

As a result, for the sake of argument, the crowdworker who fulfils the basic definition of Convention No. 177 and: (i) does not employ others; (ii) has a relationship with a platform for a period of at least several months; (iii) performs work that is coordinated with the platform users' economic activities; and, (iv) derives more than 33–80 per cent of the home work-related income from one client (or platform), could be designated as a homeworker. Alternatively, the fourth quantitative criterion could also be replaced, for instance, by: (iv) does not perform home work for any client outside of any platform. In the larger scheme of things, by fulfilling these conditions, it is supposedly confirmed that the crowdworker is not an independent home-based "enterprise". On the other hand, if the crowdworker does not fulfil these conditions, the worker can be considered economically independent; even then, the crowdworker may still be covered under Convention No. 177. The economically independent

1223. David Durward & Ivo Blohm, *The Rise of Crowd Aggregators – How Individual Workers Restructure Their Own Crowd* – 395, 395–409 (Jan Marco Leimeister & Walter Brenner eds., *Proceedings der 13. Internationalen Tagung Wirtschaftsinformatik*, Universität St. Gallen 2017). More examples of how this occurs, *see* Meredith R. Morris et al., *Subcontracting Microwork* 1867, 1867–1876 (*Proceedings of the 2017 CHI Conference on Human Factors in Computing Systems*, ACM 2017).

1224. Alain Supiot, *Beyond Employment: Changes in Work and the Future of Labour Law in Europe* 15 (OUP 2001).

1225. Aleksynska, Bastrakova & Kharchenko, *supra* n. 78, at 32.

1226. King-Dejardin, *supra* n. 1025, at 28.

crowdworker is only an independent home-based worker if the homeworker also has the necessary degree of autonomy.[1227] It is the final issue that demands our attention.

369 **The autonomy necessary** – The question of what it means for a crowdworker to have the degree of autonomy necessary to be considered an independent home-based worker is challenging. First of all, Convention No. 177 only covers crowdworkers who need to comply with the employer's specifications. Therefore, someone who sells necklaces on Etsy or has considerable freedom to develop a company logo without instructions from the employer is not even a presumptive homeworker under the "basic definition". Secondly, regarding the home-based workers that do receive specifications, certain indicators should be disregarded as indicative of an independent and entrepreneurial status. The home-based worker is allowed to use his or her own tools and materials without this affecting the status as a presumptive homeworker.[1228] Similarly, a lack of direct control or direct supervision on the crowdworker might indicate that the crowdworker is not a standard employee, but it should not exclude the crowdworker from being classified as a homeworker (*supra* no. 338).[1229] Nor does the provision of home work on an occasional basis usually affect the worker's degree of autonomy. The occasional performance of home work should not exclude home-based workers from Convention No. 177's scope, except for the limited exemption under Article 1(b) (*supra* no. 331).[1230]

370 These examples show that home-based workers' autonomy has particular qualities. As mentioned before, whether or not to value working time sovereignty – schedule control – as a factor for the determination of homeworkers' and crowdworkers' legal status is highly relevant. As explained by Howcroft and Bergvall-Kåreborn, "[c]rowdworkers exercise autonomy in that they usually choose when and for how long they wish to work, with little direct supervision of task completion".[1231] In other words, crowdworkers seem to experience autonomy along similar lines as industrial homeworkers. However, this "type of autonomy" is, arguably, not the kind of autonomy indicative of a home-based worker's independent and entrepreneurial status. To establish the crowdworker's degree of autonomy in light of Convention

1227. Such a "change in terms has some important implications as the focus of 'independence' tends to revolve around not being dependent on another while 'autonomy' centres on a state of being self-governed". François Pichault & Tui McKeown, *Autonomy at Work in the Gig Economy: Analysing Work Status, Work Content and Working Conditions of Independent Professionals*, 34 New Technology, Work and Employment 59, 63 n. 1 (2019).

1228. "Under the terms of Article 1(a)(iii), the status of homeworkers is not determined by who provides the tools and materials". ILO Committee of Experts on the Application of Conventions and Recommendations, *supra* n. 633, at 202.

1229. This follows from the overall understanding that homeworkers are not directly supervised and controlled. "As the work is undertaken outside the employer's premises, the level of supervision by the employer tends to be more restricted and limited to providing specifications". ILO Committee of Experts on the Application of Conventions and Recommendations, *supra* n. 633, at 202.

1230. Home work often has an occasional nature and as illustrated above (*supra* no. 331), the Conference consciously restricted the exemption for occasional homeworkers to persons with an employee status who occasionally perform their work as employees at home.

1231. Debra Howcroft & Birgitta Bergvall-Kåreborn, *A Typology of Crowdwork Platforms*, 33 Work, Employment and Society 21, 29 n. 1 (2019).

No. 177, one might want to focus primarily on the extent to which the crowdworker maintains "job control" (*supra* nos. 343–344).

The homeworker essentially performs outsourced tasks that employees would otherwise perform at the employer's premises. This entails that the homeworker, although physically removed, is part and parcel of the employer's business dynamics, albeit at the fringes. The factors which substantiate the homeworker's autonomy should primarily point out that the home-based worker has his or her independent business operation, however small it is, and is not the extension of someone else's. As such, the main focal point might be the nature of the work order. When the platform and user have "directive control",[1232] meaning control over the work process, and the crowdworker cannot exert any "autonomy over tasks and work conduct",[1233] the crowdworker can hardly have the degree of autonomy necessary under Convention No. 177. Indeed, as mentioned by Urzì Brancati et al., "[o]ne of the main characteristics of self-employment is that the worker acts autonomously and has a high level of discretion regarding how the task is performed. This is hardly the case for platform workers who carry out micro-tasks, as well as some transportation and on-location tasks".[1234] 371

Along these lines, for example, based on the work of Pichault and McKeown, what could be relevant to determine the degree of autonomy is whether the crowdworker: (i) receives detailed specifications;[1235] (ii) has his or her workload imposed by the platform and user; (iii) experiences weak support from the platform with no access to shared expertise, skills and a professional community; (iv) has the remuneration calculated on the basis of parameters proposed by the platform; (v) executes work through standardised work processes, or has to report on the results while at work.[1236] Based on Leimeister et al., other elements that might be important when assessing the crowdworker's autonomy are: (vi) the task's easy or complex design; (vii) the feedback mechanisms between the worker and user/platform during the work; (viii) the incentive structures in place; and, (ix) the methods applied to evaluate the crowdworker's performance.[1237] As these two publications show, it would be 372

1232. "Directive control refers to the 'mechanism by which the employer directs work tasks, specifying what needs to be done, in what order, with what degree of precision or accuracy, and in what period of time' (Edwards, 1979: 18). It is about control over the work process, which managers might describe as equivalent to supervision". Peter Cappelli & J. R. Keller, *Classifying Work in the New Economy*, 38 The Academy of Management Review 575, 584–585 n. 4 (2013).

1233. Wheatley, *supra* n. 1126, at 297.

1234. As noted by Urzì Brancati et al., "[o]ne of the main characteristics of self-employment is that the worker acts autonomously and has a high level of discretion regarding how the task is performed. This is hardly the case for platform workers who carry out micro-tasks, as well as some transportation and on-location tasks". Urzì Brancati, Pesole & Férnandéz-Macías, *supra* n. 35, at 47.

1235. One survey in the Philippines mentions this to be the case for over two-thirds of online platform workers. King-Dejardin, *supra* n. 1025, at 30.

1236. Pichault & McKeown, *supra* n. 1227, at 67.

1237. Jan Marco Leimeister, Shkodran Zogaj & Ivo Blohm, *Crowdwork – Digitale Wertschöpfung in der Wolke: Ein Überblick über die Grundlagen, die Formen und den Aktuellen Forschungsstand* 9, 26 (Christiane Benner ed., *Crowdwork – Zurück in die Zukunft? Perspektiven Digitaler Arbeit*, Bund-Verlag 2014).

interesting to discuss indicators of crowdworkers' (functional) autonomy further, potentially at the ILO level.

373 Beyond these overall indicators, there may also exist characteristics that, almost by definition, indicate that the crowdworker cannot be an independent home-based worker. One might argue, for example, that any form of crowdwork in which the identity of the worker is irrelevant, i.e. the requester offers an open call to anyone willing to complete the task, should inherently be understood not to provide the degree of autonomy necessary under Article 1(a), *in fine*. In the end, if the worker had any discretion about how to exercise the task, the employer would not engage whoever logs onto the platform first.[1238] These forms of crowdwork, which rely on whoever is willing, have been explicitly associated with digital Taylorism.[1239] Taylorism is a system in which jobs should be as simple as possible, without interactions among workers or the exercise of individual discretion/autonomy/responsibility.[1240] Since Taylorism completely opposes workers' autonomy,[1241] any platform operator that makes this its primary goal could *a priori* be suspected of working with homeworkers.

374 Other characteristics may provide a similarly "vital" indicator that workers lack the necessary degree of autonomy. When the work order demands the crowdworker to work during specific hours of the day, which for a worker on the other side of the globe might mean at night, it indicates that the worker is likewise an extension of another employer's business. Furthermore, when a change of the platform's policies directly and inevitably affects the worker's income, the worker might not have the necessary autonomy either.[1242] Similarly, the use of software that automatically tracks working time, keystrokes or monitors the worker's screen indicates that the worker

---

1238. Consider Amazon Mechanical Turk which provides micro tasks such as "[f]ind the website for a given real estate agent, then find an image of that real estate agent". Upon viewing the description of these "Human Intelligence Tasks", "the worker may choose to accept the HIT. The worker then has the allotted time to complete the HIT. While completing the HIT, the worker may choose to 'return' the HIT. (Workers often do this if a HIT turns out to have technical problems, or to take longer than they expected.) Or the worker may run out of time, in which case AMT classifies the HIT as 'abandoned'". Silberman & Irani, *supra* n. 261, at 512 and 514.

1239. "Human computation has brought Taylorism – the 'scientific management' of labor – to information work. If it continues to develop and grow, many of us 'information workers' may become human computation workers". M. Six Silberman, Lilly Irani & Joel Ross, *Ethics and Tactics of Professional Crowdwork*, 17 XRDS: Crossroads 39, 43 n. 2 (2010); Prassl, *supra* n. 110, at 52–53; Altenried, *supra* n. 1028, 145–158.

1240. Paul R. Lawrence, *The Key Job Design Problem is Still Taylorism*, 31 Journal of Organizational Behavior 412, 419 n. 2–3 (2010).

1241. "All possible brain work should be removed from the shop and centered in the planning or laying-out department". In other words, the platform user that develops the task needs to construe it in such a way that the worker has nothing to do but execute. Hans Pruijt, *Repainting, Modifying, Smashing Taylorism*, 13 Journal of Organizational Change Management 439, 439 and 445–446 n. 5 (2000).

1242. On a platform such as Crowdworker, the compensation for a task "is calculated according to the estimated average processing time as well as the level of difficulty, the length of the text, the amount of research involved or special knowledge skills required to fulfill the job. These factors are the same for all qualified Clickworkers. However, not every Clickworker will earn the same amount because of their individual routine. The faster the job gets done, the higher the targeted 'hourly wage'". When clickworker changes the way in which compensation is

is directly supervised.[1243] Although direct supervision does not necessarily exclude "autonomy" (e.g. autonomous employee), when this supervision, for instance, impacts the worker's remuneration through penalty fees, one could seriously question the independent nature of the home-based worker's activities. More broadly, these are just some examples of potentially "vital" indicators. Discussions could continue about indicators that, almost by definition, turn a crowdworker into a homeworker. This could serve to deter crowdwork platforms from engaging in certain practices.

calculated, the clickworker's income will inevitably change. Clickworker, *How Much Will I Be Paid?*, Clickworker (29 September 2020), https://www.clickworker.com/faq/.

1243. Aleksynska, Bastrakova & Kharchenko, *supra* n. 78, at 34.

Chapter 4. The Instruments on Domestic Work

SUBCHAPTER 1. THE CONVENTION'S OBJECT AND PURPOSE

Prevalence of domestic work – From cleaning the house and feeding the children to taking care of family members in need, without these efforts, society would collapse and the labour market with it.[1244] Hence, because unremunerated household work is a pillar of society, there has, accordingly, always been a demand for help in this regard. Indeed, the demand for household help has turned paid domestic work into a vital source of employment.[1245] The ILO estimates that in 2010, 52.6 million men and women classified as domestic workers.[1246] Subsequent research counted 67.1–70.1 million domestic workers in 2013.[1247] These are likely underestimates.[1248] 375

With regard to the importance of paid domestic work for a country's overall economy, it is worth emphasising that domestic workers are not as prevalent in every region. Although Europeans have easy access to domestic services, the lowest share of domestic workers is actually found in Europe and Central Asia (0.7 per cent of the total workforce). This percentage, reported in 2018, is pretty low when compared to, for example, 3.6 per cent of the total workforce in the Americas.[1249] According 376

1244. Supiot, *supra* n. 1224, at 2001, 53; Kate Raworth, *Doughnut Economics* 78- 81 (Random House 2018).
1245. This was already the case in the past. Dukes mentions that 40 per cent of women in the UK were domestic workers at the end of the nineteenth century, in addition to which also 200,000 men provided domestic services like gardening in 1902. Dukes, *supra* n. 609, at 222. The author refers to Lucy Delap, *Knowing Their Place: Domestic Service in Twentieth Century Britain* 12 and 14 (OUP 2011). *See also*, Einat Albin & Virginia Mantouvalou, *The ILO Convention on Domestic Workers: From the Shadows to the Light*, 41 Industrial Law Journal 67, 70 n. 1 (2012).
1246. ILO, *Domestic Workers Across the World: Global and Regional Statistics and the Extent of Legal Protection* 19 (ILO 2013).
1247. ILO, *Care Work and Care Jobs for the Future of Decent Work* 190 (ILO 2018).
1248. ILO Social Protection Department, *Social Protection for Domestic Workers: Key Policy Trends and Statistics* 3 (ILO 2016).
1249. 2.6 per cent in Africa, 5.8 per cent in the Arab States and 1.0 per cent in Asia and the Pacific. ILO, *supra* n. 1247, at 190.

to Blofield and Jokela, about 30 per cent of all households "are intimately involved in paid domestic work in Latin America, either as employers or as workers".[1250] In addition to regional variations, the diversity of work arrangements should also be stressed among domestic workers. As discussed below, a large share of domestic work can be described as domestic "job work"[1251] in which a domestic worker from outside the household performs services for multiple families, often for a short duration, and, possibly, but not always, on a repetitive basis (*infra* no. 404).[1252] However, very different arrangements also still exist. Research in Germany, for instance, estimated that roughly 163,000 households rely on a live-in care worker. These workers, who mostly come from Poland or other Eastern European countries, live in the household for a few weeks or months to provide nursing care.[1253] Therefore, although domestic job work has largely replaced traditional forms of domestic employment, live-in domestic work is still an important societal phenomenon, both in the Global South and North.[1254] Austria offers another example. It explicitly legalised "24-hour carers", predominantly Eastern European migrants who live-in and provide care services around the clock. The country even introduced subsidies to help households hire these carers.[1255]

377 Perhaps stimulated by subsidised governmental policies like this, the incidence of domestic work seems to have increased throughout recent decades. Growth is, moreover, not expected to stall. In Sweden, domestic work was rare during the 1970s and 1980s, amongst other reasons, because of the expansion of parental leave and the increase in day-care centres. During the 1990s and 2000s, domestic work increased again, in part stimulated by the free movement of workers in the EU.[1256] Similarly, since the 1980s, when Dutch women became more active in the labour market, increased demand for household and care services has also become

1250. Merike Blofield & Merita Jokela, *Paid Domestic Work and the Struggles of Care Workers in Latin America*, 66 Current Sociology Monograph 531, 531 and 534 n. 4 (2018).
1251. Mary Romero, *Chicanas Modernize Domestic Service*, 11 Qualitative Sociology 319, 319–334 (1988), as referred to in Pierrette Hondagneu-Sotelo, *Regulating the Unregulated?: Domestic Workers' Social Networks*, 41 Social problems 50, 51 n. 1 (1994).
1252. Domestic services are disproportionally performed on a "part-time" basis in many countries. More than half of the domestic workers have part-time jobs in Germany, Italy, Luxembourg, Spain and the United States. At the same time, one should be aware that domestic workers that work full-time for one family are still omnipresent in Latin America, for instance. Merita Jokela, *Patterns of Precarious Employment in a Female-Dominated Sector in Five Welfare States – The Case of Paid Domestic Labor Sector*, 26 Social Politics 30, 42 n. 1 (2019); Blofield & Jokela, *supra* n. 1250, at 534.
1253. Volker Hielscher, Sabine Kirchen-Peters & Lukas Nock, *Pflege in den Eigenen Vier* Wänden: *Zeitaufwand und Kosten* 95 (Hans Böckler Stiftung 2017).
1254. "In the Philippines, live-in domestic workers make up a third of all domestic workers (ILO, 2011a). In Indonesia, 1 in 10 domestic workers live in the employer's household (Tijdens and van Klaveren, 2011), while survey data gathered in the United States (2011) found that 11 % of domestic workers were live-in (NDWA survey)". Claire Hobden, *Working Time of Live-in Domestic Workers* 2 (ILO 2013).
1255. Andrea E. Schmidt, Juliane Winkelmann, Ricardo Rodrigues & Kai Leichsenring, *Lessons for Regulating Informal Markets and Implications for Quality Assurance – The Case of Migrant Care Workers in Austria*, 36 Ageing & Society 741, 742 n. 4 (2016).
1256. Catharina Calleman, *Domestic Services in a "Land of Equality": The Case of Sweden*, 23 Canadian Journal of women and the law 121, 122 and 126 n. 1 (2011).

noticeable in the Netherlands.[1257] Households' reliance on domestic workers seems to have likewise increased outside of Europe. This happened in India, where it had to do with rural-to-urban migration, unemployment among men – which forced women to find work – and the affordability of these services, making it accessible to the middle class.[1258] A "rapid increase in living standards and growing demand for a higher quality of life" has also boosted the demand for household services in China, leading approximately 25 per cent of Chinese families to look for "advanced domestic workers"; a demand that apparently cannot be met.[1259] These scholarly accounts correspond to ILO research, which confirms the upward trend. The organisation measured 19 million more domestic workers in 2010 than 1995, with the most notable increases in Latin America, the Caribbean, the Pacific and Asia.[1260] Demand is expected to continue to grow, *inter alia*, because of an ageing population, a rising percentage of economically active women and a preference for home-based care.[1261] Other reasons found in the literature related to a continued "squeeze" on the time households have left to perform domestic and care work personally, and a potential decline in public services, such as day-care centres, stimulating the demand for paid help.[1262]

Marginalised workers – Despite the prevalence of domestic work across the globe, 378
one common feature is how domestic work is characterised by a high degree of informality.[1263] These domestic work relationships are, to a significant extent, governed by customs, social hierarchies and other "non-state norms".[1264] As noted by Blackett, a lead author of the ILO's Law and Practice Report on decent work for domestic workers, domestic work is conditioned by the "law of the household workplace", not so much the law of the State.[1265] Domestic workers, or specific categories thereof, are still explicitly excluded from employment and social protection in some countries.[1266] In others, they are simply not covered in reality, without this leading to any legislative

1257. Sarah van Walsum, *Regulating Migrant Domestic Work in the Netherlands: Opportunities and Pitfalls*, 23 Canadian Journal of women and the law 141, 144 n. 1 (2011).
1258. N. Neetha & Rajni Palriwala, *The Absence of State Law: Domestic Workers in India*, 23 Canadian Journal of women and the law 97, 104–106 n. 1 (2011).
1259. Liu Minghui, *Migrants and Cities: Research Report on Recruitment, Employment, and Working Conditions of Domestic Workers in China* 41 (ILO 2017).
1260. ILO, *supra* n. 1246, at 24.
1261. ILO, *Formalizing Domestic Work* 5 (ILO 2016).
1262. Huws, *supra* n. 637, at 16; Berg, *supra* n. 104, at 88–89.
1263. Not only is the incidence of informality high in absolute terms, it manifests itself in various ways. One article describes the situation of female factory workers who are encouraged by their employers to work in the employers' home. Thomas Chambers & Ayesha Ansari, *Ghar Mein Kām Hai (There is Work in the House): When Female Factory Workers become 'Coopted Domestic Labour'*, 13 Journal of South Asian Development 141, 141–163 n. 2 (2018).
1264. ILO, *supra* n. 946, at 11.
1265. Adelle Blackett, *Everyday Transgressions: Domestic Workers' Transnational Challenge to International Labor Law* 17 and 43–45 (Cornell University Press 2019). *See also* Judy Fudge, *Everyday Transgressions: Domestic Workers' Transnational Challenge to International Labor Law*, 41 Comparative Labor Law & Policy Journal 299, 302 n. 1 (2019).
1266. Smith, *supra* n. 426, at 177–192; Virginia Mantouvalou, *Human Rights for Precarious Workers: The Legislative Precariousness of Domestic Labor*, 34 Comparative Labor Law & Policy Journal 133, 139–146 n. 1 (2012).

changes.[1267] Furthermore, even when employment protections do effectively cover domestic work relationships, domestic workers often have fewer rights, protections and recourse possibilities than regular employees.[1268]

379 Scholarship mentions many reasons for domestic workers' enduring marginalisation. In some cases, it might have to do with a country's overall labour market. For instance, as long as a country has an extensive informal economy in general, like over 80 per cent of the total workforce in Ghana around 2011, it is hard to see how a sector of the economy particularly prone to informality, such as domestic work, can be effectively formalised.[1269] In other words, the regulation of domestic work cannot be dissociated from broader labour market trends, a country's overall socio-economic conditions and cultural traditions. The 24-hour care scheme in Austria, for example, provides many families in the country with "the only affordable option to care for older relatives at home". Any future changes to the scheme bear "high political and financial risks", according to the researchers.[1270] The same is true for the Belgian system of *titres-services*, in which an agency dispatches cleaning personnel to households, who pay for the services with a voucher that has been issued and subsidised by the State. The system reaches its limits in the sense that the demand for services exceeds the number of workers available. Yet, the agencies are only profitable to a limited extent, raising questions about the system's financial viability, and, in particular, the overall cost of these subsidies for the State.[1271]

380 These very formalised forms of domestic work illustrate the struggle of domestic workers exceptionally well. Governments and other regulators are as much concerned with the price of these services for households as they are with the wages of the domestic workers involved. This observation is not meant as a critique. The cost of these government-subsidised services for households inevitably impacts whether households will revert to informal forms of domestic work.[1272] However, at the same time, this does not change the fact that domestic workers remain ensnared in a

1267. A contribution published on India in 2011, summarised the situation as "[d]iscussions abound, but progress in enacting or amending legislation is slow, reiterating the apathy of the state in providing legal protection to domestic workers". Neetha & Palriwala, *supra* n. 1258, at 118. On Asia and the Middle East, *see* Nisha Varia, *"Sweeping Changes?" A Review of Recent Reforms on Protections for Migrant Domestic Workers in Asia and the Middle East*, 23 Canadian Journal of women and the law 265, 273–276 n. 1 (2011); Minghui, *supra* n. 1259, at 26.

1268. The specific rules on domestic work can provide domestic workers with a lower level of protection than regular employees have been given. *See*, in particular, Guy Mundlak & Hila Shamir, *Bringing Together or Drifting Apart? Targeting Care Work as "Work like No Other"*, 23 Canadian Journal of women and the law 289, 289–308 n. 1 (2011).

1269. Dzodzi Tsikata, *Employment Agencies and the Regulation of Domestic Workers in Ghana: Institutionalizing Informality?*, 23 Canadian Journal of women and the law 213, 214–215 n. 1 (2011). One possibility could be through agencies, *see*, Dzodzi Tsikata, *Employment Agencies and Domestic Work in Ghana* 251, 251–263 (Judy Fudge, Shae McCrystal & Kamala Sankaran eds., *Challenging the Legal Boundaries of Work Regulation*, Hart Publishing 2012).

1270. Schmidt, Winkelmann, Rodrigues & Leichsenring, *supra* n. 1255, at 758.

1271. IDEA Consult, *supra* n. 635, at 84–85.

1272. For example, users of household platforms in Mexico and Panama are eager to find a cleaner on the platform and, then, conclude a disintermediated informal agreement with that cleaner, thus, deformalising the work relationship again. In this way, they can save on taxes etc. Clarissa E. Weber, Mark Okraku, Johanna Mair & Indre Maurer, *Steering the Transition from Informal*

socio-economic knot in which they have little bargaining power. This issue is even more complicated in countries with less formal and transparent work arrangements. The ILO's Regional Office for Arab States, for example, concluded, based on interviews with employers in Kuwait, that "[d]omestic workers living and working in Kuwait are part of a social system under which, even if existing laws were changed to protect them, they would still be vulnerable to exploitation due to the social fabric of Kuwait [in which domestic workers are not considered as real workers]".[1273] Sadly, this is not just the case in Kuwait. Interviews with employers in Jordan, similarly, "show a recurring discourse that the [migrant domestic worker] is considered 'part of the household' rather than an employee, a discourse which was used to justify limitations on the mobility of the worker and an unwillingness to give them a weekly day of leave or rest".[1274] Hobden mentions in this respect that, irrespective of the country concerned, organisers need to make domestic workers visible in order for them to pursue legislative change successfully, and, correspondingly, influence the social fabric. These workers' voices and faces need to be shared in the media and online. The public needs to be convinced that domestic work is real work with, in many instances, regular moms and dads taking on the responsibilities of the domestic worker's employer.[1275]

In addition to the obstacles related to the interrelation between domestic work and 381
society, factors related to the nature of domestic work itself also make it challenging to improve working conditions. One issue has to do with the inviolability of the home and the household members' right to privacy. The difficulty of enforcing regulations at home is compounded by households' unwillingness to become familiar with and apply employment law on their own accord, combined with easy access to informal domestic workers.[1276] Other complications have to do with the fact that relationships between domestic workers and families can become personal instead of merely professional, making these relationships subject to dynamics not seen elsewhere.[1277] Also, the largely female and racialised workforce involved,[1278] together with domestic

to Formal Service Provision: Labor Platforms in Emerging-Market Countries, Socio-Economic Review 1, 13–14 (2021).

1273. ILO Regional Office for Arab States, *Employers' Perspectives Towards Domestic Workers in Kuwait: A Qualitative Study on Attitudes, Working Conditions and the Employment Relationship* (ILO 2015)

1274. ILO Regional Office for Arab States, *Employers' Perspectives Towards Domestic Workers in Jordan: A Qualitative Study on Attitudes, Working Conditions and the Employment Relationship* 20 (ILO 2015).

1275. Claire Hobden, *Winning Fair Labour Standards for Domestic Workers: Lessons Learned from the Campaign for a Domestic Worker Bill of Rights in New York State* 23 (ILO 2010).

1276. Jennifer N. Fish, *Engendering Democracy: Domestic Labour and Coalition-Building in South Africa*, 32 Journal of Southern African Studies 107, 118 n. 1 (2006); ILO, *supra* n. 1261, at 23–25.

1277. Blofield & Jokela, *supra* n. 1250, at 533. *See also* Bridget Anderson, *Just Another Job? Paying for Domestic Work*, 9 Gender and Development 25, 27–32 n. 1 (2001).

1278. For instance, some employers would prefer "foreign-born workers" who are "perceived as submissive", whereas white women are "aggressive or opinionated", implying that foreign-born women are not. Amanda Moras, *Colour-blind Discourses in Paid Domestic Work: Foreignness and the Delineation of Alternative Racial Markers*, 33 Ethnic and Racial Studies 233, 250 n. 2 (2010). *See also* Amy Jo Murray & Kevin Durrheim, *"There Was Much That Went Unspoken":*

work's low status,[1279] and views about domestic work being "unproductive", "easy" work in a hospitable home,[1280] have all contributed to domestic workers' poor working conditions. What is more, these processes are still ongoing. Researchers, who analysed the content of publicly available ads for nannies on Craigslist in the United States, discovered that "more than one fourth (29%) of ads contained information that was actually or potentially discriminatory, while a similar percentage (27%) contained indicators that an employer may not see being a nanny as a real job".[1281]

382 Other reasons why working conditions remain poor have to do with the work's solitary nature and the little interest shown by established trade unions.[1282] Their reluctance to organise domestic workers further prevents these workers from building any real bargaining power. Something that is also impacted by the high percentage of migrant domestic workers.[1283] For instance, many undocumented migrants consider informal domestic work a viable "survival strategy".[1284] This is the case even though the situation for migrant domestic workers can be extremely dire. The Indonesian Government's decision to prevent Indonesians from working as domestic workers in Malaysia (and Saudi Arabia) because of "some particularly horrific cases of abuse" serves as a case in point.[1285] Moreover, even when the situation is less grim, migrant domestic workers still face many challenges, amongst others related to the many jurisdictions involved when working in a foreign country as well as their volatile immigration status.[1286] This interaction between domestic work and immigration is,

Maintaining Racial Hierarchies in South African Paid Domestic Labour Through the Unsaid, 42 Ethnic and Racial Studies 2623, 2625 n. 15 (2019). On gender, Paula England, *Emerging Theories of Care Work*, 31 Annual Review of Sociology 381, 382–384 n. 1 (2005).

1279. Bamu argues that the complex interplay between gender, race and class creates a perception among employers that domestic workers are not to be taken seriously, hence their work is undervalued and even regulatory compliance suffers. Pamhidzai Bamu, *Nurturing a Culture of Compliance with Domestic Workers' Rights in South Africa* 157, 191 (Darcy du Toit ed., *Exploited, Undervalued – and Essential: Domestic Workers and the Realisation of Their Rights*, Pretoria University Law Press 2013). More generally on low status, *see* ILO, *supra* n. 1261, at 26–27.

1280. Peggie R. Smith, *The Pitfalls of Home: Protecting the Health and Safety of Paid Domestic Workers*, 23 Canadian Journal of women and the law 309, 313–317 n. 1 (2011); Darcy du Toit, *Situating Domestic Work in a Changing Global Labour Market* 1, 5–9 (Darcy du Toit ed., *Exploited, Undervalued – and Essential: Domestic Workers and the Realisation of Their Rights*, Pretoria University Law Press 2013).

1281. Craig D. Lair & Christopher K. Andrews, *Advertising a Particularly Precarious Occupation: Nanny Ads on Craigslist*, 38 Sociological Spectrum 69, 82 n. 2 (2018).

1282. Neetha & Palriwala, *supra* n. 1258, at 113–115; Calleman, *supra* n. 1256, at 130–132; Helen Schwenken, *Mobilisation des Travailleuses Domestiques Migrantes: De la Cuisine à l'Organisation Internationale du Travail*, 51 Cahiers du Genre 113, 117–119 n. 2 (2011).

1283. "One of the most striking changes in domestic work in the past 30 years has been the growing prevalence of migrant work. In several regions, including Europe and the Gulf countries and the Middle East, the majority of domestic labourers today are migrant women". ILO, *supra* n. 946, at 6.

1284. Van Walsum, *supra* n. 1257, at 154–156.

1285. Juanita Elias, *The Malaysia-Indonesia Domestic Worker Dispute*, 15 International Feminist Journal of Politics 391, 392 and 394 n. 3 (2013).

1286. Judy Fudge, *Global Care Chains, Employment Agencies, and the Conundrum of Jurisdiction: Decent Work for Domestic Workers in Canada*, 23 Canadian Journal of women and the law 235, 242–244 n. 1 (2011); Varia, *supra* n. 1267, at 271–273; Clíodhna Murphy, *The Enduring*

furthermore, structured by the many intermediaries involved in posting (foreign) domestic workers. Adding an intermediary to the relationship between a worker and household can benefit workers, especially if the intermediary is a highly professional enterprise.[1287] However, intermediaries can also give rise to new forms of abuse or uncertainty.[1288] They may, for instance, obfuscate the households' obligations vis-à-vis the domestic worker, making it hard to figure out which entity bears which responsibilities.[1289]

Platforms in domestic work – When added up, this confluence of factors tends to result in precarious working conditions: wages close to the poverty line,[1290] vulnerability to violence and harassment,[1291] problematic access to social security,[1292] and ongoing use of child labour.[1293] As Jokela points out, even formalised forms of domestic work show "higher levels of precarity compared to other industries across welfare regimes and regardless of the institutional settings".[1294] However, since bad governmental policies can perpetuate this precarity,[1295] it is all the more important to pay attention to how platform operators engaged in domestic work are embedded in a country's existing domestic work industry and regulation. As mentioned in this **383**

Vulnerability of Migrant Domestic Workers in Europe, 62 The International and Comparative Law Quarterly 599, 599–627 n. 3 (2013).

1287. Smith, *supra* n. 1280, at 312. The agency, for instance, provides the domestic workers with a counterparty if they want to bargain collectively. One problem in this industry is that households will rarely, if ever, form an employers' association for collective bargaining.

1288. Manuela Tomei & Patrick Belser, *New ILO Standards on Decent Work for Domestic Workers: A Summary of the Issues and Discussions*, 150 International Labour Review 431, 437 n. 3–4 (2011).

1289. Dzodzi Tsikata, *Employment Agencies and Domestic Work in Ghana* 251, 262 (Judy Fudge, Shae McCrystal & Kamala Sankaran eds., *Challenging the Legal Boundaries of Work Regulation*, Hart Publishing 2012); ILO, *supra* n. 1261, at 14.

1290. Research on a Belgian platform – ListMinut – revealed that, while the Belgian statutory minimum wage at the time required an hourly wage of EUR 9.12, on average, workers are paid EUR 17.8 per hour for completed tasks. However, in relation to the lowest remunerated category of work, babysitting, it was only EUR 7.7 per hour. The second-lowest category were "household services, such as cleaning and ironing", which generated around EUR 10.9 an hour. Tasks related to tutoring were estimated to earn EUR 15.5 an hour, home repair EUR 18.4 an hour, and, for instance, wellness-related tasks, like hairdressing and massage, or animal care grossed more than EUR 20. One should be aware that workers are not compensated for the time spent looking for a job or travelling to the job. This makes it challenging for these workers to earn EUR 73 a day (8h x EUR 9.12). Willem Pieter De Groen, Ilaria Maselli & Brian Fabo, *The Digital Market for Local Services: A One-night Stand for Workers?: An Example from the On-demand Economy* 11–12 (CEPS 2016).

1291. Maria da Conceição Figueiredo, Fátima Suleman & Maria do Carmo Botelho, *Workplace Abuse and Harassment: The Vulnerability of Informal and Migrant Domestic Workers in Portugal*, 17 Social Policy & Society 65, 65–85 n. 1 (2018). Also, platform workers who provide household services are vulnerable. Kellen Browning & Kate Conger, *Cleaners Demand Harassment Safeguards From the Booking Service Handy*, The New York Times (10 September 2020), https://www.nytimes.com/2020/09/10/business/handy-service-cleaners-harassment.html.

1292. ILO, *supra* n. 1261, at 16–20.

1293. ILO, *Ending Child Labour in Domestic Work and Protecting Young Workers from Abusive Working Conditions* (ILO 2013).

1294. Jokela, *supra* n. 1252, at 47.

1295. *Ibid.*, 47.

dissertation's First Part, households have long relied on labour market intermediaries to find household help (*supra* no. 60). One could argue that many platforms cater to the same demand. They provide household members with the tools to outsource household work to external workers, willing to cook, clean and care for the household's residents. The dissertation's First Part argued that, unlike Uber passengers or other end-market consumers, these household members could be held responsible as employers for relying on platform workers through intermediaries (e.g. Helpling in the Netherlands, *supra* no. 60). Indeed, Eurofound is right to highlight that "[o]nline platforms have expanded the marketplace in household services for domestic users. These clients bear responsibilities towards the workers they hire".[1296]

384 In this regard, it seems that, so far, public authorities have not taken significant action to guarantee labour platforms' positive impact on this "marketplace in household services". This is unfortunate, since, for example, Albin mentions the importance of local regulations to ensure that agencies positively contribute to domestic work.[1297] Hobden and Fudge, likewise, explicitly argue that intermediaries, and, thus, also platforms, can produce beneficial and detrimental effects for domestic workers. The outcome "depends largely on the laws and policies regulating employment at large, domestic work and enterprises/agencies".[1298] For example, although platforms could formalise domestic work, it seems that this is anything but a given.[1299] Research in Mexico and Panama shows that workers and users have multiple reasons to revert back to informal domestic work once they have found a match on the platform (e.g. evasion of taxes).[1300]

385 **The spirit of the Convention** – In light of all the factors marginalising domestic workers, the ILO Convention concerning Decent Work for Domestic Workers aims to establish loud and clear: domestic work is genuine and valuable work, regardless of its particularities.[1301] The ILO's Law and Practice Report sums up this vision by describing domestic work as "work like any other" and "work like no other".[1302] The instruments adopt a human rights-based approach to counter this tendency to marginalise domestic workers.[1303] As Blackett puts it, they formulate a "human rights claim to inclusion in labor law".[1304] However, that is not all.

1296. Eurofound, *supra* n. 303, at 19.
1297. Einat Albin, *From 'Domestic Servant' to 'Domestic Worker'* 231, 249 (Judy Fudge, Shae McCrystal & Kamala Sankaran eds., *Challenging the Legal Boundaries of Work Regulation*, Hart Publishing 2012).
1298. Fudge & Hobden, *supra* n. 640, at 14–15.
1299. Gregory Randolph, Hernan Galperin & Lina Khan, *New Opportunities in the Platform Economy: On-ramps to Formalization in the Global South* (JustJobs Network 2019).
1300. Weber, Okraku, Mair & Maurer, *supra* n. 1272, at 24–25.
1301. Sandra Fredman, *Home from Home: Migrant Domestic Workers and the International Labour Organization Convention on Domestic Workers* 399, 405 (Cathryn Costello & Mark Freedland eds., *Migrants at Work: Immigration and Vulnerability in Labour Law*, OUP 2014).
1302. ILO, *supra* n. 946, at 12.
1303. Albin & Mantouvalou, *supra* n. 1245, at 72–75; Martin Oelz, *The ILO's Domestic Workers Convention and Recommendation: A Window of Opportunity for Social Justice*, 153 International Labour Review 143, 152–153 n. 1 (2014).
1304. Adelle Blackett, *Introductory Note to the Decent Work for Domestic Workers Convention, 2011 (No. 189) and Recommendation (No. 201)*, 53 International Legal Materials 250, 251 n. 1 (2014).

As indicated by Tomei and Belser, the instruments' key principles are "that domestic workers deserve protection and rights that are no less favourable than those enjoyed by other workers [i.e. 'work like any other'] [...] and that effective measures must be taken to ensure they enjoy these rights [...] [i.e. 'work like no other']".[1305] The first principle arguably reflects domestic workers "comparable worth",[1306] whereas the latter might, for instance, suggest the recognition of domestic workers' "need for differential, affirmative treatment" in light of the continued undervaluation of their work.[1307] The preamble of the Domestic Workers Convention, 2011 (No. 189), indeed, admits that "the special conditions under which domestic work is carried out [...] make it desirable to supplement the general standards with standards specific to domestic workers so as to enable them to enjoy their rights fully". This "sectoral approach" is supposed to complement the abstract appeal of the instruments' human rights-based perspective.[1308] It also makes it necessary to define what "domestic work" is and who classifies as a "domestic worker". 386

On the scope of the Convention – As regards the instrument's scope, Oelz, a senior legal specialist at the Office, has emphasised that the drafters meant to provide the Convention with a broad scope of application.[1309] Nevertheless, the drafters may have inadvertently limited the instrument's scope significantly, namely, by relying on the notion of an "employment relationship" in Article 1 of Convention No. 189 to define the concept of a "domestic worker".[1310] Some scholars have even suggested, along those lines, that agency workers and casual workers are not covered by Convention No. 189.[1311] These views signal that the scope of this instrument leaves plenty to discuss. 387

To illuminate the issue, the following Section will first discuss what it means to perform work "in or for a household or households," i.e. domestic work, after which the "unique" characteristics of domestic workers' employment relationships are discussed in Section 2. Having found that domestic workers are, indeed, bound by a "special" kind of employment relationship when compared to employees in commerce or industry, the Third Section will discuss the importance attributed by the 388

1305. Tomei & Belser, *supra* n. 1288, at 432.
1306. Adelle Blackett, *The Decent Work for Domestic Workers Convention and Recommendation, 2011*, 106 The American journal of international law 778, 783 n. 4 (2012).
1307. Adelle Blackett, *Introduction: Regulating Decent Work for Domestic Workers*, 23 Canadian Journal of women and the law 1, 14–15 n. 1 (2011).
1308. Albin & Mantouvalou, *supra* n. 1245, at 75. Albin argues that the instruments do not take this sectoral approach far enough. Albin, *supra* n. 1297, at 246–249.
1309. "Reflecting the drafters' intention that the instruments should have the broadest possible scope in order to overcome the insufficient coverage of domestic workers by other international labour standards (ILO, 2010d, p. 387), Article 2(1) provides that the Convention applies to 'all domestic workers', as defined in Article 1". Oelz, *supra* n. 1303, at 154.
1310. Fredman, *supra* n. 1301, at 408; Adelle Blackett, *Regulatory Innovation on Decent Work for Domestic Workers in the Light of International Labour Organization Convention No. 189*, 34 International Journal of Comparative Labour Law and Industrial Relations 141, 143 n. 2 (2018).
1311. Albin & Mantouvalou, *supra* n. 1245, at 71; Tonia Novitz & Phil Syrpis, *The Place of Domestic Work in Europe: An Analysis of Current Policy in the Light of the Council Decision Authorising Member States to Ratify ILO Convention No. 189*, 6 European Labour Law Journal 104, 117 n. 2 (2015).

ILO constituents to the "occupational basis" of domestic work. As it turns out, ILO constituents seemingly wanted to cover all people involved in domestic work on an occupational basis under this standard. Section 3 points out that such a broad scope of coverage would have several implications for domestic platform work. The Fourth Section, subsequently, discusses the difficulty to determine whether the employment relationship is concluded between the domestic worker and the head of a household, or between the worker and the agency, an issue that also recurs in the platform economy, where households and platforms share the employer's functions. The Fifth Section applies previous Sections' findings to two concrete examples, TaskRabbit and Care.com, highlighting what is at stake for platform workers.

SUBCHAPTER 2. THE CONVENTION'S SCOPE

The definitions in the Domestic Workers Convention, 2011 (No. 189):

> "**Article 1**
>
> For the purpose of this Convention:
> (a) the term domestic work means work performed in or for a household or households;
> (b) the term domestic worker means any person engaged in domestic work within an employment relationship;
> (c) a person who performs domestic work only occasionally or sporadically and not on an occupational basis is not a domestic worker.
>
> **Article 2**
>
> 1. The Convention applies to all domestic workers.
>
> [...]"[1312]

1. Domestic Work: Work Performed in or for Households

389 **Household work** – The Convention applies to domestic workers who, by definition, perform "domestic work" in an "employment relationship". Article 1 additionally clarifies that domestic work is work performed in or for a household or households. Consequently, to determine the scope of Convention No. 189, one needs to know what is meant by work "in or for a household or households". On their own, these words come across as far-reaching, potentially covering all the work that can be performed for a household's members. The working documents contain little details in this respect. The Office seems only to have concluded, based on the respondents' replies to its first questionnaire, that "[i]n many instances, it is suggested that the definition should include activities of gardeners, personal drivers, guards and other household-related activities, such as car washing and shopping".[1313] Surprisingly, this topic did not seem to raise any real discussions during the committee's proceedings. Publishing in the ILO's International Labour Review, Oelz refers to the same questionnaire's responses to claim that the definition takes into account the trend

1312. Art. 1 and 2 Domestic Workers Convention, 2011 (No. 189).
1313. ILO, *Report IV(2) Decent Work for Domestic Workers* 385 (ILO 2010).

of domestic workers working "for several households in parallel". It "covers the full range of household-related activities and services that support the regular functioning of the household and the well-being and development of its members. This includes indoor work, but also work that takes place outside, such as gardening, driving, shopping or supervising the family's child in a public park (ILO, 2010d, pp. 35–41)".[1314]

As such, at least from the Office's perspective, the Convention does seem to opt for 390
a comprehensive description of domestic work. Because there is no such thing as the ordinary meaning of "work in or for households", nor does the Convention's context precisely indicate what it means, a few academic articles will be used to illustrate what this might mean. Convention No. 189 derives its scope from the "household work" that households typically perform themselves, but which, in this case, is outsourced to external workers. When looking at definitions of household work, particularly Eichler and Albanese have made an effort to move beyond the usual depictions of household work, i.e. "preparing meals, doing laundry, cleaning house, shopping for groceries, doing dishes, and quite often childcare", and to clarify that household work "consists of the sum of all physical, mental, emotional and spiritual tasks that are performed for one's own or someone else's household and that maintain the daily life of those for whom one has responsibility".[1315] The authors stress that their definition includes "all care work", even "self care".[1316] Other scholars have relied on these insights to similarly define household labour as "activities, tasks, and interactions that couples engage in to maintain both family members and the household",[1317] or "as activities and tasks that individuals perform in order to maintain both other family members and the household, and that could be performed by another individual in return for payment".[1318] These academic perspectives align with the description given by the Office. As a report from 2016 on *Formalizing domestic work* notes, domestic workers "provide services and goods that are socially necessary for the maintenance of households and the wellbeing of families, in other words, tasks that are crucial for social reproduction".[1319] Similar to Eichler's and Albanese's views on household work, Convention No. 189's domestic work concept would cover some forms of "care work".[1320] However, not all the care services provided to household members might be classified as domestic work. If this were the case, a school counsellor's visit might likewise be considered domestic work because parents' emotional work is outsourced to the counsellor. With this in

1314. Oelz, *supra* n. 1303, at 153.

1315. Margrit Eichler, *Integrating Carework and Housework into Household Work: A Conceptual Clarification*, 10 Journal of the Association for Research on Mothering 9, 10 and 15 n. 1 (2008).

1316. Margrit Eichler & Patrizia Albanese, *What Is Household Work? A Critique of Assumptions Underlying Empirical Studies of Housework and an Alternative Approach*, 32 The Canadian Journal of Sociology 227, 248 n. 2 (2007).

1317. Elizabeth M. Legerski & Marie Cornwall, *Working-Class Job Loss, Gender, and the Negotiation of Household Labor*, 24 Gender & Society 447, 452 n. 4 (2010).

1318. Sophia Fauser, *Time Availability and Housework: The Effect of Unemployment on Couples' Hours of Household Labor*, 83 Social Science Research 1, 2 (2019).

1319. ILO, *supra* n. 1261, at 3.

1320. See, for example, the Committee of Experts' general survey for 2021–2022 on "Decent work for care economy workers in a changing economy" which will focus, *inter alia*, on the instruments on "decent work for domestic workers".

mind, "work in or for households" should probably not be interpreted so broadly that it covers all work for household members, wherever it takes place.

391 Indeed, it has to be emphasised that the ILO constituents, "[r]ather than defining domestic work according to tasks, [decided that] the distinguishing feature of domestic work is the workplace".[1321] The distinguishing feature of domestic work is the home, and as a result, although domestic work "is broadly understood to include tasks such as childminding, caring for older persons or persons with disabilities in their households, cooking, cleaning or ironing",[1322] the Convention, arguably, requires a connection to the physical location of the household. This would allow domestic work to encompass some forms of care work, but at the same time, the location of this social reproductive work does play a determinative role. To that extent, for this dissertation, the description of domestic work as "work performed in or for a household or households" is understood to mean that work performed for household members is domestic work if, at some point, the worker goes to the place of the household. Consequently, for example, supervising someone's child in a public park might not be classified as domestic work unless it forms part of broader childminding activities that also occur at home.

392 **Household work in the platform economy** – When this description is applied to the platform economy, the conclusion is that many platforms enable their workers to perform domestic work. In principle, Convention No. 189 targets on-demand household services such as cooking, laundering, cleaning, caregiving, tutoring, home repair, gardening, and other handyperson-like services. That means platforms, such as Care.com, TaskRabbit, Handy, SitterCity, UrbanSitter, MyBuilder, Helpling, Airtasker, TutorHub and PetSitter, are all involved in the intermediation of domestic work.

393 Furthermore, based on the descriptions of domestic work above, it is legitimate to wonder whether the Convention also covers platform workers involved in food delivery services. After all, whereas most people might think of Deliveroo, Uber Eats etc., as transportation platforms, some scholars have, in fact, classified these services as "on-demand household services".[1323] Similarly, grocery shopping on behalf of the household, after which the items are delivered to the doorstep, might likewise constitute domestic work. Consider, for example, the classification of household services in Cancedda's work. She has identified five major "sub-sectors of household services", namely childcare, care of the elderly, domestic cleaning, "catering or food services" and "domestic maintenance and gardening".[1324] The decision not to consider the transportation of food and groceries to households' doorstep as a form of domestic work would exclude one of these sub-sectors from the purview of Convention No. 189. This comes across as arbitrary in light of our prior definition of domestic work. From the ILO's perspective, it is important to settle whether Uber Eats, Deliveroo,

1321. ILO, *supra* n. 1247, at 8.

1322. *Ibid.*, 168.

1323. Robert Vaughan & Raphael Daverio, *Assessing the Size and Presence of the Collaborative Economy in Europe* 32–33 (Publications Office of the European Union 2016). *See also*, Huws, *supra* n. 42, at 132.

1324. Alessandra Cancedda, *Employment in Household Services* 8 and 23 (Office for Official Publications of the European Communities 2001).

Take Eat Easy, Foodora and others, as well as Instacart and Shipt, can be considered as intermediaries involved in domestic work. When reading the definition of domestic work literally, a food delivery courier can, indeed, be considered to perform work for a household, at least for most of the time.[1325] The courier helps out with some of the most repetitive household chores, shopping for groceries, cooking and cleaning up afterwards.[1326] Moreover, the delivery links the work to the household's location, possibly turning it into "domestic work".

2. Domestic Workers' Employment Relationships

Work like any other and no other – Having discussed the range of platforms that can be considered to organise domestic work, our attention turns towards the other conditions of the Convention's definitions. The "Convention concerning decent work for domestic workers", which is Convention No. 189's full title, has a preamble that contains relevant considerations to settle the instrument's scope. The preamble, for instance, clarifies how Convention No. 189 is "[m]indful of the commitment of the International Labour Organization to promote decent work for all through the achievement of the goals of the ILO Declaration on Fundamental Principles and Rights at Work and the ILO Declaration on Social Justice for a Fair Globalization". The Convention, in other words, fits into the overall framework to deliver decent work for all. **394**

As already mentioned, its approach thereby reflects the view, as expressed in the working documents, that domestic work is work like any other and work like no other. On the one hand, the preamble stipulates "that international labour Conventions and Recommendations apply to all workers, including domestic workers, unless otherwise provided", mentioning a range of ILO standards that have "particular relevance for domestic workers". On the other hand, the instrument's preamble also highlights some particularities under which domestic work is carried out. Domestic work continues to be "undervalued and invisible", "mainly carried out by women and girls", many of whom are particularly vulnerable to discrimination and human rights abuses because they are migrants or members of disadvantaged communities. Furthermore, the preamble admits that even though domestic workers represent a significant proportion of the national workforce (especially in developing countries), they "remain among the most marginalized". Due to these "special conditions", it is "desirable to supplement the general standards with standards specific to domestic workers so as to enable them to enjoy their rights fully". **395**

Article 1 and 2 Convention No. 189 – Article 2 of the Convention instructs that the Convention applies to all "domestic workers".[1327] As mentioned, Article 1(b) defines **396**

1325. One study reported that 16 per cent of the deliveries are made at work, with 82 per cent of them being placed from home. Carsten Hirschberg, Alexander Rajko, Thomas Schumacher & Martin Wrulich, *The Changing Market for Food Delivery* 4 (McKinsey&Company 2016).

1326. Charlene Li, Miranda Mirosa & Phil Bremer, *Review of Online Food Delivery Platforms and their Impacts on Sustainability*, 12 Sustainability 1, 8 (2020).

1327. The Convention applies to all domestic workers, except for the categories that have been excluded wholly or partly from its scope pursuant to the procedure described in the second and third paragraph of Art. 2.

the domestic worker as "any person engaged in domestic work [as discussed above] within an employment relationship". Contrary to the concept of domestic work, the "employment relationship" did not receive any detailed description. Article 1(c) only clarifies that "a person who performs domestic work only occasionally or sporadically and not on an occupational basis is not a domestic worker". Because of the importance of this "employment relationship" for the instrument's application, a crucial question is whether Article 1(c) was meant to influence our understanding of domestic workers' employment relationships, as mentioned in Article 1(b).

397 **The Employment Relationship Recommendation** – To that end, when reflecting on the meaning of an "employment relationship" in Convention No. 189, the first point that requires an explanation is the preamble's reference to the Employment Relationship Recommendation, 2006 (No. 198).[1328] Especially because this reference is not an accident, the Employer Vice-Chairperson, for example, introduced an amendment to remove the reference to Recommendation No. 198 in Convention No. 189's preamble. One reason for this was that the Employers' group had voted against this "hotly debated Recommendation" at its adoption. Secondly, the Employer Vice-Chairperson had "not seen evidence that relationships discussed in that Recommendation affected domestic workers".[1329] In other words, what does the employment relationship in a commercial or industrial context, i.e. Recommendation No. 198, have to do with employment relationships in domestic work? Although this was a legitimate remark, the Worker Vice-Chairperson opposed the Employers' amendment because the Employment Relationship Recommendation "dealt with issues such as triangular relationships, identifying the 'real employer', and differentiating employment from contracts for services".[1330] The Africa Group similarly opposed removing the reference because the relationships discussed in Recommendation No. 198, in particular concerning triangular employment relationships, also existed in domestic work.

398 Since the reference to Recommendation No. 198 was maintained, one would assume that the concept of an employment relationship in Article 1 of Convention No. 189 should be somewhat consistent with the notion developed in Recommendation No. 198.[1331] However, if the employment relationship in Convention No. 189 is understood as it is advanced in the Recommendation, the result would be for Convention No. 189 and Recommendation No. 198 to bounce the ball back and forth. Neither one provides concrete guidance on how to think about an employment relationship in the context of domestic work. Convention No. 189 largely omits doing so. As already mentioned, it only clarifies in Article 1(c) that casual domestic work is not excluded from the Convention unless it is not occupational in nature, and vice versa. Yet, because this phrasing is the result of discussions in the working group, thus behind

1328. *See, e.g.*, ILO, *Qualitative Research on Employment Relationship and Working Conditions: Preliminary Guidelines* 13-16 (ILO).

1329. Report of the Committee on Domestic Workers at the 100th Session of the International Labour Conference, Geneva, ILO, 2011, 15/18.

1330. *Ibid.*

1331. For instance, the Government member of Australia explicitly asked for this. Report of the Committee on Domestic Workers at the 99th Session of the International Labour Conference, Geneva, ILO, 2010, 12/29.

closed doors, it is unclear how this clarification precisely relates to the condition of having an "employment relationship".

Recommendation No. 198, on the other hand, was not drafted with domestic workers' employment situation in mind. Paragraph 5 of the Recommendation only stipulates that "Members should take particular account in national policy to ensure effective protection to workers especially affected by the uncertainty as to the existence of an employment relationship, including women workers, as well as the most vulnerable workers, young workers, older workers, workers in the informal economy, migrant workers and workers with disabilities". This paragraph might suggest that the Member States need to pay particular attention to domestic workers' employment status. That is because, although §5 of Recommendation No. 198 does not explicitly mention domestic workers, §7(i) of the Transition from the Informal to the Formal Economy Recommendation, 2015 (No. 204), does designate domestic workers as "especially vulnerable to the most serious decent work deficits in the informal economy". Additionally, §6 of Recommendation No. 198 stresses that Members should "take special account in national policy to address the gender dimension in that women workers predominate in certain occupations and sectors[, such as domestic work,][1332] where there is a high proportion of disguised employment relationships, or where there is a lack of clarity of an employment relationship". 399

Therefore, Recommendation No. 198 can be understood to invite the Member States to keep an eye out for the employment status of domestic workers, albeit without explicitly naming them. The problem remains, however, that the main guidelines of Recommendation No. 198 are not adapted to the context of domestic work. At its core, the instrument presents valuable indicators to identify subordination and dependence between parties to a work arrangement in industry or commerce. For example, one indicator of subordination is the fact that the work "involves the integration of the worker in the organization of the enterprise". The wording of this indicator illustrates how the instrument was not drafted with domestic work in mind because a household is not an enterprise. Furthermore, by bluntly applying Recommendation No. 198 to domestic work, there is also a risk that domestic workers' "special circumstances" will not be taken into account, something that would contradict what the preamble of Convention No. 189 claims the instruments on decent work for domestic workers intend to do. Moreover, based on our prior discussion of the rules of interpretation, one could also argue that this interaction between Recommendation No. 198 and Convention No. 189 is an excellent example of a situation in which the intention of the Conference Committee on Domestic Workers should be deemed more important than the prior conceptualisation of the employment relationship in another ILO instrument (*supra* no. 209). ILO Conventions are treaties, each of which needs to be interpreted in its own context, having its own object and purpose. As a result, 400

1332. "Considering that domestic work continues to be undervalued and invisible and is mainly carried out by women and girls, many of whom are migrants or members of disadvantaged communities and who are particularly vulnerable to discrimination in respect of conditions of employment and of work, and to other abuses of human rights". Preamble of the Domestic Workers Convention, 2011 (No. 189).

Convention No. 189's understanding of an "employment relationship" might differ from the one previously depicted in Recommendation No. 198.

401 **An inclusive employment relationship** – In light of this, did constituents intend to simply rely on the test presented in Recommendation No. 198 to identify an employment relationship for the purposes of Convention No. 189? It seems unlikely. The real issue that Convention No. 189 tries to tackle was described by the Office in 2013: "only 10 per cent of all domestic workers (or 5.3 million) are covered by general labour legislation to the same extent as other workers. In contrast, more than one-quarter – 29.9 per cent, or some 15.7 million domestic workers – work in countries where they are completely excluded from the scope of national labour legislation".[1333] The Convention acknowledges domestic workers' marginalised existence and intends to rectify it as part of the ILO's commitment to delivering decent work for all. If this is indeed the instrument's purpose, then, ILO constituents can hardly have intended for the instrument to cover the domestic workers that are already protected on account of their "employment relationship". To do so would make the Convention's "human rights-based approach" largely redundant from the moment of its adoption. The workers already covered by an employment relationship under national law, like Belgian workers engaged in *titres services*, are not the marginalised domestic workers, whose human rights are particularly at risk, such as the migrant domestic workers in Kuwait or Jordan. Instead, it must be assumed that the working group, which drafted the definitions, intended to at least deviate slightly from the traditional concept of an employment relationship in order to push the personal scope of the instrument beyond the small share of domestic workers for whom the employment relationship is not in doubt. The target population must be the larger share of domestic workers who, unjustifiably, remain fully or partially excluded.

402 One comment by the Employer Vice-Chairperson is insightful in this regard. When the EU Member States advanced an amendment to allow certain limited cases of domestic workers, i.e. "certain limited cases of employment relationship", to be excluded from the right to information on the essential aspects of the employment relationship, the Employer Vice-Chairperson objected: "Article 1 had defined domestic work as an employment relationship, how could there be different types of employment relationship?"[1334] Apparently, the EU Member States had in mind not to grant this right "for instance when an employment relationship was of very short duration or for very limited hours per week".[1335] The Government member of Bangladesh also objected, stating that this amendment "would reduce the comprehensiveness of the proposed Convention".[1336] This was a reasonable response considering that at that time, the Committee had already adopted Article 1 of Convention No. 189, which stated that only "a person who performs domestic work only occasionally or sporadically and not on an occupational basis is not a domestic worker". Therefore, it appears from this interaction that the ILO constituents seem to have intended for

1333. ILO, *supra* n. 1246, at 95.

1334. Report of the Committee on Domestic Workers at the 100th Session of the International Labour Conference, Geneva, 2011, ILO, 15/34.

1335. *Ibid.*

1336. *Ibid.*, 15/35.

work relationships of very short duration or for minimal hours per week to be covered under Convention No. 189 if there is an occupational basis. Implicitly, at least some "casual" domestic workers have the characteristics required to be classified under an employment relationship. Furthermore, although this could be a slip of the tongue, or due to the way the conversation was minuted, the Employer Vice-Chairperson explicitly equated domestic work to an employment relationship. This brings up an essential point.

This Convention aims to frame domestic work as work like any other. Keeping that 403
in mind, what could have been a clearer signal that domestic work is work like any other than to clarify that it takes place "within an employment relationship"? Lawyers usually construe a reference to an employment relationship as a condition for the application of a rule. However, in this particular case, the reference to an employment relationship may also destigmatise domestic work, de-marginalise domestic workers, and confirm that domestic workers are entitled to employment protections.[1337] From this angle, it is clear that there is more to the "employment relationship" in Convention No. 189 than meets the eye. The Convention may well take into consideration what D'Souza calls the "specificity" of domestic workers' employment relationships,[1338] although it would probably have been better if it had done so more overtly.

A "special" employment relationship characterised by commodification – Im- 404
portantly, when talking about the relationship between a domestic worker and a household, the risk of (re)commodification should be highlighted. The domestic work relationship has always been prone to commodification. Various organisations in India, for instance, still "spend substantial time and effort persuading the government, the public, and their own members to re-define 'buyers' as 'employers,' and their members as 'workers,' not 'sellers' of a service".[1339] Household members have never appreciated being held to account as employers, not even when they employ live-in domestic workers. Overcoming this aversion has arguably become an even more significant challenge nowadays. Ever since domestic employment turned into domestic "job work", domestic services have become commonplace. Domestic workers no longer work for one or a few employer(s) continuously but perform services for many households, performing a service weekly, bi-weekly, or monthly to one particular household, often in exchange for a fixed sum of money, instead of an hourly wage.[1340] The worker's aim is supposedly to find more and better jobs,

1337. Blackett, *supra* n. 1265, at 17–34.

1338. The author notes that these relationships: (i) are largely invisible because they take place in the private sphere; (ii) are characterised by an unequal balance of power between a domestic worker and the head of the household, which is unlike the unequal balance of power between an employee and employer; (iii) are covered by paternalist attitudes that disguise the perception of domestic work as a proper occupational choice; and (iv) are often executed without a precise job description. Asha D'Souza, *Moving Towards Decent Work for Domestic Workers: An Overview of the ILO's Work* 18–19 (ILO 2010).

1339. Rina Agarwala & Shiny Saha, *The Employment Relationship and Movement Strategies among Domestic Workers in India*, 44 Critical Sociology 1207, 1213 n. 7–8 (2018).

1340. Hondagneu-Sotelo refers to Romero. More specifically, Mary Romero, *Chicanas Modernize Domestic Service*, 11 Qualitative Sociology 319, 319–334 (1988), as referred to in Pierrette

potentially allowing the worker to let go of or pass on the more burdensome clients. "Under these arrangements, domestics are able to position themselves as 'experts' to sell their labor services in much the same way a vendor sells a product to various customers".[1341] The platform economy enables domestic workers to move even further in this direction, potentially leading to this perception of an "'entrepreneurial' domestic worker".[1342]

405 Domestic work can be scheduled at a minute's notice, and the app mostly deals with processing remuneration. The result is that it becomes even easier to depict household members as consumers who pay for the domestic services of an individual "entrepreneur", not employers who provide work to domestic workers. Particularly emblematic of this kind of thinking is, for example, when family members schedule a domestic worker to come and help in the household, presenting it to their family member as a sort of "gift".[1343] Looking at it from another perspective, it is often the husband in these kinds of cases who offers his wife the employ of a domestic worker,[1344] an extraordinary, unusual gift to give.

406 **Households shy away from their role as an employer** – Arguably, solid governmental policies are needed to counter this tendency to commodify domestic work, also because there are intricate reasons why household members might approach their relationship with a domestic worker from the perspective of a consumer rather than that of an employer. Some household members, for example, prefer to see their relationship with the domestic worker as a horizontal, peer-to-peer relationship instead of an instrumental, hierarchical one.[1345] Scholarship mentions a couple of interesting findings on this very issue. Murray and Durrheim describe a case study in which a

---

Hondagneu-Sotelo, *Regulating the Unregulated?: Domestic Workers' Social Networks*, 41 Social problems 50, 51 n. 1 (1994).

1341. Hondagneu-Sotelo, *supra* n. 1251, at 52.

1342. Mateescu & Ticona, *supra* n. 256, at 77. Furthermore, Ravenelle points out that although domestic platform workers could be given the freedom necessary to make them feel like entrepreneurs, as a result of policy changes by TaskRabbit, "many TaskRabbit workers stopped thinking of themselves as entrepreneurs, and began to view themselves as employees". Alexandrea J. Ravenelle, *"We're Not Uber:" Control, Autonomy, and Entrepreneurship in the Gig Economy*, 34 Journal of Managerial Psychology 269, 277 n. 4 (2019).

1343. Amanda Moras, *"This Should be My Responsibility": Gender, Guilt, Privilege and Paid Domestic Work*, 34 Gender Issues 44, 57 n. 1 (2017).

1344. To recall, "[o]nline platforms have expanded the marketplace in household services for domestic users. These clients bear responsibilities towards the workers they hire". Eurofound, *supra* n. 303, at 19.

1345. Anna Kordasiewicz, *La Relation à l'Employé vue du Côté Employeur: Le Travail Domestique des Migrantes Ukrainiennes en Pologne*, 12 Cahiers de l'Urmis 1, 8–10 (2009). According to Kordasiewicz, this desire to act as if it is a peer interaction, not so much a subordinated one, can result in "friendly professionalism". In that case, the household members acknowledge their responsibilities towards the worker in terms of pay and other working conditions, but personally refuse to exert their prerogatives in an oppressive manner because they value the personal relationship. This does not pose a problem. What does form a problem, however, is that a similar mindset can strip the work relationship of its professional/occupational character if the regulatory authorities and society at large do not emphasise the responsibilities of households when they take recourse to domestic workers. Anna Kordasiewicz, *Role-Identity Dynamics in Care and Household Work: Strategies of Polish Workers in Naples, Italy*, 10 Qualitative Sociology Review 88, 98 n. 4 (2014).

live-in domestic worker, who lives on the employer's premises, has apparent issues relating to the work, but the worker and head of the household refuse to bring them up. Contrary to regular labour contexts, where "the rights and responsibilities of both the employer and the employee are often emphasized during times of trouble", it is apparently "difficult to speak about work-related aspects of the domestic labour relationship in some cases".[1346] In another survey, Moras similarly observed that many participants who rely on external domestic workers "felt awkward actually confronting workers when they were dissatisfied".[1347] Participants were tempted to terminate the working relationship instead of confronting the domestic worker with their dissatisfaction, or they preferred to leave notes and hints. This meant that, in addition to unclear instructions about what was expected, which is frustrating for the workers, household members did not effectively correct domestic workers either. They shied away from their role as the employer in terms of supervision too. Several employers experienced a desire to be out of the house while the cleaning took place, and for those who were home, "[t]hey reported feeling uncomfortable sitting and relaxing while someone else was working in their home".[1348] Other researchers have similarly observed that particularly women seem to feel uncomfortable even by simply being at home when someone else is being paid to clean.[1349] Some even feel "guilt", as if they are not doing their part.[1350]

These qualitative insights illustrate how household members might be eager to 407
consider themselves buyers of a domestic service instead of a domestic worker's employer.[1351] Moreover, the way household members provide instructions to domestic workers, supervise their work, and control or sanction their performance is very different from the practices of regular enterprises. Therefore, if the extent to which instructions are given, supervision is exercised, and disciplinary sanctions are taken, serves as the benchmark to determine the employment status of a domestic worker, as it does in a commercial employment context, then, many domestic workers might be left without protection under Convention No. 189. Households instruct their domestic workers to clean the house or tend to the garden, plain and simple. Rarely do they receive the detailed instructions of a factory worker. Households nevertheless expect the workers to do a fine job, while the household members are perhaps off to work, hence not providing direct supervision. At the end of the day, if the work is not

1346. Murray & Durrheim, *supra* n. 1278, at 2636.

1347. Amanda Moras, *The Private Home as a Public Workplace: Employing Paid Domestic Labor*, 13 Journal of Workplace Rights 377, 387 n. 4 (2008).

1348. *Ibid.*, 390.

1349. Esther de Ruijter & Tanja van der Lippe, *Getting Outside Help: How Trust Problems Explain Household Differences in Domestic Outsourcing in the Netherlands*, 30 Journal of Family Issues 3, 23 n. 1 (2009).

1350. Moras, *supra* n. 1343, at 54–55.

1351. Many factors come together. For example, Du Toit mentions how South African households turn towards the use of "housecleaning service firms" because "[t]he emotional labour, feelings of guilt and privilege, and the sense of responsibility is something that employers no longer want to carry". David Du Toit, *Cleaning up: A Sociological Investigation into the Use of Outsourced Housecleaning Services* 193 (Stellenbosch University 2020). *See also*, Ewa Palenga-Möllenbeck, *New Maids – New Butlers? Polish Domestic Workers in Germany and Commodification of Social Reproductive Work*, 32 Equality, Diversity and Inclusion: An International Journal 557, 557–574 n. 6 (2013).

performed satisfactorily, the household searches for another domestic worker to take over. Or, in the case of platforms, a negative evaluation is given, which impacts the workers' future employment opportunities, and the household is assisted in finding another self-employed domestic worker. The point, in other words, is that the nature of domestic "job work" not only makes it prone to commodification, it also makes it prone to bogus self-employment. There is a real need to take these workers' special characteristics into account for the determination of who is and is not a domestic worker entitled to labour protections.

408 **An occupational basis** – All of the above also explains Article 1(c)'s relevance for the overall scope of Convention No. 189.[1352] One ILO flagship report presents the Convention's definitions as: "domestic work is 'work performed in or for a household or households' on an occupational basis, and a domestic worker is thus 'any person engaged in domestic work within an employment relationship'".[1353] Although the Convention itself does not explicitly make the bridge between "domestic work on an occupational basis" and "domestic work within an employment relationship", both the working documents as well as the Committee of Experts' clarifications seem to point out that this connection should, indeed, be made.

409 To start with, the Office's Law and Practice Report mentions that "[t]he Office considers that the objectives of the new instrument(s) should be to: – ensure broad coverage to reach as many domestic workers as possible [...]".[1354] However, some ILO constituents stressed in response to the first questionnaire that the notion of domestic workers should not be too broad. It "should cover only work under a contract of employment, characterized by dependence, subordination or the receipt of a salary, and exclude self-employment".[1355] As a result, even before the first round of discussions at the Conference had even started, the Office proposed to define domestic work as "work performed within an employment relationship in or for a household or households".[1356] The reference to an "employment relationship" was thereby inserted, even though the Office discerned a "broad agreement among respondents that the proposed instrument(s) should have the widest possible coverage, the main reasoning for this being that the exclusion of domestic workers from many provisions of international labour standards is among the principal causes of their decent work deficits and vulnerability".[1357] Subsequently, during the Conference's discussions in 2010, the Government member of Japan asked whether the definitions would also cover domestic workers employed by third parties. The representative of the Secretary-General responded in the affirmative, explaining "that work performed within an employment relationship included both domestic workers directly recruited by the household and also domestic workers recruited by a third party to provide

1352. "(c) a person who performs domestic work only occasionally or sporadically and not on an occupational basis is not a domestic worker". Art. 1 Domestic Workers Convention, 2011 (No. 189).
1353. ILO, *supra* n. 1247, at 168.
1354. ILO, *supra* n. 946, at 95.
1355. ILO, *supra* n. 1313, at 385.
1356. *Ibid.*, 417.
1357. *Ibid.*, 387.

services to a household".[1358] After this clarification, the EU Member States advanced an amendment that required domestic work to be performed "on a regular basis" for the worker to be considered a domestic worker. This amendment "was intended to exclude persons who, for example, worked on an occasional basis as babysitters or au pairs, and who should not be considered professional domestic workers" and "was not intended to exclude workers who worked for various employers, or on a temporary or part-time basis, or those who had different working relationships with various employers; they were all considered to be domestic workers".[1359] Because the proposal elicited quite a bit of debate, the Employer Vice-Chairperson proposed setting up a working party. This tripartite working party drafted the definitions that would end up being adopted in 2011.

When the working party's agreement was presented to the Committee, the Workers' group "wanted to put on record a number of points". According to the Workers' group, the definition: 410

> "included as domestic workers all those who worked one hour per day or even a few hours per year, people with low skills, students who worked as domestic workers for a living, as well as people who worked in multiple households. The crucial term in the definition was 'occupational basis', which was meant to exclude from the scope of the Convention people doing domestic work for pocket money but not as an occupation. All workers who performed domestic work as a living were understood to be included".[1360]

Other constituents did not refute the description given by the Workers' group. The Government representative of the United States, who was also a member of the working party, explained that "domestic work should be defined as an occupation as opposed, for example, to occasional babysitting by the daughter of one's neighbour".[1361] The Government representative of Sweden, who represented the EU at the working party, confirmed this understanding. It was not the intention "to exclude day labourers, part-time workers or those who worked irregularly as described in previous statements, if those workers were performing domestic work as an occupation".[1362] In the run-up to 2011's Committee on Domestic Workers, a proposal was made by the Office to rephrase Article 1(c), as "a person who performs domestic work only occasionally or sporadically and not as a means of earning a living is not a domestic worker".[1363] The constituents, however, quickly returned to the working group's original text, replacing "as a means of earning a living" by "on an occupational

1358. Report of the Committee on Domestic Workers at the 99th Session of the International Labour, Geneva, ILO, 2010, 12/27. This was later confirmed by the Chairperson. Report of the Committee on Domestic Workers at the 99th Session of the International Labour Conference, Geneva, ILO, 2010, 12/31.
1359. *Ibid.*, 12/27-12/29.
1360. *Ibid.*, 12/31.
1361. *Ibid.*, 12/31.
1362. *Ibid.*, 12/32.
1363. ILO, *Report IV (2B) Decent work for Domestic Workers* 8 (ILO 2011).

basis".[1364] The constituents seem not to have clarified what is understood to constitute an occupational basis.

411 Overall, these working documents indicate that the three subclauses of Article 1 of Convention No. 189 present a cohesive definition for the "domestic worker", i.e. domestic work in an employment relationship. The "occupational basis" of domestic work is foundational to this employment relationship. As such, it is, in fact, helpful to present subclauses 1(a), 1(b) and 1(c) in an integrated manner. Along those lines, the term "domestic worker" means any person engaged in or for households within an employment relationship, which is expected to be the case, unless this person only occasionally or sporadically performs domestic work and does not perform it on an occupational basis. An *a contrario* interpretation of Article 1(c) would lead to the conclusion that Convention No. 189 covers both: (i) persons who only perform domestic work occasionally or sporadically but, nonetheless, on an occupational basis; and, (ii) persons who do not perform domestic work on an occupational basis but, nevertheless, perform it regularly or frequently. Regarding the latter category, one could also suspect that persons who perform domestic work regularly or frequently do so on an occupational basis (to make a living). This turns the occupational nature of domestic work into the real touchstone for applying Convention No. 189, which matches the working party's accounts.

412 **Committee of Experts** – The clarifications made by the Committee of Experts align with this hunch. First of all, the Committee finds it important for a ratifying Member State to explicitly define "domestic work(er)" under national law. As mentioned several times, for instance, to Germany and Guyana, "because of the specific characteristics of domestic work, specific attention should be given to a definition of domestic workers and domestic work in relevant national legal instruments".[1365] The Committee's remarks seem to imply that the Convention advances a specific, stand-alone description of domestic work(ers). The Committee gave particularly concrete instructions to Ireland. In addition to stressing the importance of concrete definitions under national law, the Committee:

> "further note[d] that the Government does not indicate whether a person who performs domestic work on an occupational basis, but does so only occasionally or sporadically is considered as a domestic worker. The Committee recalls that, regardless of the type of contract held by workers providing domestic services, the definition of domestic worker laid down in Article 1 of the Convention excludes only persons who perform domestic work occasionally or sporadically and not on an occupational basis".[1366]

1364. Report of the Committee on Domestic Workers at the 100th Session of the International Labour Conference, Geneva, ILO, 2011, 15/23.

1365. Direct Request (CEACR) – adopted 2016, published 106th ILC session (2017), Domestic Workers Convention, 2011 (No. 189) – Germany (Ratification: 2013); Direct Request (CEACR) – adopted 2020, published 109th ILC session (2021), Domestic Workers Convention, 2011 (No. 189) – Germany (Ratification: 2013). Similarly, Direct Request (CEACR) – adopted 2019, published 109th ILC session (2020), Domestic Workers Convention, 2011 (No. 189) – Guyana (Ratification: 2013).

1366. Direct Request (CEACR) – adopted 2017, published 107th ILC session (2018), Domestic Workers Convention, 2011 (No. 189) – Ireland (Ratification: 2014).

The Committee reiterated its request to Ireland in 2019.[1367] This request similarly contains two distinctive elements. The first one is the indication that Article 1 "excludes only persons who perform domestic work occasionally or sporadically and not on an occupational basis". The second remarkable element is that the Convention applies "regardless of the type of contract held by workers providing domestic services". The Committee has similarly pointed out to Ecuador that "irrespective of the type of contract held by workers providing domestic services, the definition of domestic worker laid down in Article 1 of the Convention only excludes persons who perform domestic work occasionally or sporadically and not on an occupational basis".[1368] It requested Ecuador a second and third time to ensure "that persons who perform domestic work occasionally or sporadically, but who do so on an occupational basis, are covered by the guarantees established in the Convention".[1369] It did the same for Paraguay.[1370] In addition to these regulatory conversations with Ecuador, Ireland and Paraguay, the Committee has, furthermore, clarified the importance of this "occupational basis" to many of the other ratifying Member States. It repeatedly points out that the instruments cover day labourers and other precarious workers. The Committee asked the ratifying Member States such as Chile, Costa Rica, Dominican Republic, Nicaragua and Panama to amend their existing laws to this end, sometimes in quite explicit terms.[1371]

All in all, the Committee's clarifications indicate the overwhelming importance attrib- **413**
uted to this occupational basis and the insignificance of the Convention's reference to an employment relationship in comparison. So far, its clarifications seem not to have been challenged, even though the regulatory conversations with the Member States do not show that the Committee's remarks have been implemented either.

1367. Direct Request (CEACR) - adopted 2019, published 109th ILC session (2020), Domestic Workers Convention, 2011 (No. 189) - Ireland (Ratification: 2014).
1368. Direct Request (CEACR) - adopted 2015, published 105th ILC session (2016), Domestic Workers Convention, 2011 (No. 189) - Ecuador (Ratification: 2013).
1369. Direct Request (CEACR) - adopted 2019, published 109th ILC session (2020), Domestic Workers Convention, 2011 (No. 189) - Ecuador (Ratification: 2013); Direct Request (CEACR) - adopted 2020, published 109th ILC session (2021), Domestic Workers Convention, 2011 (No. 189) - Ecuador (Ratification: 2013).
1370. "Consequently, the Committee requests the Government to adopt the necessary measures with a view to amending section 2 of Act No. 5407 so that domestic workers who do not work regularly, but for whom domestic work is an occupation, are expressly included in the definition of domestic work". Direct Request (CEACR) - adopted 2019, published 109th ILC session (2021), Domestic Workers Convention, 2011 (No. 189) - Paraguay (Ratification: 2013).
1371. Direct Request (CEACR) - adopted 2017, published 107th ILC session (2018), Domestic Workers Convention, 2011 (No. 189) - Costa Rica (Ratification: 2014); "Consequently, the Committee requests the Government to adopt the necessary measures to amend section 145 of the Labour Code so that domestic workers who perform domestic work occasionally or sporadically, but on an occupational basis, are explicitly included in the definition of domestic work". Direct Request (CEACR) - adopted 2017, published 107th ILC session (2018), Domestic Workers Convention, 2011 (No. 189) - Nicaragua (Ratification: 2013); Direct Request (CEACR) - adopted 2018, published 108th ILC session (2019), Domestic Workers Convention, 2011 (No. 189) - Chile (Ratification: 2015); Direct Request (CEACR) - adopted 2018, published 108th ILC session (2019), Domestic Workers Convention, 2011 (No. 189) - Dominican Republic (Ratification: 2015); Direct Request (CEACR) - adopted 2018, published 108th ILC session (2019), Domestic Workers Convention, 2011 (No. 189) - Panama (Ratification: 2015).

It remains to be seen whether the Committee's general survey for 2022 on decent work for care economy workers will examine the comments about Ecuador, Ireland and others in greater depth. If so, it might provoke a discussion at the Conference Committee on the Application of Standards. That would be helpful to obtain a more straightforward answer to the question: does the Committee of Experts believe that Convention No. 189 covers anyone performing domestic work on an occupational basis, even if that person is technically self-employed under domestic law?

3. Domestic Work on an Occupational Basis

414 **The meaning of this occupational basis** – Although both the working documents and the Committee of Experts attribute a lot of importance to domestic work's occupational basis, none of these sources contains any specifics about what this concept entails. The only indication is that, based on how Article 1(c) is drafted, it is not necessary to regularly or frequently perform domestic work in order for it to be considered occupational. Apart from this, there is very little to build on. Whereas the English text of the Convention speaks of domestic work being performed "on an occupational basis", the French text mentions that an exemption is possible if the worker "*effectue un travail domestique seulement de manière occasionnelle ou sporadique sans en faire sa profession*". "*Profession*" in French can be translated as a profession or occupation in English.[1372] When looking at the ordinary meaning of an occupation, the *Bouvier Law Dictionary* describes an occupation as "the engagement in a job or profession".[1373] *Ballentine's Law Dictionary* describes occupation as "[a] more or less continuous or habitual engagement in a certain line of employment or industrial or business activity".[1374] *Black's Law Dictionary* defines occupation as "[a]n activity or pursuit in which a person engages; esp., a person's usual or principal work or business".[1375] One might add to these descriptions that ILO constituents seem to have associated an occupational basis with a profession that serves to make a living, delineating it from activities that are not meant to make a living (*supra* no. 411).[1376] Hence, domestic work to earn "pocket money" is not covered by the instrument. At the same time, because the Convention seems to consider anything more than sporadically or occasionally performed domestic work as covered by its regulations, the threshold of being considered an occupational, domestic worker might be relatively low. This low threshold would seem justified, considering the tendency to demean domestic work's occupational character.

415 **Beware of historical antecedents** – When determining the meaning of domestic workers' occupational character, attention must be paid to households' and the public's tendency not to perceive domestic work as genuine work because it "replaces" the

1372. Profession in the *French–English Cambridge Dictionary*, https://dictionary.cambridge.org/dictionary/french-english/profession (accessed: 28 April 2021).
1373. *The Wolters Kluwer Bouvier Law Dictionary* Desk Edition (accessed on LexisNexis).
1374. *Ballentine's Law Dictionary*, 3rd edition, 2010 (accessed on LexisNexis).
1375. *Black's Law Dictionary*, 11th edition, 2019 (accessed on Westlaw).
1376. Similarly, in standard dictionaries, an occupation is "the activity by which one regularly makes a living". *Merriam-Webster Dictionary*, https://www.merriam-webster.com/thesaurus/occupation (accessed: 28 April 2021).

work people otherwise perform themselves.[1377] For instance, a survey from 2003 in India, Italy, Sweden and Thailand revealed that:

> "domestic work is conceived as being somehow different from other work, and this is particularly clear when we look at respondent views on the rights (or their lack) to which workers in private households are entitled: 48 per cent of survey respondents did not think that domestic workers were entitled to a contract with their employer; 70 per cent thought workers should not have the right to join a trade union; 52 per cent were opposed to a right to minimum wages, and 45 per cent felt that a right to fixed working hours did not apply. [...] More generally, employers felt that labour rights were not appropriate because [domestic] workers did not need protection from them as individual employers and because such rights were inapplicable or inappropriate in the particular context of the private household".[1378]

Qualitative interviews in the United States around 2007 similarly point out that employers fail "to see their homes as workplaces".[1379] Therefore, in light of these opinions, platform workers in a domestic work context may be particularly vulnerable to their activities not being perceived as a genuine occupation.[1380]

This could, in theory, be reinforced by platforms that, for the most part, base their work relationships on short-termism and worker fungibility.[1381] Even the workers themselves might contribute to this perception. Platform workers are seemingly ashamed of their line of work, or fear that admitting it will damage their reputation and future career prospects.[1382] They choose to construe the "core part" of their "occupational identity" based on the other forms of work they often combine with platform work.[1383] If this is the case for platform workers in general, the same might be true for domestic platform workers. For all these reasons, the occupational nature of domestic platform work might be at particular risk of being denied. 416

Most likely, the extent to which this occurs will depend on the approach platform operators take. On the one hand, one could fear the worst because researchers "point out that labor platforms are strategically redefining and reinforcing cultural categories used to think about work", and so platform operators could quite easily 417

1377. Jeffrey du Preez, Claire Beswick, Louise Whittaker & David Dickinson, *The Employment Relationship in the Domestic Workspace in South Africa: Beyond the Apartheid Legacy*, 36 Social Dynamics 395, 396–397 n. 2 (2010).

1378. Bridget Anderson & Julia O'Connell Davidson, *Is Trafficking in Human Beings Demand Driven? A Multi-Country Pilot Study* 33–34 (IOM 2003).

1379. Moras, *supra* n. 1347, at 395.

1380. Philippe Auvergnon, *Le Travail Domestique sur le Chemin du Travail Décent?* 279, 296 (José Luis Gil y Gil ed., *Migraciones Internacionales e Impacto de la Crisis Económica: Compromisos de la OIT*, Juruá Editora 2013).

1381. Flanagan, *supra* n. 639, at 72–73.

1382. Alexandrea J. Ravenelle, *Just a Gig? Sharing Economy Work and the Implications for Career Trajectory* 103, 103–122 (Deepa Das Acevedo ed., *Beyond the Algorithm: Qualitative Insights for Gig Work Regulation*, Cambridge, DUP 2020). For instance, when applying for a job, workers keep it a secret that they performed platform work. Kilhoffer et al., *supra* n. 33, at 78.

1383. Huws, Spencer, Coates & Holts, *supra* n. 619, at 18–19.

brand domestic platform work as a side-gig, additional income source etc.[1384] On the other hand, it has to be emphasised that some platform operators in domestic work have actually raised awareness among households that they have responsibilities.[1385] Consequently, it could go both ways; platforms could exploit users frowning upon domestic work, or they can remind them of their obligations.

418 In this respect, what is important is how Ticona and Mateescu observe that even when "carework platforms" take the second option, encouraging clients to work with particular employment contracts, they do not necessarily enforce the regulations governing such contracts. This might be because, for promotional purposes, domestic platform work is juxtaposed against informal domestic work. It is depicted as safer and worth the premium, enticing households to transition. However, at the same time, for instance, the higher price compared to informal domestic work is something clients try to evade.[1386] To that extent, by not actively enforcing minimum wages etc., the clients benefit from the platform's functionalities and a shroud of legality, even if it means "carework platforms are not as distanced from the largely unregulated, informal markets against which they have positioned themselves as innovative departures".[1387] Indeed, despite platforms' potential to formalise and professionalise domestic work, it remains to be seen to what extent platform operators will move beyond this midway position. Platforms make domestic work visible; make it, therefore, easier to regulate, but often neglect to ensure that regulation sticks.[1388] Platform operators could play a role in not just establishing loudly and clearly that domestic work is genuine work but ensuring that public regulations cover it. Yet, in reality, because their user base has little interest in abiding by such laws, platforms might take a more ambiguous position.

419 **Does "formal outsourcing" indicate an occupational basis?** – The previous paragraphs described reasons why the occupational character of domestic platform work might end up being questioned. It pointed to the role of platforms in sustaining or countering that tendency. In this regard, the following paragraphs will argue that there are implicit reasons to expect some forms of domestic platform work to, in principle, be performed as an occupation in the sense of Convention No. 189. The argument derives from the particular trust problems that characterise domestic work,[1389] compared to other services.

420 When hiring someone to care, cook or clean, this person is invited onto private property – sometimes without the household members present – which requires trust. This trust is likewise needed from the perspective of the domestic worker. The workers enter the private space of another, opening themselves up to abuse.[1390] A

1384. Ticona & Mateescu, *supra* n. 259, at 4387.

1385. *Ibid.*, 4391.

1386. Weber, Okraku, Mair & Maurer, *supra* n. 1272, at 13–14.

1387. Ticona & Mateescu, *supra* n. 259, at 4394.

1388. "In our interviews, we found that careworkers were strongly aware of platforms' low liability to enforce fair employment relationships". *Ibid.*, 4392. *See also*, Hunt & Machingura, *supra* n. 258, at 22.

1389. De Ruijter & van der Lippe, *supra* n. 1349.

1390. Public Rights Project, *Re: Sexual Harassment of Handy Home Service Workers*, Medium (10 September 2020), https://publicrightsproject.medium.com/re-sexual-harassment-of-handy-

platform's success, inside and outside of domestic work, partially depends on the amount of trust it can generate between platform participants.[1391] However, the need to do so is arguably even more pronounced in the case of domestic work.[1392] De Ruijter, van der Lippe and Raub argue that, amongst others, due to trust issues, two kinds of suppliers provide household services. Either formal outsourcing unfolds, which means that an economic exchange takes place between the worker and household, or informal outsourcing occurs, in which case it is more of a social exchange.[1393] For the former, the worker and household do not have a pre-existing social relationship but perform the service in return for payment, whereas for the latter, primarily social obligations are created, e.g. "I take care of your children when you are on holiday, and you take care of mine when we are on holiday".

Workers who perform domestic work on a platform are, undoubtedly, part of formal outsourcing. This logically entails that households demand the platform to establish safeguards, such as insurance against theft.[1394] Outside of the platform economy, for example, referrals are essential for domestic workers to get a job because these referrals generate trust among the parties.[1395] Hondagneu-Sotelo similarly mentions that "employer networks" are the primary job finding technique for domestic workers because referrals convince households that workers are trustworthy.[1396] This is what the platform economy has partially institutionalised. Job referrals are replaced by the platform's monitoring systems, asking households to rate workers. These ratings provide prospective employers with an idea of the worker's trustworthiness. 421

Now, when the ILO constituents agreed for babysitters, who mind children in exchange for pocket money, to not be covered by Convention No. 189, they, arguably, set out to exclude "informal household outsourcing" (see, *supra* no. 411). In such cases, trust is not generated based on referrals or employer networks, which can come in the form of a labour platform, but has to do with the parties' embeddedness in social relationships.[1397] The babysitter has family ties, lives in the same neighbourhood, goes to the same sports club as the parents, and so forth. Households will typically not use a platform to reach out to their niece to babysit for pocket money. To this extent, one could wonder whether whenever a household reverts to a platform to leverage its network capacities, does this formal form of outsourcing automatically imply an occupational basis in the sense of Convention No. 189? 422

When thinking about students cycling for food-delivery platforms, one might be inclined to say no. However, the same might not be accurate for all platforms 423

home-service-workers-fec828d05fa7.

1391. Möhlmann & Geissinger, *supra* n. 233, at 27–37.
1392. Ticona & Mateescu, *supra* n. 259, at 4388.
1393. Esther de Ruijter, Tanja van der Lippe & Werner Raub, *Trust Problems in Household Outsourcing*, 15 Rationality and Society 473, 496 n. 4 (2003).
1394. *Ibid.*, 500–501. Platforms have been reported to apply a rigorous on-boarding procedure with the need to provide for psychometric or cleaning tests, letters of recommendation, reports from the local police station and so forth. Some platforms also allow the household and worker to meet first, before confirming the transaction. Hunt & Machingura, *supra* n. 258, at 27.
1395. Moras, *supra* n. 1347, at 393.
1396. Hondagneu-Sotelo, *supra* n. 1251, at 55 and 61.
1397. De Ruijter, van der Lippe & Raub, *supra* n. 1393, at 499–500.

involved in domestic work. Delivering food is a relatively straightforward activity that students feel drawn to, for instance, because it provides the opportunity to exercise. Working on a platform where a household evaluates the performance of a tutor is a very different thing.[1398] To the extent that the "gig-narrative" of persons jumping into their car to earn some pocket money is realistic for transportation platforms,[1399] the same is not true for domestic platform work. Hunt et al. mention that good ratings, tenure on the platform, and being relatively more available are the three key features to success.[1400] Eurofound, in turn, labels many domestic work platforms as on-location "worker-initiated" platform work, which is contrasted with on-location "platform-determined" work, such as food-delivery. In worker-initiated platform work, the worker and client choose one another; it is not so much the platform that dispatches a worker, as might be the case in transport and food-delivery. The first form of platform work "is highly influenced by the subjective ratings of individual clients; these affect workers' access to future tasks, as they are fully visible to potential clients".[1401] Eurofound, therefore, even recommends that users on domestic work platforms be made aware of the potential consequences of their ratings for workers' future job prospects.[1402]

424 Contrary to platform-determined platform work, in which ratings need to stay high enough to evade sanctions, workers' ratings in worker-initiated platform work need to stay high simply because those are the service providers clients choose. Research has found how "[p]rofiles with good ratings tend to be disproportionately awarded more jobs. A 'Matthew effect', in which the 'rich become richer', might be produced in the digital labour market".[1403] Others concur to the extent that "a comparatively small subgroup of workers collects almost all the rewards, leaving only leftovers to the majority of their less successful peers. Such extreme distributional inequality appears to be common on labour platforms".[1404] These dynamics arguably tilt these domestic work activities, such as cleaning, teaching and caring, in which ratings are decisive, towards the occupational end of the spectrum.

425 Based on these factors, it could be argued that most workers on domestic work platforms perform their services on an occupational basis. Jumping in a personal car or on a personal bike, after which the platform hands transport requests to the worker, is very different from maintaining an attractive profile so that clients provide access to their home to clean or take care of their children and pets. Also, although it would be helpful for surveys to focus more on this, there are some indications that many of these platform workers seem to genuinely (have) perform(ed) domestic

1398. Flanagan, *supra* n. 639, at 71.
1399. On this, *see* Rosenblat, *supra* n. 76, at 49–72.
1400. Abigail Hunt et al., *Women in the Gig Economy: Paid Work, Care and Flexibility in Kenya and South Africa* 34–35 (ODI 2019).
1401. Eurofound, *supra* n. 4, at 23.
1402. Eurofound, *supra* n. 303, at 19.
1403. De Groen, Maselli & Fabo, *supra* n. 1290, at 14.
1404. Brian Fabo, Jovana Karanovic & Katerina Dukova, *In Search of an Adequate European Policy Response to the Platform Economy*, 23 Transfer 163, 168 n. 2 (2017).

work on an occupational basis.[1405] Consequently, if some of these forms of domestic platform work are likely performed on an occupational basis, the Member States might have to take the necessary measures to ensure that when this is the case, it is performed under an employment relationship.

4. Labour Market Intermediation in Domestic Work

Households or platforms as employers – The previous Section argued that there are reasons to expect certain domestic platform workers to perform the work on an occupational basis. By extension, these platform workers may be covered by Convention No. 189. This observation would turn Convention No. 189 into an aspirational standard in the sense that once the Member State ratifies the Convention, the ratifying State intends for the employment status of all workers who perform domestic work on an occupational basis to be acknowledged. To this end, it remains an open question as to how to achieve this; between which parties in the triangular platform arrangement should the employment relationship be established? By and large, two main possibilities seem to exist. 426

Either the platform operator's terms and conditions fix – or merely allow for – a (special) employment relationship between the households and workers. This is, for instance, the case with Helpling in the Netherlands.[1406] Another possibility is for platforms to take on the role of the legal employer, which can happen in various ways. For example, in the context of home care agencies, "[o]ften it is quite important to agency clients that aides are agency employees and they, the clients, have no legal employer responsibilities: in their marketing, many agencies stress that they are the aides' employer".[1407] In a similar vein, Doty has observed how three American platforms, Hometeam, Honor and Home Hero, similarly decided to take on the role of a legal employer. The author predicted that this could occur more broadly because it is "good business" for platform operators to employ workers that deliver care (also 427

1405. Among domestic platform workers in South Africa, "73 per cent identified the platform as the main source of their earnings in the previous month. Participants in face-to-face interviews mentioned having recently undertaken other types of casual or informal work, [...]. However, paid domestic work was the most frequently cited work engaged in before joining the platform, whether live-in or day labour within private homes, sometimes obtained via an agency, and many continued to provide domestic labour through traditional means alongside gig work". Abigail Hunt & Emma Samman, *Domestic Work and the Gig Economy in South Africa: Old Wine in New Bottles?*, 15 Anti-Trafficking Review 102, 111–112 (2020). In Japan, regarding a babysitter platform, "[a]n analysis of the sitters' profiles shows that most are qualified nursery teachers and homemakers with children who have some experience in care work". Kazuki Abiru, *Status of the Gig Economy in Japan Considered from a Survey of C-to-C Babysitter Services*, 15 E-journal GEO 267, 267 n. 2 (2020).

1406. In this case, the platform may or may not be considered an employment mediator, depending on national law. Rechtbank Amsterdam: Case 7299840 CV EXPL 18-23708, *Federatie Nederlandse Vakbeweging v. Helpling Netherlands B.V.*, 1 July 2019, ECLI:NL:RBAMS:2019:4546. This makes their operations very similar to pre-digital registries. Pamela Doty, *Private Pay Home Care: New Models of Access and Service Delivery*, 27 Public Policy & Aging Report 111, 117–118 n. 3 (2017); Flanagan, *supra* n. 639, at 61–62.

1407. Doty, *supra* n. 1406, at 113.

see, *supra* nos. 261–262).[1408] Until now, it remains unverified whether this reasoning also applies for platforms that intermediate household services other than caring, such as cleaning, home maintenance and gardening.[1409] Furthermore, it is not clear if this tendency exists in every country or depends on contextual factors.[1410] Perhaps, as Hunt and Samman observe, it is true that clients search for ways to get rid of their duties as a legal employer; however, as seen in South Africa, platforms can stimulate this development without necessarily taking up the role of legal employer.[1411]

428 In any case, from the point of view of Convention No. 189, if wanted, platform operators engaged in domestic work can legally employ the workers instead of having the household conclude a (special) employment contract. This seems possible along two lines. The platform operator can regularly employ the platform worker as if the platform operator is a cleaning or gardening business with flexible work arrangements. Alternatively, the platform operator decides to employ the worker in a setup that shares employers' responsibilities and control with the household. In the latter case, it adopts a model akin to an agency under Article 1(1)(b) of Convention No. 181.

429 **Convention No. 181 and Recommendation No. 198** – Regarding the question of which entity bears the employer's responsibilities, neither the Private Employment Agencies Convention, 1997 (No. 181), nor the Employment Relationship Recommendation, 2006 (No. 198), provide any clear guidelines. Despite the Worker Vice-Chairperson's claim that Recommendation No. 198 deals with triangular employment and identifies the "real" employer (*supra* no. 398),[1412] it only contains vague instructions. Paragraph 4 mentions that national policy should at least "ensure standards applicable to all forms of contractual arrangements, including those involving multiple parties, so that employed workers have the protection they are due", and that these standards should "establish who is responsible for the protection contained therein". The instruments that most directly tackle triangular employment – Convention No. 181 and Recommendation No. 188 – similarly lack a concrete mechanism to attribute responsibilities to one party or the other.[1413]

430 **The instruments on domestic workers** – On the same track, ILO constituents have ensured that Convention No. 189 and Recommendation No. 201 on domestic workers are about as concrete as Convention No. 181 and Recommendation No. 198, which is to say not concrete at all. Article 15 of Convention No. 189 obliges the ratifying Member States to determine the conditions to operate a private employment agency

1408. *Ibid.*, 118–119. Similarly, van Doorn, *supra* n. 620, at 904; Ticona & Mateescu, *supra* n. 259, at 4392–4394.
1409. For instance, Book A Tiger in Germany, Batmaid in Luxembourg/Switzerland and Helpling in Switzerland work(ed) with cleaners that were legally employed by the platform operator.
1410. E.g. SweepSouth and Domestly in South Africa, which are described as "the 'Uber of housecleaning services'", rely on independent contractors. This leads Du Toit to remark that "[c]lients who prefer a more controlled employment relationship can opt for established housecleaning services where a tripartite employment relationship exist [sic] between clients, domestic employees and the management". Du Toit, *supra* n. 1351, at 108.
1411. Hunt & Samman, *supra* n. 1405, at 120.
1412. Report of the Committee on Domestic Workers at the 100th Session of the International Labour Conference, Geneva, ILO, 2011, 15/18.
1413. Art. 12 Private Employment Agencies Convention, 1997 (No. 181).

that recruits or places domestic workers, meaning both job-matching agencies and agencies that employ the worker.[1414] This duty calls for "laws or regulations that specify the respective obligations of the private employment agency and the household towards the domestic worker and provide for penalties, including prohibition of those private employment agencies that engage in fraudulent practices and abuses".[1415] In other words, the respective obligations need to be distributed between the agency or platform operator and household; however, how to do so is up to the Member States to decide. The working documents illustrate how ILO constituents refused to give more concrete instructions.

According to the Office, the answers to the first questionnaire pointed out that "[f]or **431** half the governments, the majority of employers' organizations and a few workers' organizations, only brokering agencies [i.e. employment mediators of type 1(1)(a)] qualify as intermediaries and, as such, have no employers' responsibilities".[1416] The Government member of Namibia, supported by the Government member of South Africa, made an interesting observation at the Conference on this very issue. The participant pointed out to the Workers' group that the Private Employment Agencies Convention, 1997 (No. 181), "appeared to set aside the obligations of the householder (as opposed to the employment agency) that might arise from a new Convention on domestic workers".[1417] These observations hint at a tension at the core of the interaction between Convention No. 181 and Convention No. 189. Convention No. 181 predominantly deals with agencies' obligations, whereas, in principle, Convention No. 189 mainly deals with the responsibilities of the "householder" in relation to the domestic worker.

Therefore, a considerable debate ensued at the Conference on the extent to which **432** it is appropriate to relieve household members of their responsibilities when a third party assumes those responsibilities. At 2010's Committee discussions, the Workers' group proposed to make agencies and households jointly and severally liable, because "[i]n triangular employment relationships where the domestic worker had been recruited or placed by an employment agency, it was not clear who the employer was, who had the obligations towards the domestic worker or which regulations would apply".[1418] The Africa Group and the Philippines were in favour. The Employers' group moved against "[i]mposing collective legal liability", mentioning that it would render the instrument "unacceptable".[1419] The Government member of Canada concurred. Canada stressed that this went much further than Convention No. 181 and Recommendation No. 198.[1420] The Government member of the United States, subsequently, proposed a "constructive" subamendment, but one that would dilute

1414. *See*, ILO, *Report IV(2A) Decent Work for Domestic Workers* 53 (ILO 2011).
1415. Art. 15 Domestic Workers Convention, 2011 (No. 189).
1416. ILO, *supra* n. 1313, at 386.
1417. Report of the Committee on Domestic Workers at the 99th Session of the International Labour Conference, Geneva, ILO, 2010, 12/39.
1418. *Ibid.*, 12/92.
1419. *Ibid.*, 12/93.
1420. The country representative did conveniently forget that, for example, the Home Work Recommendation does call for such joint and several liabilities between the employer and intermediary in respect of remuneration Para. 18 Home Work Recommendation, 1996 (No. 184).

the initial Workers' proposal. It demanded that the ratifying Member State attribute legal liability to the agency, household, or both. During the Committee discussions the following year, the ILO constituents started to work on an amendment proposed by the Employers' group, which completely revised the draft article in question. It did not refer to any form of liability or obligation.[1421] The Africa Group, therefore, proposed a subamendment to stress the need for Member States to specify the obligations of the agency and households, which the EU Member States and Canada initially opposed. The Africa Group's subamendment nevertheless passed, amongst others, because it was consistent with Convention No. 181.[1422]

433 As a result, despite some meaningful discussions during the Committee proceedings, in the end, the instruments on domestic workers do not take a position in terms of whether the householder or agency should be considered responsible. Article 15(1)(a) of the Domestic Workers Convention, 2011 (No. 189), merely stipulates that Members shall determine the conditions governing the operation of private employment agencies in order "[t]o effectively protect domestic workers, including migrant domestic workers, recruited or placed by private employment agencies, against abusive practices". Article 15 becomes interesting in light of our prior interpretation of Convention No. 181. Chapter 2 found that the instruments on private employment agencies also apply when self-employed workers receive job-matching services (*supra* no. 290). As a consequence, when reading Convention No. 181 and No. 189 together, if neither the user of the platform nor the platform operator accepts the status as the domestic worker's legal employer, the Member State might, nevertheless, have to effectively protect the occupationally involved domestic worker against the agencies' or platforms' abusive practices.

434 **Rogue platforms** – In this regard, assuming the Member State issues an appropriate and enforceable legal framework governing job-matching services for all domestic workers, the workers most at risk of suffering from abusive practices are probably the ones engaged on "rogue" platforms. The term rogue platform refers to platforms that do not submit their practices to the supervision of the authorities competent to monitor this legal framework. In the case of such a rogue platform, which does not comply with the rules on labour brokerage, it might be wise to fall back on Convention No. 189's default option. The platform users – household members – are, then, held accountable for their reliance on domestic workers. This default option is not far-fetched. For example, according to the information obtained by the Committee of Experts, under Argentinian law, "should an unauthorized situation arise in practice which is comparable to the operation of a private employment agency, the employment relationship shall be considered to be concluded with whomever the work is provided to, and the contracting third party [which resembles an agency] shall be jointly responsible with the direct employer [i.e. the household] for the obligations arising from the employment relationship".[1423]

1421. Report of the Committee on Domestic Workers at the 100th Session of the International Labour Conference, Geneva, ILO, 2011, 15/70.

1422. *Ibid.*, 15/72.

1423. Direct Request (CEACR) – adopted 2019, published 109th ILC session (2020), Domestic Workers Convention, 2011 (No. 189) – Argentina (Ratification: 2014).

Along these lines, one could stipulate that as long as the platform is not monitored appropriately, which can be indicated, for instance, through a certification scheme, the law expects the household to bear all responsibilities, e.g. for work accidents and expenses, potentially with joint liability. Such a default position creates clarity for everyone. Moreover, it might put a brake on the growth of rogue agencies and platforms because it disincentivises clients from using them. Suppose the domestic work platform is certified or accredited; in that instance, the platform operator can, then, take on the role of a domestic worker's legal employer. As shown before, there are reasons to expect that platform operators will, indeed, propose households to pass on the role as the legal employer (e.g. Doty's "good for business"-argument). Households like to transpose employer responsibilities to agencies. Moreover, because the platform or agency is already supervised, it will probably take those responsibilities as a legal employer seriously. With a lack of adequate supervision, a platform operator should arguably not be allowed to replace the householder as the domestic worker's legal employer.[1424] 435

5. Some Concrete Examples: TaskRabbit and Care.com

TaskRabbit – TaskRabbit intermediates short-term services between, on the one hand, households and businesses and, on the other, so-called "Taskers". Popular categories of services are handyman, cleaning, delivery, moving, furniture assembly and personal assistant. The platform's terms and conditions present these Taskers as independent business owners. TaskRabbit, moreover, makes clients and Taskers acknowledge that the platform does not supervise, scope, direct, control or monitor a Tasker's work. The platform operator's terms and conditions deny any responsibility or liability for the work performed. The platform essentially claims to be a job-matching platform. Users agree that using the services of TaskRabbit will generate a "Service Agreement" between the client and the tasker. Its terms and conditions for the United States note that "the formation of a Service Agreement will not, under any circumstances, create an employment or other service relationship between TaskRabbit and the Tasker, nor will it create an employment relationship between the Client and the Tasker".[1425] The same is true for Germany.[1426] 436

The question now becomes, what to make of all of this from the perspective of Convention No. 189? Consider the real-life example of a freelance writer who performs work on TaskRabbit in New York. On a regular month, she assembles IKEA 437

1424. "It is particularly problematic to leave it up to the parties to determine, through their contractual arrangements, how the relationship is characterized, or to give incentives to employers to reconfigure the relationship as an agency-worker rather than direct employment relationship. The South African experience shows that agencies can be fraudulent or precarious, with the result that even if the client pays the wages, the agency may not pass them on to the worker. For domestic workers, it is particularly important that the end-user is bound by the obligations in the Convention, regardless of whether the latter is strictly the domestic worker's legal employer". Fredman, *supra* n. 1301, at 410.

1425. TaskRabbit Global Terms of Service (Last updated: December 18, 2019), https://www.taskrabbit.com/terms (accessed: 13 August 2020).

1426. TaskRabbit Globale Allgemeine Geschäftsbedingungen (Last updated: October 2019), https://www.taskrabbit.de/geschaeftsbedingungen (accessed: 27 March 2021).

dressers, waits in line to occupy a table at a fancy restaurant for someone else, packs up someone's sweaters to move these to another house, and presses "cold-press organic juice" for someone once a week. The last gig takes about three hours every week. There is little doubt that most of these activities constitute work for another person's household in the sense of Convention No. 189. Furthermore, even a person who stands in line to guarantee a place at the restaurant for someone else is basically an on-demand servant. However, without a direct link with the home of the household members, it is unclear whether this specific gig classifies as "work in or for a household or households" under Convention No. 189 (*supra* nos. 392–394). Nevertheless, regardless of this one task, since all the other services were rendered within a timespan of one month, there is no denying that these activities are no longer "sporadic" from the point of view of Convention No. 189. Moreover, these jobs were performed "to supplement" a "freelance writing income, which was almost zero at the time", and the severance money from a previous job.[1427] Due to the repeated reliance on TaskRabbit to supplement other sources of income, the work likely qualifies as performed on an occupational basis. It serves to make a living and can hardly be described as informal "pocket money". The fact that the person in question does not consider these jobs a part of her occupational identity – an identity construed around freelance writing – does not matter. The fact that TaskRabbit calls its workers "Taskers" and promises commodified help when you need it at your fingertips, likewise, does not alter the occupational nature of this work. Ultimately, the platform operator stimulates formal forms of household outsourcing, *inter alia*, by conducting background checks, providing users with an overview of reviews, and taking care of the payment system.[1428] By excluding this kind of situation from the scope of Convention No. 189, one would essentially perpetuate what the Convention tries to address. In this regard, Convention No. 189 presents us with two options. Either the legalistic approach is taken, which means that in this particular instance, with a lack of established "employment relationship" between this Tasker and the individual households/platform (e.g. "service agreements"), the Convention does not apply. Alternatively, the aspirational approach is taken, which entails that the reference to the employment relationship in Convention No. 189 does not preclude this kind of situation from being covered if this Tasker conducts the work on an occupational basis.

438 **An aspirational approach** – The aspirational approach builds on the idea that the ILO constituents must have known that this Convention was not just meant to ameliorate the working conditions of domestic workers, who at a domestic level were already covered by an employment relationship. To raise the bar, the Convention needed to establish that domestic work should be governed by law, instead of non-State social norms, and revert the systematic exclusion of domestic workers from labour law and social protection (*supra* nos. 379–383). For instance, Article 3 of Convention No. 189 stipulates that "[e]ach Member shall take measures to ensure the effective promotion and protection of the human rights of all domestic workers, as set out in this

1427. Susie Armitage, *My TaskRabbit Gig in a Stranger's Fancy Kitchen*, CURBED (21 November 2019), https://archive.curbed.com/2019/11/21/20963418/taskrabbit-task-nyc-story.

1428. *See*, in particular, the "TaskRabbit Happiness Pledge", https://www.taskrabbit.com/pledge (accessed: 28 April 2021).

Convention". This article is hard to reconcile with the legalistic view that the instrument is only concerned with workers already in an employment relationship. These are not the domestic workers in dire need of human rights protection. Furthermore, the working documents seem to, indeed, indicate that ILO constituents wanted to push the boundaries. Some of the remarks indicate that the working group had agreed for the work's occupational basis to be considered the determinative factor for coverage (*supra* no. 411); such precise instructions are relevant for interpretative purposes, as indicated in the Subchapter on treaty interpretation (*supra* no. 238). Likewise, the Committee of Experts supports the view that the work's occupational nature is the core determinant for coverage under the Convention. From this perspective, the reference to the "employment relationship" in Article 1 of Convention No. 189 might significantly reflect the ILO constituents' view that domestic work is "work like any other", hence, in principle, performed under an employment relationship. This makes the Convention aspirational because it would aim to extend the employment relationship's scope at the country level to all persons who perform domestic work on a more than occasional/sporadic basis or perform it on an occupational basis. If this aspirational approach were to be adopted, the Convention on decent work for domestic workers would probably cover this Tasker's on-demand household services, meaning a country that has ratified the Convention, such as Germany, should find a way to ensure TaskRabbit operates using employment relationships.

Care.com – Whether the legalistic or aspirational approach carries the day matters. **439**
Care.com provides another excellent example. Sometimes described as the "Amazon.com for caregivers", the enterprise allows jobseekers to find work related to childcare, household help, pet care, tutoring, senior care, and special needs care.[1429] The terms and conditions that apply to the United Kingdom describe how "[e]ach Care Seeker is also responsible for complying with all applicable employment, anti-discrimination and other laws in connection with any relationship they establish with a Carer. Among other things, Care Seekers must verify that the Carer they select is legally entitled to live and work in the UK , and perform any other verification or other checks for the position they are hiring, such as identity, qualification, background and reference checks".[1430] When clicking on the Safety Guide for Carers, Care.com mentions that "[s]omeone hiring a nanny, housekeeper or anyone else who works in their home is typically considered their employer when the employee is not self-employed". The platform's website provides a hyperlink to a government website.[1431] Beyond the UK, the idea seems to be the same in other countries. "Care seekers" have to figure out the correct legal arrangement for their activities. For instance, the website for France mentions that whether it is for a nanny, housekeeper or other service, workers will be hired by an individual employer.[1432] The same advice is given concerning Belgium,

1429. Ticona, Mateescu & Rosenblat, *supra* n. 88, at 16.
1430. Terms of Use (Last Updated: March 6, 2019), https://www.care.com/en-gb/terms-of-use (accessed: 13 August 2020).
1431. "Safety Centre", https://www.care.com/en-gb/safety-centre (accessed: 13 August 2020); "Employing Someone to Work in your Home", https://www.gov.uk/au-pairs-employment-law (accessed: 13 August 2020).
1432. "Guides de Sécurité Pour les Intervenants", https://www.care.com/fr-fr/guides-de-securite-pour-les-intervenants (accessed: 13 August 2020).

in which case a link is provided to the government website on *"les contrats de travail domestique"*.[1433] This government website, however, immediately points out that workers who do not carry out work that is related to the physical household, e.g. cleaning, but perform "mainly intellectual work (nurse, housekeeper, etc.)" cannot conclude employment contracts for domestic work under Belgian law.[1434] This distinction is the result of the Belgian definition for domestic work-related employment contracts, which is very old-fashioned and narrow, and, according to which domestic workers must "perform mainly manual domestic work in connection with the household of the employer or his family".[1435] Therefore, most of the activities on Care.com are simply not eligible to be performed under a Belgian employment contract for domestic work. Care.com's legal advice is, in other words, not just confusing; it is flawed. Its tutors, nurses and even gardeners should, in theory, be provided with a regular employment contract,[1436] the kind used by enterprises. The chances of this happening seem rather slim.

440 When looking at this situation from an aspirational perspective, as a ratifying Member State, Belgium would do well to amend the legal framework governing these contracts for domestic work. The country should, arguably, move away from its archaic view on domestic work, in which full-time domestic workers provide manual labour (also see *supra* no. 391), by introducing a more inclusive statute.[1437] A domestic legal framework that aligns with Convention No. 189 should cover all dimensions of domestic work, including emotional and intellectual labour, if it has a real connection to the household's home. When looking at it from a legalistic perspective, however, no amendments to Belgian law seem needed. Care.com enables "domestic work", but Care.com's workers are not "domestic workers" under the Convention unless, at the domestic level, their domestic work evidently occurs "within an employment relationship". As a result, the Convention might not apply to Care.com's workforce because it seems unlikely for these carers in Belgium to conclude a regular employment contract with the household. Furthermore, Belgium would not be required to make any changes under Convention No. 189 because as long as these carers are "self-employed", the Convention does not apply to Care.com's workforce; hence, the country is not in violation.

441 **Avoid an inoperative Convention?** – By taking the legalistic approach to Article 1 of the Convention, the Convention might essentially become mostly inoperative as far as the platform economy is concerned. The platform operator's terms and conditions would point out that the worker is an independent contractor without any claims in

1433. *Ibid.*

1434. "Contrat de Travail Domestique", https://emploi.belgique.be/fr/themes/contrats-de-travail/contrats-de-travail-particuliers/contrat-de-travail-domestique?id=41959 (accessed: 13 August 2020); Inge Verdonck, *Hulp in het Huishouden: De Regeling voor Dienstboden en Ander Huispersoneel Onder de Loep Genomen*, 10 Sociale Wegwijzer 13, 13 n. 10 (2014).

1435. Section 5 Loi du 3 juillet 1978 relative aux contrats de travail / Wet van 3 juli 1978 betreffende de arbeidsovereenkomsten.

1436. Franky Blomme, *Huispersoneel: Van Dienstboden en Nannies tot Privéverpleegkundigen en (Ortho)(ped)agogische Begeleiders*, Oriëntatie 1, 9 n. 3 (2017).

1437. Stan Bruurs, *Het Welzijn van Dienstboden en Huispersoneel: Thuis op de Werkvloer*, Arbeidsrecht Journaal (2021).

relation to the platform or household, e.g. TaskRabbit, or emphasise that the platform user needs to comply with all applicable rules and regulations without enforcing any of it, e.g. Care.com (also see *supra* no. 419). This is a sobering observation considering how, in the long run, platforms may play a significant role, for instance, in long-term home care.[1438] In order to preserve the *effet utile* of Convention No. 189 (also see *supra* no. 212),[1439] meaning "that the drafters of a treaty have adopted a norm in order to be applied and, thus, the judge has to choose, among different possibilities, that interpretation which is most likely to guarantee the effectiveness of the treaty",[1440] it would seem advisable to take an aspirational approach. In such a case, the ratifying Member States, such as Belgium and Germany, would be asked to search for solutions to cover self-employed individuals on TaskRabbit and Care. com, who carry out domestic work on an occupational basis.

1438. Alisa Trojansky, *Towards the "Uber-isation" of Care? Platform Work in the Sector of Long-term Home Care and its Implications for Workers' Rights* (European Economic and Social Committee 2020).

1439. "[T]he principle of effectiveness is in reality no more than a particular application of the object and purpose test and the good faith rule and, therefore, an integral part of the general rule of interpretation laid down in Art 31". Oliver Dörr, *Article 31: General Rule of Interpretation* 521, 540 (Oliver Dörr & Kirsten Schmalenbach eds., *Vienna Convention on the Law of Treaties. A Commentary*, Springer 2012). *See also*, Gardiner, *supra* n. 694, at 480–481.

1440. Daniel Rietiker, *The Principle of "Effectiveness" in Recent Jurisprudence of the European Court of Human Rights: Its Different Dimensions and Its Consistency with Public International Law – No Need for the Concept of Treaty Sui Generis*, 79 Nordic Journal of International Law 245, 256 n. 2 (2010).

Chapter 5. Interim Conclusion: The International Labour Code Covers Platform Work

The International Labour Code – As shown, in addition to international labour standards that apply to all workers, including all platform workers (*supra* nos. 179–180), the International Labour Code also contains instruments that apply to more specific categories of workers and forms of platform work. Concerning the Private Employment Agencies Convention, 1997 (No. 181), Home Work Convention, 1996 (No. 177), and Domestic Workers Convention, 2011 (No. 189), the actual topic for debate is not whether they are relevant, but to which specific platform workers they ought to apply. 442

Private employment services – Convention No. 181 and Recommendation No. 188 tend to be interpreted narrowly. It is commonly assumed that these instruments only regulate jobseekers on the look out for an employment contract. However, this is an unfortunate assumption. These instruments regulate "labour market services" and protect jobseekers looking for "employment" through an agency or platform. There are no clear indications why this would not cover freelancers looking for job opportunities. On the contrary, these instruments' purpose and context seem to favour a broad scope of application. Moreover, if Convention No. 181 indeed covers the intermediation of contracts for personal services, what would the implication be? The instruments on private employment agencies pretty much aim to: (i) prevent agencies/platforms from abusing jobseekers and users; (ii) ensure that these services are accessible to all and not just the ones willing and able to pay fees; and, (iii) guarantee that PrEAs do not impede the proper functioning of the labour market. The prescriptions in these instruments are, arguably, desirable in the area of platform work. 443

Home work – Convention No. 177 and Recommendation No. 184 might similarly offer a helpful tool to govern home-based crowdwork more specifically. These instruments' overall aim is to regulate employers that issue home work in pursuance of their business activities. As such, the instruments undeniably target forms of crowdwork in which enterprises rely on home-based workers to run their business, 444 for example, by having them train artificial intelligence.[1441] Whether the instruments' scope of application, in fact, manages to capture these forms of crowdwork is another matter. If the instruments on home work are left unchanged, reflection is needed about what it means for a home-based crowdworker to be economically independent and autonomous. The goal should be to smartly differentiate between, on the one hand, home-based workers who use crowdwork platforms but are autonomous and economically independent and, on the other, people who are called on remotely by enterprises without running their own home-based business. It remains to be seen whether the conclusions of a potential Meeting of Experts in 2022 will pave the way to address crowdwork thoroughly. Tensions ran high when Convention No. 177 was adopted, suggesting crowdwork might likewise be a hard nut to crack.[1442] Therefore, the tripartite discussions might pivot towards decent work in the platform economy at large instead of taking a more specific measure to tackle crowdwork decisively.

445 **Domestic workers** – As shown, Convention No. 189 and Recommendation No. 201 are vital if discussions are oriented towards location-based platform work. Domestic workers have been deprived of labour and social protections for decades. It is important not to perpetuate their marginalisation under the pretext that casual job opportunities are being created to everyone's benefit. Many local platform workers effectively assist people who do not want to or cannot personally garden, clean, cook, shop or provide care. Although the Convention's definitions are somewhat ambiguous, the instrument's spirit tells us to be critical whenever workers performing such tasks on an occupational basis are depicted as self-employed workers. Therefore, notwithstanding the possibility of engaging in legal nit-picking about who is and is not captured as a "domestic worker" under Convention No. 189, for example, the designation of food-delivery couriers as self-employed workers should raise eyebrows. These workers deliver food to the doorstep of the partner restaurants' customers. They serve households, and, like many domestic workers before them, labour and social protections are deliberately withheld from them.[1443] Any discussion on local

1441. Vittoria Elliott, *Training Self-driving Cars for $1 an Hour*, Rest of World (3 August 2021), https://restofworld.org/2021/self-driving-cars-outsourcing/.

1442. For instance, the Chairperson of the Employers' group commented on the report of the Global Commission for the Future of Work, stating: "[l]ikewise, the recommendation on setting an international governance system for digital labour platforms, that sets and requires platforms and their clients to respect certain minimum rights and protection, is very challenging. We do not think that such a system of transnational rights can be established or successfully managed. On the contrary, it could be exploited or undermine certain freedoms". Transcript of the discussion of the Reports of the Director-General and the Chairperson of the Governing Body at the 108th (Centenary) Session of the International Labour Conference, Geneva, ILO, 2019, 2.

1443. This is, most notably, clear in countries such as Belgium and the Netherlands where some food-delivery platforms first operated with employees. They only subsequently decided to turn legally employed couriers into self-employed couriers. Moreover, it has been shown that alternatives are possible in practice. Some platform operators are also choosing to turn self-employed couriers into employees of some sort, denouncing their competitors for relying on bogus self-employed workers. *See, e.g.*, Drahokoupil & Piasna, *supra* n. 622; Jonathan Josephs, *Just Eat to Stop Using Gig Economy Workers*, BBC (14 August 2020), https://www.bbc.com/news/business-53780299; Luke Henriques-Gomes, *Menulog Announces Pivot Towards 'Employment Model' for All Couriers Within Coming Years*, The Guardian (12

platform work should not ignore this link between domestic work and platform work, in which much local platform work effectively comes to the rescue of household members' needs.[1444]

"Employment" – When added up, platform workers are indeed entitled to protections **446**
under multiple ILO standards. This is not just because some standards apply to all workers, or because some platform workers are employees, as a result of which, for instance, the Part-Time Work Convention, 1994 (No. 175), becomes relevant; it is evident that some platform workers are subjected to private employment services, some are homeworkers, and some are domestic workers. Consequently, any discussion on decent work in the platform economy should not pin itself down on a narrow-minded discussion about the "misclassification issue". The "employment relationship", as described in the Employment Relationship Recommendation, 2006 (No. 198), is not the only relevant concept for the classification of platform workers under the International Labour Code. ILO constituents might as well ask themselves: (i) which platform operators engage in job-matching services; (ii) which employment intermediating platform operators ought to legally employ the jobseekers that they put at the disposal of user enterprises; (iii) what does it mean for a crowdworker to be economically independent and autonomous as if it is a home-based business; and, (iv) at what point does a platform worker perform domestic work on an occupational basis?

April 2021), https://www.theguardian.com/business/2021/apr/12/menulog-announces-pivot-towards-employment-model-for-all-couriers-within-coming-years.

1444. "And it is easy to see how, after an exhausting shift at work, the plan to cook a home meal can dissolve, [...], giving into the temptation to click on the app and order a pre-cooked meal to be delivered to the door by Just Eat, Deliveroo or Uber Eats. Just as, in the past, the liberation of middle-class women from housework was bought at the expense of the labour of personally-employed servants, we now have a more widely pervasive pattern whereby the needs of the time-poor are met by the labour of the money-poor, bringing two forms of desperation into interaction". Huws, *supra* n. 42, at 134.

Part IV. A Blueprint for the Regulation of Platform Work at the International Level

INTRODUCTION

The purpose of Part IV – This Fourth Part of the dissertation deals with the question of whether current international labour standards sufficiently respond to digital labour platforms, taking into account the organisational structure of these platforms and the demands made by platform workers, and if not, what role the International Labour Organization can play in regulating digital labour platforms? To that end, Chapter 1 indicates that even though Convention No. 177, No. 181 and No. 189 apply to a significant part of the platform economy, they could, however, be deemed insufficiently responsive to platform work. The instruments apply and even contain valuable provisions but fail to influence the debate; they fail to connect to the issue. Additionally, due to the primary "regulatory object" of these instruments, i.e. private employment agencies, industrial homeworkers and typical domestic workers, the standards also insufficiently address some of the particularities associated with platform work. Based on these observations, if this is true for these instruments, one might also assume that, more broadly, the International Labour Code is insufficiently responsive to digital labour platforms. 447

As such, the question becomes what the ILO can do to regulate the phenomenon. 448
Chapter 2 intends to illustrate some of the various "pathways" through which the ILO could pursue an instrument on platform work. The standard-setting options discussed in this Chapter all relate to the instruments analysed in Part III; in other words, these are only a few examples. Each pathway has its advantages and disadvantages. The purpose of this Chapter is to illustrate that although it might be tempting to simply issue a Platform Work Convention and Recommendation, in reality, there are many more possibilities. Policymakers should weigh up the various options; a direct approach in the form of a Platform Work Convention or Recommendation might be, but is not necessarily, ideal.

Finally, Chapter 3 draws on the Decent Work Agenda from Part II, the instruments 449
analysed in Part III and the information about platform work from Part I to explore

what can be expected from an ILO instrument on platform work, irrespective of the pathway chosen. The Chapter intends to provide a "blueprint" of sorts, *inter alia*, based on the content of these existing instruments to inform discussions on future standard-setting. What is important to note in all of this is the limited ambition of this blueprint.

450 The Third Chapter only refers to the instruments highlighted in Part III, even if it is evident that countless guidelines in other ILS also matter for platform work (*supra* nos. 179–180). In this regard, although the use of only three instruments is a somewhat unfortunate constraint, it is less problematic than it might seem. Convention No. 177, No. 181 and No. 189 can be expected to mostly align with other ILS, rearranging what is said in general instruments on, for instance, working time and wages to fit the "atypical" working arrangements in question.[1445] This entails that, unlike, for example, the Discrimination (Employment and Occupation) Convention, 1958 (No. 111), Minimum Wage Fixing Convention, 1970 (No. 131), and Occupational Safety and Health Convention, 1981 (No. 155), which always deal with one specific issue like discrimination, wages or OSH, the same is not true for Convention No. 177, No. 181 and No. 189. The latter cover almost all dimensions of labour and social protection to the extent ILO constituents deemed it relevant for homeworkers, domestic workers and temporary agency workers. For this reason, since the selected instruments apply to platform work, they paint a relatively comprehensive - although inherently incomplete - picture of what can be expected from an instrument on platform work.

451 Among other reasons, because this final Chapter only covers the guidelines advanced in the instruments under consideration and not all of the principles and approaches present in the Code, this "blueprint" should be seen as merely informative and not prescriptive in any way. Part IV of this dissertation only offers a small contribution to the debates surrounding a future instrument, also because, as Chapter 1 will indicate, the existing instruments do not address issues that are critical to platform work in particular. One can think, for example, of algorithmic discrimination (*supra* no. 87), intermediaries' position of power (*infra* no. 474) or the complexity of regulating transnational work arrangements (*infra* no. 476). In the end, the existing instruments analysed in this dissertation are but one piece of the puzzle; they largely fail to address such issues. It is up to ILO constituents to figure out to what extent their content, as presented below, is helpful in addressing platform work, and in which respects new innovative solutions are needed.

1445. The preamble of the Home Work Convention formulates this most explicitly. It states: "many international labour Conventions and Recommendations laying down standards of general application concerning working conditions are applicable to homeworkers", yet, "the particular conditions characterizing home work make it desirable to improve the application of those Conventions and Recommendations to homeworkers, and to supplement them by standards which take into account the special characteristics of home work". Preamble of the Home Work Convention, 1996 (No. 177). The Convention on decent work for domestic workers similarly recognises "the special conditions under which domestic work is carried out that make it desirable to supplement the general standards with standards specific to domestic workers so as to enable them to enjoy their rights fully". Preamble of the Domestic Workers Convention, 2011 (No. 189).

Chapter 1. The International Labour Code Is Not Responsive to Platform Work

SUBCHAPTER 1. APPLICABLE STANDARDS WITHOUT AN ACTUAL IMPACT

Relevant guidelines without an actual impact – The instruments on private employment agencies, home work and domestic work apply to parts of the platform economy, and, moreover, contain relevant guidelines. Subchapter 1 offers two examples for each instrument, illustrating how some guidelines may relatively straightforwardly apply in the platform economy. If adhered to, they would have a significant effect. However, notwithstanding the theoretical importance of these six guidelines for platform workers, it is clear that, in fact, the instruments hardly influence the platform work debate at all. As such, this blatant disconnect between theory and practice indicates the unresponsive character of the instruments in question and, arguably, the International Labour Code more broadly. 452

Private employment agencies – As noted, platforms classify as private employment agencies in the sense of Article 1(1)(a) Convention No. 181 if they provide services for matching offers of and applications for paid work between jobseekers/workers and natural or legal persons that rely on these workers to undertake entrepreneurial economic activities (*supra* no. 299). Furthermore, since §23 of the Domestic Workers Recommendation stipulates that "Members should promote good practices by private employment agencies in relation to domestic workers, including migrant domestic workers, taking into account the principles and approaches in the Private Employment Agencies Convention, 1997 (No. 181), and the Private Employment Agencies Recommendation, 1997 (No. 188)", the same is, to some extent, valid for employment intermediation between platform workers and household members. 453

Therefore, all in all, the ILS on labour market intermediation would seem to cover a large share of platform work arrangements (*supra* nos. 300–302). For this reason, we should ask ourselves what the guidelines in these instruments on private employment agencies tell us about platform work. As it turns out, many of the instructions in Convention No. 181 and Recommendation No. 188 are highly relevant in the context 454 of platform work (for instance, *supra* no. 300). The examples below of data protection and the prohibition to charge fees to workers will illustrate this.

455 **Data protection** – Article 6 of Convention No. 181 remarks that processing "personal data"[1446] must be done in a manner that protects this data and ensures respect for workers' privacy. Data collection should be limited "to matters related to the qualifications and professional experience of the workers concerned and any other directly relevant information".[1447] The Recommendation is even more precise. According to §11, the platforms covered by Convention No. 181 should be prohibited from recording personal data not required for judging workers' aptitude for the job (e.g. social media, credit scores, see *supra* nos. 84–85). Furthermore, the information should, for instance, only be kept for as long as it is justified.[1448] As the Committee of Experts notes, in other words, the instruments on private employment agencies suggest keeping data collection to a minimum.[1449] This approach, moreover, corresponds with the guidelines of the ILO Code of Practice regarding the protection of workers' personal data, which were issued around the same time.[1450]

456 The ILO guidelines conflict, however, with the position taken by platform operators. As pointed out by Hauben et al., "[t]he appropriation of data is an essential part of the business model and concerns all types of platform work (low/high-skilled and on-location/online platform work), irrespective of the labour market status of the platform worker and the status of the client (consumer/company)".[1451] Particularly platforms that practice algorithmic surveillance, such as transportation network companies and food-delivery platforms, can be expected to continuously capture large quantities of data (e.g. Uber's Rides of Glory).[1452] Their algorithmic management is characterised by "prolific data collection and surveillance" as well as "real-time responsiveness" to the data.[1453] The data and metrics are fundamental to exert control over the workers and optimise the platforms' operations.[1454] Yet, "this can occur at a cost to the worker" (for instance, *supra* nos. 84–85).[1455]

1446. The processing of workers' personal data refers to the collection, storage, combination, communication or any other use of information related to an identified or identifiable jobseeker or worker. Art. 1 Private Employment Agencies Convention, 1997 (No. 181).
1447. Art. 6 Private Employment Agencies Convention, 1997 (No. 181).
1448. Para. 12 Private Employment Agencies Recommendation, 1997 (No. 188).
1449. ILO Committee of Experts on the Application of Conventions and Recommendations, *supra* n. 815, at 79.
1450. *See, e.g.*, principles 5.1 and 5.7, ILO, *Protection of Workers' Personal Data* (ILO 1997).
1451. Harald Hauben, Karolien Lenaerts & Willem Waeyaert, *The Platform Economy and Precarious Work* 21 (European Parliament 2020).
1452. "[T]he transportation app Uber analysed the movement profiles of its clients to estimate how many of them were probably having an affair. Uber called the late-night taxi rides in question 'Rides of Glory' and published statistics for different North American cities". Florian A. Schmidt, *Digital Labour Markets in the Platform Economy: Mapping the Political Challenges of Crowd Work and Gig Work* 19 (Friedrich-Ebert-Stiftung 2017).
1453. Alexandra Mateescu & Aiha Nguyen, *Algorithmic Management in the Workplace* 3 (Data&Society 2019).
1454. Alessandro Gandini, *Labour Process Theory and the Gig Economy*, 72 Human Relations 1039, 1049–1051 n. 6 (2019).
1455. Choudary, *supra* n. 63, at 10.

Furthermore, besides data's importance for business operations, platform operators' revenue strategies also contradict the ILO's guidelines. Labour platforms do not solely derive revenue from the services performed by platform workers. The collected data is also marketed to third parties. To this end, because platforms are unsure about what data will eventually prove valuable for their business, Van Doorn and Badger argue that "[p]latforms engage in constant data accumulation because of the potential value this data, once processed by their analytics software, might embody or give rise to".[1456] As a result, given data's utility to control workers, improve operations and make money off third parties, data extraction is, arguably, one of the dimensions on which platforms compete to obtain a commercial edge over competitors.[1457] This, however, is diametrically opposed to the policies previously established at the international level. To that extent, what should not be forgotten is how platforms are not unique. As Stigler contended decades ago, information is the *raison d'être* of labour market intermediaries (*supra* no. 68). It would, therefore, have made sense for an instrument on employment intermediation not to subject PrEAs to strict privacy and data protection requirements. Still, as noted two paragraphs above, the ILO constituents decided to curb PrEAs' information appetite, regardless of what this meant for their business model. 457

Similarly, the ILO's principles regarding data rights and protection could be emphasised once more, this time explicitly in relation to the platform economy. An excellent example of why this is needed is workers' "right to demand that incorrect or incomplete data be deleted or corrected" under §12 of Recommendation No. 188. When extrapolated to the platform economy, should this not imply a right to challenge incorrect or biased ratings and reviews?[1458] One could make such an argument. However, unless ILO constituents confirm it in a new instrument, there is little chance of §12 having any effect of that sort. 458

Prohibition of fee-charging – Another issue with platform operators' revenue strategy is their reliance on subscription plans and various types of fees.[1459] These fees and costs are sometimes imposed upon users. The restaurants working together with food-delivery platforms, for instance, complain that their profit margins shrink due to platforms.[1460] At other times, the fees are imposed upon workers. In the latter case, 459

1456. Niels van Doorn & Adam Badger, *Platform Capitalism's Hidden Abode: Producing Data Assets in the Gig Economy*, 52 Antipode 1475, 1477 n. 5 (2020).
1457. ILO, *supra* n. 25, at 59.
1458. Right now platform workers in France "tended to say that, while in theory it would be possible for them to dispute poor evaluations, procedures for doing so appeared limited, complex or unclear". IPSOS, *supra* n. 292. In New York, "[a]cross the board, workers complain that current performance systems lack formal processes to challenge negative customer reviews or disciplinary actions or penalties imposed by the platforms". DeVault et al., *supra* n. 263, at 22.
1459. For instance, Standing has called labour platforms "rentier entities" because they charge commissions of 20 per cent or more on all transactions. Guy Standing, *The Corruption of Capitalism: Why Rentiers Thrive and Work Does Not Pay* 213 (Biteback Publishing 2016).
1460. Maureen Tkacik, *Rescuing Restaurants: How to Protect Restaurants, Workers, and Communities from Predatory Delivery App Corporations* 8 (American Economic Liberties Project 2020).

there can be real issues as well.[1461] On some platforms, for example, the workers seemingly gain advantages by paying for a premium membership (*supra* no. 342).

460 Such practices directly conflict with the instruments on private employment agencies. Article 7 of Convention No. 181 is adamant: unless an exemption can be justified, "[p]rivate employment agencies shall not charge directly or indirectly, in whole or in part, any fees or costs to workers". Because workers regularly complain about fees in the platform economy,[1462] at least in theory, Convention No. 181's prohibition could instantly relieve them. For this reason, any future instrument must reassess and, possibly, reaffirm this principle, especially in light of the Employers' group's remarks in 2010.[1463] While discussing the Committee of Experts' general survey on employment instruments in 2010, the Employers claimed that it might be worth discarding the principle that labour market services are free-of-charge. It was suggested to focus more on preventing abuse generally. Based on what this research has found, however, that proposal should be met with scepticism. As shown, the initial regulations on labour market services were particularly hostile towards commercial agencies that charged fees. They were the ones targeted by the rules because their services were considered abusive (*supra* nos. 240–242). Moreover, once regulations eased up and started to tolerate commercial employment services, the "principle of free-of-charge" was, in fact, the only element from the prior Fee-Charging Employment Agencies Conventions deemed essential by the Committee on Private Employment Agencies (*supra* no. 269). Letting go of this principle would radically break with the past; additionally, it might have detrimental implications for platform workers, in particular.

461 **Homeworkers** – In addition to Convention No. 181, the Home Work Convention, 1996 (No. 177) also contains relevant guidelines for regulating online crowdwork. Crowdworkers seem primarily concerned about low and unstable pay.[1464] Regarding this concern, at least for the crowdworkers who classify as homeworkers under Convention No. 177, the Member State is asked to fix "minimum rates of wages".[1465] This guideline in the Recommendation implements the Convention's call to promote equality of treatment between homeworkers and other wage earners in terms of remuneration.[1466]

462 Notably, the ILO Committee of Experts has clarified that homeworkers' minimum rates of wages differ from the minimum wage. While negotiating the instruments

1461. ILO, *supra* n. 25, at 20, 78–89 and 115.

1462. Aleksynska, Bastrakova & Kharchenko, *supra* n. 78, at 28–30 and 36; McDonald et al., *supra* n. 36, at 51 and 61; Kilhoffer et al., *supra* n. 33, at 72–74.

1463. From the record of proceedings: "The Employer members also raised the question of whether the prohibition set out in Article 7 of Convention No. 181 on the charging of fees or other costs to workers by private employment agencies might have become obsolete and whether measures to control and prevent abuse might be more appropriate". Report of the Committee on the Application of Standards at the 99th Session of the International Labour Conference, Geneva, ILO, 2010, Part I/36.

1464. Sabine Pfeiffer & Sandra Kawalec, *Justice Expectations in Crowd and Platform-mediated Work*, 31 The Economic Labour Relations Review 483, 483 n. 4 (2020). *See also*, Aleksynska, Bastrakova & Kharchenko, *supra* n. 78, at 28; Berg et al., *supra* n. 23, at 56.

1465. Para. 13 Home Work Recommendation, 1996 (No. 184).

1466. Art. 4 Home Work Convention, 1996 (No. 177).

on home work, the employers' representatives and some governments opposed applying a minimum wage. According to the Committee of Experts, "[t]he reasons given for this opposition were that the instruments do not only apply to workers in an employment relationship and that many countries do not have a minimum wage".[1467] The ILO constituents, therefore, agreed to call for minimum rates instead. These rates should be fixed preferably by collective bargaining or, alternatively, through other "wage-fixing machinery".[1468] The Office seems convinced that with some adjustments, the principles to establish fair and equitable piece rates for industrial homeworkers could also be applied to online crowdwork, especially for micro-taskers.[1469] The instruments on home work might, in other words, contain valuable leads to develop a system for fair remuneration in crowdwork (also *infra* nos. 505–506).[1470]

Social security protections – Another essential guideline in the instruments on home work has to do with social security protections. Because most platform workers are classified as independent contractors, they are often solely responsible for their social security contributions. ILO research indicates that only 24 per cent of crowdworkers make contributions to their health insurance. This percentage is even lower when talking about other safety nets like pensions.[1471] Consequently, many crowdworkers do not have any coverage except for health insurance or what is offered to all citizens, regardless of occupation.[1472] **463**

Because some may be eager to present the extension of social security to these workers as a hopeless cause, it is urgent to recall that the extension of social security to industrial homeworkers is at least as, if not more, complex.[1473] Nevertheless, ILO constituents deemed it essential to highlight homeworkers' claim to "statutory social security protection" in Convention No. 177.[1474] The Recommendation calls on the Member States to extend and amend existing social security provisions, and even develop special schemes or funds for homeworkers.[1475] In this regard, if constituents considered it necessary and possible to achieve this for industrial homeworkers, there should be a convincing reason to reverse course in relation to crowdworkers, all the more because crowdwork's digital infrastructure can facilitate the transparent payment of social security contributions and the transparent accruement of benefits. **464**

To this end, the Global Commission on the Future of Work suggested developing an "international governance system for digital labour platforms that sets and requires **465**

1467. ILO Committee of Experts on the Application of Conventions and Recommendations, *supra* n. 633, at 222.
1468. Para. 14 Home Work Recommendation, 1996 (No. 184).
1469. ILO, *supra* n. 613, at 256.
1470. On the danger of leaving this unregulated: Sarah O'Connor, *Do Not Let Homeworking Become Digital Piecework for the Poor*, Financial Times (15 September 2020), https://www.ft.com/content/ab83270c-253a-4d7a-9ef8-a360d2e04aab. *See also*, Gray & Suri, *supra* n. 1027.
1471. ILO, *Job Quality in the Platform Economy* 4 (ILO 2018).
1472. Aleksynska, Bastrakova & Kharchenko, *supra* n. 78, at 39; ILO, *supra* n. 25, at 174.
1473. ILO, *supra* n. 613, at 166.
1474. Art. 4 Home Work Convention, 1996 (No. 177).
1475. Para. 25 Home Work Recommendation, 1996 (No. 184).

platforms (and their clients) to respect certain minimum rights and protections".[1476] This governance system could include coordination mechanisms for social security or even establish personal "Digital Social Security" accounts for crowdworkers.[1477] Recent documents indicate that the ILO seems to, indeed, make social security protections a priority for platform workers, mentioning that it will examine cross-national coordination options (also see *supra* no. 168).[1478]

466 **Domestic workers** – Lastly, the instruments on decent work for domestic workers also set valuable precedents. As explained above (*supra* nos. 409–414), the instruments' scope of application attributes much importance to the occupational basis of domestic workers' jobs. Platform workers providing work for household members on an occupational basis could, therefore, fall under the Domestic Workers Convention, 2011 (No. 189). This would have significant consequences, given Convention No. 189's protective ambitions.

467 **Domestic workers' safety** – Domestic workers are, for example, exposed to particular dangers, such as harassment and abuse.[1479] It is with good reason that Article 5 of Convention No. 189 obliges each Member State to "take measures to ensure that domestic workers enjoy effective protection against all forms of abuse, harassment and violence". The same ought to happen for platform workers in domestic work, who likewise endure harassment.[1480] According to the Domestic Workers Recommendation, domestic workers should have accessible complaint mechanisms at their disposal to report cases of abuse, harassment and violence.[1481] Such mechanisms are easy to establish in a platform environment; however, the competent authorities must still ensure operators take these cries for help seriously.[1482]

1476. Global Commission on the Future of Work, *supra* n. 406, at 44. For a discussion, *see* Janine Berg, Miriam A. Cherry & Uma Rani, *Digital Labour Platforms: A Need for International Regulation?*, 16 Revista de Economía Laboral 104, 122–125 n. 2 (2019).
1477. The platform would redirect a percentage of the remuneration to an international DSS-account. The accrued contributions are subsequently transferred to the crowdworker's domestic social security system. The Member States determine how those funds are distributed among the various national social security mechanisms, and what entitlements they bring about. Enzo Weber, *Setting out for Digital Social Security* (ILO 2018); Christina Behrendt, Quynh Anh Nguyen & Uma Rani, *Social Protection Systems and the Future of Work: Ensuring Social Security for Digital Platform Workers*, 72 International Social Security Review 17, 32–33 n. 3 (2019).
1478. ILO Director-General, *supra* n. 575, at 50.
1479. Da Conceição Figueiredo, Suleman & do Carmo Botelho, *supra* n. 1291, at 65–85.
1480. Public Rights Project, *supra* n. 1390; Browning & Conger, *supra* n. 1291. *See also*, DeVault et al., *supra* n. 263, at 21; Karen Gregory, *'My Life Is More Valuable Than This': Understanding Risk among On-Demand Couriers in Edinburgh*, 35 Work, Employment and Society 316, 322 n. 2 (2021).
1481. Para. 7 Domestic Workers Recommendation, 2011 (No. 201).
1482. Platform workers in general complain about the overall unresponsiveness of the platform operators' staff. Ursula Huws, Neil H. Spencer, Dag S. Syrdal & Kaire Holts, *Work in the European Gig Economy: Research Results from the UK, Sweden, Germany, Austria, the Netherlands, Switzerland and Italy* 41–42 (FEPS 2017); Berg et al., *supra* n. 23, at 79–80. Also the difficulty "to communicate in a timely and effective way" is apparently an issue across the various types of labour platforms. Andrea Broughton et al., *The Experiences of Individuals in the Gig Economy* 33 (Department for Business, Energy & Industrial Strategy 2018). *See also*, Ticona, Mateescu & Rosenblat, *supra* n. 88, at 32–33.

Furthermore, besides the risk of abuse, domestic platform workers also complain about dangerous working conditions. This can be the case for people working inside the house and – assuming this is indeed a form of domestic work (*supra* no. 394) – for people delivering objects and food to people's doorstep.[1483] Although aware that pursuing safety and health in domestic work poses particular challenges, Article 13 of Convention No. 189, nevertheless, declares that "[e]very domestic worker has the right to a safe and healthy working environment". Each Member State must take measures to ensure that this right becomes a reality.[1484] In a similar vein, platform workers would benefit from an explicit affirmation that, notwithstanding their perhaps unusual workplace, they too have the right to a safe and healthy working environment. 468

Standby time – Another critical point raised in Convention No. 189 relates to domestic platform workers' standby or on-call time. Like food-delivery couriers, who complain about excessive waiting time,[1485] other platform workers might also spend significant time waiting or searching for a gig. If it were up to the platform operator, this searching and waiting time remains unremunerated; only the time spent executing the gig counts.[1486] Interestingly, the instruments on domestic work go beyond merely advocating in favour of equal treatment between domestic workers and others in terms of working time regulations. The instruments also address the issue of domestic workers' standby time, which is not self-explanatory.[1487] 469

As evidenced in the European Court of Justice's case law, for example, it can be unclear whether waiting time or standby time should be equated to actual working time, hence, remunerated.[1488] The Convention seems to leave similar doubt. According to Article 10, "[p]eriods during which domestic workers are not free to dispose of their time as they please and remain at the disposal of the household in order to respond to possible calls shall be regarded as hours of work to the extent determined by national laws, regulations or collective agreements, or any other means consistent with national practice".[1489] The working documents suggest that ILO constituents seemingly disagreed about the meaning of this phrase. Does it mean that the ratifying Member States "shall" consider standby time a form of working time, to the extent 470

1483. Huws, Spencer, Syrdal & Holts, *supra* n. 1482, at 46; Goods, Veen & Barratt, *supra* n. 298, at 511–513; Mourelo, *supra* n. 531, at 81–82; Zhou, *supra* n. 37, at 24.

1484. Art. 13 Domestic Workers Convention, 2011 (No. 189).

1485. Veen, Barratt & Goods, *supra* n. 103, at 398–399; Gregory, *supra* n. 1480, at 326–328.

1486. IPSOS, *supra* n. 292.

1487. See, for instance, Supreme Court: Case [2021] UKSC 8, *Royal Mencap Society (Respondent) v. Tomlinson-Blake (Appellant) / Shannon (Appellant) v. Rampersad and another (T/A Clifton House Residential Home) (Respondents)*, 19 March 2021; McCann, *supra* n. 601. More broadly, Deirdre McCann & Jill Murray, *The Legal Regulation of Working Time in Domestic Work* (ILO 2010).

1488. European Court of Justice: Case C-303/98, *Sindicato de Médicos de Asistencia Pública (Simap) v. Conselleria de Sanidad y Consumo de la Generalidad Valenciana*, 3 October 2000, ECLI:EU:C:2000:528; European Court of Justice: Case C-151/02, *Landeshauptstadt Kiel v. Norbert Jaeger*, 9 September 2003, ECLI:EU:C:2003:437; European Court of Justice: Case C-518/15, *Ville de Nivelles v. Rudy Matzak*, 21 February 2018, ECLI:EU:C:2018:82; European Court of Justice: Case C-344/19, *D. J. v. Radiotelevizija Slovenija*, 9 March 2021, ECLI:EU:C:2021:182.

1489. Art. 10 Domestic Workers Convention, 2011 (No. 189).

determined by their laws and regulations, or does this phrase also allow the Member States to entirely exclude standby time from being considered working time?[1490]

471 Akin to the Committee of Experts,[1491] the Recommendation seems to express a preference for the former. It clarifies that the Member States "should" regulate the maximum standby time per week, month or year, make sure that waiting time is not conflated with rest periods, and settle the rate at which standby hours are remunerated.[1492] Although these instructions are best read keeping in mind that they may have been written to suit the situation of live-in domestic workers, who spend their lives in the employer's home, a decision to remunerate platform workers for the periods during which they "are not free to dispose of their time as they please and remain at the disposal of the household in order to respond to possible calls" would be significant.

472 **The instruments are relevant but lack impact** – In light of the six examples listed above, one could argue that the instruments analysed in this dissertation's Third Part apply and contain valuable provisions. Nonetheless, because these guidelines remain overlooked and are clearly not followed, one could simultaneously conclude that these instruments are not responsive to platform work. Platforms are not supposed to massively accumulate data or charge fees to workers under Convention No. 181. However, they continue to do so. Furthermore, certain crowdworkers deserve minimum rates of wages and statutory social security protections under Convention No. 177. Yet, there are no indications of this being implemented. Thirdly, Convention No. 189 and its Recommendation suggest remunerating on-call or standby time and protecting domestic platform workers' health and safety, but these guidelines also seemingly fall on deaf ears. Therefore, to cut a long story short, these instruments' content has little material influence over the broader platform work debate, despite the instruments' applicability. It is one reason why they could be perceived as unresponsive.

SUBCHAPTER 2. THE EXISTING INSTRUMENTS ARE NOT GEARED TOWARDS PLATFORM WORK

473 **Standards with a very different "regulatory object"** – The existing standards regulate private employment agencies, homeworkers and domestic workers. These three topics relate to platform workers' experiences (*supra* nos. 181–192), but at the same time, all three instruments mainly cover situations outside of the platform economy. For example, Convention No. 181 is very much concerned with agencies that legally employ jobseekers (e.g. TWAs), which is usually not what a platform operator intends to do (*supra* nos. 303–307). Convention No. 177 focuses predominantly on industrial

1490. Report of the Committee on Domestic Workers at the 100th Session of the International Labour Conference, Geneva, ILO, 2011, 15/95–15/96.

1491. For example, Direct Request (CEACR) – adopted 2018, published 108th ILC session (2019), Domestic Workers Convention, 2011 (No. 189) – Panama (Ratification: 2015); Observation (CEACR) – adopted 2019, published 109th ILC session (2021), Domestic Workers Convention, 2011 (No. 189) – Paraguay (Ratification: 2013).

1492. Para. 9 Domestic Workers Recommendation, 2011 (No. 201).

home work, even if it does apply to telework and other forms of digital home-based work. The instruments on domestic work are significantly preoccupied with live-in domestic workers, which makes sense because they are particularly vulnerable to severe abuse; however, domestic platform workers are in a way the epitome of domestic job work (*supra* no. 405), raising very different issues. For these reasons, all three instruments may well apply to platform workers and even contain some relevant guidelines, as shown in the previous Subchapter, but the overall regulatory approach of each instrument arose to deal with phenomena that are quite different from platform work. Hence, the existing standards do not pay much attention to what is particularly important for platform workers. The following paragraphs will give three examples of issues that an instrument on platform work would have to deal with more extensively than has been done so far.

The dominance of the intermediary – Part I of this dissertation explored the resem- **474**
blance between digital labour platforms and labour market intermediaries. During that discussion, platform operators were described as "permissive potentates" that decide to what extent the participants on their platform are allowed to control the terms of their own interactions (*supra* no. 43).[1493] What is instrumental to this end are the clauses in platform operators' terms and conditions in which the operator reserves the right to implement unilateral changes.[1494] Regardless of the legality of these unilateral changes under domestic civil and labour law, the truth is that platform operators implement unilateral changes irrespective of the will of workers.[1495] As it stands, none of the ILO instruments analysed above significantly constrains this tendency, not even the instruments on private employment agencies. One of the reasons may be because ILO instruments insufficiently acknowledge how dominant contemporary intermediaries, among others, have become due to changes in the labour market (*supra* no. 74).

Paragraph 15 of the Private Employment Agencies Recommendation somewhat **475**
exemplifies this. It prescribes that agencies, which legally employ workers, such as TWAs, should not prevent user enterprises from hiring that worker directly, not restrict their workers' occupational mobility, and not impose penalties on the worker for accepting employment in another enterprise. Agencies that merely intermediate between workers and employers without legally employing the worker were not expected to commit these practices. However, nowadays, platform operators constrain workers' mobility through legal and practical means even though they do not legally employ the worker (*supra* nos. 89–91). For such reasons, it would seem timely for an

1493. Vallas & Schor, *supra* n. 86, at 282.

1494. Kenney, Bearson & Zysman, *supra* n. 77, at 37.

1495. See, for instance, on how TaskRabbit changed its practices to the dismay of workers, Ravenelle, *supra* n. 1342, at 269–285. What is relevant in this regard is how "[t]o the question 'did you have to sign a contract with the app/platform', [respondents'] answer was predominantly 'no'". Entering a platform "was perceived more as an online registration and non-negotiable acceptance of the use terms of the platform, as opposed to a more conventional contract". IPSOS, *supra* n. 292.

ILO instrument to explicitly tackle the harmful effects of intermediaries' dominance in the contemporary world of work, which has not been done so far at the ILO level.[1496]

476 **Transnational work arrangements** – A second feature of platform work that is not given the attention it deserves is the transnational nature of some of these relationships. The current instruments on home work, for example, insufficiently acknowledge how industrial homeworkers fit into regional and global supply chains.[1497] The Convention on home work from 1996 did not address this point, *inter alia,* because the research on the interaction between home work and global supply chains only reached maturity in the 2000s.[1498] Such a broader transnational perspective on home-based work might have helped in light of the challenges crowdwork currently presents.

477 Until this point, the mechanisms to govern cross-border working relationships, including home work, have been underdeveloped.[1499] Article 8 of the Private Employment Agencies Convention, for instance, does clarify that "[w]here workers are recruited in one country for work in another, the Members concerned shall consider concluding bilateral agreements to prevent abuses and fraudulent practices in recruitment, placement and employment". It is unclear, however, whether the terminology of this guideline – "recruited in one country for work in another" – can also be understood to cover abuses and fraudulent practices in instances of so-called "virtual" or "digital" migration. These workers do not physically migrate, yet they are recruited in one country for work originating in another.[1500] Furthermore, this particular guideline refers to "bilateral" agreements. It will be up to ILO constituents to discuss whether bilateral agreements are also the appropriate method to govern crowdwork. Bilateral treaties are already being used to regulate transnational telework between certain countries, for instance.[1501] However, in the case of crowdwork, the workforce is

1496. Our discussion of the Home Work Convention also pointed out how current standards seem to insufficiently address jobseekers' potential dependency on an intermediary or platform to find employment (see *supra* nos. 359–364). Commercial law has already acknowledged platforms' significant influence over interactions between service providers and requesters. *See, e.g.*, Regulation No. 2019/1150 of the European Parliament and of the Council of 20 June 2019 on promoting fairness and transparency for business users of online intermediation services, OJ L 186, 11 July 2019.

1497. The ILO Conclusions concerning decent work in global supply chains from 10 June 2016 point out how "[m]igrant workers and homeworkers are found in many global supply chains and may face various forms of discrimination and limited or no legal protection".

1498. Harvey, *supra* n. 1011, at 2. Any revision should explore, for example, whether and how corporate social responsibility can aid homeworkers. Scholars observe that homeworkers are rarely accounted for in CSR. And if they are, lead firms ban them from their supply chain, which is not beneficial to these homeworkers. Delaney, Burchielli, Marshall & Tate, *supra* n. 1025, at 81–106; Marlese von Broembsen, Jenna Harvey & Marty Chen, *Realizing Rights for Homeworkers: An Analysis of Governance Mechanisms* (Carr Centre for Human Rights Policy, Harvard Kennedy School 2019); Farah Naz & Dieter Bögenhold, *Unheard Voices: Women, Work and Political Economy of Global Production* 75–91 (Palgrave Macmillan 2020).

1499. Paragraph 21 of the Employment Relationship Recommendation, 2006 (No. 198), is also rather brief, stressing that Member States should establish specific national mechanisms to effectively identify employment relationships in case of transnational provision of services.

1500. A. Aneesh, *Virtual Migration: The Programming of Globalization* (Duke University Press 2006).

1501. An example is between Luxembourg and France: Réponse du Ministère de l'économie, des finances et de la relance, publiée dans le JO Sénat du 01/10/2020 – page 4445 à la question

much more fluid, perhaps, with an operator intent on forging working relationships between people in many different countries. Three parties and, maybe, countries are involved: (the country of) the employer, the worker and the platform operator. These features would seemingly favour a multilateral approach, as envisioned by the Global Commission on the Future of Work,[1502] rather than a panoply of bilateral agreements, as proposed in Convention No. 181.

Distribution of responsibilities among the parties – An important third point concerns 478
the discussion about the entity responsible for platform workers' protections and entitlements. As discussed in the Chapter on private employment services (*supra* nos. 303–307), Convention No. 181 is hard to apply when neither the user enterprise nor the agency admits to being the legal employer. Its guidelines on the allocation of responsibilities between the agency and user are, moreover, only pertinent when the agency, or in this case, platform operator, accepts the role as a legal employer.[1503] Since platform operators tend not to accept that status, these rules on allocating responsibilities between agencies and users become superfluous in the platform economy. Additionally, the use of external agencies to legally employ platform workers, after which platform users engage these workers on, for example, food-delivery platforms, further complicates things (*supra* no. 186).[1504] In such instances, assuming domestic law allows for it, what entity bears the responsibility of the user enterprise? Say that Manpower legally employs the food-delivery courier; should either the restaurant or platform operator be identified as the user enterprise or both? Similar problems related to the blurring of employer responsibilities were raised in the context of home and domestic work.

Following the logic underlying the Home Work Convention, the platform's user will, 479
in principle, serve as the crowdworker's "employer" (*supra* nos. 324–326). As a result, most obligations are seemingly imposed upon the user enterprise. However, in reality, at least for industrial homeworkers, their contact person is often the intermediary, not the entity that gives out home work. The same seems to be true for many crowdworkers, who remain relatively uninformed about their actual employer; platform operators sometimes even seem to deliberately prevent communication between crowdworkers and users (*supra* no. 91). Perhaps in response to such dynamics, §18 of the Home Work Recommendation prescribes that "[w]here an intermediary is used, the intermediary and the employer should be made jointly and severally liable for payment of the remuneration due to homeworkers, in accordance with national law and practice". Yet, moving beyond remuneration, the question remains: who is responsible for the legal entitlements of homeworkers and crowdworkers? Are joint and several liabilities still an option?

écrite no. 17257 de M. Ronan Le Gleut (Français établis hors de France – Les Républicains), publiée dans le JO Sénat du 16/07/2020 – page 3241, Sénat (accessed: 28 April 2021).

1502. Global Commission on the Future of Work, *supra* n. 406, at 44. For a discussion, *see* Berg, Cherry & Rani, *supra* n. 1476, at 122–125.

1503. Art. 12 Private Employment Agencies Convention, 1997 (No. 181).

1504. *E.g.* Fairwork, *Fairwork India Ratings 2020: Labour Standards in the Platform Economy* 20 (Oxford Internet Institute 2020).

480 After all, contrary to home work, in domestic work, employers' representatives and governments refused to implement joint and several liabilities between the intermediary and household (*supra* no. 433). In principle, the household members seem to be held to account. However, as discussed in the relevant Subchapter (*supra* no. 428), household members may prefer the agency or platform to become the legal employer. This allows household members to shed their role as employers, creating an odd situation. On the one hand, turning the agency or platform operator into a legal employer is beneficial because it can professionalise domestic work. It can also benefit domestic workers, who obtain an enduring relationship with the agency, despite their many fractured relationships with various households.[1505] On the other hand, the agency or platform needs to take its role as an employer seriously. When the employer burden is lifted from the shoulders of household members, they can easily perceive themselves as consumers of household services (*supra* nos. 405–408). The household members' responsibility for the domestic worker is projected onto the agency, which is problematic whenever that agency or platform operator neglects its responsibility. For such reasons, it was suggested that as a default position, it might be worthwhile assuming that household members are the domestic workers' legal employers. This can be the case unless household members rely on an official agency or platform, in which case the agency or platform operator may be allowed to carry most responsibilities (*supra* nos. 435–436). Such a default position might put a brake on households' use of rogue agencies and platforms. However, as things stand, these kinds of reflections are not explicitly made in the instruments on domestic work.

481 In light of a future instrument on platform work, it is probably worth exploring the various implications of attributing specific responsibilities to platforms or their users in various settings, such as home and domestic work. Also, the imposition of joint and several liabilities might be a valuable option for particular responsibilities, such as workers' remuneration, in all or certain types of platform work.

482 **A lack of detail in the existing instruments** – As evidenced using these three examples,[1506] the instruments under review in this dissertation fall short in some respects, which becomes particularly apparent when applied to platform work. Therefore, in addition to the reasons stated in Subchapter 1, it is also the case that certain issues that affect platform workers, in particular, have not yet been satisfactorily dealt with. Based on these two observations, it would seem legitimate to pursue a new international labour standard. The next Chapter outlines a couple of standard-setting options in this respect. The main takeaway is that the ILO has multiple pathways to pursue an instrument. A thorough discussion should take place about which course to take.

1505. *See, e.g.*, Fudge & Hobden, *supra* n. 640.

1506. There are also other problems that could have been mentioned. What has not been dealt with in any existing instrument is, for example, the oversupply of workers that occurs on platforms. Indeed, "[b]ecause the business model of many platforms relies on supplying a large pool of service providers (workers), they create an excess supply of workers, resulting in significant underemployment for app workers and downward pressure on their earnings". DeVault et al., *supra* n. 263, at 18.

Chapter 2. Multiple Pathways to Set a Standard on Platform Work

Various options – This short Chapter outlines several ways in which the ILO could end up with an instrument addressing platform work. These options are based on findings in this study. There are, of course, many more regulatory pathways than the ones covered here. 483

Platform Work Convention/Recommendation – As things stand, a Meeting of Experts will be held on "decent work in the platform economy" in the second quarter of 2022.[1507] To get a sense of timing: this meeting is similar to the Meeting of Experts on the social protection of homeworkers from 1990 (*supra* no. 308), which propelled 1996's instruments on home work. Assuming the experts conclude, as this research does, that standard-setting action is recommendable, then the chances are that a Conference Committee will be instructed to deliberate on a new Convention or Recommendation. From the perspective of this research, such deliberations would have to acknowledge the variety of legal arrangements used in the platform economy. 484

As has become increasingly apparent throughout the years, labour law and platform work are reconcilable. Some platform operators voluntarily work with legal employees; others have been found to rely on bogus self-employed workers and have changed their approach (*supra* no. 98). Among this group of platforms that (are supposed to) work with employees, some platform operators do so consistently. In contrast, others such as Helpling rely on employees in one legal system and independent contractors in another (*supra* no. 60). This volatility – linked to bogus self-employment and differences in legal arrangements between countries – should incite ILO constituents to think about how to apply the Employment Relationship Recommendation, 2006 (No. 198), in the platform economy.[1508] As this research has stressed, what should not be overlooked in this respect is the overlap between local platform work and domestic work. An overly strict application of Recommendation No. 198 risks excluding platform workers that perform domestic work from the 485

1507. ILO Governing Body, *Composition, agenda and programme of standing bodies and meetings*, GB.342/INS/10(Rev.2) (ILO 2021).

1508. De Stefano, Durri, Stylogiannis & Wouters, *supra* n. 13.

protection they are owed (*supra* nos. 397–403). What should also not be forgotten is the issue of "disguised" temporary work agencies. Some platform operators, such as Wonolo and Temper, seem to behave like an agency of type 1(1)(b) in the sense of the Private Employment Agencies Convention without legally employing the worker (*supra* nos. 305–306). In such cases, how can we ensure that platforms with all the hallmarks of an agency of type 1(1)(b) accept their responsibilities as an employer? Finally, although many platform operators could, in fact, be required to establish an employment relationship with the jobseeker or between the jobseeker and user, some platform workers are genuinely self-employed and will remain that way. These self-employed workers can be entitled to protection, for instance, against abusive and unethical platform practices.[1509]

486 In addition to the complexity of legally addressing local app-based platform work, as evidenced in the prior paragraph, there is arguably an even more challenging question about what to do for crowdworkers. As discussed in this study, in defining the scope of protective provisions for these online platform workers, it might be more appropriate to ask whether the crowdworker has economic and functional autonomy (e.g. contrary to a homeworker), instead of searching for an employment relationship. Furthermore, as is the case for homeworkers, ILO constituents may not want to simply force existing labour and social protections for employees onto crowdworkers. They might have to find ways to extend and modify a range of protections to protect home-based crowdworkers effectively.

487 Based on these various considerations, the discussions on a Platform Work Convention/Recommendation, covering both local and online platform work, will undoubtedly be demanding. Frankly, such an effort even threatens to become too all-encompassing. ILO constituents will be asked to touch on many topics that are very sensitive at the ILO. First of all, as discussions regarding contract labour and Recommendation No. 198 have shown, deliberations on the scope of application of labour and social law are highly contentious. Furthermore, platform work is, for instance, associated with triangular employment relationships. The regulation thereof is likewise difficult at the ILO level (*supra* nos. 295–296). Employers' representatives and some governments are rather hesitant to extend protections beyond workers in a typical employment relationship; however, per definition, a lot of these discussions will aim for just that. Additionally, crowdwork is home-based and often transnational, whereas local app-based platform workers often physically move between clients without having any fixed workplace. The factual differences between the two further complicate the effort to deal with both in one instrument. Add to this governments' concern for the wishes of consumers,[1510] who like to rely on cheap household services (*supra* nos. 379–380), and the interests of business users that rely on an external

1509. The instruments on private employment agencies protect jobseekers in search of any employment from abusive and fraudulent practices by the agencies. That could similarly be the case for platform workers. Art. 10 Private Employment Agencies Convention, 1997 (No. 181); para. 4 Private Employment Agencies Recommendation, 1997 (No. 188).

1510. *See also*, Pepper D. Culpepper & Kathleen Thelen, *Are We All Amazon Primed? Consumers and the Politics of Platform Power*, 53 Comparative Political Studies 288, 288–318 n. 2 (2020).

platform workforce (*supra* no. 82), and realistically speaking, a successful outcome is anything but certain.

Platform Work Resolution – Partially because efforts to draft a high-profile standard on platform work in general may fail, alternative pathways must be explored. One idea could be to work with a Resolution. As mentioned earlier (*supra* no. 214), ILO Resolutions might fulfil the conditions to be considered a subsequent agreement capable of interpreting the provisions in pre-existing ILO Conventions. If true, it is not unimaginable to adopt an ILO Resolution on Decent Work in the Platform Economy that, for instance, clarifies how the Home Work Convention's conditions of economic independence and autonomy ought to be interpreted in a crowdwork environment. The Resolution could similarly confirm that many platform workers enjoy protections under Convention No. 181 in their capacity as jobseekers. In effect, the existing instruments, which are already applicable to platform work, such as Convention No. 177, 181 and 189, would be used to substantiate what the Member States, platform operators and users owe platform workers. Similar to what happened with the "General principles and operational guidelines for fair recruitment and definition of recruitment fees and related costs" (*supra* no. 280),[1511] such a Resolution could turn the conclusions of a Meeting of Experts into a clean and concise soft law instrument. 488

An instrument on digital employment services – Besides an approach that focuses on platform work in general, another option would be to adopt a standard on digital employment services. As already mentioned (*supra* no. 268), the Office initially intended for Convention No. 181 to implement a "shared labour market management"-approach, addressing both public and private employment services and their interaction. The proposal to adopt a holistic instrument was dismissed at the time. The Committee opted to only focus on private service providers. Because of this narrow take, there is still an opening to pick this issue up again and configure how digital labour market intermediaries, such as platforms, should work together with public authorities. Moreover, given the importance of digital employment services in the overall industry (*supra* nos. 61–64), it could be a legitimate topic for standard-setting. As mentioned before, most platforms engage in labour market services, ensuring that households and businesses gain access to an external workforce (*supra* no. 58 and 60);[1512] therefore, to the extent that there are sufficient grounds to pursue an instrument on platform work, the same would seem true for a standard on digital employment services. By not tackling platform work head-on but by proxy, it may be possible to reach an agreement if necessary. One of the potential advantages of focusing on digital employment services and not platform work as such, might be that the way in which platform users can also suffer from the practices of these operators can be highlighted.[1513] In this way, some additional support might be gained from employers and governments. 489

1511. ILO, *General Principles and Operational Guidelines for Fair Recruitment & Definition of Recruitment Fees and Related Costs* (ILO 2019).

1512. Besides, the platforms that do not classify as an LMI because they only serve end-market consumers, such as ride-hailing platforms, are, most notably, the ones under scrutiny for using bogus self-employed workers. De Stefano, Durri, Stylogiannis & Wouters, *supra* n. 13, 30–40.

1513. In case of restaurants and food-delivery, for instance, "[t]he contracts the app salespeople induced restaurants to sign in most cases included anticompetitive 'No Price Competition

490 **Crowdwork Convention** – In addition to a Platform Work Convention/Recommendation or as a stand-alone standard-setting item, the ILO could also pursue an instrument on crowdwork. A forceful standard on crowdwork might even, to some degree, be more critical at the ILO level than a more general one on platform work, the reason being that the ILO is probably the only international organisation with both a mandate specific enough to focus on such a "niche" subject and a membership broad enough to deal with crowdwork's global reach. Considering the ILO's likely importance in solving this issue, it is necessary to remark that an ILO instrument on crowdwork can take a couple of different trajectories; it is not necessarily advanced as part of a discussion on decent work in the platform economy. It could, for example, feature in a revision of the instruments on home work or come in the form of an instrument on transnational labour recruitment.

491 **Home work** – A couple of ILO reports were particularly topical given the COVID-19 pandemic. The Committee of Experts' general survey from 2020 covered home, tele- and crowdwork.[1514] The Office also published an extensive report on working from home in 2021, discussing the same topics.[1515] These studies could be consequential because they lay the groundwork for an informed decision on revising 1996's instruments on home work. Convention No. 177 has not only received few ratifications (11); the text of the instrument itself does not even explicitly refer to telework or telecommuting. Moreover, also in relation to industrial homeworkers, it has failed to cover certain vital angles such as homeworkers' role as a flexibility device in global supply chains.[1516] In light of such "shortcomings" and indications that remote work via ICT-means continues to gain importance,[1517] one could consider revising the home work instruments, emphasising the transnational component of such working relationships, as most notably present in crowdwork. By tying crowdwork to other forms of home-based work, the issue of people working from home in one legal system for a user enterprise in another could be explored more holistically, showing that crowdwork is not a "niche" subject at all.

492 **Transnational labour recruitment** – In a similar vein, regulation on crowdwork can also be decoupled from local platform work and tied to broader developments in labour recruitment. One reason to do so is that crowdwork platforms are just one form

Clauses,' requiring restaurants to keep prices the same across all food delivery apps and in-person dining". Tkacik, *supra* n. 1460, at 8.

1514. ILO Committee of Experts on the Application of Conventions and Recommendations, *supra* n. 633.

1515. ILO, *supra* n. 613.

1516. Research on the interaction between home work and global supply chains only became significant in the 2000s. Meanwhile, the ILO Conclusions concerning decent work in global supply chains from 10 June 2016 do point out that "[m]igrant workers and homeworkers are found in many global supply chains and may face various forms of discrimination and limited or no legal protection". Harvey, *supra* n. 1011, at 2.

1517. Alan Felstead & Golo Henseke, *Assessing the Growth of Remote Working and its Consequences for Effort, Well-being and Work-life balance*, 32 New Technology, Work and Employment 195, 208 n. 3 (2017); Nicholas Bloom, *How Working from Home Works out* 4–5 (Stanford Institute for Economic Policy Research 2020); Alexander W. Bartik et al., *What Jobs are Being Done at Home During the COVID-19 Crisis? Evidence from Firm-Level Surveys* 15 (Harvard Business School 2020).

of intermediary engaged in the offshoring of ICT services (*supra* no. 316). Indeed, other online businesses may emerge to satisfy the "desire to connect geographically disparate clients and workers".[1518] With this in mind, it might be wise to situate crowdwork platforms within a broader framework governing the recruitment of any (foreign) online labour, regardless of it happening through a "platform". Some examples outside of the platform economy are "gold miners" and other participants in the game industry,[1519] and "high-skilled" remote workers performing their job from another jurisdiction.[1520] Some have suggested that in the aftermath of the COVID pandemic, large numbers of jobs have become "Anywhere Jobs", which can also be filled from abroad.[1521] In light of this, the ILO might do well to adopt a broader perspective than crowdwork alone.

1518. Mark Graham, Isis Hjorth & Vili Lehdonvirta, *Digital Labour and Development: Impacts of Global Digital Labour Platforms and the Gig Economy on Worker Livelihoods*, 23 Transfer 135, 158 n. 2 (2017).
1519. Aphra Kerr, *Recruitment, Work, and Identity in Community Management: Passion, Precarity, and Play* 117, 117–135 (Juliet Webster & Keith Randle eds., *Virtual Workers and the Global Labour Market*, Palgrave Macmillan 2016); Moritz Altenried & Manuela Bojadžijev, *Virtual Migration, Racism and the Multiplication of Labour*, 4 Spheres Journal for Digital Cultures 1, 7–10 (2017).
1520. Simon Kuper, *Are Superstar Employees about to be Offshored?*, Financial Times (25 March 2021), https://www.ft.com/content/9414f45c-6f03-4b8f-85c5-537d7e4f4932.
1521. Jeegar Kakkad, Christina Palmou, David Britto & James Browne, *Anywhere Jobs, Reshaping the Geography of Work* (Tony Blair Institute for Global Change 2021).

Chapter 3. Future Standard-Setting Action by the ILO

SUBCHAPTER 1. FUNDAMENTAL COMPONENTS OF DECENT WORK

A blueprint for platform work regulation – The previous Chapter shows that ILO constituents can approach platform work from various angles. Depending on the angle, the content of the instrument will be different. Although it is futile to make concrete predictions about a future instrument's content for this and other reasons, there are, nonetheless, some aspects that can be expected to feature in a future standard, regardless of the instrument's form. This Third Chapter gives an overview of these aspects based on the ILO's normative framework from Part II and the applicable standards from Part III. The exploration limits itself to the information found in the ILO Constitution and Declarations from Part II and the instruments on private employment agencies, home work and domestic work. Many other issues deserve attention in a future instrument, but they are not raised due to a lack of any clear link to these instruments or prior discussions in this dissertation. 493

Freedom of association and effective collective bargaining – The 1998 Declaration is a central pillar of decent work (*supra* no. 133). Any instrument on decent work in the platform economy will, therefore, likely pay attention to collective rights, non-discrimination, forced and child labour. This happened, for instance, in Convention No. 177, No. 181 and No. 189. Convention No. 181 wants the Member States to ensure that workers recruited by private employment agencies are not denied the right to freedom of association and collective bargaining.[1522] Based on this article, the Committee of Experts more broadly demands measures "to guarantee that workers placed or recruited by private agencies are not denied the rights contained in [the] fundamental Conventions".[1523] When thinking about platform work, it is not redundant to reiterate this point, considering some platform operators' adversity towards collective voice and action (*supra* no. 93). Furthermore, in addition to ensuring 494

1522. Art. 4 Private Employment Agencies Convention, 1997 (No. 181).

1523. ILO Committee of Experts on the Application of Conventions and Recommendations, *supra* n. 815, at 85.

that platform workers enjoy collective rights, so they can, for instance, challenge information asymmetries on the platform (*supra* nos. 85–86), Recommendation No. 188 clarifies that private employment agencies should not make workers available to a user enterprise to replace workers of that enterprise who are on strike.[1524] ILO constituents may want to similarly stress that platform workers should not be relied upon to the detriment of the collective rights of user enterprises' workers.

495 When turning to Convention No. 177, it is evident that ILO constituents wanted to highlight homeworkers' right to establish or join organisations of their own choosing and participate in the activities of such organisations.[1525] Recommendation No. 184 asks the Member States very concretely to identify and eliminate legislative or administrative restrictions and obstacles to these rights. The organisations representing homeworkers must additionally be enabled to join trade union (con)federations.[1526] The Recommendation more broadly wants the Member States to encourage collective bargaining as a means of determining homeworkers' terms and conditions of work.[1527] Hence, in light of this policy on homeworkers, a question ILO constituents may want to ask is whether representative organisations and collective bargaining are also the methods of choice to set the terms and conditions of employment for crowdworkers?

496 Thirdly, the instruments on decent work for domestic workers might teach us something about platform workers' collective rights. Convention No. 189 calls on the Member States for the "effective recognition" of domestic workers' right to collective bargaining.[1528] This reference is relevant because effective collective bargaining in domestic work requires innovative approaches.[1529] There is, for instance, little chance of collective bargaining at the "enterprise-level" between workers and individual households. Also, on the "sectoral level", individual households rarely bond together to form a bargaining partner for the organisations representing domestic workers. An agency can be useful for these reasons because it gives the domestic workers' representatives a central and easily identifiable bargaining partner. In this regard, these experiences with domestic workers might teach us a couple of things about platform work. Notably, the ILO constituents did not give up on domestic workers' collective rights just because of the practical difficulties of implementing it in a domestic work context. It sets a clear precedent; ILO constituents can be expected to search for "effective" ways of collective bargaining in the platform economy. Additionally, as the domestic work context shows, the platform operator will sometimes be the partner of choice to bargain with, even if its users technically employ the workers. In such cases, when the platform operator becomes the bargaining partner, the users' interests will need to be considered. Assume the domestic workers associated with an agency manage to improve their working conditions by bargaining with that agency; this may well trigger the households to jump ship to another agency. Similar issues may ensue in the platform economy. Irrespective of the platform users being households

1524. Para. 6 Private Employment Agencies Recommendation, 1997 (No. 188)
1525. Art. 4 Home Work Convention, 1996 (No. 177).
1526. Para. 11 Home Work Recommendation, 1996 (No. 184).
1527. Para. 12 *Ibid.*
1528. Art. 3 Domestic Workers Convention, 2011 (No. 189).
1529. Claire Hobden, *Domestic Workers Organize – But Can They Bargain?* (ILO 2015).

or businesses, collective improvements of certain working conditions may entice users to switch to another platform. It is one reason why sectoral bargaining may be recommendable.

Non-discrimination – In addition to safeguarding collective rights, the Declaration on Fundamental Principles and Rights at Work obliges the Member States to eliminate discrimination in respect of employment and occupation, as addressed by the Equal Remuneration Convention, 1951 (No. 100), and the Discrimination (Employment and Occupation) Convention, 1958 (No. 111). Sadly, much progress is yet to be made in this regard. The platform economy displays blatant examples of discrimination. In the area of crowdwork, for instance, direct discrimination seemingly occurs based on nationality and age.[1530] The same might also be happening in local on-demand work. As noted before, the ads for nannies on Craigslist similarly showed signs of discrimination (*supra* no. 381).[1531] Furthermore, although it is less visible, users' ratings may also reproduce users' discriminatory biases against already disadvantaged workers,[1532] an issue that is also related to the harassment platform workers might endure on discriminatory grounds.[1533] In addition to these forms of direct discrimination, these platforms' algorithmic systems can also sustain forms of indirect discrimination (*supra* no. 87).[1534] **497**

In light of these examples, it is worth recalling the guidelines in the instruments on private employment agencies. First, §8 of Recommendation No. 188 clarifies that agencies – read platform operators – should not knowingly recruit, place or employ workers for jobs where they may be subjected to abuse or discriminatory treatment of any kind. It is crucial to discuss among ILO constituents whether this also presupposes that the platform operator actively monitors its users for discriminatory practices, such as biased ratings. More specifically, from a technical point of view, if platforms go to the trouble of monitoring communications between workers and users to ensure the platform operator is not disintermediated (*supra* no. 89),[1535] the operator could probably also monitor for signs of discrimination. Secondly, paragraph 9 calls on the Member States to act. They should prohibit or prevent agencies from drawing up and publishing vacancy notices or offers of employment in ways that **498**

1530. Graham et al., *supra* n. 1116, at 10; Cherry, *supra* n. 271, at 55.
1531. Lair & Andrews, *supra* n. 1281, at 82.
1532. Moore, *supra* n. 632, at 8–9.
1533. *E.g.*, Eurofound, *supra* n. 4, at 31.
1534. The ruling of a Court in Bologna gives a concrete example. At the time, Deliveroo used a system that allowed workers to pre-schedule specific time brackets, after which workers could cancel that booking up until twenty-four hours before the shift. If the worker did not cancel in time and failed to show up, it would impact that worker's "reliability index". This index would, in turn, affect the worker's chances of pre-booking good time brackets in the future. The claimants argued that such a system is conducive to indirect discrimination, for example, because it penalises workers who are sick or go on strike. Workers cannot justify their absence, leading to penalisation. Tribunale ordinario di Bologna: Case 2949/2019, *FILCAMS CGIL Bologna, NIDIL CGIL Bologna, FILT CGIL Bologna v. Deliveroo Italia S.R.L.*, 31 December 2020; Antonio Aloisi & Valerio De Stefano, *Deliveroo's Algorithm Discriminated Against Those Who go on Strike or Get Sick: "Frankly, my Rider, I Don't Give a Damn"*, il Mulino (7 January 2021), https://www.rivistailmulino.it/a/frankly-my-rider-i-don-t-give-a-damn-1.
1535. IPSOS, *supra* n. 292; Weber, Okraku, Mair & Maurer, *supra* n. 1272, at 19.

directly or indirectly result in discrimination, listing grounds such as race, colour, sex, age, religion, political opinion, national extraction, social origin, ethnic origin, disability, marital or family status, sexual orientation or membership of a workers organisation. Thirdly, §10 calls for the promotion of equality in employment through affirmative action programmes. This paragraph, likewise, offers a valuable subject for consideration. Crowdwork can help workers with a disability or another impairment to engage in work from home.[1536] Moreover, there is some tentative evidence that intermediaries, including platforms, perhaps, can boost disadvantaged jobseekers' employment chances.[1537]

499 **Forced and child labour** – As described in Part I of this dissertation, platform operators typically present their businesses as a marketplace (*supra* no. 79). Like the owner of a marketplace, operators decide who is allowed to set up shop. Some operators are rather lenient and might require only a name and some basic contact details. Others may ask for much more information, hoping to, for instance, boost trust between participants on the platform (*supra* no. 69). Especially for platforms that are open to anyone and do not adequately screen the labour supply side, issues of forced and child labour may come up. One BBC documentary, for example, uncovered how enslaved domestic workers in the Middle East are being traded through apps and platforms.[1538] Whereas this seemingly occurred on platforms that pay little attention to user profiles, issues also arise on platforms where one would expect operators to keep a close eye on the labour supply. A Milan Tribunal in Italy, for example, charged Uber Eats and affiliated recruiters for gang mastering offences involving migrant workers.[1539] This charge allegedly meant Uber Eats was involved in the "intermediary recruitment of 'workers on behalf of third parties under exploitative conditions, taking advantage of the workers' state of need' as well as to 'employ, hire or engage workers – including by the means of the intermediation activity referred to above – exploiting them and taking advantage of their state of need'".[1540]

500 Paragraph 2 (b) of the ILO Declaration on Fundamental Principles and Rights at Work declares that all Member States must eliminate all forms of forced or compulsory

1536. Berg et al., *supra* n. 23, at 40. For instance, also, cultural norms can force people to search for home-based work. This heavily affects women in certain countries. ILO, *supra* n. 613, at 154–155.

1537. *E.g.*, William T. Bielby & Denise D. Bielby, *Organizational Mediation of Project-Based Labor Markets: Talent Agencies and the Careers of Screenwriters*, 64 American Sociological Review 64, 80 n. 1 (1999); Xiangquan Zeng & Yuxue Cui, *Job Search, Labour Market Intermediaries and Employment Promotion: The Evidence from China*, 147 International Labour Review 280, 283 n. 2–3 (2008). Some raise question marks, observing that this potential might be limited. Jo Ingold & Danat Valizade, *Employers' Recruitment of Disadvantaged Groups: Exploring the Effect of Active Labour Market Programme Agencies as Labour Market Intermediaries*, 27 Human Resource Management Journal 530, 531 n. 4 (2017).

1538. Owen Pinnell & Jess Kelly, *Slave Markets Found on Instagram and Other Apps*, BBC (31 October 2019), https://www.bbc.com/news/technology-50228549.

1539. Tribunale di Milano: Decreto 9/2020, *Uber Italy SRL*, 27 May 2020; Elaine Allaby, *The Rise of Uber Eats Gang Masters is Tearing the Gig Economy Apart*, WIRED (15 February 2021), https://www.wired.co.uk/article/uber-eats-italy.

1540. Antonio Aloisi & Valerio De Stefano, *Uber Eats Facing Criminal Charges in Italy: Are We Managers or Corporals?*, il Mulino (5 June 2020), https://www.rivistailmulino.it/news/newsitem/index/Item/News:NEWS_ITEM:5256.

labour, i.e. "all work or service which is exacted from any person under the menace of any penalty and for which the said person has not offered himself voluntarily".[1541] Even if, contrary to these online slave markets, the situation of migrant workers at Uber Eats does not necessarily reach the threshold of forced or compulsory labour, the Committee of Experts has repeatedly stressed how migrant workers are particularly vulnerable to end up in compulsory labour.[1542] For this reason, since migrant labour is at risk of being exploited through these platforms,[1543] ILO constituents would do well to explore the dynamics between migrant labour and platform work, also in light of potential allegations of compulsory labour. In the case of such practices, strong sanctions are in order. For instance, Article 8 of Convention No. 181 stresses that "[a] Member shall, [...], adopt all necessary and appropriate measures, [...], to provide adequate protection for and prevent abuses of migrant workers recruited or placed in its territory by private employment agencies. These shall include laws or regulations which provide for penalties, including prohibition of those private employment agencies which engage in fraudulent practices and abuses".

Just like labour exploitation, child labour in the platform economy is another issue 501
that has not received the attention it deserves. News reports from, for instance, France and Brazil illustrate how minors use food-delivery platforms to perform work.[1544] Under Convention No. 181, the Member States must ensure that child labour is not used or supplied through platforms' private employment services.[1545] Because child labour is quite persistent in home-based work,[1546] Recommendation No. 184 also calls for specific programmes to eliminate child labour in home work.[1547] ILO constituents should evaluate whether the same is needed for crowdwork or any other type of platform work. Considering how child labour takes place on food-delivery platforms, it is also worthwhile highlighting §5 of the Domestic Workers Recommendation. It states that "Members should identify types of domestic work that, by their nature or the circumstances in which they are carried out, are likely to harm the health, safety or morals of children, and should also prohibit and eliminate such child labour". To that extent, although food delivery tends to be presented as a sporty and easy side-job, it is, in fact, a pretty dangerous occupation.[1548]

1541. Art. 2 Forced Labour Convention, 1930 (No. 29).

1542. ILO Committee of Experts on the Application of Conventions and Recommendations, *Eradication of Forced Labour* 20 (ILO 2007). *See also*, ILO Committee of Experts on the Application of Conventions and Recommendations, *supra* n. 398, at 111.

1543. Niels van Doorn, Fabian Ferrari & Mark Graham, *Migration and Migrant Labour in the Gig Economy: An Intervention*, SSRN (8 June 2020), https://papers.ssrn.com/sol3/papers.cfm?abstract_id=3622589.

1544. Marie Piquemal & Gurvan Kristanadjaja, *Plateformes de Livraison: Pour les Mineurs, une Course à l'Argent Facile*, Libération (3 May 2019), https://www.liberation.fr/france/2019/05/03/plateformes-de-livraison-pour-les-mineurs-une-course-a-l-argent-facile_1724849/; Edward Ongweso Jr, *Delivery Apps Are Using Child Labor In Brazil*, VICE (10 February 2021), https://www.vice.com/en/article/z3v5xx/delivery-apps-are-using-child-labor-in-brazil.

1545. Art. 9 Private Employment Agencies Convention, 1997 (No. 181).

1546. ILO, *supra* n. 613, at 162–163.

1547. Para. 29 Home Work Recommendation, 1996 (No. 184).

1548. "About 10 per cent of workers engaged in the app-based taxi sector and 21 per cent in the app-based delivery sector reported having experienced a work-related injury or an accident.

502 **The Centenary Declaration** – The Centenary Declaration has emphasised certain protective principles in addition to the Fundamental Principles and Rights at Work from the 1998 Declaration. Most importantly, safe and healthy working conditions have been declared fundamental to decent work (*supra* no. 154), and even if the original Universal Labour Guarantee was mostly dismantled (*supra* no. 155), the Declaration still states that "[a]ll workers should enjoy adequate protection in accordance with the Decent Work Agenda, taking into account: (i) respect for their fundamental rights; (ii) an adequate minimum wage, statutory or negotiated; (iii) maximum limits on working time; and (iv) safety and health at work".[1549] Given this recent emphasis, it seems likely for an instrument on decent work in the platform economy to deal with these forms of protection.

503 **(I) Fundamental rights** – The reference to "fundamental rights" seems to predominantly refer to the content of the 1998 Declaration; however, if wanted, it could also be interpreted more broadly. After all, as mentioned earlier (*supra* no. 125), for instance, the United Nations' Guiding Principles on Business and Human Rights single out the International Bill of Human Rights and 1998 Declaration as the two documents that present the internationally recognised human rights that all businesses, including platform operators, need to respect at all costs. As such, considering the critique that the selection of fundamental rights in the 1998 Declaration is arbitrary (*supra* nos. 127–128), why not cross-reference back to the UN's human rights instruments? Looking at Convention No. 189, for example, it calls on the Member States to "take measures to ensure the effective promotion and protection of the human rights of all domestic workers, as set out in this Convention".[1550] When drafting such a provision, it would not be out of place to refer to parts of the International Bill of Human Rights that are of particular relevance to the standard-setting topic at hand. In the case of platform work, one could, for example, think of everyone's right to "[r]est, leisure and reasonable limitation of working hours", and everyone's right to remuneration that provides "[a] decent living for themselves and their families".[1551]

504 **(II) Limitation of working hours** – Most people perceive platform work as intermittent work; hence, limits on maximum working hours are redundant. However, in reality, when the time spent searching for gigs is added to the time spent executing those gigs, even crowdworkers can have long working hours,[1552] engaging, for instance, in overwork and night work (*supra* no. 344).[1553] Moreover, contrary to expectation, ILO research finds that the average working hours for platform workers in the taxi and delivery sectors are 65 and 59 hours per week, respectively. The weekly average would peak at 82 hours for app-based taxi drivers in India and 63 hours for app-based delivery in Kenya and Lebanon.[1554] App-based food delivery also seems to be a full-time

These proportions were high in Morocco (34 per cent of app-based taxi drivers), and Mexico (47 per cent of app-based delivery workers)". ILO, *supra* n. 25, at 172.

1549. Para. III.B. ILO Centenary Declaration for the Future of Work, 21 June 2019.
1550. Art. 3 Domestic Workers Convention, 2011 (No. 189).
1551. Art. 7 International Covenant on Economic, Social and Cultural Rights, 16 December 1966.
1552. Berg et al., *supra* n. 23, at 67.
1553. Graham et al., *supra* n. 1116, at 8; Schörpf, Flecker, Schönauer & Eichmann, *supra* n. 281, at 51–52.
1554. ILO, *supra* n. 25, at 168.

occupation in, for instance, Argentina, where workers would perform 8.21 hours a day on average.[1555] Similarly, Zhou suggests that 49.5 per cent of "food-delivery drivers" work more than ten hours a day in China.[1556] Although such high levels of working hours are rare in the EU and places such as Australia,[1557] when the combination of platform work with other jobs is taken into consideration, even European platform workers "tend to have not only longer overall work schedules (including regular and platform work), but also more frequently atypical or unsocial working times".[1558] In other words, contrary to what some might expect, ILO constituents have good reasons to address excessive working hours in the platform economy. What should not be overlooked in this regard are the many hours of unpaid "working time" spent searching for work and remaining standby (*supra* nos. 469–471). Should this count as working time for the calculation of maximum hours and other entitlements?[1559]

(III) An adequate minimum wage – As mentioned most notably in the Chapter on home work, many digital labour platforms use financial incentives to increase and decrease remuneration, trying to regulate labour supply (*supra* no. 340). This takes place in local app-based platform work, such as food delivery.[1560] Kashyap and Bhatia also mention the example of Indian Uber and Ola drivers, who receive cash-based incentives if they meet a certain number of completed trips every day, including a threshold of peak-hour bookings. Due to such incentive structures, in the case of low base rates, "[m]ost drivers are 'pushed' to work round the clock to meet targets and be eligible for weekly incentives".[1561] **505**

Because of such practices, it is worth highlighting the principle of §15 of the Home Work Recommendation, 1996 (No. 184). Namely, a homeworker's piece rates should be comparable to the remuneration of a worker in another enterprise in the branch of activity and region concerned. ILO constituents could generalise this principle, allowing platforms some space to use financial incentives but, simultaneously, limiting the degree to which platform operators can toy with their piece rates due to a comparability requirement. This minimum requirement might be highly significant, considering the disparity between platform workers' earnings and people **506**

1555. Mourelo, *supra* n. 531, at 71.
1556. Zhou, *supra* n. 37, at 23.
1557. *See e.g.*, in Australia, McDonald et al., *supra* n. 36, at 56.
1558. Urzì Brancati, Pesole & Férnandéz-Macías, *supra* n. 35, at 44.
1559. The Home Work Recommendation, for example, stipulates that homeworkers should receive compensation for: "(b) time spent in maintaining machinery and equipment, changing tools, sorting, unpacking and packing, and other such operations". The time spent preparing for the actual work was meant to be remunerated. Para. 16 Home Work Recommendation, 1996 (No. 184).
1560. "For instance, incentives could constitute as much as 40–50 percent of earnings on some of the food delivery platforms; and a lower but still significant percentage for drivers of cabs (about 20 percent, based on interview data)". Fairwork, *supra* n. 1504, at 19.
1561. Rina Kashyap & Anjali Bhatia, *Taxi Drivers and Taxidars: A Case Study of Uber and Ola in Delhi*, 34 Journal of Developing Societies 169, 182–183 n. 2 (2018). Unlike in countries such as India, many people in the Global North consider Uber a side-job instead of a primary occupation. Nevertheless, even in that case, workers tend to work when remuneration is high, for instance, during lucrative bar hours. Brenton J. Malin & Curry Chandler, *Free to Work Anxiously: Splintering Precarity Among Drivers for Uber and Lyft*, 10 Communication, Culture & Critique 382, 391–392 n. 2 (2017).

performing similar "regular" employment activities. Many platform workers seem to be earning significantly less than their counterparts in the "traditional" labour market.[1562] This illustrates the need for potential solutions. As the ILO Office has remarked, countries such as the Philippines and the United Kingdom have concrete guidelines on calculating fair and equitable piece rates for industrial homeworkers. These experiences may help design time and motion studies that can be carried out in the platform economy to ensure piece rates genuinely add up to a minimum or living wage, taking into account maximum working hours and reasonable work intensity.[1563] On a side note, for these minimum rates to be established beyond the realm of legally employed platform workers, covering, for instance, crowdworkers, the tension with competition law would have to be resolved.[1564]

507 **(IV) Safety and health at work** – Since safe and healthy working conditions are fundamental to decent work, one would expect this to take centre stage during the discussions on decent work in the platform economy. The international labour standards analysed in this dissertation have some relevant contributions to make in this area (also see *supra* nos. 467–468). For example, the duty of private employment agencies to not knowingly recruit, place or employ workers for jobs involving "unacceptable hazards or risks" could be extended across the platform economy.[1565] Furthermore, protecting crowdworkers' safety and health at work seems challenging at first. However, since ILO constituents wanted to achieve this for homeworkers,[1566] one would expect the same to happen for crowdworkers. To this end, employers should, *inter alia*, inform homeworkers about any hazards that are known or ought to be known to the employer and provide the necessary personal protective equipment.[1567] A homeworker should also be able to refuse work "which he or she has reasonable justification to believe presents an imminent and serious danger to his or her safety or health" without suffering any undue consequences.[1568] As a result, if these guidelines were transposed to the platform economy, crowdworkers might

1562. ILO, *supra* n. 25, at 154–155 and 159.

1563. "A time and motion study is a 'work measurement system designed to determine the standard time for a qualified (average) worker or machine to complete a specified job at a defined level of performance'. It is conducted 'to determine whether the piece rate/production standards (quota) prescribed by the employers for their employees are fair and reasonable'". ILO, *supra* n. 613, at 206 and 256–257.

1564. *See, e.g.*, Nicola Countouris, Valerio De Stefano & Ioannis Lianos, *The EU, Competition and Workers' Rights* (Centre for Law, Economics and Society, UCL 2021). For a concrete example: Danish Competition and Consumer Authority, *Commitment Decision on the Use of a Minimum Hourly Fee*, Konkurrence- og Forbrugerstyrelsen (26 August 2020), https://www.en.kfst.dk/nyheder/kfst/english/decisions/20200826-commitment-decision-on-the-use-of-a-minimum-hourly-fee-hilfr/.

1565. Para. 8 Private Employment Agencies Recommendation, 1997 (No. 188).

1566. "National laws and regulations on safety and health at work shall apply to home work, taking account of its special characteristics, and shall establish conditions under which certain types of work and the use of certain substances may be prohibited in home work for reasons of safety and health". Art. 7 Home Work Convention, 1996 (No. 177).

1567. Para. 21 Home Work Recommendation, 1996 (No. 184).

1568. Para. 22 *Ibid.*

be able to avoid working with violent and distressing content, such as depictions of animal abuse.[1569]

Much will depend in this area on the contribution made by the individual platform operators. The intermediary can, for example, establish a mechanism with symbols that allow users to indicate what dangers specific gigs represent, or it can even have its own staff audit the gigs to verify if they accurately signal the danger. Similarly, it is much more sensible to force the platform operator to hand out protective equipment, such as an ergonomic mouse, once a crowdworker reaches a specific milestone than to impose that duty upon the individual platform user. The platform operators could, in turn, charge the enterprises that regularly rely on their services to compensate for the platform's investments in protective equipment. Indeed, as mentioned before (*supra* nos. 478–481), ILO constituents should thoroughly reflect on the entity on which these and other employer responsibilities rest. 508

In this respect, what must also be borne in mind is how various protections interrelate. Take the example of OSH, maximum working hours, and minimum piece rates. The ILO has frequently recalled that "a principal aim of establishing laws on working time is to combat the negative effects of long working hours on the mental and physical health of workers, reduce the high number of industrial accidents and standardize the practices of employers regarding working time".[1570] Working time regulation, in other words, protects workers' health and limits the risk of accidents,[1571] which is also relevant in the platform economy.[1572] From this perspective, platform operators are the entity capable of accurately monitoring working time;[1573] if required, they could even design their platform to award rest breaks when needed.[1574] Demanding individual users to keep tabs on working time limitations would seem far less effective than attributing that responsibility to a platform operator. Furthermore, since platform workers are often remunerated using piece rates (also see *supra* nos. 339–340), their work intensity and working hours will largely depend on how the piece-rate system operates. When platform workers have nothing to say about their low piece rates, which seems to happen a lot,[1575] they can do little but increase work intensity or work 509

1569. Berg et al., *supra* n. 23, at 86–87. *See also*, Dhruv Mehrotra, *Horror Stories From Inside Amazon's Mechanical Turk*, GIZMODO (28 January 2020), https://gizmodo.com/horror-stories-from-inside-amazons-mechanical-turk-1840878041.

1570. ILO Committee of Experts on the Application of Conventions and Recommendations, *Ensuring Decent Working Time for the Future* 289 (ILO 2018).

1571. This is acknowledged, for example, in Art. 6 Directive No. 2003/88/EC of the European Parliament and of the Council of 4 November 2003 concerning certain aspects of the organisation of working time, OJ L 299, 18 November 2003.

1572. ILO, *supra* n. 25, at 171.

1573. Veena Dubal, *Digital Piecework*, 67 Dissent 37, 40 n. 4 (2020).

1574. The Home Work Recommendation, for example, stipulates that "[a] deadline to complete a work assignment should not deprive a homeworker of the possibility to have daily and weekly rest comparable to that enjoyed by other workers". Para. 23 Home Work Recommendation, 1996 (No. 184)

1575. Most respondents in France "working via mobile applications reported that they rarely had a say in determining their rates of pay". IPSOS, *supra* n. 292.

more hours.[1576] High work intensity has its consequences for health and safety.[1577] It also makes little sense to impose a limit of 48-hours a week without ensuring the worker can reasonably earn an adequate minimum or living wage within that timeframe. Such a decision would ultimately erode the limitation on working hours. Therefore, one could argue that when platform workers are remunerated by the piece, limits on maximum working time and health and safety protections, more broadly, might remain somewhat elusive unless the platforms' piece rates adhere to minimum standards.[1578] Food-delivery platforms most appallingly illustrate this. Some of their piece-rate systems entice couriers to work excessive hours and break traffic rules.[1579] As demonstrated by this interaction between OSH, maximum working hours and minimum piece rates, ILO constituents should reflect on how various protections interrelate and can undercut or amplify one another in the platform economy.

SUBCHAPTER 2. THE STRATEGIC OBJECTIVES: EMPLOYMENT, SOCIAL PROTECTION, SOCIAL DIALOGUE

510 **Four strategic objectives** – Decent work encompasses four strategic objectives: (i) respecting, promoting and realizing the fundamental principles and rights at work; (ii) promoting employment; (iii) developing and enhancing measures of social protection; and, (iv) promoting social dialogue and tripartism (*supra* nos. 130 and 135).[1580] What is covered in the previous Subchapter mainly relates to the first strategic objective. Additionally, maximum working hours, minimum wages and safety and health have been recognised as particularly important without, however, just yet reaching the status of an ILO fundamental principle and right.[1581] By only dealing with the protections mentioned in the previous Subchapter, ILO constituents would hardly touch upon any of the three other strategic objectives. That would seem unsatisfactory. For an instrument to pursue decent work in the platform economy, ILO constituents also have to cover platform work's interaction with employment, social protection and social dialogue in general. The following paragraphs indicate what can be expected in that regard, based on the content of the instruments analysed in Part III and observations made in previous chapters.

1576. Graham et al., *supra* n. 1116, at 8.
1577. Eurofound, *Sixth European Working Conditions Survey – Overview report (2017 update)* 51 (Publications Office of the European Union 2017).
1578. Research is still scarce. Nevertheless, in particular, low-wage workers might suffer from piece rates. *See*, most notably, M. E. Davis & E. Hoyt, *A Longitudinal Study of Piece Rate and Health: Evidence and Implications for Workers in the US Gig Economy*, 180 Public Health 1, 5 (2020).
1579. X, *Delivery Workers, Trapped in the System*, Chuang (12 November 2020), https://chuangcn.org/2020/11/delivery-renwu-translation/; Rita Liao, *Viral Article Puts the Brakes on China's Food Delivery Frenzy*, TechCrunch (9 September 2020), https://techcrunch.com/2020/09/08/viral-article-puts-brakes-on-chinas-food-delivery-frenzy/.
1580. Para. I.A. ILO Declaration on Social Justice for a Fair Globalization, 10 June 2008.
1581. Discussions about making safe and healthy working conditions a fifth category of fundamental principles and rights at work are ongoing. ILO Governing Body, *Follow-up to the Resolution on the ILO Centenary Declaration for the Future of Work: Proposals for Including Safe and Healthy Working Conditions in the ILO's Framework of Fundamental Principles and Rights at Work*, GB.341/INS/6 (ILO 2021).

Promoting employment – The strategic objective of employment wants individuals to "develop and update the necessary capacities and skills they need to enable them to be productively occupied for their personal fulfilment and the common well-being"; enterprises should "enable growth and the generation of greater employment and income opportunities and prospects for all".[1582] When thinking of platform work, question marks can be raised about platform operators' contribution to these objectives. Notwithstanding notable exceptions, such as competitive programming platforms and some other forms of crowdwork,[1583] there is little evidence that platform work boosts workers' employability.[1584] For instance, Ravenelle suggests that some forms of platform work may hardly improve future employment opportunities. On the contrary, it might even negatively affect workers' future potential.[1585] Many platforms are underpinned by the idea that labour is a commodity, treating these workers as fungible service providers instead of individuals with their own goals and career prospects (*supra* nos. 241–243). By and large, platform operators seem unwilling to design their systems to exert the positive role intermediaries can have on workers' employment situation (for example, *supra* no. 77). 511

To counteract these trends and ensure that platforms benefit jobseekers' employability, ILO constituents might want to, among other things, pay attention to mechanisms that prevent workers from developing their careers through platforms. For instance, platform workers seem to fear mentioning their experience in platform work because it is negatively perceived (*supra* no. 416). In that case, a society-wide change in mentality may be needed. The Home Work Recommendation, for example, instructs each Member to promote recognition of home work as valid work experience.[1586] Something similar might be required for platform workers. Furthermore, one can also think of the barriers that prevent workers from transitioning to a direct employment relationship with the user enterprise.[1587] Platforms' prohibitions to disintermediate can be scrutinised, as well as workers' inability to communicate with users or receive valuable feedback (*supra* nos. 89–91). The instruments on private employment agencies already explicitly mention that agencies of type 1(1)(b) should not constrain workers' labour mobility. This might likewise be appropriate in the platform economy (*supra* no. 475). Additionally, as mentioned elsewhere (*supra* no. 341), when platform workers are new on the platform and, therefore, have unimpressive ratings and statistics, they tend to put their prices low to find gigs, potentially affecting established platform workers' income. A range of positive 512

1582. Para. I.A. ILO Declaration on Social Justice for a Fair Globalization, 10 June 2008.
1583. Barnes, Green & de Hoyos, *supra* n. 273, at 16–31; Ayomikun Idowu & Amany Elbanna, *Digital Platforms of Work and the Crafting of Career Path: The Crowdworkers' Perspective*, Information Systems Frontiers (2020); ILO, *supra* n. 25, at 185.
1584. Because some forms of platform work are characterised by low-skilled tasks with limited training, "it is questionable whether it fosters workers' employability by acting as a stepping stone to more traditional forms of employment". Eurofound, *supra* n. 4, at 60.
1585. Ravenelle, *supra* n. 1382.
1586. Para. 29 Home Work Recommendation, 1996 (No. 184).
1587. Recommendation No. 188 wants Member States to ensure that private employment agencies of type 1(1)(b) do not restrict the labour mobility of agency workers. This guideline might have to be extended beyond platform operators that correspond to an agency of type 1(1)(b). Para. 15 Private Employment Agencies Recommendation, 1997 (No. 188).

measures could be taken, such as establishing portable reputation portfolios, to overcome entry barriers to platforms.[1588] That might have benefits for the dynamics of the marketplace as a whole.

513 Besides these measures to boost people's job and career opportunities on platforms, it is just as crucial for platform workers, especially in low-skilled work, to improve their overall employment odds through training opportunities. As things stand, employer-provided training options remain limited in the platform economy.[1589] Hence, some researchers recommend policymakers "to incentivise platforms to optimise for skill-augmentation of workers, so that the worker population can gradually upskill and become capable of taking on new types of tasks requiring those skills".[1590] Furthermore, alternative training opportunities are also recommendable. A universal system of entitlements to training, such as the one proposed by the Global Commission, could significantly benefit full-time platform workers in low-skilled work with little opportunities to move on from that job.[1591] Current ILS already point out that, for example, temporary agency workers and homeworkers must have access to training.[1592] The Home Work Recommendation calls on the Member States to "provide training to improve homeworkers' skills (including non-traditional skills, leadership and negotiating skills), productivity, employment opportunities and income-earning capacity",[1593] whilst the Domestic Workers Recommendation asks Members to "encourage the continuing development of the competencies and qualifications of domestic workers, including literacy training as appropriate, in order to enhance their professional development and employment opportunities".[1594] ILO constituents may want to consider stressing the need to ensure that platform workers also have adequate access to training.

514 **Social protection** – Social protection encompasses both labour and social security protection.[1595] This strategic objective covers a lot of ground, of course. To that extent, it can be helpful to distinguish between labour and social protections that, from the ILO's point of view, ought to apply to everyone, and protections associated with employees or other specific categories of workers. The Centenary Declaration provides some indications about protections that should apply to every (platform) worker. Beyond the fundamental principles and rights at work, which are universal

1588. Skill tests and certifications could allow workers to compensate for their lack of ratings and reviews. Portable reputation portfolios could increase mobility across platforms and employers. Cedefop, *Developing and Matching Skills in the Online Platform Economy: Findings on New Forms of Digital Work and Learning from Cedefop's CrowdLearn Study* 60–65 (Publications Office of the European Union 2020). *See also*, Aloisi, De Stefano & Silberman, *supra* n. 280.

1589. *E.g.* Kilhoffer et al., *supra* n. 33, at 80; European Commission, *First Phase Consultation of Social Partners under Article 154 TFEU on Possible Action Addressing the Challenges Related to Working Conditions in Platform Work* 18–19 (European Union 2021).

1590. Cedefop, *Skill Development in the Platform Economy: Comparing Microwork and Online Freelancing* 12 (Publications Office of the European Union 2021).

1591. Global Commission on the Future of Work, *supra* n. 406, at 31.

1592. Art. 4 Home Work Convention, 1996 (No. 177); Art. 11 Private Employment Agencies Convention, 1997 (No. 181).

1593. Para. 29 Home Work Recommendation, 1996 (No. 184).

1594. Para. 25 Domestic Workers Recommendation, 2011 (No. 201).

1595. Para. I.A. ILO Declaration on Social Justice for a Fair Globalization, 10 June 2008.

(*supra* no. 127), ILO policy must promote the chances of all (platform) workers to acquire skills, competencies and qualifications.[1596] Member States are also asked to develop universal access to comprehensive and sustainable social protection (for example, *supra* nos. 463–465),[1597] and grant "adequate protection" to all (platform) workers, taking into account the fundamental components of decent work mentioned in Subchapter 1 (e.g. maximum working time, *supra* nos. 494–509).[1598] Based on all these leads, even genuine self-employed platform workers can, therefore, expect to receive some protections. Due to the vague language, however, it is unclear how long this list should be. ILO constituents might want to ask themselves whether self-employed platform workers should, for example, be protected against fee-charging and excessive data capturing (*supra* nos. 455–460). Indeed, based on Convention No. 181, it would make sense to protect all platform workers from such abusive and unethical practices, as well as unjustifiable constraints on labour mobility (*supra* no. 475).[1599] An instrument on platform work gives ILO constituents a real opportunity to extend such protections into the sphere of self-employment.

Furthermore, as Chapter 2 indicated (*supra* nos. 484–488), chances are that an instru- **515**
ment on platform work will have to account for the diversity of legal arrangements used in the platform economy. In crowdwork, for example, there may be room for platform workers that are neither regular employees nor genuinely self-employed but situated somewhere in between (i.e. homeworkers). The Home Work Convention mentions that for homeworkers, to the extent possible, the goal is to promote equality of treatment between homeworkers and other wage earners. The instrument highlights that equality of treatment shall be promoted, in particular, with regard to key areas such as: (a) collective rights, (b) non-discrimination, (c) occupational safety and health, (d) remuneration, (e) statutory social security protection, (f) access to training, (g) minimum age, and (h) maternity protection.[1600] The ILO constituents may want to re-evaluate if these areas of protection are, indeed, the ones that should be extended to platform workers who are not legal employees under domestic law but in another kind of dependent position.

It is also worth comparing this list from the Home Work Convention to the one **516**
found in the Private Employment Agencies Convention. Under the latter, temporary agency workers are legally employed and apparently entitled to more safeguards. Article 11 of Convention No. 181 also mentions the need to protect agency workers' working time and "other working conditions". Temporary agency workers should, furthermore, be offered compensation in case of occupational accidents or diseases, and in case of an employer's insolvency. Convention No. 181 also specifies that these workers are entitled to maternity benefits as well as parental protection and

1596. Para. II.A.(iii) ILO Centenary Declaration for the Future of Work, 21 June 2019.

1597. The Social Justice Declaration points out that the Decent Work Agenda aims for "the extension of social security to all, including measures to provide basic income to all in need of such protection, and adapting its scope and coverage to meet the new needs and uncertainties generated by the rapidity of technological, societal, demographic and economic changes". Para. I.A.(ii) ILO Declaration on Social Justice for a Fair Globalization, 10 June 2008.

1598. Paragraphs III.A and III.B ILO Centenary Declaration for the Future of Work, 21 June 2019.

1599. Para. 4 Private Employment Agencies Recommendation, 1997 (No. 188).

1600. Art. 4 Home Work Convention, 1996 (No. 177).

benefits.[1601] These differences between the list in Convention No. 177 and No. 181 beg the question of whether ILO constituents should even adopt a concrete position about what the key areas of protection for platform workers are. Given the various ways in which platform workers could be legally classified under domestic law and the many factual differences between platform workers, it would not seem easy to come up with one single list. Besides, such a list does not efficiently address some of the main complaints of platform workers, such as platforms' suboptimal distribution of work and the unpredictability of work, hence the instability of platform workers' income.[1602]

517 For such reasons, one could opt for a design more similar to that of the Domestic Workers Convention. The Convention does not advance any clear cut list. Instead, each article more or less addresses one element of protection that was considered particularly important for domestic workers. Such a design in which each article deals with a key area of protection allows the differences between various types of workers to be accentuated. For example, §18 in the Domestic Workers Recommendation stresses that in the event of dismissal at the employer's initiative, live-in domestic workers should be given a reasonable period of notice and time off to search for employment and accommodation. The same is not the case for external domestic workers, which can be explained by the fact that live-in domestic workers lose both their jobs and accommodation. Making these kinds of distinctions may also be relevant in the platform economy.

518 Indeed, in the case of non-discrimination, privacy or transparency requirements,[1603] there may be little reason to differentiate between self-employed and employed platform workers.[1604] In contrast, when it comes to dismissal, wage protection or working hours, various degrees of protection could apply depending on the workers' legal classification and the type of platform work. It is something upon which ILO constituents will have to reflect. Consider the example of wage protection. Although the associated ILO instruments are, in principle, only applicable to people earning wages by virtue of a contract of employment,[1605] as remarked by the ILO Committee of Experts:

> "Article 1 of the [Protection of Wages Convention] is not intended to establish a binding 'model' definition of the term 'wages', but to ensure that the real

1601. Art. 11 Private Employment Agencies Convention, 1997 (No. 181).

1602. Huws, Spencer, Syrdal & Holts, *supra* n. 1482, at 42–43.

1603. Many platform workers seem uncertain about how platforms' algorithmic systems work. *See*, IPSOS, *supra* n. 292. Self-employed platform workers have a real interest in knowing how to grow their business on the platform; transparency about how the platform functions could benefit both self-employed and employed workers.

1604. Recall the initial Universal Labour Guarantee, which did not make it to the Centenary Declaration (*supra* no. 155). It declared that: "All workers, regardless of their employment status or contractual arrangements, should be guaranteed: (i) respect for their fundamental rights; (ii) an adequate living wage; (iii) limits on maximum working hours; (iv) safety and health at work; (v) privacy and personal data protection; and (vi) scope for achieving better work–life balance, by having greater influence over their working time, in ways that respect enterprise needs and promote productive efficiency and shared benefits". ILO, *supra* n. 464, at 7.

1605. Arts. 1 and 2 Protection of Wages Convention, 1949 (No. 95).

earnings of workers, however termed or reckoned, are fully protected under national laws in respect of the matters dealt with in Articles 3 to 15 of the Convention. As recent experience has shown, especially with regard to the 'desalarization' policies practised in certain countries, the obligations deriving from the Convention with respect to the protection of workers' wages cannot be bypassed by mere terminological subterfuges, but require the extended and bona fide coverage by national legislation of labour remuneration whatever form it takes".[1606]

Along those lines, it needs to be repeated that homeworkers do not necessarily have an employment contract (*supra* nos. 313–314). At the same time, notwithstanding homeworkers' lack of "wages", the Home Work Recommendation still intends to limit the employers' discretion to make deductions from the homeworkers' remuneration.[1607] In view of this example, one could legitimately question the appropriateness of limiting protection against unjustified deductions to legally employed platform workers. In a similar vein, if the platform operator or user decides not to pay the worker without giving a reasonable justification,[1608] should that worker's employment status really matter?[1609] 519

Social dialogue and tripartism – Part II of this dissertation highlighted the crucial importance of social dialogue and tripartism within the ILO (*supra* nos. 108–111).[1610] Consequently, since social partners are so involved in the organisation itself, it is not surprising that ILS likewise confer a significant role to social partners. According to the instruments on private employment agencies, for example, the most representative organisations of employers and workers need to be consulted before making certain decisions, such as authorising agencies to charge fees to workers.[1611] Similarly, in the instruments on home work, the most representative organisations need to be consulted when designing the national policy on home work.[1612] Concerning domestic workers, the representative organisations should be consulted when searching for ways to, for instance, apply social security and OSH protections.[1613] Based on these precedents, it is safe to assume a future ILO instrument on platform work would also provide social partners with a vital role.[1614] 520

1606. ILO Committee of Experts on the Application of Conventions and Recommendations, *Protection of Wages: Standards and Safeguards Relating to the Payment of Labour Remuneration* 33 (ILO 2003).
1607. Para. 7 and 17 Home Work Recommendation, 1996 (No. 184).
1608. This happens quite often in crowdwork. *See, e.g.*, Aleksynska, Bastrakova & Kharchenko, *supra* n. 78, at 28–29.
1609. Some might argue that irrespective of employment status, "[w]orkers should have a right to contest non-payment". Berg et al., *supra* n. 23, at 107.
1610. As the ILO Centenary Declaration reminds us, social dialogue "provides an essential foundation of all ILO action". Para. II.B. ILO Centenary Declaration for the Future of Work, 21 June 2019.
1611. Art. 7 Private Employment Agencies Convention, 1997 (No. 181).
1612. Art. 3 Home Work Convention, 1996 (No. 177).
1613. Art. 13 and 14 Domestic Workers Convention, 2011 (No. 189).
1614. This is also the case in light of the more recent Declarations. The Centenary Declaration emphasises, for example, that effective workplace cooperation is a tool to ensure safe and productive workplaces. Para. II.C. ILO Centenary Declaration for the Future of Work, 21 June 2019.

521 To that extent, although most of these instruments stress the contribution of representative organisations very explicitly, we should not forget how the ILO is centred on tripartism, relying first and foremost on governments to design the economy in support of social justice (*supra* nos. 112–115). This mindset is clearly present in the instruments on private employment agencies, for instance. These agencies were granted legitimacy in return for worker protection (*supra* no. 289); the agencies did not receive a free pass. For example, pursuant to Article 13 of Convention No. 181, "[a] Member shall, in accordance with national law and practice and after consulting the most representative organizations of employers and workers, formulate, establish and periodically review conditions to promote cooperation between the public employment service and private employment agencies". Private agencies are meant to contribute to broader employment policies. Any future instrument on platform work will likely have to address similar questions: what is expected from platform operators, and how can their contribution to "decent work" and "full, productive and freely chosen employment" be secured?[1615] The public authorities are the main actor here, even if social partners are involved along the way. When drafting an instrument on platform work, ILO constituents will have to reflect on how representative organisations can make a valuable contribution to the Member State's efforts to reach the instrument's overall goals.

522 This can, for example, be illustrated in the area of enforcement. Paragraph 28 of the Home Work Recommendation mentions that the competent authority should establish dispute resolution mechanisms between homeworkers and their employers or intermediaries. ILO constituents might ask themselves, should social partners be involved in such alternative dispute resolution mechanisms? In Germany, for example, the German Ombudsman Office for Crowdworkers is made up of worker and platform representatives. The body seems to have successfully resolved platform-work-related issues through ADR,[1616] indicating that social partners can play a constructive role in this type of setup. Additionally, on a more conflictual note, platform workers could also be enabled to file complaints at the local authorities. The Private Employment Agencies Convention, for example, calls for adequate machinery to investigate complaints, alleged abuses and fraudulent practices related to platforms' private employment services.[1617] Similarly, the Domestic Workers Convention clarifies that domestic workers shall have access to an effective and accessible complaint mechanism,[1618] which could serve, in particular, to report abuse, harassment, and violence.[1619] ICT technology makes it relatively easy to file such complaints. Perhaps ILO constituents might want to ensure that trade unions have also access to these formal complaint proceedings.

1615. The ILO must direct its efforts to: "ensuring that diverse forms of work arrangements, production and business models, including in domestic and global supply chains, leverage opportunities for social and economic progress, provide for decent work and are conducive to full, productive and freely chosen employment". Para. II.A.(xii) ILO Centenary Declaration for the Future of Work, 21 June 2019.

1616. Haipeter, Owczarek, Faioli & Iudicone eds., *supra* n. 625, 23.

1617. Art. 10 Private Employment Agencies Convention, 1997 (No. 181).

1618. Art. 17 Domestic Workers Convention, 2011 (No. 189).

1619. Para. 7 Domestic Workers Recommendation, 2011 (No. 201).

Besides enforcement mechanisms that rely on the initiative of platform workers and their representatives, such as ADR and official complaints, ILO constituents could also opt for a system of licensing or certification in which the most representative organisations are involved.[1620] Since this is part of the enforcement framework for private employment agencies, we might ask ourselves whether this would also be appropriate in the platform economy. While licensing requires prior authorisation before engaging in business, which has become problematic in, for instance, Europe (*supra* no. 240), certification requires an already operational platform to register with the governmental authorities.[1621] The involvement of representative organisations in these proceedings is appropriate, amongst other reasons, because social partners can be expected to notice when a new platform starts its operations and refuses to seek certification. As a replacement for licensing or certification, Article 3 of the Private Employment Agencies Convention also offers the possibility of administering alternative regulatory systems, such as a code of conduct. The Committee of Experts claims these alternatives should be "properly and permanently enforced".[1622] Again, social partners can play a valuable role in properly and permanently enforcing codes of conduct because their members experience how a platform operates in practice, not just on paper. Lastly, the Centenary Declaration stipulates that the ILO must try to strengthen labour administration and inspection.[1623] That in itself could, indeed, be helpful given the significant role labour inspectorates have played in upholding labour protections in the platform economy so far.[1624] What should not be forgotten in this respect, however, is how trade unions have likewise lodged many court proceedings calling platform operators to account. Unions have not refrained from spending their resources on lengthy court battles.[1625] As such, they can form a valuable addition to labour inspectorates that might not always prioritise labour issues in the platform economy. 523

1620. Art. 3 Private Employment Agencies Convention, 1997 (No. 181).
1621. ILO Committee of Experts on the Application of Conventions and Recommendations, *supra* n. 815, at 62.
1622. *Ibid.*, 63.
1623. Para. II.A.(xi) ILO Centenary Declaration for the Future of Work, 21 June 2019.
1624. De Stefano, Durri, Stylogiannis & Wouters, *supra* n. 13, at 26–27. For a concrete example, *see* Leonie Cater, *Italy Demands €733M in Fines From Food Delivery Platforms*, POLITICO (25 February 2021), at https://www.politico.eu/article/italy-demands-733-million-euros-in-fines-from-food-delivery-platforms/.
1625. Johnston & Land-Kazlauskas, *supra* n. 291, at 5–6.

Chapter 4. Conclusion to Part IV

Sufficiently responsive? – The Fourth Part of this dissertation indicated that Convention No. 177, No. 181 and No. 189 are not particularly responsive to digital labour platforms. Although all three of these instruments apply to parts of the platform economy, the guidelines in these instruments seem to hardly influence the debate. This is not necessarily because of the Conventions' content. Many of the guidelines seem relevant (*supra* nos. 455–472); however, they nevertheless fail to connect to the issue. Since this is the case for three instruments that regulate phenomena that have much in common with platform work, one could expect this to be a broader issue. Indeed, the International Labour Code in general might struggle to regulate platform work effectively if none of these three instruments manages to have any real impact. Chapter 1 additionally argued that current ILS seem to insufficiently regulate specific issues that affect platform workers particularly hard (*supra* nos. 474–482). Therefore, even though multiple ILO instruments already apply to platform work, it seems reasonable to craft a new instrument. 524

Future standard-setting – What such a future instrument should look like is, of course, a very complex matter. This research suggests that a well-designed soft law instrument through the Governing Body might already accomplish quite a lot (*supra* no. 488). At the same time, a more solemn Convention or Recommendation adopted by the International Labour Conference naturally has more clout. In that case, however, experts and ILO constituents should be aware of the various regulatory pathways available to the organisation. Platform work has many links to existing instruments, providing the ILO with multiple angles to approach the regulation of platform work (*supra* nos. 484–492). 525

Regardless of the angle, Chapter 3 surveyed what could be expected from a future ILO instrument in light of the Decent Work Agenda and three instruments analysed in Part III. This way, one can get a partial idea of the ILO's role in regulating platform work. It is to be hoped that these considerations will provide some guidance for the discussions ahead, which, needless to say, will have to draw on the work of many more authors and stakeholders to design an effective response. 526

Summary of Findings and Conclusion

Part I. Labour market intermediaries and platform work – The main research question of this dissertation is: "Do current international labour standards sufficiently respond to digital labour platforms, taking into account the organisational structure of these platforms and the demands made by platform workers, and if not, what role can the International Labour Organization play in regulating digital labour platforms?" In responding to this question, the research first set out to discover what a digital labour platform is. As shown, the concept of digital labour platforms is descriptive. It points to a labour market phenomenon that has taken the legal community by storm. Yet, despite platform work's prominence in recent debates, concepts to describe it have received little thorough investigation. Most authors merely observe that platform work presupposes a form of intermediation or facilitation of interactions between different sides on a "platform", one side of which comprises workers. Such a rudimentary description seemed inadequate for this study. The general literature on platforms was, therefore, explored to come up with a more detailed understanding of what a DLP might be. A digital labour platform can, arguably, be described as a network that a platform operator algorithmically manages, intending to bring about interactions between workers and users. In light of this goal, what is, supposedly, typical for a DLP is the significant autonomy provided to workers and users to, in principle, self-determine the key terms of their interaction. 527

However, what is paradoxical in this respect is how, contrary to what might be expected following this description, many platform operators in the labour market attempt to boost their platforms' success by taking centralised control of the interactions on their platforms. On the flip side, the operator constrains the workers' and users' autonomy, for example, by predetermining the price of the service or issuing strict guidelines. These constraints lead to what has been called a "platform paradox". Platform operators preach freedom but, simultaneously, practice labour control at the aggregate level, tailoring the marketplace through incentives, and at the individual level, for instance, by sanctioning workers. What is more, the DLPs that receive the most attention from labour lawyers, unions and other stakeholders are precisely the ones that deviate most sharply from the archetype of a genuine platform, which is supposed to leave users with considerable autonomy. 528

529 Because of this description of pure or genuine labour platforms, as opposed to ambivalent platforms such as Uber, the First Part of the dissertation further explored the link between DLPs and other labour market intermediaries. The respective Chapters indicated many resemblances, suggesting that DLPs essentially fulfil the same role as LMIs. In that sense, when asked what DLPs do, it seems justified to answer that, in principle, they intermediate on the labour market. DLPs and LMIs aim to diminish transaction costs and establish networks between labour market participants. Both effectively shift risks among workers and user enterprises, which can be one of their selling points. The main difference between DLPs and LMIs seems to relate to the characteristics of the user base. LMIs connect jobseekers and workers to employers, either enterprises or households. Many DLPs practically do the same; however, some directly connect workers to end-market consumers, like car passengers. That feature of proper peer-to-peer interaction, which largely became possible due to ICT technology, might constitute the main difference between some DLPs and LMIs. On account of this, the group of DLPs that solely intermediates between workers and end-market consumers can probably not be seen as an LMI. Nonetheless, given the many labour platforms with a business or household in their user base, it is probably accurate to state that most DLPs are effectively LMIs. This finding is one reason justifying the selection of international labour standards in the Third Part of this dissertation.

530 **Part II. The ILO's normative framework** – Since the ILO's goal is to establish decent work in the platform economy, and the dissertation explores what role the ILO can play in this regard, a range of ILO policy documents on decent work itself were discussed. These policy documents provide the ILO with the "cognitive framework for its work".

531 Upon describing the ILO, the discussion, most notably, observed how the original ILO Constitution, including the Declaration of Philadelphia, remains the ILO's foundational text. Therefore, when answering the question: "what is the ILO's mandate?", our attention should principally go to the ILO Constitution. As noted by the Chairperson of the Committee on Strengthening the ILO's Capacity, the ILO Constitution still maps out the ILO's destination. The more contemporary ILO Declarations offer a compass to navigate these foundational texts; however, that does not change the fact that the ILO remains bound to ensure that "all human beings, irrespective of race, creed or sex, have the right to pursue both their material well-being and their spiritual development in conditions of freedom and dignity, of economic security and equal opportunity".[1626] Nowadays, this objective, as well as the other goals in the foundational texts, are embodied in the assertion that all workers are entitled to "decent work". To that extent, due to the ILO's universal mandate, platform workers have a legitimate expectation for the organisation to undertake action if it senses decent work deficits in the platform economy. Recent policy documents indicate that the ILO indeed acknowledges the issues that platform workers encounter, giving rise to a Meeting of Experts on decent work in the platform economy during the second quarter of 2022.

1626. Para. II.(a) ILO Declaration of Philadelphia, 10 May 1944.

Since the ILO intends to establish decent work in the platform economy, the question becomes what contribution can be expected from international labour standards, given their function at the ILO. As described, the International Labour Code can be perceived as a mechanism of fundamental importance to accomplish Member States' journey to social justice or decent work. It offers a guidebook, which the Member States are for the most part invited to follow, except to the extent to which it concerns Fundamental Rights and Principles at Work, in which case they are expected to comply. From this perspective, as far as the guidebook does not contain guidelines that are responsive to platform work, as this research contends, the suggestion would be to rewrite it. This research finds that, although many international labour standards apply to platform work, current ILS seem ill-suited to instruct the Member States on establishing decent platform work. Standard-setting action is justified. 532

Part III. The instruments on private employment agencies, home work and domestic work – Before explaining what standard-setting action could look like in Part IV, Part III first addressed the question of which existing ILS are highly relevant to the regulation of digital labour platforms. It noted in this respect how there are instruments that are applicable to all workers, regardless of their employment status. The Violence and Harassment Convention, for instance, is relevant for both self-employed and employed platform workers. On the other hand, since some platform workers are employees, all of the instruments applicable to employees also become relevant for legally employed platform workers. One can think of the Part-Time Work Convention, 1994 (No. 175), for example. Although there are, therefore, many ILS that deserve to be mentioned in future discussions on decent work in the platform economy, this research limited itself to three instruments in particular. It presented reasons why the Private Employment Agencies Convention, 1997 (No. 181), the Home Work Convention, 1996 (No. 177), and the Domestic Workers Convention, 2011 (No. 189), deserve special attention. 533

Before uncovering the purpose and scope of application of each of these three instruments, the dissertation subsequently answered the question: What rules govern ILO Conventions' interpretation? As it turns out, there are no authoritative concrete guidelines on how to interpret ILO Conventions. At the same time, it is apparent that the interpretation of ILO instruments is often conducted in a way that deviates from the VCLT's general rules of interpretation.[1627] The many reflections in this part of the dissertation on how the general rules of interpretation are applied in relation to ILO standards prove the validity of discussions at the ILO level on interpreting ILO instruments. The question of whether, for instance, clarifications of the ILO Committee of Experts in its general surveys "shall" or "should" be taken into account as contextual information is an intriguing one. However, given the sensitivity of 534

1627. For example, the so-called will of the Conference is given disproportionate attention by heavily relying on working documents. Also, due to the fundamental interconnectedness between all ILO instruments, which together set the course towards social justice, linguistic differences between these instruments may become relevant. Thirdly, the constitutional framework, as reinterpreted through the latest Declarations, may play a part, and, fourthly, the clarifications by the Committee of Experts are given a lot of credit in practice.

treaty interpretation for some ILO constituents – the word "interpretation" itself is taboo – the verdict should not be expected any time soon.

535 After discussing the rules of interpretation, the following question was answered: What is the purpose and scope of application of the instruments that are identified as highly relevant? The Private Employment Agencies Convention, 1997 (No. 181), was the first instrument to be covered. Convention No. 181 was put in context. It was meant to extend its predecessor's scope, the Revised Fee-Charging Employment Agencies Convention, which according to the Committee of Experts, already had a broad scope (e.g. applicable to labour contractors). With this in mind, the Chapter set out to see why Convention No. 181 is generally perceived as only relevant to the intermediation of employment relationships. It highlighted that this perception hinges on the interpretation given to the word "employment". However, notwithstanding the different opinions of others, based on the rules of interpretation, when put in its context, it seems wrong to interpret "employment" as meaning that only the intermediation of employment relationships and employment contracts is covered under this instrument. Instead, Convention No. 181 arguably covers any job-matching service aimed at providing a jobseeker with paid work by matching a jobseeker to a business user. Hence, it covers many digital labour platforms. For this reason, despite its flaws (e.g. lack of a mechanism to uncover disguised temporary work agencies), Convention No. 181 and its Recommendation are highly relevant to any discussion on decent work in the platform economy, not least to the debate on online crowdwork. The regulation of labour market services offers a meaningful avenue to regulate a large part of the platform economy, particularly the platform operators that are not guilty of bogus self-employment as legal employers.

536 The subsequent Chapter on the Home Work Convention, 1996 (No. 177), showed that Convention No. 177 is also a crucial point of reference for the discussion on crowdwork. Convention No. 177's application to the platform economy centres on the concepts of autonomy and economic independence. A home-based crowdworker performing tasks that result in a product or service asked for by a requester on the platform in pursuance of his or her business activity is covered by Convention No. 177, unless that crowdworker has the degree of autonomy and economic independence needed to run a home-based business. The Chapter explored under what circumstances a crowdworker could be considered (economically) autonomous. It found that a significant share of crowdworkers could be considered economically dependent on platform work. However, what is unclear is whether economic dependence on a crowdwork platform, as such, suffices for the home-based worker to be economically dependent in the sense of Convention No. 177, or whether this requires economic dependence in relation to one single platform user.[1628] Similarly, much uncertainty remains about the degree of functional autonomy required for an industrial homeworker or crowdworker to rightly be perceived as an independent contractor. The Chapter argued that some crowdworkers perform work that cannot in all reasonableness be considered to offer the level of autonomy necessary for that person to be perceived as a home-based business. Notwithstanding Member

1628. In the case of the latter, a far smaller share of crowdworkers would be economically dependent, hence, entitled to protections under Convention No. 177.

States' discretion to determine the meaning of autonomy in this area, based on the ordinary meaning of the word autonomy and the purpose of the instrument, a crowdworker on what is essentially a cognitive assembly line should be classified as a homeworker under Convention No. 177. In short, the ILO instruments on home work are undoubtedly applicable to some crowdworkers; the question ILO constituents should ponder is to which ones exactly?

Concerning local app-based platform work, many of the most prominent DLPs **537** essentially provide people with what would have universally been considered luxury services in the past – having a meal or groceries delivered to one's doorstep, or having a house cleaned by someone else used to be accessible to the privileged few only. The Domestic Workers Convention, 2011 (No. 189), was drafted to regulate this type of work in which households rely on others to perform work that sustains the household and its members. Now that platforms also offer these services to the middle-class, by extension, Convention No. 189 seems to apply to a broad range of activities on app-based platforms. However, due to how the instrument's scope was drafted, the Convention becomes somewhat difficult to apply whenever the platform operator does not explicitly engage the person performing domestic work by means of an employment relationship. This complication arises from the Convention's ambiguous language, which, to make matters worse, was drafted behind closed doors. The accounts about what was agreed in the drafting group make it crystal clear that someone performing domestic work on an occupational basis should be covered by the Convention. Yet, because of Article 1's literal wording, a black letter or legalistic approach to the instrument's scope might come to a different conclusion. The relevant Chapters have argued that such a legalistic approach would risk compromising the *effet utile* of Convention No. 189. With this in mind, the dissertation favoured an "aspirational approach" to Convention No. 189 and its Recommendation. The message of Convention No. 189 should be that if platform workers perform domestic work on an occupational basis, the Member State should ensure that this work takes place under an employment relationship. The Chapter, furthermore, pointed out that there are reasons to suspect that many domestic platform workers may, in fact, perform this work on an occupational basis, turning Convention No. 189 into a highly relevant instrument.

Synthesis of Part III – What does the way in which these three instruments apply to **538** the platform economy tell us? Arguably, it tells us, first of all, that lawyers should resist the urge to construe the scope of application of each single ILO standard around the concept of an "employment relationship" in the sense of the Employment Relationship Recommendation, 2006 (No. 198). Each ILO instrument has its own context and internal drivers, resulting in a unique scope of influence. Amongst others, due to the rules of interpretation, the International Labour Code does not have a unified concept of an "employment relationship". Moreover, even if it did, all three ILO Conventions analysed in Part III extend labour law provisions beyond the scope of a "regular" employment relationship.

Each does so in its own way: Convention No. 181 applies to job-matching, regardless **539** of any employment relationship; Convention No. 177 applies to home work relationships, which covers a larger group of workers than just home-based employees;

Convention No. 189 urges the Member States to develop their domestic notion of an employment relationship to cover occupational, domestic work. These three examples indicate that the ILO already uses multiple techniques to enlarge the scope of labour and social security law. ILO constituents can opt to apply provisions to all workers, regardless of their legal classification, instead of only employees. They can extend the instrument's application to workers that are not employees nor independent contractors, but a kind of dependent contractor (e.g. homeworkers). Thirdly, they can recommend that the Member States frame the concept of an employment relationship sufficiently broadly under domestic law (e.g. domestic workers).

540 Apart from showing that ILO constituents have multiple options to extend certain protections to platform workers, based on the findings from Part III, one might also conclude that if these existing ILO Conventions were implemented, a large share of platform workers would be covered under labour law and social security protection. For instance, dependent crowdworkers with insufficient (economic) autonomy and platform workers involved in domestic work on an occupational basis are entitled to protections under Convention No. 177 and Convention No. 189, respectively. This is a remarkable finding. In particular, because, let us say, crowdworkers on Amazon Mechanical Turk or handypersons on TaskRabbit are generally not the platform workers with the least autonomy in the platform economy. Nor do these platform operators overall exert the level of control of a transport or food-delivery platform. If these platform workers – Turkers and Taskers – are, nonetheless, covered by the ILS analysed in this dissertation, then the continued classification of platform workers in food delivery and transport as independent contractors, plainly and simply, becomes highly questionable.

541 **Part IV. Future ILO standard-setting on decent work in the platform economy** – Because these three instruments and many others, such as the Fundamental Conventions, apply to platform work, it is worth asking: Are the guidelines in these instruments responsive, considering platforms' operational structure and platform workers' demands? Chapter 1 of this Fourth Part argued that the guidelines in Convention No. 181, No. 177 and No. 189 were not responsive. This was based on two observations. First, all three instruments contain provisions that would tackle some of the complaints platform workers have or address some of the issues associated with platforms' operational structure. However, despite the applicability of these instruments and the fact that they contain such guidelines, a blatant disconnect exists between what the instruments want and what is happening in the platform economy. One could say that this is one reason why the instruments are unresponsive; they apply but do not connect to the issue. Despite their merits, they are too easily overlooked. Secondly, perhaps unsurprisingly, the existing instruments do not address some of the issues that significantly affect platform workers, while being only of limited importance to industrial homeworkers, regular domestic workers or temporary agency workers. This is a second reason why current instruments are unresponsive. More broadly, since these observations are made by applying three instruments that regulate labour market phenomena that have much in common with platform work, it is probable for the International Labour Code in general to be insufficiently responsive to digital labour platforms. Standard-setting action would

seem appropriate. At present, there are no clear guidelines on how to achieve decent platform work.

This brings us to the final question: What role can the ILO play in regulating digital labour platforms? Part IV offers a cautious answer to this question, drawing on this research's understanding of what digital labour platforms are, what the Decent Work Agenda implies, and the content of the instruments on private employment agencies, home and domestic work. It is clear that the ILO has multiple regulatory pathways; the discussions can still go in multiple directions. Irrespective of the direction taken, Chapter 3 has sketched what topics a future instrument would likely address and how the instruments analysed in Part III deal with these topics. Based on the considerations in this Chapter, it seems that even if the ILO were to simply "logically extend" the existing content of its ILS to the platform economy, it could already send a strong signal. For instance, since industrial homeworkers are covered by minimum rates of wages under the instruments on home work, prescribing a rate-fixing mechanism for dependent crowdworkers in a future instrument would make sense and, moreover, have a real impact. At the same time, although existing instruments provide principles and approaches that might still be viable, an instrument on platform work will require further innovative thinking. **542**

Indeed, the stakes are high. If ILO constituents consent, a future instrument can break new ground, amongst other things, by extending certain protections, such as maximum working hours, to all platform workers regardless of employment status, or by giving concrete shape to self-employed workers' collective rights in the platform economy. The boundaries that are shifted in this regard could serve as a precedent in future decades. At the same time, however, as was remarked in Chapter 2 of Part IV, the complexity of platform work does jeopardise the effort to regulate this subject at the international level. If standard-setting discussions manage to proceed in the years ahead, the organisation, particularly the Office, will undoubtedly be put to the test. It is hoped that the contents of this research, together with the efforts of many others, can help to pave the way for a successful outcome. **543**

Bibliography

TREATIES, LEGISLATION AND REGULATION

International and Supranational

Protocol concerning the entry into force of the Agreement Between the United Nations and the International Labour Organization, 19 December 1946.

Statute of the International Court of Justice, 26 June 1945

Treaty of Peace of Versailles, 28 June 1919.

Vienna Convention on the Law of Treaties, 23 May 1969.

European Union, Directive of the European Parliament and of the Council, No. 2000/31/EC, 8 June 2000 on certain legal aspects of information society services, in particular electronic commerce, in the Internal Market, *OJ.L.* 17 July 2000, No. 178, 1.

European Union, Directive of the European Parliament and of the Council, No. 2003/88/EC, 4 November 2003 concerning certain aspects of the organisation of working time, *OJ.L.* 18 November 2003, No. 299, 9.

European Union, Directive of the European Parliament and of the Council, No. 2006/123/EC, 12 December 2006 on services in the internal market, *OJ.L.* 27 December 2006, No. 376, 36.

European Union, Framework Agreement on Telework, 28 June 2006.

European Union, Regulation of the European Parliament and of the Council No. 2019/1150, 20 June 2019 on promoting fairness and transparency for business users of online intermediation services, *OJ.L.* 11 July 2019, No. 186, 57.

ILO, Centenary Declaration for the Future of Work, 21 June 2019.

ILO, Declaration concerning the aims and purposes of the International Labour Organisation (Declaration of Philadelphia), 10 May 1944.

ILO, Declaration on Social Justice for a Fair Globalization, 10 June 2008.

ILO, Abolition of Forced Labour Convention, 1957 (No. 105).

ILO, Discrimination (Employment and Occupation) Convention, 1958 (No. 111).

ILO, Domestic Workers Convention, 2011 (No. 189).

ILO, Domestic Workers Recommendation, 2011 (No. 201).

ILO, Employment Relationship Recommendation, 2006 (No. 198).

ILO, Employment Service Convention, 1948 (No. 88).

ILO, Equal Remuneration Convention, 1951 (No. 100).

ILO, Fee-Charging Employment Agencies Convention, 1933 (No. 34).

ILO, Forced Labour Convention, 1930 (No. 29).

ILO, Home Work Convention, 1996 (No. 177).

ILO, Home Work Recommendation, 1996 (No. 184).

ILO, Hours of Work (Industry) Convention, 1919 (No. 1).

ILO, Minimum Age Convention, 1973 (No. 138).

ILO, Night Work (Women) Convention, 1919 (No. 4).

ILO, Occupational Safety and Health Convention, 1981 (No. 155).

ILO, Part-Time Work Convention, 1994 (No. 175).

ILO, Private Employment Agencies Convention, 1997 (No. 181).

ILO, Private Employment Agencies Recommendation, 1997 (No. 188).

ILO, Protection of Wages Convention, 1949 (No. 95).

ILO, Right to Organise and Collective Bargaining Convention, 1949 (No. 98).

ILO, Safety and Health in Agriculture Convention, 2001 (No. 184).

ILO, Safety and Health in Agriculture Recommendation, 2001 (No. 192).

ILO, Social Protection Floors Recommendation, 2012 (No. 202).

ILO, Social Security (Minimum Standards) Convention, 1952 (No. 102).

ILO, Transition from the Informal to the Formal Economy Recommendation, 2015 (No. 204).

ILO, Unemployment Convention, 1919 (No. 2).

ILO, Unemployment Recommendation, 1919 (No. 1).

ILO, Violence and Harassment Convention, 2019 (No. 190).

ILO, Workers with Family Responsibilities Convention, 1981 (No. 156).

ILO, Worst Forms of Child Labour Convention, 1999 (No. 182).

ILO, Resolution concerning the 75th anniversary of the ILO and its future orientation, 81st Session of the International Labour Conference in 1994.

ILO, Resolution concerning strengthening the ILO's capacity, 96th Session of the International Labour Conference in 2007.

ILO, Resolution concerning gender equality and the use of language in legal texts of the ILO, 9 June 2011.

ILO, Resolution on Advancing Social Justice through Decent Work, 9 June 2016.

ILO, Resolution and conclusions concerning the second recurrent discussion on social dialogue and tripartism, 107th Session of the International Labour Conference in 2018.

ILO, Resolution on the ILO Centenary Declaration for the Future of Work, 21 June 2019.

ILO, Resolution on the principle of equality among ILO Member States and fair representation of all regions in the ILO's tripartite governance, 18 June 2021.

ILO, Conclusions concerning the role of private employment agencies in the functioning of labour markets, 81st Session of the International Labour Conference in 1994.

ILO, Conclusions concerning decent work in global supply chains, 10 June 2016.

UN, International Covenant on Civil and Political Rights, 16 December 1966.

UN, International Covenant on Economic, Social and Cultural Rights, 16 December 1966.

UN, Programme of Action of the World Summit for Social Development, 14 March 1995, A/CONF.166/9.

WTO, Singapore Ministerial Declaration, 13 December 1996, WT/MIN(96)/DEC.

Legislation and Regulation

Belgium, Loi du 3 juillet 1978 relative aux contrats de travail / Wet van 3 juli 1978 betreffende de arbeidsovereenkomsten.

Belgium, Loi du 5 mars 2017 concernant le travail faisable et maniable / Wet van 5 maart 2017 betreffende werkbaar en wendbaar werk.

Belgium, Convention collective de travail n° 85 du 9 novembre 2005 concernant le télétravail / Collectieve arbeidsovereenkomst nr. 85 van 9 november 2005 betreffende het telewerk.

Belgium, Décret du 13 avril 1999 relatif au placement privé en Région flamande (traduction) / Decreet 13 april 1999 met betrekking tot de private arbeidsbemiddeling in het Vlaamse Gewest.

Belgium, Décret du 10 decembre 2010 relatif au placement privé / Decreet 10 december 2010 betreffende de private arbeidsbemiddeling.

Canada, Labour Relations Act, 1995.

France, Sections L1254-1 - L1254-31 Code du Travail.

Malta, Employment Status National Standard Order, 31 January 2012.

Slovenia, Člen Zakon o delovnih razmerjih, dne 5. Marca 2013.

Spain, Ley 20/2007 del Estatuto del trabajo autónomo, de 11 de julio 2007.

United Kingdom, Employment Rights Act, 1996.

United States of America, Telework Enhancement Act of 2010.

CASE LAW AND ADMINISTRATIVE DECISIONS

Courts and Administrative Bodies

International, Permanent Court of International Justice 12 August 1922, Advisory Opinion No. 2, *Competence of the ILO in regard to International Regulation of the Conditions of the Labour of Persons Employed in Agriculture.*

International, Permanent Court of International Justice 23 July 1926, Advisory Opinion No. 13, *Competence of the ILO to Regulate Incidentally the Personal Work of the Employer.*

International, Permanent Court of International Justice 26 August 1930, Advisory Opinion No. 18, *Free city of Danzig / International Labour Organization.*

International, Permanent Court of International Justice 15 November 1932, Advisory Opinion No. 25, *Interpretation of the Convention of 1919 concerning Employment of Women during the Night.*

European Union, European Court of Justice 11 December 1997, Case No. C-55/96, *Job Centre COOP. arl.*

European Union, European Court of Justice 3 October 2000, Case No. C-303/98, *Sindicato de Médicos de Asistencia Pública (Simap) v. Conselleria de Sanidad y Consumo de la Generalidad Valenciana.*

European Union, European Court of Justice 9 September 2003, Case No. C-151/02, *Landeshauptstadt Kiel v. Norbert Jaeger.*

European Union, European Court of Justice 30 June 2011, Case No. C-397/10, *Commission européenne v. Royaume de Belgique.*

European Union, European Court of Justice 20 December 2017, Case No. C-434/15, *Asociación Profesional Elite Taxi v. Uber Systems Spain, SL.*

European Union, European Court of Justice 21 February 2018, Case No. C-518/15, *Ville de Nivelles v. Rudy Matzak.*

European Union, European Court of Justice 10 April 2018, Case No. C-320/16, *Uber France SAS v. Nabil Bensalem.*

European Union, European Court of Justice 19 December 2019, Case No. C-390/18, *X v. YA, Airbnb Ireland UC, and others.*

European Union, European Court of Justice 9 March 2021, Case No. C-344/19, *D. J. v. Radiotelevizija Slovenija.*

Belgium, Cour de cassation du 17 janvier 2002, Case No. C.98.0125.N.

Canada, Court of Appeal for Ontario 23 December 2009, Case No. 2009 ONCA 916, *McKee v. Reid's Heritage Homes Ltd.*

Canada, Court of Appeal for Ontario 27 January 2016, Case No. 2016 ONCA 79, *Keenan v. Canac Kitchens Ltd.*

Canada, Court of Appeal for Ontario 31 July 2019, Case No. 2019 ONCA 640, *Thurston v. Ontario (Children's Lawyer).*

Canada, Ontario Labour Relations Board 6 April 1977, Case No. 1977 CanLII 422, *Adbo Contracting Company Ltd.*

Canada, Ontario Labour Relations Board 2 February 2001, Case No. 2001 CanLII 6537, *Toronto Star Newspapers Limited.*

Canada, Ontario Labour Relations Board 25 February 2020, Case No. 2020 CanLII 16750, *Foodora Inc. d.b.a. Foodora.*

France, Cour de cassation du 4 mars 2020, Case No. ECLI:FR:CCAS:2020:SO00374.

France, Cour de cassation du 12 novembre 2020, Case No. ECLI:FR:CCASS:2020:SO01026.

France, Cour d'appel de Douai du 10 février 2010, Case No. 19/00137.

Italy, Corte suprema di cassazione 24 gennaio 2020, Case No. 11629/2019.

Italy, Tribunale di Milano 27 maggio 2020, Decreto No. 9/2020.

Italy, Tribunale ordinario di Bologna 31 dicembre 2020, Case No. 2949/2019.

Netherlands, Gerechtshof Amsterdam 16 februari 2021, Case No. ECLI:NL:GHAMS:2021:392.

Netherlands, Gerechtshof Amsterdam 21 september 2021, Case No. ECLI:NL:GHAMS:2021:2741.

Netherlands, Rechtbank Amsterdam 1 juli 2019, Case No. ECLI:NL:RBAMS:2019:4546.

Spain, Tribunal Supremo 25 septiembre 2020, Case No. ECLI: ES:TS:2020:2924.

United Kingdom, Supreme Court 19 February 2021, Case No. [2021] UKSC 5, *Uber BV and others (Appellants) v. Aslam and others (Respondents).*

United Kingdom, Supreme Court 19 March 2021, Case No. [2021] UKSC 8, *Royal Mencap Society (Respondent) v. Tomlinson-Blake (Appellant) / Shannon (Appellant) v. Rampersad and another (T/A Clifton House Residential Home) (Respondents).*

United Kingdom, Employment Appeal Tribunal 18 September 2001, Case No. EAT/542/01, *Byrne Brothers (Formwork) Limited v. Baird.*

United Kingdom, Employment Appeal Tribunal 21 December 2005, Case No. UKEAT/0457/05, *Cotswolds Developments Construction Ltd v. Williams.*

United Kingdom, Employment Appeal Tribunal 21 February 2007, Case No. UKEAT/0475/06/DM, *James v. Redcats (Brands) Ltd.*

United States of America, United States District Court, N.D. California 11 March 2015, Case No. 13-cv-04065-VC, *Cotter v. Lyft, Inc.*

ILO Supervisory Bodies

Observation (CEACR) - adopted 1992, published 79th ILC session (1992), Fee-Charging Employment Agencies Convention, 1933 (No. 34) - Argentina (Ratification: 1950).

Observation (CEACR) - adopted 1995, published 83rd ILC session (1996), Fee-Charging Employment Agencies Convention, 1933 (No. 34) - Argentina (Ratification: 1950).

Observation (CEACR) - adopted 2018, published 108th ILC session (2019), Home Work Convention, 1996 (No. 177) - Bulgaria (Ratification: 2009).

Observation (CEACR) - adopted 2018, published 108th ILC session (2019), Private Employment Agencies Convention, 1997 (No. 181) - Algeria (Ratification: 2006).

Observation (CEACR) - adopted 2019, published 109th ILC session (2021), Domestic Workers Convention, 2011 (No. 189) - Paraguay (Ratification: 2013).

Direct Request on submission to competent authorities (CEACR) - adopted 2013, published 103rd ILC session (2014) - Mexico.

Direct Request (CEACR) - adopted 1995, published 82nd ILC session (1995), Fee-Charging Employment Agencies Convention (Revised), 1949 (No. 96) - Spain (Ratification: 1971).

Direct Request (CEACR) - adopted 1995, published 82nd ILC session (1995), Fee-Charging Employment Agencies Convention (Revised), 1949 (No. 96) - Côte d'Ivoire (Ratification: 1992).

Direct Request (CEACR) - adopted 2009, published 99th ILC session (2010), Home Work Convention, 1996 (No. 177) - Netherlands (Ratification: 2002).

Direct Request (CEACR) - adopted 2009, published 99th ILC session (2010), Private Employment Agencies Convention, 1997 (No. 181) - Morocco (Ratification: 1999).

Direct Request (CEACR) - adopted 2010, published 100th ILC session (2011), Private Employment Agencies Convention, 1997 (No. 181) - Georgia (Ratification: 2002).

Direct Request (CEACR) - adopted 2011, published 101st ILC session (2012) Private Employment Agencies Convention, 1997 (No. 181) - Bulgaria (Ratification: 2005).

Direct Request (CEACR) - adopted 2013, published 103rd ILC session (2014), Home Work Convention, 1996 (No. 177) - Netherlands (Ratification: 2002).

Direct Request (CEACR) - adopted 2014, published 104th ILC session (2015), Private Employment Agencies Convention, 1997 (No. 181) - Morocco (Ratification: 1999).

Direct Request (CEACR) – adopted 2014, published 104th ILC session (2015), Private Employment Agencies Convention, 1997 (No. 181) – Lithuania (Ratification: 2004).

Direct Request (CEACR) – adopted 2015, published 105th ILC session (2016), Domestic Workers Convention, 2011 (No. 189) – Ecuador (Ratification: 2013).

Direct Request (CEACR) – adopted 2015, published 105th ILC session (2016), Private Employment Agencies Convention, 1997 (No. 181) – North Macedonia (Ratification: 2012).

Direct Request (CEACR) – adopted 2015, published 105th ILC session (2016) Private Employment Agencies Convention, 1997 (No. 181) – Zambia (Ratification: 2013).

Direct Request (CEACR) – adopted 2016, published 106th ILC session (2017), Domestic Workers Convention, 2011 (No. 189) – Germany (Ratification: 2013).

Direct Request (CEACR) – adopted 2017, published 107th ILC session (2018), Domestic Workers Convention, 2011 (No. 189) – Costa Rica (Ratification: 2014).

Direct Request (CEACR) – adopted 2017, published 107th ILC session (2018), Domestic Workers Convention, 2011 (No. 189) – Ireland (Ratification: 2014).

Direct Request (CEACR) – adopted 2017, published 107th ILC session (2018), Domestic Workers Convention, 2011 (No. 189) – Nicaragua (Ratification: 2013).

Direct Request (CEACR) – adopted 2018, published 108th ILC session (2019), Domestic Workers Convention, 2011 (No. 189) – Chile (Ratification: 2015).

Direct Request (CEACR) – adopted 2018, published 108th ILC session (2019), Domestic Workers Convention, 2011 (No. 189) – Dominican Republic (Ratification: 2015).

Direct Request (CEACR) – adopted 2018, published 108th ILC session (2019), Domestic Workers Convention, 2011 (No. 189) – Panama (Ratification: 2015).

Direct Request (CEACR) – adopted 2018, published 108th ILC session (2019), Private Employment Agencies Convention, 1997 (No. 181) – Albania (Ratification: 1999).

Direct Request (CEACR) – adopted 2018, published 108th ILC session (2019), Private Employment Agencies Convention, 1997 (No. 181) – Serbia (Ratification: 2013).

Direct Request (CEACR) – adopted 2019, published 109th ILC session (2020), Domestic Workers Convention, 2011 (No. 189) – Argentina (Ratification: 2014).

Direct Request (CEACR) – adopted 2019, published 109th ILC session (2020), Domestic Workers Convention, 2011 (No. 189) – Ecuador (Ratification: 2013).

Direct Request (CEACR) – adopted 2019, published 109th ILC session (2020), Domestic Workers Convention, 2011 (No. 189) – Ireland (Ratification: 2014).

Direct Request (CEACR) – adopted 2019, published 109th ILC session (2021), Domestic Workers Convention, 2011 (No. 189) – Paraguay (Ratification: 2013).

Direct Request (CEACR) – adopted 2019, published 109th ILC session (2020), Private Employment Agencies Convention, 1997 (No. 181) – Mali (Ratification: 2016).

Direct Request (CEACR) – adopted 2019, published 109th ILC session (2021), Private Employment Agencies Convention, 1997 (No. 181) – North Macedonia (Ratification: 2012).

Direct Request (CEACR) – adopted 2019, published 109th ILC session (2020), Domestic Workers Convention, 2011 (No. 189) – Guyana (Ratification: 2013).

Direct Request (CEACR) – adopted 2020, published 109th ILC session (2021), Home Work Convention, 1996 (No. 177) – Albania (Ratification: 2002).

Direct Request (CEACR) – adopted 2020, published 109th ILC session (2021), Private Employment Agencies Convention, 1997 (No. 181) – North Macedonia (Ratification: 2012).

Direct Request (CEACR) – adopted 2020, published 109th ILC session (2021), Domestic Workers Convention, 2011 (No. 189) – Ecuador (Ratification: 2013).

Direct Request (CEACR) – adopted 2020, published 109th ILC session (2021), Domestic Workers Convention, 2011 (No. 189) – Germany (Ratification: 2013).

SCHOLARSHIP

Books

ANEESH, A., *Virtual Migration: The Programming of Globalization* (Duke University Press 2006).

BEDNAROWICZ, B., *Platform-Mediated Work in the Gig Economy Through the Lens of the EU Social Acquis* (University of Antwerp 2019).

BEIRLAEN, A., *De Betekenis van de Conventies van de Internationale Arbeidsorganisatie in de Belgische Rechtssfeer 1919–1969* (Centrum voor de studie van de Belgische betrekkingen met de internationale arbeidsorganisatie 1975).

BENNER, C., LEETE, L. and PASTOR, M., *Staircases or Treadmills? Labor Market Intermediaries and Economic Opportunity in a Changing Economy* (Russel Sage Foundation 2007).

BLACKETT, A., *Everyday Transgressions: Domestic Workers' Transnational Challenge to International Labor Law* (Cornell University Press 2019).

BLANPAIN, R., *Arbeidsmarktrecht* (die Keure 2011).

BREINING-KAUFMANN, C., *Globalisation and Labour Rights: The Conflict between Core Labour Rights and International Economic Law* (Hart Publishing 2007).

BUGA, I., *Modification of Treaties by Subsequent Practice* (Oxford University Press 2018).

CHRISTENSEN, K. E., *The New Era of Home-based Work: Directions and Policies* (Westview 1988).

CODAGNONE, C., MATTHEWS, J. and KARATZOGIANNI, A., *Platform Economics: Rhetoric and Reality in the Sharing Economy* (Emerald Publishing Limited 2018).

CORTEBEECK, L., *Er Is Nog Werk: De Toekomst van Waardig Werk in de Wereld* (Lannoo 2019).

COUNTOURIS, N., *The Changing Law of the Employment Relationship: Comparative Analyses in the European Context* (Ashgate 2007).

DE HEREDIA RUIZ, I. B., *Work in the Platform Economy: Arguments for an Employment Relationship* (Huygens Editorial 2019).

DELANEY, A., BURCHIELLI, R., MARSHALL, S. and TATE, J., *Homeworking Women: A Gender Justice Perspective* (Routledge 2018).

DENEVE, C., *Internationaal Arbeidsrecht* (die Keure 2010).

DOERINGER, P. B. and PIORE, M. J., *Internal Labor Markets and Manpower Analysis* (D.C. Heath and Company 1971).

GARDINER, R. K., *Treaty Interpretation* (Oxford University Press 2015).

GHEBALI, V.-Y., *The International Labour Organisation: A Case Study on the Evolution of U.N Specialised Agencies* (Martinus Nijhoff 1989).

GERSHON, I., *Down and Out in the New Economy: How People Find (or Don't Find) Work Today* (University of Chicago Press 2017).

GOLDBERG, A. J., *Growth of Labor Law in the United States* (U.S. Department of Labor 1962).

GRAVEL, E. and CHARBONNEAU-JOBIN, C., *The Committee of Experts on the Application of Conventions and Recommendations: Its Dynamic and Impact* (ILO 2003).

GRAY, M. L. and SURI, S., *Ghost Work: How to Stop Silicon Valley from Building a New Global Underclass* (Houghton Mifflin Harcourt 2019).

HEPPLE, B., *Labour Laws and Global Trade* (Hart Publishing 2005).

HIGGINS, R., WEBB, P., AKANDE, D., SIVAKUMARAN, S. and SLOAN, J., *Oppenheim's International Law: United Nations* (Oxford University Press 2017).

HUWS, U., *Labour in Contemporary Capitalism: What Next?* (Palgrave Macmillan 2019).

HYMAN, L., *Temp: How American Work, American Business, and the American Dream Became Temporary* (Viking 2018).

ILO, *Dix Ans d'Organisation Internationale du Travail* (ILO 1931).

ILO, *Rules of the Game: An Introduction to the Standards-related Work of the International Labour Organization* (ILO 2019).

ILO International Training Center, *Guide to International Labour Standards* (ITC 2014).

JENKS, C. W., *Social Justice in the Law of Nations: The ILO Impact After Fifty Years* (Oxford University Press 1970).

KALLEBERG, A. L., *Good Jobs, Bad Jobs: The Rise of Polarized and Precarious Employment Systems in the United States, 1970s to 2000s* (Russel Sage Foundation 2011).

KOLB, R., *The Law of Treaties: An Introduction* (Edward Elgar Publishing 2016).

LA HOVARY, C., *Les Droits Fondamentaux au Travail: Origines, Statut et Impact en Droit International* (The Graduate Institute Geneva 2009).

MAUL, D., *The International Labour Organization: 100 Years of Global Social Policy* (Walter de Gruyter 2019).

MAUPAIN, F., *The Future of the International Labour Organization in the Global Economy* (Hart Publishing 2013).

McAFEE, A. and BRYNJOLFSSON, E., *Machine, Platform, Crowd* (W. W. Norton & Company 2017).

NAZ, F. and BÖGENHOLD, D., *Unheard Voices: Women, Work and Political Economy of Global Production* (Palgrave Macmillan 2020).

OSIEKE, E., *Constitutional Law and practice in the International Labour Organisation* (Martinus Nijhoff Publishers 1985).

PINFIELD, L., *The Operation of Internal Labor Markets: Staffing Practices and Vacancy Chains* (Plenum Press 1995).

PRASSL, J., *Humans as a Service: The Promise and Perils of Work in the Gig Economy* (Oxford University Press 2018).

PUIGELIER, C., HÉRIN, J.-L. and TILLHET-PRETNAR, J., *Dictionnaire Juridique* (Bruylant 2017).

RAWORTH, K., *Doughnut Economics* (Random House 2018).

RODGERS, G., LEE, E., SWEPSTON, L. and VAN DAELE, J., *The International Labour Organization and the Quest for Social Justice, 1919–2009* (ILO 2009).

ROSENBLAT, A., *Uberland: How Algorithms are Rewriting the Rules of Work* (University of California Press 2018).

ROUTH, S., *Informal Workers in India: Reconceptualizing Labour Law to Promote Capabilities* (University of Victoria 2013).

SANDS, P. and KLEIN, P., *Bowett's Law of International Institutions* (Sweet & Maxwell 2009).

SCHOR, J. B., *After the Gig: How the Sharing Economy got Hijacked and How to Win It Back* (University of California Press 2020).

SERVAIS, J.-M., *International Labour Law* (Kluwer 2011).

SINCLAIR, G. F., *To Reform the World: International Organizations and the Making of Modern States* (Oxford University Press 2017).

SRNICEK, N., *Platform Capitalism* (Polity Press 2017).

STANDING, G., *The Corruption of Capitalism: Why Rentiers Thrive and Work Does Not Pay* (Biteback Publishing 2016).

STOKKE, H., *Decent Work: Principles, Policies and Programmes of the International Labour Organisation* (University of Bergen 2015).

STONE, K. V.W., *From Widgets to Digits Employment Regulation for the Changing Workplace* (Cambridge University Press 2004).

SUNDARARAJAN, A., *The Sharing Economy: The End of Employment and the Rise of Crowd-Based Capitalism* (MIT Press 2016).

SUPIOT, A., *Beyond Employment: Changes in Work and the Future of Labour Law in Europe* (Oxford University Press 2001).

SUPIOT, A., *L'Esprit de Philadelphie: La Justice Sociale Face au Marché Total* (Seuil 2010).

SUPIOT, A., *Le Travail n'est pas une Merchandise: Contenu et Sens du Travail au xxie Siècle* (Collège de France 2019).

SUSSKIND, D., *A World Without Work: Technology, Automation and How We Should Respond* (Penguin Books 2021).

TAPIOLA, K., *The Teeth of the ILO – The Impact of the 1998 ILO Declaration on Fundamental Principles and Rights at Work* (ILO 2018).

VALTICOS, N., *International Labour Law* (Kluwer 1979).

VAN BERGEIJK, J., *Binnen bij Bol.com: Undercover bij de Winkel van ons Allemaal* (Querido Fosfor 2019).

VAN DER HEIJDEN, P. F., DE GIER, E., BOONSTRA, K., ROJER, M. and VEGTER, M., *Lexicon van Arbeidsrecht en Arbeidsverhoudingen* (Sdu Uitgevers 1997).

VAN DIJCK, J., *The Culture of Connectivity: A Critical History of Social Media* (Oxford University Press 2013).

VOGT, J., BELLACE, J., COMPA, L., EWING, K. D., HENDY, L., LÖRCHER, K. and NOVITZ, T., *The Right to Strike in International Law* (Hart Publishing 2020).

VOSKO, L. F., *Managing the Margins: Gender, Citizenship, and the International Regulation of Precarious Employment* (Oxford University Press 2011).

WOOD, A. J., *Despotism on Demand: How Power Operates in the Flexible Workplace* (Cornell University Press 2020).

Book Chapters

ACQUIER, A., *Uberization Meets Organizational Theory: Platform Capitalism and the Rebirth of the Putting-Out System* (Nestor M. Davidson, Michèle Finck & John J. Infranca eds., *The Cambridge Handbook of the Law of the Sharing Economy*, CUP 2018).

AGRAWAL, A., HORTON, J., LACETERA, N. and LYONS, E., *Digitization and the Contract Labor Market: A Research Agenda* (Avi Goldfarb, Shane M. Greenstein & Catherine E. Tucker eds., *Economic Analysis of the Digital Economy*, University of Chicago Press 2015).

AJUNWA, I. and GREENE, D., *Platforms at Work: Automated Hiring Platforms and Other New Intermediaries in the Organization of Work* (Steve P. Vallas & Anne Kovalainen eds., *Work and Labor in the Digital Age*, Emerald Publishing Limited 2019).

ALBIN, E., *From 'Domestic Servant' to 'Domestic Worker'* (Judy Fudge, Shae McCrystal & Kamala Sankaran eds., *Challenging the Legal Boundaries of Work Regulation*, Hart Publishing 2012).

ALOISI, A., *Hierarchies Without Firms? Vertical Disintegration, Personal Outsourcing and the Nature of the Platform* (Quaderni del Premio "Giorgio Rota" 2020).

ALSTON, P. and GANDOUR, J., *The ILO's Centenary Declaration and Social Justice in the Digital Age* (George P. Politakis, Tomi Kohiyama & Thomas Lieby eds., *ILO100: Law for Social Justice*, ILO 2019).

ALVAREZ, J. E., *Frameworks for Understanding the ILO* (George P. Politakis, Tomi Kohiyama & Thomas Lieby eds., *ILO100: Law for Social Justice*, ILO 2019).

AUTOR, D. H., *Studies of Labor Market Intermediation: Introduction* (David H. Autor ed., *Studies of Labor Market Intermediation*, University of Chicago Press 2009).

AUVERGNON, P., *Le Travail Domestique sur le Chemin du Travail Décent?* (José Luis Gil y Gil ed., *Migraciones Internacionales e Impacto de la Crisis Económica: Compromisos de la OIT*, Juruá Editora 2013).

BAMU, P., *Nurturing a Culture of Compliance with Domestic Workers' Rights in South Africa* (Darcy du Toit ed., *Exploited, Undervalued – and Essential: Domestic Workers and the Realisation of Their Rights*, Pretoria University Law Press 2013).

BEAUDONNET, X., *Quelques Observations sur l'Utilisation des Normes de l'OIT par les Tribunaux Nationaux* (George P. Politakis, Tomi Kohiyama & Thomas Lieby eds., *ILO100: Law for Social Justice*, ILO 2019).

BELLACE, J. R., *The ILO and Tripartism: The Challenge of Balancing the Three-Legged Stool* (George P. Politakis, Tomi Kohiyama & Thomas Lieby eds., *ILO100: Law for Social Justice*, ILO 2019).

BENJAMIN, P., *Subordination, Parasubordination and Self-Employment: A Comparative Study of Selected African Countries* (Giuseppe Casale ed., *The Employment Relationship: A Comparative Overview*, Hart Publishing 2011).

BENZING, M., *International Organizations or Institutions, Secondary Law* (Rüdiger Wolfrum ed., *Max Planck Encyclopaedia of Public International Law*, OUP 2007).

BIDWELL, M. and FERNANDEZ-MATEO, I., *Three's a Crowd? Understanding Triadic Employment Relationships* (Peter Cappelli ed., *Employment Relationships: New Models of White-Collar Work*, CUP 2008).

BJORGE, E., *The Convergence of the Methods of Treaty Interpretation: Different Regimes, Different Methods of Interpretation?* (Mads Andenas & Eirik Bjorge eds., *A Farewell to Fragmentation Reassertion and Convergence in International Law*, CUP 2015).

BLANPAIN, R., *Concluding Remarks* (W. Albeda, R. Blanpain & G. M. J. Veldkamp eds., *Temporary Work in Modern Society*, I, Kluwer 1978).

BONVIN, J.-M., *Les Valeurs Fondatrices de l'OIT et la Promotion de la Citoyenneté Sociale – Jalons Historiques et Défis Contemporains* (George P. Politakis, Tomi Kohiyama & Thomas Lieby eds., *ILO100: Law for Social Justice*, ILO 2019).

BRÖLMANN, C., *Specialized Rules of Treaty Interpretation: International Organizations* (Duncan B. Hollis ed., *The Oxford Guide to Treaties*, OUP 2020).

BRÖLMANN, C., *ILO Convention Practice: Mixed Methods in Norm-Setting for Social Justice* (George P. Politakis, Tomi Kohiyama & Thomas Lieby eds., *ILO100: Law for Social Justice*, ILO 2019).

CAMERLYNCK, G. H., *Approaches to Temporary Work. Legal Sources. Definitions and Possible Channels* (W. Albeda, R. Blanpain & G. M. J. Veldkamp eds., *Temporary Work in Modern Society*, I, Kluwer 1978).

CASALE, G., *The Employment Relationship: A General Introduction* (Giuseppe Casale ed., *The Employment Relationship: A Comparative Overview*, Hart Publishing 2011).

CASALE, G. and FASANI, M., *Labour Law and Digital Platforms* (Adalberto Perulli & Tiziano Treu eds., *The Future of Work: Labour Law and Labour Market Regulation in the Digital Era*, Kluwer 2021).

CHEN, Y., *Proliferation of Transnational Labour Standards: The Role of the ILO* (Tarja Halonen & Ulla Liukkunen eds., *International Labour Organization and Global Social Governance*, Springer 2021).

CHRISTODOULIDIS, E., *The ILO and the New 'Common Sense': Reflections on a Centenary* (Marc Bungenberg, Markus Krajewski, Christian J. Tams & Jörg Philipp Terhechte eds., *European Yearbook of International Economic Law 2019*, Springer International Publishing 2020).

CORDIER, Q., *L'Économie de Plateforme: Description d'un Phénomène d'Intermédiation* (Jacques Clesse & Fabienne Kéfer eds., *Enjeux et Défis Juridiques de l'Économie de Plateforme*, Anthemis 2019).

COUNTOURIS, N., *The Employment Relationship: A Comparative Analysis of National Judicial Approaches* (Giuseppe Casale ed., *The Employment Relationship: A Comparative Overview*, Hart Publishing 2011).

DAVIDOV, G., *Freelancers: An Intermediate Group in Labour Law?* (Judy Fudge, Shae McCrystal & Kamala Sankaran eds., *Challenging the Legal Boundaries of Work Regulation*, Hart Publishing 2012).

DAVIES, A. C. L., *ILO Convention 177 Home Work Convention, 1996 (No. 177)* (Edoardo Ales, Mark Bell, Olaf Deinert & Sophie Robin-Olivier eds., *International and European Labour Law Article-by-Article Commentary*, Nomos 2018).

DAVIES, A. C. L., *ILO Convention 181 Private Employment Agencies Convention, 1997 (No. 181)* (Edoardo Ales, Mark Bell, Olaf Deinert & Sophie Robin-Olivier eds., *International and European Labour Law Article-by-Article Commentary*, Nomos 2018).

DEACON, B., *The International Labour Organization and Global Social Governance – The 100 Year Search for Social Justice within Capitalism* (Alexandra Kaasch & Kerstin Martens eds., *Actors and Agency in Global Social Governance*, OUP 2015).

DE BROUX, P.-O., *L'Internationalisation des Droits Sociaux Fondamentaux. De la Paix Mondiale à la Justice Sociale: Les Origines de la Charte Sociale Européenne* (Sébastien Van Drooghenbroeck, Filip Dorssemont & Guido Van Limberghen eds., *Europees Sociaal Handvest, Sociale Rechten en Grondrechten op de Werkvloer / Charte Sociale Européenne, Droit Sociaux et Droits Fondamentaux au Travail*, die Keure 2016).

DEGRYSE, C., *Technological Disruption, Social Dereliction?* (Isabelle Daugareilh, Christophe Degryse & Philippe Pochet eds., *The Platform Economy and Social Law: Key Issues in Comparative Perspective*, Etui 2019)

DEINERT, O., *Equal Treatment as a Problem: Germany and Agency Work* (Edoardo Ales, Olaf Deinert & Jeff Kenner eds., *Core and Contingent Work in the European Union: A Comparative Analysis*, Hart Publishing 2017).

DELANEY, A., TATE, J. and BURCHIELLI, R., *Homeworkers Organizing for Recognition and Rights: Can International Standards Assist Them?* (Jill M. Jensen & Nelson Lichtenstein eds., *The ILO from Geneva to the Pacific Rim*, Palgrave Macmillan UK 2016).

DEVA, S. and WASZA, V., *Testbirds Software Testing Solutions in the Crowdsourcing Industry* (Werner Wobbe, Elva Bova & Catalin Dragomirescu-Gaina eds., *The Digital Economy and the Single Market*, FEPS 2016).

DE VRIES, T., Difficulties of the Interpretation of Conventions: A Judge's Point of View (Frans Pennings ed., *International Social Security Standards: Current Views and Interpretation Matters*, Intersentia 2007).

DIJKHOFF, T. and PENNINGS, F., *The Interpretation of International Social Security Standards* (Frans Pennings ed., *International Social Security Standards: Current Views and Interpretation Matters*, Intersentia 2007).

DILLER, J. M., *Social Justice, Rights, and Labour* (Dinah Shelton ed., *The Oxford Handbook of International Human Rights Law*, OUP 2013).

DINEEN, B. R. and ALLEN, D. G., *Internet Recruiting 2.0: Shifting Paradigms* (Daniel M. Cable & Kang Yang Trevor Yu eds., *The Oxford Handbook of Recruitment*, OUP 2013).

DÖRR, O., *Article 31: General Rule of Interpretation* (Oliver Dörr & Kirsten Schmalenbach eds., *Vienna Convention on the Law of Treaties. A Commentary*, Springer 2012).

DRAHOKOUPIL, J. and FABO, B., *Outsourcing, Offshoring and the Deconstruction of Employment: New and Old Challenges* (Amparo Serrano-Pascual & Maria Jepsen eds., *The Deconstruction of Employment as a Political Question: 'Employment' as a Floating Signifier*, Springer International Publishing 2019).

DURWARD, D. and BLOHM, I., *The Rise of Crowd Aggregators – How Individual Workers Restructure Their Own Crowd* – (Jan Marco Leimeister & Walter Brenner eds., *Proceedings der 13. Internationalen Tagung Wirtschaftsinformatik*, Universität St. Gallen 2017).

DURWARD, D., BLOHM, I. and LEIMEISTER, J. M., *Principal Forms of Crowdsourcing and Crowd Work* (Werner Wobbe, Elva Bova & Catalin Dragomirescu-Gaina eds., *The Digital Economy and the Single Market*, FEPS 2016).

DU TOIT, D., *Situating Domestic Work in a Changing Global Labour Market* (Darcy du Toit ed., *Exploited, Undervalued – and Essential: Domestic Workers and the Realisation of Their Rights*, Pretoria University Law Press 2013).

EWING, K., *Reflections on the ILO Centenary* (Caroline Kelly, Joo-Cheong Tham & Julian Sempill eds., *Papers from the Symposium on the Centenary of the ILO: Democracy, Labour Law and Trade Unions*, Centre for Employment and Labour Relations Law, Melbourne Law School 2019).

FREDMAN, S., *Home from Home: Migrant Domestic Workers and the International Labour Organization Convention on Domestic Workers* (Cathryn Costello & Mark Freedland eds., *Migrants at Work: Immigration and Vulnerability in Labour Law*, OUP 2014).

FREY, D. F., *Social Justice, Neoliberalism, and Labor Standards at the International Labour Organization* (Gillian MacNaughton & Diane F. Frey eds., *Economic and Social Rights in a Neoliberal World*, CUP 2018).

FUDGE, J., *Blurring Legal Boundaries: Regulating for Decent Work* (Judy Fudge, Shae McCrystal & Kamala Sankaran eds., *Challenging the Legal Boundaries of Work Regulation*, Hart Publishing 2012).

GARCÍA GUZMÁN, C., *The International Labour Organization as an Autopoietic System* (George P. Politakis, Tomi Kohiyama & Thomas Lieby eds., *ILO100: Law for Social Justice*, ILO 2019).

GARDINER, R., *The Vienna Convention Rules on Treaty Interpretation* (Duncan B. Hollis ed., *The Oxford Guide to Treaties*, OUP 2020).

GILSON, S., CANDITO, C., DEGUELDRE, M. and HAREL, L., *Regards sur le Portage Salarial* (Charles-Éric Clesse & Steve Gilson eds., *Le Travail Temporaire, le Travail Intérimaire et la Mise à Disposition de Travailleurs: Les 30 Ans de la Loi du 24 Juillet 1987*, Anthemis 2017).

HARNETT, S., *Words Matter: How Tech Media Helped Write Gig Companies into Existence* (Deepa Das Acevedo ed., *Beyond the Algorithm: Qualitative Insights for Gig Work Regulation*, CUP 2020).

HELFER, L. R., *Pushback Against Supervisory Systems: Lessons for the ILO from International Human Rights Institutions* (George P. Politakis, Tomi Kohiyama & Thomas Lieby eds., *ILO100: Law for Social Justice*, ILO 2019).

HOSS, C. and VILLALPANDO, S., *La Contribution de l'OIT au Droit des Traités* (George P. Politakis, Tomi Kohiyama & Thomas Lieby eds., *ILO100: Law for Social Justice*, ILO 2019).

HUMBLET, M. and ZARKA-MATRES, M., *ILO Standards Policy* (Jean-Claude Javillier ed., *International Labour Standards: A Global Approach: 75th Anniversary of the Committee of Experts on the Application of Conventions and Recommendations*, ILO 2002).

HUWS, U., *New Forms of Platform Employment or Crowd Work* (Werner Wobbe, Elva Bova & Catalin Dragomirescu-Gaina eds., *The Digital Economy and the Single Market*, FEPS 2016).

JAVILLIER, J.-C., *Presentation* (Jean-Claude Javillier ed., *International Labour Standards: A Global Approach: 75th Anniversary of the Committee of Experts on the Application of Conventions and Recommendations*, ILO 2002).

JESNES, K., NORDLI OPPEGAARD, S. M., ILSØE, A., HOTVEDT, M. J., ROLANDSSON, B., SALONIEMI, A., SAARI, T. and DØLVIK, J. E., *Chapter 7. Conclusion* (Kristin Jesnes & Sigurd M. Nordli Oppegaard eds., *Platform Work in the Nordic Models: Issues, Cases and Responses*, Nordic Council of Ministers 2020).

JONES, P., *Rethinking Microwork: The Invisible Labour of the Platform Economy* (James Muldoon & Will Stronge eds., *Platforming Equality: Policy Challenges for the Digital Economy*, Autonomy 2020).

KERR, A., *Recruitment, Work, and Identity in Community Management: Passion, Precarity, and Play* (Juliet Webster & Keith Randle eds., *Virtual Workers and the Global Labour Market*, Palgrave Macmillan 2016).

KLABBERS, J., *International Organizations and the Problem of Privity: Towards a Supra-Functionalist Approach* (George P. Politakis, Tomi Kohiyama & Thomas Lieby eds., *ILO100: Law for Social Justice*, ILO 2019).

KLABBERS, J., *An Accidental Revolution: The ILO and the Opening Up of International Law* (Tarja Halonen & Ulla Liukkunen eds., *International Labour Organization and Global Social Governance*, Springer 2021).

KOBAYASHI, K., NATH, S., CHEN, M. S. and MALENGA, J., *Decent Work and Economic Growth: Is NZ Business Progressing Well?* (Gabriel Eweje & Ralph J. Bathurst eds., *Clean, Green and Responsible? Soundings from Down Under*, Springer International Publishing 2019).

KOELTZ, D., *Delivering Public Employment Services: Which Model Works Best?* (Jason Heyes & Ludek Rychly eds., *Labour Administration in Uncertain Times: Policy, Practice and Institutions*, ILO 2013).

KOHEN, M. G., *Does General International Law Incorporate the Concept of Social Justice?* (George P. Politakis, Tomi Kohiyama & Thomas Lieby eds., *ILO100: Law for Social Justice*, ILO 2019).

KOHIYAMA, T. and PETROVIĆ, D., *The International Labour Code – Myth or Reality?* (George P. Politakis, Tomi Kohiyama & Thomas Lieby eds., *ILO100: Law for Social Justice*, ILO 2019).

KOTT, S., *L'OIT et la Justice Sociale (1919–2019)* (George P. Politakis, Tomi Kohiyama & Thomas Lieby eds., *ILO100: Law for Social Justice*, ILO 2019).

LA HOVARY, C., *The ILO's Supervisory Bodies' 'Soft Law Jurisprudence'* (Adelle Blackett & Anne Trebilcock eds., *Research Handbook on Transnational Labour Law*, Edward Elgar Publishing 2015).

LA HOVARY, C., *The ILO's Mandate and Capacity: Creating, Proliferating and Supervising Labour Standards for a Globalized Economy* (Henner Gött ed., *Labour Standards in International Economic Law*, Springer 2018).

LE BOUTHILLIER, Y., *Article 32 Convention of 1969* (Olivier Corten & Pierre Klein eds., *The Vienna Conventions on the Law of Treaties: A Commentary*, OUP 2011).

LEE, W., *Private Deception and the Rise of Public Employment Offices in the United States, 1890–1930* (David H. Autor ed., *Studies of Labor Market Intermediation*, University of Chicago Press 2009).

LEHDONVIRTA, V., *Algorithms that Divide and Unite: Delocalisation, Identity and Collective Action in 'Microwork'* (Jörg Flecker ed., *Space, Place and Global Digital Work*, Palgrave Macmillan 2016).

LEIMEISTER, J. M., ZOGAJ, S. and BLOHM, I., *Crowdwork – Digitale Wertschöpfung in der Wolke: Ein Überblick über die Grundlagen, die Formen und den Aktuellen Forschungsstand* (Christiane Benner ed., *Crowdwork – Zurück in die Zukunft? Perspektiven Digitaler Arbeit*, Bund-Verlag 2014).

LIEBY, T., *The Interpretation of International Labour Conventions and the Principle of 'Systemic Integration' – The Way Forward for an ILO Tribunal* (George P. Politakis, Tomi Kohiyama & Thomas Lieby eds., *ILO100: Law for Social Justice*, ILO 2019).

LIKIC-BRBORIC, B. and SCHIERUP, C.-U., *Asymmetric Governance, Labour Standards and Migrants' Rights* (Heidi Moksnes & Mia Melin eds., *Global Civil Society: Shifting Powers in a Shifting World*, Uppsala Universitet 2012).

LIUKKUNEN, U., *The ILO and Transformation of Labour Law* (Tarja Halonen & Ulla Liukkunen eds., *International Labour Organization and Global Social Governance*, Springer 2021).

LOBEL, O., *Coase and the Platform Economy* (Nestor M. Davidson, Michèle Finck & John J. Infranca eds., *The Cambridge Handbook of the Law of the Sharing Economy*, CUP 2018).

MARIQUE, E. and DE WILDE D'ESTMAEL, J., *La Fonction d'Intermédiaire des Plateformes: Une Nouvelle Clé pour Réglementer les Relations de Travail qu'Elles In-/produisent?* (Auriane Lamine & Céline Wattecamps eds., *Quel Droit Social pour Les Travailleurs de Plateformes?*, Anthemis 2020).

MATEESCU, A. and TICONA, J., *Invisible Work, Visible Workers: Visibility Regimes in Online Platforms for Domestic Work* (Deepa Das Acevedo ed., *Beyond the Algorithm: Qualitative Insights for Gig Work Regulation*, CUP 2020).

MENG, W., *Article 57* (Bruno Simma et al. eds., *The Charter of the United Nations: A Commentary*, II, OUP 2012).

MENG, W., *Article 63* (Bruno Simma et al. eds., *The Charter of the United Nations: A Commentary*, II, OUP 2012).

MESSENGER, J. C., *Introduction: Telework in the 21st Century – an Evolutionary Perspective* (Jon C. Messenger ed., *Telework in the 21st Century: An Evolutionary Perspective*, Edward Elgar Publishing 2019).

MESSENGER, J. C., *Conclusions and Recommendations for Policy and Practice* (Jon C. Messenger ed., *Telework in the 21st Century: An Evolutionary Perspective*, Edward Elgar Publishing 2019).

MILLAND, K., *Crowd Work: The Fury and the Fear* (Werner Wobbe, Elva Bova & Catalin Dragomirescu-Gaina eds., *The Digital Economy and the Single Market*, FEPS 2016).

MILMAN-SIVAN, F., *Freedom of Association in Deliberative Spaces: The ILO Credentials Committee* (Adelle Blackett & Anne Trebilcock eds., *Research Handbook on Transnational Labour Law*, Edward Elgar Publishing 2015).

MOECKLI, D. and WHITE, N. D., *Treaties as "Living Instruments"* (Michael J. Bowman & Dino Kritsiotis eds., *Conceptual and Contextual Perspectives on the Modern Law of Treaties*, CUP 2018).

MÖHLMANN, M. and GEISSINGER, A., *Trust in the Sharing Economy Platform-Mediated Peer Trust* (Nestor M. Davidson, Michèle Finck & John J. Infranca eds., *The Cambridge Handbook of the Law of the Sharing Economy*, CUP 2018).

MONTERO BRESSÁN, J., *Local Sweatshops in the Global Economy: Accumulation Dynamics and the Manufacturing of a Reserve Army* (Maurizio Atzeni & Immanuel Ness eds., *Global Perspectives on Workers' and Labour Organizations*, Springer Singapore 2018).

MORRIS, M. R., BIGHAM, J. P., BREWER, R., BRAGG, J., KULKARNI, A., LI, J. and SAVAGE, S., *Subcontracting Microwork* (*Proceedings of the 2017 CHI Conference on Human Factors in Computing Systems*, ACM 2017).

MUNDLAK, G., *Tri-Plus: Reflection on Opening the ILO's Tripartite Structure* (George P. Politakis, Tomi Kohiyama & Thomas Lieby eds., *ILO100: Law for Social Justice*, ILO 2019).

MUNTARBHORN, V., *Labour Rights, Human Rights and Challenges of Connectivity* (George P. Politakis, Tomi Kohiyama & Thomas Lieby eds., *ILO100: Law for Social Justice*, ILO 2019).

MURRAY, J., *Taking Social Rights Seriously: Is there a Case for Institutional Reform of the ILO?* (Colin Fenwick & Tonia Novitz eds., *Human Rights at Work: Perspectives on Law and Regulation*, Hart Publishing 2010).

NAKAMURA, A. O., SHAW, K. L., FREEMAN, R. B., NAKAMURA, E. and PYMAN, A., *Jobs Online* (David H. Autor ed., *Studies of Labor Market Intermediation*, University of Chicago Press 2009).

PALCHETTI, P., *Halfway Between Fragmentation and Convergence: The Role of the Rules of the Organization in the Interpretation of Constituent Treaties* (Mads Andenas & Eirik Bjorge eds., *A Farewell to Fragmentation Reassertion and Convergence in International Law*, CUP 2015).

PAUWELYN, J., *Is Globalization Finally Re-Balancing? Novel Ways of Levelling the Playing Field for Labour* (George P. Politakis, Tomi Kohiyama & Thomas Lieby eds., *ILO100: Law for Social Justice*, ILO 2019).

PELLET, A., *Le Rôle des Résolutions des Organisations Internationales à la Lumière de la Jurisprudence de la Cour Internationale de Justice* (George P. Politakis, Tomi Kohiyama & Thomas Lieby eds., *ILO100: Law for Social Justice*, ILO 2019).

PERULLI, A., *Subordinate, Autonomous and Economically Dependent Work: A Comparative Analysis of Selected European Countries* (Giuseppe Casale ed., *The Employment Relationship: A Comparative Overview*, Hart Publishing 2011).

PERULLI, A., *The Declaration of Philadelphia (DoP)* (Edoardo Ales, Mark Bell, Olaf Deinert & Sophie Robin-Olivier eds., *International and European Labour Law Article-by-Article Commentary*, Nomos 2018).

POTOCKA-SIONEK, N., *The Changing Nature of Labour Intermediation. Do Algorithms Redefine Temporary Agency Work?* (Jerzy Wratny & Agata Ludera-Ruszel eds., *New Forms of Employment: Current Problems and Future Challenges*, Springer 2020).

PRÜGL, E., *Biases in Labor Law: A Critique from the Standpoint of Home-Based Workers* (Eileen Boris & Elisabeth Prügl eds., *Homeworkers in Global Perspective: Invisible no more*, Routledge 1996).

RAMM, T., *Laissez-faire and State Protection of Workers* (Bob Hepple ed., *The Making of Labour Law in Europe: A Comparative Study of Nine Countries up to 1945*, Hart Publishing 2010).

RAMM, T., *Epilogue: The New Ordering of Labour Law 1918–45* (Bob Hepple ed., *The Making of Labour Law in Europe: A Comparative Study of Nine Countries up to 1945*, Hart Publishing 2010).

RAVENELLE, A. J., *Just a Gig? Sharing Economy Work and the Implications for Career Trajectory* (Deepa Das Acevedo ed., *Beyond the Algorithm: Qualitative Insights for Gig Work Regulation*, CUP 2020).

REGAN, D. H., *Sources of International Trade Law: Understanding What the Vienna Convention Says About Identifying and Using 'Sources for Treaty Interpretation'*

(Samantha Besson & Jean d'Aspremont eds., *The Oxford Handbook of the Sources of International Law*, OUP 2017).

ROLANDSSON, B., SALONIEMI, A. and SAARI, T., *High-skilled Platform Work in Finland and Sweden – the Case of Technical Translators* (Kristin Jesnes & Sigurd M. Nordli Oppegaard eds., *Platform Work in the Nordic Models: Issues, Cases and Responses*, Nordic Council of Ministers 2020).

SIMS, E., *Employment Policy* (Jean-Claude Javillier ed., *International Labour Standards: A Global Approach: 75th Anniversary of the Committee of Experts on the Application of Conventions and Recommendations*, ILO 2002).

SINCLAIR, G. F., *Managing the "Workers Threat": Preventing Revolution Through the International Labour Organization* (Michel Erpeldin, Burkhard Hess & Hélène Ruiz Fabri eds., *Peace Through Law: The Versailles peace treaty and dispute settlement after World War I*, Nomos 2019).

SMITH, R. and PINTO, M., *Rewriting the Rules: Gig Companies' Drive for Labor Deregulation* (Deepa Das Acevedo ed., *Beyond the Algorithm: Qualitative Insights for Gig Work Regulation*, CUP 2020).

SOMAVÍA, J., *A Stronger ILO: Meeting the Need for a Social Dimension of Globalization Through the Decent Work Agenda* (ILO ed., *Report V Strengthening the ILO's Capacity to Assist its Members' Efforts to Reach its Objectives in the Context of Globalization*, ILO 2007).

STEVENSON, B., *The Internet and Job Search* (David H. Autor ed., *Studies of Labor Market Intermediation*, University of Chicago Press 2009).

STRAUSS, K. and FUDGE, J., *Temporary Work, Agencies and Unfree Labour: Insecurity in the New World of Work* (Kendra Strauss & Judy Fudge eds., *Temporary Work, Agencies and Unfree Labour: Insecurity in the New World of Work*, Routledge 2014).

STROWEL, A. and VERGOTE, W., *Digital Platforms: To Regulate or Not to Regulate?* (Bram Devolder ed., *The Platform Economy*, Intersentia 2019).

SWEPSTON, L., *International Labour Law* (Roger Blanpain ed., *Comparative Labour Law and Industrial Relations in Industrialized Market Economies*, Kluwer 2014).

TAPIOLA, K., *What Happened to International Labour Standards and Human Rights at Work?* (Tarja Halonen & Ulla Liukkunen eds., *International Labour Organization and Global Social Governance*, Springer 2021).

THOMAS, C., OELZ, M. and BEAUDONNET, X., *The Use of International Labour Law in Domestic Courts: Theory, Recent Jurisprudence, and Practical Implications* (Jean-Claude Javillier, Bernard Gernigon & Georges P. Politakis eds., *Les Normes Internationales du Travail: Un Patrimoine pour l'Avenir. Mélanges en l'Honneur de Nicolas Valticos*, ILO 2004).

TREBILCOCK, A., *The International Labour Organization* (Michael J. Bowman & Dino Kritsiotis eds., *Conceptual and Contextual Perspectives on the Modern Law of Treaties*, CUP 2018).

TSIKATA, D., *Employment Agencies and Domestic Work in Ghana* (Judy Fudge, Shae McCrystal & Kamala Sankaran eds., *Challenging the Legal Boundaries of Work Regulation*, Hart Publishing 2012).

VALTICOS, N., *The Sources of International Labour Law: Recent Trends* (Wybo P. Heere ed., *International Law and its Sources: Liber Amicorum Maarten Bos*, Kluwer 1989).

VAN DOORN, N., *From a Wage to a Wager: Dynamic Pricing in the Gig Economy* (James Muldoon & Will Stronge eds., *Platforming Equality: Policy Challenges for the Digital Economy*, Autonomy 2020).

WATTECAMPS, C., *Quel Droit Social pour les Travailleurs de Plateformes?* (Auriane Lamine & Céline Wattecamps eds., *Quel Droit Social pour Les Travailleurs de Plateformes?*, Anthemis 2020).

WOODCOCK, J., *Digital Labour and Workers' Organisation* (Maurizio Atzeni & Immanuel Ness eds., *Global Perspectives on Workers' and Labour Organizations*, Springer Singapore 2018).

ZALE, K., *Scale and the Sharing Economy* (Nestor M. Davidson, Michèle Finck & John J. Infranca eds., *The Cambridge Handbook of the Law of the Sharing Economy*, CUP 2018).

Journal Articles

ABIRU, K., *Status of the Gig Economy in Japan Considered from a Survey of C-to-C Babysitter Services*, 15 E-journal GEO 267 n. 2 (2020).

ADAMS, Z., BISHOP, L., DEAKIN, S., FENWICK, C., MARTINSSON GARZELLI, S. and RUSCONI, G., *The Economic Significance of Laws Relating to Employment Protection and Different Forms of Employment: Analysis of a Panel of 117 Countries, 1990–2013*, 158 International Labour Review 1 n. 1 (2019).

AGARWALA, R. and SAHA, S., *The Employment Relationship and Movement Strategies among Domestic Workers in India*, 44 Critical Sociology 1207 n. 7–8 (2018).

AJUNWA, I., *Age Discrimination by Platforms*, 40 Berkeley Journal of Employment and Labor Law 1 n. 1 (2019).

AJUNWA, I., *The Paradox of Automation as Anti-Bias Intervention*, 41 Cardozo Law Review 1671 n. 4 (2020).

ALBIN, E. and MANTOUVALOU, V., *The ILO Convention on Domestic Workers: From the Shadows to the Light*, 41 Industrial Law Journal 67 n. 1 (2012).

ALBRECHT, S. L., *Industrial Home Work in the United States: Historical Dimensions and Contemporary Perspective*, 3 Economic and Industrial Democracy 413 n. 4 (1982).

ALSTON, P., *'Core Labour Standards' and the Transformation of the International Labour Rights Regime*, 15 European Journal of International Law 457 n. 3 (2004).

ALTENRIED, M., *The Platform as Factory: Crowdwork and the Hidden Labour Behind Artificial Intelligence*, 44 Capital & Class 145 n. 2 (2020).

ALTENRIED, M. and BOJADŽIJEV, M., *Virtual Migration, Racism and the Multiplication of Labour*, 4 Spheres Journal for Digital Cultures 1 (2017).

ANDERSON, B., *Just Another Job? Paying for Domestic Work*, 9 Gender and Development 25 n. 1 (2001).

ANDRIJASEVIC, R. and SACCHETTO, D., *'Disappearing Workers': Foxconn in Europe and the Changing Role of Temporary Work Agencies*, 31 Work, Employment and Society 54 n. 1 (2017).

ANWAR, M. A. and GRAHAM, M., *Hidden Transcripts of the Gig Economy: Labour Agency and the New Art of Resistance Among African Gig Workers*, 52 EPA: Economy and Space 1269 n. 7 (2020).

ANWAR, M. A. and GRAHAM, M., *Between a Rock and a Hard Place: Freedom, Flexibility, Precarity and Vulnerability in the Gig Economy in Africa*, 25 Competition & Change 237 n. 2 (2020).

ARATO, J., *Treaty Interpretation and Constitutional Transformation: Informal Change in International Organizations*, 38 The Yale Journal of International Law 289 n. 2 (2013).

AUTOR, D. H., *Wiring the Labor Market*, 15 Journal of Economic Perspectives 25 n. 1 (2001).

AUTOR, D. H., *Outsourcing at Will: The Contribution of Unjust Dismissal Doctrine to the Growth of Employment Outsourcing*, 21 Journal of Labor Economics 1 n. 1 (2003).

AZARIA, D., *The Legal Significance of Expert Treaty Bodies Pronouncements for the Purpose of the Interpretation of Treaties*, 22 International Community Law Review 33 n. 1 (2020).

BACCARO, L. and MELE, V., *Pathology of Path Dependency? The ILO and the Challenge of New Governance*, 65 Industrial & Labor Relations Review 195 n. 2 (2012).

BARACH, M. A., GOLDEN, J. M. and HORTON, J. J., *Steering in Online Markets: The Role of Platform Incentives and Credibility*, 66 Management Science 4047 n. 9 (2020).

BARNES, S.-A., GREEN, A. and DE HOYOS, M., *Crowdsourcing and Work: Individual Factors and Circumstances Influencing Employability*, 30 New Technology, Work and Employment 16 n. 1 (2015).

BARTOSIK-PURGAT, M. and JANKOWSKA, B., *The Use of Social Networking Sites in Job Related Activities: A Cross-cultural Comparison*, 5 Entrepreneurial Business and Economic Review 177 n. 2 (2017).

BAYLINA, M. and GARCIA-RAMON, M. D., Homeworking in Rural Spain: A Gender Approach, 5 *European Urban and Regional Studies* 55 n. 1 (1998).

BEHAGHEL, L., CAROLI, E. and WALKOWIAK, E., *Information and Communication Technologies and Skill Upgrading: The Role of Internal vs External Labour Markets*, 64 Oxford Economic Papers 490 n. 3 (2012).

BEHRENDT, C., NGUYEN, Q. A. and RANI, U., *Social Protection Systems and the Future of Work: Ensuring Social Security for Digital Platform Workers*, 72 International Social Security Review 17 n. 3 (2019).

BELLACE, J. R., *The ILO Declaration of Fundamental Principles and Rights at Work*, 17 International Journal of Comparative Labour Law and Industrial Relations 269 n. 3 (2001).

BELLACE, J. R., *Achieving Social Justice: The Nexus between the ILO's Fundamental Rights and Decent Work*, 15 Employee Rights and Employment Policy Journal 5 n. 1 (2011).

BELLACE, J. R., *ILO Convention No. 87 and the Right to Strike in an Era of Global Trade*, 39 Comparative Labor Law & Policy Journal 495 n. 3 (2018).

BELLACE, J. R., *The Changing Face of Capital: The Withering of the Employment Relationship in the Information Age*, 100 Bulletin of Comparative Labour Relations 11 (2018).

BELLESIA, F., MATTARELLI, E., BERTOLOTTI, F. and SOBRERO, M., *Platforms as Entrepreneurial Incubators? How Online Labor Markets Shape Work Identity*, 34 Journal of Managerial Psychology 246 n. 4 (2019).

BEFORT, S. F., *Revisiting the Black Hole of Workplace Regulation: A Historical and Comparative Perspective of Contingent Work*, 24 Berkeley Journal of Employment & Labor Law 153 n. 1 (2003).

BENNER, C., *Labour Flexibility and Regional Development: The Role of Labour Market Intermediaries*, 37 Regional Studies 621 n. 6–7 (2003).

BENTON, L. A., *Homework and Industrial Development: Gender Roles and Restructuring in the Spanish Shoe Industry*, 17 World Development 255 n. 2 (1989).

BERG, J., *Income Security in the On-demand Economy: Findings and Policy Lessons from a Survey of Crowdworkers*, 37 Comparative Labor Law & Policy Journal 543 n. 3 (2016).

BERG, J., *Protecting Workers in the Digital Age: Technology, Outsourcing, and the Growing Precariousness of Work*, 41 Comparative Labor Law & Policy Journal 69 n. 1 (2019).

BERG, J., CHERRY, M. A. and RANI, U., *Digital Labour Platforms: A Need for International Regulation?*, 16 Revista de Economía Laboral 104 n. 2 (2019).

BIELBY, W. T. and BIELBY, D. D., *Organizational Mediation of Project-Based Labor Markets: Talent Agencies and the Careers of Screenwriters*, 64 American Sociological Review 64 n. 1 (1999).

BLACKETT, A., *Introduction: Regulating Decent Work for Domestic Workers*, 23 Canadian Journal of women and the law 1 n. 1 (2011).

BLACKETT, A., *The Decent Work for Domestic Workers Convention and Recommendation, 2011*, 106 The American journal of international law 778 n. 4 (2012).

BLACKETT, A., *Introductory Note to the Decent Work for Domestic Workers Convention, 2011 (No. 189) and Recommendation (No. 201)*, 53 International Legal Materials 250 n. 1 (2014).

BLACKETT, A., *Regulatory Innovation on Decent Work for Domestic Workers in the Light of International Labour Organization Convention No. 189*, 34 International Journal of Comparative Labour Law and Industrial Relations 141 n. 2 (2018).

BLACKETT, A., *Introduction: Transnational Futures of International Labour Law*, 159 International Labour Review 455 n. 4 (2020).

BLANPAIN, R., *De Tijdelijke Arbeid*, 36 Rechtskundig Weekblad 509 n. 11 (1972).

BLANPAIN, R., *Belgian Report*, 36 Bulletin of Comparative Labour Relations 181 (1999).

BLOFIELD, M. and JOKELA, M., Paid Domestic Work and the Struggles of Care Workers in Latin America, 66 Current Sociology Monograph 531 n. 4 (2018).

BLOMME, F., *Huispersoneel: Van Dienstboden en Nannies tot Privéverpleegkundigen en (Ortho)(ped)agogische Begeleiders*, Oriëntatie 1 n. 3 (2017).

BONET, R., CAPPELLI, P. and HAMORI, M., *Labor Market Intermediaries and the New Paradigm for Human Resources*, 7 The Academy of Management Annals 341 n. 1 (2013).

BORIS, E., *Mothers, Household Managers, and Productive Workers: The International Labor Organization and Women in Development*, 14 Global Social Policy 189 n. 2 (2014).

BRAMESHUBER, E., *The 'Personal Work Relationship' in Austria*, 10 European Labour Law Journal 187 n. 3 (2019).

BRAWLEY, A. M. and PURY, C. L.S., *Work Experiences on MTurk: Job Satisfaction, Turnover, and Information Sharing*, 54 Computers in Human Behavior 531 (2016).

BRÖLMANN, C., *Law-Making Treaties: Form and Function in International Law*, 74 Nordic Journal of International Law 383 n. 3–4 (2005).

BROOK, P. and PURCELL, C., *The Resistible Rise of the Temporary Employment Industry in France*, 41 Economic and Industrial Democracy 121 n. 1 (2020).

BRUURS, S., *Het Welzijn van Dienstboden en Huispersoneel: Thuis op de Werkvloer*, Arbeidsrecht Journaal (2021).

BURCHIELLI, R. and DELANEY, A., *The Invisibilization and Denial of Work in Argentinian Garment Homework*, 71 Relations industrielles / Industrial Relations 468 n. 3 (2016).

CALLEMAN, C., *Domestic Services in a "Land of Equality": The Case of Sweden*, 23 Canadian Journal of women and the law 121 n. 1 (2011).

CAPLAN, R. and GILLESPIE, T., *Tiered Governance and Demonetization: The Shifting Terms of Labor and Compensation in the Platform Economy*, 6 Social Media + Society 1 n. 2 (2020).

CAPPELLI, P., *Career Jobs Are Dead*, 42 California Management Review 146 n. 1 (1999).

CAPPELLI, P., *Your Approach to Hiring Is All Wrong*, 97 Harvard Business Review 48 n. 3 (2019).

CAPPELLI, P. and KELLER, J. R., *Classifying Work in the New Economy*, 38 The Academy of Management Review 575 n. 4 (2013).

CHAMBERS, T. and ANSARI, A., *Ghar Mein Kām Hai (There is Work in the House): When Female Factory Workers Become 'Coopted Domestic Labour'*, 13 Journal of South Asian Development 141 n. 2 (2018).

CHEN, M. A. and SINHA, S., *Home-based Workers and Cities*, 28 Environment & Urbanization 343 n. 2 (2016).

CHERRY, M. A. and ALOISI, A., *"Dependent Contractors" in the Gig Economy: a Comparative Approach*, 66 American University Law Review 635 n. 3 (2017).

CHERRY, M. A., *Age Discrimination in the On-Demand Economy and Crowdwork*, 40 Berkeley Journal of Employment and Labor Law 29 n. 1 (2019).

CHIGARA, B., *Latecomers to the ILO and the Authorship and Ownership of the International Labour Code*, 29 Human Rights Quarterly 706 n. 3 (2007).

COASE, R. H., *The Nature of the Firm*, 4 Economica 386 n. 16 (1937).

COCKAYNE, D. G., *Sharing and Neoliberal Discourse: The Economic Function of Sharing in the Digital On-demand Economy*, 77 Geoforum 73 (2016).

COE, N. M. and JORDHUS-LIER, D. C., *Constrained Agency? Re-evaluating the Geographies of Labour*, 35 Progress in Human Geography 211 n. 2 (2010).

COONEY, S., *Testing Times for the ILO: Institutional Reform for the New International Political Economy*, 20 Comparative Labor Law & Policy Journal 365 n. 3 (1999).

CORDOVA, E., *Some Reflections on the Overproduction of International Labor Standards*, 14 Comparative Labor Law Journal 138 n. 2 (1993).

COUNTOURIS, N. and HORTON, R., *The Temporary Agency Work Directive: Another Broken Promise?*, 38 Industrial Law Journal 329 n. 3 (2009).

CULPEPPER, P. D. and THELEN, K., *Are We All Amazon Primed? Consumers and the Politics of Platform Power*, 53 Comparative Political Studies 288 n. 2 (2020).

DALENBERG, D. J., *Preventing Discrimination in the Automated Targeting of Job Advertisements*, 34 Computer Law & Security Review 615 n. 3 (2018).

DAVENPORT, T. H., *When Jobs Become Commodities*, 59 MIT Sloan Management Review 16 n. 2 (2018).

DAVIDOV, G., *Joint Employer Status in Triangular Employment Relationships*, 42 British Journal of Industrial Relations 727 n. 4 (2004).

DAVIDOV, G., *Who is a Worker?*, 34 Industrial Law Journal 57 n. 1 (2005).

DAVIES, A. C. L., *Wages and Working Time in the 'Gig Economy'*, 31 King's Law Journal 250 n. 2 (2020).

DAVIS, M. E. and HOYT, E., *A Longitudinal Study of Piece Rate and Health: Evidence and Implications for Workers in the US Gig Economy*, 180 Public Health 1 (2020).

DAUGAREILH, I., *La Déclaration du Centenaire de l'OIT: Tout un Programme!*, Droit social (2020).

DAU-SCHMIDT, K. G., *The Impact of Emerging Information Technologies on the Employment Relationship: New Gigs for Labor and Employment Law*, University of Chicago Legal Forum 63 (2017).

D'CRUZ, P. and NORONHA, E., *Positives Outweighing Negatives: The Experiences of Indian Crowdsourced Workers*, 10 Work Organisation, Labour & Globalisation 44 n. 1 (2016).

DEKAY, S., *Are Business-orientated Social Networking Web Sites Useful Resources for Locating Passive Jobseekers? Results of a Recent Study*, 72 Business Communication Quarterly 101 n. 1 (2009).

DEMIREL, P., NEMKOVA, E. and TAYLOR, R., *Reproducing Global Inequalities in the Online Labour Market: Valuing Capital in the Design Field*, Work, Employment and Society 1 (2020).

DENG, X. N., JOSHI, K. D. and GALLIERS, R. D., *The Duality of Empowerment and Marginalization in Microtask Crowdsourcing: Giving Voice to the Less Powerful Through Value Sensitive Design*, 40 MIS Quarterly 279 n. 2 (2016).

DERANTY, J.-P. and MACMILLAN, C., *The ILO's Decent Work Initiative: Suggestions for an Extension of the Notion of "Decent Work"*, 43 Journal of Social Philosophy 386 n. 4 (2012).

DE RUIJTER, E. and VAN DER LIPPE, T., *Getting Outside Help: How Trust Problems Explain Household Differences in Domestic Outsourcing in the Netherlands*, 30 Journal of Family Issues 3 n. 1 (2009).

DE RUIJTER, E., VAN DER LIPPE, T. and RAUB, W., *Trust Problems in Household Outsourcing*, 15 Rationality and Society 473 n. 4 (2003).

DE RUYTER, A., BROWN, M. and BURGESS, J., Gig Work and the Fourth Industrial Revolution: Conceptual and Regulatory Challenges, 72 Journal of International Affairs 37 n. 1 (2019).

DE STEFANO, V., *Casual Work beyond Casual Work in the EU: The Underground Casualisation of the European Workforce – And What to Do about it*, 7 European Labour Law Journal 421 n. 3 (2016).

DE STEFANO, V., *The Rise of "Just-in-time Workforce": On-demand Work, Crowdwork, and Labor Protection in the "Gig-economy"*, 37 Comparative Labor Law & Policy Journal 471 n. 3 (2016).

DE STEFANO, V., *"Negotiating the Algorithm": Automation, Artificial Intelligence and Labor Protection*, 41 Comparative Labor Law & Policy Journal 15 n. 1 (2019).

DE STEFANO, V., *Not as Simple as it Seems: The ILO and the Personal Scope of International Labour Standards*, 160 International Labour Review 387 n. 3 (2021).

DE STEFANO, V. and WOUTERS, M., *Triangulaire Arbeidsrelaties in de Platformeconomie: Een Voorstel tot een Vermoeden van Uitzendbureau*, 13 Arbeidsrechtelijke Annotaties 3 n. 3 (2019).

DE WET, E., *Governance through Promotion and Persuasion: The ILO Declaration on Fundamental Principles and Rights at Work*, 9 German Law Journal 1429 n. 11 (2008).

DEY, M., HOUSEMAN, S. N. and POLIVKA, A. E., *Manufacturers' Outsourcing to Staffing Services*, 65 Industrial & Labor Relations Review 533 n. 3 (2012).

DI RUGGIERO, E., COHEN, J. E., COLE, D. C. and FORMAN, L., *Competing Conceptualizations of Decent Work at the Intersection of Health, Social and Economic Discourses*, 133 Social Science & Medicine 120 (2015).

DOHERTY, M. and FRANCA, V., *Solving the 'Gig-saw'? Collective rights and Platform Work*, 49 Industrial Law Journal 352 n. 3 (2020).

DOTHAN, S., *The Three Traditional Approaches to Treaty Interpretation: A Current Application to the European Court of Human Rights*, 42 Fordham International Law Review 765 n. 3 (2019).

DOTY, P., *Private Pay Home Care: New Models of Access and Service Delivery*, 27 Public Policy & Aging Report 111 n. 3 (2017).

DREHER, G. F., LEE, J.-Y. and CLERKIN, T. A., *Mobility and Cash Compensation: The Moderating Effects of Gender, Race, and Executive Search Firms*, 37 Journal of Management 651 n. 3 (2011).

DUBAL, V., *Digital Piecework*, 67 Dissent 37 n. 4 (2020).

DUGGAN, J., SHERMAN, U., CARBERY, R. and McDONNELL, A., *Algorithmic Management and App-work in the Gig Economy: A Research Agenda for Employment Relations and HRM*, 30 Human Resource Management Journal 114 n. 1 (2020).

DUKES, R., *Regulating Gigs*, 83 Modern Law Review 217 n. 1 (2020).

DU PREEZ, J., BESWICK, C., WHITTAKER, L. and DICKINSON, D., *The Employment Relationship in the Domestic Workspace in South Africa: Beyond the Apartheid Legacy*, 36 Social Dynamics 395 n. 2 (2010).

EDELMAN, B. G. and GERADIN, D., *Efficiencies and Regulatory Shortcuts: How Should We Regulate Companies Like Airbnb and Uber?*, 19 Stanford Technology Law Review 293 n. 2 (2016).

EICHLER, M., *Integrating Carework and Housework into Household Work: A Conceptual Clarification*, 10 Journal of the Association for Research on Mothering 9 n. 1 (2008).

EICHLER, M. and ALBANESE, P., *What Is Household Work? A Critique of Assumptions Underlying Empirical Studies of Housework and an Alternative Approach*, 32 The Canadian Journal of Sociology 227 n. 2 (2007).

EKLUND, R., *A Look at Contract Labour in the Nordic Countries*, 18 Comparative Labor Law & Policy Journal 229 n. 2 (1997).

ELIAS, J., *The Malaysia-Indonesia Domestic Worker Dispute*, 15 International Feminist Journal of Politics 391 n. 3 (2013).

ENGLAND, P., *Emerging Theories of Care Work*, 31 Annual Review of Sociology 381 n. 1 (2005).

ENRIGHT, B., *(Re)considering New Agents: A Review of Labour Market Intermediaries within Labour Geography*, 7 Geography Compass 287 n. 4 (2013).

ESTLUND, J. and GRÖNLUND, A., *Class and Work Autonomy in 21 Countries: A Question of Production Regime or Power Resources?*, 53 Acta Sociologica 213 n. 3 (2010).

EWING, K. D., *Regulating for Decent Work and the Effectiveness of Labour Law*, 39 New Zealand Journal of Employment Relations 3 n. 2 (2014).

FABO, B., KARANOVIC, J. and DUKOVA, K., *In Search of an Adequate European Policy Response to the Platform Economy*, 23 Transfer 163 n. 2 (2017).

FAUSER, S., *Time Availability and Housework: The Effect of Unemployment on Couples' Hours of Household Labor*, 83 Social Science Research 1 (2019).

FELIN, T. and ZENGER, T. R., *Information Aggregation, Matching and Radical Market-hierarchy Hybrids: Implications for the Theory of the Firm*, 9 Strategic Organization 163 n. 2 (2011).

FELSTEAD, A., JEWSON, N., PHIZACKLEA, A. and WALTERS, S., *The Option to Work at Home: Another Privilege for the Favoured Few?*, 17 New Technology, Work and Employment 204 n. 3 (2002).

FELSTEAD, A. and HENSEKE, G., *Assessing the Growth of Remote Working and its Consequences for Effort, Well-being and Work-life Balance*, 32 New Technology, Work and Employment 195 n. 3 (2017).

FELSTINER, A., *Working the Crowd: Employment and Labor Law in the Crowdsourcing Industry*, 32 Berkeley Journal of Employment & Labor Law 143 n. 1 (2011).

FERNANDEZ-MATEO, I. and KING, Z., *Anticipatory Sorting and Gender Segregation in Temporary Employment*, 57 Management Science 989 n. 6 (2011).

FIESELER, C., BUCHER, E. and HOFFMAN, C. P., *Unfairness by Design? The Perceived Fairness of Digital Labor on Crowdworking Platforms*, 156 Journal of business ethics 987 n. 4 (2019).

FIGUEIREDO, M. D. C., SULEMAN, F. and BOTELHO, M. D. C., *Workplace Abuse and Harassment: The Vulnerability of Informal and Migrant Domestic Workers in Portugal*, 17 Social Policy & Society 65 n. 1 (2018).

FINKIN, M. W., *Beclouded Work, Beclouded Workers in Historical Perspective*, 37 Comparative Labor Law & Policy Journal 603 n. 3 (2016).

FINLAY, W. and COVERDILL, J. E., *The Search Game: Organizational Conflicts and the Use of Headhunters*, 40 The Sociological Quarterly 11 n. 1 (1999).

FISH, J. N., *Engendering Democracy: Domestic Labour and Coalition-Building in South Africa*, 32 Journal of Southern African Studies 107 n. 1 (2006).

FITZMAURICE, M., *Subsequent Agreement and Subsequent Practice: Some Reflections on the International Law Commission's Draft Conclusions*, 22 International Community Law Review 14 n. 1 (2020).

FLANAGAN, F., *Theorising the Gig Economy and Home-based Service Work*, 61 Journal of Industrial Relations 57 n. 1 (2019).

FLEMING, P., RHODES, C. and YU, K.-H., *On Why Uber Has Not Taken Over the World*, 48 Economy and Society 488 n. 4 (2019).

FORDE, C., *"You Know We Are Not an Employment Agency": Manpower, Government, and the Development of the Temporary Help Industry in Britain*, 9 Enterprise & Society 337 n. 2 (2008).

FREEMAN, D., *Homeworkers in Global Supply Chains*, 43 Greener Management International 106 (2003).

FREEMAN, H. and GONOS, G., *Regulating the Employment Sharks: Reconceptualizing the Legal Status of the Commercial Temp Agency*, 8 Working USA 293 n. 3 (2005).

FREEMAN, H. and GONOS, G., *Taming the Employment Sharks: The Case for Regulating Profit-driven Labor Market Intermediaries in High Mobility Labor Markets*, 13 Employee Rights and Employment Policy Journal 285 n. 2 (2009).

FREY, D. F., *Economic Growth, Full Employment and Decent Work: The Means and Ends in SDG 8*, 21 The International Journal of Human Rights 1164 n. 8 (2017).

FUDGE, J., *Global Care Chains, Employment Agencies, and the Conundrum of Jurisdiction: Decent Work for Domestic Workers in Canada*, 23 Canadian Journal of women and the law 235 n. 1 (2011).

FUDGE, J., *Regulating for Decent Work in a Global Economy*, 43 New Zealand Journal of Employment Relations 10 n. 2 (2018).

FUDGE, J., *Everyday Transgressions: Domestic Workers' Transnational Challenge to International Labor Law*, 41 Comparative Labor Law & Policy Journal 299 n. 1 (2019).

FUKUDA-PARR, S. and HULME, D., *International Norm Dynamics and the "End of Poverty": Understanding the Millennium Development Goals*, 17 Global Governance 17 n. 1 (2011).

FUSTER, B., LILLO-BAÑULS, A. and MARTÍNEZ-MORA, C., *Offshoring of Services as a Competitive Strategy in the Tourism Industry*, 24 Tourism Economics 963 n. 8 (2018).

GANDINI, A., *Digital Work: Self-branding and Social Capital in the Freelance Knowledge Economy*, 16 Marketing Theory 123 n. 1 (2016).

GANDINI, A., *Labour Process Theory and the Gig Economy*, 72 Human Relations 1039 n. 6 (2019).

GERBER, C., *Community Building on Crowdwork Platforms: Autonomy and Control of Online Workers?*, 25 Competition & Change 190 n. 2 (2021).

GIANELLE, C., *Labor Market Intermediaries Make the World Smaller*, 24 Journal of Evolutionary Economics 951 n. 5 (2014).

GILLESPIE, T., *The Politics of 'Platforms'*, 12 New Media & Society 347 n. 3 (2010).

GONOS, G., *The Contest over 'Employment Status' in the Post-War United States: The Case of Temporary Help Firms*, 31 Law and Society Review 81 n. 1 (1997).

GONOS, G., *"Never a Fee!" The Miracle of Postmodern Temporary Help and Staffing Agency*, 4 Working USA 9 n. 3 (2000–01).

GOODS, C., VEEN, A. and BARRATT, T., *"Is your Gig any Good?" Analysing Job Quality in the Australian Platform-based Food-delivery Sector*, 61 Journal of Industrial Relations 502 n. 4 (2019).

GÖTT, H., *Interactions between International Organizations: Approaching a Neglected Governance Dimension*, 17 International Organizations Law Review 75 n. 1 (2020).

GRAHAM, M., HJORTH, I. and LEHDONVIRTA, V., *Digital Labour and Development: Impacts of Global Digital Labour Platforms and the Gig Economy on Worker Livelihoods*, 23 Transfer 135 n. 2 (2017).

GRAHAM, M. and WOODCOCK, J., *Towards a Fairer Platform Economy: Introducing the Fairwork Foundation*, 29 Alternate Routes 242 (2018).

GRAMANO, E. and GAUDIO, G., *'New Trade Union Strategies for New Forms of Employment': Focus on Italy*, 10 European Labour Law Journal 240 n. 3 (2019).

GREGORY, K., *'My Life Is More Valuable Than This': Understanding Risk among On-Demand Couriers in Edinburgh*, 35 Work, Employment and Society 316 n. 2 (2021).

GRIESBACH, K., REICH, A., ELLIOTT-NEGRI, L. and MILKMAN, R., *Algorithmic Control in Platform Food Delivery Work*, 5 Socius 1 (2019).

GROZDANOVSKI, L., *Les Services Fournis par les Plateformes Numériques: Quelle Qualification Juridique pour Quels Enjeux?*, 139 Journal des tribunaux 449 n. 6818 (2020).

HAGIU, A. and WRIGHT, J., *Multi-sided Platforms*, 43 International Journal of Industrial Organization 162 (2015).

HATTON, E., *Gig Work: All Hustle and Little Gain*, 49 Contemporary Sociology 397 n. 5 (2020).

HAUF, F., *The Paradoxes of Decent Work in Context: A Cultural Political Economy Perspective*, 6 Global Labour Journal 138 n. 2 (2015).

HELFER, L. R., *Understanding Change in International Organizations: Globalization and Innovation in the ILO*, 59 Vanderbilt Law Review 649 n. 3 (2006).

HELFER, L. R., *Monitoring Compliance with Unratified Treaties: The ILO Experience*, 71 Law & Contemporary Problems 193 n. 1 (2008).

HENDRICKX, F., *Foundations and Functions of Contemporary Labour Law*, 3 European Labour Law Journal 108 n. 2 (2012).

HENDRICKX, F., *From Digits to Robots: The Privacy-autonomy Nexus in New Labor Law Machinery*, 40 Comparative Labor Law & Policy Journal 365 n. 3 (2019).

HONDAGNEU-SOTELO, P., *Regulating the Unregulated?: Domestic Workers' Social Networks*, 41 Social problems 50 n. 1 (1994).

HORTON, J. J. and TAMBE, P., *Labor Economists Get Their Microscope: Big Data and Labor Market Analysis*, 3 Big Data 130 n. 3 (2015).

HOUSEMAN, S. N., *Why Employers Use Flexible Staffing Arrangements: Evidence from an Establishment Survey*, 55 Industrial and Labor Relations Review 149 n. 1 (2001).

HOWCROFT, D. and BERGVALL-KÅREBORN, B., *A Typology of Crowdwork Platforms*, 33 Work, Employment and Society 21 n. 1 (2019).

HUNT, A. and SAMMAN, E., *Domestic Work and the Gig Economy in South Africa: Old Wine in New Bottles?*, 15 Anti-Trafficking Review 102 (2020).

HUWS, U., *Logged Labour: A New paradigm of Work Organisation?*, 10 Work Organisation, Labour & Globalisation 7 n. 1 (2016).

HUWS, U., *The Hassle of Housework: Digitalisation and the Commodification of Domestic Labour*, 123 Feminist Review 8 n. 1 (2019).

HUWS, U., SPENCER, N. H. and SYRDAL, D. S., *Online, On Call: The Spread of Digitally Organised Just-in-time Working and its Implications for Standard Employment Models*, 33 New Technology, Work and Employment 113 n. 2 (2018).

HYDE, A., *The International Labor Organization in the Stag Hunt for Global Labor Rights*, 3 Law & Ethics of Human Rights 154 n. 2 (2009).

IDOWU, A. and ELBANNA, A., *Digital Platforms of Work and the Crafting of Career Path: The Crowdworkers' Perspective*, Information Systems Frontiers (2020).

ILO, *Part IV: Positions on Home Work*, 8 Conditions of Work Digest 159 n. 2 (1989).

INGOLD, J. and VALIZADE, D., *Employers' Recruitment of Disadvantaged Groups: Exploring the Effect of Active Labour Market Programme Agencies as Labour Market Intermediaries*, 27 Human Resource Management Journal 530 n. 4 (2017).

IPEIROTIS, P. G., *Analyzing the Amazon Mechanical Turk Marketplace*, 17 ACM Crossroads 16 n. 2 (2010).

JÄGER, G., ZILIAN, L. S., HOFER, C. and FÜLLSACK, M., *Crowdworking: Working With or Against the Crowd?*, 14 Journal of Economic Interaction and Coordination 761 n. 4 (2019).

JAKOVLESKI, V., JERBI, S. and BIERSTEKER, T., *The ILO's Role in Global Governance: Limits and Potential*, 11 Revue Internationale de Politique de Développement / International Development Policy 82 (2019).

JARRAHI, M. H., SUTHERLAND, W., NELSON, S. B. and SAWYER, S., *Platformic Management, Boundary Resources for Gig Work, and Worker Autonomy*, 29 Computer Supported Cooperative Work 153 n. 1–2 (2020).

JENKS, C. W., *The Significance for International Law of the Tripartite Character of the International Labour Organisation*, 22 Transactions of the Grotius Society 45 (1936).

JOKELA, M., *Patterns of Precarious Employment in a Female-Dominated Sector in Five Welfare States – The Case of Paid Domestic Labor Sector*, 26 Social Politics 30 n. 1 (2019).

JOSSERAND, E. and KAINE, S., *Different Directions or the Same Route? The Varied Identities of Ride-share Drivers*, 61 Journal of Industrial Relations 549 n. 4 (2019).

JOYNER, C. C., *The United States' Withdrawal from the ILO: International Politics in the Labor Arena*, 12 International Lawyer 721 n. 4 (1978).

JURIK, N. C., *Getting Away and Getting By: The Experiences of Self-Employed Homeworkers*, 25 Work and Occupations 7 n. 1 (1998).

KAASCH, A. and SHRIWISE, A. (eds.), *Global Social Policy Digest 20.1*, 20 Global Social Policy 117 n. 1 (2020).

KALLEBERG, A. L., *Precarious Work, Insecure Workers: Employment Relations in Transition*, 74 American Sociological Review 1 n. 1 (2009).

KALLEBERG, A. L. and DUNN, M., Good Jobs, Bad Jobs in the Gig Economy, 20 Perspectives on Work 10 (2016).

KALLEBERG, A. L., NESHEIM, T. and OLSEN, K. M., *Is Participation Good or Bad for Workers?: Effects of Autonomy, Consultation and Teamwork on Stress Among Workers in Norway*, 52 Acta Sociologica 99 n. 2 (2009).

KARANOVIĆ, J., BERENDS, H. and ENGEL, Y., *Regulated Dependence: Platform Workers' Responses to New Forms of Organizing*, 58 Journal of Management Studies 1070 n. 4 (2021).

KARAOGLU, G., HARGITTAI, E. and NGUYEN, M. H., *Inequality in Online Job Searching in the Age of Social Media*, Information, Communication & Society 1 (2021).

KASHYAP, R. and BHATIA, A., *Taxi Drivers and Taxidars: A Case Study of Uber and Ola in Delhi*, 34 Journal of Developing Societies 169 n. 2 (2018).

KEITH, M. G., HARMS, P. and TAY, L., *Mechanical Turk and the Gig Economy: Exploring Differences between Gig Workers*, 34 Journal of Managerial Psychology 286 n. 4 (2019).

KING, Z., BURKE, S. and PEMBERTON, J., *The 'Bounded' Career: An Empirical Study of Human Capital, Career Mobility and Employment Outcomes in a Mediated Labour Market*, 58 Human Relations 981 n. 8 (2005).

KIVIAT, B., *The Art of Deciding With Data: Evidence From How Employers Translate Credit Reports Into Hiring Decisions*, 17 Socio-Economic Review 283 n. 2 (2019).

KLABBERS, J., *International Legal Histories: The Declining Importance of Travaux Préparatoires in Treaty Interpretation?*, 50 Netherlands International Law Review 267 n. 3 (2003).

KOHN, A., *Why Incentive Plans Cannot Work*, 71 Harvard Business Review 54 n. 5 (1993).

KORDASIEWICZ, A., La Relation à l'Employé Vue du Côté Employeur: Le Travail Domestique des Migrantes Ukrainiennes en Pologne, 12 Cahiers de l'Urmis 1 (2009).

KORDASIEWICZ, A., *Role-Identity Dynamics in Care and Household Work: Strategies of Polish Workers in Naples, Italy*, 10 Qualitative Sociology Review 88 n. 4 (2014).

KOSSEFF, J., *First Amendment Protection for Online Platforms*, 35 Computer Law & Security Review 1 n. 5 (2019).

KUHN, P. and SKUTERUD, M., *Internet Job Search and Unemployment Durations*, 94 The American Economic Review 218 n. 1 (2004).

KUHN, P. and MANSOUR, H., *Is Internet Job Search Still Ineffective?*, 124 Economic Journal 1213 n. 581 (2014).

LA HOVARY, C., *Showdown at the ILO? A Historical Perspective on the Employers' Group's 2012 Challenge to the Right to Strike*, 42 Industrial Law Journal 338 n. 4 (2013).

LAIR, C. D. and ANDREWS, C. K., *Advertising a Particularly Precarious Occupation: Nanny Ads on Craigslist*, 38 Sociological Spectrum 69 n. 2 (2018).

LANGILLE, B. A., *The ILO and the New Economy: Recent Developments*, 15 International Journal of Comparative Labour Law and Industrial Relations 229 n. 3 (1999).

LANGILLE, B. A., *What is International Labor Law For?*, 3 Law & Ethics of Human Rights 48 n. 1 (2009).

LANGILLE, B., *'Hard Law Makes Bad Cases': The International Labour Organization (Nervously) Confronts New Governance Institutions*, 32 International Journal of Comparative Labour Law and Industrial Relations 407 n. 4 (2016).

LAWRENCE, P. R., *The Key Job Design Problem is Still Taylorism*, 31 Journal of Organizational Behavior 412 n. 2–3 (2010).

LECLERC, O. and PASQUIER, T., *La Dépendance Économique en Droit du Travail: Éclairages en Droit Français et en Droit Comparé*, Revue de droit du travail (2010).

LEE, E., *The Declaration of Philadelphia: Retrospect and Prospect*, 133 International Labour Law Review 467 n. 4 (1994).

LEGERSKI, E. M. and CORNWALL, M., *Working-Class Job Loss, Gender, and the Negotiation of Household Labor*, 24 Gender & Society 447 n. 4 (2010).

LEHDONVIRTA, V., *Flexibility in the Gig Economy: Managing Time on Three Online Piecework Platforms*, 33 New Technology, Work and Employment 13 n. 1 (2018).

LEHDONVIRTA, V., KÄSSI, O., HJORTH, I., BARNARD, H. and GRAHAM, M., *The Global Platform Economy: A New Offshoring Institution Enabling Emerging-Economy Microproviders*, 45 Journal of Management 567 n. 2 (2019).

LEIBER, S., MATUSZCZYK, K. and ROSSOW, V., *Private Labor Market Intermediaries in the Europeanized Live-in Care Market between Germany and Poland: A Typology*, 65 Zeitschrift für Sozialreform 365 n. 3 (2019).

LI, C., MIROSA, M. and BREMER, P., *Review of Online Food Delivery Platforms and their Impacts on Sustainability*, 12 Sustainability 1 (2020).

LIANOS, I., COUNTOURIS, N. and DE STEFANO, V., *Re-thinking the Competition Law/ Labour Law Interaction: Promoting a Fairer Labour Market*, 10 European Labour Law Journal 291 n. 3 (2019).

LIEBY, T., *Quelques Réflexions sur l'Interprétation des Conventions Internationales du Travail par le Juge National*, Revue internationale de droit économique 5 n. 1 (2020).

LIECHTI, F., *Connecting Employers and Workers: Can Recommendations from the Public Employment Servicer Act as a Substitute for Social Contacts?*, 34 Work, Employment and Society 587 n. 4 (2019).

LINDERFALK, U., *Is the Hierarchical Structure of Articles 31 and 32 of the Vienna Convention Real or Not? Interpreting the Rules of Interpretation*, 54 Netherlands International Law Review 133 n. 1 (2007).

LOBEL, O., *The Slipperiness of Stability: Contracting for Flexible and Triangular Employment Relationships in the New Economy*, 10 Texas Wesleyan Law Review 109 n. 1 (2003).

LOPES, A. L. S. V. and GARIBALDI DE HILAL, A. V., *Autonomy at Work: The Perspective of a Group of Brazilian Skilled Workers*, 17 Latin American Business Review 289 n. 4 (2016).

LORQUET, N., ORIANNE, J.-F. and PICHAULT, F., *Who Takes Care of Non-standard Career Paths? The Role of Labour Market Intermediaries?*, 24 European Journal of Industrial Relations 279 n. 3 (2018).

LOUIS, M., *Who Decides? Representation and Decision-Making at the International Labour Organization*, 11 International Development Policy / Revue internationale de politique de développement 40 (2019).

MACNAUGHTON, G. and FREY, D. F., *Decent Work, Human Rights and the Sustainable Development Goals*, 47 Georgetown Journal of International Law 607 n. 2 (2016).

MALIN, B. J. and CHANDLER, C., *Free to Work Anxiously: Splintering Precarity Among Drivers for Uber and Lyft*, 10 Communication, Culture & Critique 382 n. 2 (2017).

MANGAN, D., *Labour Law: The Medium and the Message*, 100 Bulletin of Comparative Labour Relations 63 (2018).

MANTOUVALOU, V., *Human Rights for Precarious Workers: The Legislative Precariousness of Domestic Labor*, 34 Comparative Labor Law & Policy Journal 133 n. 1 (2012).

MARCHAL, E., MELLET, K. and RIEUCAU, G., *Job Board Toolkits: Internet Matchmaking and Changes in Job Advertisements*, 60 Human Relations 1091 n. 7 (2007).

MARUYAMA, T., HOPKINSON, P. G. and JAMES, P. W., *A Multivariate Analysis of Work-life Balance Outcomes from a Large-scale Telework Programme*, 24 New Technology, Work and Employment 76 n. 1 (2009).

MAS, A. and PALLAIS, A., *Valuing Alternative Work Arrangements*, 107 The American Economic Review 3722 n. 12 (2017).

MASTERS, P. E., *The International Labor Organization: America's Withdrawal and Reentry*, 71 International Social Science Review 14 n. 3–4 (1996).

MAUPAIN, F., *New Foundation or New Façade? The ILO and the 2008 Declaration on Social Justice for a Fair Globalization*, 20 The European Journal of International Law 823 n. 3 (2009).

MAUPAIN, F., *The ILO Regular Supervisory System: A Model in Crisis?*, 10 International Organizations Law Review 117 n. 1 (2014).

MAUPAIN, F., *A Second Century for What? The ILO at a Regulatory Crossroad*, 17 International Organizations Law Review 291 n. 1 (2020).

MBENGUE, M. M., *Rules of Interpretation (Article 32 of the Vienna Convention on the Law of Treaties)*, 31 ICSID Review – Foreign Investment Law Journal 388 n. 2 (2016).

McCAUSLAND, W. D., POULIAKAS, K. and THEODOSSIOU, I., *Some Are Punished and Some Are Rewarded: A Study of the Impact of Performance Pay on Job Satisfaction*, 26 International Journal of Manpower 636 n. 7/8 (2005).

McGAUGHEY, E., *A Human is not a Resource*, 31 King's Law Journal 215 n. 2 (2020).

MEIJERINK, J., KEEGAN, A. and BONDAROUK, T., *Having Their Cake and Eating it too? Online Labor Platforms and Human Resource Management as a Case of Institutional Complexity*, The International Journal of Human Resource Management 1 (2021).

MERKOURIS, P., *(Inter)Temporal Considerations in the Interpretative Process of the VCLT: Do Treaties Endure, Perdure or Exdure?*, 45 Netherlands Yearbook of International Law 121 (2014).

MERVYN JONES, J., *International Agreements Other Than Inter-State Treaties – Modern Developments*, 21 British Year Book of International Law 111 (1944).

MÖLDNER, M., *Responsibility of International Organizations – Introducing the ILC's DARIO*, 16 Max Planck Yearbook of United Nations Law 281 n. 1 (2012).

MORAS, A., *The Private Home as a Public Workplace: Employing Paid Domestic Labor*, 13 Journal of Workplace Rights 377 n. 4 (2008).

MORAS, A., *Colour-blind Discourses in Paid Domestic Work: Foreignness and the Delineation of Alternative Racial Markers*, 33 Ethnic and Racial Studies 233 n. 2 (2010).

MORAS, A., *"This Should be My Responsibility": Gender, Guilt, Privilege and Paid Domestic Work*, 34 Gender Issues 44 n. 1 (2017).

MUEHLBERGER, U. and PASQUA, S., *Workers on the Border between Employment and Self-Employment*, 67 Review of Social Economy 201 n. 2 (2009).

MUNDLAK, G. and SHAMIR, H., *Bringing Together or Drifting Apart? Targeting Care Work as "Work like No Other"*, 23 Canadian Journal of women and the law 289 n. 1 (2011).

MURPHY, C., *The Enduring Vulnerability of Migrant Domestic Workers in Europe*, 62 The International and Comparative Law Quarterly 599 n. 3 (2013).

MURRAY, A. J. and DURRHEIM, K., *"There Was Much That Went Unspoken": Maintaining Racial Hierarchies in South African Paid Domestic Labour Through the Unsaid*, 42 Ethnic and Racial Studies 2623 n. 15 (2019).

MURRAY, J., *Social Justice for Women? The ILO's Convention on Part-time Work*, 15 International Journal of Comparative Labour Law and Industrial Relations 3 n. 1 (1999).

NEETHA, N. and PALRIWALA, R., *The Absence of State Law: Domestic Workers in India*, 23 Canadian Journal of women and the law 97 n. 1 (2011).

NEWLANDS, G., LUTZ, C. and FIESELER, C., *Collective Action and Provider Classification in the Sharing Economy*, 33 New Technology, Work and Employment 250 n. 3 (2018).

NIKOLAOU, I., *Social Networking Web Sites in Job Search and Employee Recruitment*, 22 International Journal of Selection and Assessment 179 n. 2 (2014).

NOLLEN, S., *Negative Aspects of Temporary Employment*, 17 Journal of Labor Research 567 n. 4 (1996).

NOVITZ, T., *Engagement with Sustainability at the International Labour Organization and Wider Implications for Collective Worker Voice*, 159 International Labour Review 463 n. 4 (2020)

NOVITZ, T., *Past and Future Work at the International Labour Organization: Labour as a Fictitious Commodity, Countermovement and Sustainability*, 17 International Organizations Law Review 10 n. 1 (2020).

NOVITZ, T., *The Potential for International Regulation of Gig Economy Issues*, 31 King's Law Journal 275 n. 2 (2020).

NOVITZ, T. and SYRPIS, P., *The Place of Domestic Work in Europe: An Analysis of Current Policy in the Light of the Council Decision Authorising Member States to Ratify ILO Convention No. 189*, 6 European Labour Law Journal 104 n. 2 (2015).

OEI, S.-Y., *The Trouble with Gig Talk: Choice of Narrative and the Worker Classification Fights*, 81 Law and Contemporary Problems 107 n. 3 (2018).

OELZ, M., *The ILO's Domestic Workers Convention and Recommendation: A Window of Opportunity for Social Justice*, 153 International Labour Review 143 n. 1 (2014).

O'HIGGINS, P., *"Labour is not a Commodity" – an Irish Contribution to International Labour Law*, 26 Industrial Law Journal 225 n. 3 (1997).

PALENGA-MÖLLENBECK, E., *New Maids – New Butlers? Polish Domestic Workers in Germany and Commodification of Social Reproductive Work*, 32 Equality, Diversity and Inclusion: An International Journal 557 n. 6 (2013).

PECK, J. and THEODORE, N., *The Business of Contingent Work: Growth and Restructuring in Chicago's Temporary Employment Industry*, 12 Work, Employment and Society 655 n. 4 (1998).

PECK, J. A. and THEODORE, N., *Temped Out? Industry Rhetoric, Labor Regulation and Economic Restructuring in the Temporary Staffing Business*, 23 Economic and Industrial Democracy 143 n. 2 (2002).

PECK, J. and THEODORE, N., *Flexible Recession: The Temporary Staffing Industry and Mediated Work in the United States*, 31 Cambridge Journal of Economics 171 n. 2 (2007).

PECK, J., THEODORE, N. and WARD, K., *Constructing Markets for Temporary Labour: Employment Liberalization and the Internationalization of the Staffing Industry*, 5 Global Networks 3 n. 1 (2005).

PETICCA-HARRIS, A., DEGAMA, N. and RAVISHANKAR, M. N., *Postcapitalist Precarious Work and Those in the 'Drivers' Seat: Exploring the Motivations and Lived Experiences of Uber Drivers in Canada*, 27 Organization 36 n. 1 (2020).

PFEIFFER, S. and KAWALEC, S., *Justice Expectations in Crowd and Platform-mediated Work*, 31 The Economic Labour Relations Review 483 n. 4 (2020).

PHAN, T., *ILO Convention on Private Employment Agencies (No. 181)*, 36 Bulletin of Comparative Labour Relations 77 (1999).

PICHAULT, F. and McKEOWN, T., *Autonomy at Work in the Gig Economy: Analysing Work Status, Work Content and Working Conditions of Independent Professionals*, 34 New Technology, Work and Employment 59 n. 1 (2019).

PIETROGIOVANNI, V., *Between Sein and Sollen of Labour Law: Civil (and Constitutional) Law Perspectives on Platform Workers*, 31 King's Law Journal 313 n. 2 (2020).

PISANI, N. and RICART, J. E., *Offshoring of Services: A Review of Literature and Organizing Framework*, 56 Management International Review 385 n. 3 (2016).

POSADA, J. and SHADE, L. R., *Platform Labour Discourse: How Hyr Targets the "Bucket List Generation"*, 29 Democratic Communiqué 78 n. 1 (2020).

POTOCKA-SIONEK, N. and ALOISI, A., *'Festina Lente': The ILO and EU Agendas on the Digital Transformation of Work*, 37 International Journal of Comparative Labour Law and Industrial Relations 35 n. 1 (2021).

PRASSL, J. and RISAK, M., *Uber, Taskrabbit, and Co.: Platforms as Employers? Rethinking the Legal Analysis of Crowdwork*, 37 Comparative Labor Law & Policy Journal 619 n. 3 (2016).

PRUIJT, H., *Repainting, Modifying, Smashing Taylorism*, 13 Journal of Organizational Change Management 439 n. 5 (2000).

RADAY, F., *The Insider-outsider Politics of Labor-only Contracting*, 20 Comparative Labor Law & Policy Journal 413 n. 3 (1999).

RAI, S. M., BROWN, B. D. and RUWANPURA, K. N., *SDG 8: Decent Work and Economic Growth – A Gendered Analysis*, 113 World Development 368 (2019).

RANI, U. and FURRER, M., *Digital Labour Platforms and New Forms of Flexible Work in Developing Countries: Algorithmic Management of Work and Workers*, 25 Competition & Change 212 n. 2 (2021).

RANI, U. and SINGH, P. J., *Digital Platforms, Data, and Development: Implications for Workers in Developing Economies*, 41 Comparative Labor Law & Policy Journal 263 n. 1 (2019).

RATTI, L., *Agency Work and the Idea of Dual Employership: A Comparative Perspective*, 30 Comparative Labor Law & Policy Journal 835 n. 4 (2009).

RATTI, L., *Online Platforms and Crowdwork in Europe: A Two-step Approach to Expanding Agency Work Provisions?*, 38 Comparative Labor Law & Policy Journal 477 n. 3 (2017).

RAVENELLE, A. J., *"We're not Uber:" Control, Autonomy, and Entrepreneurship in the Gig Economy*, 34 Journal of Managerial Psychology 269 n. 4 (2019).

RAZZOLINI, O., *The Need to Go Beyond the Contract: Economic and Bureaucratic Dependence in Personal Work Relations*, 31 Comparative Labor Law & Policy Journal 267 n. 2 (2010).

RIETIKER, D., *The Principle of "Effectiveness" in Recent Jurisprudence of the European Court of Human Rights: Its Different Dimensions and Its Consistency with Public International Law – No Need for the Concept of Treaty Sui Generis*, 79 Nordic Journal of International Law 245 n. 2 (2010).

REIMERS, K, GUO, X. and LI, M., *Beyond Markets, Hierarchies, and Hybrids: An Institutional Perspective on IT-enabled Two-sided Markets*, 29 Electronic Markets 287 n. 2 (2019).

RICCA, S., *Private Temporary Work Organisations and Public Employment Services: Effects and Problems of Coexistence*, 121 International Labour Review 141 n. 2 (1982).

RIGAUX, M., *De Problematiek van de Uitzendarbeid*, Tijdschrift Sociaal Recht / Revue du Droit Social 57 n. 2 (1976).

RIS, M., *Treaty Interpretation and ICJ Recourse to Travaux Préparatoires: Towards a Proposed Amendment of Articles 31 and 32 of the Vienna Convention on the Law of Treaties*, 14 Boston College International and Comparative Law Review 111 n. 1 (1991).

RODGERS, G., *India, the ILO and the Quest for Social Justice since 1919*, XLVI Economic & Political Weekly 45 n. 10 (2011).

ROMBOUTS, S. J. and ZEKIĆ, N., *Decent and Sustainable Work for the Future? The ILO Future of Work Centenary, the UN 2030 Agenda for Sustainable Development, and the Evolution of the Meaning of Work*, 24 UCLA Journal of International Law and Foreign Affairs 317 n. 2 (2020).

ROSENBLAT, A. and STARK, L., *Algorithmic Labor and Information Asymmetries: A Case Study of Uber's Drivers*, 10 International Journal of Communication 3758 (2016).

ROSHCHIN, S., SOLNTSEV, S. and VASILYEV, D., *Recruiting and Job Search Technologies in the Age of Internet*, 11 Foresight and STI Governance 33 n. 4 (2017).

RYSSELINCK, V., *Portage Salarial: Une Idée Française Illicite en Belgique – Alternatives en Droit Belge*, 42 Oriëntations 2 n. 6 (2012).

SCEKIC, O., TRUONG, H.-L. and DUSTDAR, S., *Incentives and Rewarding in Social Computing: Praise, Pay, and Promote Crowd-member Workers to Elicit Desired Behavioral Responses and Performance Levels*, 56 Communications of the ACM 72 n. 6 (2013).

SHEVCHUK, A., STREBKOV, D. and DAVIS, S. N., *The Autonomy Paradox: How Night Work Undermines Subjective Well-being of Internet-based Freelancers*, 72 ILR Review 75 n. 1 (2019).

SCHLACHTER, M., *Trade Union Representation for New Forms of Employment*, European Labour Law Journal 229 n. 3 (2019).

SCHMIDT, A. E., WINKELMANN, J., RODRIGUES, R. and LEICHSENRING, K., *Lessons for Regulating Informal Markets and Implications for Quality Assurance – the Case of Migrant Care Workers in Austria*, 36 Ageing & Society 741 n. 4 (2016).

SCHNEIDER, N., *Intellectual Piecework; Increasingly Used in Research, Platforms Like Mechanical Turk Pose New Ethical Dilemmas*, 61 The Chronicle of Higher Education n. 23 (2015).

SCHNEIDER DE VILLEGAS, G., *Home Work: An overview*, 8 Conditions of Work Digest 3 n. 2 (1989).

SCHNEIDER DE VILLEGAS, G., *Home Work: A Case for Social Protection*, 129 International Labour Review 423 n. 4 (1990).

SCHNORR, G., *Le Travail Temporaire*, Cahier de Droit Européen 131 (1973).

SCHOR, J. B., ATTWOOD-CHARLES, W., CANSOY, M., LADEGAARD, I. and WENGRONOWITZ, R., *Dependence and Precarity in the Platform Economy*, 49 Theory and Society 833 n. 5–6 (2020).

SCHÖRPF, P., FLECKER, J., SCHÖNAUER, A. and EICHMANN, H., *Triangular Love-hate: Management and Control in Creative Crowdworking*, 32 New Technology, Work and Employment 43 n. 1 (2017).

SCHWENKEN, H., *Mobilisation des Travailleuses Domestiques Migrantes: De la Cuisine à l'Organisation Internationale du Travail*, 51 Cahiers du Genre 113 n. 2 (2011).

SEN, A., *Work and Rights*, 139 International Labour Review 119 n. 2 (2000).

SEHNBRUCH, K., BURCHELL, B., AGLONI, N. and PIASNA, A., *Human Development and Decent Work: Why some Concepts Succeed and Others Fail to Make an Impact*, 46 Development and Change 197 n. 2 (2015).

SERVAIS, J.-M., *L'OIT et le Travail Décent. La Difficile Médiation entre Croissance, Création d'Emploi et Protection des Travailleurs*, Revue de droit comparé du travail et de la sécurité sociale 71 n. 1 (2011).

SHAPIRO, A., *Between Autonomy and Control: Strategies of Arbitrage in the "On-demand" Economy*, 20 New Media & Society 2954 n. 8 (2018).

SHAPIRO, A., *Dynamic Exploits: Calculative Asymmetries in the On-demand Economy*, 35 New Technology, Work and Employment 162 n. 2 (2020).

SHEVCHUK, A. and STREBKOV, D., *Safeguards against Opportunism in Freelance Contracting on the Internet*, 56 British Journal of Industrial Relations 342 n. 2 (2018).

SILBERMAN, M. SIX and IRANI, L., *Operating an Employer Reputation System: Lessons from Turkopticon, 2008–2015*, 37 Comparative Labor Law & Policy Journal 505 n. 3 (2016).

SILBERMAN, M. SIX, IRANI, L. and ROSS, J., *Ethics and Tactics of Professional Crowdwork*, 17 XRDS: Crossroads 39 n. 2 (2010).

SKELTON, B. R. and YANDLE, B., *Piece Rate Pay*, 3 Journal of Labor Research 201 n. 2 (1982).

SMITH, P. R., *The Pitfalls of Home: Protecting the Health and Safety of Paid Domestic Workers*, 23 Canadian Journal of women and the law 309 n. 1 (2011).

SMITH, P. R., *Work Like Any Other, Work Like No Other: Establishing Decent Work for Domestic Workers*, 15 Employee rights and employment policy journal 159 n. 1 (2011).

SPRAGUE, R., *Are Airbnb Hosts Employees Misclassified as Independent Contractors?*, 59 University of Louisville Law Review 63 n. 1 (2020).

STANDING, G., *The ILO: An Agency for Globalization?*, 39 Development and Change 355 n. 3 (2008).

STANFORD, J., *The Resurgence of Gig Work: Historical and Theoretical Perspectives*, 28 The Economic and Labour Relations Review 382 n. 3 (2017).

STANTON, C. and THOMAS, C., *Landing the First Job: The Value of Intermediaries in Online Hiring*, 83 Review of Economic Studies 810 n. 2 (2016).

STIGLER, G. J., *Information in the Labor Market*, 70 Journal of Political Economy 94 n. 5 (1962).

SUDER, S. and SIIBAK, A., *Employers as Nightmare Readers: An Analysis of Ethical and Legal Concerns Regarding Employer-Employee Practices on SNS*, 10 Baltic Journal of Law & Politics 76 n. 2 (2017).

SUVANKULOV, F., LAU, M. C. K. and CHAU, F. H. C., *Job Search on the Internet and its Outcome*, 22 Internet Research 298 n. 3 (2012).

SWEPSTON, L., *The Future of ILO standards*, 117 Monthly Labor Review 16 n. 9 (1994).

SWEPSTON, L., *Introductory Note by Lee Swepston*, 37 International Legal Materials 1233 n. 5 (1998).

SWEPSTON, L., *Crisis in the ILO Supervisory System: Dispute over the Right to Strike*, 29 International Journal of Comparative Labour Law and Industrial Relations 199 n. 2 (2013).

SUPIOT, A., *The Tasks Ahead of the ILO at its Centenary*, 159 International Labour Review 117 n. 1 (2020).

SUPIOT, A., KOTT, S. and PIGUET, L., *De l'»Esprit de Philadelphie» à la Responsabilité Sociale et Environnementale des Entreprises*, 263 Revue Le Mouvement Social 153 n. 1 (2018).

SUTHERLAND, W., JARRAHI, M. H., DUNN, M. and NELSON, S. B., *Work Precarity and Gig Literacies in Online Freelancing*, 34 Work, Employment and Society 457 n. 3 (2020).

SYMONS, J., *The Legitimation of International Organisations: Examining the Identity of the Communities that Grant Legitimacy*, 37 Review of International Studies 2557 n. 5 (2011).

THERON, J, *Intermediary or Employer – Labour Brokers and the Triangular Employment Relationship*, 26 Industrial Law Journal 618 n. 4 (2005).

THOMAS, H. and TURNBULL, P., *From a "Moral Commentator" to a "Determined Actor"? How the International Labour Organization (ILO) Orchestrates the Field of International Industrial Relations*, British Journal of Industrial Relations 1 (2020).

TICONA, J. and MATEESCU, A., *Trusted Strangers: Carework Platforms' Cultural Entrepreneurship in the On-demand Economy*, 20 New Media & Society 4384 n. 11 (2018).

TODOLÍ-SIGNES, A., *Workers, the Self-employed and TRADEs: Conceptualisation and Collective Rights in Spain*, 10 European Labour Law Journal 254 n. 3 (2019).

TOMEI, M. and BELSER, P., *New ILO Standards on Decent Work for Domestic Workers: A Summary of the Issues and Discussions*, 150 International Labour Review 431 n. 3–4 (2011).

TOPEL, R. H. and WARD, M. P., *Job Mobility and the Careers of Young Men*, 107 The Quarterly Journal of Economics 439 n. 2 (1992).

TREBILCOCK, A., *A Comment on "Legitimising the Triangular Employment Relationship"*, 19 Comparative Labor Law & Policy Journal 79 n. 1 (1997).

TSIKATA, D., *Employment Agencies and the Regulation of Domestic Workers in Ghana: Institutionalizing Informality?*, 23 Canadian Journal of women and the law 213 n. 1 (2011).

TUBARO, P., *Disembedded or Deeply Embedded? A Multi-Level Network Analysis of Online Labour Platforms*, Sociology 1 (2021).

TUBARO, P. and CASILLI, A. A., *Micro-work, Artificial Intelligence and the Automotive Industry*, 46 Journal of Industrial and Business Economics 333 n. 3 (2019).

TUBARO, P., CASILLI, A. A. and COVILLE, M., *The Trainer, the Verifier, the Imitator: Three Ways in Which Human Platform Workers Support Artificial Intelligence*, 7 Big Data & Society 1 n. 1 (2020).

UNDERHILL, E., *Should Host Employers Have Greater Responsibility for Temporary Agency Workers' Employment Rights?*, 48 Asia Pacific Journal of Human Resources 338 n. 3 (2010).

VALLAS, S. and SCHOR, J. B., *What Do Platforms Do? Understanding the Gig Economy*, 46 Annual Review of Sociology 273 n. 1 (2020).

VALTICOS, N., *Temporary Work Agencies and International Labour Standards*, 107 International Labour Review 43 n. 1 (1973).

VALTICOS, N., *The ILO: A Retrospective and Future View*, 135 International Labour Review 473 n. 3–4 (1996).

VAN ACKER, L., *C-390/18 – The CJEU Finally Clears the Air(bnb) Regarding Information Society Services*, 9 Journal of European Consumer and Market Law 77 n. 2 (2020).

VAN DAELE, J., *The International Labour Organization (ILO) in Past and Present Research*, 53 International review of social history 485 n.3 (2008).

VAN DER HEIJDEN, J., *Institutional Layering: A Review of the Use of the Concept*, 31 Politics 9 n. 1 (2011).

VAN DER HEIJDEN, P., *The ILO Stumbling towards Its Centenary Anniversary*, 15 International Organizations Law Review 203 n. 1 (2018).

VAN DOORN, N., *Platform Labor: On the Gendered and Racialized Exploitation of Low-Income Service Work in the "On-Demand" Economy*, 20 Information, Communication & Society 898 n. 6 (2017).

VAN DOORN, N. and BADGER, A., *Platform Capitalism's Hidden Abode: Producing Data Assets in the Gig Economy*, 52 Antipode 1475 n. 5 (2020).

VAN ECK, S., *Employment Agencies: International Norms and Developments in South Africa*, 28 International Journal of Comparative Labour Law and Industrial Relations 29 n. 1 (2012).

VAN WALSUM, S., *Regulating Migrant Domestic Work in the Netherlands: Opportunities and Pitfalls*, 23 Canadian Journal of women and the law 141 n. 1 (2011).

VARIA, N., *"Sweeping Changes?" A Review of Recent Reforms on Protections for Migrant Domestic Workers in Asia and the Middle East*, 23 Canadian Journal of women and the law 265 n. 1 (2011).

VEEN, A., BARRATT, T. and GOODS, C., *Platform-Capital's "App-etite" for Control: A Labour Process Analysis of Food-Delivery Work in Australia*, 34 Work, Employment and Society 388 n. 3 (2020).

VEGA RUIZ, L., *Home Work: Towards a New Regulatory Framework?*, 131 International Labour Review 197 n. 2 (1992).

VELDKAMP, G. M. J. and RAETSEN, M. J. E. H., *Temporary Work Agencies and Western European Social Legislation*, 107 International Labour Review 117 n. 2 (1973).

VENEZIANI, B., *New Technologies and the Contract of Employment*, 2 International Journal of Comparative Labour Law and Industrial Relations 117 n. 4 (1986).

VERDONCK, I., *Hulp in het Huishouden: De Regeling voor Dienstboden en Ander Huispersoneel Onder de Loep Genomen*, 10 Sociale Wegwijzer 13 n. 10 (2014).

VERHULP, E., *Platformwerkers Verdienen Meer!*, Arbeidsrecht n. 1 (2018).

VON BERGEN, C. W. and BRESSLER, M. S., *Work, Non-Work Boundaries and the Right to Disconnect*, 21 Journal of Applied Business and Economics 51 n. 2 (2019).

VON BROEMBSEN, M., *Constitutionalizing Labour Rights: Informal Homeworkers in Global Value Chains*, 34 International Journal of Comparative Labour Law and Industrial Relations 257 n. 3 (2018).

VON HIPPEL, C., MANGUM, S. L., GREENBERGER, D. B., HENEMAN, R. L. and SKOGLIND, J. D., *Temporary Employment: Can Organizations and Employees Both Win?*, 11 The Academy of Management Executive 93 n. 1 (1997).

VOSKO, L. F., *Legitimizing the Triangular Employment Relationship: Emerging International Labour Standards From a Comparative Perspective*, 19 Comparative Labor Law & Policy Journal 43 n. 1 (1997).

VOSKO, L. F., *Less than Adequate: Regulating Temporary Agency Work in the EU in the Face of an Internal Market in Services*, 2 Cambridge Journal of Regions, Economy and Society 395 n. 3 (2009).

WEARS, K. H. and FISHER, S. L., *Who is an Employer in the Triangular Employment Relationship? Sorting Through the Definitional Confusion*, 24 Employee Responsibilities and Rights Journal 159 n. 3 (2012).

WEBER, C. E., OKRAKU, M., MAIR J. and MAURER, I., *Steering the Transition from Informal to Formal Service Provision: Labor Platforms in Emerging-market Countries*, Socio-Economic Review 1 (2021).

WEBSTER, J., *Microworkers of the Gig Economy: Separate and Precarious*, 25 New Labor Forum 56 n. 3 (2016).

WHEATLEY, D., *Autonomy in Paid Work and Employee Subjective Well-being*, 44 Work and Occupations 296 n. 3 (2017).

WHITE, R., *Industrial Home Work in Chicago*, 10 Social Service Review 23 n. 1 (1936).

WILLBORN, S. L., *Leased Workers: Vulnerability and the Need for Special Legislation*, 19 Comparative Labor Law & Policy Journal 85 n. 1 (1997).

WILLIAMS, A. C., MARK, G., MILLAND, K., LANK, E. and LAW, E., *The Perpetual Work Life of Crowdworkers: How Tooling Practices Increase Fragmentation in Crowdwork*, 3 Proceedings of the ACM on human-computer interaction 1 (2019).

WILLIAMSON, O. E., *The Vertical Integration of Production: Market Failure Consideration*, 61 The American Economic Review 112 n. 2 (1971).

WILLIAMSON, O. E., *The Economics of Organization: The Transaction Cost Approach*, 87 American Journal of Sociology 548 n. 3 (1981).

WIRTZ, J., FUNG SO, K. K., MODY, M. A., LIU, S. Q. and CHUN, H. H., *Platforms in the Peer-to-peer Sharing Economy*, 30 Journal of Service Management 452 n. 4 (2019).

WOLF, F., *L'Interdépendance des Conventions Internationales du Travail*, 121 Recueil Des Cours 127 n. 2 (1967).

WOOD, A. J., GRAHAM, M., LEHDONVIRTA, V. and HJORTH, I., *Good Gig, Bad Gig: Autonomy and Algorithmic Control in the Global Gig Economy*, 33 Work, Employment and Society 56 n. 1 (2019).

WOOD, A. J., GRAHAM, M., LEHDONVIRTA, V. and HJORTH, I., *Networked but Commodified: The (Dis)Embeddedness of Digital Labour in the Gig Economy*, 53 Sociology 931 n. 5 (2019).

WORONKOWICZ, J. and NOONAN, D. S., *Who Goes Freelance? The Determinants of Self-Employment for Artists*, 43 Entrepreneurship Theory and Practice 651 n. 4 (2019).

WU, Q., ZHANG, H., LI, Z. and LIU, K., *Labor Control in the Gig Economy: Evidence from Uber in China*, 61 Journal of Industrial Relations 574 n. 4 (2019).

X, *Industrial Home Work*, 58 International Labour Review 735 n. 6 (1948).

YAO, Y., *Uberizing the Legal Profession? Lawyer Autonomy and Status in the Digital Legal Market*, 58 British Journal of Industrial Relations 483 n. 3 (2020).

YAVAŞ, A., *Middlemen in Bilateral Search Markets*, 12 Journal of Labor Economics 406 n. 3 (1994).

ZENG, X. and CUI, Y., *Job Search, Labour Market Intermediaries and Employment Promotion: The Evidence from China*, 147 International Labour Review 280 n. 2–3 (2008).

ZHU, F. and IANSITI, M., *Why Some Platforms Thrive... and Others Don't*, 97 Harvard Business Review 118 n. 1 (2019).

Reports and Papers

ABBOTT, S. and GOULD-WERTH, A., *Unboxing scheduling practices for U.S. warehouse workers: Lessons from a research and advocacy roundtable* (D. C., Washington Center for Equitable Growth 2020).

ALEKSYNSKA, M., BASTRAKOVA, A. and KHARCHENKO, N., *Work on Digital Labour Platforms in Ukraine: Issues and Policy Perspectives* (ILO 2018).

ANDERSON, B. and O'CONNELL DAVIDSON, J., *Is Trafficking in Human Beings Demand Driven? A Multi-Country Pilot Study* (IOM 2003).

ANKER, R. and ANNYCKE, P., *Reporting Regularly on Decent Work in the World: Options for the ILO* (ILO 2009).

ATKINSON, J., GILES, L. and MEAGER, N., *Employment, Recruitment and the Unemployed* (The Institute for Employment Studies 1996).

AVRAM, S., *Labour Market Flexibility and Unemployment Duration: Evidence from the UK* (Institute for Social and Economic Research, University of Essex 2020).

BARTIK, A. W., CULLEN, Z., GLAESER, E. L., LUCA, M. and STANTON, C., *What Jobs are Being Done at Home During the COVID-19 Crisis? Evidence from Firm-Level Surveys* (Harvard Business School 2020).

BELLACE, J. R., *Labour Rights as the Means for Recognizing Human Rights at Work*, Universiteit Leiden (22 October 2018), https://www.universiteitleiden.nl/binaries/content/assets/rechtsgeleerdheid/instituut-voor-publiekrecht/sociaal-recht/bellace-leiden-lecture-22-oct-2018-.pdf.

BERG, J., FURRER, M., HARMON, E., RANI, U. and SILBERMAN, M. SIX, *Digital Labour Platforms and the Future of Work: Towards Decent Work in the Online World* (ILO 2018).

BIGNAMI, R., CASALE, G. and FASANI, M., *Labour Inspection and Employment Relationship* (ILO 2013).

BLOOM, N., *How Working from Home Works out* (Stanford Institute for Economic Policy Research 2020).

BOGLIACINO, F., CODAGNONE, C., CIRILLO, V. and GUARASCIO, D., *Quantity and Quality of Work in the Platform Economy* (Global Labor Organization 2019).

BÖHEIM, R. and MUEHLBERGER, U., *Dependent Forms of Self-employment in the UK: Identifying Workers on the Border between Employment and Self-employment* (IZA 2006).

BORINO, F., *Piece Rate Pay and Working Conditions in the Export Garment Sector* (ILO 2018).

BROUGHTON, A., GLOSTER, R., MARVELL, R., GREEN, M., LANGLEY, J. and MARTIN, A., *The Experiences of Individuals in the Gig Economy* (Department for Business, Energy & Industrial Strategy 2018).

CAMPBELL, I., *On-call and Related Forms of Casual Work in New Zealand and Australia* (ILO 2018).

CANCEDDA, A., *Employment in Household Services* (Office for Official Publications of the European Communities 2001).

Cedefop, *Developing and Matching Skills in the Online Platform Economy: Findings on New Forms of Digital Work and Learning from Cedefop's CrowdLearn Study* (Publications Office of the European Union 2020).

Cedefop, *Skill Development in the Platform Economy: Comparing Microwork and Online Freelancing* (Publications Office of the European Union 2021).

CHEN, M. A., *Informal Economy Monitoring Study Sector Report: Home-Based Workers* (WIEGO 2014).

CHEN, M. and SINHA, S., *Home-based Workers & Cities: India in Comparative Perspective* (*Empowering Home-based Workers in India: Strategies and Solutions*, Harvard University South Asia Institute 2016).

CHEN, Y. P., *Online Labour Platforms in China: Working Conditions, Policy Issues and Prospects* (ILO 2021).

CHOUDARY, S. P., *The Architecture of Digital Labour Platforms: Policy Recommendations on Platform Design for Worker Well-being* (ILO 2018).

Commissie Platformeconomie en Werk, *Hoe Werkt de Platformeconomie?* (Sociaal-Economische Raad 2020).

CORPORAAL, G. F. and LEHDONVIRTA, V., *Platform Sourcing. How Fortune 500 Firms Are Adopting Online Freelancing Platforms* (Oxford Internet Institute 2017).

COUËDEL, C., *Intérim et Plateforme Numérique de Mise en Relation: Les Enjeux des Nouvelles Formes d'Intermédiation*, Dalloz actualité (26 novembre 2020), https://www.dalloz-actualite.fr/flash/interim-et-plateforme-numerique-de-mise-en-relation-enjeux-des-nouvelles-formes-d-intermediati.

COUNTOURIS, N., *Defining and Regulating Work Relations for the Future of Work* (ILO 2019).

COUNTOURIS, N. and DE STEFANO, V., *New Trade Union Strategies for New Forms of Employment* (ETUC 2019).

COUNTOURIS, N., DE STEFANO, V. and LIANOS, I., *The EU, Competition and Workers' Rights* (Centre for Law, Economics and Society, UCL 2021).

DEAKIN, S., *The Contribution of Labour Law to Economic Development and Growth, Centre for Business Research* (Centre for Business Research, University of Cambridge 2016).

DEDEOĞLU, S., *Home Bounded – Global Outreach: Home-based Workers in Turkey* (ILO 2020).

DE GROEN, W. P., MASELLI, I. and FABO, B., *The Digital Market for Local Services: A One-night Stand for Workers?: An Example from the On-demand Economy* (CEPS 2016).

DE HOYOS, M., GREEN, A. E., BARNES, S.-A., BEHLE, H., BALDAUF, B. and OWEN, D., *Literature Review on Employability, Inclusion and ICT, Report 2: ICT and Employability* (Publications Office of the European Union 2013).

DELARUE, R., *De Rol van de Internationale Arbeidsorganisatie in de 21ste Eeuw* (ILO Office for the European Union and the Benelux countries 2012).

Denk Fabrik, *Eckpunte des BMAS: Faire Arbeit in der Plattformökonomie* (Bundesministerium für Arbeit und Soziales 2020).

DE STEFANO, V. and ALOISI, A., *European Legal framework for "Digital Labour Platforms"* (Publications Office of the European Union 2018).

DE STEFANO, V., DURRI, I., STYLOGIANNIS, C. and WOUTERS, M., *"System Needs Update": Upgrading Protection Against Cyberbullying and ICT-enabled Violence and Harassment in the World of Work* (ILO 2020).

DE STEFANO, V., DURRI, I., STYLOGIANNIS, C. and WOUTERS, M., *Platform Work and the Employment Relationship* (ILO 2021).

DEVAULT, I. A., FIGUEROA, M., KOTLER, F. B., MAFFIE, M. and WU, J., *On-demand Platform Workers in New York State: The Challenges for Public Policy* (ILR Worker Institute 2019).

DOBSON, B., *Gainful Gigging: Employment Services for the Platform Economy* (Reform 2017).

DRAHOKOUPIL, J. and PIASNA, A., *Work in the Platform Economy: Deliveroo Riders in Belgium and the SMart Arrangement* (Etui 2019).

D'SOUZA, A., *Moving Towards Decent Work for Domestic Workers: An Overview of the ILO's work* (ILO 2010).

DUBAL, V. B., *The Time Politics of Home-based Digital Piecework*, C4eJournal (15 May 2020), https://c4ejournal.net/2020/07/04/v-b-dubal-the-time-politics-of-home-based-digital-piecework-2020-c4ej-xxx/.

DU TOIT, D., *Cleaning Up: A Sociological Investigation into the Use of Outsourced Housecleaning Services* (Stellenbosch University 2020).

Economic Commission for Latin America and the Caribbean and International Labour Organization, *The Future of Work in Latin America and the Caribbean: Old and New Forms of Employment and Challenges for Labour Regulation, Employment Situation in Latin America and the Caribbean* (2019).

ENGELS, S. and SHERWOOD, M., *What if We All Worked Gigs in the Cloud? The Economic Relevance of Digital Labour Platforms* (Publications Office of the European Union 2019).

Eurofound, *Exploring Self-employment in the European Union* (Publications Office of the European Union 2017).

Eurofound, *Sixth European Working Conditions Survey – Overview Report (2017 update)* (Publications Office of the European Union 2017).

Eurofound, *Employment and Working Conditions of Selected Types of Platform Work* (Publications Office of the European Union 2018).

Eurofound, *Non-standard Forms of Employment: Recent Trends and Future Prospects* (Eurofound 2018).

Eurofound, *Casual Work: Characteristics and Implications* (Publications Office of the European Union 2019).

Eurofound, *Platform Work: Maximising the Potential While Safeguarding Standards?* (Publications Office of the European Union 2019).

Eurofound, *Back to the Future: Policy Pointers from Platform Work Scenarios* (Publications Office of the European Union 2020).

Eurofound, *Labour Market Change: Trends and Policy Approaches Towards Flexibilisation* (Publications Office of the European Union 2020).

Eurofound, *Telework and ICT-based Mobile Work: Flexible Working in the Digital Age* (Publications Office of the European Union 2020).

Fairwork, *Fairwork 2020: Annual Report* (Oxford Internet Institute 2020).

Fairwork, *Fairwork India Ratings 2020: Labour Standards in the Platform Economy* (Oxford Internet Institute 2020).

FARINA, E., GREEN, C. and McVICAR, D., *Zero Hours Contracts and Their Growth* (IZA 2019).

FARRELL, D. and GREIG, F., *The Online Platform Economy: Has Growth Peaked?* (JP Morgan Chase Institute 2016).

FLORISSON, R. and MANDL, I., *Platform Work: Types and Implications for Work and Employment – Literature Review* (Eurofound 2018).

FROUIN, J.-Y. and BARFETY, J.-B., *Réguler les Plateformes Numériques de Travail* (Rapport au Premier Ministre 2020).

FUDGE, J. and HOBDEN, C., *Conceptualizing the Role of Intermediaries in Formalizing Domestic Work* (ILO 2018).

FULLER, J. B., RAMAN, M., PALANO, J., BAILEY, A., VADUGANATHAN, N., KAUFMAN, E., LAVERDIÈRE, R. and LOVETT, S., *Building the On-demand Workforce* (Harvard Business School and BCG 2020).

GARBEN, S., *Protecting Workers in the Online Platform Economy: An overview of Regulatory and Policy Developments in the EU* (Publications Office of the European Union 2017).

GARBEN, S., *Tackling Social Disruption in the Online Platform Economy: Shifting the Narrative to the Benefits of (EU) Regulation* (FEPS 2019).

GARRISON JENN, N., *Headhunters and How to Use Them: A Guide for Organisations and Individuals* (Economist Books 2005).

GILBERT, A., THOMAS, A., PISSARIDES, C., AL-IZZI, H., MILLER, C. and BURNELL, E., *The Amazonian Era: How Algorithmic Systems Are Eroding Good Work* (Institute for the Future of Work 2021).

GRAHAM, M., LEHDONVIRTA, V., WOOD, A., BARNARD, H., HJORTH, I. and SIMON, D. P., *The Risks and Rewards of Online Gig Work At the Global Margins* (Oxford Internet Institute 2017).

GURUMURTHY, A., CHAMI, N. and BHARTHUR, D., *Platform Labour in Search of Value: A Study of Worker Organizing Practices and Business Models in the Digital Economy* (ILO 2021).

HAHN, J. K., HYATT, H. R. and JANICKI, H. P., *Job Ladders and Growth in Earnings, Hours, and Wages* (RePEc 2018).

HAIPETER, T., OWCZAREK, D., FAIOLI, M. and IUDICONE, F., *Final Report: Don't GIG Up!* (Directorate-General for Employment, Social Affairs and Inclusion of the European Commission 2020).

HARVEY, J., *Homeworkers in Global Supply Chains: A Review of Literature* (WIEGO 2019).

HAUBEN, H., LENAERTS, K. and WAEYAERT, W., *The Platform Economy and Precarious Work* (European Parliament 2020).

HIELSCHER, V., KIRCHEN-PETERS, S. and NOCK, L., *Pflege in den Eigenen Vier Wänden: Zeitaufwand und Kosten* (Hans Böckler Stiftung 2017).

HIRSCHBERG, C., RAJKO, A., SCHUMACHER, T. and WRULICH, M., (*The Changing Market for Food Delivery* (McKinsey&Company 2016).

HOBDEN, C., *Winning Fair Labour Standards for Domestic Workers: Lessons Learned from the Campaign for a Domestic Worker Bill of Rights in New York State* (ILO 2010).

HOBDEN, C., *Working Time of Live-in Domestic Workers* (ILO 2013).

HOBDEN, C., *Domestic Workers Organize – But Can They Bargain?* (ILO 2015).

HUNT, A. and MACHINGURA, F., *A Good Gig? The Rise of On-demand Domestic Work* (ODI 2016).

HUNT, A. and SAMMAN, E., *Gender and the Gig Economy: Critical Steps for Evidence-based Policy* (ODI 2019).

HUNT, A., SAMMAN, E., TAPFUMA, S., MWAURA, G. and OMENYA, R., *Women in the Gig Economy: Paid Work, Care and Flexibility in Kenya and South Africa* (ODI 2019).

HUNTER, D. and LESLIE, K., *Statistical Definition and Measurement of Dependent "Self-employed" Workers: Rationale for the Proposal for a Statistical Category of Dependent Contractors* (ILO 2018).

HUWS, U. and PODRO, S., *Employment of Homeworkers: Examples of Good Practice* (ILO 1995).

HUWS, U., DAHLMANN, S. and FLECKER, J., *Outsourcing of ICT and Related Services in the EU* (Eurofound 2004).

HUWS, U., SPENCER, N. H., SYRDAL, D. S. and HOLTS, K., *Work in the European Gig Economy: Research Results from the UK, Sweden, Germany, Austria, the Netherlands, Switzerland and Italy* (FEPS 2017).

HUWS, U., SPENCER, N. H., COATES, M. and HOLTS, K., *The Platformisation of Work in Europe: Results from Research in 13 European countries* (FEPS 2019).

IDB, WAPES and OECD, *The World of Public Employment Services* (OECD 2015).

IDEA Consult, *De Dienstencheques 360° Doorgelicht* (IDEA Consult 2018).

ILO, *Qualitative Research on Employment Relationship and Working Conditions: Preliminary Guidelines* (ILO).

ILO, *Abolition of Fee-Charging Employment Agencies* (ILO 1932).

ILO, *Employment Service Organisation* (ILO 1946).

ILO, *Report of the Governing Body of the International Labour Office upon the Working of the Convention (No. 34) Concerning Fee-Charging Employment Agencies (1933)* (ILO 1948).

ILO, *Revision of the Fee-Charging Employment Agencies Convention, 1933* (ILO 1948).

ILO, *The International Labour Code* (ILO 1951).

ILO, *Technical Background Document for the Meeting of Experts on the Social Protection of Homeworkers* (ILO 1990).

ILO, *Social Protection of Homeworkers* (ILO 1991).

ILO, *Report V (1) Home Work* (ILO 1994).

ILO, *Report VI The Role of Private Employment Agencies in the Functioning of Labour Markets* (ILO 1994).

ILO, *Report IV (1) Home Work* (ILO 1995).

ILO, *Report V (2) Home Work* (ILO 1995).

ILO, *Report IV (1) Revision of the Fee-Charging Employment Agencies Convention (Revised), 1949 (No. 96)* (ILO 1996).

ILO, *Report IV (2 A) Home Work* (ILO 1996).

ILO, *Report VI (1) Contract Labour* (ILO 1996).

ILO, *Report IV (2) Revision of the Fee-Charging Employment Agencies Convention (Revised), 1949 (No. 96)* (ILO 1997).

ILO, *Report IV (1) Revision of the Fee-Charging Employment Agencies Convention (Revised)* (ILO 1997).

ILO, *Report V (2A) Contract Labour* (ILO 1998).

ILO, *Report V (2B) Contract Labour* (ILO 1998).

ILO, *Report V (2B) Add.* (ILO 1998).

ILO, *Report V Strengthening the ILO's Capacity to Assist its Members' Efforts to Reach its Objectives in the Context of Globalization* (ILO 2007).

ILO, *Report IV(1) Decent Work for Domestic Workers* (ILO 2010).

ILO, *Report IV(2) Decent Work for Domestic Workers* (ILO 2010).

ILO, *Report IV(2A) Decent Work for Domestic Workers* (ILO 2011).

ILO, *Report IV (2B) Decent Work for Domestic Workers* (ILO 2011).

ILO, *Working Time in the Twenty-first Century: Report for Discussions at the Tripartite Meeting of Experts on Working-time Arrangements* (ILO 2011).

ILO, *Domestic Workers Across the World: Global and Regional Statistics and the Extent of Legal Protection* (ILO 2013).

ILO, *Ending Child Labour in Domestic Work and Protecting Young Workers from Abusive Working Conditions* (ILO 2013).

ILO, *Formalizing Domestic Work* (ILO 2016).

ILO, *Non-standard Employment Around the World: Understanding Challenges, Shaping Prospects* (ILO 2016).

ILO, *Inception Report for the Global Commission on the Future of Work* (ILO 2017).

ILO, *Synthesis Report of the National Dialogues on the Future of Work* (ILO 2017).

ILO, *Care Work and Care Jobs for the Future of Decent Work* (ILO 2018).

ILO, *Job Quality in the Platform Economy* (ILO 2018).

ILO, *Monitoring Compliance with International Labour Standards: The Key Role of the ILO Committee of Experts on the Application of Conventions and Recommendations* (ILO 2019).

ILO, *Report IV ILO Centenary Outcome Document* (ILO 2019).

ILO, *Report of the Committee of Experts on the Application of Conventions and Recommendations* (ILO 2019).

ILO, *World Employment and Social Outlook: Trends 2019* (ILO 2019).

ILO, *Teleworking During the COVID-19 Pandemic and Beyond: A Practical Guide* (ILO 2020).

ILO, *Follow-up to the Resolution on the ILO Centenary Declaration for the Future of Work: Proposals for Including Safe and Healthy Working Conditions in the ILO's Framework of Fundamental Principles and Rights at Work* (ILO 2020).

ILO, *Working from Home: From Invisibility to Decent Work* (ILO 2021).

ILO, *World Employment and Social Outlook: The Role of Digital Labour Platforms in Transforming the World of Work* (ILO 2021).

ILO and Eurofound, *Working Anytime, Anywhere: The Effects on the World of Work* (Publications Office of the European Union 2017).

ILO Committee of Experts on the Application of Conventions and Recommendations, *Report III (Part IV) Report of the Committee of Experts on the Application of Conventions and Recommendations* (ILO 1955).

ILO Committee of Experts on the Application of Conventions and Recommendations, *Report III (Part IV) Report of the Committee of Experts on the Application of Conventions and Recommendations* (ILO 1959).

ILO Committee of Experts on the Application of Conventions and Recommendations, *Report III (Part IV) Report of the Committee of Experts on the Application of Conventions and Recommendations* (ILO 1962).

ILO Committee of Experts on the Application of Conventions and Recommendations, *Labour Standards on Merchant Ships* (ILO 1990).

ILO Committee of Experts on the Application of Conventions and Recommendations, *Workers with Family Responsibilities* (ILO 1993).

ILO Committee of Experts on the Application of Conventions and Recommendations, *Protection of Wages: Standards and Safeguards Relating to the Payment of Labour Remuneration* (ILO 2003).

ILO Committee of Experts on the Application of Conventions and Recommendations, *Eradication of Forced Labour* (ILO 2007).

ILO Committee of Experts on the Application of Conventions and Recommendations, *ILO Standards on Occupational Safety and Health: Promoting a Safe and Healthy Working Environment* (ILO 2009).

ILO Committee of Experts on the Application of Conventions and Recommendations, *General Survey Concerning Employment Instruments in Light of the 2008 Declaration on Social Justice for a Fair Globalization* (ILO 2010).

ILO Committee of Experts on the Application of Conventions and Recommendations, *Giving Globalization a Human Face* (ILO 2012).

ILO Committee of Experts on the Application of Conventions and Recommendations, *Working Together to Promote a Safe and Healthy Working Environment* (ILO 2017).

ILO Committee of Experts on the Application of Conventions and Recommendations, *Ensuring Decent Working Time for the Future* (ILO 2018).

ILO Committee of Experts on the Application of Conventions and Recommendations, *Promoting Employment and Decent Work in a Changing Landscape* (ILO 2020).

ILO Committee of Experts on the Application of Conventions and Recommendations, *Report III (Part A) Application of International Labour Standards 2020* (ILO 2020).

ILO Committee of Experts on the Application of Conventions and Recommendations, *Addendum to the 2020 General Survey: Promoting Employment and Decent Work in a Changing Landscape* (ILO 2021).

ILO Committee on Freedom of Association, *Freedom of Association: Compilation of Decisions of the Committee on Freedom of Association* (ILO 2018).

ILO Committee on Standing Orders and the Application of Conventions and Recommendations, *Article 37, Paragraph 2, of the Constitution and the Interpretation of International Labour Conventions*, GB.256/SC/2/2 (ILO 1993).

ILO Committee on the Application of Standards, *Third Item on the Agenda: Information and Reports on the Application of Conventions and Recommendations* (ILO 2010).

ILO International Labour Standards Department, *Handbook of Procedures Relating to International Labour Conventions and Recommendations* (ILO 2019).

ILO Office of the Legal Adviser, *Manual for Drafting ILO Instruments* (ILO 2006).

ILO Regional Office for Arab States, *Employers' Perspectives Towards Domestic Workers in Jordan: A Qualitative Study on Attitudes, Working Conditions and the Employment Relationship* (ILO 2015).

ILO Regional Office for Arab States, *Employers' Perspectives Towards Domestic Workers in Kuwait: A Qualitative Study on Attitudes, Working Conditions and the Employment Relationship* (ILO 2015).

ILO Regional Office for Asia and the Pacific, *Asia-Pacific Labour Market Update, September 2017* (ILO 2017).

ILO Social Protection Department, *Social Protection for Domestic Workers: Key Policy Trends and Statistics* (ILO 2016).

International Bar Association Global Employment Institute and International Organisation of Employers, *International Labour Standards in the Contemporary Global Economy* (IBA 2018).

IPSOS, "High level summary of key findings", Prepared for KU Leuven, 2020.

IVANOVA, M., BRONOWICKA, J., KOCHER, E. and DEGNER, A., *The App as a Boss? Control and Autonomy in Application-Based Management* (Europa-Universität Viadrina 2018).

I-WIRE, *How Can Labour Market Intermediaries Secure Nonstandard Career Paths? An Exploratory Grid* (Independent Workers and Industrial Relations in Europe 2016).

JOHNSTON, H. and LAND-KAZLAUSKAS, C., *Organizing On-demand: Representation, Voice, and Collective Bargaining in the Gig Economy* (ILO 2018).

KAKKAD, J., PALMOU, C., BRITTO, D. and BROWNE, J., *Anywhere Jobs, Reshaping the Geography of Work* (Tony Blair Institute for Global Change 2021).

KÄSSI, O. and LEHDONVIRTA, V., *Do Digital Skill Certificates Help New Workers Enter the Market? Evidence from an Online Labour Platform* (OECD 2019).

KENNEY, M., BEARSON, D. and ZYSMAN, J., *The Platform Economy Matures: Pervasive Power, Private Regulation, and Dependent Entrepreneurs* (Berkeley Roundtable on the International Economy 2019).

KILHOFFER, Z., DE GROEN, W., LENAERTS, K., SMITS, I., HAUBEN, H., WAEYAERT, W., GIACUMACATOS, E., LHERNOULD, J.-P. and ROBIN-OLIVIER, S., *Study to Gather Evidence on the Working Conditions of Platform Workers* (Publications Office of the European Union 2020).

KING-DEJARDIN, A. M., *Homeworking in the Philippines* (ILO 2021).

LANE, M., *Regulating Platform Work in the Digital Age* (OECD 2020).

LENAERTS, K., DE GROEN, W. P., KILHOFFER, Z., BOSC, R., SALEZ, N., EICHHORST, W., ODY, M., ASKITAS, N. and MEYS, N., *Online Talent Platforms, Labour Market Intermediaries and the Changing World of Work* (CEPS and IZA 2018).

LIM, L. L., *Employment Relationships and Working Conditions in an IKEA Rattan Supply Chain* (ILO 2015).

MASMEJAN, D., *Débat Public en Ligne et Protection des Libertés de Communication* (Office fédéral de la communication 2020).

MATEESCU, A. and NGUYEN, A., *Algorithmic Management in the Workplace* (Data&Society 2019).

McCANN, D., *Temporal Casualisation and 'Availability Time': Mencap, Uber and the Framed Flexibility Model* (Decent Work Regulation, Durham University 2020).

McCANN, D. and MURRAY, J., *The Legal Regulation of Working Time in Domestic Work* (ILO 2010).

McDONALD, P., WILLIAMS, P., STEWART, A., MAYES, R. and OLIVER, D., *Digital Platform Work in Australia: Prevalence, Nature and Impact* (Victorian Department of Premier and Cabinet 2019).

McGAUGHEY, E., *Should Agency Workers be Treated Differently?* (London School of Economics and Political Science 2010).

MINGHUI, L., *Migrants and Cities: Research Report on Recruitment, Employment, and Working Conditions of Domestic Workers in China* (ILO 2017).

MOORE, P. V., *The Threat of Physical and Psychosocial Violence and Harassment in Digitalized Work* (ILO 2018).

MOURELO, E. L., *Work on Delivery Platforms in Argentina: Analysis and Policy Recommendations* (ILO 2020).

NAQEEB, B., SAIGOL, R. and AZHAR, U.-L., *Home-based Workers in Lahore, Pakistan* (WIEGO 2014).

National Endowment for the Arts, *Artists and Other Cultural Workers: A Statistical Portrait* (National Endowment for the Arts 2019).

NOLTE, G., *First Report on Subsequent Agreements and Subsequent Practice in Relation to Treaty Interpretation* (International Law Commission 2013).

NOLTE, G., *Second Report on Subsequent Agreements and Subsequent Practice in Relation to the Interpretation of Treaties* (International Law Commission 2014).

NOLTE, G., *Third Report on Subsequent Agreements and Subsequent Practice in Relation to the Interpretation of Treaties* (UN 2016).

NOLTE, G., *Fourth Report on Subsequent Agreements and Subsequent Practice in Relation to the Interpretation of Treaties* (UN 2016).

OECD, *Tax Challenges Arising from Digitalisation – Interim Report 2018: Inclusive Framework on BEPS* (OECD 2018).

OECD, *Policy Responses to New Forms of Work* (OECD 2019).

OECD, *OECD Employment Outlook 2019: The Future of Work* (OECD 2019).

OECD, *Expert Meeting on Collective Bargaining for Own-Account Workers* (OECD 2020).

OECD and ILO, *Tackling Vulnerability in the Informal Economy* (OECD 2019).

PADIN, L. and PINTO, M., *Lasting Solutions for America's Temporary Workers* (NELP 2019).

PARENT-THIRION, A., BILETTA, I., OOSTVEEN, A. and VERMEYLEN, G., *Self-employed or not Self-employed? Working Conditions of 'Economically Dependent Workers'* (Eurofound 2013).

PERULLI, A., *Study on Economically Dependent Work/Parasubordinate (Quasi-subordinate) Work* (European Parliament 2003).

PESOLE, A., URZÍ BRANCATI, M. C., FERNÁNDEZ-MACÍAS, E., BIAGI, F. and GONZÁLEZ VÁZQUEZ, I., *Platform Workers in Europe: Evidence from the COLLEEM Survey* (Publications Office of the European Union 2018).

PRASSL, J., *Collective Voice in the Platform Economy: Challenges, Opportunities, Solutions* (ETUC 2018).

RANDOLPH, G., GALPERIN, H. and KHAN, L., *New Opportunities in the Platform Economy: On-ramps to Formalization in the Global South* (JustJobs Network 2019).

REYNAUD, E., *The International Labour Organization and Globalization: Fundamental Rights, Decent Work and Social Justice* (ILO 2018).

RISAK, M. and WARTER, J., *Decent Crowdwork Legal Strategies Towards Fair Employment Conditions in the Virtual Sweatshop*, Regulating for Decent Work 2015 Conference (8–10 July 2015).

SAKURAI, K. and OKUBO, Y., *Job Seeker Trends 2015: Channels, Search Time, and Income Change* (The Boston Consulting Group and Recruit Works Institute 2015).

SCHMIDT, F. A., *Digital Labour Markets in the Platform Economy: Mapping the Political Challenges of Crowd Work and Gig Work* (Friedrich-Ebert-Stiftung 2017).

SCHWELLNUS, C., GEVA, A., PAK, M. and VEIEL, R., *Gig Economy Platforms: Boon or Bane?* (OECD 2019).

SELS, L., VANSTEENKISTE, S. and KNIPPRATH, H., *Toekomstverkenningen Arbeidsmarkt 2050 (Werk.Rapport 2017 nr.1)* (HIVA – KU Leuven 2017).

SILBERMAN, M. SIX, and JOHNSTON, H., *Using GDPR to Improve Legal Clarity and Working Conditions on Digital Labour Platforms* (Etui 2020).

SOSTERO, M., MILASI, S., HURLEY, J., FERNÁNDEZ-MACÍAS, E. and BISELLO, M., *Teleworkability and the COVID-19 Crisis: A New Digital Divide?* (Eurofound 2020).

TATE, J., *Unions and Homeworkers: Organizing Homeworkers in the Informal Sector in Australia, the Netherlands and Canada* (ILO 1993).

TAYLOR, M., MARSH, G., NICOL, D. and BROADBENT, P., *Good Work: The Taylor Review of Modern Working Practices* (2017).

TICONA, J., MATEESCU, A. and ROSENBLAT, A., *Beyond Disruption: How Tech Shapes Labor Across Domestic Work & Ridehailing* (Data&Society 2018).

TKACIK, M., *Rescuing Restaurants: How to Protect Restaurants, Workers, and Communities from Predatory Delivery App Corporations* (American Economic Liberties Project 2020).

TOMEI, M., *Home Work in Selected Latin American Countries: A Comparative Overview* (ILO 2000).

TROJANSKY, A., *Towards the "Uber-isation" of Care? Platform Work in the Sector of Long-term Home Care and its Implications for Workers' Rights* (European Economic and Social Committee 2020).

TSURUGA, I., NGUYEN, Q. A., BEHRENDT, C. and VAN DOORN, J., *Extending Social Security to Self-employed Workers: Lessons from International Experience* (ILO 2019).

United Nations, *The Corporate Responsibility to Respect Human Rights: An Interpretative Guide* (UN 2012).

United Nations, *The Millennium Development Goals Report 2015* (UN 2015).

URZÌ BRANCATI, M.C., PESOLE, A. and FÉRNANDÉZ-MACÍAS, E., *New Evidence on Platform Workers in Europe. Results from the Second COLLEEM Survey* (Publications Office of the European Union 2020).

VANDAELE, K., *Will Trade Unions Survive in the Platform Economy?* (Etui 2018).

VAN DER MEULEN RODGERS, Y. and ZUNDL, E., *The Future of Work in New Jersey: Care Workers and the Gig Economy*, Future of Work Task Force New Jersey, https://fowtf.innovation.nj.gov/downloads/resources/Rodgers_Zundl_NJ_Care_Economy_Future_of_Work_RCS.pdf.

VAN DOORN, N., FERRARI, F. and GRAHAM, M., *Migration and Migrant Labour in the Gig Economy: An Intervention*, SSRN (8 June 2020), https://papers.ssrn.com/sol3/papers.cfm?abstract_id=3622589.

VAUGHAN, R. and DAVERIO, R., *Assessing the Size and Presence of the Collaborative Economy in Europe* (Publications Office of the European Union 2016).

VERDERA, F., *Homeworkers in Peru* (ILO 2000).

VICTORIA HEIKEL, M., *Homeworkers in Paraguay* (ILO 2000).

VON BROEMBSEN, M., *The European Union's Commodification of Bulgarian Homeworkers: Regulating Informal Labour in Global Production Networks* (WIEGO 2019).

VON BROEMBSEN, M. and HARVEY, J., *Decent Work for Homeworkers in Global Supply Chains: Existing and Potential Mechanisms for Worker-centred Governance* (Global Labour University 2019).

VON BROEMBSEN, M., HARVEY, J. and CHEN, M., *Realizing Rights for Homeworkers: An Analysis of Governance Mechanisms* (Carr Centre for Human Rights Policy, Harvard Kennedy School 2019).

WEBER, E., *Setting out for Digital Social Security* (ILO 2018).

WERNER, E., BRAGA, M., FAMIRA-MÜHLBERGER, U., GERARD, M., HORVATH, T., KAHANEC, M., KAHANCOVÁ, M., KENDZIA, M., MARTIŠKOVÁ, M., MONTI, P., PEDERSEN, J. L., STANLEY, J., VANDEWEGHE, B., WEHNER, C. and WHITE, C., *Social Protection Rights of Economically Dependent Self-employed Workers* (European Parliament 2013).

ZHOU, I., *Digital Labour Platforms and Labour Protection in China* (ILO 2020).

ZHOU, M., *Pakistan's Hidden Workers: Wages and Conditions of Home-based Workers and the Informal Economy* (ILO 2017).

ZYSMAN, J. and KENNEY, M., *The Next Phase in the Digital Revolution: Platforms, Abundant Computing; Growth and Employment* (ETLA 2016).

OTHER SOURCES

Policy Documents and Memoranda

European Commission, *Proposal for Regulation of the European Parliament and of the Council on a Single Market for Digital Services (Digital Services Act) and amending Directive 2000/31/EC* (European Commission 2020).

European Commission, *First Phase Consultation of Social Partners Under Article 154 TFEU on Possible Action Addressing the Challenges Related to Working Conditions in Platform Work* (European Union 2021).

Global Commission on the Future of Work, *Work for a Brighter Future* (ILO 2019).

High-Level Panel on UN System-Wide Coherence, *Delivering as One*, A/61/583 (UN 2006).

ILO, *Protection of Workers' Personal Data* (ILO 1997).

ILO, *The Post-2015 Sustainable Development Agenda* (ILO 2013).

ILO, *General Principles and Operational Guidelines for Fair Recruitment & Definition of Recruitment Fees and Related Costs* (ILO 2019).

ILO, *Programme and Budget for the Biennium 2020–21* (ILO 2020).

ILO, *The ILO's Strategic Plan for 2022–25* (ILO 2020).

ILO Director-General, *Defending Values, Promoting Change. Social Justice in a Global Economy: An ILO Agenda* (ILO 1994).

ILO Director-General, *Decent Work* (ILO 1999).

ILO Director-General, *Reducing the Decent Work Deficit – a Global Challenge* (ILO 2001).

ILO Director-General, *Decent work for Africa's Development* (ILO 2003).

ILO Director-General, *Working out of Poverty* (ILO 2003).

ILO Director-General, *A Fair Globalization: The Role of the ILO* (ILO 2004).

ILO Director-General, *Consolidating Progress and Moving Ahead* (ILO 2005).

ILO Director-General, *Changing Patterns in the World of Work* (ILO 2006).

ILO Director-General, *Decent Work for Sustainable Development* (ILO 2007).

ILO Director-General, *Towards the ILO Centenary: Realities, Renewal and Tripartite Commitment* (ILO 2013).

ILO Director-General, *The Future of Work Centenary Initiative* (ILO 2015).

ILO Director-General, *Outcome of the Meeting of Experts on Fair Recruitment*, GB.328/INS/17/4 (ILO 2016).

ILO Director-General, *Programme and Budget Proposals for 2022–23* (ILO 2021).

ILO Governing Body, *Strengthening the ILO's Capacity to Discharge its Core Missions and Promote Decent Work for All at the Outset of the Twenty-first Century*, GB.294/2/1(Add.) (ILO 2005).

ILO Governing Body, *Outcome Document of the 108th (Centenary) Session of the Conference*, GB.335/INS/2/3 (ILO 2019).

ILO Governing Body, *Update on the United Nations Reform*, GB.335/INS/10 (ILO 2019).

ILO Governing Body, *Agenda of the International Labour Conference: Agenda of Future Sessions of the Conference*, GB.338/INS/2/1 (ILO 2020).

ILO Governing Body, *Decision Concerning the Update on the Status of Ratification of the 1986 Instrument for the Amendment of the Constitution of the ILO and Follow-up to Paragraph 3 of the Resolution on the ILO Centenary Declaration for the Future of Work*, GB.340/INS/18/1/ (ILO 2020).

ILO Governing Body, *Agenda of the International Labour Conference: Agenda of Future Sessions of the Conference*, GB.341/INS/3/1(Rev.1) (ILO 2021).

ILO Governing Body, *Decision Concerning the Agenda of the International Labour Conference: Agenda of Future Sessions of the Conference*, GB.341/INS/3/1(Rev.2)/Decision (ILO 2021).

ILO Governing Body, *Follow-up to the Resolution on the ILO Centenary Declaration for the Future of Work: Proposals for Including Safe and Healthy Working Conditions in the ILO's Framework of Fundamental Principles and Rights at Work*, GB.341/INS/6 (ILO 2021).

ILO International Labour Office, *Memorandum Sent by the International Labour Office to the German Federal Ministry of Labour and Social Affairs*, XLIX ILO Official Bulletin 389 n. 3 (1966).

ILO International Labour Office, *Memorandum Sent by the International Labour Office to the Ministry of Health and Social Affairs of Sweden*, XLIX ILO Official Bulletin 390 n. 3 (1966).

ILO International Labour Office, *Consideration of the 1986 Vienna Convention on the Law of Treaties between States and International Organizations or between International Organizations With a View to Formal Confirmation by the ILO*, 88th Session of the International Labour Conference in 2000.

ILO International Labour Office, *Implementing the Global Employment Agenda: Employment Strategies in Support of Decent Work, "Vision" Document* (ILO 2006).

ILO International Labour Office, *Report V: Strengthening the ILO's Capacity to Assist its Members' Efforts to Reach its Objectives in the Context of Globalization* (ILO 2007).

ILO International Labour Office, *Report VI Strengthening the ILO's Capacity to Assist its Members' Efforts to Reach its Objectives in the Context of Globalization: Continuation of the Discussion on Strengthening the ILO's Capacity and Possible Consideration of an Authoritative Document, Possibly in the Form of a Declaration or any Other Suitable Instrument, Together with any Appropriate Follow-up, and the Form They May Take* (ILO 2008).

ILO International Labour Office, *Background Document for the Tripartite Meeting on the Freedom of Association and Protection of the Right to Organise Convention, 1948 (No. 87), in Relation to the Right to Strike and the Modalities and Practices of Strike Action at National Level (Revised) (Geneva, 23–25 February 2015)*, GB.323/INS/5/Appendix III (ILO 2015).

ILO Legal Issues and International Labour Standards Section, *ILO Standards Policy: The Establishment and the Implementation of a Standards Review Mechanism*, GB.312/LILS/5 (ILO 2011).

ILO Legal Issues and International Labour Standards Section, *The Standards Initiative: Terms of Reference of the Standards Review Mechanism Tripartite Working Group*, GB.325/LILS/3 (ILO 2015).

ILO Standards Initiative–Joint Statement of Workers' & Employers' Groups (23.02.2015), TMFAPROC/2015/2.

ILO Standards Initiative–Government Group Statement (24.02.2015), TMFAPROC/2015/2.

International Law Commission, *Draft Articles on the Responsibility of International Organizations* (UN 2011).

International Law Commission, *Draft Conclusions on Subsequent Agreements and Subsequent Practice in Relation to the Interpretation of Treaties* (UN 2018).

IOE, *Factsheet on Committee of Experts on the Application of Conventions and Recommendations (CEACR)*, International Organisation of Employers (14 August 2021), https://www.ioe-emp.org/index.php?eID = dumpFile&t = f&f = 147483&token = 9ded6f4a8e-f5af953e3230072190122fd343d684.

Réponse du Ministère de l'économie, des finances et de la relance, publiée dans le JO Sénat du 01/10/2020 – page 4445 à la question écrite no. 17257 de M. Ronan Le Gleut (Français établis hors de France – Les Républicains), publiée dans le JO Sénat du 16/07/2020 – page 3241, https://www.senat.fr/questions/base/2020/qSEQ200717257.html (accessed: 28 April 2021).

World Commission on the Social Dimension of Globalization, *A Fair Globalization: Creating Opportunities for All* (ILO 2004).

World Employment Confederation, *A Decent Level Playing Field for Platform Work: Policy Recommendations for Sustainable Growth of Platform Work and the Provision of Quality Online Talent Platform Services* (WEC 2020).

World Employment Confederation and UNI Global, *Joint Recommendations of the EU Sectoral Social Partners for Temporary Agency Work: Online Talent Platforms, Labour Market Intermediaries and the Changing World of Work* (WEC 2018).

United Nations, *Guiding Principles on Business and Human Rights: Implementing the United Nations "Protect, Respect and Remedy" Framework* (UN 2011).

United Nations, *Report of the International Law Commission*, A/71/10 (UN 2016).

UN Economic and Social Council, *Creating an Environment at the National and International Levels Conducive to Generating Full and Productive Employment and Decent Work for All, and its Impact on Sustainable Development*, A/RES/64/135 (UN 2006).

UN General Assembly, *2005 World Summit Outcome*, A/RES/60/1 (UN 2005).

UN General Assembly, *Resolution on System-wide Coherence*, A/RES/62/277 (UN 2008).

United Nations Office of Legal Affairs, Memorandum by the United Nations Office of Legal Affairs, 2 April 1962, E/CN.4/L.610.

World Employment Confederation, *Promoting Fair Recruitment and Employment Practices: Code of Conduct*, Brussels, 2019.

Blogs and News Articles

ALLABY, E., *The Rise of Uber Eats Gang Masters is Tearing the Gig Economy Apart*, WIRED (15 February 2021), https://www.wired.co.uk/article/uber-eats-italy.

ALMENDRAL, A., *For Domestic Workers, Apps Provide Solace – but not Justice*, Rest of World (4 August 2020), https://restofworld.org/2020/migrant-workers-virtual-solidarity/.

ALOISI, A. and V. DE STEFANO, *Uber Eats Facing Criminal Charges in Italy: Are We Managers or Corporals?*, il Mulino (5 June 2020), https://www.rivistailmulino.it/news/newsitem/index/Item/News:NEWS_ITEM:5256.

ALOISI, A. and DE STEFANO, V., *Deliveroo's Algorithm Discriminated Against Those Who go on Strike or Get Sick: "Frankly, my Rider, I Don't Give a Damn"*, il Mulino (7 January 2021), https://www.rivistailmulino.it/a/frankly-my-rider-i-don-t-give-a-damn-1.

ALOISI, A., DE STEFANO, V. and SILBERMAN, S., *A Manifesto to Reform the Gig Economy*, Regulating for Globalization (1 May 2019), http://regulatingforglobalization.com/2019/05/01/a-manifesto-to-reform-the-gig-economy/.

ARMITAGE, S., *My TaskRabbit Gig in a Stranger's Fancy Kitchen*, CURBED (21 November 2019), https://archive.curbed.com/2019/11/21/20963418/taskrabbit-task-nyc-story.

AUTOR, D., *The Economics of Labour Market Intermediation*, VoxEU (30 October 2008), https://voxeu.org/article/economics-labour-market-intermediation.

BAIN, M., *A Huge Underclass of Ghost Workers Are Making your Shirts in their Homes*, Quartz (17 December 2015), https://qz.com/494818/in-much-of-the-world-the-sweatshop-isnt-a-factory-its-someones-kitchen-floor/.

BRADSHAW, T., *Just Eat Offers Hourly Wages in UK Gig Economy Shake-up*, Financial Times (9 December 2020), https://www.ft.com/content/352e3c09-7ce3-466a-b941-921f0d3906c7.

BRANDOM, R., *Sick Days: Instacart Promises a Safer Way to Shop, but Workers Tell a Different Story*, The Verge (26 May 2020), https://www.theverge.com/21267669/instacart-shoppers-sick-extended-pay-quarantine-leave-coronavirus.

BROWNING, K. and CONGER, K., *Cleaners Demand Harassment Safeguards From the Booking Service Handy*, The New York Times (10 September 2020), https://www.nytimes.com/2020/09/10/business/handy-service-cleaners-harassment.html.

CATER, L., *Italy Demands €733M in Fines From Food Delivery Platforms*, POLITICO (25 February 2021), at https://www.politico.eu/article/italy-demands-733-million-euros-in-fines-from-food-delivery-platforms/.

CNBC, *The Rise of Instacart and Online Grocery Delivery*, YouTube (13 May 2020), https://www.youtube.com/watch?v = WRc3USp1RAQ.

Danish Competition and Consumer Authority, *Commitment Decision on the Use of a Minimum Hourly Fee*, Konkurrence- og Forbrugerstyrelsen (26 August 2020), https://www.en.kfst.dk/nyheder/kfst/english/decisions/20200826-commitment-decision-on-the-use-of-a-minimum-hourly-fee-hilfr/.

DAVIES, C., *Uber "Willing to Change" as Drivers get Minimum Wage, Holiday Pay and Pensions*, BBC (17 March 2021), https://www.bbc.com/news/business-56412397.

DOOREY, D., *Who is the Employer of Temp Workers?*, Canadian LAW OF WORK Forum (27 October 2009), https:/lawofwork.ca/who-is-the-employer-of-temp-workers/.

DUBAL, V., *The Digitalization of Day Labor as Gig Work*, onlabor (7 May 2019), https://onlabor.org/the-digitalization-of-day-labor-as-gig-work/.

ECKHARDT, G. M. and BARDHI, F., *The Sharing Economy Isn't About Sharing at All*, Harvard Business Review (28 January 2015), https://hbr.org/2015/01/the-sharing-economy-isnt-about-sharing-at-all.

EFE, *Just Eat Prevé la Salida de su Competencia en España si se les Obliga a Contratar Riders*, elEconomista.es (4 October 2020), https://www.eleconomista.es/empresas-finanzas/noticias/10807488/10/20/Just-Eat-preve-la-salida-de-su-competencia-en-Espana-si-se-les-obliga-a-contratar-riders.html.

ELLIOTT, V., *Training Self-driving Cars for $1 an Hour*, Rest of World (3 August 2021), https://restofworld.org/2021/self-driving-cars-outsourcing/.

EWING, K., *Don't be Fooled, Uber is Still Dodging the Minimum Wage*, Institute of Employment Rights (17 March 2021), https://www.ier.org.uk/comments/dont-be-fooled-uber-is-still-dodging-the-minimum-wage/.

FNV, *Wet Arbeidsmarkt in Balans: Een (Zoek)tocht naar meer Zekerheid*, FNV (14 January 2020), https://www.fnv.nl/getmedia/929bd8d5-ffcf-4b64-a9f6-ecc27d745d0c/Notitie-FNV-Eerste-signalen-Wet-arbeidsmarkt-in-balans-jan2020.pdf.

GRISWOLD, A., *This is the Script Uber is Using to Make Anti-union Phone Calls to Drivers in Seattle*, Quartz (22 February 2016), https://qz.com/621977/this-is-the-script-uber-is-using-to-make-anti-union-phone-calls-to-drivers-in-seattle/.

HEILWEIL, R., *Beware of these Futuristic Background Checks*, Vox/Recode (11 May 2020), https://www.vox.com/recode/2020/5/11/21166291/artificial-intelligence-ai-background-check-checkr-fama.

HENRIQUES-GOMES, L., *Menulog Announces Pivot Towards 'Employment Model' for All Couriers Within Coming Years*, The Guardian (12 April 2021), https://www.theguardian.com/business/2021/apr/12/menulog-announces-pivot-towards-employment-model-for-all-couriers-within-coming-years.

IANNI, M., *Le Canton de Genève Remporte une Victoire Face à Uber*, AGEFI (2 December 2020), https://agefi.com/actualites/entreprises/le-canton-de-geneve-remporte-une-victoire-detape-face-a-uber.

Institut Arbeit und Qualifikation der Universität Duisburg-Essen, *Beschäftigte in Minijobs 2003 – 2019*, Sozialpolitik aktuell in Deutschland (28 April 2021), https://www.sozialpolitik-aktuell.de/files/sozialpolitik-aktuell/_Politikfelder/Arbeitsmarkt/Datensammlung/PDF-Dateien/abbIV91.pdf.

JOSEPHS, J., *Just Eat to Stop Using Gig Economy Workers*, BBC (14 August 2020), https://www.bbc.com/news/business-53780299.

KHOSROWSHAHI, D., *I Am the C.E.O. of Uber. Gig Workers Deserve Better*, The New York Times (10 August 2020), https://www.nytimes.com/2020/08/10/opinion/uber-ceo-dara-khosrowshahi-gig-workers-deserve-better.html.

KHOSROWSHAHI, D., GREEN, L. and ZIMMER, J., *Open Forum: Uber, Lyft Ready To Do Our Part for Drivers*, San Francisco Chronicle (12 June 2019), https://www.sfchronicle.com/opinion/openforum/article/Open-Forum-Uber-Lyft-ready-to-do-our-part-for-13969843.php.

KOROSEC, K., *Domino's Launches E-Bike Delivery to Compete With Uber Eats*, DoorDash, TechCrunch (13 August 2019), https://techcrunch.com/2019/08/13/dominos-launches-e-bike-delivery-to-compete-with-ubereats-doordash/.

KUPER, S., *Are Superstar Employees about to be Offshored?*, Financial Times (25 March 2021), https://www.ft.com/content/9414f45c-6f03-4b8f-85c5-537d7e4f4932.

LEE, D., *Amazon Ordered to Pay Back $61.7m After Pocketing Delivery Drivers' Tips*, Financial Times (2 February 2021), https://www.ft.com/content/92abc0ac-1c58-46a6-94d9-2c16b31aa890.

LIAO, R., *Viral Article Puts the Brakes on China's Food Delivery Frenzy*, TechCrunch (9 September 2020), https://techcrunch.com/2020/09/08/viral-article-puts-brakes-on-chinas-food-delivery-frenzy/.

LOMAS, N., *Uber Launches a Shift-Work Finder App, Uber Works, Starting in Chicago*, TechCrunch (3 October 2019), https://techcrunch.com/2019/10/03/uber-launches-a-shift-work-finder-app-uber-works-starting-in-chicago/.

LUNDEN, I., *Randstad Buys Monster for $429M as Recruitment Consolidation Continues*, TechCrunch (9 August 2016), https://techcrunch.com/2016/08/08/randstad-buys-monster-for-429m-as-recruitment-consolidation-continues/.

MEHROTRA, D., *Horror Stories From Inside Amazon's Mechanical Turk*, GIZMODO (28 January 2020), https://gizmodo.com/horror-stories-from-inside-amazons-mechanical-turk-1840878041.

NARVAIZA, Z., *Opinion of the European Economic and Social Committee on "New Trends in Self-employed Work: The Specific Case of Economically Dependent Self-employed Work" (own-initiative opinion)*, European Economic and Social Committee (29 April 2010), https://www.eesc.europa.eu/en/our-work/opinions-information-reports/opinions/new-trends-self-employed-work-specific-case-economically-dependent-self-employed-work.

O'CONNOR, S., *Do Not Let Homeworking Become Digital Piecework for the Poor*, Financial Times (15 September 2020), https://www.ft.com/content/ab83270c-253a-4d7a-9ef8-a360d2e04aab.

O'KANE, J., *Foodora to Exit Canada Just Months After Workers Won the Right to Unionize*, The Globe and Mail (27 April 2020), https://www.theglobeandmail.com/business/article-foodora-to-exit-canada-three-months-after-workers-won-the-right-to/.

ONGWESO JR, E., *Delivery Apps Are Using Child Labor In Brazil*, VICE (10 February 2021), https://www.vice.com/en/article/z3v5xx/delivery-apps-are-using-child-labor-in-brazil.

PATON, E. and LAZAZZERA, M., *Inside Italy's Shadow Economy*, The New York Times (20 September 2018), https://www.nytimes.com/2018/09/20/fashion/italy-luxury-shadow-economy.html.

PINNELL, O. and KELLY, J., *Slave Markets Found on Instagram and Other Apps*, BBC (31 October 2019), https://www.bbc.com/news/technology-50228549.

PIQUEMAL, M. and KRISTANADJAJA, G., *Plateformes de Livraison: Pour les Mineurs, une Course à l'Argent Facile*, Libération (3 May 2019), https://www.liberation.fr/france/2019/05/03/plateformes-de-livraison-pour-les-mineurs-une-course-a-l-argent-facile_1724849/.

Public Rights Project, *Re: Sexual Harassment of Handy Home Service Workers*, Medium (10 September 2020), https://publicrightsproject.medium.com/re-sexual-harassment-of-handy-home-service-workers-fec828d05fa7.

ROCHMYANINGSIH, D., *"Only Gojek Knows this Mystery"*, Rest of World (18 May 2021), https://restofworld.org/2021/only-gojek-knows-this-mystery/.

ROSENBERG, E., *Albertsons is Laying Off Employees and Replacing Them With Gig Workers, as App Platforms Rise*, The Washington Post (6 January 2021), https://www.washingtonpost.com/business/2021/01/06/vons-albertsons-doordash-prop-22-layoffs/.

SAID, C., *Uber May Stop Letting Drivers See Destinations and Name Prices*, San Francisco Chronicle (5 April 2021), https://www.sfchronicle.com/business/article/Uber-may-stop-letting-drivers-see-destinations-16078491.php.

SELYUKH, A., *Section 230: A Key Legal Shield For Facebook, Google Is About To Change*, NPR (21 March 2018), https://www.npr.org/sections/alltechconsidered/2018/03/21/591622450/section-230-a-key-legal-shield-for-facebook-google-is-about-to-change.

SEN, A., *Address by Mr Amartya Sen, Nobel Laureate in Economics*, International Labour Conference (15 June 1999), https://www.ilo.org/public/english/standards/relm/ilc/ilc87/a-sen.htm.

SPERBER, A., *Uber Made Big Promises in Kenya. Drivers Say it's Ruined Their Lives.*, NBC News (30 November 2020), https://www.nbcnews.com/news/world/uber-made-big-promises-kenya-drivers-say-it-s-ruined-n1247964.

SUNDHEIM, K., *The Internet's Profound Impact On The Recruiting Industry*, Forbes (2 April 2013), https://www.forbes.com/sites/kensundheim/2013/04/02/the-internets-profound-impact-on-the-recruiting-industry/?sh = 6ee67a327070.

UN Secretary-General, *Tackling the Inequality Pandemic: A New Social Contract for a New Era*, United Nations (18 July 2020), https://www.un.org/en/coronavirus/tackling-inequality-new-social-contract-new-era.

VAN CLEYNENBREUGEL, P., *Will Deliveroo and Uber be Captured by the Proposed EU Platform Regulation? You'd Better Watch Out…*, European Law Blog (12 March 2019), https://europeanlawblog.eu/2019/03/12/will-deliveroo-and-uber-be-captured-by-the-proposed-eu-platform-regulation-youd-better-watch-out/.

VAN GESTEL, M., *Vakbonden Slepen Flexwerkapp Temper voor de Rechter*, Trouw (22 October 2020), https://www.trouw.nl/economie/vakbonden-slepen-flexwerkapp-temper-voor-de-rechter~b3379193/.

VOLLEBREGT, B., *Flexwerkapp Gedraagt Zich als een Uitzendbureau, en dus ís het een Uitzendbureau*, Trouw (15 February 2021), https://www.trouw.nl/economie/flexwerkapp-gedraagt-zich-als-een-uitzendbureau-en-dus-is-het-een-uitzendbureau~b944edd1/.

WHITE, R. and PHILPOTT, A., *How the Ontario Labour Board Ruled Foodora Workers are "Employees" and Not Independent Contractors*, Canadian LAW OF WORK Forum (5 March 2020), https://lawofwork.ca/how-the-ontario-labour-board-ruled-foodora-workers-are-employees/.

X, *Delivery Workers, Trapped in the System*, Chuang (12 November 2020), https://chuangcn.org/2020/11/delivery-renwu-translation/.

X, *Nieuwe 'Vlaamse Uber' Zet Passagier aan de Knoppen*, De Tijd (24 February 2021), https://www.tijd.be/ondernemen/auto/nieuwe-vlaamse-uber-zet-passagier-aan-de-knoppen/10286716.html.

X, *Uber to Close its Uber Works Staffing Operations*, Staffing Industry Analysts (19 May 2020), https://www2.staffingindustry.com/Editorial/Daily-News/Uber-to-close-its-Uber-Works-staffing-operations-53856.

ZiPredactie, *Modelovereenkomst Platform Temper (Voorlopig) Verlengd*, ZiPconomy (26 May 2021), https://www.zipconomy.nl/2021/05/modelovereenkomst-platform-temper-voorlopig-verlengd/.

Index

BCLR – BULLETIN OF COMPARATIVE LABOUR RELATIONS

Vol. Author/Title/Year/ISBN

1. Roger Blanpain, *Individual Employment Contracts: Collective Agreements*, 1970.
2. Roger Blanpain, *Social Planning*, 1971 (ISBN 90-312-0018-2).
3. Roger Blanpain, *Guaranteed Income Funds*, 1972 (ISBN 90-312-0019-0).
4. Roger Blanpain, *Employee Participation at the Level of the Enterprise*, 1973 (ISBN 90-312-0020-4).
5. Roger Blanpain, *Vastheid van Betrekking: Staking en Bezetting*, 1974.
6. Roger Blanpain, *Labour Law and Industrial Relations (International Bibliography)*, 1975 (ISBN 90-312-0023-9).
7. Roger Blanpain, *Multinational Enterprises*, 1976 (ISBN 90-312-0024-7).
8. Roger Blanpain, *Worker's Participation in the European Company*, 1977 (ISBN 90-312-0044-1).
9. Roger Blanpain, *Women and Labour*, 1978 (ISBN 90-312-0077-8).
10. Roger Blanpain, *European Conference on Labour Law and Industrial Relations: Multinational Enterprises*, 1979 (ISBN 90-312-0091-3).
11. Roger Blanpain, *Job Security and Industrial Relations*, 1980 (ISBN 90-312-0147-2).
12. Roger Blanpain, Greg Bamber & Russell Lansbury, *Technological Change and Industrial Relations: An International Symposium*, 1983 (ISBN 90-312-0205-3).
13. Roger Blanpain, James Janssen van Raay & A. Moulty, *Worker's Participation in the European Community: The Fifth Directive*, 1984 (ISBN 90-654-4187-5).
14. Roger Blanpain, *Equality and Prohibition of Discrimination in Employment*, 1985 (ISBN 90-654-4215-4).
15. Roger Blanpain, *Restructuring Labour in the Enterprise: Law and Practice in France, F.R. of Germany, Italy, Sweden and the United Kingdom*, 1986 (ISBN 90-654-4283-9).
16. Roger Blanpain & E. Kassalow, *Unions and Industrial Relations: Recent Trends and Prospect: A Comparative Treatment*, 1987 (ISBN 90-654-4294-4).
17. Roger Blanpain & Marco Biagi, *Trade Union Democracy and Industrial Relations*, 1988 (ISBN 90-654-4394-0).
18. Roger Blanpain & Jelle Visser, *In Search of Inclusive Unionism*, 1990 (ISBN 90-654-4439-4).
19. Roger Blanpain, *Flexibility and Wages: A Comparative Treatment*, 1990 (ISBN 90-654-4461-0).
20. Roger Blanpain, Stephen Frenkel & Oliver Clarke, *Economic Restructuring and Industrial Relations in Industrialised Countries*, 1990 (ISBN 90-654-4488-2).
21. Roger Blanpain & Friedrich Fürstenberg, *Structure and Strategy in Industrial Relations*, 1991 (ISBN 90-654-4559-5).

22. Roger Blanpain, Amira Galin & Ozer Carmi, *Flexible Work Patterns and Their Impact on Industrial Relations,* 1991 (ISBN 90-654-4572-2).
23. Roger Blanpain, *Workers' Participation: Influence on Management Decision-Making by Labour in the Private Sector,* 1992 (ISBN 90-654-4600-1).
24. Roger Blanpain, Brian Brooks & Chris Engels, *Employed or Self-Employed,* 1992 (ISBN 90-654-4613-3).
25. Roger Blanpain & Tiziano Treu, *Industrial Relations Developments in the Telecommunications Industry,* 1993 (ISBN 90-654-4642-7).
26. Roger Blanpain & Marco Biagi, *Industrial Relations in Small and Medium Sized Enterprises,* 1993 (ISBN 90-654-4696-6).
27. Roger Blanpain & Marco Biagi, *Participative Management and Industrial Relations in a Worldwide Perspective,* 1993 (ISBN 90-654-4769-5).
28. Roger Blanpain, Jacques Rojot & Hoyt N. Wheeler, *Employee Rights and Industrial Justice,* 1994 (ISBN 90-654-4804-7).
29. Roger Blanpain & Ruth Ben-Israel, *Strikes and Lock-Outs in Industrialized Market Economies,* 1994 (ISBN 90-654-4841-1).
30. Roger Blanpain, Kazuo Sugeno & Yasuo Suwa, *The Harmonization of Working Life and Family Life,* 1995 (ISBN 90-411-0064-4).
31. Roger Blanpain & Laszio Nagy, *Labour Law and Industrial Relations in Central and Eastern Europe,* 1996 (ISBN 90-411-0298-1).
32. Roger Blanpain, *Labour Law and Industrial Relations in the European Union,* 1997 (ISBN 90-411-0527-1).
33. Taco Van Peijpe, *Employment Protection under Strain,* 1998 (ISBN 90-411-0528-8).
34. Roger Blanpain, Takashi Araki & Ryuichi Yamakawa, *The Process of Industrialization and the Role of Labour Law in Asia,* 1999 (ISBN 9-041-1104-7-X).
35. Roger Blanpain & Marco Biagi, *Non-standard Work and Industrial Relations,* 1999 (ISBN 90-411-1117-4).
36. Roger Blanpain, *Private Employment Agencies: The Impact of ILO Convention 181 (1997) and the Judgment of the European Court of Justice of 11 December 1997,* 1999 (ISBN 90-411-1118-2).
37. Roger Blanpain, *Multinational Enterprises and the Social Challenges of the XXIst Century: The ILO Declaration on Fundamental* Principles *at Work, Public and Private Corporate Codes of Conduct,* 2000 (ISBN 90-411-1280-4).
38. Roger Blanpain, Ryuichi Yamakawa & Takashi Araki, *Deregulation and Labour Law: In Search of a Labour Concept for the 21st Century,* 2000 (ISBN 90-411-1370-3).
39. Roger Blanpain, *The Council of Europe and the Social Challenges of the XXIst Century,* 2001 (ISBN 90-411-1543-9).
40. Roger Blanpain, *On-Line Rights for Employees in the Information Society, Use & Monitoring of E-Mail & Internet at Work,* 2002 (ISBN 90-411-1626-5).
41. Roger Blanpain, *The Evolving Employment Relationship and the New Economy: The Role of Labour Law & Industrial Relations,* 2001 (ISBN 90-411-1691-5).
42. Roger Blanpain, *Involvement of Employees in the European Union, Works Councils, Company Statute, Information and Consultation Rights,* 2002 (ISBN 90-411-1760-1).
43. Michele Colucci, *The Impact of the Internet and New Technologies on the Workplace: A Legal Analysis from a Comparative Point of View,* 2002 (ISBN 90-411-1824-1).

44. Roger Blanpain, *White Paper on the Labour Market in Italy: The Quality of European Industrial Relations and Changing Industrial Relations,* 2002 (ISBN 90-411-1841-1).
45. Roger Blanpain, Russell D. Lansbury & Young-Bum Park, *Impact of Globalisation on Employment Relations: A Comparison of the Automobile and Banking Industries in Australia and Korea,* 2002 (ISBN 90-411-1850-0).
46. Roger Blanpain & Antoine Jacobs, *Employee Rights in Bankruptcy: A Comparative Law Assessment,* 2002 (ISBN 90-411-1942-6).
47. Roger Blanpain, Takashi Araki & Shinya Ouchi, *Corporate Restructuring and the Role of Labour Law,* 2003 (ISBN 90-411-1949-3).
48. Roger Blanpain, *Collective Bargaining, Discrimination, Social Security and European Integration,* 2003 (ISBN 90-411-2010-6).
49. Roger Blanpain & Luis Aparicio-Valdez, *Labour Relations in the Asia-Pacific Countries,* 2004 (ISBN 90-411-2239-7).
50. Roger Blanpain & Ronnie Graham, *Temporary Agency Work and the Information Society,* 2004 (ISBN 90-411-2252-4).
51. Roger Blanpain, *The Actors of Collective Bargaining: A World Report,* 2004 (ISBN 90-411-2253-2).
52. Roger Blanpain & Michele Colucci, *The Globalisation of Labour Standards: The Soft Law Track,* 2004 (ISBN 90-411-2303-2).
53. Roger Blanpain, Takashi Araki & Shinya Ouchi, *Labour Law in Motion: Diversification of the Labour Force & Terms and Conditions of Employment,* 2005 (ISBN 90-411-2315-6).
54. Roger Blanpain, *Smoking and the Workplace,* 2005 (ISBN 90-411-2325-3).
55. Roger Blanpain, *Confronting Globalization: The Quest for a Social Agenda,* 2005 (ISBN 90-411-2381-4).
56. Roger Blanpain, Thomas Blanke & Edgar Rose, *Collective Bargaining Wages in Comparative Perspective: Germany, France, the Netherlands, Sweden and the United Kingdom,* 2005 (ISBN 90-411-2388-1).
57. Roger Blanpain & Anne Numhauser-Henning, *Women in Academia & Equality Law: Aiming High – Falling Short?,* 2006 (ISBN 978-90-411-2427-6).
58. Roger Blanpain, *Freedom of Services in the European Union: Labour and Social Security Law: The Bolkestein Initiative,* 2006 (ISBN 978-90-411-2453-5).
59. Roger Blanpain, Frans Pennings & Nurhan Sural, *Flexibilisation and Modernisation of the Turkish Labour Market,* 2006 (ISBN 978-90-411-2490-X).
60. Roger Blanpain & Boel Flodgren, *Corporate and Employment Perspectives in a Global Business Environment,* 2006 (ISBN 978-90-411-2537-X).
61. Roger Blanpain, Shinya Ouchi & Takashi Araki, *Decentralizing Industrial Relations and The Role of Labor Unions and Employee Representatives,* 2007 (ISBN 978-90-411-2583-3).
62. Roger Blanpain, *European Framework Agreements and Telework: Law and Practice: A European and Comparative Study,* 2007 (ISBN 978-90-411-2560-4).
63. Roger Blanpain, Jim Kitay, Leanne Cutcher & Nick Wailes, *Globalization and Employment Relations in Retail Banking,* 2007 (ISBN 978-90-411-2620-1).
64. Roger Blanpain, Russell Lansbury, Jim Kitay, Nick Wailes & Anja Kirsch, *Globalization and Employment Relations in the Auto Assembly Industry: A Study of Seven Countries,* 2008 (ISBN 978-90-411-2698-6).

65. Roger Blanpain & Michele Tiraboschi, *The Global Labour Market: From Globalization to Flexicurity*, 2008 (ISBN 978-90-411-2722-8).
66. Roger Blanpain, Michele Colucci & Frank Hendrickx, *The Future of Sport in the European Union: Beyond the EU Reform Treaty and the White Paper*, 2008 (ISBN 978-90-411-2761-7).
67. Roger Blanpain, Linda Dickens, *Challenges in European Employment Relations: Employment Regulation, Trade Union Organization, Equality, Flexicurity, Training and New Approaches to Pay*, 2008 (ISBN 978-90-411-2771-6).
68. Roger Blanpain, Hiroya Nakakubo & Takashi Araki, *New Developments in Employment Discrimination Law, 2008* (ISBN 978-90-411-2782-2).
69. Roger Blanpain, Andrzej Marian Wiatkowski, *The Laval and Viking Cases: Freedom of Services and Establishment v. Industrial Conflict in the European Economic Area and Russia*, 2009 (ISBN 978-90-411-2850-8).
70. Roger Blanpain, William Bromwich, Olga Rymkevich, Silvia Spattini, *The Modernization of Labour Law and Industrial Relations in a Comparative Perspective*, 2009 (ISBN 978-90-411-2865-2).
71. Roger Blanpain, Juan Pablo Landa & Brian Langille, *Employment Policies and Multilevel Governance*, 2009 (ISBN 978-90-411-2866-9).
72. Roger Blanpain, European Works Councils; *The European Directive 2009/38/EC of 6 May 2009, 2009* (ISBN 978-90-411-3208-6).
73. Roger Blanpain, William Bromwich, Olga Rymkevich & Silvia Spattini, *Labour Productivity, Investment in Human Capital and Youth Employment: Comparative Developments and Global Responses*, 2010 (ISBN 978-90-411-3249-9).
74. Greg J. Bamber & Philippe Pochet, *Regulating Employment Relations, Work and Labour Laws: International Comparisons between Key Countries*, 2010 (ISBN 978-90-411-3199-7). General Editor: Roger Blanpain.
75. Roger Blanpain, Desislava Nikolaeva Dimitrova, *Seafarers' Rights in the Globalized Maritime Industry*, 2010 (ISBN 978-90-411-3349-6).
76. Roger Blanpain, Hiroya Nakakubo & Takashi Araki, *Regulation of Fixed-Term Employment Contracts*, 2010 (ISBN 978-90-411-3356-4).
77. Roger Blanpain, William Bromwich, Olga Rymkevich & Iacopo Senatori, *Rethinking Corporate Governance*, 2011 (ISBN 978-90-411-3450-9).
78. Roger Blanpain & Frank Hendrickx, *Labour Law between Change and Tradition: Liber Amicorum Antoine Jacobs*, 2011 (ISBN 978-90-411-3424-0).
79. Roger Blanpain, Thomas Klebe, Marlene Schmidt & Bernd Waas, *Trade Union Rights at the Workplace*, 2012 (ISBN 978-90-411-3460-8).
80. Roger Blanpain, William Bromwich, Olga Rymkevich & Iacopo Senatori, *Labour Markets, Industrial Relations and Human Resources Management: From Recession to Recovery*, 2012 (ISBN 978-90-411-4004-3).
81. Roger Blanpain, Hiroya Nakakubo & Takashi Araki, *Systems of Employee Representation at the Enterprise: A Comparative Study*, 2012 (ISBN 978-90-411-4080-7).
82. Roger Blanpain & Frank Hendrickx, *Temporary Agency Work in the European Union and the United States*, 2013 (ISBN 978-90-411-4769-1).
83. Roger Blanpain, Toker Dereli, Y. Pınar Soykut-Sarıca & Aslı en-Tabaı, *Emerging Patterns of Work and Turkish Labour Market Challenges under Globalization: Readings on Labour and Employment Relations*, 2014 (ISBN 978-90-411-4983-1).

84. Roger Blanpain, Pablo Arellano Ortiz, Marius Olivier & Gijsbert Vonk, *Social Security and Migrant Workers: Selected Studies of Cross-border Social Security Mechanisms*, 2014 (ISBN 978-90-411-4770-7).
85. Roger Blanpain & Nikita Lyutov, *Workers' Representation in Central and Eastern Europe: Challenges and Opportunities for the Works Councils' System*, 2014 (ISBN 978-90-411-4746-2).
86. Roger Blanpain, Ulla Liukkunen & Chen Yifeng, *China and ILO Fundamental Principles and Rights at Works*, 2014 (ISBN 978-90-411-4984-8).
87. Roger Blanpain, *The Use of Languages and Employment Relations*, 2014 (ISBN 978-90-411-5606-8).
88. Roger Blanpain, Hiroya Nakakubo & Takashi Araki, *Protection of Employees' Personal Information and Privacy*, 2014 (ISBN 978-90-411-5608-2).
89. Roger Blanpain, Jan Wouters, Glenn Rayp, Laura Beke & Axel Marx, *Protecting Labour Rights in a Multi-polar Supply Chain and Mobile Global Economy*, 2015 (ISBN 978-90-411-5662-4).
90. Roger Blanpain & Stefania Marassi, *Globalization and Transnational Collective Labour Relations: International and European Framework Agreements at Company Level*, 2015 (ISBN 978-90-411-4748-6).
91. Roger Blanpain, Frank Hendrickx & Petra Herzfeld Olsson, *National Effects of the Implementation of EU Directives on Labour Migration from Third Countries*, 2016 (ISBN 978-90-411-6257-1).
92. Roger Blanpain, Frank Hendrickx & D'Arcy du Toit, *Labour Law and Social Progress: Holding the Line or Shifting the Boundaries?* 2016 (ISBN 978-90-411-6747-7).
93. Roger Blanpain & Frank Hendrickx, *Reasonable Accommodation in the Modern Workplace: Potential and Limits of the Integrative Logics of Labour Law*, 2016 (ISBN 978-90-411-6258-8).
94. Roger Blanpain, Frank Hendrickx & Bernd Waas, *New Forms of Employment in Europe*, 2016 (ISBN 978-90-411-6239-7).
95. Roger Blanpain, Frank Hendrickx, Hiroya Nakakubo & Takashi Araki, *The Notion of Employer in the Era of the Fissured Workplace: Should Labour Law Responsibilities Exceed the Boundary of the Legal Entity?*, 2017 (ISBN 978-90-411-8470-2).
96. Elena Sychenko, *Individual Labour Rights as Human Rights: The Contributions of the European Court of Human Rights to Worker's Rights Protection*, 2017 (ISBN 978-90-411-8629-4).
97. William Bromwich & Olga Rymkevich, *Improving Workplace Quality: New Perspectives and Challenges for Worker Well-Being*, 2017 (ISBN 978-90-411-8628-7).
98. Sarah De Groof, *Work-Life Balance in the Modern Workplace: Interdisciplinary Perspectives from Work-Family Research, Law and Policy*, 2017 (ISBN 978-90-411-8630-0).
99. Sylvaine Laulom, *Collective Bargaining Developments in Times of Crisis*, 2018 (ISBN 978-90-411-8999-8).
100. Frank Hendrickx & Valerio De Stefano, *Game Changers in Labour Law: Shaping the Future of Work*, 2018 (ISBN 978-90-411-9953-9).
101. Ivana Palinkaš, *The Legal and Institutional Framing of Collective Bargaining in CEE Countries: Between Europeanisation and Decentralisation*, 2018 (ISBN 978-90-411-9199-1).

102. Jeremy Waddington, *European Board-Level Employee Representation: National Variations in Influence and Power*, 2018 (ISBN 978-90-411-9202-8).
103. Jan Pichrt & Kristina Koldinská, *Labour Law and Social Protection in a Globalized World: Changing Realities in Selected Areas of Law and Policy*, 2018 (ISBN 978-94-035-0093-5).
104. Matthew W. Finkin, *American Labor and the Law: Dormant, Resurgent, and Emergent Problems*, 2019 (ISBN 978-94-035-0654-8).
105. Giuseppe Casale & Tiziano Treu, *Transformations of Work: Challenges for the Institutions and Social Actors*, 2019 (ISBN 978-94-035-0891-7).
106. Miguel De la Corte-Rodríguez, *EU Law on Maternity and Other Child-Related Leaves: Impact on Gender Equality*, 2019 (ISBN 978-94-035-1452-9).
107. Valeria Pulignano & Frank Hendrickx, *Employment Relations in the 21st Century: Challenges for Theory and Research in a Changing World of Work*, 2020 (ISBN 978-94-035-1764-3).
108. Matteo Bottero, *Posting of Workers in EU Law: Challenges of Equality, Solidarity and Fair Competition*, 2021 (ISBN 978-94-035-2860-1).
109. Bernd Waas & Christina Hießl, *Collective Bargaining for Self-Employed Workers in Europe: Approaches to Reconcile Competition Law and Labour Rights*, 2021 (ISBN 978-94-035-2373-6).
110. Mathias Wouters, *International Labour Standards and Platform Work: An Analysis of Digital Labour Platforms Based on the Instruments on Private Employment Agencies, Home Work and Domestic Work*, 2022 (ISBN 978-94-035-4024-5).